FOUNDATIONS OF A FREE SOCIETY

Ayn Rand Society Philosophical Studies

James G. Lennox and Gregory Salmieri, Editors

Also in the series

Concepts and Their Role in Knowledge: Reflections on Objectivist Epistemology

EDITED BY ALLAN GOTTHELF AND JAMES G. LENNOX

Metaethics, Egoism, and Virtue: Studies in Ayn Rand's Normative Theory

EDITED BY ALLAN GOTTHELF AND JAMES G. LENNOX

FOUNDATIONS OF A FREE SOCIETY

Reflections on Ayn Rand's Political Philosophy

Edited by Gregory Salmieri and Robert Mayhew

AYN RAND SOCIETY PHILOSOPHICAL STUDIES

University of Pittsburgh Press

Published by the University of Pittsburgh Press, Pittsburgh, Pa., 15260
Copyright © 2019, University of Pittsburgh Press
All rights reserved
Manufactured in the United States of America
Printed on acid-free paper
10 9 8 7 6 5 4 3 2 1

Cataloging-in-Publication data is available from the Library of Congress

ISBN 13: 978-0-8229-4548-2
ISBN 10: 0-8229-4548-7

Cover art: Ayn Rand, 1957. © New York Times Co./Getty Images.
Cover design: Joel W. Coggins

To Allan Gotthelf (1942–2013),
who was the leading light of the Ayn Rand Society
and the founding editor of this series.

CONTENTS

Note on the Series   xi
JAMES G. LENNOX

Introduction   3
GREGORY SALMIERI

Part One: Reason, Force, and the Foundations of Politics

The Place of the Non–Initiation of Force Principle in Ayn Rand's Philosophy   15
DARRYL WRIGHT

Force and the Mind   45
DARRYL WRIGHT

The Scope and Justification of Rand's Non–Initiation of Force Principle   76
DARRYL WRIGHT

Part Two: Rights and Government

Ayn Rand's Theory of Rights: An Exposition and Response to Critics   117
FRED D. MILLER JR. AND ADAM MOSSOFF

A Critique of Ayn Rand's Theory of Rights: Response to Miller and Mossoff   152
MATT ZWOLINSKI

Selfish Regard for the Rights of Others: Continuing a Discussion with Zwolinski, Miller, and Mossoff   166
GREGORY SALMIERI

Ayn Rand and Robert Nozick on Rights   193
LESTER H. HUNT

Rand (contra Nozick) on Individual Rights and the Emergence and Justification of Government   206
ONKAR GHATE

Anarchism versus Objectivism   228
HARRY BINSWANGER

Defending Liberty: The Commonsense Approach   237
MICHAEL HUEMER

Egoism, Force, and the Need for Government: A Response to Huemer   261
HARRY BINSWANGER

Part Three: Rand and the Classical Liberal Tradition on Intellectual Freedom

A Wall of Separation between Church and State: Understanding This Principle's Supporting Arguments and Far-Reaching Implications   283
ONKAR GHATE

The Arc of Liberalism: Locke, Mill, and Rand   304
ROBERT GARMONG

Part Four: The Nature and Foundations of Economic Freedom (and Its Opposite)

Economic Theory and Conceptions of Value: Rand and Austrians versus the Mainstream   327
ROBERT TARR

Mises, Rand, and the Twentieth Century   384
PETER J. BOETTKE

The Head, the Heart, and the Ethics of Capitalism: Response to Boettke   401
ROBERT GARMONG

The Aristocracy of Pull: An Objectivist Analysis of Cronyism   410
STEVE SIMPSON

Uniform Abbreviations for Rand's Works 429

References 433

Contributors 449

Index 453

NOTE ON THE SERIES

On August 30, 2013, only a few months after the publication of the previous volume in this series, Allan Gotthelf, its founding editor, passed away. From the beginning of our discussions with then University of Pittsburgh Press director Cynthia Miller in 2009, it was agreed that Allan would be the editor of the volumes in the series and that I would serve as associate editor. For the second volume in the series, we asked Gregory Salmieri to join us as consulting editor. For future volumes, Dr. Salmieri and I will play the role of series editors, and the editors of each volume will be selected on the basis of their expertise on the topic of that volume. For the present volume, then, Dr. Salmieri is joined by Robert Mayhew.

JAMES G. LENNOX
PITTSBURGH, SEPTEMBER 2018

FOUNDATIONS OF A FREE SOCIETY

Introduction

GREGORY SALMIERI

> If one wishes to advocate a free society—that is, capitalism—one must realize that its indispensable foundation is the principle of individual rights. If one wishes to uphold individual rights, one must realize that capitalism is the only system that can uphold and protect them.
> —"MAN'S RIGHTS" (*VOS* 108/*CUI* 367)

In several passages, including the one that stands as our epigraph, Ayn Rand writes interchangeably of "a free society" and "capitalism." She describes it as "a society of *traders*" ("Roots of War," *CUI* 34; original emphasis) and as an ideal that America and parts of Europe approached in the late nineteenth century, but which was abandoned and forgotten over the course of the twentieth (hence the title of her collection of essays on political philosophy: *Capitalism: The Unknown Ideal*).

> The creative energy, the abundance, the wealth, the rising standard of living for every level of the population were such that the nineteenth century looks like a fiction-Utopia, like a blinding burst of sunlight in the drab progression of most of human history. If life on earth is one's standard of value, then the nineteenth century moved mankind forward more than all the other centuries combined. ("Faith and Force," *PWNI* 89)

But, Rand thought, this free and prosperous society had never been properly understood and was rapidly being abandoned and forgotten, because the principles on which it depends were present only in a partial and implicit form in the work of early Enlightenment philosophers, and these

3

principles had been rejected by the intellectuals of eighteenth and nine-teenth centuries.

As is clear from our epigraph, Rand regarded the principle of indi-vidual rights as capitalism's indispensable foundation. Indeed, she de-fined capitalism as "a social system based on the recognition of individ-ual rights, including property rights, in which all property is privately owned" ("What Is Capitalism?" *CUI* 19). Thus, for Rand, capitalism is not simply an economic system; it is the wider system of social organization that includes the institutions of private property and a free market as ex-pressions of the same principle that guarantees the freedoms of speech, religion, and association protected by America's First Amendment. She wrote that "a free mind and a free market are corollaries" (*FTNI* 21) and that "a separation of state and economics" is needed "in the same way and for the same reasons as the separation of state and church" ("The Objec-tivist Ethics," *VOS* 37).

It is for this reason that Rand saw the advocacy of capitalism as the core of a political philosophy, rather than primarily or exclusively as a matter of economic theory. However, political philosophy is not self-sufficient; it depends on the other branches of philosophy. In particu-lar, Rand regarded the principle of individual rights as a bridge between morality and political philosophy, and she thought this principle pre-supposed deeper ethical convictions, which in turn presupposed certain metaphysical and epistemological foundations.

> I am not *primarily* an advocate of capitalism, but of egoism; and I am not *primarily* an advocate of egoism, but of reason. If one recognizes the su-premacy of reason and applies it consistently, all the rest follows." ("Brief Summary," *TO* 10:9 1089)

The first volume of the Ayn Rand Society's Philosophical Studies series, *Metaethics, Egoism, and Virtue: Studies in Ayn Rand's Normative Theory* (Gotthelf and Lennox 2011), explored Rand's defense of egoism and other aspects of her moral philosophy. The second volume, *Concepts and Their Role in Knowledge: Reflections on Objectivist Epistemology* (Gotthelf and Lennox 2013), focused on her theory of concepts, which is central to her advocacy of reason. In this third volume we turn to her political philosophy.

It is in this field that Rand's influence is most noticeable. The sixty years since the publication of *Atlas Shrugged* have seen a renewed enthusiasm for "capitalism," "free markets," "limited government," and "individual liberty," both among the general public and within academia. I put these terms in quotes because they are not always understood in the same ways by their sundry proponents, who are variously described (by themselves and others) as "conservative," "classical liberal," "neoliberal," or "libertarian." These labels are associated with different, overlapping groups of individuals, organizations, and positions, and each includes many people and ideas with which Rand emphatically disagreed; moreover, she denounced both the conservative and libertarian movements, and many members of these movements disparage her.[1]

Nonetheless, there is no denying that she has exerted an influence on present-day conservatism, and it is doubtful that the contemporary libertarian movement would exist if not for her large and passionate readership from which the movement continues to recruit. She is cited as an influence by many of those Republican politicians such as Paul Ryan, Rand Paul, and Ted Cruz who profess the most concern for limited government and free markets. The extent of her influence on late twentieth-century libertarianism can be inferred from the frequent references to her in the titles of publications from or about this movement. It is doubtful that a magazine advocating libertarian ideas would be called *Reason* if not for Rand's influence; and this influence is confirmed by its slogan "free minds and free markets," which is a paraphrase of a passage from Rand quoted earlier.[2] One sympathetic history of the libertarian movement, by Jerome Tuccille, is titled *It Usually Begins with Ayn Rand* (1971). A second, Brian Doherty's (2007) *Radicals for Capitalism: A Freewheeling History of the Modern Libertarian Movement*, takes its title from something Rand wrote in the first issue of her *Objectivist Newsletter* (1962):

> Objectivism is a philosophical movement; since politics is a branch of philosophy, Objectivism advocates certain political principles—specifically, those of laissez-faire capitalism—as the consequence and the ultimate practical application of its fundamental philosophical principles. It does not regard politics as a separate or primary goal, that is: as a goal that can be achieved without a wider ideological context.

1. On Rand's view of these movements, see Lewis and Salmieri (2016, 381–85) and the sources cited therein.

2. A Google Books search reveals that the pairing of the phrases "free mind" and "free market"—though not unheard of—was rare before Rand, and common thereafter, with many of the early 1960s instances of this pairing making reference to Rand.

Politics is based on three other philosophical disciplines: metaphysics, epistemology and ethics—on a theory of man's nature and of man's relationship to existence. It is only on such a base that one can formulate a consistent political theory and achieve it in practice. . . . Objectivists are not "conservatives." We are radicals for capitalism; we are fighting for that philosophical base which capitalism did not have and without which it was doomed to perish. ("Choose Your Issues," *TON* vol. 1, no. 1, 1)[3]

Although many conservative and libertarian thinkers take inspiration from Rand's novels and adopt some of her formulations, they rarely engage deeply with the "philosophical base" that she argued capitalism requires. Many whose passion for capitalism was ignited by her philosophical novels and essays nevertheless try to defend it solely on economic grounds. Of those who do recognize the need for a moral defense of capitalism, many dismiss her philosophy as confused or as insufficiently rigorous or simply as too controversial, and so they argue from more conventional positions in the foundational branches of philosophy—or from religion, in the case of many conservatives.

In the view of the editors of this volume, this is a mistake. Rand's unique ability to inspire people to appreciate capitalism stems from profound and nuanced insights into the facts of reality that give rise to the need for moral and political principles. These insights are easily overlooked by those who attempt to pigeonhole her into familiar categories—and who, finding that she defies such classification, assume that it is her ideas rather than the familiar categories that are confused. There must be many students of political philosophy who came to the subject with a conviction, instilled by Rand, that capitalism is the only moral social system, but who cannot articulate the basis of this conviction, and who have difficulty relating what they've gleaned from Rand with the defenses (and criticisms) of capitalism that they encounter in their courses.

I hope this book will be a resource for such students and for others interested in Objectivism or in political philosophy. It fills a significant gap in the scholarly literature on Rand. The philosophers who have put the most work into mastering her philosophical system and relating it to other positions in philosophy have generally focused on epistemology and the foundations of ethics, with the result that there has been com-

3. On Rand's formative influence on the contemporary libertarian movement, see also Burns (2009, 247–72).

paratively little quality work on her political philosophy. One sign of this is that, of the first twenty-four meetings of the Ayn Rand Society (ARS), only three concerned political philosophy.[4] By contrast, nine of our last twelve sessions have concerned political topics. This was largely because many of them were planned with the aim of generating material for the present volume, which brings together some of the most knowledgeable scholars and proponents of Rand's philosophy and puts them in conversation with other intellectuals who also see themselves as defenders of capitalism and individual liberty.

In the previous two volumes in the Ayn Rand Society Philosophical Studies series, the contributors who offered counterpoints to Rand's position held views that resemble hers in some way. This made their positions illuminating foils, and the exchanges threw some of the most distinctive features of Objectivism into sharp relief. We have followed the same approach here; but because of the factiousness that attends discussions of politics, and because of long-standing disputes about the relation between Objectivism and the various views that get labeled "libertarian," it is worth saying a little here about what the editors of this volume think unites the contributing authors and makes conversation among us profitable.

With respect to the aims of this book, what unites us is the view that there is something importantly correct (though perhaps also much mistaken) in Rand's political philosophy. This leads us to think that reflecting on this philosophy in conversation with one another can further our own understandings of what sort of society is best and why. Sadly, this view puts us in a minority within the broader scholarly community, which often looks on Rand with scorn. Because of this, there is an element of advocacy in the very project of giving Rand's ideas serious consideration, and so there is a way in which all the contributors to this volume can be regarded as comrades. It is a comradeship that extends beyond discussion of Rand to engagement with any of the loosely connected sets of thinkers and positions that are marginalized for some of the same reasons.

These are the thinkers and positions that I noted earlier are associ-

---

4. There have been several books on political philosophy by Objectivists and other authors who have thought comprehensively about Rand's philosophical system and acknowledge a deep debt to it. See, for example, Machan (1998), and some of Machan's earlier work; Smith (1995); Rasmussen and Den Uyl (1991, 2005). But even in these books, the authors do not engage as deeply and as explicitly with Rand's arguments as they do in their discussions of her ethics.

ated with such (overlapping) labels as "conservative," "classical liberal," "neoliberal," "neoclassical liberal," or "libertarian." Because most of these positions are outside the scholarly mainstream, and because they are related by various historical connections and by what my coeditor drolly terms a "dysfunctional family resemblance," proponents of these positions (and sympathetic scholars of these proponents) have some common interests and so form a loose-knit community. It does not follow from this, however, that there is any philosophical principle on which all the members of this community agree. Nor does it follow that we share any political goals or constitute any sort of movement.

Although all of the contributors to this volume think of ourselves as advocates of "liberty," our understandings of this and related terms differ. For example, some of us see (certain) anarchic societies as most fully embodying this ideal, whereas others (including the editors) agree with Rand that anarchy is a form of its antithesis; some of us (including the editors) reject the welfare state as anathema to a free society, whereas others have defended forms of state welfare spending. How one classifies such views and which of them one sees as essentially allied or opposed will depend on what issues one takes to be fundamental, and this will depend in part on where one stands on the issues themselves. Thus, it should come as no surprise that there is disagreement among us on issues of classification, terminology, and definition.[5] Readers will, of course, reach their own conclusions on such matters.

Turning now to more prosaic matters, this book consists of five parts. Part I comprises three chapters by Darryl Wright in which he treats the moral and epistemological foundations of Rand's politics by examining her view that reason cannot function under coercion, and showing how

---

5. Though many of our contributing authors have expressed opinions on these issues in other contexts, the only one to do so within the pages of this volume is Huemer, who defines "libertarians" as those who advocate for "*at most* minimal government"—i.e., a government "that is limited to protecting its citizens' negative rights, against both domestic criminals and hostile foreign governments" (237, below). This uniting of anarchism and the defense of limited government under a single concept would be reasonable if, as Huemer thinks, there is a significant commonality between these positions, which sets them apart from positions that accord a broader role to government. If not, the concept is what Rand called "a package-deal." On package-deals, see Salmieri (2016e, 297–98), Binswanger (2014, 236–39), and the sources cited in both. On "libertarianism" as a package deal, see also Salmieri (2016g); Lewis and Salmieri (2016, 381–82); Miller and Mossoff (2016, 194). Wherever one stands on the propriety of a concept defined along Huemer's lines, it should be noted that such a concept would exclude many "classical liberals" (and neoclassical liberals) who are sometimes regarded as libertarians.

this view provides the foundation for the principle that human beings must deal with one another by persuasion and trade rather than by force. The chapters are distant descendants of a paper titled "Reason and Freedom in Ayn Rand's Politics," which Wright presented at an ARS meeting in 1997. An expanded version was given as a lecture series two years later and for a time was available on audio cassette from Second Renaissance Books, but it has not been generally available for some time. I have always regarded these lectures as a high point in Rand scholarship and an important contribution to political philosophy, so I am very pleased at last to be able to make this material available to a wider audience in an improved and expanded form. The first of Wright's chapters identifies the role that the principle prohibiting the initiation of force plays in Rand's philosophy, the second elaborates and defends Rand's thesis that force "negates and paralyses" the mind, and the third examines Rand's justification for this principle and draws implications from this for its proper scope.

In the course of this exploration, Wright addresses several issues (and figures) that are prominent in the ongoing philosophical literature on libertarianism. Part II puts the central tenets of Rand's political philosophy in dialogue with this literature. The section begins with an essay by Fred Miller and Adam Mossoff expounding Rand's theory of rights and defending it against criticisms that have arisen from this literature. The essay was presented at an ARS meeting in 2014 along with Matthew Zwolinski's comments, a revised form of which follow it here. These comments raise questions about Rand's views on rights, force, and property, some of which I explore in the subsequent chapter.

The next two chapters, which derive from a 2013 ARS session, continue the discussion of Rand's view of rights, comparing her position to that of Robert Nozick. Lester Hunt considers Nozick's conception of rights as constraints on action that are grounded in respect for persons, and he suggests a view of the rationality of such constraints based on ideas from Rand and John Locke. Onkar Ghate takes a wider look at the relation between Rand and Nozik, showing how their differing views of nature, rights, and their role in political philosophy lead to different understandings of the moral justification of government and, consequently, to different responses to anarchism.

Questions about the moral foundations of liberty and the justification of government loom large in the next three chapters. The first, by Harry Binswanger, is an article from 1981 (with an addendum from 2011) in which he elaborates on Rand's objections to anarchism. The next two chapters derive from an exchange between Michael Huemer and Binswanger at a 2013 ARS session. Huemer criticizes Rand's egoism and her defense of what he calls "a minimal state." He rejects her arguments as flawed and her approach as rationalistic. In their place he recommends a defense of liberty based on what he calls "commonsense morality," and he considers briefly whether this commonsense morality favors anarchism or a minimal state. Binswanger's response discusses Rand's philosophical method and counters some of Huemer's objections to her ethical and political positions.

The seventeenth- and eighteenth-century liberal tradition that includes John Locke and the American Founders receives some attention in Parts I and II, but it moves to center stage in Part III, which focuses on the issue of intellectual freedom in this tradition and in Rand's political philosophy. Onkar Ghate examines Locke's, Jefferson's, and Madison's arguments for the separation of church and state and shows how Rand's view of the need to separate the state from both the church and the economy is an extension of their ideas. Robert Garmong argues in the following chapter that John Stuart Mill—who is the most prominent nineteenth-century exponent of the classical liberal tradition and is often cited as a champion of free speech—in fact represents a radical departure from Locke and a challenge to intellectual freedom. Garmong presents Rand as offering a response to Mill and a reinvigorated Lockean conception of liberty.

Part IV concerns Rand's relation to defenses of economic freedom by political theorists and economists—especially economists of the Austrian school. Robert Tarr argues that the essential difference between the Austrians and the classical and neoclassical schools is a distinctive conception of value, which is best articulated by Rand's characterization of value as *objective* rather than *intrinsic* (the view Tarr associates with classical economics) or *subjective* (the view he associates with the neoclassic school).

The next two chapters concern Rand and Mises. In a piece written for 2014 *ARS* sessions, Peter Boettke argues that Rand's literary portrayal and moral criticisms of socialism appeal to the "heart" and therefore provide a needed supplement to Mises's economic arguments, which appeal only to the "head." Writing in response, Robert Garmong acknowledges that there are important points of agreement between Mises and Rand, but he argues that the two are more different than Boettke allows, and that Mises's economic arguments are partially undercut by his failure to address the moral foundations of capitalism.

In the final chapter, Steve Simpson discusses Rand's view that government intrusion into the economy creates an "Aristocracy of Pull," in which officials have arbitrary power that they exercise at the behest of politically connected businesses to the detriment of their competitors. This, Simpson argues, is the true essence of the "cronyism" that many contemporary commentators on American politics decry.

Part One
REASON, FORCE, AND THE FOUNDATIONS OF POLITICS

The Place of the Non–Initiation of Force Principle in Ayn Rand's Philosophy

DARRYL WRIGHT

Toward the end of her seminal essay "The Objectivist Ethics," Ayn Rand states the following: "The basic political principle of the Objectivist Ethics is: no man may *initiate* the use of physical force against others. No man—or group or society or government—has the right to assume the role of a criminal and initiate the use of physical compulsion against any man. Men have the right to use physical force *only* in retaliation and *only* against those who initiate its use" (*VOS* 36; original emphasis). Let us call this the non–initiation of force principle.[1] The principle encompasses both the ban on initiated force and the (specifically limited) authorization of retaliatory force against initiators. Although this is Rand's basic political principle, the passage makes it clear that the principle's scope is wider than politics. It applies not only to the actions of government and the organization of societies but also, and equally, to the actions of individuals

I would like to thank Gregory Salmieri and two anonymous reviewers for helpful comments on a previous draft of this and the next two chapters.

1. For reasons that will be made clear later, I do not refer to this as the nonaggression principle, the standard designation of the core principle of libertarianism (from which movement Rand dissociated herself).

and groups both inside and outside of organized societies.[2] It is the basic political principle, for Rand, because it is in some sense the foundation of all her specifically political arguments and conclusions: not their ultimate foundation but, as we might put it, their proximal foundation—the principle nearest to politics, but wider than politics, on which (along with all of the other, deeper principles in Rand's philosophy) her political philosophy rests. The other principles that seem foundational in Rand's political philosophy are those involved in her account of individual rights. I will discuss the relation of that account to the non–initiation of force principle below.

The non–initiation of force principle itself raises a number of questions. How should it be understood? What specific kinds of actions does it prohibit? What is its justification in Rand's thought? Why is force coercive, and are there other forms of coercion, such as economic coercion? Why does Rand insist on the need for a complete ban on the initiation of physical force within human relationships, to the extent of prohibiting even many government actions that are widely regarded as legitimate, even essential, and whose status as initiations of force is controversial, such as economic regulation or redistribution? How is her principle related to the "nonaggression principle" espoused by libertarians? It would require a full-length book to do justice to all these questions, but in this chapter and the two that follow I will touch on all of them and extensively explore the core of her justification for the non–initiation of force principle.

Since Rand's approach to philosophy is holistic, a proper understanding of the principle requires us to see how it grows out of her more fundamental positions in ethics and epistemology, and this is my subject in the present chapter. Specifically, I aim to show how this principle is based in her ethics and relies on an account of the intellectual consequences of force that is shaped by her epistemological views. Accordingly, I will start by summarizing key themes from her ethics and eliciting her core argument for the main (prohibitory) part of the non–initiation of force principle. I go on to examine issues in her epistemology and end by exploring

2. I base this interpretation on the fact that Rand does not restrict the principle's scope by saying, for instance, that it only applies to governments or only within society. Peikoff acknowledges the principle's wide scope and fundamental status by discussing it in conjunction with Rand's theory of moral virtue, which in Rand's thought is epistemically prior to her political philosophy. See Peikoff 1991, 310–24.

Rand's conception of initiatory force, and some of the main forms that force can take. This exploration raises questions about the effects of force on the mind and about the scope of the non–initiation of force principle, which I discuss in the next two chapters, respectively.

1. Rand's Justification of Moral Principles

The non–initiation of force principle is a moral principle, for Rand. So let us consider how, in general, she justifies moral principles; and how, more particularly, she justifies moral principles pertaining to our treatment of others. Not all moral principles are other-directed, in her view, but some are, and this one clearly is.

On Rand's view, moral evaluation has a teleological basis. We elucidate that basis by asking why moral values are *necessary* for us. In the deepest sense, Rand holds, the need for moral values derives from the fact that we are *living organisms* of a particular kind. All living organisms must pursue specific *values*—specific goals, appropriate to their nature and needs—in order to maintain their lives; a living organism exists through goal-directed action. This is true even for plants, although their goal pursuit is not conscious and purposive, as it is for animals. Our similar need to pursue specific values in order to live is the ultimate basis, according to Rand, for all of the values and forms of evaluation that figure into our lives.

Living organisms as such do not pursue moral values, of course, nor could they. An animal relies on instinctual knowledge and values to act successfully within its environment; for example, to recognize and pursue its appropriate food and to recognize and evade predators. Further, not only does an animal's consciousness equip it with automatic values pertaining to its actions in the world but the functioning of its consciousness is itself governed by certain automatic values, in the sense that, by nature, the animal is motivated to attend to its environment and act on what it perceives; it cannot choose not to do these things. Rand writes that an animal's senses "provide it with an *automatic* code of values, an automatic knowledge of what is good for it or evil, what benefits or endangers its life. An animal has no power to extend its knowledge or to evade it. In situations for which its knowledge is inadequate, it perishes. . . . But so long as it lives, an animal acts on its knowledge, with automatic safety and no power of choice: it cannot suspend its own consciousness—it cannot choose *not* to perceive—it cannot evade its own perceptions—it cannot ignore its own good" (*VOS* 20; original emphasis). An animal cannot evade the knowledge, or act against the values, that its nature equips it with. It has no ability to act on a momentary whim, to drift purposelessly, to surrender its good in a moment of cowardice, or to neglect the work its life requires, such as seeking food or building a nest. Its genetic programming automatically maintains the right kind of relation between its consciousness and reality, setting it on a reality-oriented, purposive, consistent course, suited for maintaining the animal's life across its lifespan. External factors can threaten or destroy it, but within its power, the animal by nature does its best for itself.[3]

The integrity of the relation between an animal's consciousness and reality is protected by its genetic coding. But human consciousness, according to Rand, is volitional. Its functioning is not determined by our genetics (though its capacities and the requirements of its proper functioning are). We must create the equivalent state in ourselves—in our souls—a state that can underwrite the basic kinds of cognitive and existential actions that our lives require over their entire span. This, according to Rand, is the proper function of a moral code. Moral virtues (or principles), she says, "pertain to the relation of existence and consciousness" (*Atlas* 1018).[4] Fundamentally, Rand holds, it is our moral code that either enables us to project, produce, and achieve the range of other values, material and spiritual, that we need in our lives or prevents us from doing so.[5]

3. This might seem to ignore the so-called altruistic aspects of much animal behavior. Properly understood, however, I do not think the behavior referred to by that term contradicts any of Rand's claims about the ways in which animals function. In my view, at least for most species of animals, there is no real distinction to be made between the interests of an individual animal and the interests of its kind (species, subpopulation, or whatever the reference group might be, in a given case, for the other-regarding behavior that people have in mind by the term "altruism"). A seagull acts as a member of its kind and seeks what is good for a standard member of its kind.

4. Although she frames her ethics partly in terms of certain virtues, Rand does not make a sharp separation between virtues and principles. The virtues are specified in terms of principles, and people's characters depend most basically on the principles they are committed to. See *Atlas* 1018–21, and "The Objectivist Ethics," *VOS* 27–30 (on virtues); "Causality versus Duty," *PWNI* 133 and *ITOE* 33 (on moral principles).

5. Rand uses the terms "morality" and "ethics" interchangeably. In the narrower sense of "moral" in which Bernard Williams criticizes morality, the terms are not interchangeable, and her ethics rejects some of the features that Williams associates with what he calls "the morality system" (see Williams 1985, 177 and ch. 10). But she does not reject everything that has been identified with this narrower sense of moral. For example, she is perfectly at home speaking of moral laws—which she interprets as rational principles hypothetically linked to

Let us now consider, more specifically, Rand's views of the role of principles in ethics. Principles, in her view, are necessary for evaluating specific actions. In some sense every normative ethical theory must agree with this. We evaluate an action by bringing it under whatever principles the theory proposes as the criterion of right and wrong. Even if what is right depends, say, on what the virtuous person would do in a particular situation, this is a kind of principle.

But Rand makes a more specific claim about the need for principles. All normative ethical theories must have some overall criterion of right and wrong. But the status of secondary principles that are subordinate to this overall criterion has been contentious in teleological theories. On some views, such principles are at best rules of thumb that can be overridden by judgments about particular cases. What Rand claims, however, is that, even though the basis of her ethics is teleological, we have no way of evaluating the relation of a given action to the ultimate end independently of secondary principles. There is no way for us to simply inspect the action and determine straightaway how it relates to our lives. In order to do that, we first require broad teleological principles pertaining to the fundamental requirements of any human being's life. Since these requirements, as Rand conceives them, are moral requirements, the basic principles that we require are moral ones.

Moral principles enable us to grasp the long-range tendencies of specific ways of functioning cognitively and existentially. They provide a framework for constituting one's life so that it will be self-sustaining. In evaluating an action *morally*, the concern is not with its specific effects but with how well it fits into such a framework.

For Rand, moral principles maintain our lives in another respect also. They are a precondition of the self-esteem that one needs in order to live.[6] Animals value themselves automatically, by virtue of being constituted to act self-sustainingly. But human beings do not; self-loathing is possible for us. What determines self-esteem, according to Rand, is whether one's life fits one's own conception of a properly human life and whether that conception is grounded in the facts of human nature in such

---

the long-range requirements of a person's life—and her ethics includes conceptions of moral goodness and evil that do not reduce to the contrast between the admirable and the base but include a willful, deliberate element under the agent's direct control. Like other theorists of morality in Williams's pejorative sense, Rand sees morality/ethics as carving out a sphere of evaluation that is, in Williams's words, "immune to luck" (Williams 1981, 20).

6. On the need for self-esteem, see *Atlas* 1056–57.

a way that it can withstand the test of its being put into practice. Your self-esteem will suffer if you recognize yourself as acting against your accepted (perhaps implicitly so) moral principles or if you act on principles that you profess to accept but cannot honestly endorse, in view of their actual consequences.

The justification of specific moral principles, according to Rand, must proceed by reference to a developed account of human nature. Since the justification of the non–initiation of force principle will rely on some of this ethical content, I will briefly sketch some key elements of her account and the principles they lead to. She holds that reason—conceptual thought—is our means of survival; we must use our minds to develop the knowledge and values that our lives require, and to guide all aspects of our lives. Further, the values we require include material values, and these must be both envisioned and produced, a process that requires rational thought and purposive action at every stage and is central to a properly human form of existence.

Besides providing for our material needs, in Rand's view, rational productive activity satisfies crucial spiritual needs. Psychologically, one's basic choice is the choice to think—to activate one's mind purposively: "The choice to think or not is volitional [that is, under one's direct and immediate control, and non-necessitated]. If an individual's choice is predominantly negative, the result is his self-arrested mental development, a self-made cognitive malnutrition, a stagnant, eroded, impoverished, anxiety-ridden inner life" ("Our Cultural Value-Deprivation," *VOR* 102). If, on the other hand, one's choice is positive, one experiences a sense of control and mastery and a sense of self-esteem that flows from one's implicit awareness of oneself as functioning in humanly appropriate ways (that is, on humanly appropriate principles).

For a conceptual being, the activity of living has directly experienced spiritual value. Rand's term for this value is joy—and when it is a stable and lasting undertone of one's life, happiness. One achieves this value by living in accordance with the long-range requirements of one's survival; the individual she describes in the passage above is precluded from accessing it. In Rand's view, it is the spiritual value of living that provides the motive to live and the purpose of living. Material survival is not an end in itself for us, apart from the spiritual purposes to which it is directed; it is not an end one could choose for its own sake. Unless one could experience one's life as a value, the choice to live would be purposeless.

But choice, for Rand, always requires a purpose to motivate and direct it.[7] Material survival can be valued only as integral to (and, in that sense, for the sake of) happiness, and rational productive activity is important for us not only because it secures our material well-being but because it is the foundation of happiness.

Rand elaborates this point in answering a question about why a wealthy entrepreneur should continue to work:

> When I say man survives by means of his mind, I mean that man's first moral virtue is to think and to be productive. That is not the same as saying: "Get your pile of money by hook or by crook, and then sit at home and enjoy it." You assume rational self-interest is simply ensuring one's physical luxury. But what would a man do with himself once he has those millions. He would stagnate. No man who has used his mind enough to achieve a fortune is going to be happy doing nothing. His self-interest does not lie in consumption but in production—in the creative expansion of his mind.
>
> To go deeper, observe that in order to exist, every part of an organism must function; if it doesn't, it atrophies. This applies to a man's mind more than to any other faculty. In order actually to be alive properly, a man must use his mind constantly and productively. That's why rationality is the basic virtue according to my morality. Every achievement is an incentive for the next achievement. What for? The creative happiness of achieving greater and greater control over reality, greater and more ambitious values in whatever field a man is using his mind. . . .
>
> Man's survival is not about having to think in order to survive physically for this moment. To survive properly, man must think constantly. Man cannot survive automatically. The day he decides he no longer needs to be creative is the day he's dead spiritually. (*Answers* 29–30)

The above gives us some of the grounds for Rand's claim that rationality and productiveness are cardinal moral virtues, which express and maintain the moral values of reason and purpose. In her view, a principled approach to human survival must begin by recognizing these values and virtues. She characterizes these virtues, in part, as follows:

7. She discusses the relation of choice and purpose in the question-and-answer period following a lecture presenting a version of her essay "The Objectivist Ethics." The recording is available from the Ayn Rand Institute eStore. The relevant answer begins at 1:06:46. Her comments about choice begin at 1:08:22.

The virtue of *Rationality* means the recognition and acceptance of reason as one's only source of knowledge, one's only judge of values and one's only guide to action. It means one's total commitment to a state of full, conscious awareness, to the maintenance of a full mental focus in all issues, in all choices, in all of one's waking hours. It means a commitment to the fullest perception of reality within one's power and to the constant, active expansion of one's perception, *i.e.*, of one's knowledge. It means a commitment to the reality of one's own existence, *i.e.*, to the principle that all of one's goals, values and actions take place in reality and, therefore, that one must never place any value or consideration whatsoever above one's perception of reality. ("The Objectivist Ethics," *VOS* 28)

Productiveness is your acceptance of morality, your recognition of the fact that you choose to live—that productive work is the process by which man's consciousness controls his existence, a constant process of acquiring knowledge and shaping matter to fit one's purpose, of translating an idea into physical form, of remaking the earth in the image of one's values—that *all* work is creative work if done by a thinking mind, and no work is creative if done by a blank who repeats in uncritical stupor a routine he has learned from others—that your work is yours to choose, and the choice is as wide as your mind, that nothing more is possible to you and nothing less is human—that to cheat your way into a job bigger than your mind can handle is to become a fear-corroded ape on borrowed motions and borrowed time, and to settle down into a job that requires less than your mind's full capacity is to cut your motor and sentence yourself to another kind of motion: decay—that your work is the process of achieving your values, and to lose your ambition for values is to lose your ambition to live. (*Atlas* 1020)

Rationality, as Rand views it, is not incompatible with spontaneity and emotion, but it does require that these be informed and guided by a background of rational judgment. To simply surrender reason, to any extent, is to act blindly. Productiveness does not require constant work, but it requires a purposive approach to life and full use of one's mind; it requires that one seek to grow, both intellectually and in the range and caliber of one's activities.[8] The primary vice, for Rand, is irrationality and, particularly, any form of psychological evasion—of refusing to recognize salient facts, or attempting to distort them:

8. See, in this connection, *Atlas* 721–22.

[Man's] basic vice, the source of all his evils, is that nameless act which all of you practice, but struggle never to admit: the act of blanking out, the willful suspension of one's consciousness, the refusal to think—not blindness, but the refusal to see; not ignorance, but the refusal to know. It is the act of unfocusing your mind and inducing an inner fog to escape the responsibility of judgment—on the unstated premise that a thing will not exist if only you refuse to identify it, that A will not be A so long as you do not pronounce the verdict "It *is*." (*Atlas* 1017)

In formulating moral principles, we must suppose a context in which those principles are substantially reciprocated and set the terms for the functioning of a society. That is, we could not invalidate a principle requiring productiveness by noting that productive people fare badly in a totalitarian dictatorship since they are exploited and expropriated, whereas unproductive people will receive their rations anyway. The primary question of interest pertains to the basic at-large requirements of human survival. Discussion of emergencies or other extreme kinds of nonideal contexts, for Rand, must follow an inquiry into this primary question. The same applies to free riding; we must know the primary principles—the principles that even a free rider depends on some critical mass of others choosing to follow—in order to address that issue.

But the issue of free riding does deserve comment here, since it arises in regard to force. Productiveness may be the best principle overall, but in a society of productive people might one, as an individual, perhaps do better for oneself by free riding on others' efforts in some way or another, through conniving financial schemes, Mafioso tactics, or whatever? Mightn't some people, for instance, be able to live a wealthier and more luxurious life by such means than they otherwise could? Here I want to say something about Rand's *method* of approaching this kind of question.

This looks like a question being asked from argumentatively neutral territory. Mightn't free riding be the best way to get what one wants and needs in life? Perhaps not, but perhaps so—we must find out which. No questions seem to have been begged in raising the issue. But that's not quite true, because the framing of the issue at least comes very close to assuming that the items sought by free riders really do have value for them, with the issue being whether their means of acquiring those values are the best ones available. But this is a substantive assumption, and one that Rand, at least, rejects. On her view, the items do not have value for the free riders simply because they want them, and if they want them, say, to prove to themselves and others that they are "just as good as those rich bastards who think they're so smart," or for the sheer pleasure of denting someone else's achievements, then these items are certainly not good for the free riders, for they would fuel their character defects and play into an ultimately self-destructive way of functioning.

The usual way of posing the question about free riders assumes that the value of something, for a person, is independent of the means by which it is acquired. In Rand's view, however, something's value depends on its relation to moral principles, and to that extent depends on the means of its acquisition.[9] Something functions as a value for a person only if that person pursues and utilizes it in the course of a self-sustaining process of action. Moral principles specify the essential requirements of such a process for human beings. So, on the one hand, an item will have value for a person only if it is gained and kept by moral means; the assessment of value is dependent on a correct theory of morality. And, on the other hand, when we consider a moral question such as whether it is permissible for one to gain a given item by a certain means (say, by theft), the value of the particular item to oneself *in that action context* cannot be presupposed. For the question being asked is whether theft can be part of the process by which human beings successfully gain and benefit from values. To assume the item's value on the way to answering this question is to beg the question.

So it cannot be assumed that the specific items the free riders want (such as wealth and luxuries) are good for them. It must be asked whether their way of pursuing those things has a place in a *type of life* that is good for them, and this for Rand comes down to whether it is a life that can actually sustain them. If such a life requires the virtue of productiveness, then the answer to this question is clearly "no." But is this virtue necessary for everyone? It is true that there must be a critical mass of people who produce what the free rider seeks to consume, or else free riding cannot be a viable means of existence. It might also be said, as Rand does, that free riders eventually destroy their victims and thereby themselves— that this is the long-range tendency of their actions. But the deeper issue,

9. She applies this perspective to the virtue of honesty at *Atlas* 1019. She applies the same kind of analysis to questions of public policy in her essay "Collectivized Ethics" (*VOS* 93–99). Below, I discuss further Rand's view of moral principles and her conceptions of objective value and evaluation.

THE PLACE OF THE NON-INITIATION OF FORCE PRINCIPLE IN AYN RAND'S PHILOSOPHY   ▪   25

in Rand's view, is that free riders depend on what she calls the "sanction of the victim," the victims' acceptance of a moral code that legitimizes the free rider's exploitative activities. The code that serves this purpose, according to Rand, is "altruism," understood as a moral view that denigrates the pursuit of self-interest and requires sacrifice of self for others.[10] The acceptance of altruism, she holds, is what causes the productive members of society to tolerate legalized control and expropriation by the state for the purported benefit of those in need. (We will return to this point below, in connection with Rand's discussion of the non-initiation of force principle.) So if we are not to act blindly, with no way of grasping the long-term significance of our actions for our lives, we must reject the life of free riding. A society of morally confident productive individuals, who value their own lives and property, has no problem making crime a bad bargain for the perpetrators. And if society's members consider self-interested productive activity paradigmatically moral, as her ethical theory encourages them to do, then they will not accept legalized expropriation by the state. Even in the short run, then, free riders' success depends on their victims' inability to recognize their own moral stature—that is, their inability to recognize their own virtues as such, as well as their rejection of their moral right to live for their own sake (the very goal that purportedly underlies the free rider's own actions). In the absence of the sanction of the victim, Rand holds, the free rider's form of life cannot succeed even in the short term.[11]

These points shed light on Rand's egoism also. The sense in which she holds that it is in one's self-interest to be moral is that it is in one's interests as a human being; and in order to live a viable life each of us must define our own specific interests and values according to that standard—the principled, long-range requirements of a human life as such. Rand does not try to show the free riders (taking them and their values *just as they are*) that morality is good for them; what she tells them is that they had better change the way in which they value things and change themselves—change their basic way of functioning—if they want to live.

10. On Rand's use of the concept of "sacrifice," see "The Ethics of Emergencies" (*VOS* 49–56). On her use of altruism, see "Faith and Force: Destroyers of the Modern World," *PWNI* 83–84; also Salmieri 2016c, 136–41; Wright 2011b.

11. The "sanction of the victim" is a major theme of *Atlas Shrugged*. See especially *Atlas* part 2, chapter 4.

2. The Trader Principle versus Force

Returning to Rand's substantive ethical views, the positive counterpart to the non–initiation of force principle is what she calls the "trader principle." She writes: "The principle of *trade* is the only rational ethical principle for all human relationships, personal and social, private and public, spiritual and material. It is the principle of *justice*" (*VOS* 34). As this passage indicates, she uses the term "trade" in a somewhat broader than usual sense, so that the term encompasses both material exchange and personal relationships (such as love or friendship) that are mutually beneficial spiritually. The availability of a fully viable alternative social principle will be important in the justification of the non–initiation of force principle, since otherwise it might be held that force, whatever objections it may face, is a necessary means of human interaction.

Trade reflects a particular view of the ways in which interacting with other human beings can benefit someone's life. Fundamentally, trade made possible the development of knowledge and material values on a vastly expanded scale in contrast with what could be attained by one's own isolated action. To engage with others by trade is to participate in that process of development, and to derive one's sustenance from one's own participation. The premise of trade relationships, therefore, is that one benefits from social interaction by virtue of the opportunity it provides to sustain oneself in this way.

In trade, each person gains (in principle) from the success of others.[12] The productive abilities of one's trading partners expand one's own opportunities to specialize and to leverage the advantages of specialization to expand one's own production. In an environment of constantly expanding and diversifying productive activity, the market for one's own products expands (to the extent of one's ability to judge the market accurately). The wider and more variegated the range of other producers, the greater is one's own freedom to allow spiritual considerations—what

12. The force of "in principle" here is to exclude the sorts of missteps and setbacks that are endemic in human life simply because one's judgment is not infallible and accidents and emergencies can arise. These facts are part of the ineliminable background of human life in any configuration, but Rand makes two points about them that are relevant here: (1) metaphysically, accidents and emergencies are exceptional and can be minimized through human efforts; (2) missteps and setbacks arising from mistakes in judgment can generally be recovered from over time. These points are applicable, she holds, only in a free society, however, which protects its citizens from predation by others and otherwise leaves them able to function and provide for themselves.

one finds interesting and intellectually satisfying—to guide one's choice of specialization.

In a fully free society, Rand argues, one's participation in trade relationships makes it possible in principle to amply satisfy one's material needs and desires.[13] The development and application of one's productive abilities in a chosen area of work provides the foundation for satisfying one's spiritual needs, especially the need for self-esteem and for a sense of meaning and purpose.[14] Living as a trader thus provides a context not only for maintaining one's life but for the successful pursuit of happiness.

In trade relationships, according to Rand, there are no basic conflicts of interest among the participants. Each is free to take self-sustaining action. Moreover, since the production of material values is, in principle, unlimited, one may face competitive disadvantages in particular areas, but the success of others presents no fundamental obstacle to one's own. Since trade relationships are premised on the need to deal with others "by mutual consent to mutual advantage" (as judged by each of the parties), these relationships allow each participant to act as and be treated as an end in himself (*VOS* 34–35).

On Rand's view, trade relationships flow from and express the virtue of rationality. One of the central themes of *Atlas Shrugged* is that productive activity is rational activity. The producer must envision a product or service, evaluate it as good and beneficial, learn or devise the means of bringing it into reality (including the theoretical knowledge on which its production depends), communicate its existence to potential buyers, and organize its distribution. Each step involves an exercise of reason on some level.[15] It expresses and depends on one's capacity for abstract thought, evaluative judgment, creative imagination, long-range planning,

13. Those who, because of chance factors, are unable to do this through their own efforts must rely on support from others, but this will be true in any form of social interaction. The primary question, therefore, according to Rand, is how those of normal ability in (metaphysically) normal circumstances should maintain their lives.

14. On these issues, see *Atlas* 90, 220, 240–41, 988, 996–97. Rand argues that both art and personal relationships are necessary for satisfying other crucial spiritual needs, and that trade relationships create a social context in which the production of works of art can be sustained. Although our concern here is primarily with economic trade, Rand holds that proper, nonexploitative personal relationships are based on a spiritual analogue of trade, in which each party gains spiritual benefits from the relationship. For discussion, see "The Objectivist Ethics," *VOS* 34–35, and "The Ethics of Emergencies," *VOS* 49–56; *Atlas* 1033; Wright 2016.

15. In a highly specialized economy, most people do not perform all or even most of these tasks, and they do not perform them single-handedly but within an organization that employs many people. Nevertheless, Rand argues, each person's work counts as productive

and other, related rational capacities.[16] By facilitating specialization and division of labor, trade expands the life-enhancing process of applying reason in the world.

Further, in trade relationships, one does not expect others' automatic agreement or cooperation. In that sense, trade reflects a recognition that knowledge and value judgments are not automatic but depend on a self-initiated process of thought. A trader accepts the responsibility of making a case to those from whom she seeks agreement or cooperation—of appealing to their minds and submitting her own judgment to their rational scrutiny. This attitude constitutes the social expression of a commitment to objectivity. It reflects the view that since the acquisition of knowledge depends on the individual application of specific cognitive methods, an agreement between two people on any claim must proceed from the independent (but potentially collaborative) thinking of each party. Discussion and persuasion are the means by which trade relationships are established and maintained.

These kinds of considerations lead Rand to the conclusion that the trader principle respects and supports the long-range requirements of man's survival. Because of its connection to rationality, the trader principle is a moral principle, in her view; in upholding the principle one maintains the right basic relation of one's mind to reality. By contrast, Rand holds that the initiator of force perverts both the relation between her own mind and reality and the relation between her victim's mind and reality. We can see this from the main passage in which she discusses the non–initiation of force principle. The passage comes from Galt's radio speech in *Atlas Shrugged*, and I will reproduce it here in full:

> Whatever may be open to disagreement, there is one act of evil that may not, the act that no man may commit against others and no man may sanction or forgive. So long as men desire to live together, no man may *initiate*—do you hear me? no man may *start*—the use of physical force against others.
>
> To interpose the threat of physical destruction between a man and his perception of reality, is to negate and paralyze his means of survival;

since she must contribute something that is of value to her employer, and each person's activity demands that she use her mind in some way and to some extent. See *Atlas* 1020; "The Objectivist Ethics," *VOS* 25–29; *Atlas* 327–28; also Salmieri 2009.

16. Rand also regards artistic creation as a rational process. See *RM* chs. 1–3 and *AOF* ch. 1. Also see below, "Force and the Mind," section 1.

to force him to act against his own judgment, is like forcing him to act against his own sight. Whoever, to whatever purpose or extent, initiates the use of force, is a killer acting on the premise of death in a manner wider than murder: the premise of destroying man's capacity to live.

Do not open your mouth to tell me that your mind has convinced you of your right to force my mind. Force and mind are opposites; morality ends where a gun begins. When you declare that men are irrational animals and propose to treat them as such, you define thereby your own character and can no longer claim the sanction of reason—as no advocate of contradictions can claim it. There can be no 'right' to destroy the source of rights, the only means of judging right and wrong: the mind.

To force a man to drop his own mind and to accept your will as a substitute, with a gun in place of a syllogism, with terror in place of proof, and death as the final argument—is to attempt to exist in defiance of reality. Reality demands of man that he act for his own rational interest; your gun demands of him that he act against it. Reality threatens man with death if he does not act on his rational judgment; you threaten him with death if he does. You place him into a world where the price of his life is the surrender of all the virtues required by life—and death by a process of gradual destruction is all that you and your system will achieve, when death is made to be the ruling power, the winning argument in a society of men.

Be it a highwayman who confronts a traveler with the ultimatum: 'Your money or your life,' or a politician who confronts a country with the ultimatum: 'Your children's education or your life,' the meaning of that ultimatum is: 'Your mind or your life'—and neither is possible to man without the other. (*Atlas* 1023)

The fulcrum of argument in this passage is the compound claim that to make a demand backed by a threat of force "is to negate and paralyze [the recipient's] means of survival"—that is, her mind, her reason. I discuss each part of this claim in detail in the next chapter. But it is clear from the passage's structure that the argument rests significantly on this claim about how force works, which I will refer to as Rand's analysis of force. In the next paragraph, she argues in effect that there is a fallacy of self-exclusion involved in claims that anyone is rationally justified in initiating force. I discuss this argument below, also.

The polemical third paragraph is not unimportant, but the main part of the argument for the non-initiation of force principle comes in the fourth paragraph. This material clearly depends on the analysis of force broached in the second paragraph; it will fall flat without this analysis to support it. So our subsequent examination of the "negation" and "paralysis" claims will be important. But to have significance those claims by themselves must be utilized in a further argument, and this is what the material in the fourth paragraph does.

Rand says that, because force hampers its victims' "capacity to live," it puts them in conflict with the unalterable requirements of their survival. To this extent, its results are destructive. But she also claims that the initiation of force constitutes, for the initiator, an "attempt to live in defiance of reality." That is, she claims that the initiator defies reality by forcing others to live in conflict with what reality requires of them, if they are to survive. In what way is the initiator defying reality here? Since Rand says that "death by a process of gradual destruction is *all* that you and your system will achieve" (italics added), it is clear that she does not think the initiator can ultimately achieve any values by means of force, either for herself or for others. To obtain values from someone by coercion, the values have to exist. But the source of material values and all other human values, Rand claims, is a person's freedom to form and act on her rational judgment. A policy of force, therefore, is systematically self-undermining. It progressively weakens the very engines of value-creation on which it relies to achieve its stated goals.

This is a more capacious argument than the narrowly tailored argument against a particular sort of free rider briefly sketched above, which focused on the self-destructive nature of specific and relatively superficial motives for using force. The argument here considers what Rand regards as the essential nature of any initiation of force, in any form and on any scale, whether by private individuals or by governments. Further, the central issue, from Rand's perspective, is not just that force presents a free rider problem and thus cannot function as a principle of human interaction (along the lines of "it is always permissible to resort to force to achieve one's goals"). This idea is present in the passage, and it is true that this principle could not be the basis of a society but would have to be practiced only at the margins, or else no one would be producing the goods or earning the wealth that free riders want to get their hands on. But the passage mainly deals with a different and more fundamental issue.

It is widely recognized that if coercion goes too far (if, say, the government's economic regulations become too onerous), then producers will withdraw, since their production will no longer be profitable or even just because the regulatory compliance is exasperating. But the problem is usually presented as if it were exclusively a matter of motivation, and as if the solution to the problem were simply to ensure that regulation (or taxation or whatever) is well enough contained that the damage to economic incentives is tolerable. Similarly, it is recognized that government control of speech and the press can have a "chilling effect," destroying the incentive to write and speak. From this, the conclusion is drawn that the regulation of expression must at least be kept within certain narrow bounds.

But Rand's argument goes beyond these motivational points. What she claims is that force, including especially governmental force, has the effect of interfering with rational thought and "destroying man's capacity to live." Force, she holds, prevents its victims from doing what is *metaphysically necessary* for their survival. Further, as was noted above, since the initiator is precisely counting on the survival capacities of these victims, her act of force constitutes an "attempt to live in defiance of reality." Now Rand holds that those who live by force grasp, at some level, that they are defying reality, and yet they remain defiant. Her explanation for this is that, at the deepest level, they do not actually want to live—their fundamental motive is to destroy (*Atlas* 1013, 1024–25, 1133–46). But insofar as they go on acting, their manner of existence constitutes defiance of reality.

The fourth paragraph of the passage thus presents force as a major form of irrationality, and thus as a violation of a cardinal moral requirement. It is the irrationality of force that constitutes the basis of its moral prohibition. (The basis for its legal prohibition will be that it is only through retaliatory force that one can protect oneself from its initiation; one cannot respond to it by persuasion or by walking away.)

What does Rand's argument have to say about the victims of initiated force? If the moral objection to force is that it violates the virtue of rationality, then the damage done to the victims seems morally significant only insofar as the initiator of the force needs them intact in order to go on existing himself. There would seem then to be no sense in which the initiator had wronged *them*—only, perhaps, a sense in which he has wronged *himself*.

But Rand's ethics does have a way of explaining the wrong done to these victims. As a whole, the passage presents the initiation of force as a violation of the principles that must be observed "so long as men desire to live together." It is implicit in the argument of the passage that a social existence (living together) is desirable for human beings. The non-initiation of force principle is presented as one of the principles on which the benefits of a social existence depend. The wrong done to others lies in the violation of those principles; that is, the harm done to the victim of (initiated) force wrongs her qua violating these principles. The complaint that can be made by the victims of force against the initiators arises from the standpoint of their shared human interest in a certain kind of social interaction, which the initiation of force undermines. If human nature were different and, somehow, the good of the initiators required the sacrifice of their victims, then perhaps the latter would have no basis to complain. But if what human good requires is production and trade, then such a basis exists, and in that sense the victims have been wronged.

It might be objected, however, that there is no reason to suppose the use of coercion cannot be kept within carefully chosen limits, so it can accomplish some good without becoming oppressive and destructive. Perhaps, in a totalitarian dictatorship, the kind of widespread destruction that Rand envisions is unavoidable in the long run (and those perpetrating it are irrational in the double sense just explained). But her argument is also directed, for example, against the regulatory welfare state, which for all its coerciveness has not crippled human innovation and survival. We might cite the examples of Greece, Spain, and other advanced welfare states to argue the contrary—the trend of their policies is precisely toward the progressive impoverishment and demoralization of everyone. There is, however, a deeper point to make here also. The point of using force against others is to avoid the necessity of engaging with their *reasons* for action—regardless of those reasons' basis in reality—and to avoid the necessity of subjecting one's own reasons to critical scrutiny, in a process of discussion and persuasion. In this sense, the use of force involves a flight from reality, a wish to escape the constraints of realistic necessity; as such, it pushes against attempts to limit it. Further, the claim that force can be used to accomplish good ends, and can be limited by that objective, depends on a certain view of the good, which Rand will reject. I will return to this issue later in the essay.

The same response applies if we focus the objection on an individual who attempts to exist by force rather than on a social system. Rand says elsewhere that such "looters" drain and destroy their victims and then, as a result, destroy themselves because there is nobody left to loot (see *VOS* 25–26). Eric Mack has objected, however, that this assumes these looters must engage in wanton force, without consideration of consequences. If, instead, we suppose that they use force selectively and judiciously, so as not to destroy the productive capacities and motivations of their victims, then their method of survival looks much more viable (see Mack 2013, 113–14). But for the reasons given above, I think that Mack fails to appreciate force's internal logic. To be careful and judicious requires, first of all, respecting reality and the means by which we gain knowledge of reality; in the practical realm, according to Rand, it means defining reality-based principles of action, based on the need we have for such principles— namely, the necessity of acting by principle if we are to maintain and enjoy our lives. The looters' intolerance of discussion, persuasion, and trade reflects a deeper intolerance of this sort of rational cognition.

3. The Epistemic Background of the Non–Initiation of Force Principle

Rand's analysis of force claims that the initiation of force negates and paralyses the human mind. What this means, more specifically, is that it negates and paralyzes the mind's *cognitive* activities—its activities of thinking and acquiring knowledge (which I will often refer to as cognition, following Rand's usage). In addition, Rand makes further claims (which I outlined in the preceding section) about the relation of force and reason and the relation of force and the good. She advances this set of claims on the basis of certain views about the nature of cognition and knowledge and their role in human life. In this section, I will sketch those views, for the purpose of making her claims about force clear. My aim here is not to ascertain which specific premises are required to support which claims about force but, simply, to give an overview of the picture of thinking and knowing that informs Rand's various statements about the nature and effects of force.[17] Various elements of this picture will assume importance as we proceed.

Rand's epistemological views reflect two *realist* theses, one metaphysical and one epistemological: (1) that reality exists, and is what it is, independently of any conscious being's awareness or beliefs; (2) that this independent reality can be known and that human beings do in fact have substantial knowledge of it. In regard to the structure of knowledge, she is a foundationalist. The foundation of knowledge, for her, lies in perception, on which, in various ways, all conceptual knowledge is based.

Rand takes perceptual states to be *preconceptual cognitive states*. The

---

17. There has been some excellent recent scholarship on Rand's epistemology, to which those seeking a more in-depth discussion can refer. See, in particular, the essays by Gotthelf, Salmieri, Ghate, and Lennox in Gotthelf and Lennox 2013, part 1; Binswanger 2014; Salmieri 2016e.

conjunction of these two attributes has been thought to raise problems, because it has been assumed that preconceptual states cannot afford material for inference and therefore cannot be cognitive. This has often been seen as an insurmountable problem for foundationalist epistemologies that treat perception as the foundation of knowledge. But she argues that perception, viewed along direct realist lines, provides material for a norm-guided process of concept-formation and application, which in turn provides material for inference—particularly, inductive inference. Conceptual classifications provide the first step toward inductive generalizations about the characteristics and behavior of particular kinds of existents (and these in turn are the basis for deductive reasoning about the world).[18]

Perception provides only a highly circumscribed awareness of reality, limited to one's immediate surroundings. If we were equipped with a rich instinctual infrastructure, such that cues from the perceptual field could trigger reliable motives for self-sustaining action, then perception would be cognitively sufficient for us, as it is for animals. But since we are not so equipped, perception alone is insufficient for our needs. Concepts and conceptual knowledge, Rand holds, offer a solution to this problem. What conceptual knowledge does is expand the range of material that a human consciousness can deal with by integrating it into a manageable number of units. Integration of prior cognitive material is a feature both

---

18. In perception, Rand maintains, we are aware of *material objects and their properties*. But although she is a direct realist about perception, she rejects naïve realism. The nature of our perceptual apparatus affects perception, but what it affects is the *form* in which perceptible objects' features appear to us, not the objects of perception. Thus, in her view, perception does not trap us behind a veil of ideas that screens off real, independent objects from view.

It is from within this framework that Rand addresses questions about the proper account of perceptual relativity. Strictly speaking, she holds, it is not accurate to say (for instance) that from certain angles pennies appear elliptically shaped. Rather, we should distinguish between *perceptual awareness* and *perceptual judgment*. Perceptual awareness always has a form determined by the nature of our perceptual apparatus; we detect certain features of the world in the form of colors, for example. When one looks at a penny from an angle, the form in which one sees its shape is sensitive to the penny's spatial relation to one's eyes. But the object of (direct) perceptual awareness remains the penny itself, not some intermediary item (e.g., an "idea") generated by the interaction of the penny with one's sense organs.

We can make inferences from perceptual material and thus regard it as cognitive in a standard sense of that term, because there are norms by which to justify our classification of the object as a "penny" (and for other classifications and judgments, such as that it is made of metal, copper colored, US legal tender, etc.). Those judgments can in turn figure into inference in various ways. But perception itself—the perceptual field—does not speak to us, as it were. It does not present itself to be a certain way or purport to represent reality in a certain

of concept-formation and of ordinary and scientific induction, for Rand. A concept classifies together a potentially unlimited class of the referents to which it applies, and an inductive generalization similarly purports to identify the attributes of or relations among an unlimited set of particular instances. For instance, a statement such as "The human body absorbs vitamin D from sunlight" condenses a wide body of (ultimately perceptual) evidence and applies to an unlimited number of cases past, present, and future.

Concepts enable one to grasp all of the members of an open-ended class of referents.[19] Similarly, conceptual knowledge makes it possible to identify characteristics belonging to all of the members of a given class. In this sense, it extends one's awareness beyond the frontiers of perception. When one is aware that "All S is P," one is aware of a fact about all Ss, even though one could never be perceptually aware of all of them.[20] It is important, in this connection, to recognize that Rand understands knowledge in terms of *awareness*, not in terms of the more familiar framework of representation and belief. Knowledge, for her, is not a species of belief, to be distinguished by special marks such as truth and justification, though it can be perfectly accurate to describe someone who knows that such-and-such as having certain beliefs that are true and justified. The root conception of knowing for Rand is simply awareness—consciousness of an object—and the primary case of knowing is to be found in perceptual awareness. Propositional knowledge, knowing that something is the case, is a complex and derivative form of awareness, but it is not some-

---

way. It is not the penny that appears elliptical but the subject who (implicitly or explicitly) judges it to be so, based on a misinterpretation of the perceptual evidence.

As an objection to this analysis, it might be contended that we continue to see the penny as elliptical (or the straight stick submerged in water as bent, or the faraway tower as tiny) even after we have corrected our judgment about it. This might seem to suggest that it is perception itself that presents the penny to be elliptical (and thus misleads). But it seems to me that, if one carefully attends to one's visual field, this contention turns out to be false. If the penny continued to appear elliptical, it would appear misshapen, somewhat like the liquefying objects in a Dali painting. But that is not how it seems. (By this, I do not mean that it seems some other way, but that it does not seem like this.) It requires a special effort of selective focus to recover what about the content of the perceptual field might have led one to believe that the penny was elliptical.

19. For Rand's use of the concept of open-endedness in relation to concept-formation, see *ITOE* 17–18, 65–69.

20. When one knows fundamental truths concerning the properties or behavior of Ss, one is aware of new aspects of reality that had eluded one's grasp on less sophisticated levels of knowledge.

thing categorically different from what goes on when, for instance, you see the furniture and other items in the room you're in, or you hear the passing traffic on the street.[21]

Concepts enable one to develop abstract knowledge and values, which one can use to set goals and guide one's action. This is their great advantage over mere perception; the challenge they present is that, unlike perception, concepts are not an automatic means of awareness since, beyond the simplest cases, they must be formed and maintained by a volitional (though not always explicitly self-conscious) process. The idea, for instance, that "animals" deserve to be grouped together as a class—or that there is such a thing as a "vitamin," and that this category is importantly distinct from other categories in our thinking about metabolism and nutrition—requires a process of purposeful effort to reach and understand.

It is not a given, however, that our conceptual classifications will always be cognitively productive. Since concept-formation has a necessary function in human cognition and thereby in human life (a function we cannot do without), we can derive norms for its proper operation. The norms are relative to the purpose of expanding the scope of one's awareness and understanding, and thereby of expanding one's ability to act successfully over the normal span of a human life. More specifically, since Rand holds that the purpose of concepts is to enable us to refer to and generalize about more than could be contained in a single frame of perceptual awareness, it is by reference to that goal that she would formulate the norms by which concept-formation should be governed.

Similar points can be made about the development of conceptual knowledge. Induction and deduction require a methodology—a logic—to guide them, and the norms for these fields are ultimately to be derived from the goals of conceptual cognition. The core of Rand's claim that force negates and paralyzes thought will be that it *interferes with the implementation of these necessary cognitive methods.*

Concept-formation and conceptual cognition, then, both require a methodology in order to ensure that concepts, judgments, and theories actually do serve to expand and refine one's grasp of reality. Described in general terms, this methodology involves respecting what Rand calls *hierarchy* and *context.* Hierarchy requires ensuring that new cognitive material has the right sort of justificatory ties to the foundations of hu-

---

21. Rand thus defines knowledge not as justified true belief but as a "mental grasp of a fact(s) of reality" (see *ITOE* 35).

man knowledge in perception; context requires integrating that new material consistently with other knowledge. These, for Rand, are the primary
methods by which thought can be steered toward truth.[22]

The idea that the conceptual must be grounded in the perceptual
does not mean that every concept refers to something perceptible or that
every proposition describes perceptible states of the world. But it means
that concepts of perceptible entities are the starting point for all subsequent conceptualization and that the justification for forming even highly
abstract concepts will always ultimately trace back to our cognitive needs
in navigating through the perceptible world.[23] Further, it means that an
elementary level of perceptually based generalizations are the foundation
of all inductive knowledge. Rand regards human knowledge as having a
hierarchical structure, in that any given item of knowledge (e.g., a given
scientific principle) might be more or less far removed from these elementary inductions, requiring a longer or shorter series of prior cognitive
steps in order to reach or validate. Paying attention to issues of hierarchy involves ensuring that this epistemic support structure is properly in
place. Hierarchical relationships as Rand views them can be quite complex; they certainly do not reduce to a multiplicity of isolated chains of
inference, the links of which consist of individual claims or small sets of
claims. Two broad patterns are worth differentiating: (1) the move from
narrower principles to wider ones and (2) the move from a more generalized context to a narrower, more specialized field of study that depends
in some way on having the more general view in place. In each pattern,
the subsequent material is in Rand's sense further up the hierarchy of
knowledge, further removed from elementary perceptual observation
and generalization.

The issue of context is closely related and, although it has various aspects, pertains fundamentally to the way in which evidence is assimilated

22. On these two requirements, see Peikoff 1991, 121–41, also ch. 4.

23. This criterion certainly does not mean that every important discovery will have
ready practical application or even any such application, in the long run. The pursuit of
knowledge is in principle necessary and beneficial for human life, and that is virtually all that
the scientific enterprise and the study of the humanities requires in the way of justification,
from Rand's perspective, though by the same token there is no basis for the kind of view that
demeans the applied sciences as lesser pursuits, either. (See, in this latter connection, her
characterization in *Atlas Shrugged* of the scientist Robert Stadler, who holds a view of applied
science that Rand rejects and that she ultimately considers incompatible with the possibility
of free scientific inquiry, because it implies that the state must fund and control basic science.)
For an excellent discussion that compares Rand's view and the ancient Greeks' view of the
value of knowledge (and the relevance of Stadler to this issue), see Salmieri 2009, 229–322.

in the development of inductive knowledge.[24] Rand holds that, beyond the most elementary inductive generalizations from perception, the epistemic justification of every piece of general knowledge involves both (1) appropriate evidence and (2) a prior context of general knowledge that guides the assimilation of the evidence. The prior context of knowledge provides the framework in which new questions can be raised and new evidence evaluated.[25]

Suppose, for example, that we want to know how the ingestion of a certain substance affects the blood glucose levels of laboratory mice. We give it to the mice, say, by dissolving it in their water and, after a certain time interval, measure their levels of blood glucose. Let us say we find a large spike, compared to some baseline measurements taken before the substance was administered. Both the design of the experiment and the conclusion that the substance raised the mice's blood glucose levels obviously depend on a large body of established science. This context includes too much to list here, but we can mention the following as examples: (1) the general knowledge that food and other ingested substances can affect the blood glucose levels of and the knowledge of the time frame in which such effects can be observed (e.g., twenty minutes, two hours, three weeks, etc.); (2) the knowledge of the chemical properties of glucose and its role in mammalian biology; (3) the scientific and technological knowledge on which the procedure and equipment for measuring the mice's blood glucose levels is predicated; (4) the knowledge of how the mice's blood glucose levels should normally behave in the absence of the special substance.[26]

24. I say that this is the fundamental issue here because, for Rand, inductive knowledge is a prerequisite for the deductive application of knowledge to particular cases. Issues of context arise here, also, but for the sake of brevity I will focus on the inductive case, since this will be sufficient to explicate the aspects of Rand's defense of the non–initiation of force principle that depends on her epistemology.

25. In her view, even elementary perceptual inductions depend on a certain kind of context: they depend on implicit metaphysical premises, such as the premise that there are real and stable causal relationships, or that thoughts cannot directly control the behavior of inanimate objects, or that effects observed in the natural world have natural causes. At a relatively advanced stage of knowledge, these kinds of premises can be made precise and explicit and can be given a systematic justification, which for Rand consists in showing that the facts they identify are inherent in the very fact of (anything's) existence. I leave aside here the details of that project of justifying the most basic philosophical principles, which for Rand provide the indispensable framework for all inquiry.

26. These are among the kinds of considerations that are sometimes used to support the claim that observation is "theory-laden." Rand doesn't draw this conclusion. Since percep-

Paying attention to issues of context, for Rand, means bringing the entire relevant context of prior knowledge to bear in the assessment of evidence on any question, whether in science or ordinary life. What is the _relevant_ context—what does it contain? Rand's answer is that it potentially contains everything one already knows; that is, one cannot refuse in advance to consider the possible bearing of any item of knowledge on one's assessment of the evidence on a given issue. At every stage, the warrant for each new conclusion is that it makes best sense given the evidence available to one and _everything_ one already knows. The working out of detailed criteria for evaluating evidence in this contextualized way is a matter for epistemology and the philosophy of science, and the details can be passed over here. What is important, for purposes of this discussion, is the general principle that one must bring to bear the whole of one's prior context of knowledge. Since knowledge has an overall organizational structure, it is not a question of riffling through everything one knows; for instance, one would normally have no grounds to expect that anything pertaining to the fall of the Roman Empire would bear on data analysis in mouse studies.[27]

According to Rand, the process of acquiring conceptual knowledge, in order to take place at all, must be volitionally initiated, sustained, and directed by each thinker. Nothing can cause it to happen, she argues, except one's own choice, to the best of one's ability (a point that will be important in her discussion of force). Beyond the most elementary levels, conducting the process correctly requires some degree of self-consciousness, though in nonspecialized contexts this need not amount to formulable methodological knowledge but only to some ability to ex-

---

tion, in her view, provides preconceptual cognitive access to the world, in the manner indicated previously in the text, perceptual awareness is prior to all theory. Further, elementary perceptual generalizations depend only on having the relevant concepts and on implicit philosophical principles, where the latter are directly self-evident and depend on no other general knowledge (even though the concepts required for expressing them are highly abstract and advanced and thus could not be grasped early in one's cognitive development). All subsequent knowledge, including the knowledge of how our scientific instruments work, builds on that foundation, according to Rand. For discussion of the issues raised in the text and in this note, see Peikoff 1991, ch. 4; Peikoff 2005, lecture 1.

27. This issue has an additional, cultural aspect. Specialists in any field of inquiry properly focus on their own specialties. But the development of human knowledge also requires generalists who work across different fields and help to integrate diverse areas of knowledge. Further, Rand assigns to philosophy the important role of providing an integrating framework for all human knowledge and disseminating knowledge of appropriate standards for inquiry.

plain the grounds on which one drew a given conclusion. Over time, and all else being equal, the application of appropriate cognitive methods will lead toward increasing knowledge, but in any given case the fact that one's thinking has followed all the requisite norms does not preclude the possibility of error. Even in the face of error, however, there is a difference between the conclusions reached by a thought process that satisfies the relevant cognitive norms, on one hand, and a random guess (or a rationalization), on the other.

It is in terms of the methodological requirements of conceptual cognition that Rand understands the concept of *objectivity*. It has been common to think of objectivity as seeking a "view from nowhere," in Nagel's memorable phrase (see Nagel 1986). This model of objectivity implies that we must somehow transcend the limitations of our own cognitive equipment, which is unavoidably located in time and space. Rand argues that such a view of objectivity treats the involvement of the subject's own constitution as a "disqualifying element" in cognition and implies that objective cognition occurs magically, by no means whatsoever (*ITOE* 80). By contrast, she understands objectivity roughly as the right use of one's cognitive capacities. More specifically, what a rational conception of objectivity requires, in her view, is *basing the self-direction of one's cognitive processes on the requirements of cognition*, thereby rendering those processes suitable for the systematic acquisition of knowledge. A cognitive process that meets this description will be an objective one, and by extension the products of such a process—concepts, judgments, theories, evaluations—can also be characterized as objective.

An objective judgment, for Rand, is implicitly conditional. It is held only in consideration of the relevant evidence, background context of knowledge, and methodology (as brought to bear by the knower). This conditional status is necessary for a judgment or a theory to constitute a grasp or an awareness of reality. Without some systematic, though perhaps inexplicit, connection between judgment and these conditioning elements, the judgment is essentially an arbitrary guess and cannot constitute a *grasp* of reality, even if it happens to be accurate.

A claim endorsed in disregard of the need for a specific and appropriate method of cognition is in Rand's terms "arbitrary." It is a noncognitive assertion, whose acceptance undercuts the cognitive status of everything that relies on it. The issue here is not primarily whether one has exactly the right cognitive methods but, rather, whether the methods one uses reflect one's best (implicit or explicit) understanding of the requirements of cognition. If so, then one will have a potential basis for (eventually) correcting any methodological errors, and the conclusions that one reaches will not be arbitrary, even if some of them are false and therefore also require correction.[28] But the acceptance of a claim in isolation from context and evidence short-circuits this process, bringing cognition to a standstill. The manner in which force works to undercut the methodological integrity—the objectivity—of human cognition is by attempting to instill arbitrary claims.

This discussion has focused on Rand's views of knowledge and cognition. But some cases of cognitive paralysis will involve art and the process of creating an artwork. In Rand's view, although the function of a work of art is not to disseminate knowledge, artistic creation is a rational and, in some ways, a cognitive process. An artist creates from what Rand calls his "sense of life," which she characterizes as "a pre-conceptual equivalent of metaphysics, an emotional, subconsciously integrated appraisal of man and of existence" ("Philosophy and Sense of Life," *RM* 14). Explicit convictions are also relevant to the production of a creative work, in Rand's view. But artistic creativity relies crucially on the artist's subconsciously held view of life. It is this view that fuels and sets the terms for an artist's work and thus serves as the foundation of creative expression.

---

28. I take it that the issue of arbitrariness arises both in regard to the ideas one accepts and to the methodology one uses in reaching one's ideas. Like a claim reached by no particular method at all, a claim reached by an arbitrarily picked method (a method accepted with no sense of its basis) will itself be arbitrary, and one's acceptance of it will reflect a disregard for the need of an appropriate cognitive method. (Rand would, I think, hold that there are limits on the possible extent of nonarbitrary methodological errors. For instance, I doubt she would accept that the belief that knowledge of reality required no input from the senses could be the foundation of a nonarbitrary method.) It may seem as though there is a regress problem here. If the nonarbitrariness of a claim depends on the nonarbitrariness of the method (and not just on one's having some method or other), then does the nonarbitrariness of the method depend on one's having a further, nonarbitrary "meta-method" for reaching one's methodological principles, and so on, to infinity? I think Rand's answer would be that early methodological knowledge requires only a minimal and implicit methodology. Concept-formation at the early stages, she holds, is barely volitional, and implicit generalizations simply involve applying these concepts to what one perceives. (On volition and early concept-formation, see *ITOE* 150–51, also 144–45; "The Comprachicos," *ROTP* 54–55.) Rand did not discuss induction in any detail, but Leonard Peikoff has developed a view of induction that is based on her theory of concepts and is indicative of how she might approach the topic. On this, see Peikoff 2005, lecture 1. His account is further discussed in Harriman 2010, esp. ch. 1. See also Salmieri 2013, 66–69.

4. Initiated Force: A Brief Taxonomy

What Rand calls the *initiation of force* can take various different forms. Most of the ways of initiating force can also be ways of using force in retaliation. But I will set aside retaliatory uses of force for the time being; unless otherwise specified it should be understood that "force," "threat," "coercion," and related terms all refer to their initiatory forms. The ways of initiating force are not all on the same level theoretically; some are primary and others are included by analogy with or extension from the primary ones.

The uses of physical force that Rand is paradigmatically concerned with occur without the recipient's consent and, in most cases, against her will. Hugs, handshakes, ordinary surgical procedures, consensual sex acts, and other consensual forms of physical contact can be left to one side. The simplest cases of force are (1) direct attacks on the person (e.g., killing or doing bodily injury) and (2) physical confinement. Following Rand, we will call these cases of *direct force*.

These forms of force attack the process by which the victim maintains her life, and Rand's ethics prohibits them on that basis. Unlike other forms of wrongdoing, direct force (to the extent of its efficacy) materially interferes with the victim's ability to engage in a course of self-sustaining action. By contrast, if your spouse cheats on you or a business partner becomes irrationally hostile and defensive, you might be harmed in various ways but your ability to meet the requirements of your survival remains unhampered, as long as you can withdraw from the relationship by an act of will and thereby insulate yourself from the relationship's damaging effects.[29]

Rand is particularly concerned with threats of (direct) force, which she calls a form of indirect force. Why does a threat to use force count as an actual usage? One answer would be that it is the availability of direct force that does the work in securing compliance. By contrast, in bargaining for something one wants, one offers the other party a value in exchange, and it is this value that does the work in securing compliance. So a threat of force, unlike the offer of a bargain, relies on the possibility of force to achieve its end, and in that sense can be said to make use of, or be

---

29. This will not be the case in a legal system with extremely strict constraints on dissolving a marriage or business partnership. But I think Rand would use this as an argument against such restrictive laws. Here, though, the point is simply that the other party, whatever wrong she has done, creates no physical obstacle to withdrawal.

a use of, force. Since the use is not actual or occurrent, it can be described as indirect; thus, when a threat is considered "indirect force," we should understand the qualifier to be modifying "use" rather than "force."

These points seem to me to provide reasonable initial grounds for regarding threats of direct force as uses of force—that is, for seeing both threats and direct force as instances of one basic way of treating others that can be contrasted with the use of persuasion and trade. This classification does not in itself warrant an across-the-board moral condemnation of everything in the "force" category; that assessment depends on the substance of the argument for the non–initiation of force principle sketched in the preceding section (and the vindication of that argument through an unpacking of the claims about negation and paralysis of judgment and the full elaboration of its other steps). But this classification provides grounds for seeing both threats of force and direct force as variants of a single means of interaction. As Rand develops the concept of initiated force to encompass more complex indirect cases, she will also refine this account of the underlying similarities uniting all cases of initiated force, making it possible to identify more fundamental characteristics that confirm and support these initial grounds for the classification.

Threats of direct force can be divided into two subcategories: those demanding action ("Your money or your life") and those demanding belief (such as the forcible imposition of a religious orthodoxy). Rand's treatment of these two cases differs; in the first she argues that the threat "negates" the victim's thinking, and in the second she argues that the threat "paralyzes" the victim's thinking (to the extent that she complies with it). Notice that in both cases Rand is arguing that the threat has some effect that reaches to the victim's thinking, even though in the first case what the threat explicitly demands is only action (see, in this connection, Peikoff 1991, 313).[30] I discuss these two effects of force on the mind in the next chapter.

A fourth broad category of cases that Rand will recognize as initiations of force involve actions taken (or threatened) against private property. These include theft, breaking and entering, and trespass, and threats that rely on the possibility of these outcomes. They also include breach of

30. As will become clear below, Rand also holds that other indirect forms of force—such as threats against property or against people one values—can negate or paralyze thinking, but again the effect that ensues will depend on whether the threat demands action or belief. Further, Rand will argue that types of force that do not consist in a threat, such as confinement or seizure of property, also have the effect of negating the victim's thinking.

contract, fraud, and extortion to obtain someone's money or other property (see "The Nature of Government," *VOS* 130/*CUI* 383).[31] The inclusion of this category of cases raises a question about the order of justification in Rand's political philosophy: does the non–initiation of force principle logically precede or follow Rand's account of individual rights? (I discuss this question in "The Scope and Justification of Rand's Non–Initiation of Force Principle," below). In short, my view is that, in Rand's thought, the more basic cases of initiated force are identified and evaluated independently of and prior to the theory of rights.[32] The goal of the theory of rights is, then, to delineate principles for the formation of a society that meets the needs of man's life. The prohibitions contained in the initial specification of the non–initiation of force principle are reflected in the theory of rights, but the theory of rights also supports an expanded conception of the range of actions that violate the non–initiation of force principle.[33]

31. I take it that "extortion," in the broadest sense, encompasses any threat of force, although in its primary usage it refers to threats used to obtain a financial payment. Whether fraud and breaches of contract should be seen as forms of force is controversial; I will discuss this controversy, and relate it to Rand's views, later.

32. In my view, the specification of the non–initiation of force principle by reference to which the theory of rights is developed includes an additional class of comparatively elementary cases not yet introduced: the seizure of nonproprietary goods appropriated for use directly from nature and under one's active control. If, prior to the institution of a society with private property rights, you have gathered some apples beside you to eat, it would be an initiation of force and thus a violation of the non–initiation of force principle for someone else to seize them from you. This claim is not obvious; so in "The Scope and Justification of Rand's Non–Initiation of Force Principle" (below), I discuss the justification for it that comes out of Rand's philosophy. But what property rights will do, in Rand's account of them, is extend and objectively delineate the possible scope of a person's morally legitimate control over physical resources and other material values (including finished goods produced from natural resources and, eventually, intellectual property).

33. As I will argue later, Rand is not forced to choose between a "moralized" and a "non-moralized" account of force (contrary Matt Zwolinski's claim in his contribution to this volume, 84). We might say that her view is partially moralized, but this might be misleading, because it might suggest that she defines some cases of force in terms of rights, whereas what actually supports the classification of (say) property crimes as force, in her view, is not per se that they are violations of rights but, rather, the kind of effect that (such) rights violations have on the victim's life. Specifically, property crimes undermine a necessary aspect of human self-preservation that property rights make possible. The relevance of rights to the delineation of complex cases of force is that these *specific* negative effects would not be present in the absence of rights, since the underlying positive, life-sustaining action would not be present. This is not to say that in the absence of property rights there would not be other, equally deleterious harms to life to contend with; there surely would be.

Force and the Mind

DARRYL WRIGHT

and regards the threat to initiate direct physical force against someone as itself an (indirect) initiation of force. This is in part because
she holds that such threats themselves undermine the victim's mind
and therefore compromise the victim's life. "To interpose the threat of
physical destruction between a man and his perception of reality, is to
negate and paralyze his means of survival; to force him to act against his
own judgment, is like forcing him to act against his own sight. Whoever,
to whatever purpose or extent, initiates the use of force, is a killer acting
on the premise of death in a manner wider than murder: the premise of
destroying man's capacity to live." When Rand says that threats "negate"
and "paralyze" the mind, I take her to be making two different claims,
referring to two different and potentially separable effects of force (she
repeatedly uses both, which seems to suggest she had two different points
in mind).

To "negate" is defined by one dictionary as "to cause to be ineffective
or invalid."[1] In some places—for instance in the essay "What Is Capitalism?"—Rand substitutes "invalidates" for "negates"; she seems to treat

1. See http://www.merriam-webster.com/dictionary/negate.

these as synonyms (see *CUI* 15). The same dictionary defines "invalid" as "being without foundation or force in fact, truth, or law." There are many different senses of the term "invalid," but clearly the relevant one is that of "without force in fact." Invalidating or negating the mind (or someone's thinking) is rendering it ineffective in guiding her action. "Paralysis" is defined as "complete or partial loss of function, especially when involving motion or sensation of a part of the body." The distinction, then, is between making one's thinking ineffective as a determinant of action, on the one hand, and stopping thinking from occurring, on the other. The kind of "paralysis" in question is cognitive or psychological (not physical); its locus is the mind, not the brain.

1. Force as Negating Thought in Threats Demanding Behavior

It might seem that Rand locates the moral objection to coercive threats in the wrong place. It is obvious how physical confinement negates thinking by preventing the victim from acting on his own judgment. But Rand's main examples of negation involve overt or implied threats of force, such as a holdup, a government regulation, or taxation, and it is less obvious that threats have this effect. Although they may in some sense force the recipient to act or may restrict her freedom, we might wonder whether they invalidate her judgment, in the sense of rendering it ineffectual in action. A threat gives you options, and selecting between options seems like a paradigmatic example of carrying out your judgment in action. First, you decide which option is preferable, and then you rely on that decision in determining how you will act (see Matt Zwolinski's chapter in this volume for a version of this objection).

To grasp Rand's point, however, it is important to understand what she means by *thinking* and *judgment*, in this context. The kind of practical thinking that a human being needs to engage in is focused on one's life as a whole. Because we lack instincts, we cannot simply live moment by moment, like an animal, going with the flow of whatever we find ourselves moved to do. Like animals, human beings have specific survival needs and must live a certain kind of life, appropriate to our nature, in order to survive and prosper. To accomplish this, we require a broad context of knowledge and values, and a framework of long-range goals (having a career, raising a family, etc.), against which to make specific choices. To *think* about what to do is to assess one's options in the light of the totality of one's knowledge, values, and goals. What guides this process, to the extent that it is carried out correctly and well, are the exigencies of living a *human* life (a life consonant with the requirements of human survival and happiness) and one's own particular life, viewed as one's own chosen way of instantiating a human life.

What Rand is saying when she claims that force negates thought, I suggest, is that it negates *this* process. A coercive threat presents a choice unrelated to human requirements. Nothing in reality demands that one choose between one's money and one's life, or between the destruction of one's business and a payoff to the mafia, or as Rand will argue, between paying a fine and obeying a government regulation.[2] By compelling a choice in the face of an artificial, arbitrarily constructed alternative, a coercive threat derails reality-based practical reasoning, which is grounded in the necessity of taking specific kinds of action in order to maintain and nourish one's life. This form of necessity emerges from a metaphysically given alternative, one that is inescapable in the nature of things: the alternative faced by every living organism of life (maintained by a specific process of action) or death.

In this large and fundamental sense, giving your wallet to a thief is acting against the metaphysical requirements of human self-preservation, even though there is an obvious sense in which it is a "fact of reality" that the thief is threatening to kill you if you don't. The way we survive is by producing, consuming, and enjoying material and other values, and giving money to thieves is a drain on this process, even though it may, of course, be necessary in the face of a threat. What a threat negates or makes inoperative, then, is one's judgment as to the way of life that is necessary, given one's human nature and implemented in one's pursuit of one's own specific goals. Rand can deny, therefore, that the presence of options in a coercive threat preserves room for the kind of practical thought that requires moral sanction and protection. That kind of practical thought is excluded by coercive threats.

This reply might raise a different worry. How, then, can Rand extend the objection to coercive threats to cover cases in which the victim of the threat isn't actually thinking in this norm-laden sense? For example, how can it be extended to the kind of people whom Rand calls "second-handers," who do not think for themselves but copy others? Rand can respond to this worry. Second-handers still *need* to think, and to act

2. For discussion of this last issue, see below.

on their (authentic, first-handed) thinking (their second-handedness is a problem), and the option remains open to them to choose to think *provided they are not under force.* Force preemptively negates any actual thinking they might do (and coercing only second-handers would be no way of instilling independence).[3]

It is common to view threats of force as coercive. Rand takes the co-ercive nature of such threats for granted, but this assumption might be defended in the following way, compatibly with her basic views (I will briefly sketch a line of thinking that requires much fuller development). Coercion is a kind of necessitation. But it would be a mistake to think of natural necessities, such as the necessity of eating in order to survive, as coercive. These necessities form the baseline in relation to which certain man-made necessities—such as the necessity of handing your wallet to the mugger if you want to survive—can be distinguished as coercive. Some man-made necessities, however, have a basis in natural necessity, in the requirements of human survival. This is true, for example, of the fact that if you want to be paid by your employer, you must do your job. If this policy were not followed, employers could not remain in existence as employers, since they would have no output and thus no revenues with which to pay salaries. Man-made necessities that are based in this way on natural necessities should also be counted as part of the baseline frame-work of practical necessities with which cases of coercion should be con-trasted. In relation to this baseline, the necessity set up by a threat of force is arbitrary and unrelated to the requirements of survival. In this sense, it puts a wholly artificial kind of pressure on action and deserves to be characterized as coercive. This line of thinking would need much further development in order to be made fully clear and persuasive. But this way of explaining the coerciveness of threats of force has some initial plausi-bility, I think, and it is friendly to Rand's general perspective in moral and political philosophy. In any event, in explaining Rand's views below I will sometimes refer to threats of force as *coercive threats*, since that is clearly how she regards them.

3. We can say something similar about people who have made innocent errors in judg-ing their long-range good. Their survival and well-being will require that they correct these errors at some point. But to the extent that they are under force, any such improvements in their practical reasoning will be made ineffectual in determining their action. Thus, if it is objectionable to force those who judge correctly, it is also objectionable to force those who make errors.

2. Force and the Mind, Rand and Locke

Besides negating thought, according to Rand force can also paralyze thought. This claim is related to, but different from, an argument of Locke's in his first *Letter Concerning Toleration*. I will discuss this argument at some length, both because I think Rand would largely endorse it, and because I want to bring out the ways in which her own argument goes beyond Locke's.

Locke argues both that one cannot believe a proposition at will and that force cannot compel belief. Since it is in the nature of government to use force to achieve its ends, the control of religious belief is not among the proper functions of government (Locke 1689 [2010], 6–9). His argument has been extensively criticized, but much of this criticism seems to miss the point of his claims. Although he uses the term "belief," it is clear he is referring not just to anything that might be called a belief but to certain cognitive states that proceed from the rational consideration of evidence. Thus, it is irrelevant, for example, that the government might successfully brainwash dissenters into accepting some religious orthodoxy.[4] This, of course, can happen, and force can help bring it about. But it has nothing to do with the formation of beliefs on the basis of a "conviction in the mind," which is the kind of beliefs that Locke thinks we should have, in religious and other matters, and that he denies force can do anything to bring about (see Locke 1689 [2010], 8).[5]

A more subtle challenge to Locke's argument comes from Jeremy Waldron, in a highly influential (and in many ways excellent) critical discussion. Waldron argues that, although political power cannot be used directly to *compel* belief, it can be effective in shaping what people believe; specifically, by manipulating the "epistemic apparatus" through which beliefs are formed, the government can foster, reinforce, or inhibit people's adoption of certain target ideas (1988, 82). What he has in mind are examples such as the following. First, a person can be compelled to perceive sensory evidence supporting a claim; you can get someone to

---

4. This possibility is mentioned as an objection to Locke's argument in Mack 2013, 113–14.

5. Locke writes on the same page: "It is light that is needed to change a belief in the mind; punishment of the body does not lend light." In the *Essay Concerning Human Understanding*, Locke describes "light in the mind" as "evidence of the truth of any proposition" (see *Essay* IV 19 § 13).

believe that snow is white by forcing him to see some snow (82–83). Second, "a man may be compelled to learn a catechism on pain of death or to read the gospels every day to avoid discrimination. The effect of such threats and such discrimination may be to increase the number of people who eventually end up believing the orthodox faith" (81). Third, compulsory religious practice can be "part of the apparatus which surrounds, nurtures, and sustains the sort of intellectual conviction of which true religion, in Locke's opinion, is composed" (83). Finally, censorship can be used to inhibit the spread of heretical or otherwise unwanted ideas. Thus, Locke's argument fails to establish that it is impossible for coercion to shape belief and thus fails to show that it is irrational or unacceptable in principle for the magistrate ever to make the attempt.[6]

Waldron does not simply gloss over the distinction between beliefs acquired through a cognitive process and beliefs with other kinds of causes; for instance, he does not think that the possibility of successful brainwashing would refute Locke's argument. But at times he elides the distinction. For instance, insofar as they work through the emotions rather than through the understanding, the belief-sustaining mechanisms engaged by forced religious practice would seem to impede rather than further the process of rational consideration of evidence by which Locke thinks religious beliefs should be acquired. The possibility of activating these mechanisms by force therefore seems irrelevant to Locke's

---

6. A further issue, that I cannot consider here, is Waldron's reading of the normative import of Locke's argument. In common with many others, Waldron takes this to be an argument addressed to the magistrate and designed to show that it would be instrumentally irrational of him to use force to try to compel belief (1988, 63–65). But Waldron recognizes that this line of reasoning is also part of a larger argument that Locke makes in the *Letter* concerning the proper functions of the state (1988, 66). That being so, however, it seems possible to exonerate Locke of a charge that Waldron presses later on in his article—namely, that Locke ignores the effects of religious persecution on the victim and fails to provide a moral argument for toleration (see Waldron 1988, 85). If religious intolerance by the magistrate oversteps the state's proper functions, then arguably this intolerance morally wrongs those who are persecuted. This seems clearest if the argument for the state's proper functions is itself a moral argument; it is not always clear whether Locke's argument in the *Letter* should be read as such, though the majority of the textual evidence implies that it should be. Even if the argument establishing the state's proper functions is not itself a moral argument (establishing its *morally* proper functions), but only an argument establishing its rationally appropriate functions (the reading Waldron assumes—see 1988, 65) it seems plausible that for the state to burden a citizen in a manner that exceeds its proper functions would be to morally wrong that person. An emphasis on the victim's perspective is evident when Locke describes the upshot of his toleration argument as follows: "So at last we have people liberated from the dominion of others in matters of religion" (Locke 1689 [2010], 22).

toleration argument, which is concerned with the inability of force to compel *rational thought* or *cognition*.[7] This is not to say that Locke would regard the practices in question as irrational qua religious practices, or that he would want people to avoid them. But allowing the sheer experience of a religious service or other religious rituals to exert influence over one's religious convictions would seem to violate the epistemic norms underlying what he calls "love of truth":

> He that would seriously set upon the search of truth ought in the first place to prepare his mind with a love of it. For he that loves it not will not take much pains to get it; nor be much concerned when he misses it. . . . How a man may know whether he be so in earnest, is worth inquiry: and I think there is one unerring mark of it, viz. The not entertaining any proposition with greater assurance than the proofs it is built upon will warrant. . . . For the evidence that any proposition is true (except such as are self-evident) lying only in the proofs a man has of it, whatsoever degrees of assent he affords it beyond the degrees of that evidence, it is plain that all the surplusage of assurance is owing to some other affection, and not to the love of truth. . . . Whatsoever credit or authority we give to any proposition more than it receives from the principles and proofs it supports itself upon, is owing to our inclinations that way, and is so far a derogation from the love of truth as such: which, as it can receive no

Contrary to Waldron, both Locke and his contemporary critic Jonas Proast concur that the objective of the toleration argument is to establish that the magistrate has no *right* to use force against religious dissenters, with Proast maintaining that the argument fails to establish this conclusion and Locke maintaining that it succeeds (see Proast 1690 [2010], 55, 60–61; Locke 1690 [2010], 72, 73, 82–83, 84). In this respect, Waldron, though he presents his criticisms as an adaptation of Proast's, diverges from the latter's reading of Locke and, I believe, from Locke's text. Indeed, in defending himself in the *Second Letter Concerning Toleration* against Proast's charge (echoed by Waldron) that force can be indirectly effective in bringing about sincere religious conviction, Locke argues that such indirect effects cannot ground a right of the magistrate to use force against dissenters. The dispute with Proast, in this connection, concerns not what effects force can either directly or indirectly bring about but, rather, which type of effects are relevant to the question of what the magistrate may rightfully do. The argument, as Locke represents it here, is through and through a moral argument, which, if successful, would ground a moral objection from the victim's point of view to acts of religious persecution.

7. It might be objected also that these mechanisms can be activated only if the subject fails to subject his religious experiences to proper critical scrutiny. Although I think this point is well taken, it is not directly pertinent to answering Waldron's objection, since he acknowledges that the belief-forming effects of force are indirect. The point to emphasize, in this connection, is that by Locke's lights they do not result in the right kind of beliefs, specifically, beliefs grounded in a process of rational thought.

evidence from our passions or interests, so it should receive no tincture from them. (*Essay* IV 19 § 1)

In the *Letter*, Locke writes: "A ruler is wasting his time forcing his subjects to attend his own religious services on a pretext of saving their souls. If they believe, they will come of their own accord; if they do not believe, they will perish anyway, even if they come" (Locke 1689 [2010], 21). This might be seen as evidence that Locke overlooked the "generative and supportive" potentialities of religious practice in relation to religious belief (Waldron 1988, 82). Alternatively, however, it might be that Locke was aware of such potentialities but did not consider them relevant to the sort of epistemically rigorous belief-formation required for the "full persuasion of the mind" and the salvation of one's soul.[8] Certainly Rand would view the generative processes invoked by Waldron as being irrelevant to the question of whether force can compel thought.

8. When Locke says that to be saved you must be "inwardly and profoundly convinced in your own heart" (Locke 1689 [2010], 7)—this is Silverthorne's translation; Popple's translation reads, "fully satisfied in our own mind" (Locke 1689, 11)—of the truth of your religious convictions, I take it he means more than just you must in some sense feel fully sure that those religious convictions are true but you must in effect judge that they satisfy certain epistemic criteria. Locke thinks that it possible in principle for anyone to receive an "original revelation" from God. If the revelation occurred during a church service one had been forced by the magistrate to attend, then arguably, force would have played a role in one's acquisition of a piece of knowledge. But since the connection is purely accidental, it tells us nothing about the epistemic potentialities of force, and this kind of case is quite different from Waldron's.

In replying to Proast's criticism of his toleration argument, Locke acknowledges the possibility of various kinds of indirect effects of force on belief, but he argues that these effects are irrelevant to the question of whether the magistrate may properly use force to promote correct religious belief. To ground the claim that the magistrate may use force for a given purpose, it must be shown, Locke says, that force is by nature suited to that purpose. But this is not established simply by showing that an act of force could figure into a chain of events leading to the purpose's being accomplished. Rather, there must in some sense be a nonaccidental connection between the use of force and the achievement of the purpose (see Locke 1690 [2010], 73–74, 82–83). The distinction drawn here between those effects that properly follow from the use of force and those that at most follow only incidentally requires much elucidation. But it has intuitive plausibility. We recognize a distinction of this sort when we say, for example, that although being out in the hot sun might cause people to want more sugary drinks, and having more sugary drinks might cause them to gain weight, being out in the hot sun does not cause people to gain weight. This distinction also is crucial to Locke's toleration argument. He does not deny the existence of the kinds of indirect effects that Proast points to, but even where their result is genuine belief, Locke regards them as irrelevant to the question of whether religious persecution is rationally and morally justifiable. Mack makes a similar point (2013, 114) but construes Locke as arguing against the rationality of authorizing the magistrate's use of force, whereas on the reading taken here, the existence of a nonaccidental connection between means and end is a necessary condition of the magistrate's moral right to use force to promote belief.

What of Waldron's other examples?[9] In regard to his fourth example, Locke might argue that, by censoring certain relevant materials, the government hampers the process of weighing the evidence and "proofs" for and against one's conclusions and, thereby, hampers thought; arguably, the beliefs resulting from such a process would be epistemically deficient, from the perspective of Locke's epistemology.[10] But admittedly this is not wholly clear. Rand can put the point even more strongly: objectivity, for her, requires the wide-scale integration of knowledge—both individually and, through the division of cognitive labor, culturally. Insofar as people's access to relevant information and argument is coercively blocked, the objectivity of their thinking and thus its cognitive status are compromised. There are questions of degree here that I will not try to sort out, but the point is that, if we are interested in whether force can be used to shape thought (to steer the direction of a cognitive process), then both Locke and Rand can reasonably deny that this is what censorship accomplishes. Insofar as it is effective, its effects are to degrade rather than reshape thinking. If, for Locke, morally correct religious belief must also be epistemically correct to the best of one's ability (that is, guided by the commitments reflected in the love of truth),[11] then censorship is incompatible with the requirements of such belief.

Waldron's first example is, in a way, the most interesting. It seems hard to deny that forcing perceptual evidence on someone could lead to their having a genuinely cognitive grasp of some truth or other, such as that snow is white. It would not, of course, be the force but the perceptual

9. The kind of example as Waldron's fourth example is also emphasized by Bou-Habib 2003, who discounts many of Waldron's other criticisms of Locke's toleration argument but nevertheless concurs with Waldron that the argument is ultimately inadequate.

10. This is perhaps true only if the censored material would be relevant to a full consideration of the issue. But presumably it is precisely such relevance that would normally motivate the decision to censor the material. Further, full consideration of the evidence would seem to demand that the thinker herself make the judgment of relevance for herself, based on a process of thought (I do not think there is a regress in the offing here, because in some cases the relevance of an item will be evident, but full consideration of evidence would still require that the thinker herself grasp this relevance). Although Locke does not state explicitly that a lover of truth must attend to possible counterarguments to his views, that requirement would seem to be implicit in the criteria of assent set forth in the above passage about love of truth. Further, elsewhere in the *Essay* Locke is explicit that probabilistic reasoning must properly consider counterarguments (see IV 15 § 5) and he thinks that probabilistic reasoning is involved in some aspects of religious belief (IV 18 §§ 4, 6).

11. That seems to be the intent of his comments that morally correct religious belief depends on an "inward conviction of the mind" and one's accepting "responsibility for one's own eternal salvation," rather than attempting to believe as the magistrate prescribes (see Locke 1689 [2010], 7–8).

evidence that would underwrite the belief about snow. According to Waldron, though, the force employed achieves this end indirectly, by bringing the evidence into view. And the possibility of such an indirect use of force to compel belief is relevant to the issue of toleration, as Locke frames it.

But this strikes me as a Pyrrhic victory for Waldron. First, the example involves the automatized application of previously learned perceptual concepts, which qualifies as a thought process only in a minimal sense and is insufficient in most epistemic contexts. So it tells us little about the epistemic potentialities of force. The mental acts involved in learning these concepts, or other, more complex ones, could not have been similarly forced, even in Waldron's indirect sense, nor could the act of forging even moderately more sophisticated inductive generalizations or of applying more sophisticated general knowledge to cases. Indirect force could not make one grasp that water warps wood or that the darkening clouds mean it's time to cover the lawn furniture. Even more obviously, it could not have caused the researchers at CERN to grasp the significance of the observations that confirmed the existence of the Higgs-Boson.[12]

This line of reply is perhaps more easily available to Rand than to Locke, who sometimes seems to minimize the volitional aspects of cognition. Waldron quotes the following key passage from the *Essay*: "all that is voluntary in our knowledge is the employing or withholding any of our faculties from this or that sort of objects, and a more or less accurate survey of them: but, they being employed, our will hath no power to determine the knowledge of the mind one way or another" (*Essay* IV 13 § 2). As Waldron interprets this passage, Locke is saying that the understanding does its work automatically as soon as one turns one's attention to a bit of sensory input—for example, by looking out the window, observing the behavior of scientific instruments, reading a book, or listening to a lecture. We can choose whether to give our continued attention, but once we do, the mind's operations are independent of the will (Waldron 1988, 81). Other passages in the *Essay* lend support to this interpretation.[13] So does Locke's general tendency to model reasoning on perception, but the textual evidence is somewhat ambiguous. For one thing, it is not clear whether what Locke says about knowledge is meant to apply to what he calls "judgment," which employs probabilistic reasoning. He seems to view judgment as a more active process than knowing: "It suf-

---

12. Or appeared to; doubts have since been raised, but that is not to the point here.
13. For instance, *Essay* IV 13 as a whole tends strongly in this direction; also IV 1 §§ 1–2, 8–9.

fices that they have once with care and fairness sifted the matter as far as they could; and that they have searched into all the particulars, that they could imagine to give any light to the question; and, with the best of their skill, cast up the account upon the whole evidence: and thus, having once found on which side the probability appeared to them, after as full and exact an inquiry as they can make, they lay up the conclusion in their memories as a truth they have discovered" (*Essay* IV 16 § 1). Further, even his characterizations of knowledge sometimes seem to involve an active and volitional aspect:

> Men often stay not warily to examine the agreement or disagreement of two ideas which they are desirous or concerned to know [and could prove demonstratively]; but, either incapable of such attention as is requisite in a long train of gradations, or impatient of delay, lightly cast their eyes on, or wholly pass by the proofs; and so, without making out the demonstration, determine of the agreement or disagreement of two ideas, as it were by a view of them as they are at a distance, and take it to be the one or the other, as seems most likely to them upon such a loose survey. (*Essay* IV 14 § 3)

The "employing . . . of our faculties" to an "accurate survey" of a subject may involve more volitional activity than Waldron supposes. The sense in which belief was not under the control of the will would then be this: no mere act of will can change the beliefs acquired in the self-directed application of our faculties. This would be true even if it were not true that the operation of our faculties themselves is not voluntary.

In any event, even if Waldron is correct about Locke's view, then although the *Essay*'s account of knowledge might raise questions about the overall consistency of Locke's views in the period in which he composed the *Letter*, Rand can argue that the core of the toleration argument is sound: thinking depends on a volitional process that force—even indirect force in Waldron's sense—cannot control. This is clearly her view (see, for example, "The Comprachicos," *ROTP* 54–58; "What Is Capitalism?" *CUI* 14–15), and it comes out of her view of conceptual thought as an active, volitional process requiring norms to guide it.

Returning to Waldron's "snow is white" example, there is a further point worth noting. Although Locke does say that the understanding "cannot be compelled to the belief of anything by outward force," he does not need this broad a claim for his argument, and it seems unlikely that he had any such broad claim in mind, despite the generality of this formulation. It is instructive that in realistic cases of persecution, the goal is not to require examination of perceptual evidence. Persecution and the exhibition of perceptual evidence to support a claim belong to two radically different methodologies. Waldron sees them as combinable, but Locke evidently disagrees. In the *Essay*, he states:

> The assuming an authority of dictating to others, and a forwardness to prescribe to their opinions, is a constant concomitant of this bias and corruption of our judgments. For how almost can it be otherwise, but that he should be ready to impose on another's belief, who has already imposed on his own? Who can reasonably expect arguments and conviction from him in dealing with others, whose understanding is not accustomed to them in his dealing with himself? Who does violence to his own faculties, tyrannizes over his own mind, and usurps the prerogative that belongs to truth alone, which is to command assent by only its own authority, i.e. by and in proportion to that evidence which it carries with it. (*Essay* IV 19 § 2)

Although this passage occurs in the chapter on enthusiasm, it does not seem restricted to enthusiasts. Further, it is echoed in the contrasts that Locke draws in the *Letter* between "persuad[ing]" and "command[ing]" and between "us[ing] arguments" and "issu[ing] decrees" (Locke 1690 [2010], 8). One way to understand this passage is that Locke is telling us that this point of coercion, when directed against someone's ideas, is precisely to disengage them from evidence and logic. If this is true, then forcing someone to examine evidence for a claim (and, particularly, unambiguous perceptual evidence) would subvert the purposes for which coercion was being applied in the first place. It is not surprising, therefore, that actual cases of persecution do not resemble Waldron's "snow is white" case. To support his conclusions about toleration, Locke need only claim that the kinds of coercion that would-be persecutors are prepared to use are incapable of forcing people to think; indeed, they are designed to do the reverse.[14] Here, too, Rand would agree with Locke. As we have seen, she views the initiation of force as involving a flight from reality and from the constraints of evidence and reasoning.

14. The evidence of the *Letter* suggests that Locke would agree with this (see Locke 1689 [2010], 5, 30–31; also Locke 1690 [2010], 76), although on the surface he presents his argument as if the persecutors' aim were simply the benign one of conversion to the true religion. This is part of the reason I think it is a mistake to read Locke's argument simply as making a point about the instrumental irrationality of intolerance.

In view of the foregoing, we can deal more simply with Waldron's third example, in which coercion is used to require that certain religious texts be read. Waldron argues that such a requirement might work to increase the overall number of believers in a society. Although the effect would again be indirect, his aim is precisely to highlight the various ways in which force might be used to achieve such indirect effects on belief. By requiring all citizens to read the Gospels, for example, or the religious writings of C. S. Lewis, a Christian ruler might swell the ranks of sincere Christians, since at least some of those subject to such coercion might come to adopt Christianity of their own volition, based on their own independent reflection on these works. By requiring exposure to such material, the ruler can raise the chances that such reflection will occur.

No doubt this might happen, just as forcing people to read *Atlas Shrugged* might have the near-term effect of increasing the number of thoughtful adherents to Rand's philosophy of Objectivism. But there is again a question of consistency with the persecutor's deeper aims. The point of *forcing* someone to read some text or other is precisely to override—in Rand's terms, to negate—his judgment as to what materials warrant his attention. If it were really considered acceptable for him either to accept or reject the ideas propounded therein, according to the judgment of his own mind, then one suspects it would also be acceptable for him to refrain from reading the text to begin with.[15] There is in any event no difference in principle between the two; to reject the one is to lay groundwork for the rejection of the other. More important, in this case Rand at least and possibly also Locke can argue that everything in the outcome depends on the intellectual choices of those who are forced. The indirect effects that Waldron points to in the "snow is white" case are absent here; the mind cannot be forced, even in Waldron's attenuated sense.

3. Threats Demanding Belief: Force as Paralyzing Thought

Let us turn to the issue of force's paralyzing thought. Galt says that force "paralyzes" a man's rational judgment and, therefore, his means of survival. Leonard Peikoff unpacks this claim as follows: "if and to the extent that someone's gun becomes a man's court of final appeal, replacing the law of identity, then the man cannot think" (Peikoff 1991, 312). The first

---

15. Locke says something along these lines in the *Second Letter Concerning Toleration* (see Locke 1690 [2010], 77–78). Regarding why Locke does not consider these kinds of indirect effects relevant to whether the magistrate may use force to promote religious belief, see above.

thing to notice about Peikoff's formulation is that it is conditional. The claim is not that a threat of force somehow makes a person categorically unable to think, as if merely making a threat against someone would have this effect regardless of how the recipient responds to it. The recipient's inability to think results not from the threat alone but from the recipient's attempting to conform his thinking to whatever content the maker of the threat is trying to impose. If, for example, you're threatened with death for your atheism, then the claim would be that, if you attempt to conform to religious orthodoxy, not just in your external practice but in your *thinking*, you will not be able to think. Whereas Locke emphasizes what force cannot do (its inability to achieve a certain positive outcome), Rand emphasizes what it can and does do, specifically, bring about a certain kind of negative effect.

To explore Rand's claim about cognitive paralysis, I want to begin by presenting some examples that illustrate what I take her to have in mind by this term. Although we are interested mainly in cognitive paralysis under force, Rand's writings make it clear that the concept is not restricted to these contexts, and so some of the examples I will give do not involve any force. The first example comes from her own experience as a writer: "you are writing, and suddenly, on a given sequence or chapter, you find yourself completely paralyzed mentally. This strikes at unexpected moments" (*AON* 63). She calls this condition the squirms, and she notes that most writers suffer from it periodically. She describes it further as follows: "You find, suddenly, that your subconscious does not function. You know, consciously, what you want to say, but somehow the words do not come. . . . The squirms make you feel ignorant about writing. During such periods, I literally felt that it was impossible to write. I told myself consciously that I had written before; but emotionally, in that moment, I felt that I had lost the very concept of writing" (63–64). Rand attributes the squirms to the presence of an unresolved subconscious contradiction in a writer's intentions: "Whenever you experience the squirms, some clash of intentions occurs on the subconscious level, as if your inner circuits were tied in knots. You feel paralyzed because your subconscious is struggling with a contradiction, but since it is on the subconscious level, you cannot identify it immediately" (65). For instance, the problem could lie in "a contradiction in what you want to say about a subject" (65), which, until it is resolved, will prevent the execution of either of the two conflicting intentions. Rand describes the problem here psychologically, but it should be noted that nothing depends on the inner conflict's being subconscious. Its being subconscious makes the paralysis seem inexplicable and unresolvable. But unless the conflict were resolved in a way that allowed one's writing to proceed, the paralysis would not abate.

Here is an example in which the conflicting intentions were more readily apparent. In a recent article, Talbot Brewer recounts his efforts to oppose budget cuts affecting programs in the humanities at the University of Virginia. "Like many of my fellow professors," he writes, "I gave serious thought during the upheaval to the possibility of publishing a defense of what we do at our university. . . . I produced rough versions of possible op-eds but did not try to publish anything" (Brewer 2014, 71). Brewer explains the problem: "What paralyzed me was that my attempted defenses of the humanities seemed to fall into two categories: those that might conceivably help our cause but were not heartfelt, and those that were downright impolitic. These latter efforts were indeed doubly impolitic: . . . they pointed toward a serious indictment of the form actually taken by the humanities in my own university and in colleges and universities around the country. They were, in short, politically ineffective defenses of an ideal that, if taken seriously, would provide fresh grounds for attacking us" (71). Brewer wanted to write a defense of the humanities that was both heartfelt and politically safe. But the only line of defense that made sense to him, and thus that could be heartfelt (that is, the result of genuine thought and conviction) was a politically dangerous one. The attempt to produce a heartfelt but politically safe defense could go nowhere. His goal was to produce a defense of the humanities that he could accept as true, which meant that he had to be prepared to write whatever his assessment of the merits of the issue required. Thus, if necessary, he had to be willing to write something that could be politically damaging. The self-imposed demand for a politically innocuous defense derailed his ability to work out a sound argument for his position; it stopped his thinking.

In the kind of paralysis that Rand is discussing above, one usually solves the problem by modifying one's intentions so that, for example, one has a clearly defined and consistent plan for what to write. In Brewer's case, though, the problem was insoluble, because it was unacceptable to him to abandon either of his criteria for an acceptable article. That being so, he wrote nothing; his paralysis (on this issue) was irresolvable.

We can think of the conflicting intentions in these cases as reflecting conflicting norms that the thinker recognizes as authoritative.[16] In some cases, the authority of these norms may rest in part on personal choice, as when one selects a theme for a piece of fiction. In other cases, the norm's authority has a different source. Brewer, for example, might have considered it morally necessary to be both honest and politically responsible. In the cases of particular interest to Rand, in connection with the topic of force, the norms at issue will in part be epistemic. We will come to this below. But let us return to our examples for a while longer.

In resolvable cases of paralysis, the problem is solved by the writer's own integrity, in conscientiously clarifying his ideas and aims. In Brewer's case, Rand might see it as a testament to his rationality that he did not persist, once the impossibility of his task became clear to him. Someone else might have evaded the conflict and pushed ahead with a piece that was either hypocritical or irresponsible. Rand regards paralysis under force as warranting special attention because individual virtue cannot be the whole solution to the problem.

To see this, we can consider a case of Rand's own devising, from *Atlas Shrugged*. John Galt is being held by the authorities, who demand he produce an economic plan to save the country. He can do this, but he cannot produce a plan that will meet his captors' criterion: that there be no diminution in their own power and no lessening of government control over the economy. This case is structurally analogous to Brewer's. The required solution must be both viable as a solution and consistent with

16. I mean this point to be relatively noncommittal as to the philosophy of intention, on which Rand has no explicit view. When someone intends to A, and also when she Bs with the intention of A-ing, then it would seem that she takes *the requirements of A-ing* to be normative or standard-setting for her psychological and/or existential actions. (Taking these requirements as normative would include endeavoring to some extent to discover their content, where this was unknown to one.) Typically one has various intentions at a given time, and to take the requirements of achieving any one of them as normative does not mean regarding them as solely authoritative. Further, the grounds on which one takes the requirements of A-ing to be normative can vary; one might or might not view these norms as having independent authority, apart from one's intention to A. But if there are no criteria of any kind that one takes to be standard-setting for the success of one's actions, then it seems hard to make sense of the idea either that one intends to A or that one is B-ing with the intention of A-ing. These claims do not amount to a definition or an analysis, or even an account, of intentions or intentional action *in terms of* the acceptance of norms. Nor do the claims exclude the possibility of "pure intending," without corresponding action, since one can take the requirements of A-ing to be normative without acting on them at present; nor do they make any assumptions about the rationality of intentions. The claims seem to me compatible with widely different accounts, but, in any event, they also seem to me to be reflected in the way that Rand thinks about intentions and intentional action.

the maintenance of the statist economic structures already in place. Galt cannot produce a plan under these conditions. His mind cannot function cognitively on the task as defined. His own rationality is not in question; he is not about to sell out and assume power on the pretense that he can solve the nation's problems in a statist context. The significance of the fact that he is under force is that he cannot just walk away; his own rationality is of no benefit to him as long as his life is in the authorities' hands (except, perhaps, in that it prevents him from collaborating and enables him not to panic). This is the sense in which force has uniquely destructive effects: the paralysis that it creates becomes inescapable insofar as one is prevented from simply redeploying one's intellectual resources elsewhere. Force thus undercuts one's survival, and the survival of all those whom one might indirectly benefit through trade, in a manner that individual virtue alone cannot counteract. From Rand's perspective, a special moral principle is needed, therefore, to highlight and prohibit this unique kind of threat to human well-being.

Let us examine some real world cases of cognitive paralysis under force. The émigré Polish poet Czeslaw Milosz explores this subject extensively in his classic book *The Captive Mind*. The book chronicles the professional lives of several Eastern European intellectuals who struggled with issues of dissent and accommodation after the Second World War and the communist takeover of their country.

> The objective conditions necessary to the realization of a work of art are, as we know, a highly complex phenomenon, involving one's public, the possibility of contact with it, the general atmosphere, and above all freedom from involuntary subjective control. "I can't write as I would like to," a young Polish poet admitted to me. "My own stream of thought has so many tributaries, that I barely succeed in damming off one, when a second, third, or fourth overflows. I get halfway through a phrase, and already I submit to Marxist criticism. I imagine what X or Y will say about it, and I change the ending." (Milosz 1955, 14)

The poet quoted here describes himself as making the effort both to "write as [he] would like to" and to conform to Marxist orthodoxy, but he finds that the latter precludes the former. To write as he would like to would be to write according to his own ideas and "sense of life," his own grasp of the human condition and of his own experiences. It is this kind of writing that expresses thinking, as opposed to mere imitation, and this is what the effort to conform closes off.

The young poet's description of the method of his self-censorship is significant: he imagines what someone else will say about it. When an orthodoxy is being imposed by force, the decisions of the authorities necessarily become the criterion of orthodoxy; what is orthodox is whatever they regard as such. This is true regardless of the orthodoxy's content, since it requires judgment to interpret any proposed criterion (even, say, the principles of Newtonian physics), but the point of an imposed orthodoxy is to deny anyone besides the authorities standing to settle its interpretation. The availability of objective criteria of interpretation (as in the case of Newtonian physics) would be of no avail, since those criteria must still be applied by somebody, and disagreements among interpreters are always possible.[17] Unless the decision of the authorities is final, the orthodoxy has the status of a suggestion. Socially, the coercive imposition of an orthodoxy serves precisely to release the authorities from the requirements of objective thinking; they stand under no obligation to justify their decrees to those outside their ranks.

This is why the poet's self-censorship must be based on "what so and so would say." The attempt to conform to dialectical materialism as promulgated by the authorities deprives him of any method of judging the content of the doctrine to which he seeks to conform. That the doctrine itself is arguably arbitrary and indefinable (as Rand would certainly hold) is not the main issue. This means only that it is well suited to the purposes of dictators seeking to prevent independent thought and action. The key issue is that the imposition of a doctrine by force and the attempt to comply with it inwardly leave one with no independent means of ascertaining what one can or cannot think or say. But the criterion of "what so-and-so would say," in turn, has no firm criteria of interpretation; it is, in the end, a noncriterion, since the purpose of this form of coercion is precisely to facilitate the arbitrary use of political power. The authorities will do what they do and say what they say.

This helps us to see why, in Rand's view, investing any criterion with final authority over one's thinking, other than that of *one's own most conscientious application of objective epistemic norms*, necessarily paralyzes

---

17. The point here is not that "everything is a matter of interpretation" in the sense that there is no objective truth or objective meaning. Rand denies this. But she holds that truth and meaning must be ascertained by some method—they do not spontaneously reveal themselves to us—and there is no final authority in cognitive matters other than (for each thinker) one's own independent judgment. See "Who Is the Final Authority in Ethics" (*VOR*), which discusses this point in relation to ethics.

one's thought processes. Even an otherwise contentful criterion (as opposed to the elastic demands of a dictatorship) will become problematic if one's aim is to apply it *as so-and-so would*, since accessing its content relies on one's own application of proper epistemic methods. The criterion then becomes un-interpretable—"arbitrary," in Rand's terminology—by virtue of its lack of connection to one's own judgment. Rand's conception of objectivity is crucial to her ability to make this point. In her view, concepts and propositions can function as cognitive devices (and as guides to action) only when grasped by an individual mind employing an appropriate methodology.

The young poet's case exposes a contrast between cognitive paralysis under force and Rand's "squirms." Since Rand continued to accord final epistemic authority to her own judgment, her difficulties were localized and resolvable; in principle she could have proceeded on the basis of either one of her conflicting intentions, once she had identified them, with no problems of interpretation or arbitrariness. But the poet, once he institutes the intention to write acceptably, is unable to function creatively at all.[18] Milosz explains the issue as follows: "Whoever truly creates is alone. When he succeeds in creating, many followers and imitators appear; and then it seems that his work confirms the existence of some sort of 'wave of history.' The creative man has no choice but to trust his inner command and place everything at stake in order to express what seems to him to be true" (1955, 208). No longer alone inwardly, the poet could no longer create, either.

Milosz recounts the stories of several other writers with the same essential pattern. What had been vibrant, meaningful prose or verse becomes flat, stale, and lifeless:

> He tried to write differently, but whenever he denied something that lay in the very nature of his talent his prose became flat and colorless; he tore up his manuscripts. . . .
>
> Beta [a pseudonym] was a real writer in his stories about the concentration camp; though he questioned all man's inner imperatives, he counterfeited nothing, he did not try to please anybody. Then he introduced a single particle of politics and, like a supersaturated solution, his

---

18. Brewer's case is intermediate between the two. His writing problem was localized to the particular article he was working on, but since he in effect treated the expected political reactions of others as an epistemic criterion, he had no way of resolving the problem short of either giving up or writing something inauthentic.

writing crystallized, became thereafter transparent and stereotyped.
. . .

For all their violence and precision of language, his articles were so dull and one-dimensional that this debasement of a gifted prose-writer stirred my curiosity. . . .

The writing of articles acted on him like a narcotic. When he put down his pen he felt he had accomplished something. It didn't matter that there wasn't a single thought of his own in these articles. It didn't matter that thousands of second-rate journalists from the Elbe to the Pacific were saying exactly the same thing. He was active in the sense that a solder marching in formation is active. . . .

The lord who held him in thrall tolerated him for a while not because his songs were pleasing, for song is merely a means to an end. It was when his songs no longer served the desired end that his master knit his brows in anger. Publishers were instructed to print only those of his poems in which he demonstrated that he had reformed. The puritans rubbed their hands in glee. At last they had wrung his neck. They knew that no matter how he tried he could not reform. Deprived of their former exuberance, his poems no longer differed from verse ground out by second-rate rhymesters. (Milosz 1955, 102, 123–24, 124, 126, 182)

It can be seen in some of these examples that cognitive paralysis, in Rand's sense, is compatible with maintaining a literary output. Most of the writers whom Milosz profiles continued to write, and some became enthusiastic abettors of the communist state, out of intellectual insecurity or a desire for status. What is impeded is the ability to write fluidly, authentically, and insightfully. In practice, the writers who "convert" apply the "what would X or Y say?" standard by copying what other approved writers have said, which clearly raises a regress problem. The solution to the regress is for literary expression to be increasingly modeled on the propagandistic sloganeering of the leaders: "*The Stony World* was the last book in which Beta tried to employ artistic tools, like restraint, hidden irony, masked anger, etc., recognized as effective in Western literature. He quickly realized that all his concern about 'art' was superfluous. On the contrary, the harder he stepped down on the pedal, the more he was praised. Loud, violent, clear, biased—this is what his writing was expected to be. As Party writers (he entered the Party) began to out-bid each other in an effort to be accessible and simple, the boundary between literature and propaganda began to fade" (122–23).

In discussing the passage from Peikoff above, I noted that cognitive paralysis, for Rand, results from *complying* with a demand to conform one's thinking to an orthodoxy, not simply from the act of force. Milosz's account reflects the importance of this compliance condition. Each of his subjects passes through a period of crisis, after the imposition of censorship over the arts; he must decide how to respond to the new environment:

> If he is a writer, he cannot hold a pencil in his hand. The whole world seems dark and hopeless. Until now, he paid a minimal tribute: in his articles and novels, he described the evils of capitalist society. . . . But now he must begin to *approve*. . . . The operation he must perform on himself is one that some of his friends have already undergone, more or less painfully. They shake their heads sympathetically, knowing the process and its outcome. "I have passed the crisis," they say serenely. "But how he is suffering. He sits at home all day with his head in his hands." (Milosz 1955, 16)

For some of his subjects, the crisis resolves with a decision to comply with the artistic imperatives of Stalinist orthodoxy:

> Nevertheless, despite his resistance and despair, the crisis approaches. It can come in the middle of the night, at his breakfast table, or on the street. It comes with a metallic click as of engaged gears. *But there is no other way.* That much is clear. There is no other salvation on the face of the earth. This revelation lasts a second; but from that second on, the patient begins to recover. For the first time in a long while, he eats with relish, his movements take on vigor, his color returns. He sits down and writes a "positive" article, marveling at the ease with which he writes it. In the last analysis, there was no reason for raising such a fuss. Everything is in order. He is past the "crisis." (19)

Creatively, the results of these "conversions," as Milosz calls them (195), are as described in the earlier set of passages, but two further passages are worth including here:

> In his desire to win approbation, ["Alpha"] had simplified his picture to conform to the wishes of the Party. One compromise leads to a second and a third until at last, though everything one says may be perfectly logical, it no longer has anything in common with the flesh and blood of living people. . . .
>
> The Party constantly stresses its desire for good literature; at the

same time, it creates such a tense atmosphere of propaganda that writers feel compelled to resort to the most primitive and oversimplified literary techniques. Yet it was true that Beta *himself* wanted to devote all his time to journalism; although he was a highly qualified specialist, he seized upon work that was easy for the most ordinary drudge. His mind, like that of so many Eastern intellectuals, was impelled toward self-annihilation. (105, 124–25)

Milosz observes that in a sense these conversions had a calming effect, settling an inner turmoil: "He attains a relative degree of harmony, just enough to render him active. It is preferable to the torment of pointless rebellion and groundless hope" (Milosz 1955, 22). But this harmony is superficial. "One can survive the 'crisis' and function perfectly, writing or painting as one must," Milosz comments, "but the old moral and aesthetic standards continue to exist on some deep inner plane. Out of this arises a split within the individual that makes for many difficulties in his daily life" (21). Referring to "the apathy that is born in people, and that lives on in spite of their feverish activity," he writes:

> It is hard to define, and at times one might suppose it to be a mere optical illusion. After all, people bestir themselves, work, go to the theater, applaud speakers, take excursions, fall in love, and have children. Yet there is something impalpable and unpleasant in the human climate of such cities as Warsaw or Prague. The collective atmosphere . . . is bad. It is an aura of strength and unhappiness, of internal paralysis and external mobility. Whatever we may call it, this much is certain: if Hell should guarantee its lodgers magnificent quarters, beautiful clothes, the tastiest food, and all possible amusements, but condemn them to breathe in this aura forever, that would be punishment enough. (22–23)

With this extended characterization of cognitive paralysis and its spiritual consequences in place, I want to give a somewhat more theoretical account. We can make a distinction between occurrent and latent paralysis—between paralysis as a psychological phenomenon and as an epistemic condition. By "occurrent" paralysis, I mean the psychological condition of internal gridlock and its external expression in flat, lifeless prose.[19] By latent paralysis, I am referring to the acceptance or imposi-

---

19. The latter is also present in Rand's description of the "squirms"; she says that whatever one produces in this state sounds like the writing of a high school student (see *AON* 63–64). Although such output is characteristic of occurrent paralysis, one might also simply

tion of norms for one's intellectual-creative work that are incompatible with the requirements of cognition. In superficial cases of paralysis such as Rand's "squirms," the problematic norms are independently consistent with those requirements but in conflict with one another; the incompatibility with the requirements of cognition lies in the fact that one cannot think and create on the basis of a contradiction. In deeper cases, such as those of Milosz's subjects, one of the norms—that of conforming to Party orthodoxy—is incompatible in itself with the requirements of cognition. Rand explains occurrent paralysis in terms of latent paralysis, and the latter can be present without the former, if one simply does no intellectual work.

Latent paralysis extends as far as the reach of the underlying problematic norms. Some of Milosz's subjects might possibly have been able to work in secret, out of the reach of the demand for intellectual conformity. Galt cannot do any overt intellectual work, because he is being held by force by authorities who demand that he think in compliance with their premises. But Galt does not experience occurrent paralysis because, unlike Milosz's subjects, he does not try to think in compliance with the authorities' demands.

Since latent paralysis is the underlying condition, I will explore it further, focusing on the deep forms of it and setting aside the more superficial case of the "squirms." What is paralyzed, according to Rand, is one's ability to engage in cognitive tasks, to think and create. The source of the paralysis is the adoption of an intention that is incompatible with the requirements of cognition—specifically, the intention that one's thinking conform to a premise (theory, doctrine, text, etc.) that is accepted as authoritative independently of one's own judgment of its epistemic merits and meaning and whose authority is regarded as unchallengeable and final. The results of one's application of epistemic norms to any subject matter—and *the norms themselves*—must then be certified as consistent with the favored premise. This applies even to the conceptual identification of whatever perceptual evidence one relies on and to the norms for applying perceptual concepts.[20] Because it is held independently of one's

fail to produce anything as a consequence of one's inner gridlock. Analogously, in other intellectual and creative fields (such as science or the visual arts) the external evidence of occurrent paralysis would take the form of stale, imitative work in whatever field one practiced in.

20. We could take the point back a step further still: the thinking behind a decision to study a particular subject matter would have to be similarly scrutinized. But I will not pursue this angle here, since it introduces nothing essentially new into the analysis.

judgment, and its interpretation is therefore not amenable to one's judgment, this favored premise becomes arbitrary and uninterpretable. The setting of an intention to conform to such a premise amounts to the adoption of a general norm for thought that (a) claims regulatory authority over (1) the principles by which one reasons and makes judgments and (2) the output of their application and (b) lacks any actual content itself as a norm. Since thought requires a specific methodology, it cannot get off the ground in these conditions; if one tries to think, the result will be occurrent paralysis.

It should be emphasized that the regulatory authority of the favored premise extends to the epistemic norms by which one thinks, including those pertaining to the formation and application of concepts, to induction and theory-formation, and so forth. If these were held to be immune from regulatory oversight, then the conclusions generated by their application to perceptual evidence, at basic and advanced levels of inquiry, would be similarly immune. The favored premise or doctrine must be hegemonic in order to have any effect. And its hegemony must range over one's past and present thinking.

The issue of the arbitrariness of the favored premise is clearly central to the account of cognitive paralysis, so let us examine this further. In realistic cases of coerced thinking, this premise or doctrine is likely to be arbitrary, not just from the standpoint of the person complying with it but in principle. As official doctrines, both Nazism and Soviet and Chinese communism have turned out to be highly susceptible to adjustment in accordance with the political objectives of their enforcers. Their content is generated by political rather than epistemic considerations, and so their content is arbitrary from the standpoint of epistemic criteria.[21] What these doctrines require depends on what they are held to require by those in power. But, as noted earlier, even if the favored doctrine has some independent content that might be capable of objective interpretation, this content would become inscrutable if one attempted to conform one's mind to the doctrine as interpreted by so-and-so as a fundamental cognitive goal.

21. It would perhaps not be arbitrary strictly relative to those political considerations. But Rand would see the particular political principles underlying these considerations—and by extension the considerations themselves—as epistemically arbitrary. See, in this connection, her comments on evil philosophies as "systems of rationalization" in "Philosophical Detection" (*PWNI* 25–28).

Let us consider a possibility that seems remote from actual cases of thought control but is worth investigating for the light it sheds on the present issue. Suppose that one intends to conform one's thinking to some doctrine (D), according to *one's own* best interpretation of D's meaning, but let us assume that one has no particular grounds for accepting D as *true*.[22] It would be self-defeating for a dictatorship to allow such interpretive freedom. We could imagine instead that an individual wants, for reasons of their own, to conform intellectually to some view or other. Take, for example, a scientist or policy writer researching climate change who fears being ostracized from her professional peer group if the position she reaches differs from theirs.[23] But even voluntary conformity to a peer group must rely on the group members' interpretation of their ideas, in order to be effective; it would do no good to tell them they did not know their own minds. Consider this fanciful (not to say, ludicrous) case, then: a philosopher desires to conform all her thinking to her own best interpretation of Locke's philosophical views, as gathered from the latter's extant works. She will settle her interpretation fully, according to her own independent judgment, on the basis of a conscientious application of sound methods of philosophical historiography and then ensure from that point onward that everything she thinks is consistent with this body of ideas.

Would there be any issue of arbitrariness, or might she be able to some extent to prune her other beliefs accordingly? Clearly, if that happened, she would still have given up on the aim of having only true beliefs, and if that aim is constitutive of genuine thinking she would not be able to think. So Rand's claims about cognitive paralysis could still be supported; to start up her thinking again, it would be necessary for her to de-throne Locke from her mind. It seems to me that there would also be a deeper problem, however. The epistemic authority of a textual interpretation is derived from, and can be no stronger than, that of the methods by which it was reached, including not only the specific methods of textual

22. To make Rand's point, it need not be assumed that someone has evidence against the truth of the doctrine—only that they have no evidence for its truth, or insufficient evidence to make a confident judgment.

23. What view is held to be unchallengeable and what views the person herself might be inclined toward are immaterial to the issue here. The situation could arise for a scientist who fears such ostracism as Freeman Dyson faced (Dawidoff 2009) for challenging predictions of rapid and destructive warming. Analogously, a libertarian policy analyst might fear endorsing such predictions. (For an example of this sort of case, see Lepp 2017.)

interpretation but the general methods required for cognition as such. The interpretation cannot singlehandedly overturn its own grounds.[24] To accord authority to the interpretation, based on these grounds, is to accord authority to the grounds. Qua reflecting one's own best judgment, therefore, the interpretation cannot be taken to have the kind of hegemonic authority required for conforming to it.

We might suppose, though, that she could hive off the interpretation from its grounds and treat it in effect as a time-stamped pronouncement that must now simply be accepted unconditionally. But the interpretation has no agency of its own. Its efficacy is dependent on our philosopher's ability to think herself back into how she was seeing the texts; this would be true even if she had written the whole thing down. There would be no escaping the need for verdicts such as, "Oh, yes, that's what I was thinking; that's what I meant." But those verdicts, too, depend for their authority on the cognitive methods by which they are reached, and so the merely conditional authority of the supposedly unconditionally authoritative textual interpretation is reasserted. The notion of *conforming* to one's own interpretation of a text or body of ideas is chimerical.

If this is correct, then there is a deep problem with the attempt to conform one's thinking to *any* body of doctrine. To the extent that one takes this mandate seriously, its implementation deprives one of the tools necessary for grasping the meaning of the target ideas, even if these ideas are in principle objectively interpretable and even if they are known by others to be true. Because of this, it deprives one of any method for assessing one's past or future conclusions, in any area of one's thinking. It thus paralyzes one's thinking across the board, in the occurrent sense, insofar as one complies.

Realistic cases of political thought control or of submission to peer pressure might seem to contradict this sweeping claim. Consider, again, the climate researcher. It seems easily imaginable that she might go on functioning in her field, and it seems even more so that she might be independent minded in other areas of her thinking, such as in the management of her personal finances. I do not think that Rand has to deny this. Insofar as she can cordon off areas of her research, she can think, but to whatever extent she seeks to avoid the disapproval of her peers, her

---

24. That a certain interpretive strategy yielded a certain result might well count against the strategy in some cases. But it would not do so in isolation from a broader context, in which it could be seen, for example, that this result contradicted other well established claims. The point in the text is simply that the result could not overturn its grounds all by itself.

only available intellectual criterion is what ideas they will accept, and this criterion leaves all of her own ideas in limbo pending others' reactions; independent thinking can get nowhere. The same is true in regard to her finances. It is unlikely that she would feel any pressure to extend her conformism more widely, but if she extended it into deliberating about her finances, she could not think in that area, either. She could not think if she treated peer approval as a serious epistemic criterion. Further, even if, through compartmentalization, she segments off some areas of her thinking as independent preserves, the thinking she does in these areas will, on Rand's view, lack full objectivity and thus fall short of being a fully conceptual grasp of reality, since these latter goals require epistemic integration across the entire breadth of one's thought. Only then can one successfully expand the range of one's awareness to the scale necessary for fully effective specialized study and for the long-range guidance of one's life.

Normally, peer pressure is localized, and compartmentalization is possible. But Rand holds that it is not a viable long-range option for a person; it has psychological and existential costs, particularly in regard to one's self-esteem and one's ability to achieve the kinds of goals on which happiness depends. One needs an actively integrated, firsthand frame of reference in order to value oneself robustly and guide the overall course of one's life consistently and self-sustainingly. Culturally, the same is true. Science, the arts, economic life, and politics all require a philosophical frame of reference to protect the epistemic and moral integrity of their endeavors—that is, to enable the culture as a whole to be guided comprehensively by appropriate cognitive and moral norms. Where this kind of cultural integration is absent or deficient, Rand holds, a society drifts and stagnates amid increasing internal conflicts over basic values and standards.[25] In her view, the sort of cultural integration that is required for a thriving, life-affirming society, however, cannot be achieved through force. It must develop and be sustained as a meeting of independent minds, with each person grappling with the relevant issues on his own intellectual level and as his own needs warrant.

25. This sort of conflict is ever present in the United States and other Western countries today, and Rand would undoubtedly view it as confirming her point. She does not hold, however, that internal debate, even debate on fundamental issues, is harmful or undesirable. As I indicate presently in the text, cultural unity cannot be achieved by force, in her view, but only through the free and open discussion of ideas. It does, however, require at least a broad background of shared premises to get started. For Rand's views on these issues, see "For the New Intellectual" (*FTNI* 54–58) and "A Nation's Unity" (ARL 2: 1–3 [October–November 1972]).

Unlike peer pressure, the compliance demanded by a totalitarian dictatorship is all-embracing, although the means of enforcement may be imperfect. The intent, however, is across-the-board control over the independent mind. Milosz makes this point starkly:

> When one considers the matter logically, it becomes obvious that intellectual terror is a principle that Leninism-Stalinism can never forsake, even if it should achieve victory on a world scale. The enemy, in a potential form, will *always* be there; the only friend will be the man who accepts the doctrine 100 per cent. If he accepts only 99 per cent, he will necessarily have to be considered a foe, for from that remaining 1 per cent a new church can arise. The explanation Stalinists often advance, that this is only a *stage* resulting from "capitalist encirclement," is self-contradictory. The concept of a *stage* presupposes planning from the top, absolute control now and always. Eastern rulers are aware of this contradiction. If they were not, they would not have to present forced participation in clubs and parades, forced voting for a single list, forced raising of production norms, etc. as spontaneous and voluntary acts. This is a dark, unpleasant point for even the most passionate believers.
>
> This way of posing the problem discloses the madness of the doctrines. Party dialecticians know that similar attempts on the part of other orthodoxies have always failed. In fact, History itself exploded one after another the formulas that have been considered binding. This time, however, the rulers have mastered dialectics so, they assert, they will know how to modify the doctrine as new necessities arise. The judgments of an individual man can always be wrong; the only solution is to submit unreservedly to an authority that claims to unerring. (1955, 205)

By Rand's analysis, it might seem that people living in a regime that succeeded in imposing unreserved submission would simply freeze in place, unable to make independent judgments about even the simplest matters. I think this is an implication of her account. That this is not what happens even in the most repressive dictatorships might be seen as an indication of the practical difficulties involved in fully enforcing the demand for complete submission. This is no doubt true. But, for Rand, the problem also reflects, more fundamentally, a deep ethical truth: that the persistence of evil depends on the exploitation of the good. Evil, in her analysis, *functions* by drawing strength from the good it works to destroy. A dictatorship, for instance, has no alternative but to permit and count on some amount of independent judgment by a sufficient critical mass of its subjects in order for its economy and its institutions to operate at all.[26]

It must draw strength from the very qualities of human character that it seeks to suppress. At the same time, for the reason that Milosz presents, a dictatorship must officially forbid independent thought on principle. This is an inconsistent position, but the only form of consistent evil, in this regard, would be to ruthlessly identify and punish even the slightest show of cognitive independence, a process that, if successful, would require the extermination of everyone not driven to suicide. On Rand's view, no variant of the ethics of self-sacrifice—no code that denies one's right to live and think for one's own sake—can be practiced consistently, except through the wholesale destruction of human life. Dictatorships, therefore, can operate only through some amount of compromise of their fundamental principles; and individuals in a dictatorship can keep going only insofar as they can manage to create some private space in which to "breathe"—to live and think independently.

Because full compliance would be tantamount to self-annihilation, Milosz's subjects practice what he calls "Ketman." He says that the term is Middle Eastern in origin and refers to the practice of dissimulating about one's religious position while maintaining an inner core of apostasy.[27] The external side of Ketman Milosz describes as an elaborate and excruciating form of acting, which requires constant, exhausting self-monitoring so as to preclude any degree of revealing spontaneity. Inwardly, Ketman is the effort to quarantine some private interior space in which to work freely and creatively. This effort takes a variety of different forms, which Milosz explores. "Professional Ketman" is possible to those whose professions are of special value to the state:

> If I am a scientist I attend congresses at which I deliver reports strictly according to the Party line. But in the laboratory I pursue my research according to scientific methods, and in that alone lies the aim of my life. . . .
>
> The object [of professional Ketman] is to establish some special field in which one can release one's energies, exploit one's knowledge and sen-

26. This principle is related to Rand's principle of the "sanction of the victim," that evil requires the good's moral sanction in order to persist. This latter principle explains how the exploitation of the good is made possible; it is not fundamentally a matter of the exertion of brute force but of the willing submission of the better people, facilitated and encouraged by their acceptance of the morality of self-sacrifice. For these issues, see *Atlas* 416–83, and Peikoff 1991, 259–67.

27. He draws the term from Gobineau 1866 [1900]; see Milosz 1955, 5–21. The reliability of Gobineau's assertions about Ketman is not an issue here, since we are concerned only with Milosz's use of the term in an Eastern European context.

sibility, and at the same time escape the fate of a functionary entirely at the mercy of political fluctuations. The son of a worker who becomes a chemist makes a *permanent* advance. . . . But, most of all, chemical experiments, bridges, translations of poetry, and medical care [for example] are exceptionally free of falsity. The State, in its turn, takes advantage of this Ketman because it needs chemists, engineers, and doctors. . . . [Nevertheless,] moderation and watchfulness are indicated for those who espouse this form of Ketman. (1955, 65, 66–67)

These practitioners benefit from the state's own unavoidable inconsistency, although Milosz leaves no doubt that this compensation is inadequate to overcome the psychic and existential damage done to life in the Eastern Bloc countries.[28]

To conclude this chapter, I want to return for a moment to Rand's fiction. That her conception of cognitive paralysis is essentially similar to Milosz's can be seen from her story "The Simplest Thing in the World," which portrays the inner life of a writer in a time of personal crisis.[29] The crisis faced by Rand's character Henry Dorn is not about intellectual accommodation under communism but, rather, accommodation with a set of critics whose literary standards he despises. He wants to produce a work to satisfy these critics (unlike the novel he published previously to almost universal scorn), but he finds that he simply cannot write down to popular and critical tastes. His writing reflects the esthetic values he authentically accepts, and he has no way of writing other than to rely on and express that automatized value-context. The point is not that he couldn't theoretically shape himself into a different and less authentic person, training himself to imitate the sorts of works that win critical praise. He might be able to do that or, less drastically, learn to function as a cynical hack. But short of these measures, which his integrity prevents him from exploring, he cannot write, and by the end of the story he has given up.

Rand's narration of his interior monologue explores his creative paralysis. He wants to resume writing, but he also wants to avoid repeating the excruciatingly painful critical rejection he faced with his first novel.

28. John Galt's strike in *Atlas Shrugged* might be seen as a different form of Ketman, in which one withdraws one's most valuable abilities from society and performs only menial work, reserving one's real work for whatever private spaces one can create.
29. I first suggested that this story could be used to explicate Rand's conception of cognitive paralysis in a seminar with Leonard Peikoff in the mid-1990s. He agreed that there was a connection, but he is obviously not responsible for any errors in my reconstruction of Rand's views here.

Frustrated by his months of writer's block, he asks himself, "How does one make one's mind work? How does one invent a story? How can people ever be writers? Come on, you've written before. How did you start then? No, you can't think of that. Not of that. If you do—you'll go completely blank again, or worse" (*RM* 171–72). What he does not dare think of is the kind of book he wrote previously. That's the kind he can write, the kind that his own authentic perspective on literature and life will allow him to write, and in the course of the story he does in fact come up with the germs of several ideas for stories that would excite him creatively and have serious meaning. But he rejects each of these in turn as unacceptable, given the constraint that his work must be critically acceptable. Dorn simply cannot think himself into the mind of someone who could write the sort of book he is aiming for: "Think of Fleurette Lumm [one of the critics], he said to himself. . . . You imagine that you can't understand her, but you can, if you want to" (*RM* 171).

In a sense, he presumably could. He could practice Ketman and learn to act the part of a popular writer. Milosz's subjects are sometimes able to feel themselves into their public roles, making them second nature, the way a method actor would. They borrow and imitate, and the results are flat and mechanical, but over time the process of generating those results becomes fluid.[30] In this context, where he is not under force, his integrity prevents that choice. Further, in the story we're given to understand that any such similar subterfuge will fail. Dorn must be sincere: "It mustn't have any meaning. It must be written as if you'd never tried to find any meaning in anything, not ever in your life. It must sound as if that's the kind of person you are" (*RM* 172–73). His sense of life and esthetic values are what they are, and they are the only foundation on which he can write. Ketman is not a practical option for him. Milosz's account suggests that it would be psychologically possible, in principle, if Dorn made the right sort of effort. But Milosz also documents the psychological self-mutilation involved in such a task—a task that, in any event, means an abandonment of cognition and genuine intellectual activity.

---

30. There is a crucial difference here from actual acting, which explains why there is such a thing as good acting. An actor may feel or think herself into a role, almost seeming to become the person she portrays, but the entire process flows from and reflects her particular interpretation of the part. John Gielgud and Jonathan Price may both *be* Hamlet, but they are *different* Hamlets. For someone to approach the public side of Ketman in this way would be to fatally misunderstand it, as Milosz's subjects never do. Their performance must be indistinct and imitative. As Milosz heartbreakingly comments, "even the most intimate of individuals speak to each other in Party slogans" (1955, 52).

The Scope and Justification of Rand's Non-Initiation of Force Principle

DARRYL WRIGHT

I
n my first chapter, I discussed the epistemological and ethical framework that underlies Rand's principle prohibiting the initiations of
physical force. In my second chapter, I explored the ways in which she
thinks the initiation of force "negates" and "paralyzes" the mind, thereby
undermining human survival. This material puts us in a position to now
examine her justification for the principle, and her view that the principle
is universal in scope—excluding even initiations of force that might be
thought to be innocuous or even morally necessary. That's my project in
this chapter.

The main work will be done in sections 2 and 3. Section 1 deals with
actions that Rand recognizes as initiations of force, but which I did not
treat in the previous two chapters of this volume, because her identification of them as initiations of force presupposes the existence of property
rights and, more broadly, the entire structure of individual rights that she
defends. I sketch the justificatory steps by which these cases come to be
included under the non–initiation of force principle.

Section 2 takes up the question of whether there can be a rational
justification for initiating force, from the initiator's perspective. Section
3 deals with Rand's reasons for defending an all-encompassing ban on

the initiation of force. In doing so, she replies to the contention that initiated force can sometimes be used (particularly by the state) for good. That contention, she argues, rests on incorrect assumptions about the nature of values. Lastly, section 4 relates Rand's principle to the libertarian nonaggression principle.

1. Force against Property

The anti-initiation of force principle can be given an initial specification and defense without presupposing property rights. Direct force (consisting of attacks on the person or physical confinement) and threats thereof, by negating or paralyzing the mind, attack man's means of survival, interfering in the process by which one maintains one's life. They are morally prohibited on that basis, in conjunction with the fundamentals of Rand's ethical theory.

As Rand views them, rights are only applicable within society, though they have a justificatory basis in the requirements of man's long-range survival. But even prior to the formation of an organized society and the introduction of rights, we can conceive of a state in which, say, nomadic peoples utilize resources drawn from nature for their own sustenance. They would not have property rights in these resources, in Rand's view, but it seems to me that her views imply that they would (generally speaking) have another sort of moral claim on them, relative to which the non–initiation of force principle would apply in an extended way. Specifically, goods under one's active physical control, appropriated for use directly from nature, would be legitimately possessed, and it would be morally wrong for anyone else to obtain those goods by direct force or the threat of such. This, too, would be an act of interfering with the victim's ability to take self-sustaining action. The use of force against the person's *goods* is counted as a use against the *person* herself because self-preservation *requires* that one acquire and utilize natural resources for one's own sustenance.

In this scenario, the limits of legitimate possession would more or less correspond to the limits of what I will call *immediate control*, that is, the active maintenance of physical control over a set of resources. The boundaries of immediate control cannot be specified precisely, nor do they need to be. You would have immediate control over some apples you held in your hand, or over the same apples if you set them right beside you, guarding them vigilantly. Roughly, anything you readily could keep hold of, by repelling invaders, would be within your immediate control.

Legitimate possession would extend this far, and perhaps somewhat farther, but not much farther. There might, for instance, be various relatively clear ways of signaling the boundaries of what one had claimed for one's own use, such as by physically separating oneself and one's goods from surrounding others, but this would seem feasible only if the totality of one's possessions remained fairly small and everything was, if not within immediate reach, not far from that. I think it is possible, within Rand's framework, to view takings of such "flagged" resources within a small encampment as morally on a par with someone's wrestling the apple you are eating out of your hand or grabbing the apples you were guarding at your side (and the latter two as morally on a par with one another). Each constitutes an evident, unprovoked interference with self-sustaining action, which the non–initiation of force principle would prohibit. In each of these cases, I will say that the resources in question are under one's (relatively) immediate control.

There might also be various intermediary stages, on the way to the formation of an organized society, in which implicit conventions regulated the expansion of what is generally conceded to be the sphere of one's legitimate control, somewhat beyond the scope of what could be actively policed in the absence of such conventions. This might facilitate both the enlargement of one's possessions and the possibility of retaining control over them through brief periods of absence. I presume kinship alliances might also play a role in stabilizing possessions to some extent. But the expansion of (conceded) legitimate control would be modest at best, and more important, it would lack full objectivity. Beyond the sphere of what one has unambiguously set by, the claim to have particular natural resources left alone for one's future use and disposition would become problematic, because the link to one's needs and survival would be more tenuous. Unlike natural rights theorists, Rand does not posit natural principles by which stable, extendable, and identifiable property rights could be acquired in this state, independently of a legal framework. Since, as we will see, she also holds that there are objective moral principles by which to construct such a framework, in her view property rights will have an objective foundation (as I will discuss shortly). But these objective rights will not be *natural* rights in the usual sense. (The lack of full objectivity in the cases just envisioned would for Rand be an aspect of a wider problem about objectivity that will be important in her theory of rights.)

In any event, the non–initiation of force principle would prohibit the taking of goods under one's immediate control (or threats to do so) outside of society, even without the existence of property rights. The grounds for regarding goods under one's immediate control as legitimate possessions necessarily include *the fact of such control itself*. They also include the necessity of gaining control over natural resources in order to live, given that one must utilize resources but cannot do so without first having them in one's possession. But this general normative requirement to control and utilize resources is not sufficient on its own, for it provides no criterion for identifying a person's legitimate possessions. Bringing resources under one's control—picking an apple, gathering berries, killing an animal—is a way of incorporating them into the life processes and, in that sense, of beginning to utilize them. The fact of control—as opposed, say, to a declaration of intent ("I'm going to pick those apples tomorrow," said while pointing) or a sweeping claim of control ("The stuff over there shall be mine")—is the only thing close, in this context, to an objective demonstration that the goods claimed are actually being utilized for one's life. Its objectivity may be imperfect; there may be irresolvable gray areas, and in Rand's view, this is one reason for forming a society. But the central cases are clear enough to support a moral requirement of respecting such possessions.[1]

As we have seen, Rand's ethics holds that, even outside of society, there are valid binding moral principles to guide human interaction. The non-initiation of force principle, as elaborated so far, is one such principle. The principles of honesty and justice that Rand defends in her ethical writings would be others, as would the principle that each person is an end in himself.[2] As has been mentioned previously, the initiation of force is a unique kind of evil, for Rand, because it harms one's life in a way that one cannot extricate oneself from by a mere act of will, in the form of withdrawing from a certain relationship. For this reason, force can only be repelled by force; either one is victimized by it or, as far as possible, one forcibly retaliates. For this reason, Rand accepts the retaliatory use

1. I leave aside here whether, for Rand, there would be any further constraints on legitimate possession, such as Locke's nonspoilage condition or the so-called Lockean proviso (a proviso, however, that I think has been attributed to Locke through misinterpretation). If so, then these constraints would restrict the application of the non-initiation of force principle also. For the nonspoilage condition, see Locke, *Second Treatise of Government*, section 31. For the "Lockean proviso," see Nozick 1974, 178–82. For whether Locke held this proviso, see Waldron 1979; Tomasi 1998.

2. For discussion of these elements of Rand's ethics, see Gotthelf 2016; Peikoff 1991, ch. 7; Smith 2006, chs. 4, 6; Wright 2016, especially 163–67.

of force as morally legitimate ("The Nature of Government," *VOS* 126–27/ *CUI* 379–80).

But retaliatory force also presents moral hazards. Left to each person's individual discretion, retaliatory force can easily be misused, even when those involved all have perfectly good intentions. If somebody honestly but mistakenly believes that the apples in your possession are the ones she gathered, because hers are now missing and you were seen in their vicinity, both of you might reasonably consider yourselves entitled to use retaliatory force—she, to regain her apples; and you, to prevent her from taking yours. Similarly, suppose that somebody is holding in captivity a person she claims has aggressed against her, which the prisoner denies. Is this retaliation or enslavement? If it is retaliation, is it excessive? Outside of society, each person must answer that question for herself, and each person faces the potentially violent consequences of the answers that others reach. The decisions of others are arbitrary in a social sense; one has no means of ensuring they are reached by epistemically appropriate methods, but they will be imposed regardless. Further, they have to be, since the conscientious use of retaliatory force could hardly be expected to wait on the target's acceptance of one's justification for using it; in self-protection, one must proceed directly by one's own lights. So the retaliatory use of force is absolutely necessary and, outside of society, hazardous and (socially) arbitrary. This, then, for Rand, is a second reason for forming a society.

There is a further reason: Even aside from the problems of objectivity with respect to the scope of legitimate possession and the use of retaliatory force, the limited use of material resources envisioned so far is inadequate for meeting the long-range needs of man's life, which, according to Rand, requires production and trade under an extensive division of labor. These, in turn, require an organized society and a much-extended conception of legitimate possession. What a society can provide, through the institution of government, is credible public enforcement of social rules geared toward resolving these three problems: objectively demarcating the scope of individuals' legitimate control over material values; expanding the scope of legitimate control so that it is commensurate with the needs of man's life; and objectively controlling the retaliatory use of force.[3]

---

3. Thus, for the reasons sketched in this and the preceding paragraph, Rand's view denies that "political power is privately exercised" and insists on a conception of "political

It is in the context of thinking through the criteria by which a society should be organized—and, specifically, the moral norms that should govern it—that the concept of rights can be formed and an account of the content of rights can be developed. A person's fundamental need within a society, Rand argues, is the freedom to engage in self-sustaining action—the freedom to maintain and enjoy one's life—without coercive interference. Rights, as she understands this concept, serve to delineate the scope and contours of this necessary sphere of freedom. "A right," she says, "is a moral principle defining and sanctioning a man's freedom of action in a social context" ("Man's Rights," *VOS* 110/*CUI* 369).

This concept of rights identifies explicitly and in principle something presupposed in the justification of the non–initiation of force principle: that a person requires no moral authorization from others to engage in a self-sustaining action; correspondingly, a showing that some action by others interferes with that process is sufficient for its moral prohibition. In the initial justification of the non–initiation of force principle, this moral independence is narrowly invoked with respect to the limited class of actions by reference to which the concept of (initiated) force is first formed—direct force and the threat of such. In the account of rights, it is invoked in a much broader way, as self-preservation comes to be understood more abstractly, in terms of a long-range process centered on the conception and production of material values through specialization and trade, rather than in terms of a relatively short-range, minimally cooperative satisfaction of immediate needs. It is this complex wide-scale process of activity, for each individual, that the concept of rights is focused on and that it commends for societal protection.

legitimacy"—that is, of the rightful authority of duly constituted governments, understood as *essentially* public institutions, to make and enforce law within their territories (Freeman 2002, 139, 144). In this respect, Rand's view contrasts with many libertarian views, including Nozick's, contrary to the implication of Freeman (107). Relatedly, Rand does not hold that basic rights are alienable, such as through a putative enslavement contract, as Nozick and a number of other libertarians do. Rights, for her, function precisely to specify nonnegotiable terms of social existence that governments are tasked with applying and enforcing. This may also be the place to note (although I cannot take up the point in detail here) that Rand's view of political authority need not commit her to the view of Hart and others that subjection to political authority involves a surrender of one's private judgment to the government and its agents, which seems contrary to the spirit of her political philosophy. Rather, it might be seen as involving a recognition of that judgment's limited reach, in particular, its lack of political objectivity, such that one must not act upon it in certain ways (e.g., by privately exacting redress in a contractual dispute). For Hart's view, see Hart 1982, ch. 10. For related discussion, see Raz 1986, ch. 3.

The protection of this process—human self-sustaining action in its full form—can, in Rand's view, only be accomplished in an organized society.[4] This, I take it, is why Rand holds that, strictly speaking, the concept of rights is inapplicable outside of society, even though it is grounded in metaphysically given facts about human nature. She is explicit about this restriction in a passage that was deleted from her essay "Man's Rights": "Political rights pertain to the organization of a society, to the establishment of a social system, a government and a legal code. As such, they are validated by reference to the facts of reality: to man's nature and the metaphysical conditions of his life on earth—and they establish basic principles for the rational, morally defensible society appropriate to the requirements of man's survival."[5] Explaining this issue, Leonard Peikoff says:

> If a man lived on a desert island, there would be no question of defining his proper relationship to others. Even if men interacted on some island but did so at random, without establishing a social system, the issue of rights would be premature. There would not yet be any context for the concept or, therefore, any means of implementing it; there would be no agency to interpret, apply, enforce it. When men do decide to form (or reform) an organized society, however, when they decide to pursue systematically the advantages of living together, then they need the guidance of principle. That is the context in which the concept of rights arises. (Peikoff 1991, 351–52)

His point here, as I take it, is that without a grasp of the forms of long-range activity that a (properly) organized society makes possible the materials for a grasp of the concept of rights are lacking. Because of this, there would be no cognitive need to form the concept, either. We could

---

4. This is a substantive and controversial claim that puts her at odds with the anarchist strain of libertarianism and also with Nozick, who in this respect shares the anarchist view. Nozick considers a rather sophisticated form of social life to be possible in an environment in which multiple protective agencies compete, before the dominant association achieves its de facto monopoly of force. On these issues, see, for example, Rothbard 1982 [2002], part 3; Nozick 1974, chs. 2 and 4.

5. Ayn Rand, "Cut from 'Man's Rights,'" folder 87D, Box 29, Ayn Rand Papers, Ayn Rand Archives, Irvine, CA (hereafter cited as Ayn Rand Papers). I appeal to this passage, despite its having been deleted, because its content and the content of the adjacent material in the same document, which was also deleted, is consistent with the published version of the essay, suggesting that the deletions were mainly for reasons of length or to avoid what she considered overelaboration in the context of her periodical *The Objectivist Newsletter*. Further, in a passage I will discuss in a moment, Leonard Peikoff confirms that this was her view.

hold in mind the narrow range of prohibitions (and the reasons for them) that would comprise our grasp of the non-initiation of force principle, and this, together with fundamental principles of Rand's ethics, would be sufficient to guide our interactions with each other. Although there would be problems of objectivity in regard to legitimate possession and retaliatory force, no new conceptual innovation would be sufficient for overcoming those problems; only a move to the institution of a code of impersonally enforced legal rules (guided by moral principles in their formulation) would be capable of overcoming them. Thus, as Peikoff says, theorizing about rights would be "premature."

I will not go deeply into the content of Rand's theory of rights. The basic rights that she recognized are those of life, liberty, property, and the pursuit of happiness familiar from the writings of Locke and the American Founders, among others. But I do want to comment on the difference between property rights and legitimate possession. With the inception of property rights, legitimate possession no longer depends on what I called immediate control—the active policing of material goods and resources held in close physical proximity. Active use and development may sometimes be a necessary step to the acquisition of a property right, as in the case of the US Homestead Act in the nineteenth century. But the owner of a piece of property can maintain her right to it without policing or using it at all (although a legal code might reasonably recognize certain actions or inactions as signs of abandonment). You can leave your home while you travel but still maintain ownership of the home and all its contents and the land it sits on. Property rights enormously extend the possible scope of one's legitimate control over the use and disposal of material resources and goods. They also allow for the development of the concept of intellectual property, which has no correlate in the conditions of presocietal legitimate possession.

Prior to the formation of society, it is one's de facto control over resources together with the needs of one's self-preservation that secure one's moral claim to those resources; once property rights are introduced, the provisions of the legal code provide the objective criteria by which ownership is judged. The moral foundation remains the same: one's need to utilize material goods and resources in the process of self-preservation. Although the criteria stipulated by the law (the precise homesteading requirements, the evidence to be entered of a sale of good, etc.) cannot be deduced from the theory of rights and are properly sensitive to local and historical factors, they must be consistent with—and geared toward facilitating the satisfaction of—the general requirements of man's life with respect to production and trade. Once these criteria are properly in place, any violation of property rights is classified as an initiation of force, on the grounds that it materially interferes with someone's legitimate efforts at self-preservation. Further, all the base cases of initiated force, which are prohibited straightaway by the non–initiation of force principle, come to be seen also as violations of rights. These base cases, too, therefore, are properly subject to legal remediation in society.

Rand's account of property rights, then, provides a context for identifying new instances of initiated force—that is, new cases that, because of their similarity to the base cases, warrant inclusion in this category and a parallel moral evaluation. In her view, theft, breaking and entering, criminal trespass, and threats based on any of these potentialities, all impinge on the human life processes in essentially the same way as the primary cases of force. They impose an unchosen impediment to the process of living one's life, which must be forcibly repelled in order to be avoided. She holds a similar view regarding breach of contract and fraud, but since these cases are more complex and more controversial, I will defer discussion of them until later in this essay.

Rand is thus not in the position of having to choose between a "moralized" and a "nonmoralized" conception of force, each with its attendant problems.[6] The contrast intended here is between a definition of force that is independent of rights and one on which force consists in any action that violates someone's rights. Rather, for Rand, the base cases are identified *as instances of force* independently of moral criteria, including the theory of rights, although it is their moral (antilife) consequences that makes them salient. The non–initiation of force principle refers, in the first instance, to this class of cases. This specification of the principle forms part of the context for the development of the account of rights, which then provides a context for subsuming new cases under the non–initiation of force principle.

A similar point applies in regard to Rand's conception of political freedom.[7] In general, she understands freedom as freedom from the initiation of force; her justification for emphasizing this conception of freedom is that it expresses man's most fundamental need with respect to the

6. See Matt Zwolinski (this volume) for this criticism. Also see Zwolinski 2016. For a related criticism directed at Nozick, see Cohen 1995, 39.

7. A criticism of libertarian theories of freedom, which parallels Zwolinski's criticism of Rand, can be found, for instance, in Kymlicka 2002, ch. 4, section 4; Cohen 1995, 60–61.

terms on which she interacts with others ("What Is Capitalism?" *CUI* 8–9, 42–43). The development of this conception of freedom traces the same path as that of the concept of initiated force. Rights function to protect a form of freedom that is independently conceived, but they also expand the possible scope of one's freedom (together with the scope and range of one's life-sustaining activity). Freedom in this sense is neither an exclusively nonmoral nor a wholly moralized concept. Even if critics are correct that both of these latter two ways of understanding freedom are problematic, Rand's conception of freedom arguably circumvents these problems. She can appeal to the need for freedom (and the need to exclude force from human relationships) in justifying her account of rights, but she can also appeal to her theory of rights to support a more developed conception of freedom (and of initiated force) that supports her claims about the proper functions of government and the proper limits of government power.

2. Force and Reason

Rand's analysis of the effects of force on the mind helps us to understand her brief argument about force and reason, which we saw earlier: "Do not open your mouth to tell me that your mind has convinced you of your right to force my mind. . . . When you declare that men are irrational animals and propose to treat them as such, you define thereby your own character and can no longer claim the sanction of reason, as no advocate of contradictions can claim it." Notice that she envisions the coercive threats being directed at "men" (that is, human beings) not just at "a man." What this suggests, I think, is that she wants to examine the implications of coercion, considered as a *principle* of human interaction, the principle being roughly that it is rational or right or justifiable to coerce others as a way of achieving one's ends. Why examine the issue in this light? In Rand's view, every choice reflects implicit principles, and the logic of one's principles controls one's long-range direction and the outcome of one's choices. The reason for this is that one's only means of making sense of any given choice situation and deciding what to do is by conceptualizing it—by viewing it as a type of case that calls for a certain type of response. Complexity is possible; multiple principles can be involved, and it can sometimes be difficult to assess which principle is relevant. There can be complexity also in the task of articulating and justifying practical principles. But, according to Rand, the idea that we can make case-by-case decisions without any reliance on principle is an illusion; the source of the

86 ■

DARRYL WRIGHT

illusion is a failure to grasp the role of implicit principles in framing one's view of a situation and guiding one's decision. In her view, one will act on the principles one accepts; the choice one has is whether to make one's principles explicit and critically assess them—thereby giving one's course of action a deliberate shape—or to leave them unidentified and relinquish an important measure of control over one's life.[8]

The long-range consequences of our actions cannot be predicted in detail, according to Rand; nor does our survival and well-being require such predictions. What one needs to know is whether one is leading the right *kind* of life, the kind that accords with our nature and that can satisfy our needs. This, for Rand, depends on whether the principles one lives by accord with the requirements of human survival. In evaluating action, in her view the basic question to ask is not "What will the consequences be?" but "What are the consequences and implications of acting on the principles animating the action?"

With this preface, we can return to the passage. Rand says that when one makes a coercive threat (outside of retaliatory contexts), one "declare[s] that men are irrational animals." The meaning of this is not obvious. But I think she is referring to certain structural features of the conditions of human existence that emerge when coercion becomes a *principle* of human interaction. These structural features might be mastered by nonrational animals who can rely on the guidance of instinct, but they are inimical to the needs of a rational being.

When one makes a coercive threat, one places the recipient in circumstances that are structurally similar to those of an emergency, assuming the threat is credible and effective.[9] In both cases, there is an impending danger of significant harm to lives or property that one values unless one takes appropriate mitigating action; further, to prevent or reduce the harm, longer-range concerns must temporarily be set aside. Metaphysically, emergencies are rare, temporary events, and because human survival depends on the possibility of taking successful long-range

8. On the points covered in this paragraph, see "Philosophy: Who Needs It" (*PWNI*). Also see Leonard Peikoff, "Why Should One Act on Principle?" (audio lecture available from the Ayn Rand Institute e-store). Since Rand's views in the philosophy of mind diverge sharply from the behavioristic tendencies of the later Wittgenstein, she would not be bothered by Wittgensteinian rule-following considerations, which might seem to be a source of difficulty for her claims about principles.

9. I am setting aside trivial threats that might technically involve force, such as a threat to drop a paper clip on someone's foot if she does not do what you say.

action one could not live in a permanent state of total emergency.[10] As a principle of human interaction to be applied widely and regarded as suitable for human beings, however, coercion establishes the analogue of a state of total emergency encompassing all of one's life.

Since actual emergencies are normally rare and temporary, it is generally possible to deal with them without derailing one's commitment to long-range values and goals. Further, although it is not possible during an emergency to concentrate directly on advancing long-term goals, the values and goals we adopt in normal conditions provide an indispensable context for our choices. For instance, they guide the choice of whom or what to prioritize saving in a flood; more fundamentally, they supply the motivation to act at all. Our means of dealing with emergencies, in Rand's view, is the same as our means of dealing with "the normal conditions of human existence" ("The Ethics of Emergencies," *VOS* 54)—namely, conceptual thought. But if she is right about the nature of our need for concepts and what they do for us, then it seems doubtful that our conceptual capacities could have evolved if the normal conditions of existence facing our evolutionary ancestors were such as to preclude long-range action. Moreover, the proper development of one's conceptual capacities requires a context suitable for learning to deal with broad theoretical abstractions, fundamental issues, and wide-scale integrations of knowledge, such as those involved in a high school or university education; and a context in which long-range thinking and the projection of long-range goals are possible. One's ability to deal successfully with emergencies is parasitic upon one's possession of skills that must be cultivated in nonemergency conditions.

The principle of coercion, however, institutionalizes a short-range perspective. The necessity of protecting oneself and one's values from harm (e.g., protecting one's business from regulatory penalties) requires a shift of psychic and existential resources away from the pursuit of one's goals.[11] In this regard, the principle of coercion reduces human function-

10. Rand makes this point in her essay "The Ethics of Emergencies." See "The Ethics of Emergencies" (*VOS* esp. 54–56).

11. A recent example sticks in mind. A student who was working on an engineering project for an outside contractor commented that he and his team members were surprised at how much time they had to spend undoing and redoing plans, as one regulatory barrier after another came into view. It should be added that the process of regulatory encroachment is a gradual one, and it can ebb and flow in an environment of mixed principles such as that of the present time in Western countries. Long-range action need not be completely cut off, although it might be made much harder (as is clearly happening, to take one high profile

ing to a quasi-animal level, in the sense that animals are by nature incapable of (and have no need to engage in) long-term thinking and planning.[12] I take it that this is part of what Rand means by the claim that coercion treats its victims as "irrational animals." It treats them as beings who can function successfully without any long-range frame of reference. It might be objected that this is not the same as treating them as if they *had* no rational capacities. But Rand may believe that all of an organism's capacities are unified around its central means of survival. She expresses this view in some 1943 draft material for a book entitled *The Moral Basis of Individualism*, which she subsequently decided not to complete: "Every species of living creature survives through the exercise of that attribute which is its particular, distinguishing faculty. All its other attributes are adapted to the mode of existence set by the one which is its means of survival."[13] It is not clear whether she continued to hold this perspective later on, in *Atlas Shrugged*; nothing I can think of there specifically conflicts with it, although she may have come to believe that this was not the sort of claim a philosopher as such can properly make.[14] If she is assuming that species tend to function in unified ways, without attributes (or perhaps major attributes) that do not in some way support their means of survival, then she might take it to follow—from the fact that we had some other way of surviving, which did not require a long-range perspective—that all our attributes would be adapted to that other way, and consequently that we would not have developed reason, whose function is precisely to enable a long-range view.

If this is correct, then in adopting the principle that it is permissible

example, in the case of the regulatory response in the United States and elsewhere to Uber and Lyft). For an excellent account, focused on environmental issues, of the way in which the regulatory state undermines people's ability to act from a long-range perspective, see Nickson 2012. We are considering here how Rand views the consequences of coercion when taken as a principle of human interaction.

12. The point is not that animals spend all their time evading danger—this is clearly not the case—but that they do not act with a long-range perspective and toward long-range goals. The long-range advantages of various evolutionary adaptations in improving reproductive fitness do have a role in shaping their genetic hardwiring, but the animal has none of that in view in acting.

13. Ayn Rand, *The Moral Basis of Individualism* (partial manuscript), folder 12A, Box 32, Ayn Rand Papers.

14. In some notes made during the late 1950s she writes that philosophy should not encroach upon the proper questions of science. Ayn Rand "Objectivism: A Philosophy for Living on Earth" (draft material for uncompleted manuscript), Folder 15x, Box 33, Ayn Rand Papers.

to use coercion as a means of dealing with others, you would be effectively declaring them to be nonrational beings. Even if this didn't quite follow from your use of coercion, you would perhaps be presupposing that it is not important for them to make full use of their capacity to reason, or even to develop it much at all. Rand's point is that if you are of the same species as they are, then in dealing with others by coercion you are also presupposing something about your own nature: that you yourself are not a rational being, either—or, if she is not entitled to make this claim, at least that it is not very important for you to use your rational capacities. Either way, there seems to be a problem if you appeal to your use of your own rational judgment to support your use of coercion. Either your actions commit you to the denial of your own rationality, and thus to the denial that could have made any rational judgment; or they commit you to the view that it is not very important for you to use your judgment. In the latter case, if you are committed to holding that it is not very important that you use your judgment, then there would seem to be an inconsistency of sorts in your insisting that your judgment in this issue be accorded any weight by others.

Rand doesn't consider the possibility that those who try to rule others by force might believe they are in some way superior beings compared to those under their rule. They might believe that there are distinctly different superior and inferior human subtypes, and that it is their belonging to the superior type that justifies their rule. They would therefore not be committed to the self-application of any claims made about inferior others. But they would be committed to a flatly unjustifiable claim of superior status.[15]

3. The Scope of the Principle: Can Force Achieve Good Ends?

Rand presents the issue of force as one that must be decided in principle: either it is impermissible ever to initiate force or it is permissible without limitation. This might be challenged, particularly where governmental

---

15. Rand says the following about such claims in a radio interview: "A moral code has to be based on man's nature. Men do belong to the same species. . . . Since men are all examples of the same species, the fundamental rules of conduct, that which is common to all of them, and applies to all of them, will have to be the same. If some men are better than others, in certain talents or in certain achievements, this is merely a . . . difference of degree, not of kind. Therefore you couldn't have different rules for so-called superior or inferior men. . . . [T]he basic rules will have to be the same for all men, since they are based on the fundamentals of man's nature, not on degrees of their achievement or of their virtue" (The Ayn Rand Program, WKCR-FM Radio, December 13, 1964, as quoted in Hunt 2016, 349).

force is in question. It may seem reasonable to hold that no private individual may ever initiate force. But to apply that principle to the state
would require stripping down its functions radically, and perhaps unac-
ceptably, whereas it seems that advocates of a more extensive state are not
necessarily committed to the tenet that it may unleash coercion against
innocent citizens at will, much less that private individuals can unleash
coercion against one another. Rather, they hold that the state may properly initiate force for purposes of social policy in some contexts, but not
in others, and that there are principled ways of differentiating these contexts from one another. This kind of view is held not only by defenders of
the contemporary regulatory-welfare state, but by some classical liberals,
such as Hayek and Epstein, who propose a much scaled back state but still
one that exceeds the functions Rand's state would perform.

Rand holds that the destructive consequences of initiated force are
present, to some extent, in every case. Moreover, she holds that there is
no objectively definable intermediary principle between the principle of
complete proscription and that of unlimited use; to accept the initiation
of force at all is, by the logic of the position, to accept it as a principle with
unlimited application. I have already indicated some of her reasons for
this view. In this section, I will explore those reasons further.

We can begin by taking two issues off the table. Rand argues that the
legitimate functions of government—which are geared toward the protection of individual rights to life, liberty, and property—can and should be
financed by voluntary means (she discusses this issue in her essay "Government Financing in a Free Society," VOS). But if it were the case that no
such voluntary system were workable, then arguably, a citizen's refusal to
contribute within her means to the financing of the government's legitimate operations would deserve to be classified as an initiation of force, for
the reasons discussed in the section on force and property. The refusal to
contribute would constitute a material impediment to the effective functioning of a proper government and, thus, a threat to the rights of all.
We can draw an analogy here to the refusal to give testimony in a court
case in which one has relevant knowledge. Although there is no overt use
of force, it is unlikely that an objective rights-protecting judicial system
could be preserved in the absence of the subpoena power.[16] In the present
case, however, Rand's position is that the issue doesn't arise, since a fully
adequate voluntary means of government financing is available. If she is

16. Rand makes essentially this point about the subpoena power at *Speaking* 249.

right about this, then it cannot be argued that taxation is noncoercive nor that it is necessary in order for society to function at all.

The other issue that should be set aside involves those economic "externalities" that deserve to be considered rights violations, such as the dumping of toxic wastes or the creation of excessive noise (e.g., from aircraft around an airport). Standard accounts of externalities blur the distinction between violations of third-party rights and undesired effects that do not rise to the level of rights violations. How this distinction should be drawn can be legitimately controversial, and there's no need to enter into those issues in detail here. But it is worthwhile to indicate the principle by which Rand would want such controversies to be resolved. Properly conceived, individual rights, in her view, delineate zones of individual freedom, suitable for enabling each person in a society to take independent action in support of her own life and well-being. The scope of rights must be determined according to this general criterion. Activities that despoil private property or otherwise interfere with its use and enjoyment, for example, are prima facie to be regarded as violating rights, as are actions that create hazards to public health such as by polluting the ambient environment. The philosophical and legal issues involved in these kinds of cases—and in others where the scope of rights is at issue—are complex. But actions determined to violate rights will, on that basis, be classifiable as initiations of indirect force, in that they materially interfere with the legitimate and necessary ways in which individuals maintain their lives and well-being. Government action to correct these violations will be a form of retaliatory force.

So far, we have considered two kinds of cases in which, if coercion were legitimate, Rand's analysis would classify it as retaliatory. But this kind of analysis is inapplicable to the welfare and regulatory functions of most governments today and, also, to the abbreviated versions of these functions proposed by classical liberals such as Hayek and Epstein, all of which Rand considers illegitimate. These theorists would all see themselves as being opposed, in principle, to a totalitarian system of complete command and control. But Rand denies that initiated force *has* any limiting principles.

One means of establishing this conclusion turns out to be too quick. One might argue as follows: If it is even *sometimes* necessary and proper to *initiate* force, then we must surrender the principle that man is an end in himself. Some theorists would dispute this step, because they regard these justified initiations of force as necessary for counteracting other forms of coercion, specifically, "economic coercion." Since we considered Rand's reply to this view earlier, I will set it aside here. If we can dismiss this view then, as mentioned above, it seems to follow that, if initiated force is sometimes permissible, we must reject the end-in-himself principle. Since, in that case, man is not an end in himself, he may be freely used as a means to others' ends. Thus, in principle, there are no limits on the amount of coercion that can be permissibly unleashed against innocent individuals.

The reason this argument is too quick is that it ignores the possibility that coercion might be justified by its effectiveness in promoting the good. Such a justification, if available, would be self-limiting, since coercion would not be justified when it would not serve any good end. In this case, although individuals might not be wholly inviolable ends-in-themselves, they would not be violable at will either; there would be moral limits on how they could be treated, grounded in the mandate to achieve the good.[17] This is the view that we postponed consideration of earlier. I suggested earlier that Rand sees any initiation of force as involving a flight from reality—a flight from the necessity of offering justifications for one's goals and actions. But the view that force can be regulated by considerations of value pushes back against this claim, and so it is important to examine it carefully. Rand responds to this objection in her essay "What Is Capitalism?" and I will reconstruct her position in some detail in the remainder of this section.

Let us first distinguish two possible cases. One possibility to consider is that coercion might be used to advance some form of *impersonal good*. The relevant sense of "impersonality" is this: the good in question bears no regular relationship to the good of any individual, and it can vary inversely with the good of any given individual. There are different theories of impersonal good.[18] On some theories, impersonal good is a function

17. A variant of this kind of view would be its Kantian version: that we must respect the unconditional worth of rational beings; that doing so requires actively and unselfishly furthering their ends; and that the state can properly take action to secure for those who are worse off the basic conditions of life necessary for effectively furthering one's own ends, such as a minimum level of income, a sufficient education, and the opportunity to compete effectively for desirable social positions. Although this view is structurally different from the consequentialist variant sketched in the text, both rely on claims about value or the good to provide principle constraints on the state's initiation of force, and so I treat them under one heading.

18. See, for example, Moore 1903 [1993], ch. 1; Nagel 1986; Raz 2001; Regan 2003; Matthes 2015.

of individual good (e.g., the respective individual goods of all the members of a society). On other theories, impersonal good is sui generis. On either view, the advancement of impersonal goodwill almost certainly sometimes requires that some people's individual good be set back. Candidates proposed as "impersonal goods" have included "social good," or "the common good," or some form of inherent or unconditional value, such as that supposed by some theorists to attach to the natural world as such or to rational beings as such.

Besides the possibility of using force to further impersonal good, another important possibility to consider is that of using force to advance people's individual good. Paternalistic legislation is defended on just this basis—that it will force (or "nudge") people toward their own good.[19] The recently overturned ban on large servings of soda in New York City was defended in part as a measure to improve the health of soda drinkers, and it might seem hard to deny that individuals could potentially benefit from being prevented from consuming excessive sugar or from being required to buckle their seatbelts in the car. Again, however, if this is the case, then some ways of initiating force will be self-limiting, since it clearly is not true that whenever the government makes people's choices for them it improves their lives.

Rand points out that these views are not neutral among different theories of value. They make certain presuppositions about the nature of value, which are compatible with some value theories but not with others. She divides value theories into three broad categories, which she considers jointly exhaustive (when the possibility of mixed cases is included): the intrinsic approach, the subjective approach, and the objective approach.[20] I will not explore the soundness of this claim of exhaustiveness here, but her delineation of the three types is meant to be broad enough to cover the field. The classification of a theory in one category or another, or as a mixed view, will sometimes depend on teasing out implied commitments. The summary that follows should at least indicate why she views the classification as exhaustive.

19. For one recent account, see Thaler and Sunstein 2009.
20. For Rand's comparative analysis of the three views, see "What Is Capitalism?" *CUI* 13–18. Although she refers to these as "theories," it is clear that her descriptions of them are generic, allowing for multiple realizations of each type. In the case of the objective approach, however, she maintains that her own specific development of it is the only consistent one. Even if she is correct in this, it remains the case that the general approach might be attempted by a theorist who does not share all her substantive views about the good.

The intrinsic approach is what is usually called intuitionism, or sometimes realism, although not everything known as realism belongs in this category. It holds that value or goodness is a passively received object of our awareness, which we apprehend when we contemplate certain things, actions, character traits, or states of affairs. It exists (or subsists) as such independently of man's cognitive processes, and it carries its normative force entirely within itself; in Moore's terms, it is that which unconditionally "ought to exist" (Moore 1903 [1993], 33, 68). Correspondingly, valuing is simply the state of (passively) cognizing value.

The subjective approach denies there are any values that are independent of consciousness. More precisely, it denies this at the level of metaethics or the metaphysics of value, although some theories in this category offer a metaphysically antirealist reconstruction of claims to the effect that "such-and-such would be good even if nobody believed it to be so." But all of these theories deny the metaphysical thesis that there is a real order of mind-independent values, and the corresponding epistemic thesis that it is such values that provide the grounds for claims about the good.

Subjective theories, in Rand's sense, hold that value is projected, constructed, or expressively affirmed by human consciousness. This projective, constructive, or expressive activity is subject to no independent norms, though on some views it is subject to norms we impose on ourselves—either as individuals, as rational beings, or as culturally situated beings.[21] It will be helpful to have a term to encompass the different forms of activity that these theories focus on. I will borrow the term "noncognitive" for this purpose, using it in a broader sense than usual. Although in the standard sense, constructivist theories are not classified as noncognitivist, they share with noncognitivist theories the view that reflection on values is not fundamentally a cognitive enterprise. It is in this broad sense

---

21. For example, Kant's view that as a rational being you necessarily constrain your will by the Categorical Imperative asserts the existence of a self-imposed norm constraining the maxims one acts on. The classification of Kantian ethics as fundamentally subjectivist, which Rand herself suggests in at least one place, is compatible with her statements ascribing intrinsicist features to his ethics, because she holds that when fully worked out the intrinsic and subjective approaches "meet and blend." She argues that they have the same kinds of social consequences (to be discussed shortly), and that epistemically the intrinsic view collapses into the subjective, since in practice one's feelings become the basis for one's ascriptions of intrinsic value. On these claims, see "What Is Capitalism?" *CUI* 14–15. For some of her comments on Kant's ethics, see *PWNI* 88–89, 128–36; for comments suggesting that she regards Kant's ethics as having a subjectivist element, see "From the Horse's Mouth" (*PWNI*).

that I will say all of these approaches understand valuing in terms of the valuer's noncognitive activity. They are all "subjective" theories simply in the sense that the source of norms is within the subject. Some of these theories nevertheless also feature a Kantian conception of objectivity as intersubjectivity. From the standpoint of Rand's own conception of objectivity, though, these theories remain essentially similar in their metaethical commitments to more straightforwardly subjectivist accounts.

Above we considered two kinds of hypothetical cases that might seem to present problems for an absolute moral prohibition of initiated force: (1) those in which force can be used effectively to further impersonal good; (2) those in which an individual's own good can be advanced by coercing him. Both the intrinsic and the subjective approach can accommodate the first kind of case. Because of the way in which intrinsicist theories view the relation between values and valuing, the act of valuing has no special connection to the valuer's own good. Its object can be—and is most naturally thought of as being—something that is not good *for* anyone but just *good*, period. It is less obvious, perhaps, that the subjective approach can also recognize impersonal good. But there is nothing in the structure of these theories that demands that the subject's noncognitive activity centers on her own good; one can equally as well project, construct, or express acceptance of values of a wholly impersonal kind.

Further, there is nothing in the nature of the good, as conceived by these theories, to preclude its being achieved coercively. Although coercion bypasses the target's own long-range evaluation of her options, the good's status as such, in these theories, is not a function of the coerced person's evaluative judgments. Moreover, in Rand's view, these theories necessitate the use of force to achieve the good, because they fail to provide a suitable common frame of reference for resolving disagreements about values. The intrinsic approach leaves us with our clashing intuitions; the subjective approach has no recourse in cases where the relevant noncognitive activities lead us in different evaluative directions.[22]

22. Proponents of sophisticated forms of subjectivism (in Rand's sense) would vehemently deny this charge. Whether they would be right in denying it is a complex issue, which requires separate treatment. It is not obvious, for example, that on Gibbard's norm-expressivism or in neo-Kantian views, normative discussion must readily break down in the way that it seems destined to do very easily on, say, an emotivist conception of normative discourse. For Rand, I think the issue turns on whether the most basic elements in a substantive theory of value are provably true in a broadly realist sense of truth. Since this is denied by all the theories she would classify as subjective, I think she considers it to follow straightaway that normative discourse, when understood as these theories understand it, inevitably breaks

It may seem that intrinsicist views cannot accommodate the second kind of case. But that seems to me to be a mistake. Intrinsicism, as an ethical category, is a broad view about the metaphysics and epistemology of value. Although it is at home with conceptions of intrinsic, impersonal, inherent, and/or nonrelational value, it does not demand such a conception. An intrinsicist can hold that what is good *for* a person is good for her independently of her or anyone's evaluative beliefs and can be passively cognized as good for so-and-so by anyone who reflects properly. Similarly, for a subjectivist, just as our noncognitive activity can be focused on impersonal good so, too, can it be focused on the personal good of a human being as such or of a particular person. There is nothing in either approach's conception of the nature of value that precludes recognizing forms of value that are relative to a given individual.

A particular subjective account of personal good might turn out to hold that it is dependent on one's own value selections, and thus that the freedom to make such selections is required for the achievement of one's good. This kind of claim appears, for instance, in the works of certain mid-twentieth-century classical liberals, such as Ludwig von Mises and Friedrich Hayek. It is clear from some of Rand's comments on Hayek's political philosophy that she does not think he has a sound basis for arguing that one's good requires this kind of freedom (and, by parallel, would not think Mises does, either).[23] But she does not claim that every subjective theory must defend the use of paternalistic coercion.

down—that is, it breaks down not because of laziness or bad faith among the participants but because there is no common frame of reference for settling differences of basic principle. Further, for the reasons expressed in the text, she claims that these theories can license coercion in these circumstances. It should also be noted that, at the time Rand was writing on this subject (the mid-1960s), most of the extant subjectivist theories were of a fairly crude type. Hare had published his first two books in 1952 and 1963, respectively, and his view was much more complex than Stevenson's. But even Hare held, for a time, that moral judgment required only consistency and could have any (consistent) content at all, and that there were no criteria available for resolving disputes about basic moral standards. Rand's criticisms are directed at the simpler forms of subjectivism, although I suspect she would have had similar criticisms of the more complex forms had she been aware of them.

23. Neither Hayek nor Mises claims that one should act exclusively for one's own good, but they both hold that one's good or well-being depends on what one values, and that there is no aggregative social good for which individuals can be required to sacrifice their own well-being. In *The Road to Serfdom*, Hayek sums up the connection between his view of values and his conception of freedom: "It is this recognition of the individual as the ultimate judge of his ends, the belief that as far as possible his own views ought to govern his actions, that forms the essence of the individualist position" (Hayek 1944, 59). In her copy of this book, Rand comments on this passage: "If *that*'s the essence—this is why individualism has failed."

She does claim, however, that subjectivism presents no in-principle barrier to such coercion, and that on some forms of subjectivism, it will seem warranted: "If the subjectivist wants to pursue some social ideal of his own, he feels morally entitled to force men for their own good, since he feels that he is right and that there is nothing to oppose him but their misguided feelings" ("What Is Capitalism?" *CUI* 15). Intrinsicism, by contrast, *does* imply that what is good for you is independent of your own valuing activity, which latter is simply the passive grasp of value whose status as such is independent of your cognitive activities and choices. This is the case even though its status as a value *does* depend on how it *affects you*. It is good for you because it benefits you, and it could not be good for you otherwise. But, on the intrinsic approach, its benefiting you is independent of your evaluation of it. That something is good for you is not linked to your valuing it; rather, your valuing of it should depend on its being, independently, good for you, and it would be good for you even if you didn't value it. On this approach, Rand concludes, it will always therefore be suitable in principle to use force paternalistically.[24]

In each of the cases in which there are theoretical grounds for treating force as a possible means of achieving good ends, we can see a common pattern. The relevant good's status as good is held by the theory under consideration to be independent of the valuing activities of those who are subjected to coercion.[25] It is this feature that ensures that this good can be achieved even though an effective threat forces the subject to act apart from the full context of her values, flattening out her choices to a simple

In a further annotation, she criticizes Hayek's position (in the paragraph that ends with this statement) on the grounds that it is based on the de facto incompleteness and incommensurability of different individuals' respective scales of values, rather than on an in-principle argument that individuals are ends in themselves. See Ayn Rand Papers and *Marginalia* 151. Hayek's individualism and Rand's criticism of it cannot be fully treated here. But her marginalia make it clear she is unsatisfied with the link he forges between subjective value and individual freedom. For a broadly similar line of thinking in Mises to the one Rand criticizes in Hayek, see Mises 1949 [1966], 3–4, 92–97, 279–87, 331–33. Mises's views are not identical to Hayek's. In particular, whereas for Hayek it is the limitations on human knowledge that require each person to be "the ultimate judge of his ends," for Mises it is simply the fact that ends (and ultimate values) only exist as such in relation to the preferences of the individuals.

24. This conclusion about intrinsicism and personal good is not explicitly stated. But it seems to be implied at "What Is Capitalism?" *CUI* 15–16, in the third full paragraph, which discusses whether someone's own good can be forced on him. Rand's argument there seems to be directed at both the intrinsicist and subjective approaches. I discuss the paragraph further below, in connection with her own theory of value.

25. On subjectivist views, it is not independent of the valuing activities of those initiating force. By forcing others, they are imposing their own subjective valuations on others.

alternative between compliance and a penalty too severe to endure. The good's existence as such is not viewed as dependent on its having any particular relation to that context (see Peikoff 1991, 315).

Rand's theory of value (explored briefly in my first chapter) challenges this premise. The theory is grounded in her account of objectivity, which requires that the concepts used in any field be suitably connected to the foundation of human knowledge in perception. We must ask, therefore, how that connection is to be made for ethical concepts such as "value," "good," and "benefit."

Values are first isolated and identified as such, according to Rand, in relation to the activity of valuing, an activity we can observe in ourselves, in other human beings, and with the growth of one's knowledge in other living organisms. Grasping the process as one of pursuing values requires having some understanding of its structure; it is not something we can do simply on the basis of an awareness of the entities and physical motions involved. But we can come to understand both our own activity and the activity of other organisms as being action toward a goal, for the sake of something. In this context we can identify that which such activity seeks as "values." The appropriate definition of a "value" at this stage, according to Rand, is "that which one acts to gain and/or keep" ("The Objectivist Ethics," *VOS* 16).

To grasp a value as such—rather than just as whatever it is otherwise (e.g., a new car, sunlight, or fruit on a tree)—is to grasp it in relation to the gaining and keeping activity. But this activity is isolated as a distinctive form of action warranting special study by virtue of the way in which it is related to its object, the value. The value is not simply the outcome of the activity but its *goal*.[26] Neither the activity nor the value can be understood in isolation one from the other. The action is essentially toward the value; otherwise we would not classify it as value-seeking or goal-directed. Similarly, the goal or value is essentially an object of valuing, goal-directed activity; it has no existence as a goal or value apart from that activity.

As we saw earlier, Rand holds that the setting in which we find values and can form the concept of "value" is when we consider the lives of living organisms. A process of valuing is a *life process*. The goal that necessitates this process is life, living, and consequently it is only living organisms that pursue values. Life is inherently conditional and cannot exist except

26. In some contexts, it is helpful to distinguish between a value and a goal, but since they are closely related and the distinction between them is not important here, I treat them as interchangeable.

as a process of goal-directed, self-sustaining action. This action cannot be arbitrary; in order to *be* self-sustaining, it must be geared toward specific kinds of values, the pursuit of which both constitutes and sustains the organism's life.

These facts provide the context in which to understand the normative aspects of values. In Rand's analysis, there is no sharp separation between so-called normative and descriptive values. Normative value is present all along in the observable processes on the basis of which we can form the concept of value. But to grasp the basis of that normativity, we must understand this activity in its full context—that is, *as* the activity of living, of self-sustenance. In this context, we can say that what makes the process necessary and provides the standard for evaluating it are the requirements of the organism's particular kind of life.

Rand's definition of value refers to "gaining and keeping" the valued item. But a definition, for her, is a condensation of knowledge in terms of essentials, not a full description of what is defined (see *ITOE* ch. 5). The process of valuing includes not only action to gain and keep the value but also, crucially, the action of utilizing the value for one's life. When a squirrel puts by nuts for the winter, it values the nuts by acting to gain and keep them, but these actions would not qualify as "valuing" if they were disconnected from the goal of use—say, because of a sudden anomaly in the squirrel's neurology. Then its gathering of nuts would no longer count as goal-directed. Further, the way in which the value is used matters. Not only must the squirrel eat the nuts, but it must not overeat, and it must not eat at all when it has something more pressing to do—say, to defend itself from a predator. The squirrel has to orchestrate its use of the nuts, and all of its other activities, in a way that enables it to live. This, of course, is facilitated by its genetics in the form of its instincts.

Except for this last point, all of the foregoing is true for human beings also; we must use the values we gain and keep, and we must orchestrate our use of them in a coordinated way. Our use must be intelligent use— that is, use on the basis of knowledge and judgment rather than instinct. We must discover what values our lives require, and by what principles to gain, keep, and use them self-sustainingly. In other words, we must engage in a process of evaluation, which for us is also an aspect of the process of valuing.[27]

---

27. For conceptual, volitional, self-reflective beings such as ourselves, and for some values, valuing something also involves *enjoying* it. This is true when the value is an end in itself, such as one's life or some major value within one's life, which one pursues in part for its own

Evaluation, in Rand's view, is a cognitive process that—like any cognitive process on the conceptual level of consciousness—is subject to standards of objectivity. One such standard is the requirement to hold context; in evaluating, we must take full account of our knowledge, needs, and other values ("What Is Capitalism?" *CUI* 14–15), and we must "not regard any moment as cut off from the context of the rest of [our] life" ("The 'Conflicts' of Men's Interests," *VOS* 59). The process is also subject to the requirement that its concepts and conclusions be grounded, ultimately, in perceptual evidence. We have sketched above how Rand would ground the concept of "value" in such evidence. With regard to grounding evaluative conclusions, she holds that evaluation is a process of "teleological measurement" (*ITOE* 32–35). The process starts with a goal providing a standard of value and grades the items in its field according to how well they satisfy the standard. The goal that necessitates a choice of values, according to Rand, is that of living one's life, and the basic evaluative problem a person faces is that of choosing the principles of action and the subsidiary goals that will together constitute and sustain her life. One's major values and principles are, Rand says, both "the means to and the realization of" one's life ("The Objectivist Ethics," *VOS* 27). Thus Rand's general characterization of the objective approach to values: "The *objective* theory holds that the good is neither an attribute of 'things in themselves' nor of man's emotional states, but an evaluation of the facts of reality by man's consciousness according to a rational standard of value" ("What Is Capitalism?" *CUI* 14). We can speak of both the process of evaluation and the values it selects as "objective" when they meet the requirements of objectivity.

To bring out the reasons why this approach to value precludes force, I want to explore the way in which it holds that the status of something as a human value depends on its relation to the valuer's own evaluations. On

---

sake, such as a career or a friendship. Enjoyment is necessary for our purposive form of valuing to have a purpose. Life is an end in itself—on Rand's view, an ultimate value. But even an ultimate value, though it is the stopping point in the order of values, requires a purpose. Rand makes it clear that she thinks life has a purpose; its purpose is happiness ("The Objectivist Ethics," *VOS* 30). To hold one's life as one's ultimate value is, in part, to pursue it for the sake of one's happiness. It is sometimes awkward to speak of "use" in regard to something we enjoy. When we contemplate a work of art, for example, we aren't exactly using it, nor are we using our life when we enjoy it, though we are using our time. Perhaps the mode of interaction—the mode of assimilating the value, as it were—in such cases is not "use." But in order to enjoy that value we must engage with it psychologically in the appropriate way, and the enjoyment flows from that.

THE SCOPE AND JUSTIFICATION OF RAND'S NON-INITIATION OF FORCE PRINCIPLE

Rand's view, value judgments are to be validated by reference to mind-independent facts of reality. It might seem, therefore, as though everything we need in order to certify that something is good for a person is independent of her consciousness, and thus that it is possible after all to force someone's good on her. Depending on the state of the facts, either an item will or will not benefit someone's life, regardless of what she herself might say about it. To see why this is not the case, we must consider in greater detail Rand's conception of the relation between a value and the valuer's life.

At first, this relation can seem paradoxical. A value, on Rand's account, is that which furthers an organism's life. But its life is simply a process of pursuing and utilizing values. The seeming paradox is that we must identify the organism's life in terms of its values, but we must identify what is of value to it by reference to its life. In the case of nonhuman organisms, this circularity is not problematic since these organisms come into being with a full complement of values; they are set up to engage in self-sustaining action, so we largely find out what benefits their lives and is of value to them by finding out what they spend their time pursuing, and learning about how these pursuits maintain the organism in a position to continue them. The distinction between the organism's life and the values that benefit its life is reached through a shift in perspective; it does not reflect any actual separation.

In the case of humans, according to Rand, the situation is different, since we do not spring into being with a full set of values. We must figure out what a human life is, what should constitute it, and how to engage in a process of self-sustaining action. Because we must choose our values, there is a real problem. What is of value to me is what benefits my life, but my life is constituted by my values and the goals that I pursue, in their specific relations of greater and lesser importance. All of this has to be chosen. So there is a real question about how to make these choices. One way to put the problem is as follows: how can life be the standard of its own self-constitution?

One possible solution here is not sufficient—to view one's life simply as the stripped down automatic organic functions of one's body. That is certainly *not* something that can be taken as the goal of all one's activity. Nor is this the goal of the activity of other living organisms. The life of a deer is not simply its internal processes; its actions in the world are as much a part of its life as anything else—they are part of the goal of its overall activity. So there is no justification on the basis of strict, literal biology for stripping our conception of a human being's life down to these metabolic essentials.

The solution according to Rand, which is made possible by the field of ethics, is to conceive of our lives first (in terms of logical, not developmental priority) by reference to the abstractly formulated requirements of man's life as such. A human life, in her view, has certain requirements in terms of the principles by which it is lived, and these can be understood independently of the value choices of any given individual. But every individual, in order to live successfully, must instantiate these principles in her own life and use them as the highest-order reference point for her choices. In thinking of my life, then, I can say, first of all, that my life will be an instance of "man's life," a life that meets the long-range requirements of a human being's survival. Within that framework, I can fill in specifics, and those will in some ways be shaped by innate aptitudes and accidental facts, such as who and what one is exposed to in early life. As one gets older, one gets greater critical distance on all of this, and one can start bringing some deliberate order to one's values and pursuits, guided by an ethical framework.

The key point, as far as the discussion of force is concerned, is that your life is something you have to design by selecting the values that constitute it. Further, when you assimilate something into your life as a value, the benefit you derive from it depends on your self-sustaining utilization of it (and in some cases your ability to enjoy it). That, in turn, depends on your grasp of the ways in which this value relates to and serves the totality that constitutes your life. The benefit is not simply an impact it has on you, like the impact of the furniture polish in bringing out the beauty of the wooden dining table. Rather, the benefit is *the total effect of your active and active-minded utilization of the value toward the ends for which you selected it.*

It is now possible for us to see the reason Rand maintains, in principle, that it is impossible to force a person's good on her. To force a value on someone is not simply to make her accept something that will benefit her life, as if her life were something merely given and standing apart from her evaluations and choices. Rather, it is an attempt to force on her a conception of her life—to force on her a set of evaluations and thereby to control who she is. It is impossible to achieve someone else's good by this means, because one's good is something one has to design and bring into being through the processes of thought and action by means of which one lives. Forcing someone's good on her is really shutting down the process by which one comes to have a life, a self, and a good; and by which one assimilates, utilizes, and benefits from the good. Rand gives this analogy: "An attempt to achieve the good by force is like an attempt to provide a man with a picture gallery at the price of cutting out his eyes. Values cannot exist (cannot be valued) outside the full context of a man's life, needs, goals, and *knowledge*" (*CUI* 16).

Although I have stressed the creative aspects of coming to have a life (what Rand calls "achieving life"), in her view, the design and construction of our lives is subject to norms grounded in facts of reality, facts about man's nature and the nature of the world in which he acts. It is not a subjective process, even though it is a process that demands a great deal of complex choice. It is a process that, when done correctly, is objective.

We can also see why Rand rejects the first kind of case we considered above, in which coercion is used for the sake of an impersonal good. Her account of value rejects this concept. On her view, the good is always that of a particular living organism. So there can be no question of using force to achieve a good distinct from the good of individuals. This leaves us with Rand's original objection to the limited initiation of force: that the purpose of force is to circumvent the necessity of justifying one's ideas and goals, and thus that force is intrinsically resistant to limitation.

4. Rand and the Libertarian Nonaggression Principle

Libertarians characteristically espouse a principle of nonaggression as the foundation of their view.[28] I will focus on interpretations of the nonaggression principle, and how they differ from Rand's non-initiation of force principle. The discussion will be centered on three areas of controversy: the status of fraud, the status of breaches of contract, and the rights of parents and children.

In an influential article, James Child (1994) argues that libertarianism is incapable of justifying the legal prohibition of fraud. Libertarianism only prohibits aggression. Although fraud involves deception, it does not involve any initiation of force; both parties to the transaction freely and willingly transfer the money or goods they exchange, without duress. Neither party is threatened by the other, and neither party's goods are seized. The defrauded party may regret the transaction in hindsight, but this in itself cannot be grounds for legal intervention since remorse is a feature of many perfectly legitimate transactions. If you buy a shirt

---

28. Characteristically, but not always: see, for example, Zwolinski 2013, 2016.

marked "final sale" but then hate how it looks on you at home, there is no sound basis for legal remediation. There may be *moral* objections to obtaining money or goods by fraudulent means, of course. But according to libertarianism, it is not the state's business to enforce morality, generally, but only to enforce one specific prohibition, the prohibition on aggression. If you deceptively market a bottle of sugar pills as a remedy for depression, and someone credulously buys them from you, you have not aggressed against the buyer. You have merely deceived him. Thus, according to Child, there is no sound libertarian basis for legally proscribing fraud.[29] Further, although Rand does not classify herself as a libertarian, Child explicitly includes her views within the scope of his criticisms, arguing that she lacks a sound basis for her claim that fraud is an indirect form of force.

Child notes that it would be question-begging to reply that fraud constitutes force because it fails to secure *informed* consent to a transaction. Of course, fraud does fail to obtain informed consent, but to say this is simply point out that fraud is fraudulent. It does not provide grounds for regarding fraud as a type of force. According to Child, nonaggression does not require the informed consent of the parties to a transaction, but only their *free* consent—consent competently given without duress (without violence or threats thereof).[30]

To grasp the significance of Child's argument, it is helpful to consider Rothbard's views about the scope of the nonaggression principle. Rothbard does think that the nonaggression principle prohibits fraud, because it prohibits theft and, he argues, fraud qualifies as "implicit theft" (Rothbard 1982 [2002], 77–79). The perpetrator of fraud, he says, obtains money or goods without the owner's consent. But Child's point is that, in one clear sense, consent *has* been obtained: the transaction has occurred without overt violence or the threat thereof. This is what Child refers to as "free consent." Of course, there is another respect in which the transaction is *not* consensual: the victim does not give informed consent.

29. Child 1994, esp. 733–34. Some libertarians tried to meet his criticisms, within the framework of the libertarian nonaggression principle. See, for example, Kinsella 2003. By contrast, Zwolinski (2013, 2016) has recently argued that libertarianism should move away from taking the nonaggression principle to be uniquely foundational for the theory, viewing it instead as a presumption, to be balanced with other principles, rather than an absolute constraint on state action. In his view, the inability of the nonaggression principle to support a prohibition on fraud is one of several problems that arise when that principle is regarded as overriding all other political principles.

30. On these issues, see Child 1994, 730–31, 730n29, 732n32.

Rothbard cites the absence of informed consent as grounds for viewing fraud as a form of theft and, thus, of aggression. But since the transaction is in one respect consensual and in another respect nonconsensual, the question is which of these respects is salient for the assessment of fraud under the nonaggression principle. One way of understanding Rothbard's position would be to see him as granting that fraud secures free consent but maintaining that the absence of informed consent nevertheless makes fraud a form of aggression. In this case, the problem highlighted by Child's argument is that Rothbard provides no justification for taking the absence of informed consent to be decisive.

Alternatively (and it seems to me, more accurately), Rothbard can be understood as holding that the absence of informed consent also undermines free consent. Rothbard's view seems to be that the victim's consent *misfires* in cases of fraud. It is given conditionally, but since the relevant condition is not fulfilled (because the perpetrator of the fraud fails to perform as promised), no consent on the part of the defrauded party actually occurs. For instance, if you pay money for some good, but the good is not as it is represented by the seller, the conditions for your willing transfer of the sale price to the seller have not actually been met, and it is as if the seller had simply stolen the money from you (Rothbard 1982 [2002], 79, 134, 143). If this is correct, then fraud would be nonconsensual even in the respect stressed by Child.[31] Rothbard's claim, then, would not be that fraud constitutes aggression just because it fails to secure *informed* consent (a contention that Child would claim lacks justification) but, rather, that the defrauded party's reliance on a fraudulent misrepresentation of the transaction ensures that *no consent* (not even what Child refers to as "free consent") has been given to what *actually* transpires. It would be the absence of free consent—indeed, the absence of consent *sans phrase*—that would underwrite the claim that fraud is a form of aggression (Rothbard 1982 [2002], 143).

But Child can reply here that Rothbard's account of the mechanics of consent is stipulative and unjustified. His characterization of fraud leaves

31. It may seem that this response is immediately problematic, since it cannot plausibly be held that free consent is always undermined by the absence of informed consent. It would surely count as free consent if you bought a product that was exactly as advertised but that you had not bothered to adequately inform yourself about, such as an iPhone app that didn't do what you expected. But Rothbard can distinguish these cases; he can claim that when you buy a good, you transfer the sale price on condition that the good is as represented by the seller, but that you do not (and in a free market, cannot) attach the further condition that the good be just as you have represented it to yourself.

out of account the plain fact that the fraudulently obtained value (e.g., money or whatever) is transferred from one party to the other, and that it is transferred peaceably, without violence or threats thereof. The sheer insistence that no consent of any kind has been given just begs the question. Child does not deny that fraud is in a certain way nonconsensual for the victim. Rather, he challenges the contention that its being non-consensual in this way makes it a form of aggression, eligible for legal remediation under libertarianism (Child 1994, 730n29). It is insufficient to reply by pointing out a respect in which fraud is like theft, or to say that this similarity means that no consent has occurred. What occurs in cases of fraud is, in a way, like theft and, in a way, unlike theft. The question is whether fraud is *relevantly* similar to theft (and other forcings), such that it deserves to be classified as a form of force. Rothbard's account of fraud is insufficiently developed to resolve this question.

Child also notes that it is unhelpful to reply that fraud involves a kind of implicit breach of contract, since it is not clear that libertarianism can justify the legal prohibition of contract violations any more easily than it can justify the legal prohibition of fraud. Here Rothbard is in partial agreement with Child about the implications of libertarianism, even though he disagrees with Child on its merits. Rothbard gives the example of an actor who agrees to perform on a certain date, but then arbitrarily—"for whatever reason"—backs out (Rothbard 1982 [2002], 137). Assuming that she has received no advance but was to be paid later, she initiates no force in breaching her agreement. Only if she had received an advance would it be an act of force for her not to show up (138). But this distinction depends on Rothbard's account of fraud. If this account is flawed or incomplete, then it is not clear that he has the conceptual resources to support any contractual enforcement, consistent with the fundamental premises of Rothbardian libertarianism.

Child contends that libertarianism can support only a restricted conception of force, not the more expansive conception favored by Rand and others, on which fraud and contractual breaches count as forms of force. On the restricted conception of force depicted by Child, neither fraud nor contractual breach violates the libertarian nonaggression principle. Rothbard endorses a more expansive conception of force (though less expansive than Rand's; see below). But Child is correct in thinking that Rothbard fails to justify anything beyond the restricted conception.[32]

32. It is not clear whether Child himself accepts this conception but would simply invoke nonlibertarian principles to prohibit fraud and unjustifiable contractual breaches, or

The source of the difficulties with Rothbard's conception of aggression, it seems to me, lies in a particular way of understanding self-ownership, which in turn proceeds from Rothbard's commitment to what I will call *the autonomy of political philosophy*. By this I mean the view that political philosophy should be independent of normative ethics—that is, independent of any substantive ethical theory applicable to the whole of one's life. (Rothbard does not consider political philosophy to be independent of metaethics; see below.)

Rothbard makes it clear that he views self-ownership as ownership of one's own *body*. He argues that this ownership provides a foundation for ownership over land and other natural resources, when one labors on them, because one's labor "stamp[s]" on these resources "the imprint of one's personality and energy" (1982 [2002], 34). From this perspective, it seems natural to construe force as aggression directed (or threatened) against a person's body or against one's bodily control over one's property. Further, from the perspective of the kind of natural law metaethics that Rothbard endorses (chs. 1–4), this account of self-ownership will seem attractive, if one also makes the assumption that political principles must be independent of broader moral principles, an assumption that Rothbard explicitly makes (25).[33] If this assumption is rejected, then it is possible to think of political philosophy as being grounded in ethics; and if one first develops an overall account of the kind of life that a human being needs to lead, then political principles can be conceived of as authorizing and protecting that life. This is essentially how Rand understands the principles of individual rights. But if political principles must be autonomous natural law principles pertaining to social interactions, then we must look elsewhere for their grounds. For Rothbard, those grounds lie in one's ability to consciously and volitionally control one's body, which is an aspect of human nature that can be grasped apart from any specific normative

---

whether he would accept a conception of force more inclusive than what he thinks libertarianism can support. In referring below to Child's conception of force, therefore, I mean the conception that he attributes to libertarianism but may or may not himself accept as correct.

33. In explaining the purpose of his book, Rothbard says that he will not attempt "to elaborate a natural law ethic for the personal morality of man" (1982 [2002], 25). Although this might be seen only as indicating a restriction in the scope of his discussion rather than a view about the nature of political philosophy as a discipline, both the feasibility of such a restriction and the manner of its implementation will depend on how one views the relation of political philosophy to the rest of ethics. If political philosophy properly depends on ethics (in the way that Rand, for example, claims it does), then a work on the foundations of political philosophy can restrict its consideration of personal ethics to the essentials required for grounding the political principles, but it cannot leave personal ethics wholly out of account.

view about the kind of life that is suitable for a human being, and which might, in the context of a natural law theory, be thought to entail a right of ownership and control over one's body.

Rand, by contrast, does not formally employ the concept of self-ownership. But she does say at one point that a person is the owner of her own *life*. The contrast with Rothbard is instructive. Rothbard has a difficult time explaining why one owns one's body. Sometimes, as mentioned above, his answer is simply that it is a "natural fact" that one has control over one's bodily actions (1982 [2002], 31). But one's life has normative requirements, and it is to these requirements that Rand looks to support the thesis that a person must properly have control of her own life. Rothbard's own arguments occasionally veer in this direction, reflecting Rand's influence during his early career; he sometimes includes in the grounds of self-ownership the fact that a human being must be self-directed in order to survive (46). But the object of self-ownership remains limited to the body. Accordingly, the varieties of force remain limited to physical interferences with one's body or with one's physical control over one's legitimate property—or threats thereof.

Once we broaden our focus to the normative requirements of man's life, however, the picture changes considerably. In Rand's ethics, the basis for legal prohibition of the primary instances of initiated force is that they involve material interference with the process by which one maintains and enjoys one's life. But then the very same thing can arguably be said about breaches of contract. Thus, Rand writes: "Man cannot survive, as animals do, by acting on the range of the immediate moment. Man has to project his goals and achieve them across a span of time; he has to calculate his actions and plan his life long-range. The better a man's mind and the greater his knowledge, the longer the range of his planning. The higher or more complex a civilization, the longer the range of activity it requires—and, therefore, the longer the range of contractual agreements among men, and the more urgent their need of protection for the security of such agreements" ("The Nature of Government," *VOS* 129/*CUI* 382–83). In Rand's view, contracts are a necessity of human survival because long-range action is, and because contractual agreements are a necessity of long-range action. In this sense, a breach of contract is as much of a material interference with the action of living as wresting away someone's newly gathered apples in a state of nature. On this basis, it can be classified as an initiation of force. In arguing that contractual breaches constitute force, Rand refers only to cases in which one of the parties has already performed, and not to cases such as Rothbard's example of the actor (*VOS* 130/*CUI* 383). There is no disagreement between Rand and Rothbard on the former kinds of cases although (as noted earlier) Rothbard does not satisfactorily explain why those cases involve aggression. Rand's account of force points toward a way of filling this gap. Further, Rand also states without restriction that a breach of contract by one party "may cause a disastrous financial injury to the other," which would call for private retaliation in the absence of government (*VOS* 129/*CUI* 382). This occurs in the context of her explanation of why government is necessary and what its functions should be. Since, in Rand's view, the legitimacy of retaliation (either private or governmental) depends exclusively on whether force has been initiated, it seems to me that she would also regard the contractual breach in Rothbard's actor example as a case of initiated force. I suggest that her basic reason for this is given in the long passage quoted above.[34]

From Rand's perspective, Child's and Rothbard's conceptions of force both reflect what she calls the fallacy of the "frozen abstraction," which "consists of substituting some one particular concrete for the wider abstract class to which it belongs" ("Collectivized Ethics," *VOS* 94). Someone who equated ethics as such with one particular ethical view, such as that of Catholicism, would be using the concept of "ethics" as a frozen abstraction; "ethics" would no longer be functioning in her mind as a *concept*—that is, as an open-ended means of classification according to essential similarities, and of expanding and integrating one's knowledge— but as a cognitively barren signifier of the already known. I think Rand would see a sort of similar problem in Child's and Rothbard's conceptions of force. The source of the problem, in this case, would be the attempt to understand the concept of force independently of the background context that makes it necessary, which for Rand are the long-range requirements of man's survival and the necessity of defining an ethical code. In the absence of that context, a fully conceptual understanding of force becomes

---

34. Zwolinski writes that "it would be grossly implausible to characterize [fraud] as involving physical force or violence" (2016, 70; original emphasis). Rand would agree, I take it, that fraud does not involve violence (this seems to be part of the point of her calling it a *form of indirect force*). But she holds that fraud is to be classified as force because it amounts to essentially the same kind of interference with the victim's life as the base cases of force. Her classification reflects a more abstract conception of force than what Zwolinski refers to as the "First Punch Theory of Aggression," on which force consists exclusively of physical violence or threats thereof (see 2016, 69).

impossible, and understanding is restricted to the cases closest to the purely perceptual level of awareness—that is, to cases of aggression (including aggressive threats).[35]

Child's discussion of fraud seems premised on a similarly acontextual conception of trade. As mentioned above, he holds that in order for an exchange to satisfy the nonaggression principle, the parties must give it their "free consent." But he denies that the nonaggression principle requires *informed* consent, even the minimal degree of informed consent that would suffice to exclude fraud. You can freely consent to a purchase even if the seller is deceiving you about the product you're buying. The conditions of free consent are fulfilled provided that the parties to a transaction possess what Child calls "market competence," roughly, the capacity to make independent choices in a market setting; provided that there is no seizure or duress; and provided that each party actually transfers the items slated for exchange (Child 1994, 729–31). The latter requirement is important: If you pay for your groceries, but the supermarket refuses to permit you to take them with you when you leave, you have surely not freely consented to *that*, just because you gave over your money voluntarily. What you have consented to is a trade, not a gift, and so the conditions of free consent will not have been fulfilled unless a trade actually occurs. The parties to a transaction cannot be said to have each given their free consent to the arrangement unless each actually receives the items agreed upon.[36]

But this leaves a crucial question: how are these items to be designated? If fraud does not violate the nonaggression principle, then no representations made as to the nature of the items exchanged are relevant to whether free consent has been obtained. This would include signage in a store, product labeling information, and oral claims made before or during the transaction. For this reason, the items designated for exchange must be identified independently of any representations as to their na-

35. The contrast between Rothbard's and Rand's approaches is reflected in their terminology. Whereas Rothbard tends to speak of "aggression," Rand normally refers to "force." The term "force" is more abstract and unites a wider class of referents, whereas the term "aggression" is more concrete and suggests violence and manifest hostility. I have thus refrained from referring to Rand's principle as a "nonaggression principle." (For a similar point about the distinction between force and violence, see Smith 2013.)

36. Although Child does not emphasize this aspect of free consent, it is implied at Child 1994, 730, 731–32. He has no intention of denying, for example, that it would be a violation of libertarian principles for a seller to prevent you from taking possession of goods you had paid for.

ture, for purposes of determining whether the conditions of free consent have been met. What is exchanged, then, on Child's view, are the particular perceptible objects that change hands, considered apart from any conceptual identification of them—that is, the objects of exchange, on his account, are to be identified demonstratively, as *this* and *that*. From this perspective there would be no proper legal grounds whatsoever for seeking redress from the supermarket if an item advertised on its label, and designated on the store's shelves, as "laundry detergent" was actually motor oil.

Child's discussion of fraud presupposes this view of trade.[37] I suggest that the reason Rand readily accepts that fraud is a kind of (indirect) force is not that she has failed to grasp the true implications of her principles, as Child claims, but that she views trade very differently and would consider Child's view of it unacceptable. Just as Rand's view of force is developed within a normative context, in relation to the requirements of human life, so too her conception of trade is a normative one. We explain what trade is by explaining what it needs to be in order for it to play a certain necessary role in human life. This is not to say that the account of trade is inapplicable to real cases but, first, that what explains the features of real cases is people's grasp, in some terms, of the requirements of their lives; and, second, that divergent cases (if any) are to be regarded as anomalous and not probative as to the essential nature of trade—rather, the parties in such cases would be engaging in a self-defeating and necessarily marginal practice.

Viewed in terms of the requirements of human life, trade must be predicated on a shared conceptual identification between the parties of the items exchanged, and the conditions of free consent must be seen as including the requirement that this identification be at least substantially correct. If it was not substantially correct, then there would be grounds for complaint. Fraud would occur when the inaccuracy was deliberately perpetrated. Although there is much to sort out here in terms of details (such as what counts as "substantially"), it seems clear that trade would be of little value to us if it were conducted without regard for these conditions. The description under which one buys a product (e.g., "laundry detergent") is obviously essential to one's deliberations about what to buy, and the substantial reliability of representations made by one's trading

---

37. Again, it is not clear whether Child presupposes this view as his own, or whether the view is simply a presupposition of libertarianism as Child reconstructs it.

partners about the items one receives from them is a presupposition of any rational, purposeful form of exchange. The only way for exchange to serve a rational purpose, from Rand's perspective, is for it to facilitate the activity of producing and consuming the values that one's life rationally requires. But it could not do that if it took the impoverished form imagined by Rothbard and Child, in which consent floats free of the parties' conceptual grasp of the nature of the items they exchange, and fraudulent transactions therefore count as consensual.

It is important to note the conception of consent just sketched is a conception of what Child calls *free consent*. I am not citing the absence of *informed* consent as the basis for classifying fraud as force; Child is correct that this would be begging the question. Rather, the point is that a rational conception of free consent must be grounded in an account of the *function* of consensual transactions in human life—and that, in order for our conception of free consent to be grounded in this way, it must include an information component. I am not simply helping myself (or Rand) to the notion of informed consent, then, but providing a reason why free consent, rightly understood, requires a degree of informedness that is incompatible with fraud. If this is correct, then someone who is defrauded has not only *not* given *informed* consent to the fraudulent transaction but has not given *free* consent, in the relevant sense. I do not know whether Rand would agree with everything in this account of free consent, but her having accepted something like this account would explain why she says that fraud "consists of obtaining material values without their owner's consent, under false pretenses or false promises" ("The Nature of Government," *VOS* 130/*CUI* 383). Child views this statement as threatening to beg the question, but alternatively, we might see it as providing grounds for attributing to Rand something like the foregoing views of consent and trade, views that, it seems to me, are quite consistent with her overall approach to these issues.

Like his account of force, Child's account of trade strips the latter down to its most perceptually evident features—the visible exchange of perceptible objects. As a result, he arguably precludes a full understanding of it. For Rand, a fully conceptual understanding of trade (and on that basis, of fraud) requires viewing them in the context of the requirements of human life.

I will close this section by mentioning one other important divergence between Rand and Rothbard (though others could be added). In

Rothbard's view, parents are the custodial owners of their children. They are custodial owners (Rothbard's terms are "trustee" and "guardian") because they may not do absolutely anything to their children but must respect the children's rights, by refraining from killing or injuring them. But they are owners in that, for instance, they may freely sell their children to any willing buyers; parents, as the children's creators, are their partial owners. Further, there is no violation of the nonaggression principle involved in a parent's refusing to feed or care for her child; on the contrary, it would be a violation of the principle for anyone else to force the parent to do so or to punish the parent for not doing so (1982 [2002], ch. 14).

Rand, by contrast, does hold that parents properly have a legally enforceable obligation to provide support for their children. The source of this obligation, in her view, is that a child is absolutely dependent on adult support in order to live, and that it is the parents who have caused this state of dependency by giving birth to the child. She holds this view in conjunction with her strong endorsement of the moral and legal right of a woman to abort an unwanted pregnancy. But if a pregnancy is carried to term, the resulting child has a right to the parents' support (see *Answers* 3–4; "Of Living Death," *VOR* 58–59). Nor does Rand's theory of property rights offer grounds for regarding children as their parents' property. On her view, property rights are grounded, fundamentally, in our need to control and develop material resources, for the purpose of producing the values that our lives require. Nothing in this justification for property rights is applicable to children. Although one's creative activity can have relevance in determining the scope of property rights, Rand does not consider the sheer act of creation, outside of the context in which property rights are necessary, to confer a property right to whatever one has in any sense created. Indeed, in the case of children, the act of creation is the source not of a property right but of the parents' obligations to their child.[38]

The non–initiation of force principle grows out of Rand's entire philosophy. Metaphysically, in her view, the initiation of force amounts to a

---

38. In defending his view, Rothbard appeals with some justification to the natural rights tradition. But as discussed earlier, Rand's view of rights in a key respect stands outside that tradition, even though the rights she recognizes are similar to those recognized by Locke and other natural rights theorists.

flight from reality. Epistemically, it deprives rational thought of method or purpose; socially, it represents a rejection of the necessity of offering justification for one's ideas and goals; and ethically, it contradicts the long-range requirements of human survival and well-being. Politically, the full articulation and implementation of the non–initiation of force principle depends on a correct understanding of individual rights. It is this enmeshment in a wider philosophical context that allows Rand's principle to avoid the disturbing implications of Rothbardian libertarianism.

Rand held that there were two principles the acceptance of which constituted the "'basic minimum' of civilization" ("For the New Intellectual," *FTNI* 58)—the precondition of civil public discussion and peaceful coexistence. One was the principle that no one may initiate force against others. The other was the principle that public discussion must be based on rational argument and not on appeals to emotion. Her analysis of force helps us to see why she considered these principles to be tightly linked.

Part Two
RIGHTS AND GOVERNMENT

Ayn Rand's Theory of Rights

An Exposition and Response to Critics

FRED D. MILLER JR. AND ADAM MOSSOFF

A yn Rand created a comprehensive philosophic system ranging from metaphysics to aesthetics—the philosophy she called Objectivism. Yet many people think of Rand primarily as a political theorist; as a result, she is often identified as a libertarian who defends limited government. Rand, though, identifies herself as a "radical for capitalism."[1] She disavows any association with the political movement of libertarianism.[2] Her primary reason for rejecting libertarianism is that, for Rand, politics is not a primary: political principles, even such foundational political principles as the prohibition against the initiation of force, are not irreducible axioms.[3] Thus, she maintains that "Objectivism advocates certain political principles—specifically, those of laissez-faire capitalism—as the consequence and the ultimate practical application of its fundamental philosophical principles" ("Introduction," *CUI* vii).

Rand's commitment to capitalism as the only moral sociopolitical

1. See, for example, her 1963 letter to William M. Jones, Professor of English at the University of Missouri, in *Letters* 602.
2. This is discussed in some detail in Miller and Mossoff 2016.
3. Rand explains that "The basic political principle of the Objectivist ethics is: no man may *initiate* the use of physical force against others" ("The Objectivist Ethics," *VOS* 36).

system—and by "capitalism" she means "full, pure, uncontrolled, un-regulated *laissez-faire* capitalism" ("The Objectivist Ethics," *VOS* 37)—is based on her prior commitment to the principle of individual rights. But the moral principle of individual rights is not a primary either. This prin-ciple is derived from more fundamental philosophic principles, such as "a theory of man's nature and of man's relationship to existence" (*CUI* vii). Rand summarizes her theory of rights as follows:

> The source of man's rights is not divine law or congressional law, but the law of identity. A is A—and Man is Man. *Rights* are conditions of exis-tence required by man's nature for his proper survival. If man is to live on earth, it is *right* for him to use his mind, it is *right* to act on his own free judgment, it is *right* to work for his values and to keep the product of his work. If life on earth is his purpose, he has a *right* to live as a rational being: nature forbids him the irrational. (*Atlas* 1061)

In this essay we shall explicate this succinct summary statement of Rand's theory of individual rights, identifying it as the "synoptic statement." The main point of this statement has often been misunderstood. Although her further statement that "the source of rights is man's nature" ("Man's Rights," *VOS* 111/*CUI* 370) indicates that she shares some common ideas and ideals with the natural rights philosophers, especially John Locke, whom she admires ("Theory and Practice," *CUI* 150), it will become ev-ident that her theory differs from traditional natural rights theory in important respects. Moreover, as we shall see, prominent critics of her theory fail to recognize the degree to which she radically departs in both form and substance from modern and contemporary accounts of rights.

1. Rand's Theory of Individual Rights

A peaceful society in which individuals have productive and flourishing lives is possible only if individual rights are protected from the initiation of physical force. The concept of rights thus provides the logical transition from the moral principles guiding an individual's actions to the principles guiding his relationship with others.[4] "Individual rights are the means of subordinating society to moral law" ("Man's Rights," *VOS* 108/*CUI* 367; emphasis redacted). The primary function of rights according to Rand is to define and sanction a man's freedom of action in a social context.

4. In our exegesis of Rand's text, we follow her own practice (current at her time) of using "man" and "his" to refer to all human beings regardless of gender.

Today, this may seem like an obvious intuition to many people. On the one hand, economic prosperity, technological innovation, and a high standard of living have been achieved, and even the poor are well-to-do by historical standards, in the United States, the first country in history explicitly founded on the principle of individual rights. On the other hand, the destruction, wars, organized mass murder, and other horrors perpetrated by modern governments that have consistently denied individual rights—totalitarian regimes such as Nazi Germany, the Soviet Union, the People's Republic of China, and Khmer Rouge, and theocratic regimes such as the Taliban's Afghanistan and the Islamic Republic of Iran, to name just a few—have made clear that such sociopolitical associations can be inimical not just to human flourishing but to human life as such.

But Rand does not base any aspect of her philosophy of Objectivism on intuitions, and her theory of rights is no exception. Rand rejects intuitions in philosophical analysis and refuses to ground abstract ideas on rough approximations of what feels right based on packaging together a haphazard amalgam of facts, undefined concepts, and the conventional wisdom of the day.[5] Her unique method of philosophical analysis is always to return to first principles, asking questions and seeking to develop a rational explanation for the ideas that an "intuition" assumes as given.

In Rand's ethical theory, she first asks, "*Why* does man need a code of values?" ("The Objectivist Ethics," *VOS* 14; original emphasis). Thus in her political theory, she first asks: Why do people need rights? What facts give rise to the concept of rights and the moral limitations that this concept imposes on the use of force in society? In answering these questions through methodical rational analysis, Rand concludes that "the source of rights is man's nature" (VOS 111/*CUI* 370) and, as such, the moral concept of individual rights refers to "conditions of existence required by man's nature for his proper survival" (*VOS* 111/*CUI* 370; quoting *Atlas* 1061).

Accordingly, the concept of individual rights rests on Rand's conception of human nature and on her ethical theory—that humans are rational animals and that it is proper for individuals to act and to acquire the values comprising a flourishing rational life—but these topics are beyond the scope of this paper. Here, it must be sufficient to recognize that people are not born with either the physical capabilities or the existing knowledge necessary to acquire even the basic values that make possible

5. See "The Objectivist Ethics," *VOS* 15.

a mere physical existence, such as food, clothing, and shelter. More fundamentally, the necessary physical capabilities and objects—such as the basic tools necessary to hunt or grow food, to make clothing, or to build homes—must first be conceived by the human mind and then created through deliberate productive action. Even then, humans still do not have the innate knowledge of how to use a bow and arrow, wield a hammer, operate a sewing machine, or use a computer. They must learn further how to use these tools properly in order to create and secure the values necessary for life. In brief, humans are rational animals, which means that they must acquire knowledge of how to live—the knowledge of what is necessary to live and the further knowledge of the methods for producing and using the values that make this life possible.

These are incontrovertible facts of human nature, and a moral code that justifies living a *human life* means that the actions that support this life must be justified as well. As Rand recognizes, the basis of rights is not Divine Law (God) or human law (Congress), but the basic conditions of human nature—that individuals must be left free to take the necessary mental and physical actions to sustain a flourishing life proper to a rational animal. This thesis concerning the basis of rights has two fundamental implications that are essential to the justification for individual rights.

First, normative principles such as individual rights are conditional propositions, not categorical imperatives. As Rand recognizes in the metaethical foundation of her moral theory, "It is only the concept of 'Life' that makes the concept of 'Value' possible" ("The Objectivist Ethics," *VOS* 16; quoting *Atlas* 1013). If one wants to live, then one must engage in the actions necessary to achieve the values that sustain one's life.[6]

This radical insight by Rand into the nature of the concept of "value" in her ethical theory leads to her equally radical explanation about the conceptual hierarchy of rights. Rights refer to the requirements of human nature and what is necessary for an individual to live as a rational animal in society with other people. Thus, just as *life* is the foundation for ethical theory, the *right to life* is the foundation of all rights. "There is only *one* fundamental right (all the others are its consequences or corollaries): a man's right to his own life. Life is a process of self-sustaining and self-generated action; the right to life means the right to engage in self-sustaining and self-generated action—which means: the freedom to take all the actions required by the nature of a rational being for the support,

6. See *VOS* 16–17; Binswanger 1990.

the furtherance, the fulfillment and the enjoyment of his own life" (*VOS* 110/*CUI* 369). This is what Rand means when she writes that "If life on earth is his purpose, he has a *right* to live as a rational being" (*Atlas* 1061), as rights define the full scope of freedom of action necessary for one to live (and living for humans is the life of a rational being).

This leads to the second implication of Rand's ethical theory for her theory of rights: man's mind is the fundamental source of the values that sustain his life, and thus rights secure the necessary freedom to think and act as a rational animal. Aristotle first recognized that men are rational animals.[7] On the basis of Aristotle's tremendous accomplishment in identifying the essential nature of man, Rand states an important corollary: "The action required to sustain human life is primarily intellectual. Everything man needs has to be discovered by his mind and produced by his effort. Production is the application of reason to the problem of survival" ("What Is Capitalism?" *CUI* 8). Since man is a rational animal, then this implies that his "mind is his basic means of survival" (*CUI* 7).

Rand's discovery of the fundamental nature of what it means to live a human life defines what an individual's right to life requires of other people in society when they act individually or act through delegated agents in political institutions. In sum, the rights to liberty and property are *logical corollaries* of the right to life, because to live requires that one be able to undertake the thought and action necessary to sustain one's life; ergo, "the right of liberty means freedom of individual decision, individual choice, individual judgment and individual initiative" (*Journals* 354).

In the most basic sense of the physical conditions of life, one cannot create a farm on which to grow food, build a home, and trade with others unless one has the *freedom to think* about the importance of these values (food), the *freedom to discover* how to achieve these values (learn the principles of husbandry, mechanical engineering, etc.), and has the *freedom to act* on this knowledge to create and use these values (cultivating land, domesticating farm animals, manufacturing tools and machines that make farming possible, etc.). To deny individuals the freedom to think and act is to deny them their ability to live their lives in the only way that they can as human beings. Rand writes that, "for every individual, a right is the moral sanction of a *positive*—of his freedom to act on his own judgment, for his own goals, by his own *voluntary, uncoerced* choice" (*VOS* 110/*CUI*

---

7. See, for example, Aristotle, *Nicomachean Ethics* 1.17.1098a7–8: "the function of man is an activity of soul which follows or implies a rational principle" (Ross trans.).

369). There can be no right to life without the right to liberty to take the necessary life-sustaining actions required to think and to create the values that comprise a flourishing human life.

Given the conceptually hierarchical relationship between the rights to life and liberty and the way these rights sanction the value-creating actions necessary to live, it is unsurprising that Rand ultimately concludes: "The right to life is the source of all rights—and the right to property is their only implementation. Without property rights, no other rights are possible" (*VOS* 110/*CUI* 369). An individual living on an island would still need to think and to produce the values necessary to sustain his life. If he wants to live, he would be morally right to think rationally about the facts of his nature as a rational animal and how to survive given his surrounding conditions. If he wants to live, he ought to identify fecund soil and cultivate it (produce a farm), create the tools necessary to grow food (a plow, hoe, etc.), learn how to grow food (corn, wheat, etc.), and so on. The values that he produces to sustain his life are his "property." In society, this individual has the "right to property"—that is, the freedom to acquire, use, and dispose of these same values. He has the moral claim to be free from coerced interference by other people in his choices and actions to produce the values (property) required to live a flourishing life.

The rights to life and liberty define and sanction the freedom of action necessary to sustain one's life, and one has the right to property in the values that one produces to sustain one's life or that one obtains through trading other produced values. Rand concludes: "no rights can exist without the right to translate one's rights into reality—to think, to work and to keep the results—which means: the right of property" (*Atlas* 1062). To grasp the concept of the right to property is to understand what it means to have the right to life and liberty, and vice versa.[8]

Significantly, Rand is not saying that the right to property is a moral claim to an object: like all other individual rights, the right to property secures only freedom of action in a social context (*VOS* 110/*CUI* 369). Specifically, the right to property secures the freedom that is necessary for a man to practice the virtue of productivity—creating the values necessary

---

8. In this respect, Rand challenges most virtue-based theories of civil society, which typically argue that the government must coercively inculcate virtue in its citizens. As evidenced by Rand's political theory, it is not necessary for a virtue-based political theory to be antagonistic either to individual rights generally or to the right to property specifically. See, for example, Miller 2006 (explaining how Aristotle's theory of virtue ethics may be compatible with political freedom).

for him to live. Thus, as a consequence of Rand's understanding of the connection between property and the virtuous actions that create values, she defines the right to property as "the right to gain, to use and to dispose of material values" (*VOS* 111/*CUI* 370).[9]

Rand's insights into human nature and her development of her ethical theory lead her to the conclusion that the rights to life, liberty, and property define the sphere of freedom of action for an individual to live a flourishing life in society.[10] As Rand writes in the synoptic statement quoted at the beginning of this article, "If man is to live on earth, it is *right* for him to use his mind, it is *right* to act on his own free judgment, it is *right* to work for his values and to keep the product of his work" (*Atlas* 1061). Rights are moral principles that have a necessarily interrelated two-fold function: they sanction (approve) the freedom necessary for someone to take the thought and action required to live a flourishing life, and they sanction (prohibit) third parties in interfering with these actions. The social experience of rights is therefore *negative*: people respect another person's rights by "abstain[ing] from violating them" (*VOS* 110/*CUI* 369). But this negative exclusivity should not be divorced from what gives this exclusivity its meaning and import; rights first define and sanction an individual's freedom in acting to live.

This leads to the conclusion that many theorists and commentators assert as the foundational premise in their political theory: the prohibition on the initiation of force in society. Today, this is known among libertarians as the "nonaggression principle." One commentator has re-

---

9. See also "The New Fascism: Rule by Consensus": "The right to property is the right of use and disposal" (*CUI* 227). Significantly, this is similar to the classic definition of the right to property in American law; see, for example, *McKeon v. Bisbee*, 9 Cal. 137, 142 (1858): "Property is the exclusive right of possessing, enjoying, and disposing of a thing"; *Eaton v. B. C. and M. R. R.*, 51 N.H. 504, 511 (1872): "Property is the right of any person to possess, use, enjoy, and dispose of a thing" (quoting *Wynehamer v. People*, 13 N.Y. 378, 433 [1856]).

10. Rand recognizes that there is a wide range of individual rights beyond the rights to life, liberty, and property. Throughout her writing, she recognizes many derivative rights, such as the right to self-defense (*Atlas* 1063), contract ("Collectivized Rights," *VOS* 119; "The Nature of Government," *VOS* 129/*CUI* 382), free trade ("Man's Rights," *VOS* 114/*CUI* 373–74), freedom of speech (*Journals* 384, 367; *ARL* 2:23 [August 1973], 230), freedom of the press (*ARL* 3:2 [October 1973], 251–56; *ARL* 2:23 [August 1973], 230), a fair trial ("The New Fascism: Rule by Consensus," *CUI* 230), vote ("Representation without Authorization," *VOR* 233), privacy (*Letters* 622), abortion (*ARL* 4:2 [December 1975], 382), and the pursuit of happiness (*VOS* 114/*CUI* 373). According to Rand, these and many other rights are all "corollaries" of "a man's right to his own life" (*VOS* 110/*CUI* 369).

ferred to the nonaggression principle as the "basic libertarian idea" (Huebert 2010, 3).[11]

Rand agrees that force should be banished from human relationships,
but she does not consider this to be merely a *political* principle; rather, it is
a more fundamental insight in *ethical* theory. She recognizes that physical
force breaks the necessary causal connection between the rational mind
and the world in which this mind functions, identifying facts and guiding
the actions necessary to create and use values for a flourishing life. Force
turns the conditional propositions of a moral code into deontological imperatives that require one to act regardless of the facts, one's knowledge,
or one's values. In brief, a person compelled to act under physical coercion
is no longer a moral agent. "Values cannot exist (cannot be valued) outside the full context of a man's life, needs, goals, and *knowledge*" (*CUI* 16).
Thus, as Rand summarizes this fundamental normative insight about the
basic conditions of social interaction between people: "Force and mind
are opposites; morality ends where a gun begins" (*Atlas* 1023).

Since the concept of rights defines the scope of freedom an individual
must use his mind and to act to achieve the values necessary for life, then
coercion is the only way that someone can be prevented from acting according to his rights: "To violate man's rights means to compel him to act
against his own judgment, or to expropriate his values. Basically, there is
only one way to do it: the use of physical force" (*VOS* 111/*CUI* 370). Social
disapproval, economic disadvantages, and other forms of persuasion can
only succeed in influencing an individual if one *thinks* that such things
are important and accepts them as such, but a gun or other form of physical coercion is the only thing that removes independent thought from the
equation in an individual's action.

On the basis of her recognition of the evil of the initiation of force in
her ethical theory, Rand makes the equally pioneering insight in political
theory that the initiation of force is the sine qua non in violating individual rights, such as a mugger stealing a wallet, a thief stealing a computer
from one's home, or the government taxing wages. In all such cases, the
individual's thoughts and actions with respect to how to live one's life are
made moot—a gun and the threat of death intercede between the indi-

11. Huebert explicitly identifies the nonaggression principle as the proposition that "anyone should be free to do anything he or she wants, as long as he or she does not commit acts
of force or fraud against any other peaceful person" (2010, 4). Murray Rothbard framed this
proposition as a purely negative injunction: "no man or group of men may aggress against the
person or property of anyone else" (1973 [2006], 27).

vidual's mind and the actions one should take to achieve one's values in living the life one seeks for oneself.[12] Rand points out the inherent contradiction in using force to achieve an alleged moral good, such as those who claim that they have a "right" to force others to think or act in whatever way is deemed important for the "public good": "There can be no 'right' to destroy the source of rights, the only means of judging right and wrong: the mind" (*Atlas* 1023).

But recognizing that the prohibition on the initiation of force is a core principle in ethical theory—Rand even acknowledges that it is "the basic political principle of the Objectivist ethics" ("The Objectivist Ethics," *VOS* 36)—does not mean that this proposition is the *foundation* on which to derive other political principles regardless of the moral concepts and principles that give it meaning.[13] In fact, what Rand shows is that the concept of individual rights is not derived from the principle prohibiting the initiation of force but, rather, is derived from the same facts and moral concepts from which the principle of the evil of the initiation of force is derived in her ethical theory—the nature of man as a rational animal, the concept of value, the conditional nature of moral propositions. This gives the full meaning to Rand's statement (quoted above) that "Individual rights are the means of subordinating society to moral law" (*VOS* 108/ *CUI* 367).

Rand conceives of "rights" as principles sanctioning the actions required by man's nature for his survival in a social context. Individual rights make it possible for the virtuous man to live in organized society, in which he is free to think and to act in creating, using, or disposing of the values that comprise a flourishing life. Rand captures this basic truth in the final sentence of the synoptic statement: "If life on earth is his purpose, he has a *right* to live as a rational being: nature forbids him the irrational" (*Atlas* 1061).

It is only when an individual's rights are secured against others that he can interact with other men peacefully and for mutual benefit. "A civilized society is one in which physical force is banned from human relationships—in which the government, acting as a policeman, may use

12. Rand writes that "Man's rights can be violated only by the use of physical force. It is only by means of physical force that one man can deprive another of his life, or to enslave him, or rob him, or prevent him from pursuing his own goals, or compel him to act against his own rational judgment" ("The Nature of Government," *VOS* 126/*CUI* 379).

13. In his earlier writings, for instance, Tibor Machan argued that "Political ideas [can] be supported in isolation from their underpinnings" (1980, 23).

force *only* in retaliation and *only* against those who initiate its use" (*VOS* 112/*CUI* 371). Rand's radical theory of rights explains why all men, as rational animals who must think and act to create the values necessary for life, have "unalienable rights" including the fundamental rights to "life, liberty and the pursuit of happiness" proclaimed in the American Declaration of Independence.

2. Objective Rights versus Natural Rights

Rand's theory of rights is similar in both method and content to the theory of natural rights that inspired the Founding Fathers to create the first country expressly founded on a moral principle—the principle of rights eloquently stated in the Declaration of Independence.[14] In fact, Rand's distinctive method of philosophical analysis—starting from facts and first principles—is similar to the argument in John Locke's *Second Treatise of Government*, a book that revolutionized political theory by returning to first principles to determine what Locke calls the "Original of Political Power" (§ 1, 268).[15] Given the shared ideals in their respective political theories, it is important to differentiate Rand's theory of individual rights from Locke's theory of natural rights. This is necessary not only to make clearer what are her unique contributions to political theory but also because of persisting confusions about her theory of rights (exemplified in the philosophical critiques discussed below).

Rand's theory of rights resonates with ideas advanced by natural rights philosophers and especially by Locke. Both Rand and Locke believe that rights are a nonsubjective moral standard because they both believe the concept of rights is derived from human nature.[16] Rand believes that "the source of rights is man's nature" (*VOS* 111/*CUI* 370), and Locke believes that it is a "Law of Nature," which is "Reason," that "no one ought to harm another in his Life, Health, Liberty, or Possessions" (*Second Treatise* § 6, 271). Rand further agrees with Locke when he writes

14. The Declaration of Independence states for the very first time in the history of the formation of new political state that individual rights are the moral justification for political states as such: "We hold these truths to be self-evident, that all men are created equal, that they are endowed by their Creator with certain unalienable Rights, that among these are Life, Liberty and the pursuit of Happiness.—That to secure these rights, Governments are instituted among Men, deriving their just powers from the consent of the governed."

15. Locke, *Two Treatises of Government* (1690 [1988]), 1. Citations will be given parenthetically in the text, with section number (marked by §) followed by page number in this 1988 edition.

16. "Locke was seeking to justify a system of morality by grounding the moral law in something objective" (Yolton 1958, 483).

that a proper government is created by individuals to secure "the mutual *Preservation* of their Lives, Liberties and Estates" (§ 123, 350). Since the function of government is to secure rights against "dangerous and noxious Creatures [who] are not under the ties of the Common Law of Reason" (§ 16, 279), they both understand that the essence of governmental action is coercion.[17] Rand thus agrees with Locke's significant insight that if "a Robber break into my House, and with a Dagger at my Throat, make me seal Deeds to convey my Estate to him, ... [t]he Injury and the Crime is equal, whether committed by the wearer of a Crown, or some petty Villain" (§ 176, 385).[18]

Underlying his political theory, Locke's moral theory is implicitly individualistic (although this remark has some qualifications, which will be discussed shortly), and this explains why he is able to formulate the principle of *individual rights* in his political theory. Accordingly, he repeatedly states in the *Two Treatises* that "the Fundamental Law of Nature [commands] Man . . . to be preserved," and that the Law of Nature is grounded in man's "strong desire of Self-preservation" (§ 16 and *First Treatise* § 86, 205).[19] Again, Rand agrees: "Rights are conditions of existence required by man's nature for his proper survival" (*VOS* 111/*CUI* 370). And, like Rand, Locke reveres the rational human mind that can discover truth and virtue.[20] His "mixing labor" theory of property reflects his belief that production of values is key to a flourishing human life.[21]

But there are important differences between Rand's theory of rights

17. As Rand put it, "The nature of governmental action is: *coercive* action" ("America's Persecuted Minority: Big Business," *CUI* 43). See also "The Nature of Government" (*VOS* 133–34/*CUI* 386–87).

18. Elsewhere in the *Second Treatise*, Locke writes: "Hence it is a mistake to think that the supreme or legislative power of any commonwealth can do what it will, and dispose of the estates of the subject arbitrarily, or take any part of them at pleasure" (§ 138, 361). In *A Letter Concerning Toleration*, Locke similarly writes that "Absolute liberty, just and true liberty, equal and impartial liberty, is the thing we are in need of" (1689 [1824], 2).

19. On the moral duty of self-preservation, see also Locke's statements in the *Second Treatise* that "Every one . . . is *bound to preserve himself* and not to quit his Station willfully," and that "the [Natural] Law . . . was made for my Preservation" (§ 6, 271, and § 19, 280). In the *First Treatise*, Locke argues that "Reason, *which was the Voice of God in him*," teaches man to labor and use things in the world in "pursuing that natural Inclination he had to preserve his Being" (§ 86, 205).

20. In the opening passages of *An Essay Concerning Human Understanding* (Locke 1690 [1979]; hereafter cited as *Essay*), Locke writes that "Since it is the Understanding that sets Man above the rest of sensible Beings, . . . it is certainly a Subject, even for its Nobleness, worth our *Labour* to enquire into" (*Essay* I 1 § 1). Ultimately, according to Locke, this inquiry and thought produces the "Information of Virtue" (I 1 § 5).

21. See Mossoff 2013, 294–307.

and Locke's theory of natural rights. While these may be differences among friends, they are important because they concern the validity of the principle of individual rights. At root, there are two fundamental errors committed by Locke that undermine his ability to justify morally the value-creating activities that comprise the underlying justification for the rights to life, liberty, and property. The first has to do with the ultimate justification for why rights are valid—that rights define the freedom necessary for a rational person to create the values that comprise a flourishing life. The second has to do with the nature of the concept of individual rights, which is not a fact of human nature itself but, rather, a conceptual identification—a moral principle—that refers to the factual conditions necessary for how people should live together in society.

First, with respect to the foundation for rights, Rand explains that moral principles, such as the virtues of rationality and productivity, are conditional propositions inferred from the facts of life and the nature of man as a rational animal. This is the fundamental identification by Rand in the synoptic statement that "If man is to live on earth, it is *right* for him to use his mind, it is *right* to act on his own free judgment, it is *right* to work for his values and to keep the product of his work" (*Atlas* 1061). Locke also implicitly understands that individual rights secure the freedom necessary to live and to produce the moral values necessary to live a flourishing life—what he repeatedly refers to in the *Second Treatise* as the "Conveniences of life" (see §§ 34, 37, 44).[22] But Locke does not rationally explain why life is the moral foundation that justifies both the concept of value and the concept of rights.

Within the *Two Treatises*, Locke makes two separate but related assertions about why life is the proper moral standard on which to ground the theory of natural rights. First, he espouses a version of psychological egoism. In the *First Treatise*, he writes that "God . . . made Man, and planted in him, as in all other Animals, a strong desire for Self-preservation" (§ 86, 205).[23] Thus, humans cannot help but act for their preservation and, hence, our moral and political theory must account for this basic inescapable fact. As an alternative explanation for why life is the moral standard,

22. See also Mossoff 2013, 299–303.
23. Alternatively, other natural law philosophers, such as Samuel Pufendorf, argue that God constructed man's moral psychology such that he would be inclined toward sociableness, which then serves as the foundation for natural law obligations. See *De Jure Naturae et Gentium Libri Octo* 2:3.vi, where Pufendorf states that "God has appointed for man a sociable nature" (1672 [1934], 188).

Locke offers a deontological account of the Natural Law such that it enjoins men to act for their self-preservation: "Men [are] all the Workmanship of one Omnipotent, and infinitely wise Maker. . . . Every one as he is *bound to preserve himself,* and not to quit his Station willfully; so by the like reason . . . [he] may not . . . impair the life, or what tends to the Preservation of the Life, the Liberty, Health, Limb or Goods of another" (*Second Treatise* § 6, 271). According to this alternative account, the Natural Law *simpliciter* commands that man should preserve himself (and incidentally respect the rights of others).

With these two assertions, Locke was covering his bases, grounding rights in both a descriptive fact (psychology) and a normative ought (God's commands), which thus provided as complete as possible a justification in his context of the fundamental moral principle that one should live, which is the moral basis for justifying the principle of the right to life, liberty, and property. Thus, according to Locke, the moral foundation for individual rights rests on two assertions: a deontological normative principle that one ought to preserve one's life,[24] and the factual claim that the "strong desire of Preserving his Life and Being" that was "Planted in him, as a Principle of Action by God himself" (*First Treatise* § 86, 205).[25] At root, these two claims are not really distinct from each other. In both cases, the ultimate moral proposition that one ought to live and thus one has a right to life is equivalent to the proposition that this is a duty created in or imposed on man by God—as the "Maker" both of human psychology and of the "Law of Nature."

When Rand states that the "source of man's rights is not divine law or congressional law" (*Atlas* 1061), she and Locke are in agreement on the latter claim but not the former, and this is a key aspect of her unique contribution to the definition and justification of individual rights. Locke understands in some important respects that moral and political theory should strive to justify the moral ideal of a flourishing life lived in accordance with human nature, but he builds his arguments on a partially theistic foundation. This ultimately leads him astray.

24. Locke writes: "The *State of Nature* has a Law of Nature to govern it, which obliges every one: And Reason, which is that Law, teaches all Mankind, who will but consult it, that being all equal and independent, no one ought to harm another in his Life, Health, Liberty, or Possessions" (*Treatises* 2:6). Later, he claims that "natural Reason" and "Revelation" each independently and consistently lead to the same conclusion that individuals "have a *property* in several parts of that which God gave to Mankind in common" (2:25).

25. Note also: "God makes him *in his own Image and after his own Likeness*" (*First Treatise* § 30, 162 alluding to *Genesis* 1:26).

The absence of a properly identified, fact-based foundation for his moral theory leads him to inconsistent moral arguments, and it ultimately undermines his justification for rights as such. For instance, in *Some Thoughts Concerning Education and Of the Conduct of the Understanding*, Locke argues that the Christian maxim "we should love our neighbor as ourselves" is a "fundamental truth" on par with Isaac Newton's scientific laws of mechanics, which is consistent with his view of God as the maker of human nature and as the ultimate source of moral obligation (1693 [1996], 222–23). But Locke never fully confronts the inherent tension, if not outright contradiction, between his claim that faith-based altruism is a fundamental moral law and his claim that reason and self-preservation are the foundation of moral and political theory.

For instance, Locke asserts in the *Second Treatise* that, once one's own self-preservation is not in jeopardy, God commands that "ought he, as much as he can, *to preserve the rest of Mankind*" (§ 6, 271), but this raises more unanswered questions. Is this merely a secondary duty, and if so, how does this square with his claim that altruism is a "fundamental truth"? Locke also states (as quoted above) that just as one ought to preserve one's own life, "so by like. . . reason" one ought not to "impair the life, or what tends to the Preservation of the Life, the Liberty, Health, Limb or Goods of another" (§ 6, 271). Unfortunately, Locke does not spell out what the "like reason" is that would support these two very different conclusions (a point that the libertarian philosopher Michael Huemer alleges is a fault with Rand's theory of rights, as will be discussed below).

Indeed, how does one reconcile the moral injunction to preserve others with the moral injunction that one ought to live a flourishing life? This is not a rhetorical question or merely a concern imposed externally on Locke's political theory, because Locke repeatedly raises and leaves unanswered this question throughout the *Two Treatises*. For instance, in the *First Treatise*, he admits, as did Hugo Grotius before him, that there is a right to "Charity," by which those in "extream want" can rightly claim "a Title to so much out of another's Plenty" as needed because "God requires him to afford to the wants of his Brother" (§ 42, 170).[26] Where does the right to property end and another's right to claim that property under

---

26. Hugo Grotius calls it a "right of necessity" and explains that, "if a man under stress of such necessity takes from the property of another what is necessary to preserve his own life, he does not commit a theft." *De Jure Belli ac Pacis Libri Tres* 2:2.6 (1625 [1925] 193).

the "right to charity" begin?[27] Moreover, in the *Second Treatise*, Locke expressly limits the property that can and should be earned through one's own productive labor on the condition that one can only rightly claim this property as long as "there is enough, and as good left in common for others"—what is now known as the "enough and as good" proviso (§ 27, 288). Both the right of charity and the "enough and as good" proviso seem to be based on his premise that God created man, the universe, and the Law of Nature—a premise grounding his ethical theory in (unjustified) injunctions of the Bible that conflict in both substance and method with his factually based, reasoned explanations for self-preservation and individual rights.[28]

Without a proper moral foundation in the actual facts of human nature (and grounding instead the fundamental moral obligation in the handiwork of God), Locke lacks a thoroughly and consistently rational and inductive account of a theory of rights. This weakens his theory by leading him to proffer inconsistent moral obligations involving an individual's social duties to others—duties that could be and have been used to justify violations of rights in the name of more fundamental moral obligations to others. Locke, for instance, fudges on the morality of taxation, claiming that it can be justified by the "consent of the majority."[29] And although Locke does not expressly endorse the concept of eminent domain, it was first defined and justified by his fellow natural rights philosophers Hugo Grotius and Samuel Pufendorf, and subsequent legal theorists un-

27. Unlike Locke's "right of charity," Grotius develops express conditions and limitations on his "right of necessity," answering this question in part. *De Jure Belli* 2:2.7–9 (1625 [1925]). This makes the "right of necessity" look less like a *moral claim* to charity and more like the *legal claim* to necessity that functions as an affirmative defense in tort law. Still, Grotius, like Locke, leaves unaddressed the tension in the two conflicting ethical principles of individualistic egoism and altruistic collectivism. See also Tuck, who recognizes that "Grotius was . . . the first radical rights theorist," but that Grotius's work also "is Janus-faced, and its two mouths speak the language of both absolutism and liberty" (1979, 71, 77–79).

28. This is also reflected in his writings outside of the *Two Treatises*, such as his willingness to place the Christian maxim of loving one's neighbor on a par with Newton's scientific laws of mechanics (Locke 1693 [1996], 222–23).

29. The full passage reads: "It is true governments cannot be supported without great charge, and it is fit that every one who enjoys his share of the protection should pay out of his estate his proportion for the maintenance of it. But still it must be with his own consent—i.e., the consent of the majority, giving it either by themselves or their representatives chosen by them; for if any one shall claim a power to lay taxes on the people by his own authority, and without such consent of the people, he thereby invades the fundamental law of property, and subverts the end of government" (*Second Treatise* § 140, 362).

derstandably saw no conflict between eminent domain and Lockean political theory.[30] Locke's lack of a consistent and rational foundation also opened the door to the critics of individual rights, who focused on this as a way to undermine the moral claims of individuals to have their rights respected in the face of calls for the "public good." The best exemplar of this is Jeremy Bentham's famous attack on natural rights theory as "nonsense on stilts."[31]

This leads to the second difference between Rand's theory of rights and Locke's theory of natural rights, which is related to the lack of a proper foundation for the concept of rights. Since Locke thinks rights are a "Law of Nature," rooted in deontological-type injunctions directly from or the by-product of the work of God in making the world, then he ultimately thinks of rights as *intrinsic* in human nature. This is in fact what Locke really means by *natural* rights. He even believes that fundamental moral concepts, such as "value," are intrinsic in nature, as evidenced by his famous farming example of "mixing labor" (see *Second Treatise* §§ 40, 43). Through several iterations of this example, he keeps increasing the amount of value contributed by the productive labor of the farmer, concluding ultimately that labor accounts for 99.9 percent of the total value of the farm and its produced goods, such as wheat (§ 43, 298). Thus, according to Locke, there is always some nonproduced value that intrinsically exists in nature before an individual identifies and transforms the world into the produced items that serve a flourishing life or, in Locke's terminology, "improved the conveniencies of Life" (§ 44, 299).

Locke's intention is right and laudable, but the lack of precision and clarity in the moral concepts employed in his argument undermines achieving his ultimate goal. In fact, Locke never defines the moral concept of "value" that serves as the fulcrum in his moral theory and in his theory of rights. Even lacking an express definition, he is mistaken in supposing that there are values in the world that exist independently from the actions undertaken to sustain one's life, even if that preexisting value is only 0.1 percent of the total value in the farm. As Rand recognized, it is untrue that fallow land qua land is a value. It is only land; a descriptive fact of the world. This descriptive fact is converted into a normative value

30. William Blackstone, in his justly famous *Commentaries on the Laws of England*, endorses a Lockean account of natural rights and limited government together with eminent domain. See Blackstone 1765 [1979], 134–35. For Grotius's and Pufendorf's justification for eminent domain, see Miller and Mossoff 2016, 191, 203nn19–20.

31. In "Anarchical Fallacies" (1796). See Bentham 1844, 91.

only after an individual undertakes the necessary intellectual and physical efforts to use the land as a farm, employing the skills necessary to till the soil, plant and grow crops, and then harvest the crops for food. The value in the farm is not 99.9 percent the result of productive labor; rather, 100 percent of the value is the result of human thought and action. The value exists entirely in the identification, creation, and use of the farm.

This is significant, because Locke's concession that some value intrinsically exists in the world independently of human interests or actions undermines his justification for individual rights, especially his justification for the right to property. According to Locke, each man can claim as his property the value that he has created, but since he admits that not all value arises solely from productive activities, then we are left with an important, unanswered question: How do we account for the unproduced value in property that preexisted productive labor, as the laborer does not seem to have a rightful claim to a property right in this portion of the good, according to Locke's own property theory? Although Locke considers this unproduced, preexisting value to be de minimus, constituting only one tenth of one percent, this does not change the import of this question concerning the *moral* foundation of a property right that is predicated on the creation and use of values that serve a flourishing life.

In fact, this lacuna has generated substantial criticism, which uses this assumption of unproduced, preexisting value against Locke's justification of property rights.[32] Robert Nozick, for instance, argues that Locke cannot adequately distinguish between the value created by labor and the value that preexists the labor and to which one lacks any moral claim. He claims that Locke's concept of property is fundamentally incoherent (Nozick 1974, 174–75). Although Nozick misrepresents the nature of the "mixing labor" argument in this (in)famous criticism of Locke,[33] his critique has traction because there is a sense in which Locke is confused about the concept of value—he implicitly defines value as something *intrinsic* in the natural world that was itself created by another moral agent (God).

---

32. The assumption that there is some intrinsic value in nature apart from any human thought or action is common, even among the critics of Rand's concept of property rights. See, for example, Mavrodes, who writes: "There is plenty of wealth . . . which was never produced by any human being at all. . . . Within our present system it is a fact that land, minerals, timber, etc.—regardless of whether we call them wealth or something else—will be the functional equivalents of wealth" (1972, 256).

33. See Mossoff 2013, 289–90; Mossoff 2002, 155–64.

Despite his lack of a precise definition of value and his unsuccessful grounding of this fundamental normative concept either in deontological commands by God or in a type of psychological egoism, Locke developed a comprehensive, integrated justification for the rights to life, liberty, and property, as well as the corollary that it is the moral function of government to secure these rights. These are some of the important points of agreement between Locke and Rand, and for this reason Rand respects Locke's achievements as a natural rights philosopher. Locke's influence on the creation of the American Republic, the first country formed on the moral principle that the government serves to protect individual rights is undeniable.[34] Thomas Jefferson wrote of the Declaration of Independence that "all its authority rests then on the harmonizing sentiments of the day, whether expressed in conversation, in letters, printed essays, or in the elementary books of public right, as Aristotle, Cicero, Locke, Sidney, etc."[35] Rand similarly recognizes this monumental achievement and the importance of such philosophers as Aristotle and Locke. "It took centuries of intellectual, philosophical development," she writes, "to achieve political freedom. It was a long struggle, stretching from Aristotle to John Locke to the Founding Fathers" ("Theory and Practice," *CUI* 150).

3. Philosophical Critics of Rand's Theory of Rights

Rand's theory of rights, along with her entire philosophy of Objectivism, has met with widespread resistance among academics. Many of them have simply ignored or dismissed her views, no doubt because they are repelled by her individualistic ethical theory and her principled justification of laissez-faire capitalism. However, her theory of rights has also been criticized by leading academic philosophers who are in general sympathy with her ethical and political conclusions, including, most notably, Robert Nozick (1971), Eric Mack (1984), and Michael Huemer (2002). In contrast to uninformed and less charitable critics, Nozick, Mack, and Huemer attempt to take her writings seriously, offering interpretations of her main claims together with reconstructions of her arguments for them. All three of them, notwithstanding, find Rand's arguments unsound and her theory of rights indefensible.

---

34. Rand writes that "The most profoundly revolutionary achievement of the United States of America was *the subordination of society to moral law*" (*VOS* 109/*CUI* 368).

35. Letter from Thomas Jefferson to Henry Lee, May 8, 1825, in Koch and Peden 1944, 719.

Although Nozick, Mack, and Huemer are accomplished scholars who have produced other work worthy of study, as we shall explain, their critiques of Rand are misdirected, the result of taking passages out of context and reconstructing arguments with little or no support in Rand's texts.[36] More important, the source of these misinterpretations is a failure shared by all three critics to grasp the radical character of Rand's thought. In brief, they all fail to recognize the degree to which she breaks from the conventional philosophical concepts and methodologies that are employed by most academic philosophers today. The result is that they impose an alien conceptual framework on her theory of rights, thereby producing the very incoherence they accuse Rand of committing in her philosophical analysis of this foundational political principle. Nozick, Mack, and Huemer raise three main objections against Rand's theory of rights: first, that she invalidly infers rights from the moral rightness of actions; second, that she invalidly derives individual rights from the claim that man is an end in himself; and third, that the two primary moral principles underlying her political theory—egoism and rights—are fundamentally at odds with each other. These three critiques will be examined in turn.

Criticism 1

This criticism is that Rand invalidly infers the existence of rights from the moral rightness of actions. It is advanced by Mack, who claims "that [Rand's] arguments show a failure to understand well the character of rights," because she does not recognize that rights secure freedom not just for right actions, but most important, for wrong actions as well (Mack 1984, 150). He bases this critique in the synoptic statement from *Atlas Shrugged* quoted above:

> The source of man's rights is not divine law or congressional law, but the law of identity. A is A—and Man is Man. *Rights* are conditions of existence required by man's nature for his proper survival. If man is to live on earth, it is *right* for him to use his mind, it is *right* to act on his own free judgment, it is *right* to work for his values and to keep the product of his work. If life on earth is his purpose, he has a *right* to live as a rational being: nature forbids him the irrational. (*Atlas* 1061)

36. In the case of Nozick this point is amply demonstrated in Den Uyl and Rasmussen 1978.

Mack takes this passage to be arguing "that various types of unimpeded action and acquisition are right for individuals as conditions of their respective proper survival and that, therefore, each individual has a right to engage in these unimpeded actions and acquisitions" (Mack 1984, 152).

As a preliminary matter, it bears noting that Mack does not respect the text of the synoptic statement. This is important, because a failure to read the text as written—recognizing the propositions within their appropriate context and meaning—naturally leads one astray. For instance, the synoptic statement contains no term such as "therefore" or "consequently" to indicate that the conclusion that "man has a right to live as a rational being" is deduced by Rand as a matter of formal logic from the premise "it is right for man to live rationally." Moreover, the synoptic statement does not refer to *action* as "conditions of existence required for man's nature for his proper survival"; rather, it is *rights*—that is, the freedom from coercion such that one can take actions. This lack of precision in respecting the text of a philosophical argument, especially one presented in such a succinct format as the synoptic statement, easily leads to misunderstanding and strawman attacks, as we will soon show.

Since Mack assumes that Rand purports to deduce the existence of rights directly from the moral rightness of actions, he objects that Rand's theory of rights fails to account for two important and related features of individual rights: first, that "a person can have a right to do something it is not right for him to do," and second, that there are "differences between claiming that an action is morally right and claiming that the agent has a right to perform it" (Mack 1984, 151). A theory that is "oblivious" (to use Mack's characterization of Rand's theory of rights) to these important conceptual features of rights would certainly be indefensible—but this is not Rand's theory of rights. Each of Mack's two objections will be examined in turn.

The first of Mack's objections is that Rand's argument implies that individuals have only the right to do what is morally right but not the right to do wrong. Mack states that "if we have read this [synoptic statement] from *Atlas Shrugged* correctly, Rand's argument for rights has the consequence that persons only have the right to do what is right" (Mack 1984, 153).[37] But, as already pointed out, Rand does not claim that individ-

---

37. Mack also believes that this conclusion is implied by Rand's characterization of the right to life as "the freedom to take all the actions required by the nature of a rational being for the support, the furtherance, the fulfillment and the enjoyment of his own life" (Mack 1984, 153).

ual rights are deduced from, and thereby limited solely to, the morally correct actions necessary to live. As noted, it is Mack who rewrites Rand's text by inserting a "therefore" into her summary of her theory of rights.

Even if this misreading of Rand's argument did not occur, Mack's criticism still suffers from a more fundamental flaw. In brief, it equivocates between two separate arguments: (1) the induction of a moral principle, and (2) the scope of application of that principle once it is placed in its appropriate philosophical context with other political principles, such as the additional moral principle that one is prohibited in society from initiating force against others. The justification for a moral principle, as represented by the facts that give rise to it, does not define solely the application of this principle, especially when this principle must be integrated with other facts and principles. In political theory, rights are a fundamental principle that define the scope of one's freedom of action, and the nonaggression principle is an equally important principle that defines the scope of one's interactions with others. It is thus possible that one might abuse one's freedoms to engage in unethical behavior, such as engaging in an irrational act of self-destruction by entirely destroying one's mind or body with drugs solely on a whim, but as long as one is not initiating force against an innocent person one is not violating other people's rights.

Even more important, the *justification* for rights is not that people can or should do wrong, but that they need rights in order that they can do right—that is, so that they can live and flourish. Mack fails to recognize Rand's radical philosophical justification for rights by implicitly imposing on her the conventional understanding and justification for rights today that individual rights are necessary in order to do wrong. The "right to do wrong" is a widespread intuition about the reason we have rights, but as with Rand's return to first principles, it is not valid to ground any philosophical principle in intuitions. What does it mean that one has a "right to do wrong"? Obviously, it cannot be that one has a right to do wrong by stealing, committing fraud, killing, or otherwise violating other people's rights. This would turn the concept of "rights" into a contradiction. The only plausible meaning of the "right to do wrong" is that it means wrongs that don't entail the violation of other people's rights, but this fact is already accounted for by the moral principle that one should not initiate the use of force against others.

In this respect, the "right to do wrong" at best represents the fallacy of the package deal.[38] At worst it is arguably an *anti-concept*, because it is "an unnecessary and rationally unusable term designed to replace and obliterate some legitimate concept."[39] The correct principle is not that one has a "right to do wrong" but, rather, that one has *"the right to disagree"* with others in society. Rand explains this point as follows:

> Since knowledge, thinking, and rational action are properties of the individual, since the choice to exercise his rational faculty or not depends on the individual, man's survival requires that those who think be free of the interference of those who don't. Since men are neither omniscient nor infallible, they must be free to agree or disagree, to cooperate or to pursue their own independent course, each according to his own rational judgment. Freedom is the fundamental requirement of man's mind. . . . The right to agree with others is not a problem in any society; it is *the right to disagree*. ("What Is Capitalism?" *CUI* 8, 11)

The proper scope of the application of rights is that each person has a right to disagree with others, which is a necessary corollary of recognizing the fact that people are not omniscient. As long as neither person initiates force against the other as a result of this disagreement, they are respecting each other's rights. This exposes the fallacy of the "right to do wrong." That one is wrong is not what matters; it is that each person is left free from coercion when disagreements occur. In brief, it is not a matter solely of each person literally acting within their rights but also of each person acting to respect other people's rights that creates a peaceful, productive, and flourishing society.

If two individuals, Jones and Smith, have "the freedom to take all the actions required by the nature of a rational being," this means they are each free to act according to their own judgment without interference even when they disagree, provided neither initiates force against the other. Jones would not be able to exercise this freedom if his judgments and decisions could be overruled by Smith's judgment that Jones is doing something wrong, and conversely Smith would be unable to exercise his judgments and decisions if he could be forcibly overruled by Jones.

---

38. The fallacy of package-dealing, a fallacy first identified by Rand, is defined in an editor's footnote by Leonard Peikoff, as follows: "'Package-dealing' is the fallacy of failing to discriminate between crucial differences. It consists of treating together, as parts of a single conceptual whole or 'package,' elements which differ essentially in nature, truth-status, importance or value." (*PWNI* 24).

39. Ayn Rand, "Credibility and Polarization," *ARL* 1:1 (October 11, 1971), 1.

There can be no right to disagree if Smith has the authority to review, nullify, and coercively impede the judgments and decisions of Jones, or vice versa. (And, we might well ask: From where is Smith supposed to derive such authority?)

This shows that Mack's counterexample to Rand's theory of rights is misplaced. He posits the following scenario as revealing the alleged incoherence of Rand's theory: If Jones were freely to amuse himself by playing a solitary game of Russian roulette, this would not be an action "required by the nature of a rational being for the support, the furtherance, the fulfillment and the enjoyment of his own life. . . . It follows from this that the freedom to perform this action is not included within Jones's rights" (Mack 1984, 153). Mack's conclusion, though, does not follow from Rand's theory of rights. According to her theory, Smith and Jones have the right to disagree as a necessary corollary of their rights to life and liberty—that is, to exercise their respective freedoms and act accordingly without interference from others. Thus, neither has the right to interfere with the other's actions on the grounds that the other has made mistaken, reckless, or even dishonest choices (provided, of course, that these actions do not initiate force against the other person). Even if Smith deems Jones's action to be irrational and antilife, this does not give Smith the right to forcibly interfere. Unethical actions that harm no one but oneself, whether done dishonestly or as a result of an honest mistake, are not a justification for coercion by others—for, as Rand recognized, to claim otherwise contradicts the very basis for rights, the rational mind guiding one as a moral agent in one's life.[40]

The second of Mack's objections is that Rand's argument fails to establish that individuals are obligated not to violate the rights of others. Mack further contends that Rand's theory of rights is unsound, because "to establish that a person is right to do x is neither to establish that he has a right to do x nor to establish that others have a right that he do x. . . . For having a right includes having a moral claim *against other people* that they act or not in certain ways" (Mack 1984, 151). On this basis, Mack argues that Rand misunderstands the nature of the obligation imposed by rights on others not to interfere in the actions that are positively justified by one's right. According to Mack, "Rand seems to tie an individual's rights to do some action to the *usefulness* of his being in some

---

40. See the discussion above of Rand's recognition of the contradiction of forcing people to be good.

condition or his doing some action for man's life," but whether Jones has a right against Smith to do x does not depend on whether doing x is in fact useful to either Smith or Jones (155).[41] As Mack puts the point: "Rights and their correlative obligations involve *deontological* claims, i.e. moral claims about how persons must (or must not) be treated that are not determined by the consequences of persons being so treated" (155–56). Thus, he concludes that "people's rights cannot directly be read off from some truth about their proper ends" (156).

Rand does explicitly state that an individual's rights involve obligations on the part of his neighbors, albeit "of a *negative* kind: to abstain from violating his rights" ("Man's Rights," *VOS* 110/*CUI* 369), and on this basis Mack reasons that to the extent that Rand's concept of rights has any coherent meaning, it is because she implicitly and "steadily employs" a deontological notion of rights. He admits that Rand "never explicitly acknowledges it" (perhaps because of her criticism of Kant's deontological ethical theory), but he believes he has successfully hoisted Rand on her own anti-deontological petard when he points out that her claims "that man is a 'sovereign individual who owns his own person' and that no man is a 'natural resource' at the (rightful) disposal of others"—that a violation of an individual's rights entails treating him as a "sacrificial animal" rather than as an "end in himself"—are necessarily deontological categorical imperatives, of the sort espoused by Kant.[42]

Finding linguistic similarities between claims made by Rand and Kant does not prove that her normative arguments are implicitly deontological any more than it proves that finding some linguistic similarities between Rand and Plato would prove that she subscribes to Plato's theory of Forms. The point is to ask whether the propositions represented by these linguistic phrasings—the concepts and broader context of the philosophical system in which they are made—are the same. Clearly they are not.

In fact, Rand explicitly rejects deontology—as she explains in many of her writings, but most clearly in her essay "Causality versus Duty." Here, she distinguishes between obligation and duty. Rand defines "duty" as "the moral necessity to perform certain actions for no reason other

---

41. In saying this, Mack is suggesting Rand infers that one has a right to perform an action from the mere fact that it is instrumental to one's goals. This is a misrepresentation of Rand's view of the role of rights, as we shall see below.

42. Mack 1984, 156, citing "What Is Capitalism?" (*CUI* 10), and "The Objectivist Ethics" (*VOS* 32).

than obedience to some higher authority, without regard to any personal goal, motive, desire or interest" (*PWNI* 129).[43] Kant, according to Rand, is "the arch-advocate of 'duty'" because he maintains that moral duties, such as his famous "categorical imperative," are "legislated" by "pure practical reason" without regard for any goals resulting from a person's inclinations, emotions, and desires (129–30). "Obligation," in contrast, refers to the necessity imposed by nature pursuant to one's own choices; in brief, a moral obligation reflects the hypothetical necessity that Rand maintains is at the core of all proper ethical theories, as she describes in the following passage:

> Life or death is man's only fundamental alternative. To live is his basic act of choice. If he chooses to live, a rational ethics will tell him what principles of action are required to implement his choice. If he does not choose to live, nature will take its course.
>
> Reality confronts man with a great many "musts," but all of them are conditional; the formula of realistic necessity is: "You must, if—" and the "if" stands for man's choice: "—if you want to achieve a certain goal." You must eat, if you want to survive. You must work, if you want to eat. You must think, if you want to work. You must look at reality, if you want to think—if you want to know what to do—if you want to know what goals to choose—if you want to know how to achieve them.(133)[44]

Here Rand makes it clear that moral obligation takes the form of a hypothetical necessity: "You must do X, if you want to achieve Y," for example. It does not take the form of a categorical imperative: "You must do X (regardless of what you want)," for example. It is curious, then that Mack quotes this very passage in his critique of Rand's theory of rights, but he somehow misses the significance of Rand's distinction between deontological duties and the moral obligations that can and should arise for rational individuals.

Contrary to Rand's explanation, Mack does not think it possible to justify moral obligations between individuals in society, such as the non-aggression principle and the principle of individual rights, without these obligations having a necessarily deontological character. He thus concludes that Rand's express denial of deontology results in an incoherent

---

43. *PWNI* 129–36 (all the following quotes in this paragraph are from this essay).

44. It bears observing that Rand's distinction between duty and obligation corresponds roughly to Kant's distinction between "categorical imperatives" and "hypothetical imperatives."

theory of rights, because she cannot account for the social obligation of refraining from the initiation of force, which is the sine qua non according to Rand of violating individual rights. But this conclusion of incoherence is of Mack's own creation, resulting from his imposing on Rand's theory of rights (and on her broader ethical theory) his own conception of what he thinks is the only possible moral argument available to justify respect for rights.[45]

Setting aside the explicit issue of taking Rand's theory of rights out of context, her claim that "man is an end in himself" is similar to the second formulation of Kant's categorical imperative.[46] And this raises an interesting question of the role this proposition plays in her justification for individual rights. This leads us to the second criticism of her theory.

Criticism 2

The second criticism is that Rand invalidly derives individual rights from the claim that man is an end in himself. Nozick raises this criticism in response to the following passage in "The Objectivist Ethics": "The basic *social* principle of the Objectivist ethics is that just as life is an end in itself, so each living human being is an end in himself, not the means to the ends or the welfare of others—and, therefore, that man must live for his own sake, neither sacrificing himself to others nor sacrificing others to himself. To live for his own sake means that *the achievement of his own happiness* is man's highest moral purpose" (*VOS* 30). Nozick then asks the question: "Supposing that it is granted that living as a rational being is, for each person, a value, how do we get to some *social* conclusion about people's rights?" (Nozick 1971, 292). Nozick understands Rand's principle that man is an end in himself to have two applications, ethical egoism (man

45. Mack regards "Causality versus Duty" as misguided and fundamentally inconsistent with her other writings on ethics. In particular he finds it inconsistent with her fundamental argument in "The Objectivist Ethics" that life is "an ultimate goal, an *end in itself*," which "makes the existence of values possible" (*VOS* 17). But unless one is imposing on Rand a deontological conception of ethical obligations, which is an alien concept in her ethical theory, then there are no inconsistencies between her respective writings on ethics. For instance, Mack charges that Rand "slips into the view that *all justification* (not just for actions) is hypothetical" (1984, 135). As explained above, this is no "slip" by Rand, as her entire ethical theory is predicated on hypothetical obligations that derive from the basic factual requirements of life and the values that sustain it. This is but one more example of how it is Mack, and not Rand, who creates the very incoherencies that he imposes on her theory of rights.

46. *Groundwork for the Metaphysics of Morals* (1785 [2002]): "Act so that you use humanity, as much in your own person as in the person of every other, always at the same time as end and never merely as means" (Ak 4:429; Wood translation [2002, 46–47]).

must live for his own sake and not sacrifice himself to others) and inter-personal obligation (man must not sacrifice others to himself). According to Nozick ethical egoism is the primary application and interpersonal obligation secondary.

Nozick offers the following reconstruction of Rand's argument (slightly abbreviated here):

1. For each person, the living and prolongation of his own life is the greatest value for him.

2. Each person should (most of all) pursue the maintenance of his life as a rational being.

3. Each person has a right to do what he should (most of all) do.

4. Each person should not violate another person's rights.

5. To sacrifice another person or treat him as a means is to violate his rights.

6. One should not sacrifice another person or treat him as a means.

Nozick apparently believes Rand to be arguing that, since an individual should perform self-interested acts, this somehow generates rights against another individual not to interfere. Nozick thus views step (3), the inference that introduces rights, as the crucial step in this reformalized presentation of her theory.

In response to the further move from step (3) to step (4), though, he makes the following criticism: "If we assume that rights are not to be violated, and others should not forcibly intervene in the exercise of someone's rights, then argument is needed to the conclusion that a person does have a right to his own life, that is, that others shouldn't intervene in it, even granting that its maintenance is *his* highest value" (Nozick 1971, 302n7). He does not think that Rand supplies this argument. He suggests that Rand's argument might be plausible if one has "a vision of a morally harmonious universe in which there are no irreconcilable conflicts of duty, of shoulds, and in which if you should do something, I shouldn't forcibly prevent you from doing it. But no conclusive arguments have been offered for such a vision" (294).

The main problem with this critique is that Rand's justification for rights does not follow the deductive steps that Nozick presents as her alleged argument; for instance, she does not deduce directly from the principle of rights that others should not violate rights. To the contrary, Rand's inductive methodology is to integrate two separate principles—

the political principle of individual rights and the ethical principle that the initiation of force is evil—and derives the conclusion that the initiation of force is prohibited because it is anti-mind and thus breaches the rights of the individual who is seeking to live a rational, flourishing life. Similar to Mack, Nozick imputes to Rand an argument both for and from the principle of rights that she is not making.

Just as Mack fundamentally misunderstands Rand's philosophical justification for individual rights, Nozick seems to be erroneously imputing to Rand his own notion of rights as "moral side constraints" entailing correlative deontological obligations, as he argues in his famous monograph *Anarchy, State, and Utopia*. In this work, Nozick defends a libertarian theory of the minimal political state. His political theory is essentially neo-Lockean; he assumes that individuals have natural rights not to be coercively interfered with, which they possess in a state of nature devoid of political institutions and which must be strictly observed by political officials as well as by private individuals. Nozick does not follow Locke in basing natural rights on the Natural Law, which is correlative with and grounded in Divine Law (see section 2 above), but Nozick never makes clear *how* he thinks that natural rights and other Lockean principles are to be justified once Locke's theistic framework is jettisoned. He simply postulates rights or entitlements by an appeal to intuition, revealing the same lack of concern with establishing a rational, moral foundation for individual rights that characterizes the similar invocation of the "nonaggression principle" by other libertarians.[47]

Also, just as Mack incorrectly reconstructs Rand's justification for rights within an alien philosophical framework that imposes on her a commitment to deontology that she expressly and consistently rejects, Nozick appears to assume that Rand must be defining rights as a type of deontological principle that she purports to derive from the self-regarding moral obligations of individuals. The assumption is that, since Rand is not a utilitarian, she must by necessity be defending a deontological theory of rights. But this is clearly a misreading of Rand's theory of rights.

For instance, a deontological moral duty is categorical and universal regardless of context, but these two essential characteristics of deontological moral claims directly and explicitly contradict Rand's definition of a right. We have already established the first point, that Rand rejects the concept of categorical duty. As for the second point, Rand states that

47. See above the discussion of the libertarian nonaggression principle in section 1, above.

"A 'right' is a moral principle defining and sanctioning a man's freedom of action in a social context" (*VOS* 110/*CUI* 369). The significance of the phrase "in a social context" in this definition is lost on both Mack's and Nozick's recasting of her theory of rights as an inconsistent form of deontology. She explains this qualification as follows: "'Rights' are a moral concept—the concept that provides a logical transition from the principles guiding an individual's actions to the principles guiding his relationship with others—the concept that preserves and protects individual morality in a social context—the link between the moral code of a man and the legal code of a society, between ethics and politics. *Individual rights are the means of subordinating society to moral law*" (*VOS* 108/*CUI* 367; original emphasis).

Rights are a moral principle defining proper social relationships. Just as a man needs a moral code in order to survive (in order to act, to choose the right goals, and to achieve them), so a society (a group of men) needs moral principles in order to organize a social system consonant with man's nature and with the requirements of his survival. Although Nozick and Mack both focus on Rand's claim in the synoptic statement that "the law of identity" is "the source of man's rights," they fail to understand the context that gives meaning to this claim. For Rand, "rights" are not intrinsic metaphysical features of human nature; neither are they deontological commands. They are moral principles based on the facts that, as rational animals, humans require freedom in order to think and to act in creating and pursuing the values that comprise a flourishing life. Thus, the only proper sociopolitical system is one in which individual rights are respected—in which it is possible for humans to coexist and cooperate within a social context as individual moral agents. Rights are moral principles that apply not to individuals in abstraction but only to individuals "in a social context."[48]

In sum, Nozick attributes to Rand a deontological philosophical

---

48. Leonard Peikoff explains the significance of the delimiting concept of a "social context" in Rand's unique definition of rights:

> If a man lived on a desert island, there would be no question of defining his proper relationship to others. Even if men interacted on some island but did so at random, without establishing a social system, the issue of rights would be premature. There would not yet be any context for the concept or, therefore, any means of implementing it; there would be no agency to interpret, apply, enforce it. When men do decide to form (or reform) an organized society, however, when they decide to pursue systematically the advantages of living together, then they need the guidance of principle. This is the context in which the principle of rights arises. If your society is to be moral (and therefore practical), it declares, you must begin by recognizing

framework in which the principle of rights (which also appears to be equated with the ethical principle prohibiting coercion) is simply deduced through "pure" a priori–type reasoning from a prior commitment to the ethical theory of egoism. Such a view of rights may be consistent with Nozick's own belief that individuals possess "natural rights" in the state of nature—that is, outside of organized society—and thus these are some type of universal, categorical duties possessed by people, regardless of context. But this is not Rand's theory of rights, nor is it a proper characterization of her ethical theory of egoism (though that is a topic beyond the scope of this paper).

Criticism 3

The third criticism is that the theoretical foundations for Rand's two moral principles—egoism and rights—are fundamentally at odds with each other. Michael Huemer disagrees with Nozick's and Mack's claims that Rand derives her theory of rights directly from her ethical egoism. Huemer observes: "Conspicuously absent from Rand's discussions of what rights one has and of the importance of rights is any appeal to EE [i.e., Ethical Egoism]" (Huemer 2002, 268). However, Huemer believes that the absence of egoism from Rand's theory of rights instead reveals the allegedly real flaw in her justification for rights: He charges that Rand's ethical egoism is inconsistent with her advocacy of rights.

Employing a method of interpretation like Mack's and Nozick's approaches in critiquing Rand's theory of rights, Huemer reframes Rand's ethical and political principles that she presents in "The Objectivist Ethics" into a summary statement of what he refers to as Rand's two principles of nonsacrifice:

P1: I should never sacrifice myself for the benefit of others.

P2: I should never sacrifice others for the benefit of myself.

He argues that P1 is a corollary of ethical egoism (Huemer 2002, 260) and that P2 follows from the principle that individuals have rights that should not be violated.[49] From this reformulation of Rand's theory into his P1 and

the *moral requirements* of man in a social context; i.e., you must define the sphere of sovereignty mandated for every individual by the laws of morality. Within this sphere, the individual acts without needing any agreement or approval from others, nor may any others interfere. (1991, 351–52)

49. He writes that P1 represents the proposition "The only good reason I can ever have for doing (or not doing) anything is that it would serve (or interfere with) my own interests" (referring to the citations on "Individual Rights" in *Lexicon*, 212–17).

P2 principles of nonsacrifice, Huemer then makes the following critique: "While these principles are logically consistent with each other, there is a deep tension between them in the context of the Objectivist ethics. The tension consists in the fact that Rand gives arguments in support of P1 and P2 that contradict each other, that depend on contradictory assumptions, and/or that are extremely implausible empirically. The result is that while the conjunction of P1 and P2 is logically coherent, Rand's defense of it is not" (259).

Huemer's argument is more fundamental and complex than that of Mack's or Nozick's, and thus it requires some explanation. His main point is that the two principles he ascribes to Rand presuppose inconsistent assumptions about the nature of value. His argument can be summarized as follows: P1 (i.e., ethical egoism) is true only if value is essentially *relative to the agent*, because sacrificing oneself to others would require giving up what is of value to the agent for the sake of something else that is valuable to someone else but not to the agent himself. Hence, P1 assumes that value is essentially relative. However, there are only two ways of justifying P2 (i.e., the principle of rights). On the one hand, one might adhere to the agent-relative concept of value and argue that an individual can never achieve what is valuable to him by sacrificing others to himself. This has the advantage of basing P2 on the same concept of value as P1, but the problem is that it relies on "Rand's claim that sacrificing others, or violating others' rights, would always harm the agent's own interests," which Huemer finds "extremely implausible empirically" (2002, 265). He offers as counterexamples the many political regimes throughout history that maintained their existence by exploiting their subjects and the even greater number of criminals who have profited at the expense of their victims. On the other hand, P2 could be deemed to assume that an agent should respect others' rights because each individual's life is an end in itself. This argument might be sound if an individual's life, insofar as it is an end in itself, is an *absolute* value that everyone else is obligated to respect. The problem with this is that absolute value contradicts the agent-relative value assumed by P1: How could an individual's life be of value in an *absolute* sense and not merely be of value *relative* to that specific individual?[50] Huemer concludes that Rand is caught on the horns of a dilemma in arguing for P2: she must either rely on an implausible empirical

---

50. As is clear from this summary, Huemer's argument relies on a distinction between agent-relative and absolute value. His distinction corresponds roughly to a distinction that Rand makes between different theories of the good in "What Is Capitalism?" (*CUI* 13–15).

claim or invoke an absolute conception of value that necessarily conflicts with the agent-relative conception underlying her ethical egoism. In either case, her theory fails for either empirical or logical reasons.

Similar to Mack's and Nozick's critiques, Huemer's claim that Rand's theory of rights falls prey to a dilemma is a problem of his own making. Huemer's two principles (P1 and P2) might be suggested by Rand's above-quoted statement that "man must live for his own sake, neither sacrificing himself to others nor sacrificing others to himself" ("The Objectivist Ethics," *VOS* 30).[51] As has been shown, however, Rand's *meaning* of and *justification* for this proposition are entirely different from Huemer's. In the context of Rand's philosophy, one will search in vain in her essays for anything akin to a statement of P1 or P2 as the type of all-encompassing principle that Huemer claims them each to be. In brief, Huemer reduces Rand's theory of rights to incoherence because he himself injects into Rand's theory the very contradictory concepts and ideas that produce this result.

The fundamental problem is that Huemer's reconstruction of Rand's theory of rights leads him to make claims within ethical theory that Rand rejects, but again, a full defense of her ethical theory and its central concepts and principles is beyond the scope of this paper. Thus, we can only identify the ways in which Huemer directly contradicts the moral principles that define the philosophical context in which Rand justifies the principle of individual rights. Any theory torn from its supporting philosophical context obviously loses any claim to meaning or coherence, and this is exactly what occurs in Huemer's critique. We find two main difficulties with Huemer's critique.

Huemer's "absolute value" corresponds to what Rand calls the *intrinsic* theory of the good: "the good is inherent in certain things or actions as such, regardless of their context and consequences, regardless of any benefit or injury they may cause to the actors and subjects involved" (13). However, Huemer's "agent-relative value" does not correspond to what Rand calls the *subjective* theory of the good—that is, "the good bears no relation to the facts of reality, that it is the product of a man's consciousness" (14). Rand contrasts both the intrinsic and the subjective theories of the good with what she calls the *objective* theory of the good—that is, "the good is an aspect of reality in relation to man" (14). This is important because Huemer's description of value as "relative" can be misleading because "relative" often suggests "subjective." Therefore, it should be kept in mind throughout this discussion that "relative" as used by Huemer takes the place of "objective" as used by Rand and not that of "subjective." See Smith 2006, 25–33, for a helpful discussion of Rand's theory of value.

51. Huemer's two principles also bear a linguistic resemblance to Galt's Oath: "I swear, by my life and my love of it, that I will never live for the sake of another man, nor ask another man to live for mine" (*Atlas* 1069).

First and foremost, Huemer's claim that P1 (prohibiting self-sacrifice) is justifiable only if it rests on a claim of subjective or relative values directly contradicts Rand's concept of objective value. In fact, her explanation in her metaethics of why values are objective is not just fundamental to her ethical theory. It is an essential and fundamental insight that animates all of her normative analyses.[52] Moreover, her explanation of how value is objective is an original argument itself, and thus it does not mean that values are intrinsic in nature nor that they are deontological commands that apply to all individuals regardless of context or purpose. In misunderstanding this fundamental concept in Rand's ethical theory, Huemer thus mistakes the nature of the obligations imposed by rights, and he believes he finds contradictory statements by Rand about these obligations—statements that reflect both absolute and agent-relative conceptions of value—but this is only because he has failed to identify the moral concepts and principles that Rand is relying on to explain the derivative sociopolitical principle of rights.

Second, and as a result, because Huemer fails to understand the basic moral concepts that comprise Rand's justification for rights, such as value and how Rand induces the meaning of this term from the facts of life, he also fails to understand Rand's argument that "the rational interests of men do not clash" (*VOS* 34). Based on his assertion in the first horn of his dilemma that people do in fact flourish and succeed from sacrificing others, he further argues that this is also an implausible empirical claim (assuming, as he does, that all value is agent-relative). On this point, Huemer is joined by Nozick, who makes a similar critique. Nozick sees Rand as falling in "the optimistic tradition" (1971, 295) espoused by Plato in the *Republic* who argued that there it is never advantageous for an individual to act unjustly.

It is unnecessary to recount Rand's entire explanation of and justification for her view that there are no real conflicts of interest among rational men that she presents in her essay "The 'Conflicts' of Men's Interests." She is clear in this essay that she is presupposing both the facts she has identified about human nature and the ethical principles she induces from these facts. It is noteworthy that Rand concludes this essay with the following injunction: "All of the above discussion applies only to the relationships among rational men and only to a free society" (*VOS* 64). Ignoring this crucial and explicit qualification, Huemer poses as a

---

52. See Allan Gotthelf, "The Morality of Life," in Gotthelf and Salmieri 2016.

counterexample a welfare state in which some individuals gain unearned benefits by means of government taxing the income of producers, which is hardly what Rand would regard as "a free society" (Huemer 2002, 265). Thus Huemer (like Nozick) completely misses the point of her argument. Without these necessary premises, it is unsurprising that her conclusion appears to lack support, just as the twentieth floor of a building would collapse to the ground if the underlying nineteen floors were first removed.

Conclusion

The purpose of this paper has been to explicate Rand's theory of rights, to contrast it against similar theories such as the theory of natural rights, and to respond to some of the critics of her theory. Her critics understandably recognize the significance of the synoptic statement in *Atlas Shrugged* that "the source of man's rights is . . . the law of identity," as this indeed provides the key to understanding the radical nature of Rand's theory of rights. But the synoptic statement also cannot be read out of context, as it presupposes Rand's earlier insights into human nature, the concepts she induces in her metaethics, and ultimately the ethical principles that serve as the vital premises in her justification for individual rights. This is all necessary to completely understand her definition of a right as "a moral principle defining and sanctioning a man's freedom of action in a social context" (*VOS* 110/*CUI* 369).

It is also necessary to understand the significant points of departure between Rand and the philosophers with whom she is most closely associated, such as Locke. To raise a point from Rand's epistemology, the essence of concept formation consists of both differentiation and integration—of recognizing the genus and differentia that give proper meaning to a concept.[53] As she writes in the synoptic statement, the "source of man's rights is not divine law," and this is the essential difference between her theory of rights and the natural rights philosophers such as Locke who ultimately ground human nature in a world created by a moral agent (God).

Once Rand's theory of rights is understood in its proper philosophic context, it further becomes clear why her critics have misunderstood her theory and its justification. They have redefined her basic concepts, by imposing on her argument philosophical premises and alien categories

---

53. *ITOE* ch. 2 (Concept Formation). See also Peikoff, who explains the essential role of differentiation and integration in the Rand's theory of concepts (1991, 4–81).

that she expressly considered and rejected, such as "deontological obligation" and "absolute value." They have thereby failed to grasp the radical
nature of her methodology in inducing the political principle of rights
and integrating this principle with the ethical principle that one should
not initiate force against others. We do not claim that Rand's theory of
rights is necessarily complete in that it leaves no unanswered questions,
nor do we deny the need for critical examination of her arguments. We do
insist, however, that a correct understanding of her theory of rights must
proceed from an appreciation of its radical character in both its philosophic method and content.

A Critique of Ayn Rand's Theory of Rights

Response to Miller and Mossoff

MATT ZWOLINSKI

I've been asked to contribute to this volume in the role of a critic. It's a necessary role, I suppose. And one to which the training of an academic philosopher lends itself rather well. But it's also a deservedly disreputable role. The critic qua critic is not unlike a parasite, drawing his succor only to the extent that he can succeed in sapping it from someone else. Like a mosquito, or a state, the critic produces nothing of value itself. He lives, instead, off the productive activity of others.

Nevertheless, it is the station to which I have been assigned, and I will do my best to discharge the duties attached to it faithfully. Accordingly, the vast bulk of my comments will be negative in nature. I will probe for logical weaknesses, ambiguities, and equivocations and do my best to poke a few holes in the very fine essay that Fred Miller and Adam Mossoff have created.

Before I do, though, I would like to begin by noting, for the record, the important role that Ayn Rand's thought has played in my own life. It's no exaggeration to say that without Ayn Rand, I would never have thought of seriously studying philosophy, let alone making a career of it. I was a sophomore in college studying computer science when a friend recommended that I read *The Fountainhead*. And from the moment I picked it up it was not too long at all before I switched my major to philosophy, started my own "Students of Objectivism" club, and enthusiastically devoured everything I could get my hands on related to Ayn Rand's thought. Her ideas were an inspiration for me—and remain so today. And while I no longer consider myself an Objectivist, I have tremendous respect for the philosophy Ayn Rand created.

I also have a great deal of respect for the work that both Mossoff and Miller have done in developing and extending those ideas, both in the paper under consideration and in the many other thoughtful and thought-provoking papers they have written on this and related subjects. Their paper on Rand's theory of rights, I think, is an especially important and helpful piece. Not only does it set out with admirable clarity the way in which Rand herself conceives of rights and their fundamental philosophical justification, it also does a very fine job of showing how radically distinct Rand's theory of rights is from other superficially similar theories espoused by non-Objectivist libertarian philosophers. Whether one agrees with Rand's theory or not, this paper provides a tremendously useful service in making clear just where the points of contention are.

Mossoff and Miller's paper provides rich food for thought and discussion. But in my comments here, I want to focus on just three issues: first, the relationship between rights as liberties and rights as claims; second, the Objectivist claim that the mind is the ultimate source of all values and its relation to the justification of property rights; and third, the nature and justification within Objectivism of the nonaggression principle. I have chosen these three issues because they seem to me to highlight some of the most fundamental differences between Rand's theory of rights and the ways in which both most academic philosophers and non-Objectivist libertarians think about rights. I bring them up here not so much because I hope to convince Miller and Mossoff, or other Objectivists, that Rand's view is mistaken. Instead, I have the more modest goal of simply helping both parties to the debate to become a little bit clearer about where exactly the differences between them lie.

Liberties and Claims

In her "synoptic statement" on rights, Rand makes the following series of claims: "If man is to live on earth, it is *right* for him to use his mind, it is *right* to act on his own free judgment, it is *right* to work for his values and to keep the product of his work. If life on earth is his purpose, he has a *right* to live as a rational being: nature forbids him the irrational." Rightly or wrongly, this passage is going to trigger alarm bells in the mind of most contemporary analytic philosophers who read it. And so it is no surprise that two of the three objections that Miller and Mossoff consider are related to this passage, or at least to the basic idea that it expresses.

The alarm bells are going to be triggered by the fact that Rand is using the word "right" in two very different senses in this passage. The fact that she does this is not *necessarily* a problem, of course. As long as both Rand and her readers are clear about this fact, and about the distinct meanings attached to the different uses of the word, this sort of thing is perfectly fine. If I tell you that I was fishing on the riverbank when I remembered I needed to go downtown to make a deposit at the bank, you all know perfectly well what I mean, and neither logic nor clarity of communication is offended in any way.

The problems start in when one or both parties are *not* clear about the difference in meaning. When this happens, there's a danger of sliding between one meaning and the other without really noticing. And when that happens, faulty logic can be easy to slip into. Banks have money. And rivers have banks. But you'd be making an error to conclude that you could go digging for dollars in the bank of the San Diego River.

In her synoptic statement, Rand uses the word "right" three times to refer to what analytic philosophers call the "deontic status" of certain kinds of actions. To say that an action is "right," in this sense, is to say either that the action is *permissible* (i.e., that it is not wrong), or more strongly, that it is *obligatory* (i.e., that it would be wrong *not* to do). So, for example, when Rand says that it is right for man to work for his values, she seems to mean *at least* that it is not wrong for him to do so, and perhaps more strongly that it *would* be wrong for him not to do so.

Rand's fourth usage of the word "right," however, is significantly different. When she says that man "has a *right*" to live as a rational being, she is not merely saying that it *is* right for man to live as a rational being. She is saying that man *has* a right to live as a rational being. And these are two very different claims.

To have a right is to have a certain kind of *claim* against others.[1] That claim could be a purely *moral* one (in which case the right is a *moral* right), or it could be one enforceable by law (in which case it is a *legal* right). It could be a claim against others that they perform certain positive actions such as repaying a debt (in which case it is a *positive* right),

1. See Hohfeld 1913.

or it might simply be a claim that others *refrain* from performing certain kinds of actions such as taking one's property without one's consent (in which case it is a *negative* right). The important point, for our purposes, is that rights are claims *on other people.* To say that A has a right against B doesn't say much at all about what it would be wrong or right for A to do. What it says, instead, is that it would be wrong for B to act (or fail to act) toward A in certain ways. If A has a right, then as a matter of moral logic, some other person B must have a corresponding obligation.

And this is where many philosophers are going to see a gap in Rand's argument. Where do these obligations come from? Claims about what rights one has, and hence claims about what obligations other people have, do not *follow* as a matter of logic from claims about what it is morally right for one to do. The fact that your life is a value to *you* does not logically entail that *I* have an obligation to allow you to live it. There's a logical gap there. And it is a gap that, as Michael Huemer notes (2002), seems especially large for a political philosophy built on egoist foundations. For, if egoism is correct, then your life is a value to *you*, but not necessarily any value at all to *me*. All value is agent-relative, and so we cannot appeal to the *impersonal, agent-neutral* (or "intrinsic") value of human life to explain why people have an obligation to respect our right to life. To what, then, can we appeal?

There is an obvious strategy for the Objectivist to pursue in response to this question. But it is oddly one that, so far as I can tell, Miller and Mossoff never mention in their paper. The strategy is this. Rather than saying that person A's rights follow from facts about A himself—what his values are, what it is right for him to do, and so on—we argue that they follow from facts about person B—the person who has an obligation to respect those rights. So, instead of saying that A has a right to life because A's life is valuable to A, we say that B has an obligation to respect A's right to life because doing so is in some way valuable *for* B *himself.*

This, after all, seems the most natural way of justifying rights in an egoistic philosophy. You have an obligation to respect my rights not (primarily) because it is good for *me*, but because it is good for *you*. Such a strategy avoids the worries about equivocation and logical gaps that I raised earlier. It does, however, raise other questions and difficulties of its own.

For instance, if the claim is that B should respect A's rights because doing so is good for B, one thing we'll want to hear more about is precisely *how* it is supposed to be good for B. There seem to be two possible approaches to answering this question, both of which are represented in some of the things Rand herself had to say about rights.[2] On one approach, call it the *instrumental* approach, *B* ought to respect *A*'s rights because doing so is an effective means for *B* to achieve his own independently defined set of values. One finds a rather crude version of this approach in Hobbes—the reason one has not to kill one's confederates in the state of nature is that doing so is likely to get *you* killed, too.[3] But it is also an approach with some historical precedent in the tradition of Ancient Greek eudaimonism for which Rand professes such respect—specifically in the Epicurean approach to interpersonal morality.

Far more common among the Ancient Greeks, however, was a different approach to thinking about the way in which other human beings ought to figure in to our own rational deliberation. On this more common approach, which we can call the *constitutive* approach, respect for the rights of others is not merely an effective strategy for pursuing our own independently defined and agent-relative good. Rather, respect for the rights of others is a *constitutive part* of our own good. The reason Howard Roark doesn't cheat his customers isn't just that he doesn't want to be caught and punished. It's because cheating his customers—even if he gets away with it—would *not be good* for him. Whatever money he gained by such cheating either would not be a value for him at all or at least would not be a value sufficiently great to outweigh the damage that his cheating does to his own moral character.

When Michael Huemer charges that Rand's reconciliation of egoism and rights depends upon claims that are "extremely implausible empirically" (2002, 259), I suspect it is because he assumes that Rand must be thinking about the connection between these two ideas in purely instrumentalist terms. And if that really *was* the only or primary way in which Rand thought about them, then Huemer would have a point! It *is* unlikely that respect for the rights of others will in *all* circumstances (even in all *social* circumstances) be the best *means* for achieving our own independently defined ends. And at any rate, it doesn't seem as if a *principled* commitment to respect for the rights of others could or should really depend upon contingent circumstances in the way the instrumental approach requires it to be. Respect for the rights of others might be a good rule of thumb for promoting one's self interest on the instrumental view. But a rule of thumb is not a moral principle.

2. See, for a brief discussion, Long 2010.
3. See Hobbes, *Leviathan*, ch. 15.

Of course, constitutive approaches face their own challenges too. *Why* should the rights of others be thought to be a constitutive part of my own good? What if I don't care about those others? I think that there are some promising responses to these questions available to the defender of the constitutive approach.[4] But for now, I don't want to explore those questions in any further detail. My point for now is that *something* like this approach seems the most promising way of reconciling Rand's egoism with her theory of rights. And so I was surprised to see no discussion of it in Miller and Mossoff's paper.

Mind, Value, and Property

As Miller and Mossoff note, Ayn Rand held that value is *objective*, not intrinsic or subjective. Value is not inherent in the world itself, apart from man's relation to it. Nor is it *purely* the product of man's mind. It is, rather, "an aspect of *reality* in *relation* to man" ("What Is Capitalism?" *CUI* 14; emphasis added). And specifically in relation to man's *mind*.

For Rand, "man's mind is the fundamental source of values that sustain his life" (Miller and Mossoff, above, 121).[5] Physical stuff by itself can be no aid in man's survival unless it is first understood by the mind and then put to work through deliberate, rational, productive action. Before man figured out what to do with it, crude oil was a pollutant, not a value. It was the human mind that transformed oil from an annoyance into a resource.

I think that there is a tremendously important insight in this analysis of value. But I also think it's possible to stretch that insight too far. And, unfortunately, I think that both Rand herself and Miller and Mossoff in their paper are guilty of doing precisely this.

Consider Miller and Mossoff's analysis of Locke's famous discussion of agricultural value. According to Locke, the great bulk—indeed, 99.9 percent, in his final analysis—of the value produced by agriculture is accounted for by the *labor* that goes into it.[6] By contrast, the contribution of unimproved land is de minimis—just 0.1 percent. Locke intended this example to serve as a kind of shocking demonstration of the relatively high value of labor compared to land. But for Miller and Mossoff, and for Rand as well, 0.1 percent is still too high. "It is untrue," they write, "that fallow land qua land is a value" (132). "The value in the farm is not 99.9 percent

4. See, for example, Long 2000.
5. All references to Miller and Mossoff are to their essay in this volume.
6. See John Locke, *Two Treatises of Government* 2:5 §§ 37–44.

the result of productive labor; rather, 100 percent of the value is the result of human thought and action. The value exists entirely in the identification, creation, and use of the farm" (133).

Now, there's one sense in which what Miller and Mossoff are saying here seems clearly correct. Stuff without a valuer is not a value. Therefore, without the human mind and the human action to which it gives rise, 100 percent of the value that we find in agriculture today would not exist. Therefore, 100 percent of that value is due to the human mind. Notice, however, that exactly the same argument could be made, mutatis mutandis, with respect to land! All the valuers in the world cannot produce value without some *object* to value. Therefore, without the natural resource of land (or some other suitable substitute), 100 percent of the value that we find in agriculture today would not exist. Therefore 100 percent of that value is due to land!

This, I think it is sufficiently obvious, is not the most helpful way of thinking about these issues. Even if it's true that nothing of value would exist without the human mind, it's equally true that nothing (or at least *almost* nothing) of value would exist without physical resources for the mind to operate on. Both the human mind and physical resources are thus necessary for the production of value. Objective value is an aspect of reality in relation to man. So without the reality, or without the man, there is no value.

This is not merely an abstract philosophical point. As Mossoff and Miller (and Locke) recognize, it has important implications for a host of practical issues, including in particular the justification of property rights. If natural resources have no value in themselves, then individuals who claim exclusive property rights over those resources do not thereby deprive their fellow human beings of anything of value. And thus, it would seem, the justification of private property rights is rendered far less problematic. After all, if the sole source of the value of my land is *my* mind, why should *you* have any claim on it? The value of my land derives entirely from *me*, so I am not really depriving you of anything to which you would otherwise have had access when I put a fence around it.

As helpful as such an argument would be in justifying strong rights of property, however, it simply does not work. Even if we accept Rand's idea that natural resources have no *intrinsic* value in themselves, we must nevertheless recognize that they are a *necessary component* in the production of value. And so when we take those natural resources and put a fence around them, we *are* depriving others of something important. We are depriving nonowners of the liberty they once possessed to use that resource in their *own* productive activities. We are imposing upon them an obligation to refrain from using that resource without our consent—an obligation that we will enforce with the use of physical violence, if necessary. And this calls for justification.

I am an enthusiastic supporter of property rights. And thus I do believe that such justification can be provided. But—and here I return to my earlier point about rights and egoism—providing a justification to *B* of *A*'s property right in *X* would seem to require doing more than simply showing how such rights are good for *A*. Since *A*'s property right imposes an obligation on *B*, we need to show how such an obligation is good for *B* as well. If *A*'s property right in *X* is good for *A* but bad for *B*, then for *B* to respect that right would be an act of self-sacrifice and fundamentally incompatible with his rational pursuit of his own self-interest.

How could *A*'s appropriation of *X not* be bad for *B*? Well, as both Locke and Nozick noted, and as David Schmidtz has more recently argued (1994), original appropriation helps to convert negative-sum games into positive-sum games. In a world in which nothing is privately owned, Tragedies of the Commons are common, and individuals face strong incentives to make quick and often inefficient use of natural resources before somebody else uses them first.[7] Private property, in contrast, provides owners with an incentive to make productive improvements in what they own. People build structures, till fields, and plant crops because *they* are able to reap the benefits these actions generate. But as private property gives rise to trade, specialization, and the division of labor, these private benefits spill over onto nonowners as well. Most of us alive today have never engaged in a single act of original appropriation. By the time we arrived on the scene, all the land had been taken. But it would be a mistake to think of ourselves as victims—ripped off by the people who got here first. As Schmidtz says (1994, 45), original appropriation is not the prize. Prosperity is the prize, and when it comes to prosperity, latecomers win big.

This strikes me as a useful way of thinking about the justification of property. Even so, it's worth noting that most thinkers who have pursued something like this approach, including Locke and Nozick themselves, have concluded that the justification of property has its limits. It's true that *A*'s appropriation of *X normally* has spillover benefits for *B*. And

7. See Hardin 1968.

so normally that act of appropriation will be justifiable to *B* in terms of his or her own self-interest. But what about when it isn't? What if *A* gets greedy and decides to appropriate *all* of a vital scarce resource, leaving *B* with nothing? Can *A* come to acquire all of the land surrounding *B*, thus "trapping" *B* and demanding extortionate payment before allowing *B* to cross *A*'s land? For Locke and Nozick and those who follow in their footsteps, these kinds of questions led to the adoption of a proviso that limits acts of permissible appropriation to those that, in Locke's language, "leave enough and as good for others" or, in Nozick's, do not "worsen the position" of others.[8]

Nozick himself thought that the "free operation of a market system will not actually run afoul of the Lockean proviso" (1974, 182), and so as a practical matter the differences between his view and a nonproviso view of property might be small. But even so, the proviso plays an important role in the underlying *justification* of property for Nozick (and for Locke). For them, the proviso was essential to ensure that a system of property rights would serve the interest of *all* persons, not just the interests of those lucky, fast, or perceptive enough to be original appropriators.

So here's where this leaves us. Physical resources, I have argued, even if they are not "values in themselves," are nevertheless necessary preconditions of value. This means that people cannot effectively act to pursue and create values without access to physical resources. And this, in turn, means that there is at least a prima facie conflict of interest inherent in the appropriation of property. Every time a resource is appropriated as private property, there's one less resource left for *me* to appropriate, and one less opportunity for me to create and pursue my *own* values. For an egoist moral philosophy, this represents a challenge. If *A*'s appropriation of *X* is to be justified, on egoist terms we must show not only that this appropriation is compatible with *A*'s self-interest but with *B*'s as well. I think that there are several strategies available for doing precisely this. But they are not strategies that, as far as I can tell, either Miller and Mossoff, or Rand herself, ever pursue. I'm curious to know why not, and what alternative strategy they endorse instead for dealing with this problem.

The Nonaggression Principle

As Miller and Mossoff note, Ayn Rand endorses a form of the libertarian "nonaggression principle," which holds that the use of force should properly be banished from human relationships. Unlike some libertarians,

8. Locke, *Two Treatises* 2:5 §§ 27, 33; Nozick 1974, 174–82.

however, Rand views the nonaggression principle as an *ethical* principle, and not merely a political one.[9] Moreover, it is an ethical principle that, for Rand, is grounded in more fundamental philosophical considerations about human nature and the nature of value.

For Rand, force is evil because it prevents individuals from acting according to the dictates of their own reason. Thus force violates man's fundamental right to life—his right to act in pursuit of his values according to his own judgments, uncompelled by the judgment of any other. As Rand puts it, "To violate man's rights means to compel him to act against his own judgment, or to expropriate his values. Basically, there is only one way to do it: the use of physical force" ("Man's Rights," *VOS* 111/*CUI* 370).

For Rand, and for Miller and Mossoff's interpretation and defense of Rand, the nonaggression principle plays an import role. Rand appears to see the nonaggression principle as *defining the scope* of man's rights—one has the right to live as one wishes *provided* one does not initiate force against any other human being. And Miller and Mossoff appeal to the nonaggression principle to, among other things, rebut one of the criticisms leveled against Rand by Eric Mack. Mack (1984) had argued that Rand seems to be committed to holding that individuals have the right to do what is morally right but not the right to do what is morally wrong. In response, Miller and Mossoff claim that Rand's theory of rights must be understood *alongside* the nonaggression principle, which they describe as an "equally important principle that defines the scope of one's interactions with others" (137). One might abuse one's rights by acting in a way that is morally wrong, but so long as one does not initiate force against others, it is not permissible for others to compel you to act rightly by initiating force against you.

For Rand, then, "the basic political principle of the Objectivist ethics is: no man may *initiate* the use of physical force against others" ("The Objectivist Ethics," *VOS* 32). But how exactly are we to understand the meaning of the key term "force" in this principle? Without a clear understanding of this key concept, we cannot know how to apply the nonaggression principle, nor can we understand the role that such a principle ought to play in a broader ethical and political theory.

Traditionally, libertarians and Objectivists have taken one of two broad approaches to defining "force." One approach, which we can call

---

9. Murray Rothbard seems to have wavered between viewing it as a broad ethical principle with legal implications and viewing it as a strictly legal principle. Walter Block consistently interprets it as a legal principle only.

the "moralized approach," defines force in terms of an underlying theory of *rights*. The other approach, the "nonmoralized approach," defines force in a way that makes no essential reference to rights or other moral terms. To see the difference, imagine a case in which *A* violates *B*'s rights but does so without so much as physically touching *B*. Perhaps *B* leaves his car unlocked on the street, and *A* lets himself in and drives away with it. Has *A* initiated force against *B*? If we accept the nonmoralized definition of force, we will have to say "no." After all, *A* didn't touch *B* at all. The only way we can explain the way in which *A*'s action affects *B* is in terms of the *property right B* has in his car. But if *this* is our basis for claiming that *A* has initiated force against *B*, then we are implicitly relying on a moralized definition of force. *A*'s action initiates force against *B* *because* it violates *B*'s (moral) rights.

It matters a great deal which of these understandings Objectivists rely on to inform the nonaggression principle. But neither understanding is entirely without its own peculiar difficulties. If, for instance, we accept a nonmoralized definition of force, then we abandon the tight, conceptual connection between force and the violation of rights and must accept the possibility that some rights violations will not involve the initiation of force, *and* the possibility that some cases of the initiation of force will not involve rights violations. And this means that we must take seriously the socialist argument that property rights *themselves* involve the initiation of force.[10] After all, if I put a fence around a piece of land and threaten to arrest anybody who walks across it without my consent, it certainly *looks* like I'm initiating force when I grab a peaceful trespasser and slap a pair of handcuffs on him. The only way to deny that my action constitutes the initiation of force, it seems, is to argue that it was really the trespasser who *initiated* force. But that move is available only if we abandon the nonmoralized conception of force and adopt a moralized understanding instead.

Suppose we do that. Adopting a moralized definition of force allows us to explain why the individual who steals someone's car *is* initiating force, and why the landowner who enforces his property right *isn't*. So, so far, so good. But the moralized approach to force comes with a serious drawback of its own. For if we define the initiation of force in terms of the violation of rights, then we *cannot* define the violation of rights in terms of the initiation of force, lest we be guilty of circular argument. In other words, if we say that force is just any activity that violates individual rights, we cannot turn around and then say that our rights are to be un-

10. G. A. Cohen is the most famous proponent of such arguments. See Cohen 1995, 2011.

derstood in terms of freedom from the initiation of force. And we cannot, as Miller and Mossoff do, appeal to the nonaggression principle as an *independent moral principle* that can be brought in *alongside* Rand's theory of rights to buttress that theory against critiques such as those made by Eric Mack.

Both ways of understanding force, then, appear to generate problems for Rand's use of the nonaggression principle. And it is not clear to me, from Rand's writings or from Miller and Mossoff's paper, which of them Rand herself adopts.

Rand's frequent references to the way in which physical force severs the connection between man's mind and his actions seems to me to suggest a nonmoralized understanding. In these passages, it seems as though Rand is describing a certain "natural kind" of behavior (i.e., forceful behavior), making the empirical claim that this kind of behavior is the only kind of behavior that undermines an individual's ability to act according to his own rational understanding of the world and of his values, and then, from these premises, drawing the normative conclusion that this sort of behavior violates individual rights.

But I don't think this argument will work, either. First, it's not clear to me that what we usually regard as force really has the kind of effects that Rand, Miller, and Mossoff claim it does. Miller and Mossoff write that actions that initiate force, "such as a mugger stealing a wallet," render moot "the individual's thoughts and actions with respect to how to live" their lives (124). In cases such as this, they claim, "a gun and the threat of death intercede between the individual's mind and the actions one should take to achieve one's values in living the life one seeks for oneself" (125).There's something to this analysis, I think. But it raises a lot of questions that neither Miller nor Mossoff nor, as far as I know, Rand herself ever answers. Suppose a criminal who is about to rob a bank points his gun at you and tells you he'll shoot you in the kneecap unless you stab the bank guard in the chest. Does his threat of violence prevent you from acting in accordance with your own reason? Well, strictly speaking you still have *some* choice. You can either do what he says or you can get shot in the knee. So it's not as though you've been reduced to the status of an *object*. It's not as though you have, as Miller and Mossoff suggest, lost all moral agency altogether. (This, incidentally, is why the criminal law would hold you liable if you did what the gunman said, despite his threat of force. Duress is no defense to the charge of murder.)[11] If the gunman picked you up and *threw*

11. See Dressler 2006, ch. 23.

you at the guard, *then* we would have a genuine case of what Aristotle described as "compulsion," and here it really would be appropriate to say that you have not *acted* as an agent at all—rather, you were *acted upon*.[12] But most cases that we describe as force aren't like that. What makes the gunman's action wrong is not that he *eliminates* your capacity for choice but that he wrongfully limits it. You *should* be able to refrain from stabbing the guard *and* keep your kneecap intact. Instead, you are forced to choose one or the other.

But once we recognize that force merely *limits* choice, we face a second problem: that of distinguishing between those limitations of choice that are *rights-violating* from those that are not. A tree that falls across your path and prevents you from going where you want to go prevents you from acting as you might have wanted to act, too. But none of us would say that the tree has violated your rights. Why not? A fallen tree might prevent your free movement just as much as me forcefully interposing my body between you and where you want to go. If we regard one of these as a rights violation and the other as not, we will have to explain the difference on the basis of something other than their respective effects on the agent's choice, since those effects are, by hypothesis, identical. Here's another example. Suppose a black man in a racist town is denied the right by every business owner to step foot upon their property or do business with them in any way. The black man accordingly cannot buy food, cannot find a place to sleep, cannot rent a car to drive out of town, and so on. Have his rights been violated? Certainly, his choices have been restricted. His capacity to live according to his own reason has, it certainly seems, been impeded. Indeed, impeded to a much greater degree than it would be impeded if a thief stole twenty-five cents out of his pocket. I assume, however, that neither Rand nor Miller and Mossoff would hold that the actions of the business owners were a violation of his rights. But I'm less clear as to *why*.

Their paper does touch on this issue, however, very briefly. At one point, they write that "Social disapproval, economic disadvantages, and other forms of persuasion can only succeed in influencing an individual if one *thinks* that such things are important and accepts them as such, but a gun or other form of physical coercion is the only thing that removes independent thought from the equation in an individual's action" (124). But I simply do not see how this argument is supposed to help. For

---

12. Aristotle, *Nicomachean Ethics* III 1–5.

starters, and as we have already seen, a gun does not *remove* independent thought from the equation. It merely limits it, unjustly. But once this fact is recognized, we can't distinguish between the gunman's action and, say, "economic disadvantages" in the way that Miller and Mossoff suggest. If a boss threatens to fire his female employee unless she sleeps with him, Miller and Mossoff seem to suggest, this can only succeed in influencing her if she *thinks* having a job and being able to afford food and a place to sleep is important. But, of course, the gunman's threat to shoot you in the knee unless you stab the bank guard can only succeed in influencing you *if* you *think* having an intact kneecap is important! I don't want to deny, of course, that there *are* important moral differences between threatening to fire someone and threatening to shoot them. The question isn't whether there's a difference, but what the correct philosophical analysis of that difference is. And the analysis offered by Miller and Mossoff in this case simply doesn't work.

Conclusion

Miller and Mossoff have given us an exceptionally helpful paper on Ayn Rand's theory of rights. Part of what makes it so helpful is that it is written with such clarity that a critic of that theory, like me, can easily see exactly where he disagrees with it. I have spent a good deal of time in these comments elaborating upon those disagreements. But I hope that Miller and Mossoff, and readers of this volume, will take my comments in the way they are intended—as an invitation to open the door to conversation rather than as an attempt to slam it shut. I think that both Objectivists and non-Objectivist academic philosophers can only benefit from the kind of conversation Miller and Mossoff have started with their paper. And, in the spirit of the trader principle, I look forward to what I am sure will be many mutually beneficial conversations about these topics, both in the pages of this volume, and beyond.

Selfish Regard for the Rights of Others
Continuing a Discussion with Zwolinski, Miller, and Mossoff

GREGORY SALMIERI

att Zwolinski characterizes his critique of Rand's theory of rights, which he wrote in response to Fred Miller and Adam Mossoff's presentation of the theory, as an invitation to further conversation between Objectivist and non-Objectivist philosophers. I would like to continue the conversation by addressing what I take to be the central question running through the critique: Why (if at all) is it in an individual's interest to respect the rights of others? Rand's own discussions of rights focus on an individual's need for the liberty that rights "define and sanction." This focus, which Miller and Mossoff follow in their presentation, highlights the benefits to an individual of having his rights respected rather than how he benefits from respecting the rights of others. Zwolinski finds this puzzling and suggests that it stems from a lack of attention to rights' character as *claims* that impose moral obligations on others to respect them. As an ethical egoist, Rand must have held that any obligation to respect rights (or to do anything else) stems from the interest of the obligated individual, so Zwolinski considers whether Rand might have held (or whether Objectivists should adopt) either of two traditional lines of argument by which philosophers have sought to ground obligations in self-interest.

The second section of Zwolinski's critique narrows the focus to property rights, asking how an individual's right to a given resource can be justified to other individuals on whom the right poses "an obligation to refrain from using that resource without [the owner's] consent." How can it be in the nonowners' interest to acknowledge such an obligation? The third and final section of his critique asks whether Rand's understanding of force is prior or posterior to her theory of rights, raising problems for both alternatives.

Rand's understanding of force and the wrongness of initiating it is part of the moral theory that forms the context for her theory of rights. It is because her discussions of rights presuppose this context that they do not focus on why it is selfish to respect the rights of others. These discussions are addressed, not to an individual deliberating about how to treat others but to people deliberating jointly about the terms on which they will interact as a society.[1] This joint deliberation presupposes other moral principles about human interaction (including the principle prohibiting the use of force) for which she offers straightforwardly egoistic justifications. Respecting rights is simply the means by which a group of individuals each of whom is selfishly committed to these principles can implement them on a societal scale.[2]

Thus, in order to understand why Rand thinks it is selfish to respect rights, we must consider why she thinks it is selfish to live by these prior principles. Because her reasons do not fall into either of the two traditional lines of argument that are often regarded as the only ways of es-

---

1. One can see this if one attends to the context of the paragraph from Galt's speech that Miller and Mossoff (118, above) call the "synoptic statement" of Rand's theory of rights. In the preceding paragraph, Galt discusses how he and his fellow strikers will rebuild America's political system; and in the subsequent paragraph, he discusses what happens to society when men do not "choose man's survival as the standard of their morals and their laws"—i.e. when they do not base their societies on the concept of rights (*Atlas* 1061–62).

2. Rasmussen and Den Uyl (1991, 2005) emphasize this role for rights when they describe them as "meta-normative principles" that are the basis for law rather than regular "normative principles" that guide individuals in their interactions with others. They think that Rand leaves ambiguous which sort of principles rights are (1999, 111), but they credit her with the insight (central to their own view) that rights provide the link between individual morality and a legal code (2005, 265). I am not convinced that there is a need for this distinction between two sorts of principles, or that the sorts are mutually exclusive (as Rassmussen and Den Uyl seem to regard them), but there is certainly a difference between viewing rights primarily as principles governing an individual in his actions with respect to others and viewing them primarily as principles concerning the organization of a society. Rand (like Rassmusen and Den Uyl) conceived of rights in this second manner, whereas many of her critics (including Zwolinski) conceive of them in the first manner.

tablishing that it is self-interested to live morally, I'll begin with a brief discussion of how Rand's view of self-interest and its relation to morality differs from these traditional views. Next, I'll turn to two related moral principles that are the core of Rand's social philosophy: the trader principle and the anti-force principle.[3] After discussing these principles and their egoistic justification, I'll discuss how the concepts of rights, including property rights, enable individuals to implement these principles.

This agenda amounts to sketching an answer to Zwolinski's central question in the form of an unrepresentative summary of Rand's ethics and politics—a summary that recapitulates the structure of her system, while focusing on several issues where Zwolinski engaged with Miller and Mossoff and emphasizing some connections between these issues. I had intended this chapter to be a reply to Zwolinski's critique, but my goal of bringing out the connections between the issues took me into topics that aren't addressed in his paper or in Miller and Mossoff's and the chapter swelled beyond the size appropriate to a reply; so I present this as a next step in what I hope will be an ongoing conversation with Zwolinski, Miller, Mossoff, and others.

Rand's Egoism as Opposed to the Instrumental and Constitutive Approaches

Zwolinski writes that "there seem to be two possible approaches" to arguing that an individual benefits from respecting the rights of others. The first approach, which Zwolinski calls "instrumental," is to argue that respecting rights is valuable as "an effective means for [the individual] to achieve his own independently defined set of values" (156, above). The second approach, which he calls "constitutive," is to argue that "respect for the rights of others is a *constitutive part* of our own good" (156).

These two approaches correspond to a widely assumed dichotomy between two ways in which an item can be good (or valuable): the item can be good *instrumentally* (i.e., because it has some good consequence

3. Rand doesn't refer to the principles by these names in print, but she referred to "the trader principle" by this name in notes and correspondence (see *Journals* 584, 650; *Letters* 498). What I'm calling Rand's "anti-force principle" is sometimes identified with the "non-aggression principle" or "nonaggression axiom." This terminology (which is used by Miller and Mossoff and by Zwolinski [123 and 153, above]) looms large in the libertarian literature that grew out of Murray Rothbard, who likely adapted his version of the principle from Rand. Darryl Wright (103–14, above) explains why this terminology is unfortunate, but Wright's preferred name for the principle ("the non–initiation of force principle") is a mouthful, so I've adopted "anti-force principle" for short.

distinct from itself) or it can be good *intrinsically* (i.e., in itself, apart from its consequences).[4] These ways of being good are supposed to be jointly exhaustive and mutually exclusive; some items might be good in both ways (as Plato argued that justice was); but even in such cases, the item's intrinsic value is supposed to be distinct from its instrumental value.[5]

Rand held that life is an "end in itself" and that "an organism's life is its *standard of value*: that which furthers its life is the *good*, that which threatens it is the *evil*" ("The Objectivist Ethics," *VOS* 17–18). She identified the standard of moral value as "*man's life*, or: that which is required for man's survival *qua* man" (*VOS* 25).[6] Her moral code consists in a set of values, virtues, and principles that she argued a human life requires.

Some commentators who have presupposed the dichotomy we've been discussing have thought that there are only two coherent positions Rand could have held about how the contents of her moral code are related to life. According to the first of these positions, values and virtues are instrumentally valuable to an individual as mere means to his *survival*, without themselves being constituents of the life that they help to sustain. This position is a version of what Zwolinski calls the instrumental approach, but it is an instrumental approach to morality as a whole rather than specifically to respecting rights (which is only one part of morality). According to the second position, which is a version of the constitutive

---

4. This dichotomy has been drawn in various terms. One text that introduces it in the terms I'm using here is Hospers 1961 (104–38), which Rand commented on in a letter to Hospers (*Letters* 561). "Instrumental value" is sometimes called "extrinsic" value, and (what I'm here calling) intrinsic goodness is sometimes called "final goodness" or "ultimate goodness" or being an "end in itself." In some contexts, calling something intrinsically good means that it is valuable apart from any relation to a valuer, but my use of the term here is not meant to foreclose the possibility that there are agent-relative intrinsic values. In fact, I think that there are no intrinsic values of either sort (agent-relative or agent-neutral) and that the view that a certain value is intrinsic always stems from dropping part of the context presupposed in its identification as a value. Rand wrote that this identification "presupposes an answer to the question: of value to *whom* and for *what*" (*VOS* 16). An agent-neutral, intrinsic value would be something that is valuable apart from its value to anyone for anything, whereas an agent-relative intrinsic value would be one that is valuable to someone but not for anything.

5. Socrates takes this position on justice at the beginning of Book 2 of Plato's *Republic* (358a), which may be the first text to introduce the distinction between intrinsic and instrumental values (though these are not the terms Plato uses). Socrates spends the rest of the work defending this position.

6. In this formulation and many others, Rand uses the word "man" to refer to any member of the human species, regardless of sex and age. This generic use of "man" and of masculine pronouns was common when Rand was writing, and it figures prominently in the philosophical tradition—especially in the Aristotelian and Enlightenment traditions on which Rand draws. Think of such titles as Ethan Allen's *Reason: The Only Oracle of Man* (1785),

approach, an individual's good or ultimate value isn't his literal survival but his leading a distinctively human sort of life that includes moral virtue. This sort of life and the constituents that distinguish it from other ways in which a human being might live are supposed to be valuable intrinsically rather than because of any contribution they make to survival. Some commentators have ascribed one or the other of these two positions to Rand, and others have seen her as confused or indecisive between the two.[7] None of these interpretations survives a careful reading of Rand's corpus, once one dispenses with the assumption that the two positions in question jointly exhaust the possibilities. And indeed, the whole alternative between intrinsic and instrumental values that lies behind these positions is incompatible with Rand's way of thinking about values.

Rand argues that the concept "value" (or "good") arises and is meaningful only in the context of an organism acting to sustain its life. This life, which is the organism's ultimate value, is "a process of self-sustaining and self-generated action" (*VOS* 16). The process consists in the pursuit of the various items and conditions that the organism needs (given its

Thomas Paine's *The Rights of Man* (1791), and Louise Ropes Loomis's collection of Aristotle's works, *On Man in the Universe* (1943). However, this generic use of masculine language has since fallen out of favor, because it reflects the view—now widely rejected as sexist—that the adult male is the paradigm case of a human being (see Miller and Swift 1976; Moulton 1981; Warren 1986; Little 1996). This development has left the language without a term that functions grammatically as "man" does in many philosophical works—a singular term by which one can refer to a human being abstractly and discuss things that hold true of each human being in virtue of human nature. Philosophers working in the Aristotelian tradition today often use "the human," intending this phrase to be understood as phrases like "the mallard" or "the great white shark" are understood when used in connection with animal species. There is now a growing literature on how such phraseology should be understood (see especially Foot 2001, 29–36, 46–47; Thompson 2008). Perhaps this is, on whole, the best terminology to adopt for such purposes. In any case, in passages where I am expanding on or interacting with Rand's texts, I retain her use of the generic masculine language.

7. Rasmussen (2002, 2006, 2007a, 2007b) attributes the constitutive approach to Rand or at least thinks this is the most promising line along which to develop her thought. Mack (1984, 2003), Badhwar (1999), and Long (2000, 2010), all charge Rand with some sort of confusion on this point, but they regard the constitutive approach as the more promising strand. Badhwar and Long (2016) attribute (what I'm here calling) the instrumentalist interpretation to Thomas and Kelley 1999, Gotthelf 2000, and Smith 2000. But each of these sources notes some of the features of Rand's position (discussed below) that differentiate it from the instrumentalist view. (See Thomas and Kelley 1999, 78n17; Gotthelf 2000, 83; Smith 2000, 74, 130–48.) Consequently, I think it is a mistake to attribute the instrumentalist interpretation to these commentators, though they do not explicitly reject this interpretation. Some more recent pieces are more explicit about how different Rand's approach is from both traditional approaches. (See Gotthelf 2016, 78–81, 90–92; Salmieri 2016c, 132–36; Wright 2005, 2008, 2011a.)

nature) to carry on performing the relevant process. These items or conditions are the organism's values.[8]

To see why this view is incompatible with a dichotomy between intrinsic and instrumental value, consider whether a plant's carrying out the process of photosynthesis is good (i.e., valuable) for the plant *instrumentally* or *intrinsically*. Photosynthesizing is only good for the plant because it produces chemical energy, which the plant needs to survive, and so we might see the process as valuable instrumentally. However, what it is for the plant to survive is for it to continue carrying on a set of activities that includes photosynthesis, and this might lead us to think of photosynthesis as an intrinsically valuable constituent of the life to which the plant's instrumental values are mere means. And yet, photosynthesis is a constituent of the life that is the plant's ultimate end precisely because of the causal contribution it makes to sustaining this life.

The same is true of all the activities that make up part of any *process of self-sustaining self-generated action*. Such a process is literally a means to itself, such that each component action is a constituent of the process's end precisely by being a means to this end.[9] The actions are not valuable as means to anything wholly distinct from themselves, nor are they valuable apart from their effects. Instead, each is valuable as *a causally contributing member of a self-sustaining whole*. For the same reason, the life that is an organism's ultimate end should be understood to include the organs, conditions, instruments, and relationships that it acts to achieve and that make its continued activity possible. On Rand's view, to be valuable at all is to be valuable *to* some organism *for* the sake of some role it plays in the process of self-sustaining action that is the organism's life. This view precludes the possibility of anything's being valuable either instrumentally or intrinsically, if we take these terms to be absolute and mutually exclusive. Rather than being either instruments or constituents, all values are *instrumental constituents*—that is, *organs*—of a life.

This is not to say that all of an organism's values are equal. Some are central to its life and irreplaceable, others are peripheral and fungible,

---

8. See "The Objectivist Ethics," *VOS*; Peikoff 1991, 206–19; Gotthelf 2016, 73–81; Wright 2011a; Smith 2000.

9. It is this fact about life that Rand thinks makes it an end in itself and so an ultimate value. "Metaphysically, *life* is the only phenomenon that is an end in itself: a value gained and kept by a constant process of action" (*VOS* 18). So, for her, even an organism's life isn't intrinsically valuable to it, if that means that the life is valuable to the organism *apart from the life's aims and effects*, for part of what it is for the life to be an end in itself is that the life aims at (and effects) its own existence over time. (On this last point, see Binswanger 1992.)

and many lie somewhere between these extremes. In the case of a tree, a particular leaf or twig or a particular episode of photosynthesis would be peripheral and fungible; the tree's trunk and its ability to photosynthesize would be central and irreplaceable; and between these extremes would fall such values as the tree's boughs and the several species of pollinating insect that it attracts by means of its flowers and uses to propagate itself.

Likewise, a human life will include peripheral and fungible values, such as particular tools or meals or jobs or acquaintances (as well as particular bodily cells and particular episodes of metabolic activity) that could be easily replaced. It may also include some concrete values that are central enough to the person's life to be irreplaceable, such that losing them would permanently and significantly impair and imperil his life (including by undermining his will to live). A person's career or spouse or child may fall into this category.

Among the central and irreplaceable values to any organism will be the process by which it selects the other values it needs to pursue and thereby coordinates its activities into a self-sustaining whole. Nonhuman organisms accomplish this by innate (physiological or psychological) mechanisms that function automatically. Human beings, by contrast, direct our lives by the faculty of reason, which is why Rand regards it as "man's basic means of survival" (*VOS* 25). Since reason does not function automatically, a human being does not automatically value his own life or know how to preserve it; indeed, he does not automatically value or know anything at all.

Morality, for Rand, is a body of knowledge that guides a human being in the formation and pursuit of the sort of values human beings need to survive, and all of the virtues and values that Rand specifies as constituents of "Man's Life" earn their place by making a crucial contribution to survival.[10] Rationality is the fundamental virtue, because reason is our fundamental means of survival—the faculty by which a human being knows the world and by which he can conceive of and pursue values that can integrate his actions into a self-sustaining whole. The other virtues (independence, integrity, honesty, justice, productiveness, and pride) specify forms of cognition and action that rationality entails.

Thus morality plays the role in human life that is played in other species by the innate mechanisms that coordinate their actions into a

10. For discussion of the contribution each makes, see Peikoff 1991, 250–324; Gotthelf 2016, 81–87, 92–96; Smith 2006.

self-sustaining whole. As such, morality is a fundamental means to a human being's survival and, therefore, an essential constituent of a human life. This, of course, applies only to the correct moral code—the one that takes man's life as its standard and is correctly grounded in human nature. A person who acts in accordance with some other morality, or who lives amorally, is analogous to a diseased organism whose system of self-direction is compromised. To whatever extent (and in whatever domains) this is true of an individual, his actions are self-destructive rather than cohering into a self-sustaining whole. Of course, many people survive for whole human lifespans even though they often act immorally, just as many survive across whole lifespans with physiological disorders; but in both sorts of cases, the defects are not the cause of the person's survival, nor are the defects aimed at life. Only insofar as an individual is acting morally is he pursuing his life at all, and only to this extent can anything be of value to him.

I have made similar points about Rand's view of virtue in the past and they have sometimes been met with objections that seem to me to miss the point.[11] At the risk of belaboring the issue, I think it will be clarifying to respond to one of these objections here. Roderick Long (2016) writes:

> If virtues are constitutive elements of the ultimate end *because* of their causal contribution to that end, then their instrumental role must be logically prior to their constitutive role. In other words, the end to which virtues make a causal contribution cannot *already* be characterized as having those virtues as constituents. It would be circular to say that *this* is valuable because it contributes to *that*, if *that* is already conceptualized as including *this*. Hence the life to which virtues are *constitutive* means must be a more richly and thickly characterized version of life than the life to which virtues are initially identified as *instrumental* means—leaving Rand with the problem of deciding *which* of these two versions of life to identify with the ultimate end.

Notice that this same reasoning could be applied to the case of photosynthesis as follows:

> If photosynthesis is a constituent of a plant's life *because* of its causal contribution to life, then its causal contribution must be logically prior

---

11. My previous expositions include Salmieri 2016d, 8; 2016a, 60–62; 2016c, 134–36; and 2016f.

to its constitutive role; hence the life of which photosynthesis is a *constitutive* means must be a more richly and thickly characterized version of life than the life to which photosynthesis is initially identified as *instrumental* means.

What would the less "rich" and "thick" characterization of life be to which we would then identify photosynthesis as an instrumental means rather than a constituent? Perhaps we could characterize life in terms of the processes by which the chemical energy produced by photosynthesis is used to power the plant's other activities. But then these processes too are "instrumental" to the other activities, so we'll need an even poorer and thinner characterization of life, and any characterization we produce will be subject to this same objection, unless it is so impoverished and emaciated as to exclude reference to any vital processes whatsoever, in which case it won't be a characterization of *a life* at all.

To adequately understand the phenomenon of life we must grasp that there are complex activities in which each component is a means to the continuation of the whole. Such complexes cannot be analyzed into unidirectional teleological relations: breathing may be for the sake of cellular metabolism, but so too (in a breathing organism) is cellular metabolism for the sake of breathing. Each vital process both depends on and contributes to the whole that comprises them all. There are "thicker" and "thinner" characterizations of life only in the sense that a life can be characterized with different degrees of specificity. We can talk about life in general, or about the plant form of life, the fern form of life, or the life of a particular fern, but there are no teleological relations between the more and less abstract characterizations of life. A particular fern has the features it does in order to sustain its own life, not to sustain some generic plant life (or life-in-general). Once one grasps this, one sees that there is no basis for the absolute distinction Long insists on between "instrumental" and "constitutive" means (or between the instrumental and constitutive "roles" of any given means). When explaining what a particular vital process contributes to a life, one can and should characterize the life in a way that doesn't make reference to that process, but this does not imply that the items named in this characterization of the life are ulterior in value to the process being explained.[12] Thus, in validating the moral values and

12. How such explanations should be structured is an interesting issue both in ethics and in the philosophy of biology. My own nascent thinking on this issue (which is sketched above and in Salmieri 2016a, 58–63) takes its inspiration from Jim Lennox's (2010) interpre-

virtues by indicating how they enable us to fulfill more obvious survival needs like those for food and shelter, Rand does not imply that a life characterized solely in terms of the fulfillment of these needs is the ultimate value and that morality is valuable only as means to a full stomach.

The preceding should make clear that Rand's approach to moral philosophy is not vulnerable to the first of the objections that Zwolinski levels against the instrumental approach. She does not turn moral principles into mere rules of thumb to be followed only in those circumstances where they are the most effective means to secure a meal or a buck. Rather, on Rand's view, moral principles are part of our means of evaluating such concrete ends, such that no such end pursued immorally could be of any value.[13]

However, Rand's approach does share with the instrumental approach the challenge of establishing that her moral principles are really fundamental causal contributors to an individual's survival, such that, in violating them, a person necessarily acts against his own life. However, facing this challenge is an asset. Too often what ethicists present as universal moral principles are just their personal preferences or prejudices (or those of their society or social class). This is particularly true of many of the things that the Ancient Greek eudaimonists, who are the paradigms of the constitutive approach, regard as intrinsic constituents of the good life.[14] To be objective, an approach to ethics needs to identify a standard by which we can tell whether a proposed moral principle is genuine, and it needs to show how this standard follows from the facts that give rise to the need for morality. Such versions of the constituative approach as have been developed provide no such standard by which to determine whether something is a genuine constituent of the human good.

In any case, it is not as difficult as Zwolinski implies to establish *principles* concerning the impact that different sorts of action will have on one's life. Even Hobbes's instrumentalist egoism, though crude, provides more than rules of thumb to which a shrewd operator might find exceptions. Hobbes notes that certain sorts of action (theft, murder, etc.)

---

tation of Aristotle's conception of a "*bios*" (or way of life) and from Tore Boeckmann's (2007) concept of a "core combination" in esthetics. Boeckmann's concept is itself an integration of Rand's concept "plot-theme" (on which see "Basic Principles of Literature," *RM* 76–78) and the view expressed by Roark in *The Fountainhead* (12) that a building must be designed around "one central idea."

13. See Wright's discussion of this issue above, 17–25.

14. On this point, see Salmieri 2016f.

necessarily put their perpetrators into a state of enmity with any society to which they might belong; he grasps that because a society's resources are incomparably greater than that of any individual's, any perpetrator of such actions is more likely than not to be discovered and punished; and so Hobbes concludes that an individual would be foolish to expect to profit by perpetrating such actions.[15] This is why, as Plato also recognized, people who live unjustly rarely if ever escape punishment in the long run, and why any who do escape punishment do so by luck, rather than by savvy.[16] The crudeness of Hobbes's position lies, not in his argument that crime doesn't pay but in his assumption that, simply because criminals want loot, the loot would be good for them if only they could get away with it. According to Rand's more sophisticated view, an item is good for an individual only if he rationally pursues it for the sake of some contribution that he understands it could make to his life; and moral principles are part of the means by which such contributions are understood, so no item pursued in disregard of morality can be a value.

The Selfishness of Trade and Self-Destructiveness of Force

The values that a human being needs in order to survive and prosper must be discovered and produced by a rational process that can be performed only by human beings as individuals, each aiming at his own life. It is a process that can be performed on an ever-expanding scale, progressing from caves, berries, and fire to skyscrapers, fine cuisine, and nuclear energy. Each human being benefits from other human beings' success at this process, but only so long as he treats them "as independent equals" to be dealt with "by means of a free, voluntary, unforced, uncoerced exchange—an exchange which benefits both parties by their own independent judgment" ("The Objectivist Ethics," *VOS* 35).

This is an important respect in which human beings are different from other organisms. The members of any nonhuman species are fundamentally in competition with one another for the inputs to their survival process. Whatever cooperation there may be among members of the species (e.g., among bees in a certain hive or between a pair of mated birds)

---

15. See Hobbes, *Leviathan* 15.4–8.

16. Plato's Socrates, after spending nine books of the *Republic* arguing that (even apart from their consequences) justice is intrinsically good for its possessor and injustice is intrinsically bad, insists in Book 10 (613b–14a) that just people do in fact reap fine and secure benefits from the good reputation they earn, and that unjust ones are usually eventually caught and punished.

takes place in the context of a broader competition with other species members over scare resources. This is not true for human beings. Rather than competing for the wild berries from the same plant generation after generation, we can learn to cultivate plants. Rather than competing over a fixed stock of arable land, we can clear forests to make more land available, and we can discover ever better techniques for producing more food from the same land. When our soil is exhausted, we can learn how to fertilize it, and when supplies of known fertilizers are depleted, we can discover new fertilizers or learn to synthesize them from atmospheric nitrogen. It is in this way that an ever increasing number of human beings have survived on earth, with a growing standard of living.

As Rand puts it, "the rational interests of men do not clash" (*VOS* 34). Of course, people do often come into conflict: wars have been fought over land and other resources, and individuals often find themselves at loggerheads. But, far from being a necessary, inherent feature of the process by which human beings survive, such conflicts are *deviations* from the human form of life. Such deviations are commonplace because the knowledge of how to lead a human life is not automatic: it had to be discovered, and once discovered, it needs to be continually applied by conscious effort. When people live rationally, their interests are fundamentally harmonious. There is still competition for such things as jobs, customers, and romantic partners, but Rand argues that such competitions take place in the context of a shared recognition that "man's self-interest can be served only by a nonsacrificial relationship with others" (*VOS* 34).[17] Galt explains the implications of this for how to deal with others:

I deal with men as my nature and theirs demands: by means of reason. I seek or desire nothing from them except such relations as they care to enter of their own voluntary choice. It is only with their mind that I can deal and only for my own self-interest, when they see that my interest coincides with theirs. When they don't, I enter no relationship; I let dissenters go their way and I do not swerve from mine. I win by means of nothing but logic and I surrender to nothing but logic. I do not surrender my reason or deal with men who surrender theirs. I have nothing to gain from fools or cowards; I have no benefits to seek from human vices: from stupidity, dishonesty or fear. The only value men can offer me is the work of their mind. (*Atlas* 1022–23)

17. On these issues, see also "The 'Conflicts' of Men's Interests" in *VOS*.

A nonsacrificial relationship is one of *trade*, in which each interaction leaves both parties better off and able to derive further benefits from one another (and from third parties) in the future. By contrast, any interaction in which one person is sacrificed for the sake of the other brings at best short-term gains while undermining the person who is the source of the gain and thus rendering him less able to provide benefits in the future. This is the case even if the sacrifice is made voluntarily, and this is part of why mooching (attempting to live off of others' voluntary sacrifices) is irrational. It amounts to diverting time and energy from the task of creating life-sustaining values to the task of draining those who do produce them. The ill effects of mooching, however, are limited to the moochers themselves and to those productive people who unjustly choose to associate with them. Because of this, moochers can be safely ignored by those who know better than to support them. This is not true of people who seek to drain productive people *by force*.

Although traders offer values and moochers do not, both leave it up to others whether to enter into a relationship with them. If the other party to a prospective relationship declines, his life continues on as it would have if he had never encountered the trader or the moocher. To use force against someone, by contrast, is to impose oneself on someone *against his will* and, thereby, to interfere with his ability to direct his life. This makes those who initiate force a threat to all rational people—one that they cannot tolerate and against which they must retaliate.

> Whatever may be open to disagreement, there is one act of evil that may not, the act that no man may commit against others and no man may sanction or forgive. So long as men desire to live together, no man may *initiate*—do you hear me? no man may *start*—the use of physical force against others. (*Atlas* 1023)

"To deal with men by force," Rand writes, "is as impractical as to deal with nature by persuasion" ("The Metaphysical versus the Man Made," *PWNI* 44). The seeming best case scenario for the *looter* (the initiator of force) is that she is able to extract some material item from her victim or coerce him into performing some service that he would not have performed willingly. But this "success" leaves the looter no better off than a moocher: she's attained a short-range goal via a means that damages the source of the values on which her life depends. The more fully she brings the victim under her power, the more she disrupts his ability to lead a human life and to conceive and create the sort of values that the looter needs from him.

This is why societies with slave labor are much less prosperous than otherwise similar free societies, and societies with controlled economies are less prosperous than otherwise similar societies with freer economies. It is also why an industrial revolution occurred in nineteenth-century America and England, when for the first time (despite the profound injustices that persisted in both societies) a critical mass of humanity was free enough that many individuals could discover new knowledge, produce new values, and catalyze one another's achievements on an ever expanding scale. As Onkar Ghate discusses (211–219, below), this was made possible by a profound philosophical advance: the realization that a society must free its members from force, and the discovery of some of the means by which this can be accomplished.[18]

The impracticality of preying on one's fellow human beings is more easily recognized on an individual level than on a societal level. A predator not only damages those who produce the values on which his life depends (as a moocher does), he makes enemies of them, giving them every reason to devote their minds and resources to the task of finding and destroying him. Predation is not a crafty strategy; it's a myopic lunging in the service of a whim, with no thought given to the long-range consequences of one's actions or of whether they cohere into a life that can sustain a human being across a human lifespan. Rand explains:

> The men who attempt to survive, not by means of reason, but by means of force, are attempting to survive by the method of animals. But just as animals would not be able to survive by attempting the method of plants, by rejecting locomotion and waiting for the soil to feed them—so men cannot survive by attempting the method of animals, by rejecting reason

---

18. I have indicated why it is counterproductive for one individual to loot another in the context of a free society and why free societies are more prosperous than unfree ones. The case of a comparatively free member of a society in which other members are unfree—for example, a white man in the American South during the antebellum or Jim Crow periods—raises additional questions that I cannot try to resolve here. It should be clear why I think such a person would be benefited by his society's being freer, but this leaves unanswered such questions as: What place should making his society freer have in his hierarchy of values? To what extent can he take part in the society without being complicit in its evil? And how do the answers to these questions relate to his self-interest? The answers will surely differ depending on how free or unfree the society is, and just what role the individual in question plays in it.

and counting on productive *men* to serve as their prey. Such looters may achieve their goals for the range of a moment, at the price of destruction: the destruction of their victims and their own. As evidence, I offer you any criminal or any dictatorship. ("The Objectivist Ethics," *VOS* 25–26)

I have already alluded to Rand's view that initiating force "negate[s] and paralyze[s]" reason, which is the human means of survival. I won't say much more about this position here, because Darryl Wright treats it extensively (and excellently) in "Force and the Mind" in this volume; but I should weigh in on one point where I agree with Zwolinski's criticism of Miller and Mossoff. Some of their formulations suggest that a person under threat of force ceases to be able to think or to choose at all, and that this is what differentiates force from other ways in which one person might seek to influence another. Inducements such as "social disapproval, economic disadvantages, and other forms of persuasion," they write "can only succeed in influencing an individual if one *thinks* that such things are important and accepts them as such, but a gun or other form of physical coercion is the only thing that removes independent thought from the equation in an individual's action" (above, 124). Zwolinski responds (correctly in my view) that a gunman's threats can influence us only because we think it is important not to be shot, and he notes that there are things we would choose not to do even at gunpoint, because we think doing them is worse than getting shot.

Even when threatened, unless we are paralyzed by terror, we remain free to think about how awful the demands are, how credible the threats are, and whether there is any way to resist. But all such thinking is *short-range* deliberation about how to address an imminent threat rather than the long-range and creative thinking needed to conceive and realize new values and to integrate the pursuit of these values into a life that can sustain one across a human lifespan. As Wright argues, force paralyses reason in that it is impossible to project and pursue such values within the constraints set by a gunman's shifting decrees, and it negates reason in that it renders moot deliberation about how one would proceed if one were free of these constraints. It is this long-range creative reasoning that directs a human life, and this sort of reasoning requires freedom from force.

Consequently, although there are ways in which one can reason in the presence of force (including about how to deal with the fact that one is under force), I think there is a crucial difference between other people's initiations of force and other facts about one's environment that one must negotiate when deciding how to act. Zwolinski assimilates the initiation of force to these other factors, treating force, natural phenomena, and nonforcible actions by other people all as facts that can "limit" or "restrict" choice. He writes as though the effect on a traveler is the same if she is prevented from taking a certain path, no matter whether it is because the path is barred by a highwayman, because it is obstructed by a fallen tree or ferocious animal, or because a shopkeeper refuses to sell her equipment she would need to make her way along it.[19]

In fact, the shopkeeper is no obstacle to the traveler at all; he is simply not an aid until and unless the traveler can persuade him to become one. Even if his refusal to deal with her is irrational and unjust (as for example if it is motivated by prejudice), she is no worse off than she would be if he and his shop (and equipment) didn't exist at all.

The highwayman, the fallen tree, and the ferocious animal are all obstacles to the traveler. But unlike the tree and the animal, which are not acting by choice or capable of reasoning, the highwayman has chosen to initiate force upon the traveler rather than reasoning with her. Moreover, he remains capable of reasoning and will likely attempt to reason with her in the context established by his initiation of force. To negotiate the situation successfully, she must keep in mind that his imposition of force on her is not some impersonal fact about which the two of them can reason jointly. It is something he is *doing to her* instead of dealing with her by reason. His initiation of force takes them outside the context in which joint deliberation, common planning, and genuine agreement are possible, for these forms of interaction presuppose that each party regards the other as *someone to interact with* rather than as *something to act upon*.[20]

This is what separates physical force and other means by which one person might try to influence another. A consensual (or voluntary) interaction between two people is one in which each party has the option to participate or not; and if one chooses not to participate, he can carry on with his life without any interference from the other. Thus, so long as the parties continue to interact, they do so based on some *agreement* (at least as to the terms of the interaction), and this provides a context for further joint reasoning. A forced (or coerced) relationship, by contrast, is one in which one party acts upon the other without his consent.

19. This example is intended to combine several of Zwolinski's examples (or slight variants of them) into a single case. I deal with some of his examples more directly below.

20. The error of regarding someone else's initiated force against you as on par with a fact of nature is a recurring theme in the third part of *Atlas Shrugged* (esp. 917, 1102).

Zwolinski gives two examples that are essentially similar to that of the shopkeeper who refuses to help the hiker. The first concerns a male employer who threatens to fire a female employee unless she sleeps with him. The second example concerns "a black man in a racist town" where all the businesses are closed to him so that he "cannot buy food, cannot find a place to sleep, cannot rent a car to drive out of town, and so on" (164). Each of these cases involves a severe injustice, but it is not an initiation of force because the unjust parties do not deprive their victim of anything other than the benefits that could have come from a relationship with them.[21] If the employer did not exist, then neither would the job the woman presently holds, so in (wrongly) firing her or threatening to do so, he leaves her in no worse a position than she would have been in if he had not come into her life.

The case of the black man in the racist town is under-described, but let's suppose that the man is a motorist who has broken down on the interstate just outside of the town, and let's further stipulate that he can somehow be confident that none of the townspeople will assault or rob him. In this case, although he would have been much better off had he broken down outside of a town populated by better people, the townspeople's shunning him leaves him no worse off materially than he would have been if there were no town there at all. But, of course, our stipulation is absurd. In any actual community so racist that all the businesses would be closed to a stranded black motorist, the motorist would have every reason to fear for his safety; for such communities would include many people who would not hesitate to assault him, and the local authorities would be likely to overlook such crimes.[22] This illustrates a point that we will explore in the next section: in order for an individual living among others to be free of force, the society must be organized in accordance with certain principles. Thus, although the business owners' refusal to deal with the black motorist is not per se an initiation of force against him, it is a strong indication that he has entered a community where is subject to force.

(I assume that Zwolinski's choices of examples are not accidental. The racist and sexist practices the examples reference were outlawed in the United States by Title II of the Civil Rights Act of 1964. Though the

21. It might be objected that what the unjust party does in these cases is an affront to his victim's dignity, and this is surely true, but such affronts do not amount to *depriving* the person of dignity or of anything else.

22. On such communities, see Loewen 2005; see esp. 228–29 on the fates of inadvertent visitors to such towns).

Act also nullified many state laws that Rand viewed as gross violations of rights, she opposed the Act because she saw Title II as violating property rights and as therefore representing the intrusion of force into what would otherwise be voluntary relationships.[23] If Rand's understanding of force and its application to this case is correct, we would expect Title II to have the effect of reinforcing racial and sexist prejudices by negating and paralyzing individuals' ability to judge one another objectively in the context of business relationships. Whether the Title has in fact had this effect is a difficult historical question.[24])

In saying that the injustices in Zwolinski's examples are not initiations of force, I do not mean to minimize them. The initiation of force is not the only evil, and some actions that involve no force are more vicious in their motivation and more destructive in their effects than are some forcible actions.[25] A betrayal or insult from someone one loves, for example, can be more ill-motivated and more harmful than a punch or

23. For Rand's discussion of the Act, see "Racism," *VOS* 156–57 (also 153–54). It should be noted that she emphatically rejected the other argument that some proponents of civil rights gave for opposing the Act—namely, that the Jim Crow laws, however despicable, were within the legitimate authority of the states and so could properly be overturned only at the state or local level, and not by the federal government. She wrote that the state laws mandating segregation, "should have been declared unconstitutional long ago" (*VOS* 153) and that "it is proper to forbid all discrimination in government-owned facilities and establishments" (*VOS* 156). Clearly, then, she agreed with Title III of the Act, and perhaps with Titles I and IV–VI as well. But, evidently, she regarded Title II as sufficiently bad to make the Act as a whole "the worst breech of property rights in the sorry record of American history in respect to that subject" (*VOS* 157), despite the fact that the other titles eliminated unconstitutional state laws that she saw as "abrogating the citizens' individual rights" (153).

24. To answer the question by empirical research, one would need to find a way to separate the effects of Title II from those of the other titles (especially Title III). Without doing this, one could only assess the effect of the Act as a whole, and even here, there are difficulties. The Act was one effect of a broader cultural movement against racism and sexism. No doubt there are many respects in which racism and sexism (or at least their most overt expressions) have diminished since 1964, but it is hard to tell how much of this change is because of the Act and how much because of other effects of the cultural movement. It is difficult also to project how history would have unfolded if this movement had sought to fight private discrimination solely via private means such as boycotts. Moreover, it is not clear how to measure the rate at which racism and sexism are diminishing (assuming that they are), and it is not obvious that the diminution has been faster since 1964 than it was in the decades preceding it. Finally, there are many other confounding factors, most notably the effects of the "wars" on poverty and drugs.

25. That this is Rand's view should be evident from *Atlas Shrugged*. Consider James Taggart's spiritual exploitation of his wife, Cherryl. He exercises no force against her, but this is one of the episodes through which Rand explores the depth of his evil, and his actions precipitate Cherryl's suicide. (See *Atlas* 868–907.) Similar remarks apply to Rearden's family.

a picked-pocket, and the unjust acts in Zwolinski's examples are worse both in their motivation and in their intents than are many assaults or robberies. What distinguishes the initiation force from other wrongs is not the scale of the wrong or its motivation, but its nature. An initiation of force is an *intrusion* (however minor or benignly intended) into an individual's life, whereas other wrongs (however major or malicious) are not.[26] Other wrongs can be fought in other ways, but to maintain the integrity of one's own life, one must be ready to answer force with force, and in order to live together as a society, we must organize ourselves in such a manner as to free each of us from force. It is for this purpose that the concept of "rights" is necessary.

Rights as the Means to a Consensual Society

I've discussed force now for some time without much reference to rights. Zwolinski raises a dilemma about the relation between these two concepts. Either "force" (or "physical force" or "physical coercion") is to be understood in terms of rights or it is to be understood independently of it. If force is to be defined as activity that violates rights, then it would be circular to consider (as Rand does) whether a certain action involves initiating force to determine whether it violates rights. But, unless force is defined in this way, Zwolinski thinks, many actions that Rand thinks violate rights (especially property rights) will turn out not to involve initiations of force, and so attempts to enforce these rights (e.g., forcibly evicting trespassers) will be initiations of force.[27]

   As I understand it, to exercise physical force is simply to act on some-

---

26. My thinking on the issues discussed in this paragraph owes a lot to discussions with Onkar Ghate as we were preparing a series of lectures on political philosophy. For his treatment of some of these issues in that lecture series, see Ghate 2017 3:09–11:40.

27. Note that the issue Zwolinski raises here is structurally the same as the one he raises with regards to the relation between moral action (specifically, respecting rights) and self-interest. In each case, his challenge amounts to asking whether a certain principle of Objectivism is meant to be analytic or synthetic. If it's analytic, it can be established with necessity a priori, but it is uninformative; if it's synthetic, then it is contentful but we can't be confident that it's true. If what Rand means by "self-interest" includes following certain principles she calls "virtues," then, by those definitions, virtue will be self-interested; but this scheme doesn't give anyone any reason to act virtuously, and it has no defense against anyone who builds different principles (or none at all) into his definition of "self-interest." Likewise, if "initiation of force" just means "whatever violates rights," then it will necessarily be true that all and only initiations of force violate rights, but this tells us nothing about which actions are rights-violating initiations of force. On the other hand, if self-interest is defined independently of the virtues, then it's an empirical question (a matter of observed patterns of cause and effect) when virtue promotes self-interest, and it's doubtful that it does so all the time. Likewise, if force isn't defined in terms of rights, it's a doubtful empirical question

one without her consent—to *interfere* in her life. That there is such a phenomenon can be understood without the concept of rights, and often instances of this phenomenon can be recognized without recourse to the concept.[28] However, in many contexts we need the concept of "rights" in order to distinguish between consensual interactions and initiations of force. This is not because of a lack of clarity in the meaning of "force" but because the boundaries of an individual human life are often unclear, particularly in cases involving the complex interactions among individuals living together in a society. The principle of rights enables us to define these boundaries and thereby to grasp that certain actions that do not involve bodily contact nonetheless intrude into someone's life.

A life includes not only the activities taking place within an organism's body but also the organism's complex interaction with its environment. This process often involves incorporating materials into the organism's life without incorporating them into its body. Consider, for example, a chipmunk's store of nuts. Its role in the chipmunk's life is analogous to the role played in bears' lives by the fat they grow during the fall to sustain them through the winter. Both bears and chipmunks find food when it is readily available and store it for later use. A chipmunk's store is external to its body, whereas a bear's is internal, but this does not make the store any less a part of the chipmunk's life: the store, just like the fat, is something the organism creates and maintains for the sake of the role it plays in sustaining its life.

The same is true of the many life-sustaining values human beings create. Rand stresses this point, often analogizing such creations to bodily organs.[29] But, whereas the hoarding and building behaviors of other an-

whether force is always involved in rights violations. On Rand's rejection of this dichotomy and the implications of this rejection for her philosophical methodology, see Peikoff's "The Analytic Synthetic Dichotomy" (in Rand, *ITOE* 88–121) and Salmieri 2016e.

28. This is not to say that the concept of "force" (even in these cases) includes no moral content, as Zwolinksi suggests the concept of force would if it were not defined in terms of rights. The facts that make it necessary to form concepts distinguishing between voluntary interaction and force are the same facts that make the one sort of action moral and the other immoral. This is true also with such pairs of concepts as "honest" and "dishonest," "just" and "unjust," or "rational" and irrational." In all these cases the grasp of the relevant concepts is simultaneous with the grasp of a moral principle advocating one form of action and condemning the other. The facts on which the concepts and principle are based are causal facts about the requirements of human survival and the causes and effects of various sorts of action.

29. The hero of *Anthem*, for example, likens the electric light he invents to a part of his body: "this wire is as a part of [my] body, as a vein torn from [me], glowing with [my] blood" (*Anthem* 61). Similarly, in *Atlas Shrugged*, Dagny Taggart compares having to leave Taggart

imals are instinctive and fixed, the faculty of reason enables human beings to create values in ways that are unlimited in their variety and complexity. When people share a common environment, they interact with it and with one another in intricate and overlapping ways that make the boundaries of individual lives difficult to determine. As a result, one cannot undertake complex projects without fear of interference by (even well-intentioned) others. In order for people who share an environment to ensure that all of their interactions will be consensual, leaving each free to lead his own life by his own judgment, we must *demarcate* the boundaries of our lives. This means explicitly identifying a range of activities that each individual can take unilaterally without intruding on anyone else's life, and recognizing that interference by anyone else in these activities constitutes force initiated against him. This is the function served by the concept of rights.

Rand defines "a right" as "a moral principle defining and sanctioning a man's freedom of action in a social context" ("Man's Rights," *VOS* 110/ *CUI* 369). To say that an individual has a right to his life is to endorse his freedom "to take all the actions required by the nature of a rational being for the support, the furtherance, the fulfillment and the enjoyment of his own life" ("Man's Rights," *VOS* 110/*CUI* 369). Other rights, which are derived from the right to life, specify some of the requisite freedoms. In particular, the right to "the pursuit of happiness" specifies that the individual needs the freedom to set his own purpose in life (rather than being subordinated to the purposes of others), the right to liberty specifies that he needs to be free to determine unilaterally the means by which to achieve this purpose, and the right to property specifies that he needs to be free "to gain, to keep, to use and to dispose of material values" (*VOS* 110–11/*CUI* 370).

These rights serve as guides to people in the formation of a government and legal system through which an individual's rights can be further specified by defining procedures for such things as the acquisition and transfer of property and the formation, dissolution, and adjudication of contracts. Absent such a government, the boundaries between one person's life and another's are ill defined, with the result that there is only a very small range of activity a person can safely take without expecting to

Transcontinental to having "her legs amputated" (*Atlas* 56); and, when the legislature in *Atlas Shrugged* passes a law that requires Rearden to divest himself of some of his businesses, he recognizes "that they had slashed part of his life away and that he had to be ready to walk on as a cripple" (214).

come into conflict with others. A legal system that implements and elaborates the concept of rights brings nuanced clarity to the distinction between voluntary and forced interactions. This enables progressively more complex and more intricately interconnected forms of human action. The result is an ever grander scale of life available to every individual.

With this in mind, let's consider Zwolinski's example of a stolen car. How, he asks, does a thief who drives away with an unattended car initiate force against the owner, whom she doesn't even touch? As Zwolinski points out, we need the concept of rights—specifically, property rights—to see this as a case of initiation of force. But what we understand by means of this concept is that the car is a non-bodily part of the owner, such that to interact with it against his will is to attack him. The process by which the car came into existence involves a staggeringly complex nexus of interpersonal relationships, and it is because of the owner's precise role in this nexus that the car belongs to him.[30]

The concept of rights is part of our means of conceiving of these relationships, bringing them about, and protecting them. It enables us to recognize that, though the car is not part of the owner's body, it stands in the same broad relation to his life as do his legs: it came into existence through his vital activity (in particular, his role in the market economy), in order to serve his need for transportation. Driving off with the owner's car is like breaking his legs, and the concept of rights enables us to see that these two actions are alike in precisely those respects that make the latter action an initiation of force. Thus, though the distinction between consensual interaction and the initiation of force isn't defined in terms of rights, the concept of rights enables us to apply this distinction to subtle and complex cases, and thereby to create and maintain the institutions needed to cohabitate voluntarily while living the interwoven, grand-scale lives of which human beings are uniquely capable.[31]

Some of Zwolinski's other examples concern ownership of land and

---

30. Read (1958) famously discusses how the creation of a simple pencil from raw materials drawn from distant parts of the earth requires the work of "millions of human beings . . . no one of whom even knows more than a very few of the others." Consider how many times more people must be involved (directly or indirectly) in the creation of an automobile.

31. In these respects, rights stand to force as inference rules stand to logical validity. We can grasp the distinction between valid and invalid inferences before we know any inference rules, and indeed our grasping this distinction is a precondition for understanding any inference rules. However, there are many cases in which we need to use the inference rules to determine whether an inference is valid or invalid, and there are complex arguments that we are only able to form or entertain at all because we have an explicit knowledge of inference rules.

other resources that—unlike the car in the example just discussed—would exist even apart from people and the concept of rights. "When we take those natural resources and put a fence around them," he writes, "we are depriving nonowners of the liberty they once possessed to use that resource" and "imposing upon them an obligation to refrain from using that resource without our consent—an obligation that we will enforce with the use of physical violence, if necessary" (159). This force is retaliatory, only if using the resources without our consent constitutes an initiation of force against us. But if it does constitute force against us, Zwolinski thinks, it can only be because it violates the obligation imposed by our property right, and so force will be defined in terms of rights.

Life as such involves incorporating materials from one's environment into oneself. When a deer eats a berry, the berry becomes part of the deer, and its calories can no longer be accessed other than by eating or harnessing the deer. Yet, it is clear (I take it) that someone who kills or harnesses the deer is acting on the deer, whereas someone who eats a wild berry in the deer's neighborhood is not. A farmer's act of tilling a plot of land in the wilderness, thereby transforming it into a farm, is like the deer's act of eating the berry.[32] Both are cases of an organism incorporating something into its life. Therefore, someone who trespasses onto the farm is imposing on the farmer's life (perhaps endangering her crops, etc.), even

32. In conceiving of a use for the land and doing the work to transform it, the farmer creates the land as a value. Miller and Mossoff write that, in such cases, 100 percent of the farm's value is due to the farmer, and they criticize Locke for allowing that even 0.1 percent of the value is contributed by the land. Zwolinski interprets Miller and Mossoff's claim as resting on the fact that the work of the human mind is a necessary condition for the land to have any value at all, but he points out that the existence of the land is also a necessary condition. I don't think this is the right way to interpret their argument. The role of the mind in the land's being valuable is not that of a mere necessary condition. It is the agent that creates an actual value out of land that is only potentially valuable. Although it is true that, once a person does this, the land does not remain as an unowned item out of which someone else might forge a value. But it does not follow from this that the person has thereby diminished the stock of potential value in the world, leaving fewer opportunities for future human beings to create values. Something qualifies as a potential value only relative to some method or other of using it to sustain human life, and human beings are forever discovering new methods to make use of new things (or to make use of old things in new ways), thus the stock of potential values is ever increasing. This is true even in the case of land. Far from there being a static quantity of land to own, we find or create new land to be owned and new sorts of property rights for existing land. For example, people now own land formed by reclamation from bodies of water (like lower Manhattan, Boston's Back Bay, parts of Singapore, and much of the Netherlands), and in the future they may own land on the sea floor or on the surface of the moon; moreover, in addition to the sorts of property rights to land that were recognized in the seventeenth century, we now recognize mineral rights and air rights.

though, at an earlier time, he could have walked onto the same patch of land without affecting the farmer at all. The reason he may not enter the land anymore is the same reason he cannot eat a berry that's already been eaten by someone else: the item is no longer there to be made use of other than by making use of the person.

Thus I agree with Miller and Mossoff in thinking that there is no special problem of justifying the initial acquisition of property to anyone. The person who first transforms an item into a value by incorporating it into his life thereby owns it. But this is not to deny that there are difficult questions concerning initial acquisition and property rights. For, unlike the difference between eaten and uneaten berries, the difference between owned and unowned land is not always obvious; nor is it obvious by which actions a person can incorporate land (or anything else) into her life. Moreover, the relevant sorts of actions may change as human beings discover new ways of living that make use of land and other elements of nature in new ways. Because of these facts, we face continual questions about who owns what and about how ownership of various sorts of resources can be established.

As I see it, the central question is how a person can objectively mark off something as his, and how much he can be entitled to claim by an initial act of creation. Could the first person who invented agriculture, for example, thereby claim at a stroke all the land in the world for his farm? What about all the land of the specific sort he knew how to grow crops on? Or is what he's entitled to claim as property not the land (or not much land), but the technique of farming? I'm skeptical that philosophy can provide uniform abstract answers to such questions outside of the context of the legal system of a specific society. What it can provide is a principle of property rights that each society must intelligently tailor to its own circumstances.

The principle is that when a person finds a way to make something that was previously useless and unowned serve his life, his exclusive domain over the relevant values should be recognized by society and protected. The person who invented agriculture didn't have any way to cultivate the whole earth, to serve as a landlord over it, or even to license others to use his discovery for a fee; he wasn't in a position to even conceive of such uses for his discovery. What he had learned to do was to turn a certain patch of land into a farm; so, when he did this, that patch of land became his, by right. Others then owned the farms they created by the methods they learned from him; and, over time, systems of government and legal doctrines were developed to recognize and protect these rights (however imperfectly). As the division of labor became more advanced, the kinds of property that could be created and exploited (and the conditions needed to do this) became more complex, and so the need arose for mechanisms to register deeds, patents, copyrights, trademarks, and so on.

The process will continue as technology progresses, giving rise to new forms of property. Corresponding to each new form of property will be a new way in which one person can initiate force upon another. But, however remote these rights violations may be from the perceptibly obvious case of bodily assault, what it is for them to be initiations of force remains the same. They are instances of intruding against someone's will into the process by which he produces and enjoys the values by which he sustains his life. Thus, when faced with the question of whether some newly declared putative right really is a right, we can answer by determining whether violating it would constitute intruding in this manner into anyone's process of self-sustaining, self-generated action.

Once a rational individual living by the moral principles we have been discussing recognizes that the proposed right is genuine (such that to violate it would be to initiate force against someone else), he sees that respecting the right is in his interest. The principles enable the individual to see that the life in which his interest consists is (and is sustained by) a process of reason and production and that this process benefits from trade with other people who are engaged in this same process. Thus the individual understands that he has nothing to gain from anyone's sacrifice and that he has everything to lose from the introduction of force.

This policy of respecting the rights of others does not mean that there is no circumstance in which the individual would violate a right. A respecter of rights can recognize that there are exceptional, emergency, borderline, and marginal cases in which it is appropriate for an individual to violate a right. What it means to say that the action still violates a right is that the action imposes on someone else's life (however justifiably or marginally). The government should recognize this fact and have mechanisms to compel the perpetrator to recompense the damaged individual. What it means for an individual to respect rights, even while violating a right, is that he recognizes the legitimacy of the right, voluntarily makes any restitution he deems appropriate given the circumstances, recognizes the legitimate authority of the courts to determine whether more compensation or punishment is owed, and submits willingly to the government enforcement of the courts' decisions.

For example, a person stranded and starving in a remote area near someone else's vacant and well-stocked cabin might reasonably break into the cabin and eat the food; but when he is out of danger, he should offer to pay for the food and for any damage he might have done to the property. Moreover, if he lives in a society with reasonably objective laws, he should submit willingly to the judgment of the courts, if the owner files suit or a prosecutor brings charges.[33]

Similarly, in Zwolinski's example of a black man stranded in a racist town, it may be appropriate for the man to borrow a townsperson's phone without permission and use it to summon help from the next town. For the man to respect rights in this circumstance would mean his making a good faith effort to return the borrowed property, and his recognizing the authority of an objective judicial system to treat his action as a crime and/or tort. Part of what it would mean for the judicial system to be objective is that it could be counted on to consider the extenuating circumstances and the triviality of the crime, and not to discriminate on the basis of race.[34] The further a judicial system departs from objectivity, the less obliged individuals are to recognize its authority, and the less applicable the principle of respecting rights becomes, since the principle presupposes a context in which one is recognized as an independent equal.[35]

These two examples involve emergencies; but even in ordinary cases, it is consistent with respect for rights to occasionally engage in what one thinks are trivial, nondamaging trespasses or to occasionally breach a contract on the understanding that one is liable for damages in so doing. One of the benefits of a legal system that provides the means for adjudicating disputes and rectifying them proportionately is that it relieves one of the need to be persnickety about whether a contemplated action involves a minor violation of anyone's rights. What morality demands of

33. Joel Feinberg (1978, 102) memorably described the plight of such a "stranded backpacker," and the example has been considered in subsequent discussions of the scope and absolutism of property rights, such as Lomasky 1991 and Gaus 2012.

34. Of course, as indicated above, in any actual community so racist that no business owner would deal with the motorist, the motorist could not count on the judicial system to be objective. Too often members of racial minorities have reason to distrust law enforcement and the courts even in communities where there is little overt racism.

35. This point raises many questions about how we ought to conduct ourselves, given that the legal systems under which we all live fall short of objectivity, and given that the brunt of the resulting injustice is often born by members of particular groups (defined along racial, sexual, ideological, financial, or other lines). These are pressing questions, but I cannot pursue them here.

an individual is not legalistic caution never to step on anyone's toes but, simply, a selfish regard for others.

Such a regard consists in recognizing (in thought and action) that other human beings are individuals who must lead their own lives for their own sakes; that the values one seeks from others derive from and depend on their living in this way (rather than their living as a means to one's own ends); that one can, therefore, benefit only from consensual, nonsacrificial relationships with them; and that the principle of rights and a government to implement it are needed to banish force from society and to make all relationships consensual. It is this recognition that makes respect for rights a selfish value.

Ayn Rand and Robert Nozick on Rights

LESTER H. HUNT

M y contribution to this discussion of Robert Nozick and Ayn Rand will inevitably be somewhat off center. Having just finished writing a book on Nozick's political philosophy, I am at present far more competent to instruct people about his views than to do so with regard to hers. Accordingly, the bulk of my comments will be about him, and my comments on her will be somewhat impressionistic in tone, making little pretense at scholarly meticulousness. My ultimate aim is to discuss a point of contrast between the two philosophers. I argue that Rand's position on one important issue, or at least a position that is in the spirit of her philosophy, is a stronger one than his position on the same issue, and that indeed this can be argued to some extent on the basis of principles that Nozick himself might accept.

Both Rand and Nozick base their arguments for their political principles on moral grounds. Neither of them thinks of the political, as Nozick would put it, as "a completely autonomous realm" (1974, 6). For both philosophers, the realm of politics, like the rest of human life, is subject to moral judgment, and moral principles that are to be applied to political agents are the same as the ones that apply to ordinary human beings. The state and its representatives, according to both of them, are not a unique breed apart from the rest of us.

From here on, however, they seem to sharply part ways. If the moral is the foundation of the political, what is the foundation of the moral? To this question, Rand clearly has answers. She thinks of herself as a systematic thinker, in the sense that her ideas exhibit a definite logical structure: some are based on others and are based ultimately on certain clearly identified first principles. Nozick's philosophical method seems very different. Like many contemporary "analytic" philosophers, he typically takes an approach that might be called "methodological intuitionism," in that he appeals to reader's moral judgments, typically in response to concrete hypothetical cases, and builds his case on these judgments, which he assumes will be the same as his own. Although the political argument is based on ethical ideas, his ethical thinking itself seems to be foundationless (see Nagel 1975).

This impression, though I suspect it is widely shared, is an illusion. It is actually not true that Nozick offers no theoretical basis for his ethical principles. The most important substantive ethical idea in his *Anarchy, State, and Utopia* (an idea with which Rand would stand in broad agreement) is what he calls "the libertarian constraint." This idea, as he puts it, "prohibits aggression against another"—that is, it prohibits the initiation of force (Nozick 1974, 33). Roughly speaking, it prohibits the use of force—except in response to action that is wrong in the same way that force is wrong, action that violates rights. He offers a "formal argument" (identified as such in the index) for this principle. He also calls it an "argument from moral form to moral content" (34). As we will see in a moment, it involves ideas that place his moral thinking close to that of Immanuel Kant and, thus, in sharp contrast to the forthrightly naturalistic position taken by Rand.

Nozick points out that rights, as we typically think of them, have a feature that is puzzling. A right, he says, is a moral concern that can be interpreted in more than one way. To put it in terms of an example, suppose that in our community some terrorists capture six innocent people, holding them hostage, and that they convince us they will begin executing their hostages one at a time unless we hand over to them one other member of the community, someone they were not able to get their hands on so easily, someone who happens to be, like the hostages, perfectly innocent. Suppose we are certain that if we did this, this one person would be executed, but the other six would be released. If we do comply with their demands, we will save five lives. Suppose, further, that capturing this one person and giving him or her to terrorists is the only way we can save these lives. Should we? Most people of whom I have asked this question say no—and by a wide margin! Why? One way to put the most likely answer would be to say that we think of this person as having a right to life. But what sort of moral concern is this right to life, exactly?

After all, the six hostages have a right to life as well. If the non–violation of rights is so important, why don't we treat it as a goal (or, as Nozick sometimes puts it, an "end-state") to be maximized? And if we do not treat the non–violation of rights as a goal, in this sense, what other sort of moral consideration can a right be? Nozick's answer is that we can treat rights as what he calls "side constraints" or, more simply, "constraints."

But what sort of moral concern is a constraint? Nozick insists that a constraint cannot be explained as a special sort of goal. A goal is something that we seek. A constraint is a principle that denies us certain means in the pursuit of our goals. To say this, though, only sharpens the issue somewhat. Why, in our conduct toward our fellow human beings, does it make sense to observe constraints? Why not simply maximize our goals?

At this point Rand's way of thinking veers sharply off the path that Nozick is treading, as she would reject this question, at least in the form in which I have stated it. As an ethical egoist, she holds that pursuing a goal—the best life for oneself—is exactly what we should be doing. Individual rights, as long as they are genuine rights, do not deny us any means—that is, any genuine means—of pursuing this ultimate goal.[1] As Nozick thinks of them, a decent person's commitment to observe these moral considerations necessarily includes a willingness to do so even if they do require one to forgo to some extent the achievement of one's goals, including goals that are very important. I think it would be a mistake, however, to assume that because Nozick's treatment of the issues raised by this question is irrelevant to anyone who approaches these issues on the basis of egoistic premises, that he is grappling with a problem they simply do not have to face. It is true enough that a consistent ethical egoist who recognizes individual rights does not think that such rights deny him what he ultimately wants, but I will argue in a moment that, assuming that one observes rights as a matter of principle, an egoistic po-

---

1. This feature of the issue, which I had previously overlooked, was brought to my attention by Onkar Ghate in our exchange at the 2014 Eastern Division meetings of the American Philosophical Association on which this essay is based.

sition does raise a problem to which some of Nozick's discussion is indeed relevant.

Nozick, as I say, does attempt to answer the question of why it makes sense to observe constraints, and he does so in widely separated sections of chapter 3 of his book. One is the section for which the question actually serves as it title: "Why Side Constraints?" The other is titled "What Are Constraints Based On?"

In the former section he frames the issue that lies behind the problem about rights and constraints in quite general terms: "Isn't it irrational to accept a side constraint C, rather than a view that directs the minimization of violations of C? . . . If nonviolation of C is so important, shouldn't that be the goal? How can a concern for the nonviolation of C lead to the refusal to violate C even when this would prevent other more extensive violations of C? What is the rationale for placing the nonviolation of rights as a side constraint upon action instead of including it solely as a goal of one's actions?" (Nozick 1974, 30).

As he points out in a later book, *The Nature of Rationality*, during the twentieth century there were great advances in our theoretical understanding of "individual rationality and rational interactions among people" in such technical fields as "decision theory, game theory, probability theory, and theories of statistical inference" (1993, xv–xvi). I would add microeconomics to this list, and the branch of economics known as "value theory." Generally, the conception of rationality involved in these fields of investigation amounts to seeing it as maximizing (or optimizing or satisficing) the expected value of the results of one's actions. Although they do not rest on single-goal theories like old-fashioned hedonism and classical utilitarianism, nor indeed on ethical egoism, these fields are in effect goal-based, in that they treat rationality as a function of the expected value of goals that are achieved by one's actions. This means that, according to the best, most powerful theories of rationality available to us, to knowingly forgo an action that would produce more net value than any alternative action is simply irrational. But if one accepts a side constraint, one will sooner or later be doing precisely that. One would expect that a principle that puts methods and means to achieving goals out of one's reach would eventually mean that one achieves fewer of one's goals. How can this be rational?

Nozick's attempt to resolve this issue is based not so much on an analysis of constraints, nor yet on an attempt to replace or revise the maximizing (or optimizing, etc.) conception of rationality, as on an account of the subject matter to which side constraints apply. Moral constraints make sense because they are about persons, and persons are special. If we were to drop constraints and use the standard of violation minimization, we would be working a profound change in the moral status of the human individual: "Side constraints reflect the underlying Kantian principle that individuals are ends and not merely means: They may not be sacrificed or used for the achieving of other ends without their consent. Individuals are inviolable" (Nozick 1974, 30–31).

Exactly how do side constraints, as he puts it, "reflect" this "Kantian principle"? Probably the greater part of his answer is to be found in this often quoted statement in the "Why Side Constraints?" section:

> Side constraints express the inviolability of persons. But why may not one violate persons for the greater social good? Individually, we each sometimes choose to undergo some pain or sacrifice for a greater benefit or to avoid a greater harm: We go to the dentist to avoid worse suffering later; we do some unpleasant work for its results. . . . In each case, some cost is borne for the sake of the greater overall good. Why not, *similarly*, hold that some persons have to bear some costs that benefit other persons more, for the sake of the overall social good? But there is no social entity with a good that undergoes some sacrifice for its own good. There are only individual people, different individual people, with their own individual lives. Using one of these people for the benefit of others, uses him and benefits others. Nothing more. What happens is that something is done to him for the sake of others. Talk of an overall social good covers this up. (Nozick 1974, 32–33)

Here, as throughout the book, Nozick is thinking of utilitarianism as his principal opponent in the realm of ethics. He is rejecting it on the grounds that the one really powerful reason for adopting it rests on a false assumption. This powerful reason rests in part on the conception of rationality that I have just been discussing, which holds that what makes an action rational is that it can be expected, based on available evidence, to maximize the good. The utilitarian identifies this good with the collective good, the good of everyone, added together. In Nozick's view, this would only be a strong argument if there were some being that benefits from this collective sum, which is not the case. Rights, as constraints on maximizing behavior, function to block the sacrifice of the interests of the individual for the sake of the alleged interests of the group.

This, though, is at best only a partial answer to the question about how it makes sense to recognize constraints. So far, Nozick has only argued for one negative feature of constraints, that they do not allow sacrificing individuals to the group, and he has done so on the basis of a negative feature of human beings, which is that they do not add up to a collective super-entity. How can it be rational, more generally, to forgo goal-pursuit by observing constraints on the pursuit of those goals?

This is the issue he treats in the section "What Are Constraints Based On?" There, he discusses the old questions: What sorts of beings have rights? What is the feature on the basis of which they are entitled to the sort of consideration we give to beings that have rights? He lists features that, according to one traditional proposal or another, are supposed to answer this question: (1) sentience and self-consciousness; (2) rationality, or the capacity to use abstract concepts; (3) possessing free will; (4) being a moral agent, or having the capacity to follow moral principles; and (5) having a soul. With the possible exception of the last item on the list, he faults them all for failing to meet a requirement that he thinks any theory of this sort must meet: "It would appear that a person's characteristics, by virtue of which others are constrained in their treatment of him, must themselves be valuable characteristics. How else are we to understand why something so valuable emerges from them? (This natural assumption is worth further scrutiny)" (1974, 48).

At first sight, the "natural assumption" does not seem intuitively appealing. Why can good things only be explained by other good things? Perhaps he means that the characteristic we seek must be valuable in order to explain why it results in such a *transfer* of value from the rest of us to that person. Respecting the rights of others means, in Nozickean terms, forgoing many opportunities to advance one's own goals, or at least being prepared to forgo them. This is what it means to view rights as constraints. This raises a problem that any theory of moral constraints must also eventually face, one that we have already posed, which is that constrained behavior seems to mean forgoing value. How can this be rational? I would like to suggest that, though Nozick does not explicitly deal with the issue of the rationality of constraints in the section on what constraints are based on, he does say some things that can help reduce the urgency of that problem.

He says that, in addition to the traditional list of not-particularly-valuable characteristics, we need "an intervening variable M" for which these features constitute necessary conditions. Actually, in his discussion of this issue, he focuses on items 2 through 4—rationality, free will, and moral agency. He brings the soul (item 5) back into the discussion in a way that gives it a different status from the other features, while sentience (number 1) for some reason drops out of the picture (though one could say that he addresses it later, in the section of chapter 3 on the moral status of animals). While being based in some way on these features, M must also have a "perspicuous and convincing" connection to constraints, so that it illuminates both the constraints and the features on which they allegedly are based (1974, 49).

These three features, he says, unite to form another important feature of persons: the capacity to form long-term plans and to guide one's life on the basis of a chosen overall conception of it. The moral importance of this feature, he says, is to be found in the fact that it leads to another important feature, namely, meaning: a "person's shaping his life in accordance with some overall plan is his way of giving meaning to his life" (Nozick 1974, 50). He explicitly leaves open the question of whether these two features are identical (that is, whether meaning simply *is* having a plan) or whether long-term planning is only a necessary condition of the creation of meaning. He also leaves open the question as to which of the two features is supposed to be M, or whether they both are. He ends by raising questions about how meaning is related to the content of moral constraints. Is it that the behavior that violates a person's rights is incompatible with their having a meaningful life? Or should we construct something like utilitarianism, but with meaningfulness as the maximand instead of happiness? Or does the notion of meaning enter ethics, as he says, "in a different fashion"—apparently meaning some fashion other than determining the content of the moral constraints.

Nozick is sometimes misunderstood on this point.[2] He is not saying we can derive ethical content from the notion of a meaningful life. This, however, leaves the point of this section of *Anarchy, State, and Utopia* somewhat obscure. It seems clear enough that he wants M to explain constraints. But if it doesn't explain their content, just how does it explain them? I suggest that it might shed explanatory light on the rationality of

---

2. Narveson (1988, 167) attributes to him the idea that a being with feature M "would just obviously accord libertarian rights to all other M-beings." This is not Nozick's position. Narveson also tells us that the M stands for "Meaningfulness." Actually, Nozick never tells us what M is short for, if anything.

having constraints at all. This possibility becomes a little more apparent if we consider something that Nozick does not seem to notice: There are other candidates for M in the history of ethics in addition to the one that he offers. Interestingly, they tend to have certain things in common.

First, consider the criteria for M that Nozick has lain down. There are the two I have already mentioned, that the items on the traditional list of features (at least the three that get the focus of his attention) should be necessary for M, and that M should shed some sort of explanatory light on constraints. In addition, he says that, because M (whatever it is) satisfies the first criterion, it should also help to explain why people have traditionally "concentrated on" these features. He also mentions, as an interesting characteristic of his own version of M, that it has the "feel" of something that might help to bridge the gap between "is" and "ought," as it seems to "straddle" the boundary between them. He does not lay this down explicitly as a characteristic that M must have but it makes sense to suppose it is, given that constraints are "oughts" and the traditional features they are supposed to be based on seem to be pure "ises."

One philosopher who has explicitly argued that there is a certain trait of persons that meets most of Nozick's criteria is Immanuel Kant. This is hardly surprising, as Nozick's ethical views in *Anarchy, State, and Utopia* are, as I have said, in the Kantian tradition. However, Kant's version of M is interestingly different from Nozick's. Kant's version of M, the all-important characteristic, is that of being a source of the moral law. More precisely, Kant thought that the moral law springs from pure reason and that each person is an instance of "rational nature." Kant argues explicitly that rationality, free will, and moral agency (in Nozick's sense) are necessary components of the trait that gives a person this special status. In addition, it is at least arguable that Kant's notion of Pure Practical Reason can explain why people think these features are ethically important, and also that it straddles the is/ought divide. As to the light it might shed on constraints, I will get to that in a moment.

Some might wonder at this point if M-traits are, so to speak, "for Kantians only," that they only have any point within the framework of a more or less Kantian moral theory. I would say that their application and relevance is much wider than that. I think one can easily sketch out another example of a possible M-trait, one that can give us a theory that is a good deal more naturalistic than those of Nozick and Kant. This view seems to me to be more or less in the spirit of some of the arguments that

John Locke gives in favor of property rights and also, more closely, in the spirit of Ayn Rand's account of rights.[3]

The view I have in mind can be roughly summarized as follows: Humans, unlike all other animals, must produce the wherewithal to live. Other animals live by consuming portions of their environment. The deer consumes grass, and the wolf pack consumes the deer. Even the hunter-gatherer way of life, the closest that human life comes to the pure consumption way of life of other animals, involves producing weapons, tools, clothing, and shelter. With the advent of agriculture, humans turned to producing their food as well. Radically altering their environment, they constantly respond to unforeseen effects. Rather than respond to the same situations in the same way or with a finite repertory of behavioral responses, as other animals do, they constantly develop new and better solutions to problems. In other words, they do not merely react to the environment (which eventually becomes to a large extent their own creation), they have ideas about it and develop new ideas. Because all this effort aims at producing things to be used by human beings in their efforts to survive and flourish, it results in material that is indeed very valuable to humans, sometimes large masses of such material. This attracts the attention of human predators who would live off the productive efforts of others. That threatens productivity itself, which requires social cooperation of increasingly complex sorts. The human predator thus poses a problem, surely one of the most serious problems, for human survival itself. But humans have long had a crucial part of the solution to this problem, or this productivity would never have reached its present level in the first place: There are norms protecting the productive against predators and enabling the social cooperation that productivity requires. Many of these norms can be interpreted in Nozickean terms as constraints.

These three versions of M differ in important ways. Kant's version, unlike Nozick's and the Randian/Lockean one I have imagined, carries heavy metaphysical baggage. On the other hand, the Rand/Locke version and that of Kant have implications as to the content of the constraints, while that of Nozick probably does not. One thing I think they *all* have in common is, however, the explanatory light they can shed on moral constraints. The sort of illumination I have in mind is of a very particular

3. Locke, *Two Treatises of Government*, 2:5. For the most relevant passages in Rand, see *VOS* chapter 1, "The Objectivist Ethics" (esp. 36–37); chapter 12, "Man's Rights" (esp. 108–15); and chapter 14, "The Nature of Government" (esp. 126–27). See also her *CUI* chapter 1, "What Is Capitalism?" (esp. 18–20).

sort. Notice that each of them attributes a sort of value to persons. The characteristics they attribute to persons—giving meaning to things, being a law-giver, being a creator—are all attributes that traditionally belong to the divine. I would not want to lean too hard on this way of putting the point, but it does suggest something about the kind of value we are attributing to M-beings. This is not the sort of value that one has as a means to an end. This sort of value is not a matter of the uses the being might serve but, rather, of what attitudes are appropriate toward it. Traditionally, the attitudes appropriate toward the divine include reverence and worship. The idea of reverencing or worshiping persons, simply as persons, might seem odd, but Rand did once describe the "sense of life" embodied in *The Fountainhead* as "man-worship."[4] In addition, there are other attitudes that might be appropriate to a being that possesses only a mere touch of divinity, such as respect. Respect (*Achtung*) was in fact Kant's word for the attitude he believed was appropriate to beings with his version of M.

What could this have to do with the problem of the rationality of constraints? Notice that there is an aspect of the problem that really is an issue about the appropriateness of attitudes. The general problem about the rationality of constraints rests on the fact that constraints are obstacles to achieving our goals. If you consistently conform to a constraint then—sooner or later, and perhaps very often—there will be some increment of value that you will not achieve, but that you could have achieved if you had violated the constraint. In Nozick's way of understanding constraints, this might well be an on-the-whole and in-the-long-run loss of achievable value. This is an issue about the rationality of action, and it is the sort of rationality that the value-maximizing conception of rationality is about. But actions are not the only sort of thing that can be rational or irrational. We can ask whether it is rational to do a certain thing, but we can also ask whether it is rational to fear bats, to love people who do not love us in return, or to hope for resurrection and eternal life. These latter sorts of questions are not directly about action. They are about attitudes. In particular, they are about whether a given attitude is appropriate to its object.

The attitude-appropriateness issue, where side constraints are concerned, is based on the fact that, though it is true that side constraints such as individual rights are obstacles to achieving one's goals, this is not

4. "Introduction," *Fountainhead* ix.

how a morally decent person sees them.[5] Suppose that I see you have un-knowingly dropped a fifty-dollar bill, which I could easily pick up unde-tected and walk away with. Instead, I hand it to you. I could have spent it on things that I value, but I forgo whatever good I would thereby have reaped because such behavior would violate your rights. Yet if I am a de-cent person, I do not at that moment perceive your rights as obstacles to my achieving good things.

One might think that this is a truth about constraints and not about M-beings, such as persons. Perhaps decent people never see constraints as frustrating obstacles. But this is not true. Imagine that you are driving to work, worried that you might arrive late, and a traffic signal turns yellow, then red just a shade too early for you to slip through the intersection. You might well feel that you have confronted an annoying obstacle to achieving one of your goals. This is so, despite the fact that you recognize you mustn't cross against a red light—in fact, it is *because* of this very fact, since your recognition of this constraint is precisely the obstacle you face. Yet it is hard to imagine looking at the rights of persons in this way, although in a way they are, from a Nozickean point of view, obstacles of the same sort.

Persons and traffic signals are alike in that both represent to us con-straints on our conduct, but they are also profoundly different. The var-ious versions of M offer explanations of the difference. Each can be used as a basis for attributing to persons the peculiar sort of value that Kant called "dignity," while denying it to a mere mechanism such as a traffic signal. Individual rights can be seen as imposing costs upon us, but hu-man beings, as we see it, are *worth it*; so much so that we do not ordinarily see these effects as costs at all.

Perhaps the Nozickean problem of the rationality of constraints can be solved by connecting the problem about the rationality of constrained action with the other sort of rationality, the rationality of attitude-appropriateness. If one has a certain attitude, considerations can be plau-sible reasons for action though they do not appear from another perspec-tive to be reasons at all. From the perspective of the value-maximizing conception of rationality, constraints do not make sense as reasons for action. From the perspective of respect for persons grounded on some version of M, they do. Perhaps a solid case for the rationality of that atti-tude can solve, or *dis*solve, the problem of the rationality of constraints.

5. I discuss this phenomenon more elaborately in Hunt 1997, 171–75.

Now back to an issue I broached earlier on: if ethical egoism implies that rights are not really constraints, what value do any of these considerations have from that point of view? To some extent, I suppose the proper answer to this is obvious, from things I have said more recently. The relevance enters the picture if and when the egoist recognizes rights, as the Rand-style egoist does. Regardless of what one thinks of the ultimate grounding of individual rights, respecting the rights of others always means forgoing opportunities for the advancement of one's goals in the short run. Of course, the rights-respecting egoist views the matter from a larger, more inclusive viewpoint, from which one can see that one is not forgoing value at all. But what exactly is this larger view? If it is simply the long-run view, then the theory would be that refraining from violating individual rights is something that always involves accepting short-term deficits for larger long-term benefits. This seems to raise the same problem that is faced by the constraint view, albeit in a milder form. It is still true that one could spend the money one does not steal on things that one now desires. This is not a matter of philosophy but of undeniable fact. Yet consciousness of this fact, as such, does not seem to be reflected in the psychology of what we ordinarily think of as a decent person. Just as we normally do not perceive such things as the acceptance of net loss, or possible net loss, incurred in the name of observing a constraint, so we do not perceive them as a matter of incurring short-term deficits either. Naturally, the ethical theorist is perfectly capable of revising this commonsense view, of declaring it to be wrong, at least in part. Yet the revision that the theory would be making in this case does not seem right. The notion of incurring short-term deficits does not ring true as an account of the way rights are related to value. There seems to be more to it than can be brought to light by a short-term-versus-long-term analysis. What more might there be? Here Nozick's discussion of the need in ethical theory for an M-type feature is helpful. More precisely, what is helpful is the possibility it yields for supporting a view of the value of persons as rights-holders. This sort of value, whether we think of it in terms of man-worship or of respect, is a sort of value that exists in the present: there is no delayed gratification involved, no waiting needed.

In addition, there is a fact that I think is implied by things I have already said but perhaps should be made explicit: not only does the problem Nozick's version of M is meant to solve have a close cousin that is still a problem for the Randian egoist, but the Locke/Rand version of the solution is arguably superior to those posed by both Nozick and his predecessor, Kant. First, it is at least on the same footing as the two others with respect to the two criteria for M that he lays down: it sheds a certain explanatory light on constraints by connecting them with value, and it helps explain why traditional ethical theory has concentrated on the items in Nozick's original list: most obviously, items 1 through 4. Obviously, the vision of "man the producer," as we might call it, uses and integrates the ideas of consciousness, rationality, choice, and the capacity to follow moral principles. It also has the other desirable feature he mentions, of "bridging" the "is/ought" divide. "Producer," here, does not mean simply one who causes something, just anything, to come into existence, but one who brings about things that are useful to human beings in their struggle to survive and flourish. When we bring this concept into our theories, we enter the realm of value. As I have pointed out, this version of M is superior to Kant's in its relative lack of purely speculative assumptions and is superior to Nozick's in that it does seem to have very broad and substantial implications for the actual content of rights and other moral principles. Just as production and predation are definite things, so the selection of principles that protect the one against the other is a far from arbitrary process. However the details might be worked out, what we have seen here is that it also invests the whole of morality with a meaning and a value it would not otherwise have: not an irksome necessity but a framework for human greatness.

Rand (contra Nozick) on Individual Rights and the Emergence and Justification of Government

ONKAR GHATE

N ozick's political position in *Anarchy, State, and Utopia* (Nozick 1974; hereafter *ASU*) might seem similar to the political position argued for by Rand in the 1950s and 1960s, in works such as *Atlas Shrugged, The Virtue of Selfishness,* and *Capitalism: The Unknown Ideal,* all three of which are listed in *ASU*'s bibliography (358). Both philosophers in some sense support the "night watchman state of classical liberal theory" (*ASU* 25), and both view its justification as resting essentially in the principle of individual rights. The use of this principle as the foundation for proper government they trace back to Locke (Nozick's special emphasis) and to America's Founding Fathers (Rand's special emphasis).

But although the similarities in position and argument are real, I think the differences swamp the similarities, particularly in terms of their fundamental approaches to political philosophy and their conceptions of individual rights. Attending to these differences sheds light on each thinker's viewpoint and helps generate thought about political philosophy as such and the principle of individual rights in particular. In any case, these basic differences are my focus. That they are my focus, however, should not be taken to mean that I think the similarities are nonexistent or uninteresting. I will take up four main issues, contrasting Rand's less-well-known perspective on these to Nozick's perspective in *ASU*: state-of-nature theory, the philosophical status of the principle of individual rights, answering objections from the individual anarchist, and the need in political philosophy for a radically new moral foundation.

State of Nature Theory

Nozick classifies his approach to political philosophy as a state-of-nature theory. Rand does not so classify hers. The difference is significant.

Roughly put, to project a state of nature is to project a period of humankind's existence in which people interact pre-government. A state-of-nature theory analyzes what human life is like in a state of nature and why government could/would/should emerge from it. This analysis is thought to (help) explain the features of a proper state and to (help) justify it.

Nozick acknowledges that his story of how a proper state could/would/should emerge from his projected state of nature is not historically accurate, but history is not his purpose. He also seems aware of the fact, although he does not emphasize it, that his projected state of nature itself is not a depiction of any historical period, not even in broad strokes. Looking at the issue from the standpoint of explanatory political theory, Nozick states the first point this way: a "theory of a state of nature that begins with fundamental general descriptions of morally permissible and impermissible actions, and of deeply based reasons why some persons in any society would violate these moral constraints, and goes on to describe how a state would arise from that state of nature will serve our explanatory purposes, *even if no actual state ever arose that way*" (*ASU* 7, original emphasis). His explanatory purpose here is to show that the features and principles governing a proper state are fully derivable from the nonpolitical—in this case, from moral concerns and principles.

The attempt to show this, Nozick realizes, meshes with a major concern of his from the standpoint of political philosophy, which is to answer the individual anarchist. "Since I begin with a strong formulation of individual rights, I treat seriously the anarchist claim that in the course of maintaining its monopoly on the use of force and protecting everyone within a territory, the state must violate the individual's rights and hence is intrinsically immoral. Against this claim, I argue that a state would arise from anarchy (as represented by Locke's state of nature) even though no one intended this or tried to bring it about, by a process which need not violate anyone's rights" (*ASU* xi).

It is informative to ask why Nozick takes this approach to answering the anarchist. Why not argue *directly* that the governmental actions that the anarchist claims violate the individual's rights are not in fact violations of those rights? Why does Nozick argue *indirectly*, arguing that, from a stateless period of existence, a state that performs the actions in question would emerge by a process that need not have violated anyone's rights? And why is it important that the state's emergence be *unintended*? I suspect that one of the main reasons Nozick takes the approach he does is that it was a conversation with the economist-anarchist Murray Rothbard that "stimulated his interest in individualist anarchist theory" (*ASU* xv). One can see in *ASU* an attempt to use Rothbard's framework against himself. If Nozick can show Rothbard that by an invisible hand—that is, by the "market forces" that Rothbard allegedly prizes—persons in a stateless existence, in which their individual rights are generally recognized and respected by themselves and others, would or could create a state through a series of rights-respecting steps, even though no one was trying to, then Rothbard's objection to the state dissolves.

In contrast to all this, Rand does not ground her position in state-of-nature theory, and she rejects the idea that a proper state does or can emerge unintentionally, by an invisible hand. Her reasons for doing so, as we will see, center on her very different conception of individual rights. Like Nozick she does address the anarchist's objections, but she answers them directly.[1] Before discussing these crucial points of difference, however, it is helpful to establish some points of contact. Even though Rand is not offering a state-of-nature theory, she does agree with some of the reasons that are often thought to motivate such a theory; and, using a projection somewhat similar to a state of nature, she does stress the importance to political philosophy of considering the individual alone, outside of society. To set the proper context, let us consider three factors that often motivate state-of-nature theory.

One goal often sought by political thinkers in projecting a state of nature is to help show that neither government nor society is a moral authority whose pronouncements, in laws or conventions, determine what is morally good or evil. If it is clear that in a scenario in which a state or social system does not yet exist, moral distinctions would neverthe-

---

1. It should be noted that although Rand does discuss anarchy in her writings about individual rights and government, and she is familiar with some of the arguments of Rothbard and other contemporaneous anarchists, she regards the advocacy of anarchy by alleged capitalists and freedom fighters as, at best, a "naïve floating abstraction" that amounts to support for some form of despotism. See "The Nature of Government" (*VOS* 131); Peikoff 1991, 371–73.

less still exist, this highlights the idea that the source of morality lies elsewhere. This is a point on which Nozick and Rand agree, but neither uses a state of nature to emphasize the point. The priority of the moral to the political is an *assumption* of Nozick's projected state of nature: it is a scenario in which individuals largely follow moral principles but are ignorant of states and governments, which do not yet exist. Rand does emphasize the nonsocial nature of morality, but her chosen projection is not individuals interacting in a stateless period of existence but, rather, an individual alone on a desert island: "it is on a desert island that he would need [morality] most" (*Atlas* 936).

A second value often sought by political thinkers in projecting a state of nature is to help draw attention to both the positives and negatives that governments can bring. Nozick and Rand regard this as a real value, though in slightly different ways. In projecting his state of nature, in which individuals generally act morally, Nozick seeks to contrast "the best anarchic situation one reasonably could hope for" with life governed by a proper state. "If one could show that the state would be superior to this most favored situation of anarchy . . . or would arise by a process involving no morally impermissible steps, or would be an improvement if it arose, this . . . would justify the state" (*ASU* 5). This contrast helps isolate the benefits that the best state can bring as well as any accompanying negatives. I think Rand would agree that it is useful to contrast stateless periods of human existence with various forms of the state, but she does not think of anarchy as a stable situation to which one should make comparisons.[2] Moreover, she thinks that political philosophy rests on a deeper question than Nozick recognizes.

What Nozick calls the fundamental question of political philosophy—"Should there be any state at all?" (*ASU* 4)—is not for Rand the first question. The first question is why should an individual seek a social existence? And then, why, more specifically, should he value an organized society with other individuals, many of whom are strangers? What are the benefits obtainable in society and on what terms? It is a crucial but later question whether those terms include the formation of a government and, if so, what kind of government. Thus Rand begins her article "The Nature of Government" by stressing that a social environment is most conducive to a human being's survival because it makes possible a vast increase in knowledge and trade. The pursuit of these benefits of social existence

---

2. See "The Nature of Government" (*VOS*); Peikoff 1991, 371–72.

helps establish the fundamental principles that should govern organized social life, including why and what kind of government is needed. In setting up the issue in this way, Rand's first point of contrast is again not individuals interacting in a stateless period of existence but an individual alone on a desert island (*VOS* 125–26).

The third value often sought by political thinkers in projecting a state of nature is to highlight the metaphysical requirements of the individual's survival. This is a point of vital emphasis for Rand, and I think for Locke—but not for Nozick. Here too, however, for Rand the better contrast to civilized life is not the individual interacting with other individuals in a stateless period of existence, but Robinson Crusoe acting alone on a desert island. By asking us to strip away the many conveniences of organized society, to think of an individual standing alone and trying to survive in reality, this projection helps us isolate the necessary, inescapable conditions of self-preservation—conditions that organized society should heed and protect. And by focusing on an individual standing alone, this projection helps one appreciate that the individual can preserve himself even when others are acting in self-destructive ways.[3]

The reason that these issues about self-preservation are so important to Rand is that her ethics stresses that the quest of morality is the quest for self-preservation. "Do they tell you that the purpose of morality is to curb man's instinct of self-preservation? It is for the purpose of self-preservation that man needs a code of morality" (*Atlas* 928–29). Any morally proper form of social or political organization should recognize this fundamental point. Both *Atlas Shrugged* and *The Fountainhead* emphasize that self-preservation is an individual affair; that an individual must learn to face nature alone, as if on a desert island; that there exists unalterable survival requirements, and that life in society does not and cannot change these, only obscure them. In her later nonfiction Rand argues that a proper social system will explicitly identify and respect the survival requirements of the individual, which on her view is precisely what the principle of individual rights does and why it is the foundational principle of political philosophy. "The social recognition of man's rational nature—of the connection between his survival and his use of reason—is the concept of *individual rights*" ("What Is Capitalism?" *CUI* 9; original emphasis). And this means that *"Individual rights are the means of subordinating society to moral law"* ("Man's Rights," *VOS* 108).

3. See "What Is Capitalism?" (*CUI*, especially 1–12).

To sum up the context now established, Rand like Nozick thinks morality precedes politics and that proper government must be grounded in and derived from moral principle. Rand like Nozick thinks that it is important to pay careful attention to both the positives and negatives that governments can bring, though she thinks the first question of political philosophy is not why should there be a state but why should the individual seek social organization. However, Rand, like Locke but unlike Nozick, thinks that the issue of self-preservation is foundational to the principle of individual rights, that this principle is *explicitly* based on the morally crucial idea that the individual survives by reason, and that it is *explicitly* formulated to subordinate society and government to moral principle. This last point will be central to what I discuss in the remainder of the essay.

The Philosophical Status of the Principle of Individual Rights

For Nozick, individual rights are moral principles that can be reached and grasped outside of society, in a state of nature; certainly, they are not inherently political. The persons interacting in Nozick's projected state of nature have knowledge of their rights, including of at least aspects of these rights' exercise and implementation, but no knowledge of states or governments. If they had such knowledge—if, for instance, they had some knowledge of better and worse forms of government—the idea of offering an invisible-hand account of the emergence of a state would be problematic. For Rand, by contrast, the moral principle of individual rights *is inherently political*. For Rand, therefore, Nozick's projected state of nature embodies a contradiction. Let us explore why.

To begin, Rand as I have said views the principle of individual rights as *explicitly* formulated to subordinate might to right and to reconstruct government, placing government on a firm and proper base. She regards the principle of individual rights as the foundation of the American experiment and, because of the success of the Revolution and the promise of the Declaration of Independence, holds that "an ideal social system had once been almost within men's reach" ("Introduction," *CUI* viii). The explanation of the creation of the United States is not an invisible hand. Far from it. The creation of the United States required lengthy, sustained, conscious thinking about government and the individual's relation to the state, thinking that dates back to at least the early part of the Enlightenment. Among other subjects examined, such as history and law, this meant developments in both ethics and political philosophy. In ethics, there was a conscious focus on the importance of self-preservation and the conditions that individual self-preservation requires. In political philosophy, there was a rethinking of the purpose of government and a shift from viewing government as master of the individual to viewing it as the individual's servant. For Rand, this thinking culminates in the Declaration of Independence and the US Constitution, documents created by a process that is diametrically the opposite of unintended.

At the core of this new philosophical thinking was the principle of individual rights, which Rand maintains is simultaneously a moral and a political principle. It lies at the border of ethics and political philosophy. Its dual nature is important. Crucial to the formulation of the principle is some understanding of the fact that ethics is about an individual's basic relationship to reality: morality is essentially individual and nonsocial. But there are enormous values the individual can gain from life in society. A proper social system will be one within which the individual can lead a moral life and gain the benefits of social existence while avoiding the potential harms. The principle of individual rights is the conceptualization of the fundamental conditions that a proper government and social system must meet, a specification of the sphere in which the individual must be sovereign and free to act, a sphere determined by the nature of morality and, underneath that, by the nature of reality and the nature of human beings. (As mentioned earlier, one purpose in projecting a state of nature may be to help isolate these moral and metaphysical conditions.)

Here is Rand setting out her full conception of the principle's foundation, in a formulation that integrates the metaphysical, moral, social, and political nature of rights:

> The source of man's rights is not divine law or congressional law, but the law of identity. A is A—and Man is Man. *Rights* are conditions of existence required by man's nature for his proper survival. If man is to live on earth, it is *right* for him to use his mind, it is *right* to act on his own free judgment, it is *right* to work for his values and to keep the product of his work. If life on earth is his purpose, he has a *right* to live as a rational being: nature forbids him the irrational. Any group, any gang, any nation that attempts to negate man's rights, is *wrong*, which means: is evil, which means: is anti-life. (*Atlas* 972)

As this passage suggests, for Rand the principle of individual rights is formed in the context of thinking about the individual's life in society. Rand's formal definition of individual rights captures the fact that they do not exist ready-made in nature and are not arrived at simply by an individual's moral self-reflection. They are principles that must be consciously formulated and delineated by new, systematic thinking about *morality*, *society*, and *government*: "The principle of man's individual rights represented the extension of morality into the social system—as a limitation on the power of the state, as man's protection against the brute force of the collective, as the subordination of *might* to *right*." And then her formal definition: "A 'right' is a moral principle defining and sanctioning a man's freedom of action in a social context" ("Man's Rights," *VOS* 109–10).

To first reach the idea and then to properly formulate the principle of individual rights, Rand regards as momentous achievements. The mature principle integrates a vast amount of knowledge in terms of philosophical essentials: a metaphysical-epistemological recognition that the individual survives by the independent exercise of his rational mind, a moral recognition of the importance of self-preservation, and a political recognition of the benefits of life in society along with its potential dangers, including careful philosophical, political, legal, and historical consideration of how to organize society and government in order to systematically achieve the benefits of social organization and avoid the dangers. The principle of individual rights is an explicit, *new* conceptualization of the proper foundation for an organized society and its government. "The concept of individual rights is so new in human history," Rand writes, "that most men have not grasped it fully to this day" ("Man's Rights," *VOS* 111). This perspective on the principle of individual rights as a wide-scale philosophical-historical integration is not Nozick's perspective in *ASU*.

And this I think is why Rand would maintain that Nozick's projected state of nature embodies a contradiction. For Rand there is no such possibility as a number of individuals existing prior to the creation of any state yet, somehow, in possession of knowledge of their "individual rights" and of (some) knowledge of how to secure and protect these rights. When thinking about stateless periods of human existence one should think about actual stateless periods of human existence (as Locke did), such as the existence of some of the tribes inhabiting parts of North America prior to the arrival of European settlers. Nozick's state of nature is much too civilized, too much unlike tribes and similar forms of historical existence before the creation of a state. If we are really projecting a time before a state existed, we must not think of persons as explicitly grasping that they have a right to life, liberty, property, and the pursuit of happiness and must not think of them as going around hiring different protection agencies and buying insurance contracts and the like. There is a reason, according to Rand, that the political knowledge *and* the moral knowledge of pre-state tribes are at a relatively primitive stage. Knowledge of both of these fields grows together.

For Rand, as I have said, the principle of individual rights represents a lengthy integration of knowledge. Much of this knowledge presupposes the existence of an organized, civilized society in order for it to be acquired. And some of this knowledge is itself the product of detailed observation and analysis of various types of social systems, states, and governments, in order to understand and conceptualize what is good and bad in their functioning. So although the principle of individual rights stands above politics, as its ruling and foundational principle, this does not mean for Rand that the principle can be formed prior to the establishment of various forms of social or political organization and moral reflection upon their positives and negatives. The state of nature Nozick projects embodies a distortion of the progression of humankind's knowledge—a violation, in Rand's terminology, of the hierarchy of human knowledge.

What difference does this make to Nozick's argument? It means that, from Rand's perspective, Nozick's goal of showing "that a [proper] state would arise from anarchy . . . even though no one intended this or tried to bring it about, by a process which need not violate anyone's rights" (*ASU* xi) is wrongheaded. For if the idea is to try to explain how clashing tribes would or could, by morally legitimate steps, unintentionally create the United States of America, the attempt is hopeless. To put it bluntly, there is no such thing as a bunch of clashing tribes unintentionally creating the Declaration of Independence and then the Constitution of the United States. If, on the other hand, the idea is to try to explain how a group of mostly virtuous individuals *possessing rich moral knowledge,* which extends all the way to a knowledge of the principle of individual rights, would unintentionally create, by rights-respecting steps, an ideal government, the approach is also hopeless. In a pre-state existence, these individuals could not have the knowledge that Nozick is projecting them to have. Or, if they *did* possess this complex knowledge (if one imagines transplanting thousands of eighteenth-century Americans, familiar with the doctrine of the rights of the individual, onto a virgin content), their creation of a government would not be unintentional but *intentional.* In trying to answer Rothbard on his own terms, Nozick has gone astray.

There is a further, related way in which, from Rand's perspective, Nozick's acceptance of Rothbard's terms significantly distorts understanding of the principle of individual rights. Following Rothbard, Nozick treats free trade and force—that is, voluntary exchanges of goods and exchanges of blows—as similar activities. Thus, supposedly, in a state of nature we have a *free* market in which individuals hire competing protection agencies and buy insurance contracts, just as today we have a free market in which individuals hire competing real estate agents. And just as we can explain, say, the emergence of money by an invisible-hand process from individual, voluntary barter transactions, so we can explain, by similar "free market forces," the emergence of a proper state from the hiring of competing protection agencies. For Rand, however, free trade and force are essentially different activities, and this kind of comparison does not make sense. For Rand, to try to conceptualize voluntary exchanges in the terminology of coercion is a grave error (e.g., "the Super Bowl ad forced me to buy a can of Pepsi" or "a hungry man is not free")—and so too is the attempt to conceptualize coercion in the terminology of voluntary exchange (e.g., "private protection agencies are 'competing' on a 'free market' and 'customers' will 'shop around'").[4]

In its simplest form, free trade is a voluntary exchange of goods— for example, of three oranges for four apples, between two individuals who both think they will benefit from the exchange. If either individual does not like the proposed terms of trade, if he thinks his three oranges are worth more than four apples or his four apples are worth more than three oranges, *he can walk away and remain as he was.* To force someone, on the other hand, is to bypass his will, to remove or override his choice in the matter. When you are coerced, you cannot walk away. If you try, you will be beaten up, detained, fined, imprisoned, or shot. Until force is extracted from a social interaction, until both parties are reasonably assured that the other is not going to resort to force, it is difficult for them to know if an interaction or exchange is voluntary. Consider a real example. When I was a child my family drove through a part of Ethiopia that was effectively stateless and mostly deserted. A smiling man with a rifle slung over his shoulder came up to our car, asking for something, we were not sure what. We eventually settled on giving him a banana. Did we give it

---

4. For one aspect of Rand's discussion of this issue, including the distinction she makes between economic power and political power, see "America's Persecuted Minority: Big Business" (*CUI*). See also Peikoff 1991, 402–6; Binswanger 2011.

to him freely or were we coerced? To this day, it is impossible for *us* to decide. Exchange and free exchange are very different things. *Extracting force* from social interactions, as we will see, is a crucial way of understanding what for Rand a proper government accomplishes.

And it is I think some rudimentary grasp of the distinctive nature of force—of force's awesome destructive power—that helps explain mankind's creation of nonideal forms of social organization, including nonideal governments and states, from an early historical age.[5] A state qua state is already a relatively sophisticated attempt to put the destructive power of force under moral control, to subordinate might to right. For Rand, fully to subordinate might to right is a difficult problem and even a beginning, partial solution counts as an achievement:

> The evolution of the concept of "government" has had a long, tortuous history. Some glimmer of the government's proper function seems to have existed in every organized society, manifesting itself in such phenomena as the recognition of some implicit (if often nonexistent) difference between a government and a robber gang—the aura of respect and of moral authority granted to the government as the guardian of "law and order"—the fact that even the most evil types of government found it necessary to maintain some semblance of order and some pretense at justice, if only by routine and tradition, and to claim some sort of moral justification for their power, of a mystical or social nature. ("The Nature of Government," *VOS* 132)

From this perspective of trying to subordinate might to right, the achievements of the Renaissance and more so of the Enlightenment stand as towering accomplishments: the development of an individualistic moral outlook and of a deep understanding of the evil of initiated force as an interference with an individual's ability to reason, combined with a systematic formulation of the means of extracting force from organized society. For Rand this knowledge develops together and forms a unity. The more one understands the power of the individual's rational mind, the more egoistic one's moral principles will become; the more one understands morality as egoistic, the more one understands the paramount importance of forming and following one's rational judgment; the more one understands the evil of initiated force, the more one understands

---

5. To use force in retaliation against the initiators of force is, Rand writes, "to destroy destruction" (*Atlas* 937).

that it is an attempt to circumvent and incapacitate an individual's rational judgment; and the more one understands these issues, the more one will be led to formulate and propagate the moral-political doctrine of the rights of the individual. The *explicit, conscious* political goal becomes not a "free-market competition" in using force but the systematic extraction of force from social interactions. "The precondition of a civilized society," Rand writes, "is the barring of physical force from social relationships—thus establishing the principle that if men wish to deal with one another, they may do so only by means of *reason:* by discussion, persuasion and voluntary, uncoerced agreement" ("The Nature of Government," *VOS* 126).

All of this means that for Rand, although the terms and conditions of human survival in reality, upon which the principle of individual rights is based, exist in historical periods prior to the establishment of government, the principle itself does not. Before people begin to formulate the issue, even if only in preliminary terms, it is premature to speak in terms of securing and protecting the rights of the individual. To formulate the individual's fundamental rights—his rights to life, liberty, property, and the pursuit of happiness—requires much thought. It requires conceiving of and formulating a range of activities in which the individual in society *should* be sovereign and why. Within this sphere of protected actions, the individual will be free to act without anyone's permission or approval and can claim, in the name of self-defense, that others in society be prohibited from encroaching on this sphere. It then requires defining the *types* of action that constitute encroachment and what *sorts* of penalties and prohibitions should ensue. To then translate this set of fundamental rights—all derived from the individual's right to life—into a full set of legal rights and principles, so that it is clear to each individual, in concrete terms and in individual cases, when he is acting within his rights and when he would be encroaching on the rights of others, as well as what does and does not constitute self-defense in the name of his rights, is itself an enormous task. Such a complex body of law is an achievement of decades and centuries.

Prior to all this being defined and codified (that is, prior to the formulation and implementation of the principle of individual rights), it is often difficult to know what counts as morally proper action in regard to others. In a state of nature, for instance, it often is difficult to say whether one does or does not have a moral right to do something. Nozick remarks that the status of procedural rights is unclear in a state of nature (*ASU* 56,

96)—and in his projected state of nature their status certainly is unclear. For when one is thinking about procedural rights, one is thinking about the procedures that it would be legitimate for organized society, legal institutions, and government to follow—but people in Nozick's projected state of nature have no knowledge of government. And my point is that the unclear status of procedural rights in Nozick's state of nature is, for Rand, the status of the principle of individual rights *as such* in a stateless period of human existence. No thinking has yet been done or principles formulated to define proper social interaction and the basic terms of social organization. As a result, it would often not be clear to an individual when he is acting within a sphere of action in which, morally, he should be sovereign and when he is encroaching on the same sphere of another person. Nor would it be clear what constitutes appropriate self-defense.

For example, suppose that in a state of nature you have domesticated a pig. A person from a neighboring tribe then takes your pig and eats it. Can you, morally, kill the perpetrator? Can you seize something from him in compensation? Everything of his? What about from the person he is living with (his spouse or child)? What about from other immediate family members, from distant relatives, or from any member of his tribe? What if you do not know who the perpetrator is? Can you go to the neighboring tribe and search every hut? Or, to take a different scenario, suppose that Robinson Crusoe and Friday live as strangers on an island, and Crusoe invents a new kind of spear with which to hunt. Morally, can Friday copy the design? If not, what does Crusoe have a moral right to do in self-defense if Friday does copy it? Or suppose that Friday discovers oil or invents a radio. To what, precisely, does Friday have a moral right and what, precisely, can he do in its defense?

Nozick seems to treat such (nonprocedural) questions as having definite answers in a state of nature; for Rand, this distorts the truth. Indeed, what projecting a state of nature helps one appreciate is how unclear the boundaries (to use Nozick's term) are of morally proper and improper interaction and the vital need to define, politically, the sphere of action in which the individual is sovereign. This, I think, is one of the reasons that Rand defines a right as "a moral principle *defining* and sanctioning a man's freedom of action in a social context" (my emphasis).

Individual rights don't exist ready-made in nature, to be copied down like the Ten Commandments. Nor do they arise from reflection about morality in the absence of sustained, systematic thinking about questions of proper social and political organization. Individual rights require careful thinking about how the metaphysical requirements of the individual's survival, the fact that his basic means of survival is reason, are to be secured and respected in society. The task of explicitly formulating these principles and their implementation, of systematically subordinating might to right and of extracting force from human relationships, Rand views as a highly purposeful, intentional endeavor. These principles are not reached by an invisible hand. This, as we have now seen from a few different angles, is a radical difference between Nozick's and Rand's conception of individual rights.

The Individual Anarchist

The fact that for Rand the principle of individual rights is inapplicable in a state of nature—that answers to many questions about what one has a moral right to do in regard to other persons are indeterminate until the principle has begun to be formulated and implemented—shapes her answer to the individual anarchist. She does not try to answer him indirectly, as Nozick does, by showing how "free-market forces" would lead moral individuals by an invisible hand to create a statelike institution. Rand does not think a pre-state social existence is a *free* market, precisely because the principle of individual rights has not been formulated and implemented and force has not been extracted from social interactions. Instead, she answers the individual anarchist directly.

The first part of *ASU* largely addresses two kinds of concerns raised by the individual anarchist. The first concern is that any government will itself violate the rights of the individual, by "redistributing" wealth or taxing its citizens. In regard to such concerns, Rand argues that a proper government would not and need not have such power: it would not have the power to "redistribute" wealth, to conscript its citizens into military service, to tax them, and so on.[6] A proper government is not and need not become a legalized criminal gang. The second concern is that any government, by establishing a monopoly on the use of force (that is, by extracting force from social interactions), thereby deprives individuals who choose *not* to delegate their right of self-defense from independently exercising this right—and this is a violation of the rights of these individuals. To this concern Rand argues that in a society that is seeking to define and secure

6. For the issues of "redistributing" wealth and of taxation, see her essays "Man's Rights," "The Nature of Government," and "Government Financing in a Free Society" in *VOS*; for the issue of the military draft, see her essay "The Wreckage of the Consensus" in *CUI*.

the rights of the individual, an "independent" (to use Nozick's term) has no such right of independent exercise.

An individual does have, according to Rand, a moral right of self-defense, a moral right to take action to protect his other moral-political rights, but none of these rights is sharply defined (or definable) in a state of nature. A society that is explicitly endeavoring to formulate and codify such principles into law is striving to do three things: (1) to define clearly the rights of the individual, the sphere of action in which he is sovereign; (2) to define clearly what does and does not constitute interference with these rights and so is or is not prohibited; and (3) to define clearly what does and does not constitute action in self-defense when one believes one's rights have been violated. All of this is crucial to extracting force from social interactions and creating a free market and a free society. One important aspect of this difficult task is to make the principles and their implementation clear, known, stable, and predictable, in part by removing individual discretion insofar as possible. But more widely, a proper government, Rand argues, "*is the means of placing the retaliatory use of physical force under objective control—*i.e., under objectively defined laws" ("The Nature of Government," *VOS* 128; original emphasis). Accomplishing this has many facets.

For instance, in order for it to be knowable and in principle predictable when retaliatory force will be used in human society, why, and in what ways, or in order for an individual not to be subject to multiple and inconsistent attempts to use force, or in order for an individual not to be subject to double jeopardy and the like, the use of retaliatory force must be made as robotic as possible. Its use should not be at the discretion of an individual, even if that individual acts rationally.[7] A government has to hold a monopoly on the legal use of force, Rand argues, "since it is the agent of restraining and combating the use of force; and for that very same reason, its actions have to be rigidly defined, delimited and circumscribed; no touch of whim or caprice should be permitted in its performance; it should be an impersonal robot, with the laws as its only motive power" ("The Nature of Government," *VOS* 128). For this robot to be functioning morally, there must be objective laws that define and control the government's own functioning, processes, and procedures:

---

7. And the discretion that remains to government officials, such as deciding whether to press charges in a borderline case, exists to render the use of retaliatory force more objective and deliberative, not less.

The retaliatory use of force requires *objective* rules of evidence to establish that a crime has been committed and to *prove* who committed it, as well as *objective* rules to define punishments and enforcement procedures. . . . If a society left the retaliatory use of force in the hands of individual citizens, it would degenerate into mob rule, lynch law and an endless series of bloody private feuds or vendettas. If physical force is to be barred from social relationships, men need an institution charged with the task of protecting their rights under an *objective* code of rules. (*VOS* 127)

On Rand's view, therefore, I think the "independent" who says he chooses not to delegate his right of self-defense is free to say this. But nevertheless, and leaving aside emergencies for the moment, he has no moral right as an individual to so act—that is, to resort to the use of force, *even if he asserts that he is using force in self-defense.* In the specified context, the *only* valid form of exercising his right of self-defense is to make use of the principles and legal apparatus that has been set up in the name of defining, securing, and protecting the rights of the individual. An "independent" would have a legitimate objection that he is being prohibited from exercising his right of self-defense only if he were banned from making use of the governmental apparatus that has been erected—as, for instance, was the case for "colored" people in the Jim Crow South.

Somewhat similar to Rand's argument here is Nozick's argument that a dominant protective association would, morally, have to compensate independents for prohibiting to them individual acts of self-defense and that the least expensive way of providing this compensation would be to extend its protective services to them. However, as already discussed, Rand thinks it is misguided to speak of dominant protective associations emerging on a free market pre-government: absent a proper government there exists no free market. Moreover, she thinks that the establishment of a proper government does not interfere with an "independent's" right of self-defense, so there is no issue of compensation. To the contrary, it would be the first time anyone and everyone's right of self-defense is actually defined and secured. Further, although Rand is arguing that any individual must be able to make use of the government's apparatus to defend his rights against criminal trespass or governmental encroachment, she argues that private, contractual agreements occupy a different status.[8]

8. See, especially, Rand, "Government Financing in a Free Society" (*VOS*).

This is how Harry Binswanger formulates the point, in an article that Rand read and of which she approved: "A proper government functions according to objective, philosophically validated procedures, as embodied in its entire legal framework, from its constitution down to its narrowest rules and ordinances. Once such a government, or anything approaching it, has been established, there is no such thing as a 'right' to 'compete' with the government—i.e., to act as judge, jury, and executioner. Nor does one gain such a 'right' by joining with others to go into the 'business' of wielding force" (Binswanger 1981, 12).[9] In other words, from the perspective of a society that has erected a government that approaches a proper one (such as today's US government) an individual who directly uses force rather than appeals to the government to use force on his behalf (for example, by submitting a stolen goods report or launching a lawsuit for damages) is *initiating the use of force even if he claims that he is acting in self-defense.* He is engaged in action he has no *moral* right to take, given the alternative available to him. And this remains true even if he is robbed, and even if in this particular case he would carry out a better investigation of the robbery than would the police. The issue of what his alternative is—namely, appeal to government—is important: exceptions will be carved out in law when this alternative is unavailable. As Binswanger writes, "a proper government does not prohibit a man from using force to defend himself in an emergency, when recourse to the government is not available; but it does, properly, require him to prove objectively, at trial, that he *was* acting in emergency self-defense" (12).[10]

So although Rand, like Nozick, rejects the objections of the individual anarchist, she does so for different reasons and from a very different conception of individual rights, which ultimately stems from a different moral perspective.

Moral Radicals

This last point, that Nozick's and Rand's moral perspectives are different, raises large and fundamental issues. Nozick regards individual rights as side constraints on the pursuit of (moral and political) goals; Rand regards them as conditions required for the individual's survival and hap-

---

9. In his editor's preface to *The Ayn Rand Lexicon*, Binswanger states that Rand read and approved of this article (*Lexicon* x).

10. The issue of when a group of individuals has a moral right to try to institute a better form of government is, for Rand, a separate issue, which I leave aside here. See, for instance, "Collectivized 'Rights'" (*VOS*).

piness, which is the goal of morality, and, agreeing with the Declaration of Independence, she regards them as themselves forming the goal of politics and government: "to secure these rights, governments are instituted among men." Nozick seems to ground his conception of individual rights in a Kantian framework (*ASU* 30); Rand emphatically rejects the Kantian approach to morality.[11] But as interesting as these issues are, I must leave them aside. By way of conclusion, I want to take up one difference in their moral perspectives, a difference especially relevant to the genesis of the principle of individual rights and to what is needed today to resurrect the principle. For Nozick was trying to resurrect Locke's moral-political approach and Rand was trying to resurrect that of the Founding Fathers.

According to Rand the source of the Enlightenment's achievement is also the source of its vulnerability. At its best, the Enlightenment put forth the conviction that a rational morality can be formulated, one that would accord a fundamental place to the individual's self-interested pursuit of his own happiness and welfare.[12] This conviction, which you could state as a focus on the importance of self-interest or self-preservation or the individual's life and happiness in this world, led to the formulation of the individual's fundamental rights—the rights to life, liberty, property, and the pursuit of happiness—as principles that would, in the sphere of politics and government, properly subordinate might to right. The development of the principle of individual rights helped lead to the idea that the initiation of force is a special evil, an attempt to negate the very possibility of an individual pursuing a moral life, and therefore as something that had to be extracted and banished from society. To implement this goal required careful formulation and definition of the individual's full legal rights and of constitutions and legal codes that would secure and protect these rights. But the Enlightenment project did not fully succeed because its thinkers did not formulate a new moral code of self-interest.

11. For Rand's rejection of the Kantian approach to morality, see her essay "Causality Versus Duty" *PWNI*. See also Peikoff 1982, especially ch. 4.

12. Locke in his *Essay Concerning Human Understanding* contends that morality is capable of rational demonstration (3:11 § 16; 4:3 §§ 18–20), and in the *Second Treatise* he gives a crucial moral place to the individual's goal of preserving himself, arguing that people (should) form political societies in order to help each member achieve this goal (*Two Treatises* 2:2 §§ 6–15). More generally, the Enlightenment outlook placed great importance on the pursuit of happiness and on rationality and truth-seeking as the individual's means to attaining happiness; it celebrated science, industry, merchants, and profitable trade to mutual advantage, helping establish the foundations of industrial capitalism; and it challenged the ideas that sensuality, self-regard, and pride are sins. See Gay 1966, 184–85; Gay 1969, 45–51, 194–201.

Rand, I think, saw it as one of her philosophical tasks to formulate a new moral code worthy of the Enlightenment's political achievements, capable of philosophically grounding the free society envisioned by the best of its thinkers. She stated the theme of her most ambitious work, *Atlas Shrugged*, as "the role of the mind in man's existence—and, as corollary, the demonstration of a new moral philosophy: the morality of rational self-interest" (*FTNI* 97).

Now in one way Nozick agrees with Rand here. He says near the beginning of *ASU* that the "completely accurate statement of the moral background, including its underlying basis, would require a full-scale presentation and is a task for another time. (A lifetime?) That task is so crucial, the gap left without its accomplishment so yawning, that it is only a minor comfort to note that we here are following the respectable tradition of Locke, who does not provide anything remotely resembling a satisfactory explanation of the status and basis of the law of nature in his *Second Treatise*" (*ASU* 9).

But in another way, this issue highlights a fundamental difference in approach between Nozick and Rand. As Nozick says, he proceeds in a way similar to Locke, trying to derive political conclusions without presenting a moral theory, though he does offer more in this regard than does Locke in the *Second Treatise*. Rand, on the other hand, thinks that the Enlightenment project had to fail; that without a new morality that fully rejected the Christian emphasis on self-sacrifice, the Enlightenment's new conception of government could not be fully defined or defended; and that this is the philosophical lesson to draw from the abandonment of the moral-political doctrine of the rights of the individual in the nineteenth and twentieth centuries.[13] So as a philosopher one should not now proceed in the way Locke proceeded a few centuries ago.

It may be that what explains Rand's and Nozick's different approaches here is that Rand thinks a *radical* moral alternative to what currently predominates must be formulated, whereas Nozick does not think this. In Lester Hunt's interpretation of *ASU*: "the basic argumentative strategy of the book is to appeal to shared common-sense moral intuitions. He turns the moral part of common sense against the political part. If he has correctly identified common-sense morality, and if his argument is a cogent one, this would be an important achievement, even without his

---

13. See Rand, *FTNI* 3–58, and "Man's Rights," "Collectivized Ethics," and "Collectivized 'Rights'" in *VOS*.

giving an independent defense of these moral intuitions. It would present most of his readers with a challenge to which they can only respond by changing their views, either about morality or about the realm of the political" (2015, 10). This is a plausible reading of *ASU*, so let me conclude by briefly sketching why I think Rand would reject this argumentative strategy as a proper approach. I will leave aside the more general issues that I think Rand would challenge: the very notion of "moral intuitions" and the appeal to so-called commonsense moral views as philosophical resting points, even if only temporary ones. Instead I will focus only on a conflict of ideas that she sees running through Western history and that she thinks shapes what people today regard as "common sense" in moral matters.

Rand would agree that it is true, particularly for Americans, that you can appeal to moral ideas which many Americans hold to help convey to them the attractiveness of a free society. This is because America is the nation forged by the Enlightenment; embedded in its ideals, institutions, and outlook, Rand maintains, is an individualistic, egoistic moral perspective. But one can also appeal to more explicit moral ideas Americans hold in order to establish the evil of a free society. So, for instance, many Americans will be suspicious of a massive new prescription drug "benefit," because it is a scheme to redistribute wealth from those who earned it to those who did not; but this opposition is effectively disarmed when explicitly told that such a program is moral to enact, because we are our brother's keeper. Rand labels the source of these explicit moral ideas the mystical-altruistic-collectivist axis in ethics, which she argues is in the ascendency after the Enlightenment. Without exposing and challenging this approach and the moral code that results, and proposing a new and radical alternative, she thinks the fight for individual rights is doomed. What Nozick's argumentative strategy amounts to is telling people that they accept some moral reasons for supporting a free society—while ignoring the fact that they accept more fundamental moral reasons for supporting its elimination. This split is the problem in America today.

As an illustration of this difference in argumentative strategy, let me give one example. In the first part of *ASU*, Nozick spends almost no time arguing for the evil of the initiation of physical force. For Rand, this omission, though perhaps understandable given Nozick's perspective, is fatal. From Nozick's perspective, it is understandable so long as he regards it as a "common-sense moral intuition" that initiating force is wrong. And it certainly is true that you can point to a bully beating up a child at school for his lunch money and say that this is the initiation of force and that it is bad—and most people will agree with you. But, philosophically speaking, Rand holds that to think that anything like this is sufficient to establish what the initiation of force is and why it is wrong is to fail to understand the history of morality.

Rand argues in her essay "What Is Capitalism?" that if one understands the two kinds of epistemological approach shaping the viewpoints that dominate ethics, one will see that they *both* require and sanction the initiation of physical force in pursuit of the good. The first epistemological approach, which she calls the intrinsic theory, "holds that the good resides in some sort of reality, independent of man's consciousness"; the second approach, which she calls the subjectivist theory, "holds that the good resides in man's consciousness, independent of reality." She then continues:

> The intrinsic theory and the subjectivist theory (or a mixture of both) are the necessary base of every dictatorship, tyranny, or variant of the absolute state. Whether they are held consciously or subconsciously—in the explicit form of a philosopher's treatise or in the implicit chaos of its echoes in an average man's feelings—these theories make it possible for a man to believe that the good is independent of man's mind and can be achieved by physical force.
>
> If a man believes that the good is intrinsic in certain actions, he will not hesitate to force others to perform them. If he believes that the human benefit or injury caused by such actions is of no significance, he will regard a sea of blood as of no significance. If he believes that the beneficiaries of such actions are irrelevant (or interchangeable), he will regard wholesale slaughter as his moral duty in the service of a "higher" good. It is the intrinsic theory of values that produces a Robespierre, a Lenin, a Stalin, or a Hitler. It is not an accident that Eichmann was a Kantian.
>
> If a man believes that the good is a matter of arbitrary, subjective choice, the issue of good or evil becomes, for him, an issue of: *my* feelings or *theirs*? No bridge, understanding, or communication is possible to him. Reason is the only means of communication among men, and an objectively perceivable reality is their only common frame of reference; when these are invalidated (*i.e.*, held to be irrelevant) in the field of morality, force becomes men's only way of dealing with one another. If the subjectivist wants to pursue some social ideal of his own, he feels morally entitled to force men "for their own good," since he *feels* that he is right

and that there is nothing to oppose him but their misguided feelings. (*CUI* 14–15)

What is needed, Rand argues, is a new, fully objective epistemological approach in morality; only this can explicitly identify the evil of the initiation of force and systematically uproot it. Far from being a commonsense idea, the evil of the initiation of physical force is a new and major philosophical conclusion, which overturns centuries of received opinion in ethics. This new moral perspective Rand holds was somewhat explicit in the formulation of the principle of individual rights but was never made fully explicit and consistent, because it was never properly grounded philosophically. These points are what she is trying to establish, and it helps explain why her focus in philosophy is moral and epistemological, not political.

And this is but another illustration of the main point of this essay. From Rand's perspective, Nozick's state-of-nature approach to individual rights empties the principle of much of its distinctive content and fails to see its explicit formulation and political implementation for the radical achievements that they were. A government dedicated to protecting individual rights was not and could not have been a product of an invisible hand. The principle of individual rights, along with its implementation as the foundational principle of government, represents a radically new and conscious attempt to subordinate might to right, premised on a faltering new conception of what is morally good. Historically and philosophically, it should be understood and defended as such.[14]

14. I would like to thank the editors of this volume for their comments on an earlier version of this paper as well as Douglas B. Rasmussen, who commented on the version I presented at the 2016 annual conference of the Association for Private Enterprise Education.

Anarchism versus Objectivism

HARRY BINSWANGER

Q: A government has a legal monopoly on the use of physical force within its borders. What is the answer to the "libertarian" anarchists who claim that to maintain this monopoly a government must initiate force in violation of the rights of those who wish to defend their own rights or to compete with the government by setting up private agencies to do so?

A: The anarchist claim merits discussion only to illustrate the sort of self-defeating contradictions generated by *anti-philosophical* movements, of which the so-called libertarians are a prime example.

A proper government is restricted to the protection of individual rights against violation by force or the threat of force. A proper government functions according to objective, philosophically validated procedures, as embodied in its entire legal framework, from its constitution down to its narrowest rules and ordinances. Once such a government, or anything approaching it, has been established, there is no such thing as a

Author's note: This chapter combines "The Q&A Department," *The Objectivist Forum* 2.4 (1981): 11–14, which Ayn Rand read and of which she approved, and a lightly edited addendum from my post dated July 18, 2011, on *The Harry Binswanger Letter* (www.hbletter.com).

"right" to "compete" with the government—that is, to act as judge, jury, and executioner. Nor does one gain such a "right" by joining with others to go into the "business" of wielding force.

To carry out its function of protecting individual rights, the government must forcibly bar others from using force in ways that threaten the citizens' rights. Private force is force not authorized by the government, not validated by its procedural safeguards, and not subject to its supervision. The government has to regard such private force as a threat—that is, as a potential violation of individual rights. In barring such private force, the government is retaliating against that threat.

Note that a proper government does not prohibit a man from using force to defend himself in an emergency, when recourse to the government is not available; but it does, properly, require him to prove objectively, at a trial, that he was acting in emergency self-defense. Similarly, the government does not ban private guards; but it does, properly, bring private guards under its supervision by licensing them and does not grant them any special rights or immunities: they remain subject to the government's authority and legal procedures.

The attempt to invoke individual rights to justify "competing" with the government collapses at the first attempt to concretize what it would mean in reality. Picture a band of strangers marching down Main Street, submachine guns at the ready. When confronted by the police, the leader of the band announces: "Me and the boys are only here to see that justice is done, so you have no right to interfere with us." According to the "libertarian" anarchists, in such a confrontation the police are morally bound to withdraw, on pain of betraying the rights of self-defense and free trade.

Regarding the purported betrayal, one can only respond: if this be treason, make the most of it.

In fact, of course, there is no conflict between individual rights and outlawing private force: there is no right to the *arbitrary* use of force. No political or moral principle could require the police to stand by helplessly while others use force arbitrarily—that is, according to whatever private notions of justice they happen to hold. "There is only one basic principle to which an individual must consent if he wishes to live in a free, civilized society: the principle of renouncing the use of physical force and delegating to the government his right of physical self-defense, for the purpose of an orderly, objective, legally defined enforcement. Or, to put it another way, he must accept *the separation of force and whim* (any whim, including his own)" ("The Nature of Government," *VOS* 129; original emphasis).

The basic questions that the antiphilosophical "libertarians" ignore or evade are: what is the nature and source of individual rights, and how are these rights to be implemented? Only by answering these questions can one proceed to consider what is or is not proper self-defense in concrete cases. But the answers to these questions are far from self-evident. To establish even the general principles on which the detailed, concrete administration of justice depends requires political and legal philosophy (and the metaphysics, epistemology, and ethics these fields presuppose). The "libertarians" take a shortcut: they plagiarize Ayn Rand's principle that no man may initiate the use of physical force and treat it as a mystically revealed, out-of-context absolute. This one principle, deprived of its philosophical base, is expected to replace jurisprudence, constitutions, legislatures, and courts. Then they imagine that the rest of us are obligated to accept, on faith, any gang's promise that their use of force will be "retaliatory."

Bear in mind that, in fact, those who would be granted the right to enforce their own notions of just retaliation include leftists who consider government intervention in the economy to be retaliation against business activities that the leftists view as "economic force." Then there are the terrorist groups who claim that random slaughter is "retaliation" against "Zionist imperialism," "British rule," and so on. Are we to assume that the country will have been converted to "libertarianism" before anarchism is instituted? Very well. One wing of the "libertarians" holds abortion to be murder; in their view, force against women who have abortions is retaliation in defense of the right to life. Another wing welcomed the New Left rioters of the 1960s, including the Black Panthers, as liberators who were retaliating against "state coercion." How will the principle of no initiated force—in a philosophical vacuum—resolve disputes of this kind?

In any society, disputes over who has the right to what are inescapable. Even strictly rational men will have disagreements of this kind, and the possibility of human irrationality, which is inherent in free will, multiplies the number of such disputes. The issue, then, is How are political and legal disputes to be settled: by might or by right—by street fighting or by the application of objective, philosophically validated procedures?

The most twisted evasion of the "libertarian" anarchists in this context is their view that disputes concerning rights could be settled by "competition" among private force-wielders on the "free market." This claim represents a staggering stolen concept: there is no *free* market until after force has been excluded. Their approach cannot be applied even to a baseball game, where it would mean that the rules of the game will be defined by whoever wins it. This has not prevented the "libertarian" anarchists from speaking of "the market for liberty" (i.e., the market for the market).

By their talk of "competition" in the context of government, these "libertarian" anarchists endorse the statists' equation of production and force (see "The Nature of Government"). "Competition" is an economic, not a political, concept; it refers to the voluntary exchange of values, not to the exchange of gunfire.

Behind the puerile fantasies of "market solutions" to political and legal disputes lies the collectivist notion that the ideas of the individual are determined by social institutions, so that once the "proper" social institutions have been established, "the people" will automatically agree on political and legal issues, and government will no longer be necessary. In the Marxist version of anarchism, once a socialist economy has "conditioned" men to altruism, they will automatically act according to the principle "from each according to his ability, to each according to his need." In the "libertarian" version, once a capitalist economy has been established, rational selfishness will become automatic, and "the market" will act to resolve whatever short-lived disputes still arise. In the words of one of the "libertarians": "Legislation forcing the parties [in a dispute] to submit to binding arbitration would be unnecessary, since each party would find arbitration to be in his own self-interest. Nor would it be necessary to have legal protection for the rights of all involved, because the structure of the market situation would protect them" (Tannehill and Tannehill 1970, 92).

In any irreconcilable dispute, at least one party will find that its view of justice is stymied. Even under anarchy, only one side will be able to enforce its ideas of where the right lies. But it does not occur to the anarchists that when one of their private "defense agencies" uses force it is acting as a "monopolist" over whomever it coerces. It does not occur to them that private, anarchistic force is still force—that is, the "monopolistic" subjection of another's will to one's own. They are aware of and object to the forcible negation of "competing" viewpoints only when it is done by a government. Thus, their actual objection to government is not to its "monopolistic" character but to the fact that "A government is the means of placing the retaliatory use of physical force under objective control— that is, under objectively defined laws" ("The Nature of Government").

The real target of the anarchists' attack is *objectivity*. Objectivity requires one to prove that one is acting within one's rights; they do not want to be held accountable to anyone for anything—not even regarding their use of physical force. They damn governmental retaliation because it is objective; they demand to be "free" to use force on whim.

In the philosophical battle for a free society, the one crucial connection to be upheld is that between capitalism and reason. The religious conservatives are seeking to tie capitalism to mysticism; the "libertarians" are tying capitalism to the whim-worshipping subjectivism and chaos of anarchy.

To cooperate with either group is to betray capitalism, reason, and one's own future.

Addendum, added in 2011

There are two further, though lesser, arguments for anarchism that I also want to answer.

The first might be called "the argument from moral freedom." This argument holds that it is wrong to impose morality by force, which government, as a monopoly, necessarily does, since it is on moral grounds that it prohibits "competitors." The alternative to imposing morality by force, it is claimed, is letting a thousand flowers bloom—that is, nonmonopolizing "defense agencies," each attracting, voluntarily, "customers" who patronize whichever agency has the moral outlook they find most congenial.

But this ignores the fact that we are not concerned with shopping for shoes but, rather, with "shopping" for wielders of physical force. Force is not a market good; force *is* "monopolistic": it is the subjugation of another's will to your own. Force is the opposite of permitting dissent. By its nature, force is the imposition of value judgments—the coercer's ideas about what ought to be. This remains true whether the wielder of force is called "the government" or "Joe's defense agency."

If one must avoid imposing moral ideas by force, then one must renounce force altogether—that is, practice pacifism. Like all arguments against the monopolization of force, "the argument from moral freedom" reduces to an advocacy of pacifism. Pacifism is the most nearly consistent form of anarchism. Few anarchists, however, realize this. They implicitly assume that there is such a thing as physical force that lets dissenters go their own way.

Let me concretize this. If someone shoots at me and I shoot back, I am using force to impose my morality—the moral rightness of my defending my life—on the gunman shooting at me. To avoid imposing my morality by force, I could only try to *persuade* him not to kill me. I could not use defensive force against him. The non–initiation of force principle is itself a moral principle. Individual rights are moral principles. Is it wrong to use retaliatory force to "impose" freedom and to protect rights?

This points to the equivocation in the phrase: "imposing morality."

It is indeed wrong for the government to "impose morality" in the sense of trying to force men to be virtuous. But that is not what a proper, limited government does: its coercive "imposition" of morality is retaliatory force used to protect freedom. It is indeed in the name of morality that the government "imposes" freedom: freedom is what makes virtuous action *possible*. But only the free choice of the individual can make virtue *actual*. Virtue cannot be coerced.

For example, it is wrong for the government to make men go to church or to stop them from going to church; it is right for the government to wield retaliatory force to secure their freedom to make this choice for themselves. Force used to maintain freedom is force used to "impose morality" to that extent. This is true whether the force is wielded by the government, a private group, or an individual. Again, the only alternative is not merely the absence of government but the absence of retaliatory force—that is, pacifism.

The failure of "anarcho-capitalists" to see this brings me to a second point: *anarchism is a product of and expression of collectivism*.

"Anarcho-capitalists" fail to see the pacifist implications of their position because they think in terms of groups instead of individuals. They think in terms of "defense agencies" and picture many "competing" (i.e., conflicting) agencies. These anarchists could not avoid the pacifist implications of their positions if they realized that both a government and a "defense agency" is just a group of individuals. When reduced to the level of individual-to-individual interactions, it becomes clear that "not imposing morality by force" means no *individual* can use force to defend himself—as in my example of not shooting back at someone who starts shooting at you.

If we abandon the collectivized mind-set, we see that anarchism would mean any individual can "take the law into his own hands." But when he uses what he feels to be retaliatory, and thus, morally justified, force, he is taking exactly the same action to which anarchists object when it is taken by a government: attempting to forcibly exclude the "competing" use of force by the initiator of force (e.g., the gunman). If it is morally proper for an individual to defend himself by force, it is morally proper for him to band together with others to do so—that is, to form a government.

The same facts that make individual self-defense moral—that is, the right to self-defense—makes governmental force moral if it is used in defense of the rights of individuals.

Government is not a collective super-organism. It is the agent of those individuals who establish and support it, by delegating their right of self-defense to it. If those individuals have the right to defend themselves, then the government, as their agent, has the right to wield retaliatory force on their behalf. Only a collectivized mentality can hold that the police, acting on my behalf, cannot forcibly exclude "competitors" but a "defense agency" can. Put it this way: a proper government is a defense agency, and to carry out its mission it can't let "competitors" (other gangs) use unsupervised force.

The telling difference between a proper government and a private defense agency is that a proper government is placed under objective control. Thus, nonpacifist anarchists object not to retaliatory force but to placing retaliatory force under objective control. Their objection is to objectivity.

The second argument of "anarcho-capitalists" is the argument from history: governments have always grown beyond their proper limits, so we must assume they inevitably do so.

This argument ignores *why* government has grown. The cause is: bad philosophy. Particularly, altruism. The history of the United States shows exactly this. Our government has grown beyond its proper limits because Americans have thought that it *ought to*.

It is men's *ideas* that rule their actions and their politics. It is not the power lust of politicians but the philosophical ideas of the citizenry that have caused the expansion of state power since the founding of this country. The power lust of politicians would be impotent in a society whose citizenry—and intellectuals—understood the Objectivist political philosophy.

Does anyone think that a power-luster who got into Galt's Gulch would have any chance of succeeding? End of story.

And if one holds that the majority of men are too irrational to ever see that their own self-interest requires a free society, then one must simply give up and retreat to a deserted island. One cannot consistently advocate any ideas—including anarchism—if the vast majority will not listen to reason. We see here a variant of the contradiction in Plato's doctrine of the philosopher-king. Plato held that "the masses" are inherently incapable of distinguishing true philosophic ideas from trickily presented false ones, as promulgated by the Sophists of his time. Yet, inconsistently, Plato held that the ideal society would be one in which the military would enforce the right philosophy (i.e., Plato's) on the populace. But how would the military know who is the right philosopher to follow? How would they know which philosopher to obey? And what would make the populace submit to the rule of those military men? On Plato's pessimistic view of the average man, no philosopher-king could ever come to power or stay in power.

In the same way, if "the masses" are too irrational to keep government within its proper bounds, they are too irrational to keep "defense agencies" to the task of actual defense.

One final wrinkle. "Anarcho-capitalists" claim that "the market" would keep defense agencies in check. (This idea represents a collectivist view of the market.) But remember: what is up for grabs here is whether or not there will be a market. When the society is turned over to warring gangs, the race goes to the bloodiest, not to the best producers.

And that is one more aspect in which the "anarcho-capitalists" are actually statists: they equate the dollar and the gun, production and force. The Left claims that "concentrations of wealth" on the market are coercive. The "anarcho-capitalists" claim that coercion is just another service on the market. But both are wrong: voluntary exchange has nothing in common with coercive interactions.

Production must be kept strictly separate from destruction. A business deals in the creation of goods and services to offer on a free market; a coercer deals in destruction. The proper use of destruction is to combat destruction—to wield retaliatory force against the initiators of force. But retaliatory force is still destruction, not production. There is no such thing as "the market for force-wielding." For there to be a market in the first place, those who would simply seize goods must be met with force. The benefits of a free market presuppose that freedom has been established. Market mechanisms can't establish or protect the preconditions of there being a market.

"Anarcho-capitalism" is a contradiction in terms. Capitalism can exist only where rights are protected, including property rights. To protect rights, criminals who initiate force must be met with retaliatory force. But the wielding of retaliatory force itself must be placed under objective control, by a constitutionally limited government with objective law. Otherwise, what results is not "competing defense agencies" but civil war.

That war will be won by the gang with the most ruthless and most powerful army. Under anarchy, might, not right, determines what the "laws"
will be.

In terms of current events, anarchism means Lebanon or Somalia.
To link such horrors with the benevolence and prosperity of capitalism
is obscene.

Defending Liberty
The Commonsense Approach
MICHAEL HUEMER

> Capitalism stands its trial before judges who have
> the sentence of death in their pockets. They are
> going to pass it, whatever the defense they may
> hear; the only success victorious defense can pos-
> sibly produce is a change in the indictment.
> JOSEPH SCHUMPETER

1. The Need for a Philosophical Defense of Liberty
1.1. Capitalism, Minimal Government, and Libertarianism

A *minimal government* is one that is limited to protecting its citizens'
negative rights, against both domestic criminals and hostile foreign governments, where these rights are understood primarily as rights against
coercion and fraud. Such a government would need a police force, a court
system, a military, a small number of political leaders (legislators and
president), and nothing else. Needless to say, no government in the world
is anything close to minimal in this sense. Existing governments fund
schools, roads, the arts, space exploration, and scientific research. They
control the supply of money and the delivery of first-class mail. They license television and radio stations, subsidize farms, and bail out failing
banks. They regulate what drugs people may use, what kinds of medical
care may be provided and by whom, how food may be labeled, what wages
one may pay, and how large a company may be. All of these things go beyond the range of the minimal state.

  Libertarians advocate *at most* minimal government. Libertarians
divide into two classes. Minimal state libertarians ("minimal statists"),

The epigraph is from Schumpeter 1942 [1975], 144.

including Ayn Rand and her followers, advocate minimal government.[1] Libertarian anarchists (or "anarcho-capitalists"), on the other hand, advocate no government.

Capitalism is a logical corollary of libertarianism. It is an economic system based upon free markets and private property. Both minimal statists and libertarian anarchists advocate this economic system.

What is the best way to defend libertarianism? Should political liberty be defended chiefly on economic grounds, on moral grounds, or something else? And does the best defense of liberty lead to minimal statism or anarchism? These are the questions I aim to answer in what follows.

1.2. Economic and Philosophical Arguments for Capitalism

Most criticisms of libertarianism are criticisms of capitalism. Over the past century and a half, capitalism has been reviled for a wide variety of alleged failings, both practical and moral. It has been accused of being inherently exploitative, of generating vast inequality, of destroying freedom, of being economically unstable, of destroying the natural environment, of causing imperialism, and of wasting valuable resources, among other things.

Defenders of capitalism have often rested their case on practical, economic arguments: capitalism is relatively economically efficient under most circumstances; for a variety of reasons, it tends to lead to much greater preference-satisfaction than systems based on governmental control.[2] Sometimes, the defenders of capitalism appeal to more traditionally moral arguments, as in Ayn Rand's appeal to individual rights or Robert Nozick's comparison of wealth redistribution to slavery.[3] But generally speaking, the economic arguments seem to predominate among contemporary defenders of liberty. This may be due to a conviction that economic arguments are more objective, more conclusive, or simply more persuasive than philosophical arguments.

I believe this is both a logical and a rhetorical mistake. It is a logical mistake because some discussion of moral and political values is necessary for a cogent defense of capitalism and political liberty in general. Not

---

1. Since Peter Schwartz's "Libertarianism: The Perversion of Liberty" (1988), some Objectivists object to being labeled "libertarians." Nevertheless, their views satisfy the definition of the political philosophy of libertarianism (not to be confused with the Libertarian Party or the current libertarian movement) given in the text. See Hsieh 2003 for discussion.

2. See Mises 1922 [1951]; Friedman 1990; Friedman 1989.

3. See "What Is Capitalism?" *CUI* 10–11; Nozick 1974, 169–72.

every criticism of capitalism is based upon an economic error; at least some criticisms correctly identify, at least in broad outline, real effects of capitalism. This is the case with what is perhaps the most influential criticism, the criticism that capitalist societies harbor great inequalities of wealth. To decide whether capitalism is desirable or just, we must know not only what effects capitalism produces but what effects are desirable or just. Does the alleviation of inequality, for example, justify state intervention into an otherwise capitalist system? Nor is philosophical discourse in this area doomed to subjectivity or mere guesswork; there is a philosophical case for liberty that is at least as strong as the economic case. This fact, I hope, will emerge in the following discussion (see section 4).

But why is it a *rhetorical* mistake to rely on economic rather than moral arguments for liberty? Rhetorically, one might think it best to avoid such controversial areas as moral philosophy when possible and to portray one's arguments as resting instead upon some more scientific, "objective" body of knowledge such as economics. Economists are often in a position to offer something close to mathematical proofs, based upon general theories of rational action, of certain factual claims about the effects of government policies—that minimum wage laws cause unemployment, that import quotas harm the domestic economy, and so on. Won't arguments of this kind have greater persuasive power with most audiences than appeals to something so intangible as justice and morality?

The answer, as Ayn Rand recognized, is almost certainly not. Granted, if one is addressing a room full of economists and mathematicians, then economic arguments are likely to have greater persuasive force than moral arguments. But for almost any other audience, the case is quite the opposite. There are two main reasons for this. First, *most people do not think like economists.* Most people find the typical moral argument much easier to follow than the typical economic argument. Thus, one argument against deficit spending is that the state has no right to impose trillions of dollars of debt on future generations of taxpayers just so that the government can provide services to the current generation without having to raise taxes now. Another argument is that deficit spending doesn't really stimulate the economy as Keynesians claim, because government spending crowds out private investment. Whether one agrees with either of these arguments or not, the former is much easier for most people to understand; it is much closer to how we think in ordinary life.

Second and more importantly, *people will not accept a social system that violates their moral sense.* Any reflective defender of capitalism must sooner or later come to wonder at the continuing impotence of the economic arguments for capitalism. How have arguments for protectionist trade barriers managed to survive so long after Ricardo refuted them? Why do people call for greater government intervention whenever government error has created a crisis? Why do they continually believe that more government regulation of industry is needed, despite the weight and variety of evidence of the failure of government management?

Joseph Schumpeter had the right of it: contemporary intellectuals are determined to convict capitalism of some grievous offence. It does not matter if you refute a dozen economic fallacies. There will always be more, because the driving force is not economic confusion. The driving force is the sheer *antipathy* that most intellectuals feel toward capitalism. As long as that antipathy remains, more fallacies can always be concocted to rationalize it.

What is the root of the antipathy toward capitalism? This antipathy, I believe, is chiefly moral in origin. Partly, it is the sense that it is *unfair* that some people—who appear not greatly superior to other men—should wind up holding vast wealth while others have barely enough to eat. A purely capitalist society seems coldhearted and selfish. And there is a sense that it would be *wrong* for the government, which is responsible for the structure of society, to make some suffer unfairly when the government could easily create a fairer and more compassionate distribution of society's wealth by simply increasing its tax rate and generously giving the extra revenue to the poor. These are paradigmatically philosophical ideas. And so it is to philosophy that we must turn for the remedy, if these ideas are to be uprooted at all.

2. Ayn Rand's Defense of the Minimal State
2.1. Freedom from Government

Ayn Rand was clear in her belief that the ultimate foundation for any successful defense of capitalism had to be the ethical theory of *egoism*, the view that the correct action in any situation is always the most selfish action. She held it an error to defend capitalism for the sake of its contributions to the common good. Capitalism and altruism, in her view, were fundamentally incompatible.[4]

Why did Rand endorse egoism? Unfortunately, the interpretation of

---

4. See "The Objectivist Ethics," *VOS* 36–38, and "The Obliteration of Capitalism," *CUI* 204–5.

Rand's argument is highly controversial, and it is impossible to give any clear and explicit statement of the steps of the argument that would be generally accepted. But the key move seems to occur in this passage:

> There is only one fundamental alternative in the universe: existence or nonexistence—and it pertains to a single class of entities: to living organisms. . . . It is only a living organism that faces a constant alternative: the issue of life or death. Life is a process of self-sustaining and self-generated action. If an organism fails in that action, it dies; its chemical elements remain, but its life goes out of existence. It is only the concept "Life" that makes the concept of "Value" possible. It is only to a living entity that things can be good or evil.[5]

She goes on to explain that ethics, as a field of knowledge, exists because human beings, alone among known organisms, must consciously identify the actions necessary to preserve their lives. The function of ethics is the identification of the general principles of action that intelligent beings must follow to sustain their lives.[6]

I cannot discuss all interpretations of the argument here, so I will simply state very briefly what I make of it.[7] The best I can make of it is that Rand starts from the correct observation that an individual organism will die if it does not take certain actions, and infers that, for that organism, those actions are *good*. She further assumes that nothing *else* is good, apart from the things that sustain the organism's life. To infer that action A is good for S from the premise that A is required to sustain S's life, one must apparently presuppose that S's life is good for S.[8] It thus appears to me that, if Rand had an argument for egoism, this argument had at least two starting premises:

1. For any living thing, S, S's life is good for S.
2. For any living thing, S, nothing other than S's life is intrinsically good, neither *for* S nor in an agent-neutral sense.

I find no further argument for these premises in Rand's corpus.

From the principle of egoism, Rand claims to derive a constellation

---

5. *Atlas* 939, quoted in "The Objectivist Ethics," *VOS* 15–16.
6. See "The Objectivist Ethics," *VOS*.
7. For further critical discussion, see Huemer 1996 (section 5) and 2005a.
8. Failing that, one must at least assume that *if A sustains S's life, then A is good for S.* Whether we substitute this slightly weaker claim for the claim that S's life is good for S makes no difference to any of the subsequent arguments in the text.

of closely related political principles, pertaining to the notions of sacrifice, individual rights, aggression, and force. Here I will simply state one principle that plays a particularly prominent role in the defense of capitalism. This is what libertarians sometimes call the Non-Aggression Axiom: "The basic political principle of the Objectivist ethics is: no man may *initiate* the use of physical force against others. . . . Men have the right to use physical force *only* in retaliation and *only* against those who initiate its use" ("The Objectivist Ethics," *VOS* 36; original emphasis).[9] Hence, it follows that nearly all governmental policies (those that go beyond the activities of the minimal state) are wrong. A few examples will suffice to explain the logic:

I. Individuals who ingest recreational drugs are not thereby using force against anyone else. The state, in arresting and imprisoning such people, deploys physical force against them. Thus, drug prohibition constitutes an initiation of force on the part of the state, which is morally impermissible.

II. Welfare programs take money from the wealthy and give it to the poor. This redistribution is effected through threats of physical force, including actual physical force deployed against those who fail to turn over to the state the funds demanded of them. Since this is an initiation of force by the government, it is morally impermissible.

III. Immigration laws involve the state in using force to expel people who reside in the country without the government's permission. Mere presence in a certain broad geographical region, with the consent of the property owners whose land one uses (for example, landlords who agree to rent an apartment to one) does not constitute a use of force against anyone. Therefore, immigration restrictions involve the state in wrongfully initiating force against immigrants.

2.2. *Against the Anarchists*

Rand held that the only feasible way to protect individual rights was through a government. In most of her discussion of the subject, her image of anarchy seems to be that of a system entirely lacking in laws, courts, or any organizations for the protection of individual rights. This of course is not the proposal of anarcho-capitalists, who envision a system of com-

9. The appellation "Non-Aggression Axiom" derives from the broader libertarian discourse rather than from Rand herself.

peting courts and protection agencies. In the interests of space, I will here assume familiarity with the anarcho-capitalist proposal on the part of the reader.[10]

Where Rand briefly considers anarcho-capitalism, her chief objections appear to be twofold. First: a system of competing protection agencies would quickly devolve into interagency warfare. Whenever customers of different agencies had a dispute, the customers would demand that their agency fight on their behalf.[11] Second: anarcho-capitalism cannot provide *objective* laws, instead leaving law dependent on human whims.[12] This objection goes by very quickly in Rand. Harry Binswanger explains it in more detail:

> A proper government functions according to objective, philosophically validated procedures, as embodied in its entire legal framework, from its constitution down to its narrowest rules and ordinances. . . .
>
> [T]here is no conflict between individual rights and outlawing private force: there is no right to the *arbitrary* use of force. No political or moral principle could require the police to stand by helplessly while others use force arbitrarily—that is, according to whatever private notions of justice they happen to hold.[13]

The argument seems to be that a (proper) government is objective, whereas competing protection agencies are nonobjective. What do Rand and Binswanger mean by "objective" in this context? I believe the idea is that a proper government applies force in accordance with *correct* or *rationally justified* moral principles. In contrast, Rand and Binswanger believe, private protection agencies would apply force in accordance with false or unjustified moral beliefs, or perhaps mere whims.

3. Difficulties with Rand's Defense of the Minimal State
3.1. The Perils of Relying upon Ethical Egoism

There are two salient problems with relying upon ethical egoism for the defense of capitalism. First, ethical egoism is obviously false. Now, in rejecting egoism, I am not denying that self-interest plays a role in proper moral judgments, or that it is proper for a person to have some regard to his own interests. What I am denying is that self-interest is all that mat-

---

10. See Huemer 2013 for a relatively full exposition and defense of the system.
11. See "The Nature of Government," *VOS* 127/*CUI* 380; compare Nozick 1974, 15–17.
12. See "The Missing Link," *PWNI* 59.
13. Binswanger 1981 (original emphasis; reprinted in this volume).

ters. Similarly, I do not hold that an individual should exist solely for others, or that helping others is the only thing that matters morally. I *do* hold, however, that the interests of others have some intrinsic moral weight. Thus, I think that in deciding what to do, an agent should typically take into account *both* his own interests *and* those of others.[14]

The issue of ethical egoism has been discussed at length elsewhere,[15] so here I will just briefly summarize one sort of argument:

3. If ethical egoism is true, then for any action A that I can perform, if A provides a net benefit to me (compared with every alternative), then I should do A.

4. Therefore, if ethical egoism is true, then if A provides a trivial net benefit to me—say, equivalent to the value of a dime—while causing horrific agony and death for four million innocent people, I should do A.

5. It is not the case that, if A provides a trivial net benefit to me while causing horrific agony and death for four million innocent people, I should do A.

6. Therefore, ethical egoism is false.

The idea here is to test whether one really thinks that self-interest is all that matters, or whether—as I have suggested—the interests of others have *at least some* moral weight. Thus, the argument asks the reader to weigh a *tiny* benefit to self against a *vast* harm to others. I count on the reader to find it absurd that the tiny self-benefit would outweigh the vast other-harm.

To resist this argument, one would have to reject at least one of steps 3–6. Premise 3 is true by the definition of "ethical egoism," so that is not in dispute. Statement 4 is a straightforward deduction from 3, and conclusion 6 a straightforward deduction from 4 and 5, so those steps cannot be in dispute either. So the only step that one could dispute is premise 5. An egoist might claim that 5 is false because ethical egoism is true. I, on the other hand, claim that egoism is false because premise 5 is true. How is such a dispute to be resolved?

As mentioned above (section 2.1), Rand's argument for egoism rests on at least two starting premises, roughly as follows:

14. I also am not claiming that everyone matters *equally*, and I am not claiming that consequentialism is the correct kind of moral system. I am only claiming that the interests of others sometimes have some proper weight, intrinsically, in deciding what one ought to do.

15. See Rachels 2003; Huemer 1996 (section 5), 2002, 2005a.

1. An organism's life is good for that organism.

2. Nothing else is intrinsically good.

My argument, on the other hand, rests on the single starting premise 5. Which is a more plausible starting point: "one shouldn't torture and kill four million people to obtain a trivial benefit," or "the only intrinsic value for anyone is one's own life"? Only a sociopath could find the latter more plausible.

Be that as it may, the second problem with relying upon ethical egoism is this: almost everyone firmly rejects it. From a rhetorical standpoint, it seems like a mistake to attempt to persuade an audience of a controversial thesis (the justice of capitalism) by relying upon a theory (egoism) that is not just controversial but in fact disdainfully rejected, with almost complete confidence, by virtually everyone.

Perhaps if one had some incredibly persuasive argument for the widely rejected thesis, then it might be feasible to first convince one's audience of that thesis and then proceed to address the original controversy. But in fact, whatever one thinks of the merits of Rand's argument for egoism, it is scarcely open to question that the argument is utterly unpersuasive to almost everyone who hears it. *Some* people—generally those who agree with Rand about virtually everything else—find her egoist argument highly persuasive. Based on my own experience, however, when the argument is presented to professional philosophers or undergraduate students (whether through Rand's original presentation or through Tara Smith's restatement),[16] hardly anyone, either among experts or among lay people, finds the argument at all persuasive. This suggests that appealing to ethical egoism is not the most likely way of convincing most people to support capitalism. Indeed, attempting to defend capitalism on the basis of egoism is likely to do more to *discredit* capitalism in the popular mind than to promote it.

3.2. *The Non-Aggression Axiom*

There are two main problems with relying upon the Non-Aggression Axiom to defend minimal government. First: the Non-Aggression Axiom entails anarchism. Government, by definition, holds a monopoly on the services it provides.[17] It maintains this monopoly through the use of force

---

16. "The Objectivist Ethics" (*VOS*); Smith 2000, ch. 4.

17. From Weber 1946, 78 (original emphasis): "The state is a human community that (successfully) claims the *monopoly of the legitimate use of physical force* within a given territory." See also "The Nature of Government": "A government is an institution that holds the

against anyone who attempts to compete—that is, anyone who attempts to provide the same services as the government. Now, either the provision of these services constitutes aggression, or it does not. If it constitutes aggression, then, by the Non-Aggression Axiom, government is unjustified. But if it does *not* constitute aggression, then to use force to prevent other people from providing these services is itself to commit aggression. In other words, if the state violates rights, then it must be abolished; if the state does not violate rights, then it can have no valid objection to other organizations doing the same thing as the state is doing.[18]

Note what I am *not* here suggesting. I am not suggesting that it is acceptable for private entities to use force in just any manner they choose. There are *some* exercises of force that are justified, and others (the great majority) that are not justified. If you believe in government at all (whether you support a minimal state or something larger), you must think that these justified uses of force include at least some cases in which force is deployed against someone who previously violated others' rights, in order to impose punishment or extract compensation from the perpetrator of the rights violation. In such circumstances, the perpetrator presumably does *not* have a right not to have force used against him. Now, you might think, plausibly, that some special procedural conditions must be satisfied; for example, perhaps the perpetrator must have been given a fair trial, using certain highly reliable procedures; perhaps the perpetrator must have been given an impartial jury of their peers, and so on. *Whatever* your view is of the circumstances that justify coercion, the question is, why may not a private entity, instead of the state, exercise coercion against a rights-violator *in exactly those circumstances*? By hypothesis, in doing so the private party would not be violating the perpetrator's rights.

Some believe that the state must prohibit such private action because private protection agencies would pose too high a *risk* of committing rights violations; the state may therefore respond to the creation of such agencies as to a threat of unjust coercion.[19] This suggestion fails to avoid my argument: either the state itself poses an undue risk of unjust coercion, or it does not. If it does, then we are justified in using force to abolish the state. If it does not, then an organization that does the very same thing the state does would not pose an undue risk of unjust coer-

exclusive power to *enforce* certain rules of social conduct in a given geographical area" (*VOS* 125/*CUI* 378; original emphasis).

18. See also Childs 1969.

19. See Binswanger 1981; Nozick 1974, 54–56, 88–90, 101–8.

cion. To have an enforceable monopoly, the state must not only prohibit exceptionally risky or corrupt protection procedures; the state must prohibit *any* competitors, no matter how closely the competitor's procedures match those of the state itself. A competing agency might be enforcing *exactly the same laws*, using *exactly the same procedures* for determining guilt or innocence as the government, and the government would still have to forcibly shut down that agency—otherwise, the state does not claim a monopoly. This makes it very difficult to claim that the state is not an aggressor.

The second problem with the Non-Aggression Axiom is that the "axiom" is uncontroversially false. Again, here is Rand's statement of the principle: "[N]o man may *initiate* the use of physical force against others. . . . Men have the right to use physical force *only* in retaliation and *only* against those who initiate its use." ("The Objectivist Ethics," *VOS* 36.) Here is the first counterexample. Suppose Sally knows that Jon is going to kill her. (This *might* be because Jon *threatened* to kill Sally, or it might be for other reasons; e.g., Jon might have tried his hardest to conceal his intentions, but accidentally left evidence of his plan, which Sally has discovered.) *As yet*, however, Jon hasn't used force against Sally. The above statement of the Non-Aggression Axiom entails that Sally must wait for Jon to use force first; then, if she is still alive, she may retaliate. Obviously, Objectivists do not believe this; they believe one may use force to prevent unjust violence by others. But this simply is not what the above quotation says. "Defense" is what one does to *prevent* oneself from being harmed; "retaliation" is what one does *after* one has been harmed. And what the above quotation actually says is that one may only use force in *retaliation*. Of course, this is easily remedied. We may simply say: A person may use physical force only (1) to prevent someone else from initiating its use, or (2) in retaliation against those who initiate its use.

Here is the second counterexample. Jon and Sally have a contract: Sally will give Jon an eye exam (she is an optometrist), in exchange for which Jon will mow Sally's lawn. Sally holds up her end of the deal, but then Jon reneges; he refuses to mow Sally's lawn. Sally files a lawsuit against Jon. Nearly everyone, Objectivists and libertarians included, agrees that (if there is a state) the state may force Jon to either mow Sally's lawn or pay Sally some sort of compensation for the breach of contract. But at no point in this story did Jon use or threaten to use physical force against Sally. So the state would be initiating the use of force against Jon, where doing so is not necessary either to prevent or to retaliate for anyone's use of force.

Rand once tried to assimilate breaches of contract to cases of coercion, writing: "A unilateral breach of contract involves an indirect use of physical force: it consists, in essence, of one man receiving the material values, goods, or services of another, then refusing to pay for them and thus keeping them by force (by mere physical possession), not by right—i.e., keeping them without the consent of their owner" ("The Nature of Government," *VOS* 130/*CUI* 383). This is very implausible on its face. Some observations: (a) On this account, one can be engaged in "the use of force" while sitting completely inert, in a field thousands of miles away from anyone else. (b) On this account, the use of force consists in one's keeping "by mere physical possession" the goods that the other party provided. But in my example, there are no goods that Jon is in physical possession of, and I don't know what it means to "keep" an eye exam. It is similarly bizarre to claim that Jon is exerting force by "keeping" his lawn-mowing ability. (c) On this account, "physical force" is not a physical concept but a moral concept: if I hold goods that I am *justly entitled to*, I am not using force; but if I hold goods that I am *not justly entitled to*, then I am using force. This undermines the attempt to use the Non-Aggression Axiom to criticize left-wing advocates of wealth redistribution. The central claim of these thinkers is that justice requires wealth redistribution;[20] thus, one would have to *first* show that their central thesis is false *in order* to show that they are advocating the initiation of force.[21]

Here is the third counterexample. This time, there are no relevant agreements between Jon and Sally. Jon, however, has been spreading false and malicious rumors about Sally, accusing her of killing patients to sell their organs on the black market. Jon's slanders greatly damage Sally's reputation, harming both her social relations and her business interests. Sally sues Jon. Again, almost everyone, Objectivists and libertarians included, agrees that the state may award damages to Sally and enforce this judgment coercively if necessary. But again, Jon has not initiated force against Sally in this example (words are not force), nor has he threatened to do so, nor has he broken a contract with Sally.

Here is the fourth counterexample. Sally has accidentally dropped her wallet on the street. Jon picks up the wallet, takes one hundred dollars

20. See for example, Rawls 1971 [1999]; Cohen 1989.
21. Compare William Edmundson's claim that government is not coercive (1998, ch. 4) because "coercion" is a normative concept, and the government's actions are morally justified.

out of it, and then leaves the wallet on the street. In this case, no use of physical force against Sally was required, since Sally was not present to defend her wallet. Nor was Jon breaking a contract, since he never agreed not to rob Sally. Nor was he committing libel or slander. Nevertheless, if the government catches Jon, they may compel him to return Sally's money.

Here is the fifth counterexample. Sally, through no fault of her own, finds herself in danger of starvation. Jon has plenty of food that he doesn't need, but he irrationally refuses to give any to Sally, not even in exchange for any amount of money. There is no other food Sally can get to in time to save her life; her only option to avoid starvation is to forcibly take away some of Jon's food. In this case, nearly everyone believes Sally would be justified in doing so.

Taking account of all of these examples, we should modify our formulation of the Non-Aggression Axiom to read as follows: A person may use physical force only (1) to prevent someone else from initiating its use, (2) in retaliation against those who initiate its use, (3) to enforce a contract, (4) to enforce compensation for libel or slander, (5) to enforce property rights, or (6) to preserve one's life or other extremely important interests in an emergency. Now do we have a correct moral principle? Perhaps. But this principle is too complex to be a useful tool for refuting more expansive conceptions of the role of government. A leftist might wonder why, given the number of clauses already included in the principle, one may not add one more clause to deal with the case where the use of force is necessary to prevent the poor from suffering severe hardship or to remedy inequality in the distribution of wealth.

3.3. *Proper Government and Improper Anarchy*

Turning at last to the objections to anarchy, how would disputes between customers of competing protection agencies be resolved in an anarcho-capitalist society? Whereas Objectivists believe these disputes would be resolved through violence, anarcho-capitalists argue that agencies would instead resolve disputes through private arbitration. Briefly, the reason for this is that arbitration by a neutral third party is widely regarded as a much easier, less costly, and more just method of resolving disputes than resorting to physical force. Physical force generally results in much greater overall costs, even for the party who "wins" the conflict, than almost any peaceful method of dispute resolution; indeed, the costs are very often greater than the total value that was in dispute to begin with.

The workings of private security and arbitration have been discussed at length elsewhere, along with responses to a wide variety of other potential practical objections to anarchism, so here I will simply refer the reader to that literature, to which Rand provides no response.[22]

Turning now to the argument that government is needed to establish objective control over the mechanisms of coercion, what is the status of Binswanger's statement that a proper government is objective? Is this an empirical claim? Can we find some proper governments and observe whether they function according to objective, philosophically validated procedures?

The answer is no, because on discovering that a government does not function according to objective principles, Binswanger would declare that it was not a *proper* government. In fact, probably no proper government has ever existed. The phrase "a proper government" refers rather to a hypothetical entity. Given this, it is unclear how the superiority of proper government over improper anarchy gives us grounds for preferring government over anarchy. Why may not the anarchists also introduce a hypothetical *proper* anarchy, in which the competing protection agencies all function according to objective, philosophically validated procedures, just as Binswanger's proper government does?

But this clash of hypothetical scenarios would not be intellectually productive. What matters is what can be expected to happen under alternative proposed social structures, given realistic assumptions about human nature. In either type of social system, human beings will exercise their judgment. We do not face a choice between a world in which coercion is wielded by humans and a world in which coercion is wielded by some infallible superhuman force. The choice is only one of whether to rely upon the judgments of the members of a single organization or to rely upon the judgments of the members of a number of distinct and competing organizations. There is no reason to believe that only a monopolistic force-wielder can have rational or reliable moral beliefs.

Anarchist theorists have given reasons for believing that competing protection agencies would be more likely to resolve disputes justly than government courts. Very briefly, the main point is that, when the government fails in its function, it need fear no loss of its "customer" base, since citizens have no one else to turn to for protection and dispute resolution;

22. See Friedman 1989, especially chapter 29; Rothbard 1973 [2006], especially chapter 12; Huemer 2013, especially chapters 10–11.

nor need it fear loss of revenues, since it can simply tax people at whatever rate it chooses.

Democratic enthusiasts claim that (in a rational and decent society) the democratic process ensures the integrity of government, since leaders who act wrongly will be voted out of office. But there is a crucial reason why market mechanisms tend to be much more effective than democratic mechanisms for bringing about positive change: if I determine that a business is not providing the value I expect and I decide to switch brands, I thereby *get* the new brand. I receive the goods the new company offers. But if I determine that a politician is not providing the value I expect and I decide to support another politician, I do not thereby get that new politician. I still get whomever the majority votes for, and my decision to switch my vote makes no difference at all, except in the incredibly unlikely event that the other voters are exactly tied. As a result, it pays one to be informed and rational in making market purchasing decisions, whereas it does not pay to be informed and rational in making political (e.g., voting) decisions.[23] This point is commonly recognized by defenders of capitalism seeking to explain why, for example, government provision of shoes would be much worse than market provision of the same product. What is commonly overlooked is that the same dynamics apply to *any* goods or services that might be provided either by the state or by competing private businesses.

4. Toward a Credible Defense of Liberty
4.1. Commonsense Morality and the Rejection of Authority

So far, I have rejected a purely economic defense of political liberty, and I have rejected philosophical defenses based upon either ethical egoism or the Non-Aggression Axiom. What is left?

What is left is a defense of political liberty based upon commonsense morality. Many libertarians (including Objectivists) seek to ground their political views in an overarching, abstract ethical or metaethical system.[24] However, it is seldom noted that no such system is needed to defend liberty to an audience of ordinary people, since the moral intuitions of ordinary people already support liberty in a more simple and direct manner. Of course, most people's *political* views are highly antilibertarian.

---

23. For a fuller discussion of this and related issues, see Caplan 2007b; Huemer 2013, section 9.4 and chapter 10.
24. See *VOS*; Narveson 1988; Rothbard 1973 [2006].

Nevertheless, most people's intuitions regarding ordinary, interpersonal morality—the norms governing interactions between individuals—are far more consistent with a libertarian political philosophy than with the political views most people actually hold. To see the point, consider three issues on which libertarians hold controversial views:

I. *Recreational drugs:* The current US policy of drug prohibition involves the state in forcibly taking captive drug users and sellers and confining them in dangerous and extremely unpleasant conditions (prison) for extended periods of time, often for years at a time. A majority of Americans support this policy, particularly for the "harder" drugs such as cocaine and heroin. Yet hardly anyone, even among those who wish to see *the state* continue its prohibition policy, would think it proper for a private individual to kidnap people at gunpoint and hold them captive for years at a time in retaliation for their private recreational ingestion of unhealthful substances. Almost anyone would regard it as seriously wrong for any nongovernmental agent to engage in the sort of behavior in which the state is presently engaged.

II. *Wealth redistribution:* A large majority of Americans favor at least some government programs designed to take money from taxpayers and redistribute it to some favored group—for example, welfare, financial aid to college students, social security, Medicare. But hardly anyone would support a private organization's behaving in the same manner. If Oxfam were to begin demanding contributions and threatening to kidnap and imprison anyone who dared defy their demands, hardly anyone would regard this behavior as morally acceptable. This is so despite the fact that Oxfam's programs are far more socially beneficial than those of the state.

III. *Immigration:* A large majority of Americans favor fairly strict legal restrictions on immigration, and most believe the state is justified in forcibly deporting illegal immigrants. But hardly anyone thinks that a private individual may declare who may or may not reside in the country (on *other* people's property) and then kidnap at gunpoint anyone whom the individual has not granted permission to reside in the country in order to forcibly expel them from the land.

These examples should make the pattern clear. The difference between libertarians and nonlibertarians lies not in any unusual libertarian beliefs about interpersonal ethics but merely in the fact that libertarians are unusually consistent in their application of commonsense morality. Libertarians believe that what is wrong for a private individual or organization to do is also wrong for the state to do. Nonlibertarians believe that the state possesses a special dispensation, a right to deploy force in a stunning array of circumstances in which it would clearly be wrong for anyone else to deploy force. This special dispensation is known as "authority"—the state may coerce individuals, it is thought, because the state possesses authority over everyone else.

I cannot here discuss all the philosophical defenses of authority that have been offered. Suffice it to say that (a) there is a prima facie problem for anyone who, while recognizing the serious moral objections to coercive behavior of the kinds discussed above when that behavior is carried out privately, nevertheless wishes to maintain that the same behavior is morally permissible and desirable when carried out by a government; and (b) all of the extant attempts to justify this ethical double standard are open to compelling objections, as I have argued elsewhere.[25] This approach to defending libertarianism is what I refer to as the commonsense approach.

4.2. Rhetorical Superiority of the Commonsense Approach

I claim that all existing accounts of political authority conflict with firm, commonsense moral intuitions and that, furthermore, the rejection of political authority drives us to some form of libertarianism. Suppose I am right about that. Then we can defend political liberty without relying upon any general account of the nature of morality, any comprehensive moral theory, nor even any general theory of coercion. The defense of liberty does not require us to *reject* such general theories; it is consistent with a wide variety of ethical and metaethical theories.

There are two closely related reasons why the commonsense approach is rhetorically superior to approaches that rely upon general ethical or metaethical theories. The first reason is that the commonsense approach immediately puts statists on the defensive. When confronted with the tension between their moral attitudes toward private coercion and their attitudes toward political coercion, nonlibertarians face a burden of explaining and justifying this double standard. It is they who must devise a theory—a theory of authority—and defend this theory from objections. In contrast, the theoretical approaches commonly favored by other liber-

25. Huemer 2013, part 1.

tarians unwisely put the advocate of liberty in the defensive posture at the start, for it is the libertarian who winds up having to articulate a general theory, devise arguments for the theory, and defend the theory against all manner of counterexamples and other objections.

Second, the theoretical approaches typically require the assertion of premises that simply are not obvious to most people. For instance, the premise that nothing other than one's own life can be intrinsically good for one, or the premise that morality must be based upon a social contract, or the premise that it is always wrong to initiate the use of force. One is going to have to work quite a bit to convince most people that they really must accept these abstract claims. The Randian defense of capitalism is particularly ill-fated, as it can only succeed once we have convinced the audience to adopt ethical egoism and thus to radically depart from the fundamental moral beliefs that have been held by nearly everyone in nearly every society throughout all of recorded history. Granted, inductive inferences from history are fallible; nevertheless, the historical record would seem to suggest, whatever one may think of the merits of the theory, that general conversion to ethical egoism is not exactly one of the more likely of future cultural developments.

The commonsense libertarian faces much easier going, since he relies upon moral premises that the audience is already inclined to accept. No one has to give up their religion, adopt a new comprehensive philosophical system, radically revise their values, or reject the putative wisdom of virtually all the moral thinkers of the past. All I am asking my audience to do is to apply to the state the same moral standards that they already apply to every other agent.

4.3. *Epistemic Superiority of the Commonsense Approach*

The commonsense approach to promoting liberty may be good strategy, but is it good philosophy? Or would we be better off trying first to settle matters of abstract theory, so that we might then deduce our moral judgments about more concrete issues from the correct general theory? Our commonsense ethical intuitions, after all, may be misguided. Won't we be more reliable if we check these intuitions against a philosophical theory?

The questions of the preceding paragraph embody a widespread and fundamental epistemological confusion, the same fallacy that characterizes rationalistic philosophies in general. The fundamental fallacy of rationalism is the idea that human knowledge proceeds from the abstract to the concrete, from the general to the specific; that one arrives at particular judgments by applying pre-given abstract rules to particular circumstances. The evidence of human experience stands almost uniformly against these assumptions, in virtually every area of human intellectual endeavor. In the sciences, one does not begin with an abstract theory and then use it to interpret experiences. If one wants to develop a theory, one begins with a large collection of concrete facts; patterns may emerge and explanations may suggest themselves, once one has collected a sufficient body of background facts. One's theories must conform to and be driven by the concrete facts, not the other way around. It is not that one uses data to winnow down the list of permissible theories. When we begin investigating some area, we typically do not even have a list of possible theories to start with—or if we do, that list will almost certainly not include the correct theory, or the theory that we are ultimately going to wind up with. For example, it is not as though the ancient Greeks rejected quantum mechanics because they didn't have enough evidence for it. The ancient Greeks did not *consider* quantum mechanics; it could not have occurred to them, because they did not have data that even suggested it as a possibility. No one even thought of the modern interpretations of quantum mechanics until we had data that those interpretations could explain.

Much the same is true in mathematics, despite the fact that mathematical knowledge is commonly presented to students in the form of axiomatic systems. Historically, mathematical axiomatizations postdate the recognition of large bodies of particular mathematical facts, which the axioms are then used to systematize. For example, people used arithmetic long before Peano's axioms were discovered. The ancient Greeks knew that one plus one was two, with no help from Peano, who arrived thousands of years later. Euclid's *Elements*, often held up as the paradigm of an axiomatic mathematical system, did not emerge from Euclid's brain in the form it is presented. Geometry began in ancient Egypt and Babylon as an unsystematic collection of empirical principles concerning lengths, angles, areas, and volumes, millennia before Euclid arrived on the scene. The Greeks changed the methodology of geometry from one of trial and error to one of logical deduction, and Euclid gathered together theorems from a variety of sources (adding some new proofs of his own) to produce the *Elements*.[26] Again, human knowledge proceeds *from* the concrete and specific *to* the abstract and general, not the other way around. Only once we have knowledge of a variety of relatively concrete truths firmly in mind may we profitably proceed to devising a general theory.

26. See Burton 1995, chs. 2–4.

The same is true in philosophy. In epistemology, for example, one does not (if one is wise) begin from some general, allegedly self-evident theory of knowledge and thence merely draw out the implications of this axiomatic theory for each of the major areas of knowledge. This procedure is the origin of philosophical skepticism.[27] Rather, one must begin with a variety of examples of knowledge—I know where I live, when Napoleon was defeated, how many planets are in the solar system, and so on—and from there attempt to explain what knowledge is and how it may be gained *such that these examples are accounted for.* Similarly, if we wish to arrive ultimately at some general theory of ethics, we must start from a variety of relatively concrete, particular ethical truths. It is those who proceed in the opposite direction—declaring some general, abstract theory and then demanding that the particular facts conform to it—who are responsible for the mountains of failed (and often absurd) theories that dominate the landscape of the history of philosophy. The history of science is similarly littered with false aprioristic theories. Fortunately, in modern times scientists learned to improve their methodology so as to put the concrete facts first. Philosophers have yet to learn this.

In the history of philosophy, what percentage of the theories that have been embraced by one philosopher or another have actually been *correct*? No one knows the exact answer to this, but something between 0 and 5 percent would be a fair guess. The vast majority of philosophical theories that have been embraced are presently rejected by the vast majority of philosophers, and there are very few if any nontrivial philosophical theories that are generally accepted. Knowing this, our estimate of the reliability of philosophical theorizing in general must be very low.

"But," one might say, "this time is different, for I have one very special theory. This theory has been conclusively *proven*, starting from self-evident axioms! None of those failed theories of the past were actually proven." What if we were to look through the history of philosophy and consider just the philosophical theories *that have been thought conclusively proven by their proponents*—what percentage of *those* theories were actually correct? Almost anyone familiar with the history will agree that the answer is, again, very low. Spinoza thought that his entire metaphysical system was deductively proven from self-evident axioms and definitions. Descartes thought he had proved the existence of God, with 100

---

27. The pattern is clearly seen in the cases of such philosophers as David Hume (1748 [1975]) and Peter Unger (1975).

percent certainty, from self-evident axioms. Aquinas had not one but five "proofs" for the existence of God. Plato "proved" the immortality of the soul.[28] And none of these was a stupid man; these were some of history's greatest thinkers. For a present-day philosopher, then, to declare that he has *proved* (this time for real!) some extremely controversial thesis should naturally occasion a certain degree of skepticism on the part of any observer—including the philosopher himself—who is not utterly naive.

Is the conclusion here one of despair? If philosophers are so bad at identifying the truth, if the things we regard as self-evident are usually false, should we simply give up on identifying any important philosophical truths?

That conclusion would be too hasty (and, as it is itself a philosophical claim, self-defeating). Natural science fumbled around with *utterly false* theories, theories that we now know were nowhere even remotely close to correct, for thousands of years before finally decisively embarking on the path of progress.[29] The proper conclusion is that philosophy stands in need of methodological reform and that philosophers must proceed much more cautiously, particularly when it comes to sweeping, abstract generalizations, than we have to date. Philosophers should attempt to follow in broad terms the path of intellectual progress in all other areas: the path from the specific and concrete to the general and abstract. (Notice, incidentally, that my methodological recommendation is self-supporting: I did not arrive at it by deducing it from some general axioms about knowledge. I arrived at it through reflection on a variety of specific instances of human knowledge acquisition, a few of which are mentioned above.)

The commonsense approach to political philosophy is epistemically superior to the rationalistic approach for three closely related reasons. First, the commonsense approach begins from concrete, specific moral judgments rather than sweeping, abstract generalizations. As I have been discussing, this is a more reliable method in general.

Second, the commonsense approach begins from premises that are logically weaker than the premises typically used in rationalistic ap-

---

28. Spinoza, *Ethics*; Descartes, *Meditations on First Philosophy*; Aquinas, *Summa Theologica* I a.2.3; Plato, *Phaedo*.

29. I have in mind here the theory that the fundamental elements of the physical world are earth, air, fire, and water; that diseases are caused by imbalances of the four bodily humours of blood, phlegm, black bile, and yellow bile; that bodies fall to the Earth because they are striving to regain their natural place; that the stars are pinpricks in the firmament; and so on. For a useful review of ancient and medieval science, see Lindberg 1992.

proaches. When I deploy the premise, for example, that it would not be permissible for a private individual to kidnap and imprison a neighbor simply because the neighbor was ingesting unhealthful substances, my premise is compatible with a wide range of possible ethical and metaethical theories. An Objectivist can accept this premise, but so can a Christian, a Kantian, an Aristotelian virtue theorist, or a contractarian. Because it is consistent with so many theoretical possibilities, the commonsense premise is more likely to be true than any of those general theories. Because erroneous judgment is such a widespread problem in philosophy, it is important to proceed as cautiously as possible, and this means taking the *logically weakest premises* that one can, consistent with arriving at a conclusion on the question one wishes to investigate (in this case, the proper political system). To insist on a grand theory that answers all controversial questions is to needlessly expose oneself to a *much* greater risk of error.

Third, as a general rule, claims that are highly controversial or even counterintuitive tend to be less reliable than claims that are obvious and uncontroversial. The commonsense approach starts from premises that strike almost everyone, including almost all the experts in the field, as obvious. The rationalistic libertarian defenses tend to start from claims that are much less widely accepted, often claims that strike most people as obviously *false*, such as the claim that only one's own life can be of value. A rational person does not reject a proposition of which he is more strongly convinced, solely on the basis of premises of which he is *less* convinced. Therefore, the failure of most people to be convinced by rationalistic arguments for libertarianism is not merely a psychological failing but a manifestation of epistemic rationality. And so the commonsense approach is not only rhetorically but *epistemically* superior.

5. Anarchy or Minimal State?

One "disadvantage" of the commonsense approach is that it does not enable us to deduce the complete structure of the ideal society on the basis of just a few simple philosophical sentences. We cannot say, for example, "The state by its nature initiates aggression; therefore, we must have anarchy, no matter the consequences!" Though I argued above (section 3.2) that the Non-Aggression Axiom entails anarchism, this is *not* my argument for anarchism. To decide between anarcho-capitalism and the minimal state, we will require a large body of knowledge—knowledge from social psychology, history, economics, sociology, and philosophy. The fact that all states initiate aggression against individuals is an important consideration in favor of anarchy, but it is only one among many considerations that must be weighed.

The reason for this is that commonsense morality is not absolutist. Commonsense morality holds that it is *generally* wrong to treat other human beings in certain ways—for example, to deploy violence against them or to use their property without their permission. But almost everyone also intuits that such prima facie wrongful behavior *can* be justified in extreme circumstances, as when it is necessary to prevent something *extremely bad* from occurring. For instance, almost everyone judges it permissible to borrow a person's car without the owner's permission if doing so is necessary to take someone to the hospital in the case of a serious medical emergency.[30] Therefore, in deciding whether a minimal state is justified despite its aggressive character, we need to determine whether the minimal state is in fact necessary to prevent something extremely bad from happening, something much worse than the aggression committed by the state.

Many believe that this is in fact the case. Critics of anarchism have often held that an anarchist society would immediately devolve into a war of all against all, leaving everyone much, much worse off than the inhabitants of the average state, to say nothing of a well-designed state.[31] Defenders of anarchism maintain, on the other hand, that a well-ordered anarcho-capitalist society is possible, in which there would be significantly *lower* rates of violence and crime—and that the members of such a society would be more prosperous, freer, and in general much better off than the members of any feasible governmental society. To decide between limited government and anarchy, we must determine what the consequences of an anarcho-capitalist system would actually be. If statists are correct in their assessment of these consequences, almost no one would say that anarchy was the right social system; if the anarchists are correct in *their* assessment, almost everyone would.

This matter, obviously, is not to be resolved here. As I say, it is a complex question whose resolution must draw upon a wide range of knowledge from a variety of disciplines. A book-length treatment would be more appropriate than a paragraph.[32] My immediate point is simply to

30. This example is from Wellman 2005, 21.

31. See Hobbes, *Leviathan* (1651), ch. 13; Rand, "The Nature of Government" (*VOS* 127/ *CUI* 380).

32. Again, see Huemer 2013, part 2.

renounce the rationalistic approach of deducing either anarchism or statism from some simplistic philosophical theses asserted as axiomatic.

But despite what I have just said, the case for *libertarianism*—that is, the argument that we ought not to have anything *more* than a minimal state—is more easily made on the basis of more limited and widely known premises. Almost everyone, I contend, already knows enough to figure out that libertarianism is correct. The reason for this is that the advocates of a more expansive state—for instance, those who support welfare programs, drug laws, and immigration restrictions—do not even *claim* any reasons for these policies that would serve to justify the level of coercion involved according to commonsense morality. In other words, the arguments supporting an expansive state over a minimal state differ in one crucial respect from the arguments supporting government over anarchy: In the arguments for government in general, the alleged consequences of anarchy are so bad that almost everyone would intuitively judge the need to avoid such consequences as sufficient grounds to justify coercion, *even without any general assumption of political authority*; thus, the debate comes down to whether those consequences would really occur. But in the arguments for an expansive state, the reasons given for going beyond the minimal state (for instance, the health harms of drug use, the need to help the poor send their children to college, the fiscal and economic impacts of immigration) typically are *not* strong enough that, in commonsense morality, they would justify coercion on the part of any private agent. The belief that the state possesses a special sort of authority is thus required in the case of the arguments for the expansive state, whereas it is not needed in the case of the arguments for the minimal state. Thus, to arrive at a libertarian political philosophy, all we need do is reject the doctrine of political authority.

Egoism, Force, and the Need for Government
A Response to Huemer

HARRY BINSWANGER

Professor Huemer's paper is important because it squarely and clearly challenges key tenets of Objectivism. In so doing, it reveals how different Objectivism is from some of the other views that Huemer (and many others) package together with it under the label "libertarian."[1] I will confine my comments to the topics of egoism, force, and anarchism, but first I will respond to his final section on methodology.

Methodology

Since my comments on the paper's methodology are going to be negative, let me begin by observing that Rand and Huemer have a common enemy here: Rationalism. Rand, like Huemer, completely rejects the methodology of Rationalism—which she understands to be the "claim that man obtains his knowledge of the world by deducing it exclusively from concepts, which come from inside his head and are not derived from the per-

These comments are based on those delivered on an earlier draft of Huemer's paper at the Ayn Rand Society meeting in San Francisco, March 30, 2013. The author wishes to acknowledge the helpful editorial suggestions provided by Gregory Salmieri.

1. See Gregory Salmieri's discussion of the concept "libertarian," in the introduction to this volume, 6–8.

ception of physical facts" (*FTNI* 30). Deduction presupposes induction, because deduction is the process of applying inductively acquired generalizations "downward" to less general issues. Induction, based on and checked by perceptual observation, is, Objectivism holds, the primary means of acquiring knowledge. "Man's senses are his only direct cognitive contact with reality and, therefore, his only *source* of information. Without sensory evidence, there can be no concepts; without concepts, there can be no language; without language, there can be no knowledge and no science" ("Kant Versus Sullivan," *PWNI* 90).[2] Objectivists regard concept-formation as key to the advance of knowledge, and concept-formation, Rand writes, "is, in essence, a process of induction" (*ITOE* 28). The root here is Objectivism's commitment to the primacy of perception over concepts, which means: (1) perception is prior to and independent of concepts, (2) concepts are dependent on perception, (3) perception is the given, and (4) perception is the standard for judging the conceptual. As I stress in *How We Know*:

> Knowledge begins with perception and builds up hierarchically from perception. The first "upward" step is concept-formation, a process that starts with the perceived similarity of two or more perceived objects. The next step upward comes with the formation of higher-level concepts, in the required hierarchical order. One cannot have a higher-level concept without the lower-level ones on which it rests, and the first-level concepts are formed from perception. . . .
>
> When we subsume something under a concept, that is a "downward" step, one that cashes-in on the cognitive power gained in previous upward steps. To say "Socrates is a man" is to apply the concept "man" to him—which presupposes one has formed the concept "man." The very purpose of ascending the hierarchy of knowledge is to use the knowledge, to apply it, which means applying it back to perceptual reality. In cognition, too, what goes up must come down.
>
> The purpose of concepts is conceptual identification. The purpose of theory is practice. The purpose of consciousness is successful action in the world.
>
> The same progression from the perceptual to the more abstract applies to the hierarchy of propositions and to the hierarchy of inferences.

2. See also my extensive discussion of knowledge as "bottom up" rather than "top down" (Binswanger 2014, chapter 11).

The progression is always: from perception to the more abstract (for the sake of subsequent downward application to concretes). . . .

Induction from perceptual observation is the essential means of gaining new knowledge. Though deductive steps often appear as intermediaries in the process, the overall progression is inductive—bottom-up. (Binswanger 2014, 371–72)[3]

Rand's political conclusions are based on her theory of ethics, which she arrived at *inductively*. In fact, the entire content of Objectivism is inductively based (see Leonard Peikoff's lecture series "Objectivism through Induction" [1998]).

But that Rand and Huemer have a common enemy does not mean that they are methodological allies. Despite his statement that "human knowledge proceeds *from* the concrete and specific *to* the abstract and general," the *working* methodology of his paper is that hoary false alternative to Rationalism: Empiricism. Rand opposed both Rationalism and Empiricism with equal fervor. By "Empiricism" here I mean the methodology of a myopic immersion in isolated concretes, refusing to conceptualize, refusing to abstract, refusing to integrate into the wider context—that is, ironically refusing to engage in *induction*. Induction, for Objectivism, is a process of abstraction and logical integration.[4] The result is not just some after-the-fact commentary on knowledge already sufficient in itself but an integrated *system* of principles that enables one both to understand the reasons underlying the earlier conclusions and to define the context in which they apply or do not apply. For example, to explain Kepler's laws of planetary motion by reference to Newtonian mechanics is to grasp the causes of the regularities Kepler formulated and to be able to extend them to all cases of orbital dynamics (and much more). The essentials involved in the progression from observation to abstraction, generalization, and systematization—the essentials of logic—are these: treating each conclusion not as an isolated proposition but as an integral part of the full *con-*

---

3. See also Peikoff 1991, 52–55, 90–91; Peikoff 2012, chapters 7–9; his lecture courses 1998 and 2005; as well as Salmieri 2005 and 2009 (which explain how the heroes in *Anthem* and *Atlas Shrugged*, respectively, use induction to reach philosophic principles).

4. Rand wrote very little on induction as such. I extrapolate what I say here from what she wrote about concept-formation, and on epistemology generally. Rand's best student and interpreter, Leonard Peikoff, developed a theory of induction in the Objectivist tradition, which is presented in the first chapter of Harriman 2010. See also the references given in the previous note.

text of a growing system of knowledge and recognizing that this system has a *hierarchical* structure, with some judgments supplying the means of grasping others.[5] It is context and hierarchy that are most conspicuously absent from Huemer's approach. He treats Objectivism not as a philosophy, but as a flat collage of independent propositions, as we will see.

The paper proceeds by ripping Rand's conclusions out of context, depriving them of their grounding in observation, and rendering their meaning indeterminate. This licenses Huemer to interpret Rand's conclusions in ways that are incompatible with the text and that Rand would not endorse. Sometimes Huemer constructs arguments of his own for her positions—arguments that are inspired only loosely, if at all, by anything Rand said and that contradict her own methodology. Then he finds unpersuasive the arguments he has substituted for her own. Finally, he attacks the resulting straw man by raising out-of-context, sometimes science-fictional, examples meant to show that Objectivism is unrealistic. I turn now from issues of method to those of content.

Ayn Rand's Egoism

As Huemer observes, Rand provides a moral argument for capitalism that rests on ethical egoism. For Rand, egoism is not a primary but a corollary implication of what value *is* (its dependence on life). In the introduction to *The Virtue of Selfishness*, she writes (x):

> The choice of the beneficiary of moral values is merely a preliminary or introductory issue in the field of morality. It is not a substitute for morality nor a criterion of moral value, as altruism has made it. Neither is it a moral primary: it has to be derived from and validated by the fundamental premises of a moral system.
>
> The Objectivist ethics holds that the actor must always be the beneficiary of his action and that man must act for his own rational self-interest. But his right to do so is derived from his nature as man and from the function of moral values in human life—and, therefore, is applicable only in the context of a rational, objectively demonstrated and validated code of moral principles which define and determine his actual self-interest.

5. The corresponding injunctions of the Objectivist epistemology are to *integrate* and to *reduce to perception*. On integration Rand writes, "No concept man forms is valid unless he integrates it without contradiction into the total sum of his knowledge" (*Atlas* 1016); and Peikoff writes, "Proof is a form of reduction . . . a process of establishing a conclusion by identifying *the proper hierarchy of premises* . . . terminating with the perceptually given" (1991, 138; and also chapter 4).

There is no separate argument for egoism, and the passage from Galt's speech that Professor Huemer quotes as Rand's "argument for egoism" is in fact her argument that life is the root of values because it is precisely the relation of things to life that makes them of value. Egoism falls out as a corollary. Value pertains to a relationship between an organism's actions and its survival needs—an organism's *own* actions and *its own* survival needs. Given this view of the nature of value, effects on other organisms can indeed have value-significance for the acting organism but only insofar as these effects redound upon itself.[6] The same is true for the actions of the specific organism that philosophy is concerned with: man.[7] I am here speaking metaphysically about the nature of value as such; other people— to the extent they are rational—are an immense value to one's life (see more on this, below).

Assuming we now understand what Rand's argument actually seeks to establish, let me turn to inspect that argument. The essential point is this: only life makes possible an objective, nonarbitrary distinction between value and disvalue, or good and bad. This is because all value-concepts pertain to goal-directed action. ("A value is that which one acts to gain and/or keep" [*Atlas* 1012].) And goal-directed action presupposes something being at stake for the agent, something that it can gain or lose in the action. Apart from the beneficial or harmful effects of action back on the agent, there is no way to distinguish goals, values, good, and so on from anything else. This is the point of her immortal robot example ("The Objectivist Ethics," *VOS* 16): a robot that moves around but (hypothetically) cannot be affected by any of the consequences of its activities could have no values. Nothing is at stake for it.

The essential step in Rand's argument is one unaccountably elided from Professor Huemer's quotation: "The existence of inanimate matter is unconditional, the existence of life is not: it depends on a specific course of action" (*Atlas* 1012; quoted in "The Objectivist Ethics," *VOS* 15).

It is the *conditionality* of life upon action that creates good-for and bad-for. An animal strives to gain the food it needs to survive; that's why

6. See Binswanger 1990, 1992; Peikoff 1991, 189–93, 206–20; Gotthelf 2016, 74–81; Smith 2000, 84–111; Smith 2006, 19–48.

7. I follow Rand in using "man" in the gender-neutral sense to name the human species. On the controversy over this usage, see Salmieri's discussion in "Selfish Regard for the Rights of Others," 169n6, above. Given Rand's very explicit and developed ideas concerning gender, sex, and psychosexual identity, and her consciously ironic description of herself as "a male chauvinist" (*Answers* 106), she almost certainly would have strongly opposed the current trend toward gender-neutral language; see "About a Woman President" (*VOR*).

it hunts or grazes. It is this need to act that creates the basis for our evaluation of things as good for or bad for any living organism. (The additional distinction between *morally* good and *morally* bad arises, Rand holds, where there is volitional choice.) Apart from an agent's need to act to achieve certain things, there is no *objective* basis for distinguishing between success and failure, benefit or harm, good or evil. And "need" here means "that which is required for continued existence." Thus we see the connection of value, through need, to the continued existence of the agent.

Note the context in which Rand makes her famous statement: "There is only one fundamental alternative in the universe: existence or nonexistence." The context is the dependence of values upon alternatives—or, as I put it, on something "being at stake." Existence or nonexistence is the only fundamental *value-generating* alternative. We can find an unlimited number of other alternatives in the universe: being red or not being red, being here or being there, and so on. But those are alternatives within existence, and they have *value-significance* only to the extent that they affect the acting organism's chances of survival—that is, of continuing to exist. In the simplest terms, if being red means easily being seen by a predator, that's *bad* for the potential prey; but it's *good* for the predator. The application to man of this basic biological issue—life versus death—requires recognizing man's specific means of survival: his reasoning mind, which operates volitionally. Although all values arise from facing survival needs, *moral* values arise from facing survival needs with a volitional (conceptual) consciousness. "To remain alive, [man] must think. But to think is an act of choice. . . . [M]an is a being of volitional consciousness. Reason does not work automatically. . . . [F]or you, who are a human being, the question 'to be or not to be' is the question 'to think or not to think'" (*Atlas* 1012). Egoism, again, is a corollary of the fact that value is a relation between an agent's action and his own life. Consequently, to deny egoism is to deny the value-relationship as such. It is to hold that it doesn't matter what the effects of one's choices are on oneself. But "doesn't matter"—to whom and for what? To "matter" is to matter to an acting organism, and the mattering is the benefit or harm to that organism.

Accordingly, every non-egoist code (altruism being the paradigm case) is parasitic upon egoism, epistemologically. A child could not form the normal concepts of "good" and "bad" if, from the beginning of his life, he was taught those terms in an anti-egoist fashion, with "good" meaning that which harms him and "bad" meaning that which causes him to gain. If parents brought up a child to understand that "good" means things like being spanked, having his toys taken away from him, losing to others in games, and failing in school, he would come to use the word "good" as we use "bad" (and likewise for learning "bad"). This is a consequence of the fact that the root and fundamental meaning of good is "pro-life"—one's own life. There is no way to learn value-concepts except in relation to one's own pleasure and pain, joy and suffering, well-being or injury, life or death.

But the situation is not symmetrical. Egoism is not epistemically dependent upon altruism. One does not have to learn moral concepts by reference to self-sacrifice. (The culture of Ancient Greece, though intensely focused on morality, made little or no appeal to self-sacrifice.) Nor does one have to learn moral concepts by reference to God's will, utilitarian considerations, environmental impact, the categorical imperative, or any other non-egoist (and, by implication, anti-egoist) conception. Everyone, simply to survive, must act and think some of the time and in some respects on the premise of egoism. But there is no parallel requirement that a person think or act counter to egoism.

Professor Huemer's criticism of egoism is two-pronged. One prong seems devoted to avoiding challenging people's preconceptions. He comes perilously close to saying: "Egoism isn't true because very few people believe it is true." He casts this as a rhetorical or "marketing" issue, but we must remain exquisitely sensitive to the difference between what "sells" and what is a logically valid case.[8]

Elsewhere, Professor Huemer has argued that what everyone believes is quite likely to be true.[9] And this is indeed the case—but only for issues quite close to the perceptual level. One must distinguish abstract and difficult issues from simple, concrete ones. Everyone recognizes that the sky is blue. Everyone recognizes that two plus two equals four. But issues of moral judgment are quite abstract, and very few people approach the subject of morality by making independent, rational judgments. The vast majority conform to what they have been taught or what is held in their culture. This is the same way they proceed in regard to religion. People don't accept the doctrines of religion because they have become convinced by

8. In regard to marketing, I have to take strong exception to the implication that the Objectivist approach to persuading people of capitalism is not effective. Ayn Rand has converted more people to capitalism than any other author in the last two hundred years, and without her there would be no "libertarian" movement.

9. Huemer 2005b.

the ontological argument, or any of the other mildly tricky arguments for God that have been cooked up over the centuries. They believe in God because they *want* to believe, and one of the main reasons they want to believe is that the others in their subculture believe it. The same is true of altruism—except that, in contrast to the issue of God's existence, the history of philosophy offers amazingly little in the way of arguments, even bad ones, purporting to explain why a man should live for others.

And living for others is what altruism means. If you don't agree, that's a subject for discussion, but please accept that it is what Ayn Rand and Objectivism mean by altruism, and it is that idea that we Objectivists are opposing. Ayn Rand writes: "The basic principle of altruism is that man has no right to exist for his own sake, that service to others is the only justification of his existence, and that self-sacrifice is his highest moral duty, virtue and value" ("Faith and Force," *PWNI* 61).[10]

Now, as a matter of sociological fact, the vast majority of people hold mixed, contradictory views on the role of self-interest in morality. To some extent and in some moods, the common man espouses the doctrine drilled into him since childhood: that one's moral worth is gauged by the extent of the sacrifices one makes for others, and that any self-interested action is, at best, mere "prudence," an amoral concession to "practicality." At other times (at least in America), he admires selfish virtues such as independence and productive achievement, and he is proud of his ability to provide for his own well-being. So, contra Professor Huemer, it is not the case that the common man has some sort of clear recognition that altruism (or some other anti-egoist code) is right and egoism is wrong, in the way he has a clear recognition that the sky is blue. In short, the (very abstract) question of what is the proper system of morality cannot be answered by appeal to "common belief" or "our intuitions."

I turn now to the second prong of Professor Huemer's attack on egoism: the incredible example of an egoist choosing to get a dime's worth of value (or net value) at the cost of "horrific agony and death for four million innocent people."

Moral judgment requires knowledge—knowledge of motives, causes, effects, and context. But we are given none of that for this example. We are not told whether the dime-saver causes the deaths of the four million, or whether he merely fails to prevent them. If the former, Rand's

---

10. On how altruism so defined relates both to conventional moral thought and to the history of moral philosophy, see Salmieri 2016c, 136–41.

morality of rational self-interest does not permit it (and in fact regards mass murder as the most horrendous evil). Anyone with an elementary familiarity with Objectivism knows that it advocates inviolable individual rights—and does so because the reign of rights is necessary for anyone to achieve his self-interest.[11] The underlying facts are available to the simplest, least educated man. It is not in order to sacrifice themselves to others that millions of the world's poor stream to America, the country symbolizing individual rights; it is to advance their own lives that they come here, even at great cost. They come to live under a political system that (in its original conception) implements the moral principle that no man may prey upon others.

Frederic Bastiat summarized well the reason why respecting others' rights is to everyone's self-interest. He pointed out that there are three alternatives: (1) everyone plunders everyone, (2) some plunder others, (3) no one plunders anyone. The first leads to universal destruction; the second is contradictory, involving a double standard; the third is to the interests of every individual (*The Law* [1850/2007], 16).[12]

Rand went deeper, explaining why rights are "conditions of existence required by man's nature for his proper survival" (*Atlas* 1061). Rights are pro-life because reason is man's basic means of survival, and reason cannot operate under force. But his paper does not even mention this issue, even though it is the foundation of the entire social-political structure of Objectivism.

Instead of confronting the reasoning behind the Objectivist ethics and politics, this paper deals in (alleged) counterexamples. Counterexamples as such have very limited value, and no value unless: (1) one uses clear, center-of-the page examples (versus the dime example), and (2) one identifies the meaning of the counterexample—the principle behind its being a counterexample, so that the generalization being attacked cannot be defended by making adjustments to the application of the principle. Huemer's counterexamples do not meet these requirements. This failure marks one way in which the paper reads as polemical advocacy rather than scholarly investigation and criticism.

Now let's consider the dime example, not as a case of mass murder but as a case of refraining from preventing the deaths. In this case, the

---

11. See Wright's three chapters and Ghate's two chapters in this volume.

12. Rand held that universalizability is a necessary condition for morality—while vehemently rejecting that it is a sufficient condition (à la Kant).

issue of rights violation does not arise, and the issue is whether the man has a moral obligation to have prevented the deaths and whether doing so would have been counter to his self-interest. Professor Huemer poses the example in terms of a *net* benefit of a dime's worth of value. But this means that the man has a slightly higher value that he gains or keeps by not averting this particular catastrophe. What value the man is to gain or keep—a value that slightly exceeds the (immense) value of saving four million lives—is simply not specified. Does he, for instance, *save* a different set of four million lives, plus gets a dime? Or does the egoist have to choose between his own life and that of the four million? Is it four million people in North Korea, whom he will never meet nor interact with, and who are living a subhuman existence under that communist dictatorship—or do the four million include his friends, family, and his wife? Although masked by the little word "net," the alleged counterexample is completely undefined and consequently shows nothing.

Here is a less unrealistic example. A man faces the choice of spending his money to save his own life, or donating that money to save the lives of three strangers in a distant land. Egoism would demand that he save his own life. But this is not contrary to "common sense."

Professor Huemer's idea of what egoism would require derives from his, not Rand's, formulation of egoism: "for any action A that I can perform, if A provides a net benefit to me (compared with every alternative), then I should do A." This kind of approach renders "net benefit" subjective and indeterminate. Ethics does not consist of cost-benefit analyses; ethics identifies and applies *principles* of action. Contrast the range-of-the-moment, contextless approach of the formula given above with Rand's explication of her standard of morality: "Man's survival qua man": "'Man's survival qua man' means the terms, methods, conditions and goals required for the survival of a rational being through the whole of his lifespan—in all those aspects of existence which are open to his choice" ("Objectivist Ethics," *VOS* 26).

Is indifference to other people consistent with those "terms, methods, conditions, and goals"? Are other people—not Adolf Hitler, but people in general—a value to one another or not? Well, of course they are. Where would anyone be without others to learn from, trade with, and find friends and romantic partners among? It would be a terminally warped conception of man's life qua man which held that a rational being is better off alone on a desert island than in midtown Manhattan. Here is a *principled* approach:

The two great values to be gained from social existence are: knowledge and trade. Man is the only species that can transmit and expand his store of knowledge from generation to generation; the knowledge potentially available to man is greater than any one man could begin to acquire in his own lifespan; every man gains an incalculable benefit from the knowledge discovered by others. The second great benefit is the division of labor: it enables a man to devote his effort to a particular field of work and to trade with others who specialize in other fields. This form of co-operation allows all men who take part in it to achieve a greater knowledge, skill and productive return on their effort than they could achieve if each had to produce everything he needs, on a desert island or on a self-sustaining farm. ("The Objectivist Ethics," *VOS* 35–36)

Rand would have agreed with Spinoza, another egoist, when he wrote: "There is no single thing in Nature which is more profitable to man than [another] man who lives according to the guidance of reason."[13] She would have agreed because not only is it entirely consistent with Objectivism, it is obviously true. So, in terms of a code of moral *principles*, based on man's survival qua man, morality absolutely requires valuing the lives of other people (though not above one's own).

In any case, there is no need to resort to science-fictional, puzzling cases; there are real-life examples all around us. Bill Gates and Warren Buffet call upon their fellow billionaires to give away the bulk of their fortunes, not to some specific cause that they argue is worthy but to *any charity at all*. Clearly the premise here is that spending the fortune is good so long as one doesn't spend it on oneself, one's business, or one's loved ones. Many people, obviously, share this belief, but what does this show? Only that many people have accepted the altruist morality. But what we want to know is: Should they have? Is there any *rational* basis for it?

In regard to at least semi-realistic examples, commonsense beliefs extend only to the result—that a man should choose this way, not that way—not to the abstract principle that identifies the *reason* for that result. Common sense does not have a position on whether, for instance, a given choice should be made because man is a value to man or because there is a deontological obligation to do so. In these (artificial) examples, when the man on the street is asked *why* a person should choose one result over the other, he would be likely to answer by giving memorized platitudes, or quoting from the Bible. But we as philosophers can deal with the issue

13. *Ethics* IV, Prop. XXXV, Cor. 1 (Spinoza 1667 [1949], 212).

on a rational, principled level. And, coincidentally (speaking of a dime's worth of value) Ayn Rand has identified the principle involved:

> Do not hide behind such superficialities as whether you should or should not give a dime to a beggar. That is not the issue. The issue is whether you *do* or do *not* have the right to exist *without* giving him that dime. The issue is whether you must keep buying your life, dime by dime, from any beggar who might choose to approach you. The issue is whether the need of others is the first mortgage on your life and the moral purpose of your existence. The issue is whether man is to be regarded as a sacrificial animal. Any man of self-esteem will answer: "*No.*" Altruism says: "*Yes.*" ("Faith and Force," *PWNI* 61)

Altruism is not the only non-egoist moral theory, but the fundamental divide is between the egoist view that moral value is a relationship between the agent's life and the consequences of his choices and any view holding that moral value consists in something else. Morality is either pro-life or anti-life. The form of anti-life—whether giving up one's life to one's neighbors, to God, or to a categorical imperative—is secondary. Altruism is merely the form of anti-life morality that is most popular at present in Western culture. Throughout most of human history and throughout the Islamic world today, the reigning moral code is supernaturalism: submission to God's will. The "commonsense beliefs" of most men throughout most of history is that the decision of whether the four million are to live or die is to be determined by consulting a sacred text or some charismatic leader. But altruism is the main alternative to egoism in our culture, and history has shown how little value its practitioners place on human lives: we must not forget the one hundred million people murdered under communism, an ideology founded on ruthlessly implementing the altruist dictum "From each according to his ability to each according to his need." In world-scale practice, altruism has demonstrated itself to be, in Ayn Rand's damning charge, "a morality of death." What else could a morality that severs "value" from "life" be?

Force

I turn now to Huemer's social-political disagreements with Objectivism. Here I need to move more quickly, but fortunately I will be able to do so, because the issues he raises are discussed in other essays in this volume.[14] The two issues involved are (1) the nature of force and (2) anarchism.

---

14. See Wright's first chapter and Ghate's two chapters in this volume.

Rand repeatedly criticized the libertarians for treating the non–initiation of force principle as if it were an axiom, observing that it is a quite derivative principle, requiring a complete philosophic base. Her egoism is an important part of this base, as Huemer acknowledges when he writes: "From the principle of egoism, Rand claims to derive a constellation of closely related political principles." However his description is misleading, in that it suggests Rand simply deduces the relevant principles *directly* from egoism. In fact, her thought proceeds from the point about the relation between value and life (discussed above) to the principles of man's nature qua man, and from there to egoism, and from there to virtue, and from there to social ethics, and from there, finally, to politics. Some such step-by-step progression is required in order to justify condemning and prohibiting the initiation of physical force. Those libertarians who oppose the initiation of physical force typically resist even discussing basic philosophic issues. They take refuge in the idea that the evil of initiated force is self-evident, axiomatic. Huemer even refers to the "Non-Aggression Axiom." But treating a derivative principle as an axiom merely deprives it of its grounding in reality and turns the principle into a subjective preference or an article of faith.[15]

In responding to the five challenges to this principle raised by Professor Huemer, I have to assume the Objectivist philosophy as my base. Let me just give the principle involved in answering each. My comments are not ad hoc adjustments but elucidations of how the same principle applies to different contexts. Darryl Wright's three chapters in this volume stress the need for understanding force and rights in the context of the requirements of man's optimal, long-term survival.

1. The first example concerns having to wait for force to be used: as Wright explains, above (42–43), the threat of force *is* force. Indeed, threats are the main form that coercion takes. The government compels obedience to its laws by means of threats. Of course, those threats are backed up by hands-on force, but the reason that we pay our taxes is not that the IRS has actually taken it out of our bank accounts.

2. Wright (above, 106–12) also explains why breach of contract is force. Professor Huemer says that in refusing to perform a contracted-for service, Jon did not use physical force against Sally. But clearly Jon did use force: he obtained a *material* value from Sally (her eye-examination

---

15. For Rand's view of what it is to be an axiom, see *Introduction to Objectivist Epistemology*, ch. 4. For her view on why only according to the objective theory of the good, not the subjective or intrinsic, is the initiation of force morally wrong, see "What Is Capitalism?" (*CUI*).

service) without her consent—that is, without giving her the form of payment (lawn-mowing) that was her condition for consenting to the deal. Obtaining a *material* value from another without making the agreed-upon payment is force. The situation is the same as if Jon had held a gun to Sally's head to force her to perform the medical service. An eye doctor certainly has a property right in her services: they are hers to supply or withhold as she sees fit. And Sally did not consent to supply her services for free. Jon has caused her to take physical actions to which she did not consent. That is physical force. (Note that without the physical element [the physical act of performing an eye exam], the case would not involve physical force. If Jon tries to impress Sally by falsely telling her that he is a tennis pro, even if he succeeds in deceiving her, the mere hearing and believing of the lie does not constitute being subjected to physical force. In the legal terminology, fraud requires material damages.)

More generally, force against property is force. Property has to be acquired by physical action. To deprive a man of the product of his property-earning actions is to have made him function as a slave: to have labored for the benefit of someone else, involuntarily.

3. Defamation. Rand thought that a person has a sort of property in his reputation. Someone who impersonates me in order to sell to customers impressed by my reputation is, in effect, stealing this property from me (as well as defrauding the customers). And someone who defames me is damaging this property. The idea that a person can have property in his reputation follows from Rand's view that the basis for a property right is an individual's creation of something that is of material value.[16] However, the specific application of this principle to the realm of reputation has not been worked out in detail.

4. Stealing a wallet. As explained by Wright (77–85), Miller and Mossoff (122–23) and Salmieri (185–89), force against property is force. This point is absolutely essential to understanding and defending individual rights. As Rand wrote in several places, "Without property rights, no other rights are possible."

5. Stealing in extremis—so as to prevent starvation. This is subject to Rand's charge of context-dropping. Why is Sally starving? Why does she have no recourse? Why can she not offer to Jon to clean his house or take his clothes to the dry cleaner in exchange for the food that Huemer stipu-

---

16. See the discussion of this view in the present volume in the chapters by Wright, Miller and Mossoff (132–33), and Salmieri (189–90).

lates Jon does not need? Why is Jon the only source of food for Sally? Why are there no jobs for Sally, no family or friends, and no private charity?

Depending on how we answer all these (unaddressed) questions, some cases of stealing in extremis may be justified morally, even if they properly fall within the scope of laws against theft. Sally could steal the food, then accept the legal penalty. But even if the law makes an exception for such in extremis cases, incredibly rare as they would be under laissez-faire capitalism, it would in no way challenge the principle of individual rights and the non–initiation of force. Rand has written on how individual rights are absolute, but *contextually* absolute, and they do not apply in what she calls "a metaphysical emergency," such as in lifeboat situations ("The Ethics of Emergencies," *VOS*). And it is just such a "lifeboat" case one would have to construct if one is to make the example plausible.

Force is actual or threatened nonconsensual physical contact with another's person or property. Man's survival qua man depends on his use of his mind, but in each of these examples one party is acting in a way that negates or paralyzes the mind of the other.[17]

Anarchism versus Limited Government

In answering Rand's objections to "competing governments," Professor Huemer states: "arbitration by a neutral third party is widely regarded as a much easier, less costly, and more just method of resolving disputes than resorting to physical force." Voluntarily submitting to arbitration can be effective in resolving some types of disputes, but it cannot substitute for the criminal law. And arbitration is unthinkable outside the context of an established, accepted government that protects private contracts and simply secures the peace. The idea that voluntary arbitration provides a general means of resolving human conflicts is contradicted by the vast spread of human history, which has been characterized by constant warfare, both across borders and within (the American Civil War, which was between competing governments, resulted in six hundred thousand deaths). Even today, the idea that people would be satisfied with a cost-benefit approach flies in the face of worldwide jihadism, with its cry of "death to the infidel!" The Islamic advocates of imposing blasphemy laws on the citizens of Europe and America are hardly deterred by a consideration of "costs." Nor are plain Mafiosi, who go on murdering each other despite the "costs."

17. See Wright's second contribution to this volume (45–75, above).

Professor Huemer refers to anarchist "literature, to which Rand provides no response," citing, inter alia, David Friedman.[18] As it happens, I had a long discussion with Friedman in the late 1970s, in which he advanced to me exactly this cost-benefit argument. He maintained that it would pay competing "defense agencies" to have "treaties" among themselves to avoid the costs of warfare. I was not entirely satisfied with my response to Friedman in this conversation, so, soon thereafter, I posed this question to Ayn Rand in personal conversation, asking whether these "treaties" among "competing governments" would work. Without hesitation, she replied: "You mean like at the UN?" Since I was painfully familiar with the long, hopeless record of the UN's attempts to bring peace through intergovernmental arbitration and agreement, the point was vividly clear to me. By whom or what would interagency agreements be *enforced*? If they were truly binding, then the agreeing agencies would constitute a government; if not, then they would be meaningless.

The idea that the establishment of competing governments would lead evil people to somehow be converted to the rational calculation of their self-interest is a variant of the Marxist notion that the "mode of production" determines ideology. This is one reason why anarchism is a theory of the left, not of liberty. Rand always maintained that anarchism is a collectivist ideology.

Objectivism holds that predation upon others is against men's rational self-interest—that it is, in fact, self-destructive. That point is essential to the defense of freedom and free markets, and I assume Professor Huemer agrees with it, since he appears to advocate capitalism, at least economically. But the self-destructiveness of initiated force has never stopped some men from resorting to it, and no change in the "mode of production" will do so. Men's actions are caused by their ideas, not by economic conditions.

18. Although Rand did not reply to this literature per se, she did briefly address this line of thought in her 1973 article "The Missing Link." She refers to those on the right who "intend to preserve capitalism, they claim, by replacing it with anarchism (establishing 'private' or competing' governments, i.e. tribal rule)." And she adds, "These rightists' distance from reality may be gauged by the fact that they are unable to recognize the actual examples of their ideals in practice. One such example is the Mafia. The Mafia (or 'family') is a 'private government,' with subjects who chose to join it voluntarily, with a rigid set of rules rigidly, efficiently and bloodily enforced, a 'government' that undertakes to protect you from 'outsiders' and to enforce your immediate interests—at the price of your selling your soul, i.e., of your total obedience to any 'favor' it may demand. Another example of a 'government' without territorial sovereignty is offered by the Palestinian guerrillas, who have no country of their own, but who engage in terrorist attacks and slaughter of 'outsiders' anywhere on earth" (*PWNI* 59–60).

Professor Huemer advances a new (at least to me) idea on behalf of anarchism. It amounts to this: if it is right that the government wield retaliatory force, it cannot be wrong for vigilantes to do so. I counter with: if it is right for a man to drive his car, it cannot be wrong for others to drive it. Obviously, the fact that it is right for one person, or one agency, to do something does not necessarily mean it is right for another person or agency to do the same thing. It depends on *why* it is right for the relevant agent to do the thing. In the case of driving that particular car, part of what makes it right for the man to do it is that it is *his* car. Similarly, the fact that a constitutionally limited government, operating under objective law, is morally entitled to use retaliatory force does not mean that everyone else is morally entitled to do so. It does not legitimize lynch mobs, vigilantes, the Mafia, jihadists, abortion-clinic bombers, or any private "business" enforcing its own "law" at gunpoint.[19]

Huemer supposes that a private "business" of force-wielding could, like a proper government, act objectively. But objectivity is more than the formal requirements of procedure. Objectivity is a commitment to the truth, independent of biases, incentives, and motives.[20] And public objectivity, as opposed to one's private knowledge of one's own intentions, requires that any onlooker have good evidence of the unbiased nature of the party wielding force. But each of the competing private militias would be deriving its income from its "customers" and thus would have a direct, financial interest in using force to advance the interests of its "customers"—at the expense of "customers" of other "defense agencies."

Under a governmental system, the government is the agent of all citizens, providing each with "equal protection under the law" and equal representation. Under "anarcho-capitalism," each private militia would be the agent of just those who are paying it, as attorneys today are of their clients. The proposal to put coercion "on the market" means: "Let's arm the lawyers."

The idea of lawyers with guns, tanks, police, and troops is bad enough, but there's more: these private militias would be judges, legislators (or fatwa-issuers), and executioners wrapped up in one. The militias would be owned by an individual or group and operated for their private profit. Any money they receive in "damages" would go into the owners'

19. Regarding abortion, it is highly relevant to note that a great many libertarians, including Ron Paul, are anti-abortion. These people regard abortion as murder. What "treaty to minimize costs" can be drawn to cover this issue?

20. See Smith 2015.

pockets. Whatever outward semblance of objectivity they would adopt, genuine public objectivity would be impossible under such a setup.

Above I put "business" in scare-quotes because I do not want to commit one of the central fallacies of anarchism: the equation of production with force. I cover this in my article against anarchism (see "Anarchism versus Objectivism," this volume), which Professor Huemer cites. Government is not a "business," and does not provide "a service." Government is force, a gun. "Competition" does not apply to the wielding of force: that is conflict, not competition. Keeping force and production absolutely separate, never confusing the two, is a fundamental requirement of defending capitalism. The equation of economic power with political power is the number one weapon of the left.[21] It is frightening that people who see themselves as defenders of capitalism make this equivocation, and it is another way in which anarchism, properly, belongs on the left.

Ultimately, anarchists who oppose monopoly government have to end up as pacifists. This is because *all force is monopolistic.* (Even in the economic realm, "monopoly" means a business protected from competition by force, not merely a single-seller.)[22] There is no such thing as force that lets dissenters go their own way. Force does not tolerate "to each his own." Force is precisely the attempt to subjugate another's will to one's own. If force in self-defense is justified, this *means* that monopolizing an interaction is justified. If I use force to defend myself against an aggressor, I am not trying to persuade him—I am attempting to stop him from acting as he chooses.

If the government monopolization of force were wrong, so would be the private use of force by individuals. The argument against government's monopoly on force is thus an argument against self-defense, and it leads to pacifism. And, in practice, pacifism in international relations is almost forced upon anarchists, since they can have no solution to the problem of national defense.[23]

If any region were to try to implement "anarcho-capitalism," it would soon be invaded and taken over by some aggressive, statist nation. Domestically, anarchism also would pave the way for dictatorship: "When

---

21. See Rand, "America's Persecuted Minority: Big Business" (*CUI*), and Binswanger 2011.

22. See Binswanger 2005; Daniels 2005.

23. One "anarcho-capitalist," Harry Browne (1973, 83), claimed that the absence of government is actually an advantage: no foreign power would invade an anarchist region, he wrote, because there would be no domestic government to surrender!

force is the standard, the murderer wins over the pickpocket" (Francisco's "money speech" [*Atlas* 413]). The downward spiral would begin when any proper "protection agency" refrained from shutting down a "competing" agency that picks pockets—perhaps in the form of imposing a small tax on those who trade with its "customers."

Ayn Rand's argument against "competing governments" is: "*A government is the means of placing the retaliatory use of force under objective control*—i.e., under objective law" ("The Nature of Government," *CUI* 331; original emphasis). This is a philosophically deeper perspective on Locke's description of "the end of civil society" as being "to avoid and remedy these inconveniences of the state of nature which necessarily follow from every man being judge in his own case." In a footnote, Locke goes on to quote Hooker: "no man might in reason take upon him to determine his own right, and according to this own determination proceed in maintenance thereof, inasmuch as every man is towards himself, and them whom he greatly affects, partial; and therefore that strifes and troubles would be endless except they gave their common consent all to be ordered by some whom they should agree upon, without which consent there would be no reason that one man should take upon him to be lord or judge over another" (Hooker, *Eccl. Pol.* I § 10).[24] One man or one agency wielding private force (except in an emergency when recourse to governmental protection is unavailable) is "taking the law into his own hands." This constitutes an *objective threat* to every other man. Again, the threat of force is force. Other men cannot know how and when a vigilante gang or "competing protection agency" will use force. Therefore, in banning the extragovernmental, unregulated use of force, the government is *retaliating* against this threat.

"Objectivity" is a concept that includes the fact that man acquires knowledge by specific means. He cannot read the minds of other men and so cannot automatically know the basis on which they will use force. In "Anarchism vs. Objectivism" (this volume), I give this concretization: "Picture a band of strangers marching down Main Street, submachine guns at the ready. When confronted by the police, the leader of the band announces: 'Me and the boys are only here to see that justice is done, so you have no right to interfere with us.' According to the 'libertarian' anarchists, in such a confrontation the police are morally bound to withdraw, on pain of betraying the rights of self-defense and free trade." One

24. *Second Treatise of Government*, section 89, and section 90, footnote 2.

could well add the case of an Islamic "protection agency," dedicated to enforcing Sharia law, announcing, "We are only here to see that the Will of Allah is done."

Conclusion

The overall thrust of Huemer's paper is to advocate a certain form of promoting capitalism. Let's not, he says, tie capitalism to egoism because people won't go for that (and with good reason, he thinks). It's not good marketing. Let's sell to them on the basis of what they already value: commonsense decency.

But the only way to succeed in "marketing" capitalism is to get people to understand that every individual has inalienable *rights*. And rights are incompatible with altruism. A person whose life belongs to the needy cannot claim to own his own income—it would belong by right to those who need it more than he.

Nor can an altruist use the non–initiation of force principle to defend capitalism. If altruism were true, the have-nots would be the proper owners of the wealth of the haves. According to the altruist code, government welfare programs are *retaliation* against the "exploiters" who are wrongly in possession of money that belongs to the needy—*because* they are the needy.

The morality of egoism, in contrast, holds that each individual's life is his own, that he is not born in debt to anyone, that he exists for his own sake, not as the moral slave of others, and that *therefore*, no one has a claim on his life, time, thought, or energy.

That is the base of rights, and rights are the base of capitalism.

Part Three
RAND AND THE CLASSICAL LIBERAL TRADITION ON INTELLECTUAL FREEDOM

A Wall of Separation between Church and State

Understanding This Principle's Supporting Arguments and Far-Reaching Implications

ONKAR GHATE

The explicit separation of church and state is a vital new principle of the American experiment in freedom. The most philosophical of America's Founding Fathers, Jefferson and Madison, certainly viewed it in this way. As did Ayn Rand, who in political philosophy saw herself as securing and extending the foundation built by these Enlightenment thinkers in the Declaration of Independence and the Constitution of the United States. Rand described herself politically as a radical for capitalism and, when briefly expanding on her position, would often make the following comparison: "When I say 'capitalism,' I mean a full, pure, uncontrolled, unregulated *laissez-faire* capitalism—with a separation of state and economics, in the same way and for the same reasons as the separation of state and church" ("The Objectivist Ethics," *VOS* 37).[1]

Rand's comparison, however, would now increasingly fall on deaf ears. Americans today, far from being able to extend the reasons supporting church-state separation to the economic realm, have little understanding of this principle or of the arguments advanced by Locke, Jeffer-

---

1. See also Rand, "Introducing Objectivism" in *VOR* 4. For her description of herself and Objectivists as radicals for capitalism, see "Choose Your Issues," in *TON* vol. 1 no. 1, 1.

son, Madison, and others in its favor. This is the topic of my essay. I begin by examining today's confused popular debate about the proper relation between church and state, and why almost no one in America upholds a "wall of separation" between the two anymore. Most of the rest of the essay then focuses on the actual principle of church-state separation and why a "wall of separation" is an appropriate metaphor for the principle and its supporting arguments. I conclude with a brief discussion of why Rand thought both that the principle extends to the economic realm and that this extension is vital to the full, consistent case for freedom.

The Popular Debate about Church-State Separation

Perhaps the easiest angle from which to see the confusion in today's American debate is this: people are debating a metaphor with little to no understanding of the abstract principle for which it is a metaphor. I distinguish three major factions sparring in this debate, which I call the Religionists, the Secularists, and the Compromisers.

The metaphor of "a wall of separation between church and state" is usually traced back to Thomas Jefferson's 1802 letter to the Danbury Baptist Association, though one certainly can find earlier uses of similar imagery. The US Supreme Court famously expanded on Jefferson's metaphor a century and a half later in *Everson v. Board of Education*: "The clause against establishment of religion by law was intended to erect 'a wall of separation between church and state.' . . . That wall must be kept high and impregnable. We could not approve the slightest breach."[2] But if this is *all* one has to guide one's reasoning—a metaphor and no principle—numerous questions will arise that seem to throw the idea into doubt and disrepute.

For instance, with the description of the wall as "high and impregnable," the implication seems to be that the church is completely walled off from the state and the state is completely walled off from the church. Never the two shall meet. How can this be proper? It seems to imply that the government cannot intervene in religious ceremonies or set foot on church property no matter the circumstances. But what if a church is practicing some ritual of human sacrifice? What if, on church grounds, boys are being raped? Or, to take much less disturbing examples, what if a church's bells are ringing throughout the night or a mosque is loudly broadcasting prayers in the early morning? Do neighbors have to put up

---

2. Hugo L. Black's majority opinion in *Everson v. Board of Education* (Dreisbach 2002, 100).

with the noise, with no recourse to the government, because church is completely walled off from state? Surely not. Church grounds are not a separate country, as some view the grounds of an embassy.

So, most people think, the church cannot be *completely* walled off from the state. What about in the other direction? Is the state completely walled off from the church? If it is, does this mean that if a person becomes a member or an official of a church, he can no longer work in government? Does it imply that religious people should not make political arguments or engage in public advocacy? Some people in the debate seem to hold this. Those trying to defend the separation of state *from* church will often say that religion is a private matter, which should not be brought out in public. The "public square," as they put it, using another metaphor, should be "neutral" and "religion-free." As President Obama stated their view, they think you have to "leave your religion at the door before entering into the public square." But this is wrong, Obama said. Did Martin Luther King violate the Constitution when he, often in religious terms, protested governmental oppression of blacks? Should the government have jailed those who advocated for the abolition of slavery in religious language? Should their appeals have been ignored? If the answer to these questions is "No," then, many Americans conclude, the state is also not *completely* walled off from the church, politics from religion.[3]

But if the First Amendment does not erect a wall of separation between church and state, high and impregnable, what exactly does it do? What does the metaphor mean? This is the focus of the debate. One faction—often labeled "the Religious Right," but which I call the "Religionists," in part because this faction cuts across the (blurry) left-right political spectrum—frequently asserts the following: The First Amendment creates freedom *for* religion. It prevents the government from persecuting religion. The state cannot stop someone from preaching or practicing his religion by fining or imprisoning him. On this interpretation, the "free exercise" clause is the heart of the First Amendment.[4] It creates a *one-way*

---

3. Obama 2006. Importantly, Obama also added that the separation of church and state "is critical to our form of government because in the end, democracy demands that the religiously motivated translate their concerns into universal, rather than religion-specific, values. It requires that their proposals be subject to argument, and amenable to reason. If I am opposed to abortion for religious reasons but seek to pass a law banning the practice, I cannot simply point to the teachings of my church. I have to explain why abortion violates some principle that is accessible to people of all faiths, including those with no faith at all." I will come back to a similar point later in the essay.

4. The First Amendment reads: "Congress shall make no law respecting an establishment of religion [the 'establishment' clause], or prohibiting the free exercise thereof [the 'free

wall of protection for churches against the power of the state. All the "establishment" clause means, by contrast, is that the state cannot erect one church as *the* state-sanctioned and supported church of the United States. This leaves many powers still in the hands of the federal government to aid and support religion and religious groups—just as the government today aids and supports autoworkers, the unemployed, and banks deemed too big to fail.

But many people object to the Religionists' interpretation of the First Amendment. It permits much too much intermingling of religion and politics, they contend, and thereby violates the rights both of nonbelievers and of people whose religious beliefs do not enjoy governmental aid and support. A different interpretation of the First Amendment, and of the wall of separation it creates, is needed. This is supplied by the faction typically labeled "the Secular Left"—so the basic debate is supposedly between the Religious Right and the Secular Left. But for reasons similar to why I prefer the term "Religionists," I rename this second group the "Secularists." What do the Secularists claim that the First Amendment means? It means freedom *from* religion.

Why do we need freedom from religion? Because religion has been a source of strife, discord, warfare, and tyranny throughout history, particularly when religion wielded political power. So we have to say to religion: hands off government. You cannot get any taxpayer money to support your religious organizations or programs; the government is not going to display your religious symbols in its buildings; the government is not going to begin the day in governmental schools with religious prayers; in short, the government is not going to allow any believers to use the law to "impose [their] narrow morality on the rest of us." This quote is from a flyer handed out by the Freedom From Religion Foundation, in which it is also stated, "Not only is it un-American for the government to promote religion, it is rude." The public square, Secularists say, must be religion-free.

The heart of the First Amendment, on this interpretation, is the "establishment" clause, which not only prohibits one church from being established as the state-sanctioned and supported church of the United States, but also prohibits any funding of churches or religious organizations and any involvement of religion in government. It creates a *one-way* wall of protection for both the government and the "public square"

exercise' clause]; or abridging the freedom of speech, or of the press; or the right of the people peaceably to assemble, and to petition the Government for a redress of grievances."

against the power of the church. The "free exercise" clause, by contrast, is secondary. As a citizen, you are free to practice your religious beliefs in *private*. But do not bring them out in public, into the "public square." In effect, the Secularists treat religion as many people treat sex: so long as it is voluntary and consensual, do whatever you want behind closed doors but do not display it in public, because no one else wants to hear it and no one else wants to see it.

To this, of course, the Religionists have a response. They say to the Secularists, in effect, that when you tell us that religion is a private matter not to be brought into the "public square," what you are declaring is that our religious beliefs are dirty laundry not to be aired in public. Who are you to decide this? The "public square" can contain anything in it, no matter how crazy or disgusting—it can contain Hippies, Communists, and pornography—but not a display of the Ten Commandments. It can contain the Piss Christ but not the nativity scene. Governmental schools can teach Marxist pseudohistory and "diversity training" but not prayer or faith-based opposition to gay marriage. Attacks on religion are permitted, but not acknowledgments of it. This, the Religionists say, is unjust—a violation of our rights to free exercise and free expression—and must stop.

Enter the Compromisers, which I suspect is the largest faction numerically. The Compromisers say that we live in a "pluralistic," "multicultural" society, and what we need to do is *balance* the interests, rights, and values of members of competing factions. Obviously, there is no wall of separation between church and state, high and impregnable, *in either direction*. At most, to quote the words of Justice Burger—who, notice, is still speaking in metaphors and images—there is a line of separation which, "far from being a 'wall,' is a blurred, indistinct, and variable barrier depending on all the circumstances of a particular relationship." Others talk of a "very permeable wall," a wall "punctuated by checkpoints," and a wall "with a few doors in it."[5] On this interpretation of Jefferson's metaphor for what the First Amendment accomplishes, *there is no principle which it symbolizes*. There are only ongoing compromises and concessions made in the hope of satisfying opposing factions.

Is there freedom *for* religion, as the Religionists demand? Yes, answer the Compromisers. America is a predominantly religious country. America has a public religion, which it is appropriate if not crucial for the

5. Chief Justice Warren Burger in *Lemon v. Kurtzman* 1971 (Dreisbach 2002, 89; descriptions of the wall, 91).

federal government to recognize. As Jon Meacham, former managing editor of *Newsweek* states the point: "public religion is consummately democratic. When a president says 'God bless America' . . . each American is free to define God in whatever way he chooses. A Christian's mind may summon God the Father; a Jew's, Yahweh; a Muslim's, Allah; an atheist's, no one, or no thing. Such diversity is not a prescription for dissension. It is part of the reality of creation" (2007, 3). What is the problem, the Compromisers in effect wonder, if one's fellow Americans look at one suspiciously when one declares: "No thing bless America?" What is the problem if one is simply forced to acknowledge the reality of creation?

But is there also freedom *from* religion, as the Secularists demand? Yes, the Compromisers answer again. We need some religion in government, but not too much; obviously, we must not go to extremes. After all, Meacham tells us, the great problem of the twentieth century was totalitarianism, but so far the great problem of the twenty-first century is: extremism (2007, 17). How we are to know the proper amount of religion in politics is, of course, left unspecified.

We now have before us the contours of America's popular cultural debate about church-state separation, a debate between the Religionists, the Secularists, and the Compromisers. I submit that no members of these factions understand what Jefferson's metaphor of a wall of separation between church and state means because no one understands the principled, philosophical position that the metaphor is meant to capture. And having lost sight of the principle and its supporting arguments, people today are increasingly abandoning the metaphor as unhelpful and misleading, thereby letting crumble this crucial pillar of American freedom. It is past time to take a look beyond the metaphor to the principle it encapsulates and the arguments on behalf of that principle.

The Locke-Jefferson Case for Church-State Separation

I regard Locke's *A Letter Concerning Toleration* (1689) as the seminal text for the American separation of church and state, and will treat it as such.[6] Jefferson and Madison were familiar with Locke's *Letter* and echo its language and arguments. They do, however, extend and generalize the argument in certain ways, particularly Jefferson, the Founding Father who is my focus here.

In essence Locke's is a jurisdictional argument: if one understands

6. In the following references to the *Letter*, page numbers refer to Locke 1689 [1824].

the proper and limited jurisdiction and powers of a church *and* the proper and limited jurisdiction and powers of a state, one will recognize that there exists a wall of separation between church and state. Observe that we are already well beyond the terms of today's cultural debate. Neither the Religionists nor the Secularists nor the Compromisers speak much about the proper delimited purpose and functions of the state. Today many people seem to think that the state can do virtually anything, so long as it respects and follows a democratic process. Someone who holds this will never accept or even understand the principle of church-state separation. If the state can provide medical insurance, bail out banks, fund the research of professors, and set the curriculum of primary and secondary governmental schools, why can it not also ban prayers in the schools it runs, aid faith-based charities, and fund a Billy Graham? If the government's powers are virtually unlimited, then it can legitimately control virtually anything, so long as it follows the appropriate procedures; it is a mistake to think of it as, in principle, walled off from any area of life.

In contrast to this, Locke is concerned with defining and justifying the state's proper purpose and functions, which in his view are highly delimited. His basic goal in the *Letter*, he tells us, is to identify the limited jurisdictions of both state and church: "I esteem it above all things necessary to distinguish exactly the business of civil government from that of religion, and to settle the just bounds that lie between the one and the other" (1689 [1824], 9–10). When Locke accomplishes this, his conclusion is that "the church itself is a thing absolutely separate and distinct from the commonwealth. The boundaries on both sides are fixed and immovable. He jumbles heaven and earth together, the things most remote and opposite, who mixes these societies" (21). It is certainly natural to describe Locke's conclusion here as being that a wall of separation exists between church and state. With this basic framework in mind, let's turn to his argument.

First, Locke has a definite conception of what the proper scope of government is. The state is not a Leviathan with unlimited power. It is an institution created by individuals to protect each person's natural rights—to secure, on earth, each individual's life, liberty, health, and property (10). The state's legitimate powers are derived from this basic purpose. True, Locke does often speak of the public good, and it is not obvious that this notion is reducible to securing the rights of all the individuals involved. Nevertheless, the essence of his view remains that the state is created to protect the rights of the individual. A proper state, Locke argues in the

Letter, does not have the power to tell us how best to live our lives in this world. The decisions of how to maintain our health and estate, to use Locke's examples, are up to us: our own thought, judgment, reason and action (22–23).[7] And if the state does not have this kind of power over our lives on earth, he says, it certainly does not have it in regard to the next world. As Locke puts it, the power of the state "neither can nor ought in any manner to be extended to the salvation of souls" (10).

This is Locke's view of the proper jurisdiction and delimited power of the state: its function is nothing more and nothing less than to secure the rights of the individual citizens. Now consider a church. A church is simply a voluntary association of individuals who have chosen to come together to worship God in a certain fashion. We are all free to form or join a church, if we agree with its teachings, and free to leave, if we disagree (13–14). As a voluntary association in civil society, a church has no power to use force. Like any other voluntary association, it must use persuasion, argument, exhortation. Given this, Locke thinks there is not much reason for state and church to come into contact—any more than there is reason for state and, for example, voluntary chess clubs to come into contact. Consider why.

The job of the state, as we have seen, is not to take care of our lives in this world or of our souls in the next world. Both jobs are our responsibility, and we must possess the freedom of *thought and action* to carry them out. This implies that the state qua state has no business trying to teach, let alone to enforce, any *doctrines* about how to take care of our lives in this world or the next. The "business of law is not to provide for the truth of opinions, but for the safety and security of the commonwealth, and of every particular man's goods and person" (40). An aspect of this point is that the state also has no role in trying to ensure that citizens are *acting as though* they believed that this or that idea were true—that, for example, they are *acting as though* a carbohydrate-rich diet is superior to a protein-rich one or that Luther's version of Christianity is superior to Calvin's (18–19). Indeed, Locke holds that the attempt to enforce religious conformity is particularly wrongheaded. As is the case for any idea, we cannot *coerce* someone into understanding and accepting an idea he does not grasp firsthand to be true; all we can do is make him mouth the words or act as though he believed the idea. But in the case of religious doctrines, God obviously would grasp the hypocrisy of someone just mouthing the

---

7. Locke's is a fundamentally nonpaternalistic view of government.

words or acting as though he believed them, and therefore it is particularly wrongheaded to think that we can save a man's soul through coercion (10–11). Thus the state is not charged with the task of propagating or enforcing any doctrines, including religious ones, and in this respect will not come into contact, let alone conflict, with churches.

A church, on the other hand, *is* concerned with doctrine, specifically doctrines about the next world and salvation. But as a voluntary, private association it is *not* concerned with protecting an individual's rights and worldly goods from encroachment by the actions of others—that is what the state properly does, as the agency of coercion. In essence, therefore, the state has no business scrutinizing what goes on inside a church qua church—and a church has no business trying to wield the state's coercive power. There exists, in principle, a wall of separation between state and church. But this principle does not mean that church and state are literally cut off from each other, with no contact at all. In particular, a church is not like the grounds of a foreign embassy.

Basically, Locke argues that for any action which does not violate the rights of an individual, *every* individual or voluntary association of individuals is free to perform that action, including a church. But for any action that does violate the rights of the individual, *no* individual or group is free to perform that action, including every church (34–36). Thus, to use Locke's examples, a church can sacrifice a calf as part of a religious ceremony. But it cannot sacrifice a human being (34). And when the state intervenes in a church's affairs to stop human sacrifice, it is not policing religious doctrine but only protecting the rights of an individual against actions that encroach upon them. In other words, the state does not care *why* a church is trying to murder a person, whether it be for religious reasons or not; it only cares *that* a church is trying to murder someone, irrespective of the reason.

This broaches a wider issue. Locke notes that many people think state and church must come into constant contact and become intertwined because both state and church seek to promote morality and moral action. But they do this in fundamentally different ways, Locke argues (41–43).

First, churches may promote morality only by voluntary means. To live a good life in this world, and certainly with a view to our eternal happiness, requires that we be inwardly convinced that what we are doing is right—and that we are doing it precisely because it is right. This conviction cannot be coerced. We must have liberty of conscience. So a church, like every other person and association, must respect the individual's right of conscience: in the realm of morality a church can try to teach and persuade, but it must not reach for a sword.

Second, the morality and goodness of one's own life is not at the mercy of other people's choices. In this world we should not care, Locke says, if our neighbor lives a bad life. We should not care if he eats too much, spends too much on remodeling his house, or drinks his money away in a bar. The pain and suffering from his errors and irrationalities will be his, not ours. Our rights and freedom to live remain intact. Likewise, Locke says, why should we care if our neighbor is committing sins against God and thus jeopardizing his soul in the next world? That is his problem, not ours; he is the one going to hell, not us. So long as we retain the liberty of conscience to ensure that what we are doing is right, we are safe; no recourse to government is necessary.

This implies that, third, the state promotes morality only in the sense of protecting the rights of the individual, including his liberty of conscience. In effect, the state preserves the conditions in which we can each live a good life, but we then, as individuals, have to take advantage of those conditions. Thus Locke's position is that even though both church and state are concerned with promoting morality, they must do so in fundamentally different ways. A church is concerned with teaching and propagating moral doctrines; the state is not. The state is concerned with protecting by force an individual's rights, including liberty of conscience; a church is not. And so long as an individual's rights are respected, he need not worry about the moral stature of others in regard to this world or the next. State and church therefore remain fundamentally separate, each in a principled way walled off from the other.

This is Locke's basic account of the principle of church-state separation in his *Letter.*

I now want to highlight two crucial ideas that Locke is counting on for his argument, in order both to appreciate the scope of the argument and, much more importantly, to indicate why Locke would be so concerned, from the perspective of establishing a proper government, to separate church from state. The first, obvious point is that Locke's argument rests on him having an account of natural or individual rights and of the state's essential function as securer and protector of these rights; both of these issues are discussed in the *Second Treatise*, though the latter issue more so than the former. The second and less obvious point is that Locke's argument rests on a definite conception of what religion and God are. This point is worth exploring in a bit more detail.

Locke, as we have seen, argues that the salvation of one's soul is independent from other people's actions. This viewpoint conflicts with many other religious approaches. What would happen, for instance, if I told a Taliban leader that he should stop beating up women for showing their skin? I point out to him that even if these women are sinning against God it has no effect on him and the salvation of his soul. Now if this Taliban warrior decided to answer me instead of immediately slitting my throat, I think he would answer thus: "Of course it affects me! God demands obedience from everyone. He demands that we all carry out His will. If I don't enforce obedience to Allah by everyone, He will strike me down!" If I replied that God does not want blind, unreasoning obedience, that a woman has to be inwardly persuaded that God would want her to cover up, and that this reasoned conviction has to be why she will not show her skin in public—how would the Taliban leader answer me? "Reasoned conviction? Persuasion? She has to be convinced by reasons and evidence!? I didn't need these things to embrace Islam! Why should she? What she needs is to fear and obey. And my knife is pretty effective at generating fear and obedience!"

Now, of course, I don't think this sort of religious mentality is restricted to the Taliban; it has characterized many religious movements across the centuries. But it is not Locke's attitude; his approach to religion is light-years from this type. Locke does believe in God and in two worlds, but each world is rational and orderly. For Locke, in effect, God is a powerful but rational overlord. Reason constrains Him. Locke's attitude in the *Letter* is basically that God would not be so unreasonable as to make the salvation of our souls depend on blind faith or on the choices and actions of other people, over which we have no control. To do so would be to create an irrational universe.

For Locke, our lives in this world are between each of us and nature. We each have to use our reason to work and produce and live well; so long as our rights are protected, we need not be concerned with the choices and actions of other people and the mess they may make of their own lives. Similarly, our lives in the next world are between each of us and God. In regard to this realm too we each have to use our reason and conscience to do what we think is right. And we need not be concerned with the religious choices and actions of other people, including any sins against God that they may commit, because a rational God would never make the salvation of our soul depend on preventing or rectifying other people's sinful actions. Thus the root of Locke's particular approach to religion is the supremacy he gives to reason. He is not at the point of discarding faith entirely. But he subordinates it to reason. "Reason must be our last judge and guide in everything."[8] And this emphatically includes matters of faith. "Reason and faith [are] not opposite, for faith must be regulated by reason" (*Essay* IV 17 § 24). But if faith is not the opposite of reason, what is it?

Basically, faith is the acceptance of an idea as true because God has revealed it. Revelation means getting a message from God, which cannot contradict reason but which can supplement it. But even if God sends the message directly to you—you have to rationally judge whether the message is in fact from God. Locke suggests that it is pretty hard to get the evidence necessary to be convinced that God is communicating with you. Why is it so hard to be rationally convinced of this? Because there are two other possibilities. It could be Satan who is communicating with you. Or, and Locke suggests this is the much more typical case, it could just be a whim of yours, that you really, really want to believe—and so you pretend to yourself that it is the word of God. This last is an aspect of what Locke calls Enthusiasm, which he dislikes. He hates all those people who, devoid of rational arguments for their position, "cry out, *It is a matter of faith, and above reason*" (*Essay* IV 18 § 2). About this Tertullian kind of religious mentality (namely, the "We believe it because it is absurd" crowd) Locke says, in his sober way, that this "is a very ill rule to choose their opinions or religion by" (§ 11).

Locke further argues that it is this kind of mentality—a mentality that betrays its own rational nature, a mentality that subordinates reason to whim—that will coerce others. This kind of person, Locke says, "does violence to his own faculties, tyrannizes over his own mind, and usurps the prerogative that belongs to truth alone." The kind of person who abuses and tyrannizes his own mind, will abuse and tyrannize the minds of others. As Locke asks rhetorically: "Who can reasonably expect arguments . . . from him in dealing with others, whose understanding is not accustomed to [arguments] in dealing with himself?" (*Essay* IV 19 § 2).

This I think is a profound insight. And it points to both the deeper reason and the deeper way in which Locke separates church *from* state. The very purpose of the state is grounded in reason—for Locke, man's

---

8. *Essay Concerning Human Understanding* (1690; hereafter cited parenthetically in the text as *Essay*) IV 19 § 14.

natural rights are connected to the fact that man is a rational being. And the formulation and execution of laws, Locke stresses in the *Second Treatise*, must be done in accordance with reason. There is no room for Enthusiasm in how the coercive power of the state will be deployed in society. To give Enthusiasm such room would be to create a government with arbitrary power and thereby to descend into tyranny. The extent to which churches and religions are dominated by Enthusiasm (and Locke seems to think this happens a fair amount) is the extent to which it is vital to ensure that churches and religions have no say in controlling or directing the use of force in society. Government must be the province of reason, not Enthusiasm.

With all this in mind, let us turn to Jefferson and Madison's implementation of the principle of church-state separation. They build on this entire Lockean philosophical foundation. They accept Locke's principle of church-state separation and extend it. They essentially agree with Locke that the state's proper jurisdiction is to protect the rights of the individual from encroachment by the actions of others, and nothing more. A proper and limited state, therefore, as the point was often expressed, takes no cognizance of religion. They also essentially agree that religion is a personal matter between oneself and God—between "me and my Maker" as Jefferson often states the point; other people's sins are their problem, not yours. They agree that religion and blind faith are unnecessary to run a proper government and a threat to it; only the idea of individual rights and the guidance of reason are needed. And they agree that reason has supremacy over faith. They demand the freedom to follow the dictates of conscience, as it was often expressed. To them this means to follow reason and (moral) conviction, and not to be coerced. An individual's conscience, properly, should yield only to evidence and arguments, not Enthusiasm.

Where they extend Locke's argument is specifically in regard to the idea of liberty of conscience, of which I think Jefferson has the most profound grasp. He seems to see most clearly that the issue of liberty of conscience is, more fundamentally, the issue of freedom of thought, or intellectual freedom, as such. The fundamental issue is the government's power to persecute or to establish, to penalize or to promote—that is, to police—*ideas* as such. Religious and moral ideas are but an instance of this. An implication of this fact, as both Jefferson and Madison realize, is that contra Locke a proper government does not *tolerate* this or that idea or voluntary association, religious or otherwise. The government possesses no power to outlaw any idea or voluntary intellectual association, however morally "intolerable" the idea or association may be. The use of the phrase "religious toleration" at best obscures this fact and at worst implies that a proper government does possess such power—as it still does for Locke: in his *Letter* atheists are not to be tolerated.

On the Jeffersonian view, by contrast, the government's jurisdiction, to use Locke's term, is not ideas but actions, period. In the letter in which Jefferson coins his metaphor of a wall of separation between church and state, he writes that "the legislative powers of government reach actions only, and not opinions."[9] He states elsewhere that even though ideas produce actions, the state can intervene only when "principles break out into overt acts against peace and good order."[10] The government's proper power extends "to such acts only as are injurious to others. But it does me no injury for my neighbor to say there are twenty gods or no god. It neither picks my pocket nor breaks my leg."[11] Further, he says, our civil rights do not depend "on our religious opinions, any more than our opinions in physics or geometry."[12] He argues that it is not the state's prerogative to establish ideas about religious matters, or ideas about proper medicine and diet, or ideas about physics, such as censoring Galileo's discoveries or establishing Descartes's theory of vortexes. Jefferson maintains that intellectual freedom requires—in his language—that the operations of the mind are not subject to the coercion of the laws.[13]

Thus Jefferson holds that it is no accident that the First Amendment contains the content that it does, and that it addresses not just religion, but freedom of speech and freedom of the press as well, because what the First Amendment is doing is protecting intellectual freedom as such. Whatever violates any aspect of the First Amendment, Jefferson writes, "throws down the sanctuary which covers the others."[14]

With all of this in mind, Locke's articulation of both the principle of church-state separation and the arguments in its support together with Jefferson's broadening of the principle's scope and meaning, let us consider again Jefferson's metaphor of a wall of separation. Fundamentally, it means more than the idea that a wall of separation exists between church

9. Thomas Jefferson, "A Wall of Separation" (quoted in Church 2004, 130).
10. Thomas Jefferson, "Virginia Statute for Religious Freedom" (Church 2004, 76).
11. Thomas Jefferson, "Notes on the State of Virginia" (Church 2004, 51–52).
12. Thomas Jefferson, "Virginia Statute for Religious Freedom" (Church 2004, 76).
13. Thomas Jefferson, "Notes on the State of Virginia" (Church 2004, 51–53).
14. Thomas Jefferson, Draft of "The Kentucky Resolutions" (Dreisbach 2002, 63).

and state; it means that a wall of separation exists between the state and, to use Jefferson's language, man's opinions, religious or otherwise. To say that the church is walled off from the state is a shorthand way of saying that *the state is to take no cognizance of an individual's ideas, religious or otherwise.* The state's concern is only with an individual's actions, specifically with any actions that trespass on the rights of other individuals, irrespective of the particular ideas generating those actions. The state should neither penalize nor tolerate nor promote *any* ideas—it should be fundamentally unconcerned with and neutral toward the ideas individuals hold. And from the other direction, to say that the state is walled off from the church, means that a citizen, including any voluntary association of them, such as a church, is *walled off from using the state's coercive power either to penalize or to promote ideas, religious or otherwise.* If an individual wants to hinder or support an idea, he must argue his case with others and try to persuade them to adopt the idea—not enact a law. Moreover, to say that the state is walled off from the church means there is no room for faith to dictate the terms, purpose, or functioning of government; these are solely the province of reason.

Whether Jefferson (and Madison) consistently held to this position and its logical implications and applications is a separate issue, which I am not here focusing on; I believe, for instance, that just as there is a contradiction in Locke's basic argument in his *Letter* and its attitude toward atheists, so there is a contradiction between Jefferson's argument for church-state separation and his support for public education. Although I will briefly return to this issue below, my central point is to capture the principle that Jefferson was advancing. His metaphor of a wall of separation *is* meant to capture a principled position, which he argues for by extending and generalizing Locke's basic argument in the *Letter.*

Rand's Development of the Locke-Jefferson Case for Separation

As Jefferson (and Madison) sought to deepen, broaden, and render more consistent Locke's argument for church-state separation, so Rand seeks to do the same with theirs. On her account the principle rests, fundamentally, on the need to embrace reason as an absolute in both thought and action.

This means, first, that whereas Locke and Jefferson give supremacy to reason over faith and posit a supernatural realm governed by rational considerations, Rand discards all appeal to faith and the supernatural. Neither Locke nor Jefferson is able to demonstrate that God or a supernatural dimension exists, let alone that God is a rational overlord and that religious morality is an affair exclusively between "me and my Maker." In the end, the existence of God and a supernatural realm must be accepted on faith. And as we have seen, someone like a Taliban warrior whose "faith" tells him something very different about the nature of God and of religious morality will reject the notion that God is constrained by reason and that He does not command us to intervene coercively when other people sin. Rand eliminates from the argument for church-state separation all appeals to the supernatural and to faith, even if it is only a faith that somehow "supplements" reason. She argues that the notion of the supernatural—of something "transcending" existence, identity, causality, and human consciousness, that is, of something "transcend- ing" nature—is incoherent.[15] And reason permits no "supplementation" by faith. On her view, it is never rational to embrace an idea or perform an action without some evidence supporting the idea or action. Faith, she maintains—"belief unsupported by, or contrary to, the facts of reality and the conclusions of reason"—"is the negation of reason."[16] Accordingly, Rand dismisses all knowledge claims that rest directly or indirectly on the notion of the supernatural as attempts to integrate the incoherent, and she places all faith-based assertions into the special category of the arbitrary.[17]

For Rand, therefore, even more so than for Jefferson, the issue is not religious freedom, as though there were some special freedom pertaining to a supernatural realm and to (supplementary) guidance by faith. The issue is intellectual freedom. The argument for freedom rests solely on the nature and requirements of reason to grasp and navigate this (natu- ral) world. Nor does Rand appeal in her argument to the "rights" or "dic- tates" of conscience. Insofar as these dictates pertain to the supernatural and supposedly supplement reason, Rand rejects their existence. Insofar as these dictates refer to choice in accordance with moral principles and convictions, Rand regards this as an *aspect of reason*. Going further than Locke (and Madison and Jefferson), she views "the will" as an aspect of the faculty of reason and views moral knowledge as a species of scien- tific knowledge: ethics is a science that studies and defines the fundamen-

15. See especially *Atlas* 947–59; *ITOE* ch. 6; "The Metaphysical versus the Man-Made" (*PWNI*). See also Peikoff 1991, ch. 1.

16. *Playboy* interview (March 1964), quoted under the entry "Religion" in *Lexicon*.

17. On the attempt to integrate the incoherent, see *ITOE* ch. 5; on the Arbitrary, see the entry "Arbitrary," in *Lexicon*. See also Peikoff 1991, ch. 5.

tal values an individual must seek and the fundamental virtues he must practice in order to thrive.[18]

Thus when Rand writes ("What Is Capitalism?" *CUI* 17) that reason and force are opposites—that a "rational mind does not work under compulsion; it does not subordinate its grasp of reality to anyone's orders, directives, or controls; it does not sacrifice its knowledge, its view of the truth, to anyone's opinions, threats, wishes. . . . Such a mind may be hampered by others, it may be silenced, proscribed, imprisoned, or destroyed; it cannot be forced; a gun is not an argument. (An example and symbol of this attitude is Galileo.)"—it is important to keep in mind that for Rand this principle encompasses both science and morality.

It encompasses both, because for Rand, as I have said, reason and will are not two separate faculties. Rather, the faculty of reason sets an individual's goals and values and determines the ways in which he will pursue them, all of which is done by a volitional process of thought and subsequent action:

> Reason is the faculty that identifies and integrates the material provided by man's senses. It is a faculty that man has to exercise *by choice*. Thinking is not an automatic function. In any hour and issue of his life, man is free to think or to evade that effort. Thinking requires a state of full, focused awareness. The act of focusing one's consciousness is volitional. Man can focus his mind to a full, active, purposefully directed awareness of reality—or he can unfocus it and let himself drift in a semiconscious daze, merely reacting to any chance stimulus of the immediate moment, at the mercy of his undirected sensory-perceptual mechanism and of any random, associational connections it might happen to make.[19] ("The Objectivist Ethics," *VOS* 22)

The attempt to coercively override or bypass a person's will *is* the attempt to override or bypass his reason. Or, looking at the same issue from a positive perspective, the choice to activate his conceptual mind and embrace reason—as against evading the facts of reality and the need for thought—is, according to Rand, the root of moral good and evil. The central principle of Rand's philosophy is that reason is man's basic

---

18. See "The Objectivist Ethics" (*VOS*) and "Who Is the Final Authority in Ethics?" (*VOR*).

19. There certainly are precursors of the idea that reason operates volitionally in Locke's writings.

means of survival. The essence of morality is the acceptance of reason as an absolute, the passionate quest for knowledge and the commitment to enact this knowledge in the pursuit of one's own life and happiness. The root moral choice, the existence of which grounds a valid notion of conscience, is the choice to think or not. To betray one's conscience *is* to betray one's mind:

> You who speak of a "moral instinct" as if it were some separate endowment opposed to reason—man's reason *is* his moral faculty. A process of reason is a process of constant choice in answer to the question: True or False?—*Right or Wrong?* . . . A rational process is a *moral* process. You may make an error at any step of it, with nothing to protect you but your own severity, or you may try to cheat, to fake the evidence and evade the effort of the quest—but if devotion to truth is the hallmark of morality, then there is no greater, nobler, more heroic form of devotion than the act of a man who assumes the responsibility of thinking. (*Atlas* 935)

Coercion, then, for Rand is a negation of an individual's reason, will, *and* moral conscience because these are all perspectives on the unity that is a properly functioning rational faculty. As Rand briefly summarizes her point, "Force and mind are opposites; morality ends where a gun begins" (*Atlas* 936). On this approach, the concept of individual rights is formulated precisely to extract coercion from human relationships. The concept is grounded not in the supernatural, Rand argues, but in the "social recognition of man's rational nature—of the connection between his survival and his use of reason" and thus "preserves and protects individual morality in a social context" by defining the areas in which the individual must be sovereign, free to think and act—free to reason and produce.[20]

From this fundamental perspective, Rand maintains, the arguments for intellectual freedom and economic freedom share the same root: the requirements of the rational mind to guide the individual. In the realm of thought, this means that the government must not have the power to penalize or promote ideas. As Rand expresses the principle, in terms similar to Jefferson's, "Since an individual has the right to hold and to propagate any ideas he chooses (obviously including political ideas), the government may not infringe his right; it may neither penalize nor reward him for his ideas; it may not take any judicial cognizance whatever of his ideology. . . . Ideas, in a free society, are not a crime."[21] Rand explicitly extends this

---

20. "What Is Capitalism?" (*CUI* 9) and "Man's Rights" (*VOS* 108).
21. "'Political' Crimes" (*ROTP* 176).

principle to the entire realm of thought, including education, scientific research, and the arts, arguing that governmental schools, governmental funding of scientific research, and governmental funding of the arts violate the individual's right to intellectual freedom.[22] Thus she rejects both Locke's claim that the government should not tolerate atheists and Jefferson's desire to establish public schools in part so that the people would have the education necessary to safeguard their liberty. In order for the entire realm of ideas to be fully free from coercion, the government must have no power in any way to penalize or *promote* ideas as such, even if those ideas are necessary for proper government or civilization itself. A "proper government is based on a definite philosophy," Leonard Peikoff writes in presenting Rand's conception of intellectual freedom, "but it can play no role in promoting that philosophy" (1991, 367).

The same essential point follows, Rand maintains, in the realm of production: the government must not have the power to penalize or promote any form of economic activity or organization. This is why she says that there should be a separation of economics and state in the same way and for the same reasons as the separation of church and state. The root of industrial production, Rand argues, is abstract thought. "Production," she writes, "is the application of reason to the problem of survival" ("What Is Capitalism?" *CUI* 17). "Have you ever looked for the root of production? Take a look at an electric generator and dare tell yourself that it was created by the muscular effort of unthinking brutes. Try to grow a seed of wheat without the knowledge left to you by men who had to discover it for the first time. Try to obtain your food by means of nothing but physical motions—and you'll learn that man's mind is the root of all the goods produced and of all the wealth that has ever existed on earth" (*Atlas* 383). For thought fully to be free, Rand argues, the realm of production must be free. Or, stating the same point negatively, all governmental controls over and interventions into the individual's productive activities (and of his ensuing consumption and voluntary trading) *are instances of penalizing or promoting ideas.*

Take the Food and Drug Administration (FDA) as an example. Among the FDA's activities are determining which drugs a doctor can legally prescribe, which drugs a patient can purchase, and how a company must test and manufacture pharmaceuticals. What if an individual doctor *thinks* that a particular drug, although banned by the FDA and not

22. See "The Comprachicos" (*ROTP*); "Tax Credits for Education" (*VOR*); "The Establishing of an Establishment" (*PWNI*); "Let Us Alone!" (*CUI*).

without risks, is worth the risk for a particular set of patients? The doctor is not free to act. What if, within this set of patients, some of them *judge* that they would like to take the drug? They are not free to act. What if a company *argues* that the way the FDA wants it to test its drugs is wasteful? Or what if it *concludes* that there is a better way to test for safety or efficacy? Or what if it has *invented* a whole new process of manufacturing pharmaceuticals, unapproved by the FDA? It is not free to act. In prohibiting actions like the taking of an experimental medicine, the government is effectively banning the *thought processes and ideas* that generate the action and is discarding the principle that reason is the individual's basic means of survival. And in promoting (commanding) actions such as how to manufacture a drug, the government is effectively proscribing alternative thought processes and ideas that could generate alternative productive actions.

The freedom to produce is a crucial aspect of the individual's rights to life, liberty, property, and the pursuit of happiness. If the purpose of individual rights is to preserve and protect individual morality in a social context, the two realms that, above all else, must be protected are those of thought and production. Politically, there should exist a separation of church and state (the issue of intellectual freedom) and, *for the same reasons*, there should exist a separation of economics and state (the issue of economic freedom).

And the idea of "separation" designates the same thing in the economic sphere as in the intellectual sphere—that is, the spheres should be separated in the same way. To say that there is a separation of state *from* economics is to say that the state is walled off from taking cognizance of another aspect of man's life-sustaining activities: not only of his abstract thoughts but also of his productive actions. The state neither tolerates nor persecutes nor promotes any form of production or trade. It is not the state's prerogative to decide whether it should tolerate that Microsoft includes an Internet browser within its operating system—or to decide whether to persecute a firm because it consulted some competitors when setting what prices it would charge—or to decide whether to promote domestic automakers or individual homeowners. All of these activities should be left to the voluntary decisions of the individuals involved. And it is certainly not the prerogative of the state to act as a central planner, trying to "control" and "steer" the entire economy by, say, manipulating the money supply. The job of the state is to secure and protect the individual's ability to think, produce, and trade, not to try to curtail this activity or to direct it toward some allegedly noble goals that transcend the individual's own life and pursuit of happiness. Only if the state is so restricted is the individual's rational, productive mind truly free.

From the other direction, to say that there is a separation of economics from state is to say that *every* economic actor—be it an employer or an employee, a capitalist or a consumer—is walled off from using the state's coercive power to stop economic activity he dislikes or to *promote* economic activity he likes. No one can enact his *economic doctrines* into law. No one can declare that given my economic views, there should be tariffs on foreign steel producers and subsidies for US corn producers; or that a merger between AT&T and T-Mobile should be legally prevented but a merger between HP and Compact should be allowed; or that gold should be outlawed as money. If a citizen wants to try to implement his economic views and theories, he must do so privately and voluntarily, seeking as necessary the agreement and cooperation of other individuals. He can stop buying foreign steel and try to convince others to do the same; he can donate his money to US corn producers; he can stop using gold as money and encourage others to do likewise; he can set up a voluntary socialist commune and try to persuade other people to join. But what he cannot do is use the power of the state to override the productive judgment and activities of others. Only if one's fellow citizens are so restricted from gaining control of the coercive power of the state is one's rational, productive mind truly free.

For Rand, therefore, freedom forms a unity whose roots are the full requirements of man's rational mind. As she states her point in a crucial formulation: "*Intellectual* freedom cannot exist without *political* freedom; political freedom cannot exist without *economic* freedom; *a free mind and a free market are corollaries*" (*FTNI* 25). This principle, that a free mind and a free market are corollaries, Rand regards as the full philosophical extension of the reasoning that led, first, to the principle of church-state separation. Seen from this perspective, the principle that a free mind and a free market are corollaries is the culmination of the Enlightenment's intellectual quest for freedom.

The Arc of Liberalism
Locke, Mill, and Rand
ROBERT GARMONG

Although in America Ayn Rand's ideas are most often cited favorably by self-described conservatives or libertarians, in historical terms she is heir to the tradition of liberalism. The word "liberal" comes from the same root as the word "liberty," so a "liberal," etymologically and historically, was someone who believed that protecting freedom is the fundamental role of the state. Different versions of liberalism differ according to how they define liberty, yet all claim to share the view that liberty is at the heart of government.

In the eighteenth and early nineteenth centuries, under the influence of John Locke and his early followers, a "liberal" meant a defender of both economic freedom and intellectual freedom, or to paraphrase Rand, "free markets and free minds." To put it in contemporary terms, the early liberals defended the socioeconomic system that would later be known as laissez-faire capitalism, including both rights to free trade and rights to freedom of expression and personal liberty.

By the mid-twentieth century in America, on the other hand, liberalism had come to mean the defense of social or political rights such as freedom of speech, and self-professed liberals considered the right to property and economic freedom to be less important. FDR's "Four Freedoms" included what he called "freedom from want" and the "freedom from fear" (Roosevelt 1941). The new conception of freedom, as Roosevelt envisioned it, may entail government support for arts and ideas that can't support themselves in the marketplace. Later, under LBJ and Nixon, it encompassed federal antidiscrimination laws and even reverse discrimination via federal contractor quota requirements (Affirmative Action). Nowadays, "freedom" may require protection from "triggers" and other felt offenses.

Today's liberals seek to liberate what they regard as personal choices, while expanding the role of government in the economy. For example, they support the right of a same-sex couple to marry, but not that of a baker to opt out of baking their wedding cake. Liberalism's transformation from a movement that defended freedom across the board to one that rejects economic freedom illustrates the importance of political philosophy and the need for Rand's insights in that field. The three key thinkers whose ideas essentially shaped the arc of liberalism—from full-throated defense of freedom to today's opposition to free markets, and (hopefully) back to thoroughgoing defense of free markets and free minds—are John Locke, John Stuart Mill, and Ayn Rand. Others have played important parts in the development of liberal political thinking, but these three thinkers were the ones who most fundamentally defined and redefined liberty, and thus liberalism—and thus, the course of Anglo-American politics itself.

As US Representative Chester Bowles famously declared in the late 1950s, "We Are All Liberals Now" (Bowles 1959). This was a significant overstatement, but there is a sense in which it is nearly true. Even "conservatives"—who by definition seek to "conserve" existing institutions—in an American context follow an essentially "liberal" political culture. America was founded on classical liberal principles, so American conservatives can claim a basis in a classical liberal, freedom-based political theory. The crucial question, though, is which definition of liberty, and therefore of liberalism, is to be accepted.[1]

John Locke's Classical Liberalism

The idea of liberalism, in its classical sense, was best defined by John Locke. Locke was the premier philosopher of liberty in the eighteenth

1. It is worth noting that Rand distances herself from the terms "liberal" and "conservative," typically putting each term in scare quotes to indicate that these are not precise labels but, in her term, package-deals of disparate political views.

century, and the chief inspiration of America's founders. Locke's defense of liberty, which Darryl Wright adroitly summarizes in "Force and the Mind" in this volume, is most fundamentally rooted, not in the *Second Treatise of Government* but in his *Essay Concerning Human Understanding* and his *Letters Concerning Toleration*. The key argument was presented the First *Letter*.

Locke considered the individual, or any free association of individuals, to have the absolute right of assembly and speech. Any noncoercive behavior, he thought, was part of one's freedom. A church, for example, has the right to excommunicate members who fail to follow its practices and teachings, as long as it does not subject its lapsed members to "rough usage," by which Locke means "damnifi[cation] in body or estate." For, he says in *A Letter Concerning Toleration*, "all force . . . belongs only to the magistrate, nor ought any private persons, at any time, to use force; unless it be in self-defense against unjust violence" (Locke 1689 [1824], 17).

Thus, he defined the line between the ethical and the political spheres in terms of coercion: a church, or presumably any other association or individual, may choose whichever moral standard it wishes, may associate with or refuse to associate with whomever it wishes, so long as it does not engage in violence toward those of whom it disapproves. It is only the "magistrate"—that is, the government—that has force at its disposal, and it should use force only to protect the individual against force. The distinction between the sphere of morals and the sphere of politics, for Locke, hews to the distinction between the coercive and the noncoercive. The "magistrate"—the government—uses and ought to use force to protect the rights of citizens. All other institutions use only the power of persuasion.

To put Locke's case for liberty in its most fundamental terms, freedom is a requirement of the independent, rational mind, without which it cannot function. Locke argues that the power available to government, the power of coercion, cannot secure genuine intellectual agreement. It can produce silence and nodding acquiescence, but not true understanding. And without understanding, agreement is illusory.

Locke's immediate focus in the *Letters Concerning Toleration* is the belief in religion, an idea that I would argue is actually rooted in the irrational "Enthusiasm" that Locke condemns in his *Essay Concerning Human Understanding* (Locke 1690 [1979], IV.19). Nevertheless, Locke's argument about religion has broader implications. Although couched in narrow terms as a freedom of religion (and then, only freedom of non-

Catholic religions), his arguments apply equally to all intellectual dissent.[2] Because of this, they lay the groundwork for all freedom, including the right to property.

Locke argues that proper belief depends upon "light and evidence"—that is, empirical evidence and logical inference. He argues that without evidence, and without reason, belief is meaningless. In religious terms, one's soul will not be saved merely because one *claims* to believe in the one, supposedly true God; one must actually comprehend the reasons for such belief.

Locke argues that genuine belief in any proposition requires comprehension of the reasons supporting it. This is an activist epistemology: to believe a proposition, in the full sense of the word "believe," means to have taken the appropriate mental actions to understand and process its evidence and its relationship to all the other truths one has comprehended. Otherwise, what one has is not belief but "hypocrisy" (Locke 1689 [1824], 11).

According to Locke, one cannot be said to believe propositional content until one is aware of some facts that *justify* the belief. Locke writes: "No man can so far abandon the care of his own salvation as blindly to leave it to the choice of any other, whether prince or subject, to prescribe to him what faith or worship he shall embrace. For no man can, if he would, conform his faith to the dictates of another. All the life and power of true religion consists in the inward and full persuasion of the mind; and is not faith without believing" (Locke 1689 [1824], 11). Locke's rhetoric somewhat obscures the radical nature of his point. He might seem to be making a merely normative point that "true religion" has more "life and power" if it is based on "inward and full persuasion." However, the literal meaning of his point is that "no man *can*" believe an idea simply because another person believes it, even "if he would." Locke's point is not that one *should not* accept an idea without understanding the evidence for it. The point is that one *cannot*, in the meaningful sense, believe that for which one does not at least minimally understand the evidence.

Locke certainly realizes the too real possibility of people framing

---

2. In a view that was dominant among Anglo-American Protestants until John F. Kennedy's 1960 speech on Catholicism, "Address to the Greater Houston Ministerial Association," Locke believed that the pope was, uniquely among religious leaders, also a political leader who ruled a foreign country (the Vatican). Therefore, Locke argued that Catholics could not be loyal to England's monarch. This was not due to religious doctrine but to what Locke considered a purely political consideration.

their viewpoints based on others' beliefs rather than on observation and reason—that they may "judge of things by men's opinions" rather than "opinions by things" (Locke 1706 [1824], § 24 363). Indeed, he complains, "that by which men most commonly regulate their assent, and upon which they pin their faith more than anything else . . . is, *the opinion of others*." His point is that such assent is not properly to be termed "understanding, but a species of ignorance" (Locke 1690 [1979], IV.15 § 6).

Merely professing to agree with a proposition does not stand as proof that one has made the "full and exact inquiry" demanded by the truth. Locke argues that "the external profession and observation, if not proceeding from a thorough profession and approbation of the mind, is altogether useless and unprofitable" (Locke 1689 [1824], 16). As long as one cannot literally force a mind to think, external profession is the only thing that censorship can mandate. "For," as Locke wrote in an earlier essay, "punishment and fear may make men dissemble; but, not convincing anybody's reason, cannot possibly make them assent to the opinion."[3] Hence, Locke concludes that censorship, even granted that it is exercised in the interest of true ideas, cannot promote understanding of the truth. (For a thorough explication of these points, the reader should look to Wright, "Force and the Mind," this volume.)

As Wright has argued, Locke's defense of liberty is impressive, yet incomplete. Among other problems with Locke's argument, although he shows that coercion is not a proper basis for belief, he does not demonstrate that coercion is *uniquely* destructive of the mind.[4]

John Stuart Mill's Redefinition of Liberty

John Stuart Mill made an argument that was akin to Locke's, in treating independence as an epistemological requirement of truth and understanding. But there is a crucial difference: Mill defined the "moral coercion of public opinion" as akin to literal coercion. In doing so, he undermined the crucial distinction between ethics and politics.

John Stuart Mill's path from classical liberal to dissenter is well-known. Mill began life as a defender of capitalism. In his teens, he worked with his father, James Mill, to render David Ricardo's ideas about economics into James Mill's *Elements of Political Economy*. John Stuart Mill

---

3. "An Essay on Toleration" (1667), in Goldie 1997, 155.

4. I have some reason to believe the Third and Fourth *Letters Concerning Toleration* contain some stronger arguments on this topic, but they have never been widely read, and they have not been analyzed in detail to this day.

claimed to have "no higher ambition than that of treading in his [James Mill's] steps" as a defender of free speech, as of economic freedom.[5]

However, in later years he came to disavow James Mill's confidence in free markets, as well as in the so-called marketplace for ideas. The early editions of John Stuart Mill's *Principles of Political Economy* were supportive of the free market, but he later added the notorious "Chapters on Socialism," which propose experimenting with socialist schemes in order to see if they could be made to work. While not a thoroughgoing endorsement of socialism, this was a major departure from the commitment to economic freedom that had characterized his father's generation of liberals.

However, Mill's flirtation with socialism was not his fundamental departure from the liberalism of his father and of Locke. Mill's fundamental departure was this argument that the concept of liberty itself requires a fundamental redefinition. This redefinition entails an activist state that can and must intervene in private, noncoercive actions among individuals. In this way, Mill undermined the Lockean concept of liberty and justified the state's involvement in what Locke would have considered to be purely private moral choices.

The key text that defines contemporary liberalism, in contradistinction to Lockean classical liberalism, is Mill's slender volume *On Liberty*. In his *Autobiography*, Mill described it as "a kind of philosophic textbook of a single truth, which the changes progressively taking place in modern society tend to bring out in ever stronger relief: the importance, to man and society of a variety in types of character, and of giving full freedom to human nature to expand itself in innumerable and conflicting directions" (Mill 1874, 7:20).

That "single truth" is what later thinkers termed Mill's "Harm Principle": the idea that others should "interfere" with the liberty of the individual only in order to prevent him from harming others. Mill introduced the principle as follows:

> The object of this Essay is to assert one very simple principle, as entitled to govern absolutely the dealings of society in the way of compulsion and control, whether the means used be physical force in the form of legal penalties, or *the moral coercion of public opinion*. That principle is, that

5. "Law of Libel and Liberty of the Press" (1825), in Robson 1984, 4. In the same article Mill claims "That truth, if it has fair play, always in the end triumphs over error, and becomes the opinion of the world," a view he would later reject (Robson 1984, 8).

the sole end for which mankind are warranted, individually or collectively, in interfering with the liberty of action of any of their number, is self-protection. That the only purpose for which power can be rightfully exercised over any member of a civilized community, against his will, is to prevent harm to others. (Mill 1859, 1.10)[6]

This statement represents a radical, intentional break with the earlier liberalism of John Locke.

John Stuart Mill opens *On Liberty* with the claim that "a different and more fundamental treatment" of the nature and extent of liberty was required by the exigencies of the nineteenth century. In the past, the concept of liberty had been defined as a protection from government, especially from despotism. However, borrowing the concept "the tyranny of the majority" from Alexis de Tocqueville's *Democracy in America*, Mill argues that "when society is itself the tyrant, . . . its means of tyrannising are not restricted to the acts which it may do by the hands of its political functionaries" (Mill 1859, 1.1).

It is the latter category, nongovernmental restrictions on "liberty," that Mill intends to establish as meaningful. Although, he says, tyranny of the majority is often "vulgarly" considered to begin and end with the state, this is too limited an understanding of freedom (Mill 1859, 1.1). Without the concept of social "tyranny," Locke's theory of rights and the separation of powers would be adequate for the defense of liberty. But in Mill's own day, he claims, "social tyranny" is "more formidable than many kinds of political oppression, since, though usually not upheld by such extreme penalties, it leaves fewer means of escape, penetrating much more deeply into the details of life, and enslaving the soul itself" (Mill 1859, 4.4).

Mill claims that a better appreciation for the true grounds of liberty will allow a better, more subtle application of state power. Under the current system, he claims, "there is a considerable amount of feeling ready to be called forth against any attempt of the law to control individuals in things in which they have not hitherto been accustomed to be controlled by it; and this with very little discrimination as to whether the matter is, or is not, within the legitimate sphere of legal control; insomuch that the feeling, highly salutary on the whole, is perhaps quite as often misplaced as well grounded in the particular instances of its application."[7]

6. Here and in what follows I cite *On Liberty* by chapter and paragraph number.
7. Mill to Harriet Taylor Mill (January 29, 1854), in Mineka and Lindley 1972, 141–42.

This means, by implication, that the government should do more than it is currently doing "perhaps quite as often" as not. Government should expand, as a means of protecting "liberty." Although Mill does not give many examples of this necessary expansion, he does argue that there should be a governmentally funded, secularized intellectual establishment modeled after the Church of England.[8] He also argues for universal, state-mandated education, which was not in itself a radical idea among liberal thinkers of the day, having been advocated by Thomas Jefferson, among others (Mill 1859, 5.12). However, as I shall argue later, the implications of his view are much broader than Mill lets on and explain much of the current state of American politics.

As a matter of rhetorical strategy, Mill focused his attention on those applications of his theory that were, at the time, relatively uncontroversial among liberals. His plan was to raise concern for what he termed "the independence of the individual," defined as the absence of social pressuring. Once the principle was established, public policy would follow suit.

In a letter to his wife, Harriet Taylor Mill (whom Mill considered almost a coauthor of the book, though she died before it was completed and therefore could not get authorial credit), Mill called *On Liberty* "concentrated thought—a sort of mental pemmican." Pemmican is a tough, jerky-like food invented by Cree Indians that had to be chewed heavily or even boiled in stew before it could be consumed. Likewise, Mill expected that the value of *On Liberty* could only be extracted after considerable processing and chewing by "thinkers, when there are any after us."[9]

Mill's avowed purpose in *On Liberty* was not to defend a separation between the spheres of government and of ethics but, rather, the exact opposite: he intended to collapse the two. He claims that the concept of self-regarding immorality is a mistake, and he argues that gambling, frequent drunkenness, and other forms of dissolution, which had previously been regarded as "self-regarding vice," are not per se immoral. The only "vices" that Mill regards as per se immoral are those that result directly in harm to others—vices such as "Cruelty of disposition; malice and ill-nature; that most anti-social and odious of all passions, envy; dissimulation and insincerity, irascibility on insufficient cause, and resentment

8. This idea is defended in the early newspaper article "Attack on Literature" (1831), in Robson and Robson 1986, 318–27. This essay was published shortly after Mill's recovery from the mental crisis that had much to do with reshaping his views in later life. The same idea is elaborated in much more detail in the article on "Coleridge," in Leavis 1980, 39–66.

9. Mill to Harriet Taylor Mill (January 29, 1854), in Mineka and Lindley 1972, 141–42. The last phrase is a rather striking indication of his own self-image.

disproportioned to the provocation; the love of domineering over others; the desire to engross more than one's share of advantages (the *pleonexia* of the Greeks); the pride which derives gratification from the abasement of others; the egotism which thinks self and its concerns more import- ant than everything else, and decides all doubtful questions in its own favour" (Mill 1859, 4.6). It is, he says, only when a person's conduct harms others, that it "is taken out of the self-regarding class" and becomes "amenable to *moral* disapprobation in the proper sense of the term" (Mill 1859, 4.6; my emphasis). Mill is not drawing a distinction between that which is amenable to political control and that which is merely a moral is- sue. Rather, he is arguing that both ethics and politics are entirely defined in terms of those actions that harm others.

James Mill's Optimistic Assumptions

James Mill, John Stuart Mill's father, had discussed intellectual freedom with an optimism that the younger Mill would later reject. Discussing the freedom of the press, James Mill argued that it could be relied upon to produce truth. Although he contemplated the possibility that discus- sion of ideas would entrench established opinions, he argued that free- dom from government coercion would be sufficient to cure the "mental disease" of conformity to wrong and hidebound ideas.[10]

James Mill held an optimistic attitude toward the free market for ideas, which might be compared to the economist's notion of "efficient markets." "Every man, possessed of reason, is accustomed to weigh ev- idence, and to be guided and determined by its preponderance. When various conclusions are, with their evidence, presented with equal care and with equal skill, there is a moral certainty, though some few may be misguided, that the greater number will judge aright."[11] While John Stu- art Mill holds that truth has an advantage over falsehood in a free com- petition, he sees his father's idea that the victory of truth over falsehood is a "moral certainty" (whatever that means) as a fantasy. As long as people have free will, there can be no certainty that truth will win—just as there is no certainty that the "best" product will win in the marketplace.

John Stuart Mill later came to reject his father's optimism about the free market in economics, as well as in ideas. With regard to economics, he wrote:

10. James Mill, "Liberty of the Press," in Ball 1992, 109.
11. James Mill, "Liberty of the Press," in Ball 1992, 121.

There are many things which free-trade does passably. There are none which it does absolutely well; for competition is as rife in the career of fraudulent presence as in that of real excellence. Free trade is not upheld, by any one who knows human life, from any very lofty estimate of its worth, but because the evils of exclusive privilege are still greater, and what is worse, more incorrigible. But the capacity of free trade to produce even the humblest article of a sufficient degree of goodness, depends on three conditions: First, the consumer must have the means of paying for it; secondly, he must care sufficiently for it; thirdly, he must be a sufficient judge of it. (Mill 1859, 2.17)

With regard to these latter two considerations, especially, Mill was deeply skeptical. He had little confidence that the average consumer of thought cared sufficiently for the truth or could judge it accurately. He wrote that "the dictum that truth always triumphs over persecution," which was widely held by liberal thinkers, "is one of those pleasant falsehoods which men repeat after one another till they pass into commonplaces, but which all experience refutes. History teems with instances of truth put down by persecution" (Mill 1859, 2.17). (Note that John Stuart Mill is accepting essentially the same view as James Mill, but on its flip side. Whereas James Mill argued that the economic free market for goods and services is defensible because it *automatically* leads to the best possible outcome, the younger Mill argues that the free market lacks worth because it does not. Neither considered the possibility that the free market is an epistemological tool for discovering information about goods and services or about ideas.)

John Stuart Mill does consider discussion to be generally efficacious in refuting errors. He owns that "wrong opinions and practices gradually yield to fact and argument," though they do so only to the extent that they are given a full hearing (Mill 1859, 2.7). But he does not believe that freedom of speech will necessarily bring about the triumph of new, true ideas.

Social Tyranny of the Majority

Mill is a consequentialist, and his argument about intellectual freedom is dependent upon his view of its consequences. He argues that "opinion, on this subject, is as efficacious as law; men might as well be imprisoned, as excluded from the means of earning their bread" (Mill 1859, 2.19). If other people's unfavorable opinion of you is strong enough to prevent you from earning your bread, you might as well be punished by force of law and coercion. Hence, the possibility that social pressure might lead to negative consequences would, for Mill, alter the landscape of political theory.

It is likely that the experience of James Mill looms large in his son's thinking. An intellectual at odds with the majority of the public, yet attempting to feed a growing family on the proceeds of his writing alone, the elder Mill felt acute pressure to present his ideas in a way that soft-pedaled those views that "could not prudently be avowed to the world," particularly his atheism and political radicalism (Mill 1874, 44).

Despite having largely supported himself as a writer from the age of thirty, James Mill made no significant political or economic pronouncements until his writing career was well enough established that he could feel more confident in stating unpopular views. Although he later plunged into political activism, he never ceased to urge on his son, and to practice in his own writings, reticence with regard to his religious skepticism. Atheism in the nineteenth century was an opinion James Mill considered the public especially unprepared to consider with level-headed seriousness. The feeling of repression that resulted from "this lesson of keeping my thoughts to myself, at that early age," was likely a precursor to John Stuart Mill's later view that freedom requires more than the mere absence of coercion (Packe 1954, 11).

John Stuart Mill, however, went beyond his father's reticence, and argued that "though usually not upheld by such extreme penalties, [social tyranny] leaves far fewer means of escape, penetrating much more deeply into the details of life, and enslaving the soul itself" (Mill 1859, 1.4). Governments, no matter how large, are limited in scope; but when one's peers judge and condemn, Mill suggests, they are much more difficult to avoid (they leave "fewer means of escape"). Furthermore, each private individual or group may have as many points of attack as they have moralistic viewpoints: one attacks premarital sex; another is a prohibitionist; another is antigay. Styles of dress and personal adornment, home and garden, artistic interests, which books are appropriate to read, miscegenation—all have been subjected to intense social pressure across the years.

Furthermore, Mill suggests, merely governmental coercion does not "enslave the soul itself." Just as Locke had argued that coercion cannot change a person's mind, so Mill seems to believe that a person who is effectively silenced by coercion can and likely will continue to believe his or her heretical ideas. Mill argues, with Locke, that being the object of repression often serves to entrench the heretic all the more.[12] Without open

12. Cf. "An Essay on Toleration" (1667), in Goldie 1997, 156.

and unstigmatized discussion, Mill says, heretical opinions (which he is here assuming to be erroneous) "continue to moulder in the narrow circles of thinking and studious persons among whom they originate" (Mill 1859, 2.19). He argues that censorship increases, rather than decreases, people's tendency to cling to their sects.

Governments tend to censor only those ideas that are already socially unpopular and stigmatized, but Mill argues, "it is that social stigma which is really effective," not the governmental coercion (Mill 1859, 2.23). "Our merely social intolerance kills no one, roots out no opinions, but induces men to disguise them, or to abstain from any active effort for their diffusion. . . . [W]ithout the unpleasant process of fining or imprisoning anybody, it maintains all prevailing opinions outwardly undisturbed, while it does not absolutely interdict the exercise of reason by dissentients afflicted with the malady of thought" (Mill 1859, 2.19). When "society itself"—that is, one's peers—are the ones demanding conformity, Mill thinks, the individual has a powerful incentive to acquiesce: most people do not want to be pariahs. The desire to conform to society is so strong, Mill suggests, that most people will never develop their own independent views in the first place. The first goal of society in these instances, he says, is not to suppress dissent but to prevent it from forming (Mill 1859, 1.5).

Whereas "the unpleasant process of fining or imprisoning" dissidents may call forth a backlash, Mill suggests, social pressure at the hand of the kindly inquisitors who constitute one's friends and neighbors merely provokes its victims to cave in. "Where public opinion is sovereign," Mill writes elsewhere, "an individual who is oppressed by the sovereign does not, as in most other states of things, find a rival power to which he can appeal for relief, or, at all events, for sympathy" (Mill 1848 [1909] V, IX § 3).

In what may be a bit of historical irony, John Stuart Mill's break from his father's sanguinity about the influence of social pressure upon the individual stems at least partly from premises inherited from the psychological theories of Jeremy Bentham and likely James Mill himself. Among the impulses to action, the elder utilitarians had held, the desire for the approval of others is one of the strongest.[13] It is thus the case that social pressure can exert a great deal of compulsion on the individual who is its subject.

James Mill had written that "where there is no motive to attach a man to error, it is natural to him to embrace the truth."[14] But John Stuart Mill

13. Bentham, *The Principles of Morals and Legislation*, ch. X, § XXII.
14. James Mill, "Liberty of the Press," in Ball 1992, 121.

notes that, when the majority of society believes the same idea, the desire for approval *produces* a motive to attach a person to that idea, whether the idea be true or false. The fear of conformism was a lasting theme of Mill's life. It appears, for instance, in an early newspaper article on freedom of expression. There, he regards as a peculiar defect of the age "the mental cowardice which prevents men from giving expression to their conviction, and the insincerity which leads them to express what they do not think."[15] We can see this same concern about conformism in Mill's views on sectarianism, which are reported by his friend the socialite and memoirist Caroline Fox (1882, 115): "The spirit of sect is useful in bringing its own portion of Truth into determined prominence, and comfortable in the repose it must give, to be able to say, I am sure I am right; on the other hand, it not only walls up the opinions it advocates within the limit of its own party, but it is very apt to induce a pedantry of peculiarity and custom, which must be injurious to Truth." It may not be an exaggeration to say that the project of *On Liberty* is to secure the blessings of free discussion, while avoiding that "pedantry of peculiarity and custom" that is the pitfall of sectarianism.

Political Implications of Mill's Theory

Let us now pause and take stock of what we have from John Stuart Mill. He has argued that, at least in his contemporary world, freedom from coercion is inadequate to the requirements of liberty; for there is an even greater threat to liberty—namely, "social tyranny," or the tendency of other private individuals to harm one in punishment for actions that do not harm others. How might this threat manifest itself?

Consider the case of a gay man in the 1990s in America, when sodomy was (generally) not punished by law but was still widely reviled as immoral and indecent. A gay person who did not harm any nonconsenting others might be subjected to significant harm because of his sexual preference. Most importantly, he could be fired from his job, and he could be refused rental housing. He may be denied the opportunity to buy a home, if the seller is afraid of the social stigma from selling to a gay man. Let's assume that he lives in a place where such denials are common, and he will face significant long-term difficulties as a result of coming out as gay.

15. "The Debate on the Petition of Mary Ann Carlile" (1823), in Robson and Robson 1986, 21.

Mill would have to say that this is a form of "social tyranny." The man has harmed no nonconsenting others, yet he has faced significant harm as a result. He must choose between the repression of living in the closet and the loss of livelihood and living space. How, then, should the man respond? Mill suggests three levels of response.

The first is "remonstrating with [the person with whom one disagrees], or reasoning with him, or persuading him, or entreating him" (Mill 1859, 1.18). One may give the person "considerations to aid his judgment," and may even have them "obtruded on him," but in the end "he himself is the final judge" (Mill 1859, 4.4). Thus the gay man could attempt to argue people out of their prejudices against him. In the case of actions that do not harm others, such remonstrations are one's only recourse. However, in the current case, further actions would be available.

One can apply Mill's second level of response, "the moral coercion of public opinion." This is the same sort of "coercion" that is being wrongly applied to the gay man himself. According to Mill, such "coercion" is wrong only when it is applied to that which does not harm others. Just as governmental coercion may be applied to prevent or punish a thief, so "the moral coercion of public opinion" may be applied to punish someone who has used this sort of coercion to harm another. Thus, for example, defenders of the harmed gay man may organize a boycott of the employer who dismissed him for being gay.

But once those expedients are exhausted, what then? In this case, what Mill terms "civil penalties" are in order. This is the flip side of Mill's equation of private, noncoercive actions with governmental coercion: both may be applied in response to "moral coercion." Mill himself did not chew very extensively on the pemmican of On Liberty. He left that for "thinkers, when there are any after us." And indeed there have been many who have followed on Mill's path.

The 1964 Civil Rights Act in America was a triumph of Millian liberalism. On one hand, it ended governmental discrimination against minorities, which had been a blatant violation of the idea that "all men are created equal" and endowed with equal rights. But with the same stroke of the pen, it prohibited private individuals or companies from discriminating against minorities.

Rand penned an impassioned essay titled simply "Racism," in which she roundly excoriated racism and all racist policies as "the lowest, most crudely primitive form of collectivism" (VOS 147–57). Yet she argued against the Kennedy-Johnson Civil Rights Bill as "a gross infringement of individual rights" (*VOS* 156). "It is," she argued, "proper to forbid all discrimination in government-owned facilities and establishments: the government has no right to discriminate against any citizens. And by the very same principle, the government has no right to discriminate *for* some citizens at the expense of others. It has no right to violate the right of private property by forbidding discrimination in privately owned establishments. No man, neither Negro nor white, has any claim to the property of another man. A man's rights are not violated by a private individual's refusal to deal with him" (*VOS* 156). (It should be obvious that Rand's use of the term "Negro" was in accordance with common practice at the time and bore no racist intentions.) Rand objected to the whole realm of antidiscrimination laws and antidiscrimination agencies. The entire contemporary notion of "freedom" is a legacy of Mill's breakdown of the barrier between ethics and politics, between coercion and the feeling of social pressure.

Mill versus Rand

Rand writes that all human interactions should operate on the same moral basis as economic trade, each party trading value for value, neither sacrificing his own value for the sake of the others, nor sacrificing their value for his sake.

Consider a purely economic case: Suppose a man wishes to rent his garage apartment to a Muslim family from Saudi Arabia. He knows the family well, having worked with the husband during a time in the Middle East. They can afford the rent, he knows they will pay him on time and take care of the unit, they plan to stay there for a long time, and so on. It is, let's presume, a perfectly rational decision given the available pool of renters and his constellation of values, needs, and financial considerations. In other words, to rent them his apartment would be the best possible trade of value for value between him and the renters. Now let us consider three fundamental ways this trade could be disrupted.

One is a purely irrational decision. Suppose on the night before the rental contract was to be signed, he sees a documentary about 9/11. He becomes enraged, calls the family, and tells them they cannot rent the apartment. His next renters are late with rent, trash the apartment, play loud music—and he spends years regretting his decision not to rent to the Saudi family. Clearly this was an irrational decision, but it is a purely ethical issue: no one forced him to make the wrong choice, and he must bear the blame by himself.

Another way a trade can go wrong is through coercion. Suppose on the day before the family was to move in, the US government announced that all Muslims' residence visas and work permits are revoked, and they must leave the country. Now he has no choice but to rent to the bad tenants, or to no one at all.

But there is a third category of reason the trader principle can be violated: irrational social pressuring. Suppose the man tells his boss he's about to rent to a nice Middle Eastern couple. The boss frowns and says "I'm sorry, but I lost my brother and my son fighting in Iraq. There's no way I'm going to pay you to keep a roof over the head of a bunch of Muslims. You think about it over the weekend, then you can tell me on Monday whether or not you're submitting your resignation." The man goes home shaken and uncertain.

After work, he bumps into his preacher at the supermarket. "Surely," he thinks, "a man of God will approve of my taking in a family that needs a home." The minister shakes his head and says, ruefully, "I spent some years ministering to an expatriate community in Saudi Arabia. The persecution they put good Christians through, not to mention preachers of the faith, is ungodly. You do as you wish, but I would find it difficult to minister to a family with Muslims in their home. You wouldn't be welcome in my church."

When he gets home, his wife is extremely upset. She tearfully tells him that, since word spread that they were introducing a Muslim family to the neighborhood, she has been asked not to return to her social clubs, and none of the neighbors' children are allowed to play with their kids. Reluctantly, the man calls his would-be tenants and tells them that he cannot rent them the apartment.

Of course, in today's America it would be illegal for a landlord to refuse to rent to a valid tenant for reasons of race, ethnicity, or religion. Nor would the man's boss be legally allowed to fire him for a reason unrelated to his job performance. Mill would consider this to be the triumph of his view of liberty: no longer would the community be allowed to place such onerous control on the landlord, nor he on potential tenants.

These examples were a reality not too many years ago for people in many minority groups. Minorities in terms of race, religion, lifestyle, country of origin, and so on—all have suffered tremendous harm as a result of actions that did not harm others (such as religious observance), or even for something that wasn't an action at all (such as the color of their skin).

Rand draws a bright line between coercive and noncoercive methods of dealing with others—in her terms, between force and persuasion. But why should the line be drawn there? Why not at any action that harms innocent others? ("Innocent" here means those who have not themselves caused harm to others.) Why shouldn't discrimination, excommunication, and other forms of private harm be considered tantamount to coercion? Without an answer, the classical liberal standard of Locke, which holds that coercion—and only coercion—is to be prohibited from social relations, would be mistaken or at least incomplete.

Rand's Response to Mill

Rand argues that man's rights can be violated only by the use of physical force. Consider the victim of Mill's social pressuring. Consider the gay person, or the person who wishes to rent an apartment to the Muslim couple, or the Muslim couple themselves. Mill would say that they face considerable harm because of their condition. But is their situation analogous to that of a victim of coercion? We must first consider the reason for their condition.

In the second chapter of this volume, Wright provides some great examples to consider. From the perspective of responding to Mill, the most challenging is the example of Talbot Brewer, who "censored" himself rather than publish an editorial that would either (1) contain politically unpalatable ideas, or (2) undercut his own political views. Likewise, Wright envisions a "climate researcher" who fears being "ostracized from her professional peer group," or even a case she considers "fanciful (not to say, ludicrous)": "a philosopher desires to conform all her thinking to her own best interpretation of Locke's philosophical views, as gathered from the latter's extant works. She will settle her interpretation fully, according to her own independent judgment, on the basis of a conscientious application of sound methods of philosophical historiography and then ensure from that point onward that everything she thinks is consistent with this body of ideas" (69–70, above). But this may not be so fanciful. Indeed, Rand herself suffered from sycophantic followers who attempted to mimic her ideas and borrow her reputation.

Consider a thinker who believes he must conform his ideas to the dominant orthodoxy, or else he cannot be hired, his career will be at an end, and his long and expensive education will have been wasted. This is not an arbitrary prospect, but the reality faced by many thinkers on the "Right" in academia today. It is in fact an extremely difficult situation.

However, consider the difference between that person's situation and the situation faced by someone under actual coercion.

It is instructive to contrast Mill's conception of "harm" with Rand's concept of "physical force." Physical force is rooted in literal force such as battering a person, or physically removing his property (theft), or physical restraint (kidnapping, slavery, and so on). "Coercion" means that one might be imprisoned, be physically beaten, or have one's property stolen for one's beliefs. None of this pertains to an academic dissentient.

"Harm," on the other hand, is a much more nebulous concept, and one that Mill himself fails to define clearly. Some commentators (e.g., Skurupski 1989, 342) have been led to think Mill has no consistent definition of "harm" at all, but if so that would be a fatal error. If the so-called harm principle is to have any use, it must be applicable in practice. It must therefore be possible to define what is and is not a "harm."

In some places Mill (e.g., 1859, 1.19) seems to speak of "harm" as any infliction of pain—which is itself, in the utilitarian definition, a concept subject to question. In utilitarian terms, "pain" includes any negative emotions: dissatisfaction, frustration, or discomfort. This is an overly broad definition of harm, since it would suggest that a woman who failed to return an unrequited love was "harming" her would-be boyfriend.

In the final analysis, Mill considers someone to have been "harmed" by his having been denied "certain interests, which, either by express legal provision or by tacit understanding, ought to be considered as rights" (Mill 1859, 4.3; compare 4.6, 10, 15). These "rights" are defined in utilitarian terms, as those interests that it is best for society to protect, and therefore there may be questions about which specific interests they should include. They include such things as livelihood, housing, and any other institutional "good offices" (Mill 1859, 4.6). This may include a job, a position in community or political leadership, or perhaps something such as an apartment.

But consider what this means, to the victim of social pressuring. He's been denied a job, an apartment, a family association, or some other benefit because of something he has done that caused no violation of another person's rights. What has he lost?

At worst, he has been denied an advantage that he should (in full justice) have been given. Someone failed to give him the value-for-value trade he should have given. But nothing has been *taken* from him. His life is essentially the same as if the other person had never existed in the first place. He can go on to write books for a public audience, give lectures to business leaders, or do innumerable other things as a public intellectual. This in fact is what Rand herself did, though she was, of course, a woman with talents beyond the ordinary. Others, such as Mortimer Adler, have managed to make a living as intellectuals without university portfolios.

I will interject here a personal anecdote, because it is relevant. When I first met the woman who is now my wife, Ma Lei, she informed her father, in the way that is appropriate for a Chinese courtship. He absolutely forbade her to have a foreign boyfriend, but she defied him. She told him—I was later informed—"If you don't allow me to marry this man, I will never marry anyone, and I will never give you a grandchild."

Here is a key case of "social coercion," in Mill's sense. If there were ever a society in which "social coercion" should be effective, it is China—and if there were ever a relationship in which it should be effective, it should be between father and daughter. And yet, against all the odds, she bucked her father's opinion. (And for the record, her father and I are now the best of friends.) A Chinese father holds the ability to visit his daughter with tremendous stress and social anxiety if she disobeys his will, but he cannot legally harm her in any physical way, imprison her, or take her property. Compare this with coercion. In some countries, a father whose daughter betrayed his will could have her whipped, stripped of any property she had been promised, or even stoned to death.

The difference here is not merely one of severity, it is a difference of principle. In the case of moral pressuring, the "harm" done is psychological, its impact dependent upon the individual's receptiveness or the lack thereof. Compare this with coercion, which is a radically different situation. Chinese university professors live in fear that they will have their lives and property stolen from them if they express ideas contrary to the government. It's not that they may lose this one particular job; the government may make it illegal for any employer to hire them. There is no justice, no rectitude, no alternative: they are unemployable, by government decree.

It is important to note that politics is downstream from ethics. Rand views independence as a moral virtue—that is, a quality of character necessary for the achievement of a fundamental value, the primacy of one's own rational thinking. Rand's hero in *The Fountainhead*, Howard Roark, says that an independent person "does not function through" other people. The formulation that follows is crucial: "He is not concerned with them in any primary matter. Not in his aim, not in his motive, not in his thinking, not in his desires, not in the source of his energy" (*Fountain-*

head 683). The independent person is focused on his or her own vision of reality, not that of others. His or her motives, reasoning, emotional life, and fundamental source of passion for living all come from himself or herself, not from others.

Rand would never claim that companionship and cooperation are irrelevant to one's happiness. But they are not fundamental to it, nor is it possible to achieve happiness or well-being by placing another person's judgment above one's own. The person subjected to coercion has no choice but to place the other's judgment and values above his own. The person subjected to social pressuring has a choice. He may cave in and become a second-hander (to use Rand's term from *The Fountainhead*) or resist and retain his or her independence.

The conceptual muddiness that comes from blurring this line can be seen in the battle lines of every university or other frontier of the culture war. Once offense is considered tantamount to coercion, it becomes essentially impossible to adjudicate cases of conflicting claims of "harm." If a conservative student expresses disapproval of gay marriage, for instance, is that "the moral coercion of public opinion" against her gay classmates? On the other hand, if her gay classmates object to her viewpoint, is that "moral coercion" against her? As the past twenty years or more of academic wrangling have shown, there is no good way to settle these cases as long as one holds that social pressuring is akin to coercion and subject to the same strictures.

So when John Stuart Mill argues that "the moral coercion of public opinion" is tantamount to actual coercion, he is tilting against a windmill. The bright line, the definition that should and must be upheld, must be between force and persuasion. Coercion—physical force—of any kind is on one side of the line, while persuasion—even irrational or bullying persuasion—is on the other side.

John Locke had made a true, yet not fully validated, assertion that coercion and only coercion could destroy thinking. John Stuart Mill took advantage of Locke's lacuna to argue for a significant expansion of the realm of the state. Ayn Rand provided a philosophical argument that fulfilled Locke's promise, for the first time fully grounding the prohibition on coercion in both ethics and epistemology. This is why I regard liberalism as an arc, from Locke to Rand, with an interruption by Mill. The full and explicit defense of freedom, and the liberal conception of man as the rational being, was promised by John Locke, and delivered by Ayn Rand.

Part Four
THE NATURE
AND FOUNDATIONS
OF ECONOMIC FREEDOM
(AND ITS OPPOSITE)

Economic Theory and Conceptions of Value

Rand and Austrians versus the Mainstream

ROBERT TARR

Ayn Rand is best known in contemporary culture for being an intransigent defender of capitalism. She always insisted, however, that "I am not primarily an advocate of capitalism, but of egoism; and I am not primarily an advocate of egoism, but of reason. If one recognizes the supremacy of reason and applies it consistently, all the rest follows" (*TO* 1089). She was adamant that capitalism had to be defended on philosophic grounds: "I want to stress that our primary interest is not politics or economics as such, but 'man's nature and man's relationship to existence'—and that we advocate capitalism because it is the only system geared to the life of a rational being" ("Introduction," *CUI* vii).

Understanding the basic nature of value is crucial to understanding capitalism, Rand thought. A rational being must be a rational valuer, and she held that conventional theories of values and of evaluation did not treat these as rationally derived. These theories fall into two basic categories, which Rand called "intrinsic" and "subjective." In contrast, she defined and defended a new category: a new concept of objective value. She writes: "Capitalism is the only system based implicitly on an objective theory of values—and the historic tragedy is that this has never been made explicit" (*CUI* 15). She made this base explicit in her essay "What Is Capitalism?" (*CUI* ch. 1).

Every theory of economics necessarily assumes at its base a particular conception of the nature of value. I aim to examine how the different conceptions of value have been assumed by different economic theories, and how these shaped the theories. Classical economics assumed and was shaped by an intrinsic theory of value, while modern mainstream neoclassical economics was shaped by a subjective theory. More controversially, I argue that Austrian economics was shaped by *implicitly* assuming an objective conception of value (in Rand's sense). It is the elements of an objective conception of value embedded in their theories that explain why Austrian economists reach a (largely) proper understanding of the nature of capitalism (from Rand's perspective) and are rightly viewed as the preeminent advocates of capitalism in the economics profession.

Ayn Rand: Value Deriving from Conceptual Knowledge

One of Rand's main intellectual goals was to define a rational ethics. In her essay "The Objectivist Ethics," she writes:

> Most philosophers have now decided to declare that reason has failed, that ethics is outside the power of reason, that no rational ethics can ever be defined, and that in the field of ethics—in the choice of his values, of his actions, of his pursuits, of his life's goals—man must be guided by something other than reason. By what? Faith—instinct—intuition—revelation—feeling—taste—urge—wish—*whim*. Today, as in the past, most philosophers agree that the ultimate standard of ethics is *whim* (they call it "arbitrary postulate" or "subjective choice" or "emotional commitment")—and the battle is only over the question of *whose* whim: one's own or society's or the dictator's or God's. Whatever else they may disagree about, today's moralists agree that ethics is a *subjective* issue and that the three things barred from its field are: reason—mind—reality. (*VOS* 15)

Rand begins her ethics with a conception of value grounded in goal-directed action: "'Value' is that which one acts to gain and/or keep" (*VOS* 16). She traces the phenomenon of goal-directed action to the fundamental nature of living organisms: that living organisms in order to survive must systematically pursue goals aimed at preserving their lives. But while plants and animals have their goals (their values) automatically prescribed for them, man, as a volitional conceptual being, does not.[1] Man's basic means of survival is his conceptual faculty:

> Man cannot survive, as animals do, by the guidance of mere percepts. . . . He cannot provide for his simplest physical needs without a process of thought. He needs a process of thought to discover how to plant and grow his food or how to make weapons for hunting. His percepts might lead him to a cave, if one is available—but to build the simplest shelter, he needs a process of thought. No percepts and no "instincts" will tell him how to light a fire, how to weave cloth, how to forge tools, how to make a wheel, how to make an airplane, how to perform an appendectomy, how to produce an electric light bulb or an electronic tube or a cyclotron or a box of matches. Yet his life depends on such knowledge—and only a volitional act of his consciousness, a process of thought, can provide it. ("The Objectivist Ethics," *VOS* 23; quoted in "What Is Capitalism?" *CUI* 7)

For Rand, values are conceptual: "Man's actions and survival require the guidance of *conceptual* values derived from *conceptual* knowledge" (*VOS* 21). But this involves two distinct types of thought process: conceptual thought to discover knowledge of facts and conceptual thought to form values. Or: a thought process aimed at discovering the facts of reality (including facts about man's needs), and a distinct type of thought process aimed at integrating these facts so as to conceive goals and devise plans for achieving them. The first category of thinking (discovering factual knowledge) is widely recognized. The latter category (conceptual, *goal-directed* thinking) is less so. Rand emphasized the role of *creative* thinking in forming and achieving goals.

After describing the enormous complexity of the conceptual integrations necessary for identifying *factual* knowledge of reality, Rand writes:

> Yet this is the simpler part of his psycho-epistemological task. There is another part which is still more complex.
>
> The other part consists of applying his knowledge—i.e., evaluating the facts of reality, choosing his goals and guiding his actions accordingly. To do that, man needs another chain of concepts, derived from and dependent on the first, yet separate and, in a sense, more complex: a chain of normative abstractions. While cognitive abstractions identify the facts

---

1. Following Rand's usage, I use "man" and "mankind" to refer to human beings and humankind.

of reality, normative abstractions evaluate the facts, thus prescribing a choice of values and a course of action. Cognitive abstractions deal with that which is; normative abstractions deal with that which ought to be (in the realms open to man's choice). (*RM* 6)

Goal-directed thinking crucially depends on factual knowledge but is distinct from it. The facts, by themselves, do not automatically dictate what goals man should pursue nor what steps (what means, what conceptual plans) will achieve them. It takes a separate, and different, process of thought to conceive and achieve goals.

The type of conceptual thinking involved in goal-directed thinking (of creatively conceiving goals and creatively integrating means to ends) Rand calls "teleological measurement":

> In regard to the concepts pertaining to evaluation ("value," "emotion," "feeling," "desire," etc.), the hierarchy involved is of a different kind and requires an entirely different type of measurement. It is a type applicable only to the psychological process of evaluation, and may be designated as *"teleological measurement."* . . . Teleological measurement deals, not with cardinal, but with ordinal numbers—and the standard serves to establish a graded relationship of means to end.
>
> For instance, a moral code is a system of teleological measurement which grades the choices and actions open to man, according to the degree to which they achieve or frustrate the code's standard of value. The standard is the end, to which man's actions are the means.
>
> A moral code is a set of abstract principles; to practice it, an individual must translate it into the appropriate concretes—he must choose the particular goals and values which he is to pursue. This requires that he define his particular hierarchy of values, in the order of their importance, and that he act accordingly. Thus all his actions have to be guided by a process of teleological measurement. (*ITOE* 32–33)

For fully rational, conceptual evaluation to be possible, an individual's values must form a consistent, integrated harmony. This is an important principle of Rand's ethics: that one must do the hard thinking to *integrate* all of one's goals into a consistent whole, to avoid working at cross-purposes (one must know that the pursuit and achievement of one goal won't contradict and negate another goal). This integrated hierarchy must be applied to the evaluation of every particular goal, plan, action, or object. It is only by having all one's goals integrated in this fashion that one can rationally assess what will in fact advance one's goals or sabotage them. But the only way to know this is to trace all the complex indirect links and causal chains to assess the consequences for *all* of one's goals. For this reason, Rand continues:

> (The degree of uncertainty and contradictions in a man's hierarchy of values is the degree to which he will be unable to perform such measurements and will fail in his attempts at value calculations or at purposeful action.)
>
> Teleological measurement has to be performed in and against an enormous context: it consists of establishing the relationship of a given choice to all the other possible choices and to one's hierarchy of values. (*ITOE* 33)

Such an integration can only be done by reference to an *ultimate* standard, which, for Rand, is man's life. By tracing the causal consequences of all one's goals (and all their means of achievement) to the ultimate consequences they entail for one's life (and weighing them and integrating them accordingly), one can have a fully integrated *conceptual* justification of all one's goals.

For Rand, then, value (in the case of man) crucially depends on and embodies conceptual knowledge. Value requires the conceptual identification of the causal role that an object or action can play, within an integrated plan, aimed at achieving a goal (with the ultimate goal being the individual's life). To "evaluate" *is* to engage in this sort of thought process.

In contrast to views that treat fact and value as radically different categories, Rand writes: "Knowledge, for any conscious organism, is the means of survival; to a living consciousness, every 'is' implies an 'ought'" (*VOS* 24). This does not mean, for Rand, that the "ought" follows as a direct or *automatic* implication from the "is." A separate (and different) process of creative thought is required to identify the value implications of "what is."

To concretize this distinction: Everyone has had experience with the type of person who has (or can easily get) all the *factual* information he needs, and yet who is passive or paralyzed in action. Often he is paralyzed in action precisely because he hasn't chosen to engage in a *goal-directed* thought process—that is, to conceive a goal and devise a plan to achieve it. This type of thought process doesn't happen automatically; the facts by themselves don't mandate what to do.

Rand's *Atlas Shrugged* is replete with illustrations of this issue. Her positive characters regularly engage in goal-directed thinking, conceiving new goals and constantly making the effort to devise new plans to achieve their goals. In contrast, the negative characters do *not* engage in creative goal-directed thinking and do not have or pursue any creative goals. Most often they subsist in passive mental lethargy, merely reacting (usually emotionally) to whatever facts and circumstances happen to hit them. The worst characters actively evade awareness of important facts and circumstances, precisely to avoid grasping the need for action and for the thought processes to guide it. This point, in fact, forms part of the central theme of *Atlas Shrugged*: the role of reason in man's life, which includes, importantly, the role of reason in conceiving and achieving goals that further man's life.

Without Rand's conception of values as essentially embodying conceptual knowledge, knowledge is separated from value, giving rise to the "is-ought" gap. In contrast to her conceptual view of value (which she designates as "objective"), Rand defines two main categories of theories that exclude conceptual knowledge from value, which she designates as "intrinsic" and "subjective":

> The *intrinsic* theory holds that the good is inherent in certain things or actions as such, regardless of their context and consequences, regardless of any benefit or injury they may cause to the actors and subjects involved. It is a theory that divorces the concept of "good" from beneficiaries, and the concept of "value" from valuer and purpose—claiming that the good is good in, by, and of itself.
>
> The *subjectivist* theory holds that the good bears no relation to the facts of reality, that it is the product of man's consciousness, created by his feelings, desires, "intuitions" or whims, and that it is merely an "arbitrary postulate" or an "emotional commitment." . . .
>
> The *objective* theory holds that the good is neither an attribute of "things in themselves" nor of man's emotional states, but an *evaluation* of the facts of reality by man's consciousness according to a rational standard of value. (Rational, in this context, means: derived from the facts of reality and validated by a process of reason.) The objective theory holds that *the good is an aspect of reality in relation to man*—and that it must be discovered, not invented by man. Fundamental to an objective theory of values is the question: Of value to whom and for what? An objective theory does not permit context-dropping or "concept-stealing": it does not permit the separation of "value" from "purpose," of the good from beneficiaries, and of man's actions from reason. (*CUI* 13–14)

The subjective theory of value holds that value is rooted in some conscious phenomenon in the mind of the subject, detached from any facts of reality (e.g., Hume's view or the hedonic utility of Utilitarians); it is rooted in consciousness without reference to a mind grasping reality. The intrinsic theory holds that value is something inherent in existential objects (or actions); it is rooted in reality, without reference to a mind grasping reality. In contrast, Rand's conception of objective value is fundamentally about *a mind grasping reality*. Although not denying the wide variety and complexity of different theories of value, it's Rand's view that in each case somewhere along the line, implicitly if not explicitly, all intrinsic theories *ultimately* rely on the individual "just knowing" what's good, while all subjective theories ultimately rely on the subject "just feeling" what's good. Completely left out of each case is any sort of *rational* process of forming values. It is precisely this issue that Rand has in mind when she asserts that "most philosophers agree the ultimate standard of ethics is whim."[2]

In defining her intrinsic/subjective/objective trichotomy, Rand conceptualizes the terms differently from the traditional objective/subjective dichotomy. This can be a source of confusion, particularly when we apply her ideas to economics. In the traditional dichotomy, "objective" designates a phenomenon that is in reality independent of consciousness; while "subjective" denotes a phenomenon that is "subject-dependent"—that is, a phenomenon that depends on the subject's consciousness in some form. Rand uses the term "intrinsic" to denote theories that view knowledge or values as mind-independent features of reality. Meanwhile, the category of "subjective," as often used in economics, lumps together the views of value that Rand calls "subjective" and "objective." For Rand, "subjective" designates conscious phenomena that are unconnected to reality, and "objective" designates conscious phenomena that represent *deliberate, conceptual, mental integrations* of facts of reality. Both can be construed as "subject-dependent," but they differ fundamentally in their connection to reality. (I use the terms "subjective," "objective," and "intrinsic" in Rand's meanings of the terms, unless otherwise noted.)

Both the mainstream neoclassical school of economics and the rival Austrian school are traditionally considered "subjective value" schools in contrast to the "intrinsic value" perspective of classical economics. I believe that the stark differences between these two schools of thought

2. According to Rand, "A 'whim' is a desire experienced by a person who does not know and does not care to discover its cause" (*VOS* 14).

334

ultimately trace back to different conceptions of value: the neoclassical school assumes a purely subjective conception of value, while the Austrian school *implicitly* assumes an objective conception of value. While it's true that for both schools value is *subject-dependent*, their stark differences trace to the fact that the neoclassical school conceives value in purely subjective and thus nonrational terms, and the Austrians broadly (and implicitly) have a view of value as involving conceptual knowledge to conceive ends rationally and to integrate means to ends. Unfortunately, the traditional category of subjective value confuses many later Austrians, too, such that they come to view value as rooted in subjective consumer preferences; this muddies but does not destroy their implicitly objective conception of value.

Later thinkers in the Austrian school often talk about "subjective knowledge."[3] But this idea again is meant only to emphasize subject-dependence, that each individual has his own particular, finite context of knowledge that guides his actions (he cannot be presumed to know things he has no way of knowing, in contrast to mainstream assumptions of "perfect knowledge"). The Austrian idea, generally, is only meant to convey this subject-dependence and not the philosophic idea that one can only know "things-as-they-appear-to-us" (i.e., only the phenomena of our own consciousness).[4] Essential to the Austrian theory of the market process is precisely that the individual *learns* new knowledge about reality (and about the goals, plans, and actions of other people), such that he comes to increasingly conform to reality. He forms new evaluations accordingly; new goals, plans, and courses of action. When Austrians use the term "subjective," then, in most contexts the proper way to understand it is simply as "subject-dependent."

Another potential confusion to avoid is that, for Rand, the values required by man's life do not solely refer to physical or material needs. In her view, man's conceptual consciousness has a specific identity with its own needs and requirements, which, if not fulfilled, will lead to impaired functioning. But since man's conceptual faculty is his basic means of survival, impaired conceptual functioning means impaired *survival*. Thus, the needs of man's consciousness are just as real, just as important, and

3. A more detailed discussion of this issue, with a focus on Hayek and Mises, will be addressed in a later section.
4. A few Austrian thinkers do explicitly commit to the view that knowledge is subjective in this philosophic sense.

just as objective as man's physical needs.[5] Rand's view contrasts with the view that grounding the concept of value in the biological life of man necessarily makes value purely about satisfying man's *physical* needs.[6] There appears to be a wide range of things that men "subjectively" like and pursue, but which don't seem to have any connection to his physical survival, such as poetry, music, philosophic discussion, and so on. Rand's view is that all such "spiritual" values (e.g., art or philosophy) *do in fact* have crucial survival value for man.[7] Even pleasure itself, for Rand, is an objective need that stems from man's metaphysical nature as a living organism.[8] Far from mere subjective likings, the needs of consciousness are objective needs that man must discover and fulfill as much as any physical needs.

A further issue to mention is Rand's category of "optional value." Within her category of "objective value," there is a wide range of optionality. Shoes, for example, are an objective value to man's life; but, in most cases, the particular color of shoes does not make a difference and can be whatever the wearer chooses. This kind of issue is often used in economic theorizing to illustrate that value is "subjective"; but Rand's view is that the proper way to conceptualize it is in the category of "optional," within the wider category of objective value.[9]

The issues of spiritual values and optional values have motivated economists to conceptualize value in purely subjective terms, suggesting that value, as far as economics is concerned, simply denotes whatever someone likes and pursues, period. It is true that anything someone seeks to obtain on the market (for whatever reason) will lead to the formation of prices—which are then subject to some form of economic explanation. This is true even for cases of irrational/immoral products (drugs, prostitution, etc.), which are *objective disvalues* in Rand's view. But this manifestly does *not* mean that a subjective conception of value is necessary or

5. She writes, for example: "Man's consciousness is his least known and most abused vital organ. Most people believe that consciousness as such is some sort of indeterminate faculty which has no nature, no specific identity and, therefore, no requirements, no needs, no rules for being properly or improperly used. . . . The fact [is] that man's consciousness possesses a specific nature with specific cognitive needs" (*VOR* 101).

6. For example, see the discussion of this type of view in Kirzner 1976, 32–37.

7. See *RM* for Rand's theory on the connection of art to man's survival, and see *PWNI* for the connection of philosophy to man's survival.

8. See Nathaniel Branden, "The Psychology of Pleasure" (*VOS* ch. 6). "Pleasure, for man, is not a luxury, but a profound psychological need" (*VOS* 71).

9. See Peikoff 1991, 323 for discussion of this point.

sufficient for economic theory (as will be argued in detail in the balance of this essay).

For Rand, the concept of "objective" designates conscious phenomena that represent deliberate, conceptual, mental integrations of facts of reality. A full understanding of this concept requires an understanding of the epistemological nature of these conceptual integrations.[10] Rand's view is that a concept represents a mental grouping of referents, according to definite criteria, to form a new mental integration. This mental grouping is a creative, fact-based act that results in a new (previously nonexistent) mental product. The facts of reality alone do not automatically dictate how to form the appropriate conceptual integration of those facts. It takes *creative* effort to identify the criteria for grouping that are required by the nature of the referents, of the human mind, and of the cognitive purpose one is trying to fulfill.

At a higher level, this is what all creative problem-solving involves: mentally manipulating the elements of a problem until one discerns a new way of *integrating* them so as to solve the problem. Three aspects of Rand's view are important to emphasize. First, it takes volitional effort on the part of the individual to initiate and sustain such a thought process, or else thinking does not take place. Second, the resulting integration is something *new* that is formed in the mind of the thinker (it would not exist without his efforts). Third, a new integration is *creative*; it is not an automatic result algorithmically written on his mind from a mere surveying of the facts. These are all inseparable aspects of the single act of creative thinking—volitional, creative formation of a new mental integration—but it's important to emphasize them separately.

It's exactly mental integration of this type that Rand thinks lies at the root of *production*. Production is the production of value, and value (for Rand) crucially involves conceptual knowledge; which means, at root, that it involves a conceptual mental integration. For Rand, "production is the application of reason to the problem of survival" (*CUI* 8). Rand regularly stresses, throughout her novels and her nonfiction essays, that the root of all production is an idea, a creative mental integration: "Whether it's a symphony or a coal mine, all work is an act of creating and comes from the same source: from an inviolate capacity to see through one's own eyes—which means: the capacity to perform a rational identification—which means: the capacity to see, to connect and to make what had not been seen, connected and made before" (*Atlas* 782–83).

10. For a detailed discussion of Rand's theory of concepts, see *ITOE*.

To identify value is to engage in the process of teleological measurement discussed above—that is, goal-directed thinking aimed at conceiving a new end and forming new integrations of means. Forming a new integration in this way *is* the root value-creating activity. Although a plan must be executed for a value to be achieved in reality, it's the formation of the mental integrations guiding this action that is the root source of the value.

An entrepreneur starting a new venture needs to conceive a vision and discover what integration of inputs can achieve the vision he seeks to produce. Given his estimation of the potential value of the product, he consciously imputes value to the inputs, each one based on its respective contribution to the output. The inputs are neither "intrinsically valuable" nor "intrinsically productive." By themselves, they have no value and no use. The only value they have is the value the entrepreneur *conceives* them to have, given their role within some plan he has devised, to achieve some value he has conceived, based on the facts he has identified.[11] The inputs only have a "productive use," because the entrepreneur consciously seeks to *use* them in some particular role.

The view of production, then, is a teleological one. Production of value stems from the mental conception of a goal and the conceptual integration of a plan to achieve that goal. The fundamental, root act of production is the volitional, creative formation of these conceptual mental integrations.

As with any mental integration (for Rand), the three points mentioned above apply. The integration underlying production is a direct result of the volitional thinking of the producer. It is a *new* phenomenon (it wouldn't exist at all but for the producer's mental effort). And it is *creative* (it's not "intrinsic" in the facts of reality, to be algorithmically or automatically imprinted in his mind, but is the result of a creative thought process). These are the factors that underlie Rand's fundamental justification of why a producer is the fundamental *cause* of production of value, and thus why, in justice, he fully deserves the value he produces.

This is the view of production from an *objective* conception of value. If value is conceived as intrinsic or subjective, however, then value does *not* essentially involve any mental work. Instead, all value is simply "given" to the mind, quite apart from any deliberate conceptual act (value

---

11. To the extent that the inputs he is contemplating using already have economic value, it's only because *other* entrepreneurs have consciously imputed value to them, given the role those inputs play in *their* plans aimed at their productive goals.

is "just known" or "just felt"). On these conceptions of value, there is no room for any mental integration to play a role, no room for the mind to *do* anything in producing value per se. If conceptual knowledge is not involved, then value cannot be something rationally created by the mind; it cannot be some *new* mental integration that the thinker brings into existence; and it is not the result of any volitional mental effort on the part of the individual.

What does this imply for a view of production? A teleological view of production is impossible on intrinsic or subjective conceptions of value since they exclude a view of valuing in terms of conceiving ends that guide the creative integration of means. But the only real alternative is an "efficient cause" view of production, where the value of output is deemed to stem entirely from the inputs to a production process (raw materials, labor, machines, etc.). In this view, the producer plays no fundamental role in creating value; at best, he is merely a deterministic cipher passively reacting to circumstances. There is nothing for him *to* do, since all production stems directly (and effectively "automatically") from the factors of production themselves; they are the source and cause of value.[12] These sorts of views have been important in mainstream economic theory, but they are antithetical to Rand's view of production.[13]

Production also effectively comes to be conceived as static. If production of value doesn't fundamentally stem from conceiving goals and creatively integrating means, then there is no room to account for a *process* of creating such new mental integrations, as the driver of progress in production. Scientific and technical knowledge may be acknowledged as one of the input factors to production, but there is no recognition of the distinct process of goal-directed thinking to identify the *value* of integrating factors of production (including technical knowledge) into a given pro-

---

12. The fundamental role of the producer or businessman is the "entrepreneurial" role—that of conceiving a vision and devising plans to realize it and bring it to fruition. There are other economically distinct roles that may be combined in the same person, such as manager/supervisor or provider of capital. These latter roles fit perfectly well into an efficient-cause view of production as "inputs" or factors of production. Typically, therefore, the role of the businessman is reduced to only these. In contrast the entrepreneurial role, by its nature, is necessarily excluded from an efficient-cause view of production and can only be captured in a teleological view of production.

13. Rand illustrates (in a critical fashion) efficient-cause views of production in various places in *Atlas Shrugged*; for example, that production is just a matter of "muscles" (labor), or that a factory, or a machine, or a motor can be intrinsically (and hence automatically) productive regardless of who owns or directs it.

cess of production. Any innovations in technical knowledge are therefore conceived as occurring completely independently from any value considerations; they occur exogenously to economic production (in this view), and are then simply "automatically" reflected in production. Production itself is just the static process of output stemming from given and known input factors rather than a continuous process of new *value*-integrations.

As discussed above, factual knowledge alone does not automatically dictate how to integrate those facts into goals and plans. But this whole category of a distinct process of goal-directed thinking is precisely what drops out on intrinsic or subjective conceptions of value. The three different conceptions of value (intrinsic, subjective, objective) lead to fundamentally different views of production in economic theory (as argued below): a view where goal-directed thinking is central to production (as in the Austrian school) and a view where goal-directed thinking is absent from production (as in classical and neoclassical economics).

Rand's advocacy of capitalism was based on her view that it embodies an objective conception of value: "Of all the social systems in mankind's history, *capitalism is the only system based on an objective theory of values*" (CUI 14; original emphasis). It is only capitalism, in her view, that guarantees men the freedom to produce. It is only with capitalism that production (production of value) is truly *possible*, because it is only capitalism that protects the root mental act of the creative formation of goals and plans and the freedom to act on them. There are three elements fundamental to the functioning of capitalism: the entrepreneur, profit-seeking, and competition. In Rand's view, all three of these center around the view of production as the creative formation of conceptual goals and plans.

The function of the entrepreneur is preeminently to engage in the process of creatively conceiving new productive goals and integrating the means to achieve them. Rand writes: "The professional businessman is the field agent of the army whose lieutenant-commander-in-chief is the scientist. The businessman carries scientific discoveries from the laboratory of the inventor to industrial plants, and transforms them into material products that fill men's physical needs and expand the comfort of men's existence" (FTNI 23). In other words, the fundamental role of the businessman is to take *factual* knowledge and figure out what *value* it can serve. It is precisely the businessman's role to engage in goal-directed thinking so as to form the conceptual integrations necessary for identifying and achieving value.

Profit is the reward for successfully discovering new value opportunities, and it pertains precisely *to the discovery.* Once knowledge about value opportunities becomes widespread and widely implemented, the profit is competed away and disappears. The only way to consistently earn *new* profits is to continually engage in a process of discovery of new value opportunities.

Competition, for Rand, is effectively competition in this type of cognition. The competitive race is at root the race to create new value. One's "advantage" over competitors is precisely the creation of new products valued more highly by the market, or the discovery of how to better integrate factors of production to higher-valued uses—knowledge that competitors do not possess. For Rand, the fundamental issue is the creative evaluation and grasp of new opportunities, however, not the competition per se. She writes: "Competition is a by-product of productive work, not its goal. A creative man is motivated by the desire to achieve, not by the desire to beat others" ("The Moratorium on Brains," *ARL* 8).

What context then does Rand's philosophy set for economics? What facts of reality give rise to the science of economics? We've seen how her concept of objective value shapes her concept of production, and how production of value is central to man's life and survival. For an isolated individual (e.g., Robinson Crusoe), there is no further problem or question about production, beyond what philosophy describes. Crusoe needs to engage in a constant process of thought to discover factual knowledge about reality and to integrate this knowledge into values—that is, to conceive the goals that will sustain his life and to devise integrated plans for achieving these goals. For Crusoe, all the knowledge he needs in order to evaluate what to produce is in principle accessible to him. Since he is thinking, valuing, and producing for his *own* needs, given his own context and knowing full well his own integrated set of goals, there is no additional issue for him beyond the problems of conceptual thought and evaluation that we have already discussed.

Production under the division of labor introduces an entirely new question and problem. Under the division of labor, most people spend most of their time producing value for others. But since a value (for Rand) stems from a conceptual conclusion reached by an individual mind (within its own context of knowledge and integrated hierarchy of values), and since we can't directly know the minds of others (nor think nor value for them), how are we to know what others value? How are we to evaluate what to produce, what *counts* as production? It's possible to engage in *physical* production under the division of labor, while not producing value (when the objects created turn out not to be valued by others or are valued less than the inputs used to create them). General Motors may physically produce cars; but if the company is losing money, then it's engaged in value *destruction*, not production.

In a small self-sufficient village, this problem of production might be solved by direct communication. The blacksmith can approach the cobbler and commission directly what he wants. But in today's complex economy, goods are produced by strangers, often halfway around the world and by a long chain of production. And yet, we can walk into any local shoe store and usually find just the pair that suits us. How does this work? This is the basic task of economics: to detail the principles and processes by which this value problem is solved; to explain how it is that we can come to know about the values of others, such that we can successfully evaluate what to produce. To explain this interpersonal integration of knowledge of others' values is to explain the interpersonal integration of production under the division of labor.[14]

Rand's fundamental approach to all ethical, political, and economic questions is always the radically individualistic perspective, the perspective of the individual. For her, the correct perspective for economics would be: How am I (the individual) to evaluate what counts as production under the division of labor? This must be the fundamental starting point for economics. She categorically rejects any perspective on economics that operates from an aggregate or societal-level perspective, such as "how to most efficiently allocate society's resources." She designates this sort of collectivist perspective as the "tribal premise," which, she writes, "leads . . . to a baffling sort of double standard or double perspective in their way of viewing men and events: if they observe a shoemaker, they find no difficulty in concluding that he is working in order to make a living; but as political economists, on the tribal premise, they declare that his purpose (and duty) is to provide society with shoes" (*CUI* 6).[15] For Rand, the correct perspective from which to approach economics *is* the perspective of the shoemaker trying to make a living.

14. I don't mean to suggest that Rand explicitly formulated the fundamental question of economics in these terms (she never really discussed it), but I believe this way of conceiving the economic problem follows fairly naturally from her views. My statement of the problem is informed by the way in which the modern Austrian school *does* explicitly conceive the economic problem, which I think is basically consistent with Rand's ideas. The reasons for this basic consistency are explored later in the essay.

15. See her extended discussion of "tribal premise" in *CUI*, ch. 1.

It is Rand's conviction that an intrinsic or subjective conception of value will necessarily lead to a view of society as organized around collective goals. This logically leads to an aggregate, tribal perspective on society, including in economics.[16] In contrast, an objective conception of value logically leads to a radically individualistic perspective on society, and in economics. We won't have space to pursue this point in depth, other than to note that mainstream economics, in both its classical (intrinsic value) and neoclassical (subjective value) variants, has consistently maintained a tribal perspective in economics. Only the Austrian school, operating implicitly with an objective conception of value, has approached a radically individualistic perspective similar to Rand's. This is most consistently expressed in Mises's theoretical system, in *Human Action* (1949 [1996]).

Mainstream Economics: Value Sundered from Knowledge
Classical Economics: Intrinsic Value

The various economic thinkers in the classical period of economics were united by a shared intrinsic conception of value. The Physiocrats, who are precursors to this period, represent an extreme version of intrinsic value in economics. They considered *only* agriculture and extractive industries to be "productive," because it is only in these sectors that we end up with physically more material than we start with. We plant a handful of grain; we harvest a bushel. Manufacturing, in contrast, is "nonproductive," because it simply involves the rearrangement of preexisting matter. A carpenter making a chair will simply form preexisting wood into a new shape, without thereby bringing into existence a greater *quantity* of wood or any other substance. The rearrangement contains nothing "new," nothing "more" than the sum of the inputs (including labor) that went into constructing it.[17] The concept of production is therefore effectively construed in *metaphysical* terms; production simply represents the creation or acquisition of physically more matter. Obviously, there is no room for any element of creative mental integration in this concept of production.

This view of production was rejected by Adam Smith (and all subse-

16. See *CUI* 11–15, for her discussion of how intrinsic and subjective conceptions of value underlie and necessarily lead to the concept of "common good."

17. Mises, for example, writes that "the French Physiocrats contended that all labor was sterile unless it extracted something from the soil. Only cultivation, fishing and hunting, and the working of mines and quarries were in their opinion productive. The processing industries did not add to the value of the material employed anything more than the value of the things consumed by the workers" (Mises 1949 [1996], 141).

quent classical thinkers). For Smith, production is fundamentally about rearranging matter to be more *useful* to man. Production (in broad terms) is the production of some sort of value. But what is the nature of this value? Smith begins by noting that the concept of value is used in two distinct meanings: "use value" and "exchange value" (Smith 1776 [1981], 44). The use value of an object is the usefulness that it has to man, such that we can say (for example) that "food is useful to sustaining man's life" or "clothing is useful for protecting man from the elements." Exchange value, in contrast, is the economic value that something has, the goods that can be acquired for it in trade. Although Smith maintains that an object must have use value in some degree as the *condition* for it to have any exchange value (useless things will command nothing in exchange), he quickly rejects the idea that the use value is the *source* and cause of an object's specific exchange value. Smith's famous diamond-water paradox illustrates the difficulty: "The things which have the greatest value in use have frequently little or no value in exchange; and on the contrary, those which have the greatest value in exchange have frequently little or no value in use. Nothing is more useful than water: but it will purchase scarce any thing; scarce any thing can be had in exchange for it. A diamond, on the contrary, has scarce any value in use; but a very great quantity of other goods may frequently be had in exchange for it" (44–45).

In talking about use value, Smith briefly opens the door to the possibility of a conception of value in terms of an individual rationally evaluating the use of an object toward his goals; but the door is quickly shut. For Rand, the concept of value "presupposes an answer to the question: of value to whom and for what?" (*VOS* 16). Smith does not conceive usefulness in terms of the concrete use of a specific object to a particular individual's conceived goals (i.e., there is no "to whom" or "for what"). Rather, he construes "usefulness" only in abstract terms, for "man" in general. There is a valid perspective from which to say, for example, "food is useful to man." But this broad, abstract perspective on use value cannot be applied to explain the *specific* economic value of specific concrete objects. In trying to do so, one is implicitly led to conceiving the usefulness (e.g., of food) as some sort of reified "usefulness," inherent in and intrinsic to all the concrete instances of it. If "food" has the abstract usefulness it is said to have, then every concrete unit of food must have the same abstract usefulness. But then, every identical unit of food must be conceived as having the same *value*.

By framing "usefulness" in terms of abstract, universal, *factual* knowledge, Smith ignores from the outset the category of creative goal-directed thinking. This puts him squarely in an intrinsic conception of value. If every physically identical unit of a good must have the same abstract factual usefulness, then the use value is something intrinsic in the object. This follows inescapably if one tries to form a concept of "value" without involving the question "to whom and for what."

The diamond-water paradox makes clear that we can't look to abstract usefulness as an explanation of economic value. Where then to look? If value doesn't stem from the use of an object, it can only derive from the elements used to construct the object. One of the earlier general observations in economics was that the price of an object tended to gravitate to its cost of production. Smith turns to look for the source and determination of exchange value in the cost of producing an object.[18]

Every produced object has its "natural price," Smith thought, corresponding to its cost of production, to which its market price is inevitably drawn. The cost of production explains the natural price of an object, and the natural price is the systematic explanation for market prices and price tendencies. The task of a theory of value, then, is to trace back the chain of costs of a product to the ultimate sources and explanations of these costs, in order to explain exchange value.

The "natural price" of any object traces to the three main types of inputs that serve to produce it: labor, capital, and land. The wages of labor, the interest on capital, and the rent of land used in producing an object constitute its cost and thus explain its natural price. But this only leads to the further question: What determines the prices of labor, land, and capital? Each of these in turn must have its "natural price," explained in terms of *its* cost. But this means tracing each of these back to antecedent factors, with an ultimate grounding in *physical* facts of reality. Wage levels, for example, were often explained in terms of the "subsistence" wage (i.e., the wage needed to just barely sustain a family of four and thus reproduce the labor force without increasing it). In similar ways, classical economists traced the natural price of each factor of production back to its own idiosyncratic roots.

While the details of these views were never satisfactorily solved by

---

18. While it's commonly believed that classical economists held a labor theory of value, it's more accurate to view the theories as "cost of production" theories. It's true that labor was often the largest cost, but classical thinkers never succeeded in fully reducing the cost of all goods to labor only. Either way, the overall conception of value is the same—that value is intrinsic to an object and derives from the inputs that serve to produce it.

classical economists, the overall conception of value necessarily led to a particular conception of production. If production is production of exchange value and if exchange value derives from cost, then the inputs must be the *cause* of the value of the output. "Production" can only be conceived as the transmission of intrinsic value *from* the inputs *to* the output. If value is intrinsic in objects, then for the same reason, "productiveness" (production of *value*) has to be seen as something intrinsic in the factors of production. We see this view in all the classical thinkers. As one example, Jean-Baptiste Say's writings show the regular use of terms such as "productive agents," possessing intrinsic "productive powers," which consist in being able to "communicate" or "annex" value to a finished product.[19] Ultimately, this perspective reduces to a physical conception of production; it is the physical resources and physical actions that are fundamentally responsible for production. Such a view is necessarily implicit in an intrinsic conception of value: if intrinsic value inheres in each object, then each physically identical object must have the same value—making value coextensive with the physical object.

A view of production centered on the physical causation of inputs transforming into output is necessarily an "efficient-cause" view of production, contrasting directly with Rand's "teleological" view of production. This leaves no room for the creative origination of goals and the creative integration of means as the root of production (of value-creation). There is no element of goal-directed thinking at all, since, in an intrinsic value conception, value is not fundamentally conceived in terms of goals and plans. There is no element of conceptual knowledge involved in the concept of value and, thus, no fundamental role for the creative mind to play in production of value.

Classical treatises typically include large sections on production, but the discussion invariably focuses heavily on *physical* aspects of production such as climate, the fertility of soil, the characteristics of the labor force, the dynamics of population, and so on.[20] Some classical thinkers did discuss knowledge as being relevant to production, but any such discussion was only of factual scientific or technological knowledge, and the *value* of such knowledge was simply assumed implicitly to be obvious and intrinsically given. Thus, while classical economists *seem* to be talking a

19. See Say's *Treatise of Political Economy* (1803 [1855]).
20. See, for example, Say 1803 [1855] or Mill 1848 [1909]; in both, a large section on production forms "Book 1" of the respective treatises.

great deal about production, they are not in fact talking about production in Rand's meaning of the concept—as a process rooted in the creative formation of new *value* integrations.

What then is the fundamental issue or question of economics? Given the classical conception of value, it cannot be the evaluation problem we posed before: how to know what others value in order to evaluate what counts as production under the division of labor. Value inheres in objects themselves. In order to know what counts as production of value, then, one need only look to the intrinsic value of the object itself. If one produces a particular physical object, then ipso facto the object has the intrinsic value indicated by its "natural price." For Smith, the fundamental question of economics was the "Wealth of Nations," the question of how to maximize the aggregate production of intrinsic value—that is, of physical goods (per capita), given a nation's aggregate resources. From Rand's point of view, this is an example of the tribal perspective in economics: conceiving the fundamental economic problem in terms of aggregates, and in seeking the achievement of a particular aggregate result.

During the classical period, careful distinctions to arrive at precise concepts of profit and entrepreneurship were only in the process of emerging. But it would be impossible, on an intrinsic conception of value and an efficient-cause view of production, to arrive at anything like Rand's conception of profit as the reward to the creative formation of new value-integrations, or her view of the entrepreneur as the creator. There is no role for the entrepreneur as the fundamental producer of value in the economy, when all value stems intrinsically from input resources.

Neoclassical Economics: Subjective Value

The generally acknowledged turning point between classical economics and modern economics was the "marginal revolution," the independent and near simultaneous discovery of the marginal utility principle by William Stanley Jevons, Carl Menger, and Leon Walras, in the early 1870s. Each of these three thinkers has his own approach to and perspective on the issue, but the core idea in each of them was to fundamentally shift the conception of value from being intrinsic in the object to stemming from the subject (the individual valuer). Classical economists failed to reach this perspective by construing "use value" in abstract terms, as a generalized sort of "use" for "man" in general. The essence of the marginal revolution was to construe "use value" in terms of a *concrete* use of a *particular* unit of a good, for a specific individual. Instead of the perspective that "water" is useful to "man's life," the marginalist focus is on the particular glass of water in front of me, and what particular use it can presently serve *to me*. Importantly, this must take into account my present context—that is, what quantity of water I already possess or have already consumed. If my thirst is fully slaked, the water may serve no use and thus have no value to me. If I am thirsty, but I have a ten-gallon container of water beside me, then again this *particular* glass of water is not of great value to me (if it spills, I can easily replace it). But if I'm in the desert, I may value an equivalent glass of water as high as my life itself. Thus all value arises only within an individual's particular context and pertains to the specific use he has for a particular good.

With this fundamental shift in perspective, Smith's diamond-water paradox is effectively solved, and use value is fully reconciled with exchange value. "Water" is less valuable than "diamonds," in normal circumstances, because it exists in sufficient quantity that any additional units have little or no value. Thus, the exchange value of water is low or nil.

From this perspective, physically identical units of a good, rather than being viewed as having identical value (as on the intrinsic value perspective), are viewed as having *different* value, depending on the context. Not only will physically identical units of a good have different value to different people, they will have different value to the *same* person at different times and even different (higher or lower) value to the same person at the *same* time. Each glass of water relieves my thirst more; so each subsequent glass is less useful and less valuable to me.

The principle that each additional unit of a good will be valued less than the prior one is the crucial principle of diminishing marginal utility. With this principle in hand, economists explain downward-sloping demand curves—and (with an analogous principle) upward-sloping supply curves. This grounds the fundamental explanation of *all* prices in terms of the intersection of supply and demand, providing a much more unified and systematic theory of price than classical theories could achieve.

Menger, Jevons, and Walras all shared the common conception that value is subject-dependent. But this category obscures two fundamentally different ways in which value can be dependent on a subject: it can be conceptualized as dependent on the subject's *thinking* or on the subject's *feelings* (or "whims"). In Rand's view, these belong in two separate categories: objective value and subjective value.

For Rand, as we've noted, the concept of value presupposes a "to whom" and "for what." The crux of the shared conception of value of Menger, Jevons, and Walras (in contrast to Classical economists) is that it includes a "to whom" (value as subject-dependent), but a critical difference arises in the "for what."[21] For Jevons, "value depends entirely upon utility," and "Utility must be considered as measured by, or even as actually identical with, the addition made to a person's happiness. It is a convenient name for the aggregate of the favourable balance of feeling produced—the sum of the pleasure created and the pain prevented" (Jevons 1888, 45). With Jevons, the "for what" is the individual's pleasure (and absence of pain)—that is, the hedonic utility of the Utilitarians. Value is subject-dependent because it is the subject who feels pleasure. Jevons therefore tends to express and explain the law of diminishing marginal utility in terms of pleasure. While he briefly and tangentially refers to particular uses of objects, his explanation of diminishing utility centers on notions such as the physiological experience of "satiation" or on observations that the same stimulus continuously applied tends to result in diminishing intensity of pleasure, and so on.

For Menger, in contrast to Jevons, the "for what" of a good is that it fulfills a *conceived goal* and is conceptually recognized as doing so. Menger accounts for value in terms of an individual having conceptual knowledge of an object's causal connection to achieving his—the valuer's—goals. Thus value is "subject-dependent" for Menger because it is the subject who conceives the goal, and it is the subject who possesses the knowledge of the relationship of the object to his goal. This type of view falls into Rand's category of *objective* value.

Menger's conception of "usefulness" does not simply devolve into pleasure; usefulness maintains the meaning of a causal relationship of a means to a goal. We can see the difference in emphasis with an example of how the Austrians present the marginal value concept. Eugen von Böhm-Bawerk, a follower of Menger, illustrates the concept with the example of a farmer laying up five sacks of grain for the winter (1891 [1930], 149–50). The first sack he plans to use to stave off starvation (and thus has the value of life itself to him); the second sack he plans to use to become hale and hearty, to have the energy to work; the third sack he plans to use to feed his cow; the fourth sack he plans to use to make alcohol; the fifth sack he plans to use to feed his pet parrot. Each of these is treated as a con-

---

21. My contrast of the different conceptions of "subject-dependent" value will here center on Jevons and Menger. Walras shares with Jevons a purely subjective conception of value, but I won't examine here his particular version, or how he arrives at it.

ceived goal, and the farmer is viewed as consciously planning the use of the sacks of grain according to the importance of each goal to his life. The law of diminishing marginal value is explained, not in terms of some progressive sensation of satiation, or of diminishing pleasure, but by the fact that the farmer deliberately and consciously plans the use of each sack to serve his most important goals first, and then to use each subsequent sack to serve progressively less important goals. It is this conscious evaluation of the importance of each goal to his life (and the planned use of each unit accordingly) that causes each subsequent unit to be valued less. I'll examine Menger's conception of value in more detail in the next section but, for now, note that the idea that value is "subject-dependent" ("subjective" in the sense of this term most often used by economists) masks that Menger and Jevons in fact have fundamentally different conceptions of value, which lead to radically different economic theories.

Jevons's use of a subjective conception of value, conceived in terms of hedonic utility, is further cemented by another consideration: "It is clear," he writes in the introduction to his famous book, "that Economics, if it is to be a science at all, must be a mathematical science" (1888, 3). The fact that the new approach to economics operates with a *marginal* conception of utility (Jevons thinks) clearly invites the use of differential calculus: "As the complete theory of almost every other science involves the use of that calculus, so we cannot have a true theory of Economics without its aid" (3). Bentham had already conceived "utility" as lending itself to an arithmetic of pleasures and pains; Jevons now wants to develop the differential calculus of pleasures and pains.

But reducing all value to a single cardinal mathematical scale in this way negates any possible role for conceptual integration in valuing. Rather than viewing things in terms of an individual pursuing a complex of conceptually integrated goals (representing his vision of his life plan), Jevons reduces it all to a single goal, a single motivation, a single homogeneous axis of "utility," which varies only quantitatively (and thus is mathematically tractable). But to do this is to eject from consideration the element of *conceiving* goals and the rich conceptual integrations of means to ends—that is, it excludes any element of teleological integration. All of that is collapsed into a single cardinal axis, where objects are simply to be ranked flatly along a single scale according to their utility (the amount of pleasure they evoke, in fact or in expectation).[22]

---

22. This is not to deny that, on the objective view, values can be ranked against each other ordinally, but this is only achieved as the result of integrating them into a rich hierar-

Subsequent economic thinkers eagerly pushed forward the mathematicization of economics, but they came to reject Jevons's conception of value in terms of hedonic utility, deeming irrelevant whatever psychological activities might be occurring in the consciousness of the subject. All that is needed for economic theory (it was thought) is to know that the individual exhibits a preference for one thing over another. The prevailing view came to be that what goes on inside the mind of the valuing individual is irrelevant to economics; all that matters is his "revealed preference." But this is just a further expression of a subjective-value conception (in Rand's sense). Whether value is pleasure or value is revealed preference, it is *not* seen to stem from or depend on the conceptual thought processes of the individual. Value is not viewed as embodying knowledge, and this is in fundamental contrast to Rand's objective conception of value. Implicit in the views of these economic thinkers, then, is that value is fundamentally sundered from knowledge.

As far as economics is concerned, then, the preferences or values of individuals are to be treated as simply "given." Preferences are not something that depend on or emerge from anything in the economic realm but, rather, form part of the "data" from which economic reasoning *begins*. The source of these preferences, and any changes in them, can only be treated as exogenous to economics.

With a new concept of value, the developing neoclassical school of economics was necessarily led to a new view of production and its place in economics. For the classical economists, production was a central topic; production was viewed as the "efficient cause" process of producing intrinsic value (which effectively meant the production of physical goods, since intrinsic value is coextensive with the physical good). But with value now conceived as a subjective emanation from a consciousness, production came to have a less central place in economic theory. W. C. Mitchell writes: "Nowadays [1934] economics is thought of as centering primarily not on the problem of production but on that of value and the distribution of income." In fact, "in many a modern treatise there is no separate discussion of production. The subject which was the very center of Adam Smith's interest gets incidental rather than systematic treatment. What the theorist has to say is broken up into bits" (Mitchell 1967, 37–38).

On Rand's objective conception of value, where thought is directed at

---

chical structure (a process that involves a great deal of complex thinking and choosing), not as a result of having a flat uniform mathematical axis for measuring values.

conceiving goals and integrating means to ends (teleological integration), production is seen as clearly a value issue. In fact production is, at root, the achievement of these sorts of conceptual value-integrations. But if the concept of value is conceived in purely subjective terms, there is no room to subsume any element of conceptual integration—or a creative teleological thought process—under the concept of value. If value is fundamentally conceived in terms of pleasure or revealed preference, it's difficult to see how the activities of production per se can be considered *value* issues.

Production, then, has to be conceived purely as an issue of *factual* knowledge. The complex integrations of factors of production must be conceived only in terms of scientific/technical knowledge, not involving any value questions. Any integration of productive factors essentially reduces to studying their factual properties, and their proper integration is only a matter of having the right technical knowledge. The integration involved is not viewed as fundamentally involving any process of *evaluation*.

But (as discussed) facts alone cannot tell us how to integrate those facts into a conceived goal, nor how to integrate means into a plan to achieve it. Scientific and technical possibilities, alone, cannot tell us how best to *use* them and combine them. This issue goes to the heart of the differences between the Austrian school and the neoclassical school (see below).

The subjective concept of value therefore leads us to this fundamental split. "Value" is conceived as subjective consumer preference, without any knowledge element, and "production," therefore, is conceived purely in terms of factual knowledge, with no value element. It is this fundamental split that causes *both* consumer values and production to drop out of economic theory. Both are treated as exogenous to economics, simply as "given" data for economics and thus the starting point for economic reasoning. The source of (and change in) subjective consumer values is considered to be a matter perhaps for psychology or sociology, but not economics. The integration of productive factors is taken as a purely technical matter, not a value matter, and thus also is not a concern for economics.

What then is economics fundamentally about? What is the fundamental problem of economics? According to Jevons: "Pleasure and pain are undoubtedly the ultimate objects of the Calculus of Economics. To satisfy our wants to the utmost with the least effort—to procure the greatest amount of what is desirable at the expense of the least that is undesirable—in other words, *to maximise pleasure*, is the problem of Economics" (1888, 37). We are left with a mathematical optimization problem. With given consumer preferences, given production functions, and known resource availability, the only task left to economics is to mathematically solve for the matrix of prices and quantities that will maximize utility.

This mathematical solution point is the "equilibrium" point. The equilibrium framework becomes the fundamental framework of analysis for mainstream neoclassical economics. As Kirzner (who will later disagree with it point for point) describes the framework:

> The focus of attention, in this view of the task of price theory, is thus on the *values of the price and quantity variables*, and in particular on the set of values consistent with *equilibrium* conditions. In investigating the consequences of a particular market structure, this approach examines the associated pattern of equilibrium prices, costs, and outputs. In investigating the consequences of a particular change in taste, or technology and the like, it examines the equilibrium conditions after the change, comparing them with those before the change. The very efficiency of the market system as an allocator of society's resources is appraised by examining the allocation of resources at equilibrium. In investigating the desirability of particular government policies, this approach appraises the effects of the changes these policies will bring about in the equilibrium situation. In all this the emphasis is on the *prices* and *quantities* and, in particular, on these prices and quantities as they would emerge under *equilibrium* conditions. (Kirzner 1973, 5)

A crucial assumption in order to mathematically solve for this equilibrium point is that all knowledge be given. The economist must assume "perfect knowledge" (of consumer preferences, technology, resource availability) in order for there to be any sort of determinate mathematical solution to the problem. One simply cannot solve a system of simultaneous equations if some equations are left out, or their functional form is not known, or some variables are missing. Correspondingly, in this view, there is not much to talk about *other* than the equilibrium point. Given the starting data, the only determinate point *is* the equilibrium point. A disequilibrium state could take any form; there is no *systematic* account that can be given of it, other than to say there should be a tendency for the prices and quantities to return to the determinate equilibrium point. What is the nature of that "tendency" to equilibrium, as a process? Mainstream economics has had little success finding much to say about that.

From the perspective of the mainstream neoclassical school, the fundamental problem of economics is not a problem of knowing what others value in order to evaluate what counts as production—in contrast to Rand and (as we'll see later) the Austrians. There can be no such problem, when all knowledge is simply assumed given. But if we assume "imperfect" knowledge (unknown consumer preferences, unknown production functions, unknown resource availability), then we effectively destroy the basic framework of neoclassical economics as the mathematical description of the equilibrium state. Neoclassical economics would simply have little to say in that case.[23] We can note in passing that the fundamental neoclassical focus on describing equilibrium states—taking an aggregate view of the economy and fundamentally viewing it in terms of achieving some aggregate result (equilibrium)—is another example of what Rand calls the tribal perspective in economics.

The view of man that is embedded and assumed in the neoclassical framework is what Kirzner calls the "Robbinsian maximizer" or "Robbinsian economizer" (Kirzner 1973).[24] In this view, the individual, operating with given ends and known means (including full knowledge of all the ways the means can be technically combined), has only to mathematically optimize the allocation of means to ends in order to maximize utility. There is no room for the creative formation of new evaluative conceptual integrations in this view. There is no room for creatively conceiving new goals; all ends are given. There is no room for creatively integrating new plans (discovering new means or new combinations of means) to better achieve one's goals; all integrations of means are assumed in advance. There is no creative conceptual thought process required (or possible) at all. The "rationality" of economic man, in this view, is simply to run the mathematical algorithm to deterministically calculate the quantitatively optimal choice, a choice that is already implicit in the given data. In other words, the mental processes of Robbinsian economic man are, point for

23. Neoclassical economics does sometimes try to account for uncertainty or "imperfect" knowledge, but only in terms of *known* probability distributions. Algorithmic methods can still mathematically deduce equilibrium outcomes from these. For Austrians the relevant category is what they call "sheer uncertainty" or "sheer ignorance" (i.e., so-called unknown unknowns). It is this category, for Austrians, that makes mathematical equilibrium analysis inapplicable, and that gives rise to creative thought and discovery as the essence of what economics must fundamentally grapple with.

24. Named for Lionel Robbins, who formalized the neoclassical definition of economics in 1932: "Economics is the science which studies human behavior as a relationship between given ends and scarce means which have alternative uses" (1932, 16).

point, the direct antithesis of Rand's view of teleological thinking—of an individual creatively conceiving new goals and new conceptual integrations of means. Robbinsian economic man is effectively a deterministic puppet, dancing to the tune of the "given" data. But this is no accident; it follows logically from a subjective conception of value.

Production is treated in an analogous manner. In the branch of economics known as the "theory of the firm," the firm's basic problem is also merely a deterministic quantitative optimization problem. With given production functions (the particular functional relationship of how input resources can be combined), and facing a given and known demand curve, the production problem that the firm faces is merely to choose the quantity of each input resource to use, and the quantity of output to produce, in order to maximize profits. The real problem of production— creatively conceiving a productive goal (a new product or service), and the creative formation of a rich integration of all the complex interrelated aspects of production in order to achieve that goal—is simply assumed away as "given."

The consequences of the neoclassical concept of value pervade every element of economic theory. It's widely recognized, for example, that the market economy is driven by a striving for profits. Tellingly, neoclassical economics has had a hard time capturing or explaining this fact in its systematic body of theory.

In a nonequilibrium world, there are price discrepancies; thus opportunities abound for "entrepreneurial profits"—that is, opportunities for someone to creatively seek out and exploit price differences in order to earn profits. In an equilibrium world, however, all knowledge is already assumed given. All production techniques are already discovered and implemented, and all markets are perfectly clear at the equilibrium price. There are no price discrepancies, and hence no room for entrepreneurial profits.[25] This isn't of much concern to theorists. Paul Samuelson, writing in an early edition of his famous textbook, explains:

> In addition to wages, interest, and rent, economists often talk about a fourth category of income: profit. Wages are the return to labor; interest the return to capital; rent the return to land. What is profit the return to? Economists do not always agree on the answer. A graduate student recently checked over a number of modern textbooks and came up with 14

25. In equilibrium, there is still an interest return on capital, and returns from risk premia; but no entrepreneurial profits.

different answers! What shall we do? Examine all 14 answers? Add a fif-
teenth? The obvious thing is to give a common-sense description of what
people generally mean when they speak of profits. Let us call a spade a
spade. If profit is a miscellaneous catchall category, let us recognize it as
such. (Samuelson 1955, 583)

In other words, profit is essentially an unimportant phenomenon, a left-
over residual that we can discuss casually without needing to give a *systematic* account of it, as a central part of economic theory.

With markets at equilibrium, and no real concept of entrepreneurial profit, it is no surprise that the concept of the entrepreneur effectively
drops out of neoclassical theory as well. There is simply no room for him,
no analytic role. At equilibrium, there is no entrepreneurial innovation.
Any innovation that does occur is viewed as a scientific or technological
matter, occurring exogenously to economics. In the face of such innovation, the task of economics is simply to mathematically reoptimize with
the new data, in order to determine a new equilibrium point. But the entrepreneur is not a scientist or an engineer; this is not the type of innovation he engages in. From Rand's point of view, his innovation consists in
creatively forming new value-integrations, innovation in terms of conceiving new goals and creatively seeking to better integrate means to ends.
Since the subjective value concept of mainstream neoclassical economics
logically excludes this category of thinking, there is simply nothing for
the entrepreneur to do in the neoclassical framework.

The existence of a problem is recognized by theorists. Baumol (1968)
lamented: "In more recent years, while the facts have apparently under-
scored the significance of [the entrepreneur's] role, he has at the same
time virtually disappeared from the theoretical literature" (64). But, he
continues, "it is not difficult to explain his absence" because "obviously,
the entrepreneur has been read out of the model. There is no room for
enterprise or initiative. The management group becomes a passive cal-
culator that reacts mechanically to changes imposed on it by fortuitous
external developments over which it does not exert, and does not even
attempt to exert, any influence. One hears of no clever ruses, ingenious
schemes, brilliant innovations, of no charisma or of any of the other stuff
of which outstanding entrepreneurship is made; one does not hear of
them because there is no way in which they can fit into the model" (Baumol 1968, 66–67).

Baumol and others have tried to make room for the entrepreneur in the neoclassical model, often trying to model him as an input factor of production susceptible to supply-demand analysis, but such attempts inevitably fail to capture the essence of what the entrepreneur is and the range of what he does. Revisiting the issue more recently, Bianchi and Henrekson (2005) ask, in the title of a paper: "Is Neoclassical Economics Still Entrepreneurless?" Echoing Baumol, they locate the problem at the heart of the neoclassical paradigm: "The reason for this disregard of entrepreneurship is not a denial of its relevance for economic development and the organization of economic activity. The reasons are methodological: the entrepreneur and the entrepreneurial function largely elude analytical tractability" (2005, 1). After systematically surveying "the different mainstream/neoclassical modeling techniques that have been used in order to capture the entrepreneurial function in the economy" (1), they find the situation essentially unchanged: "We conclude that an individual real-world entrepreneur, even if highly stylized, cannot at present be modeled in mainstream economics, since he or she *does* elude analytical tractability. In this sense, the neoclassical entrepreneur is (still) not entrepreneurial" (22).

Finally, with the market at equilibrium, the concept of competition becomes problematic. In Rand's view, entrepreneurs strive for profits by striving for new value-integrations (new goals and new integrations of means) to identify profit opportunities, winning away customers by providing better products and/or lower prices. The competitive race *is* the ceaseless search for such new value-integrations, and the competitive advantage one gains is precisely in achieving them ahead of others.

In the neoclassical equilibrium framework, however, with the assumption of "perfect knowledge" there is no possibility of any such competition. Everything is already discovered, and nothing changes. There are no new goals to seek, all possible combinations of means are already known, and production simply consists in the endless, rote repetition of the same activities. There simply cannot be any competition in seeking new goals and plans, when all such integrations are assumed given in advance.

For neoclassical economics, the concept of competition logically has to be reconceptualized in equilibrium terms. Rather than denoting a *process*, competition necessarily comes to denote a particular *state* of affairs, at equilibrium. The earliest important neoclassical conception of competition was the theory of "perfect competition." For a state of perfect competition to exist, there must be a large number of buyers and sellers, such that no individual can influence the price (all are "price-takers"), and all knowledge must be given. Thus, rather than denoting a process whereby an individual gains the advantage over competitors by creatively forming new value-integrations ahead of others, perfect competition comes to denote a situation where *no one* has any advantage over anyone else. As Hayek pointed out in a key paper criticizing the then-emerging new concept of competition:

> The theory of perfect competition . . . has little claim to be called "competition" at all and . . . its conclusions are of little use as guides to policy. The reason for this seems to me to be that this theory throughout assumes that state of affairs already to exist which, according to the truer view of the older theory, the process of competition tends to bring about (or to approximate) and that, if the state of affairs assumed by the theory of perfect competition ever existed, it would not only deprive of their scope all the activities which the verb "to compete" describes but would make them virtually impossible. (1948, 92)

And yet, while competition is redefined to be the *opposite* of its normal meaning, Hayek continues, "the general view seems still to regard the conception of competition currently employed by economists as the significant one and to treat that of the businessman as an abuse."[26]

As with the classical view of production, the neoclassical view of production amounts in the end to an "efficient cause" view of production—not because value is intrinsic in production (classical economists), but because value is *irrelevant* to production. Production is viewed as emerging (in effect) "automatically" from inputs (with factual, scientific/technical knowledge as one of the inputs), rather than stemming from creatively formed new *value*-integrations. Entrepreneurial profit drops out because it is the return *to* such new value-integrations; and the entrepreneur disappears because he is the *creator* of the value-integrations.

Austrian Economics: Objective Value

There is a fundamental commonality between Rand and the Austrian school, grounded broadly in a shared objective conception of value (only

26. The perfect competition model has been followed by many successor theories of competition in neoclassical economics, but the root issue and root problem remain the same. In focusing on equilibrium states, knowledge has to be assumed as given (in one way or another), and thus competition is not conceived in terms of *the discovery and evaluation of knowledge*.

implicit in Austrian theory), which leads the Austrian school to recognize the centrality of knowledge to evaluation, and thus to make the creative integration of knowledge, in forming goals and plans, the very heart of their economic theory. However, to begin with, it should be noted that Rand would disagree, on philosophic grounds, with many of the ideas of various thinkers in the Austrian school. She disagreed vehemently, for example, with Hayek's political arguments in defense of capitalism, which she thought granted too much to collectivist premises.[27] She disagreed with many of Mises's philosophical statements, particularly his wider framework of "praxeology."[28] She also rejected some of Mises's economic concepts (for example, "consumer sovereignty").[29] There is no evidence that she ever read Menger, whose famous book was largely inaccessible in its original German edition and was published in English for the first time only in 1950.

We should note also that the Austrian school encompasses a diversity of views on many topics, and it would be impossible to survey them all. Nevertheless, I believe there *is* a core set of fundamental underlying ideas that unites the Austrian school as a school, and it centers on an *implicitly* objective conception of value. I've tried to highlight here those elements that I think best cohere with this underlying conception of value, and to show how this set of ideas is broadly consistent with Rand's views. Since the objective conception of value is only implicit in Austrian economics, and only imperfectly recognized and imperfectly applied by different thinkers, I will highlight some elements more starkly and more in Rand's terms than any Austrian thinker does, so it is not the case that any partic-

27. See Rand *Letters*, 308. I have found no evidence that she ever commented on Hayek's specifically economic work, and it seems unlikely that she read any of it.

28. Nathaniel Branden's review of Mises's book *Human Action*, published in *The Objectivist Newsletter* under Rand's supervision, states: "In justice to Professor Mises' position and our own, it must be mentioned that there are many sections of *Human Action* with which Objectivists cannot agree. These sections pertain, not to the sphere of economics as such, but to the philosophical framework in which his economic theories are presented. We must take the gravest exception, for example, to the general doctrine of praxeology; to the assertion that all value-judgments are outside the province of reason, that a scientific ethics is impossible; to the disavowal of the concept of inalienable rights; and to many of the psychological views expressed." Nevertheless, the otherwise glowing review concludes: "Notwithstanding these reservations, the book is of the first rank of importance, eminently deserving of careful study. It is a major economic classic. As a reference work, it belongs in the library of every advocate of capitalism" (*TON* vol. 2, no. 9, 34).

29. See *Marginalia* 105–41 for Rand's marginal notes on portions of *Human Action*. On the issue of consumer sovereignty in particular, see *Marginalia* 132, 137.

ular Austrian thinker can be expected to agree in every respect with my presentation.

The objective conception of value is only implicit in Austrian economics, because Austrians explicitly place themselves in the "subjective value" category, along with neoclassical economics. This prevents them from tracing their differences with the neoclassical school to a fundamentally different concept of value. Instead, they characterize their differences in a variety of ways: that Austrians view knowledge as "subjective" (subject-dependent), where neoclassicals view it as universally given and known; that Austrians focus on the market process, where neoclassicals focus on equilibrium; and so on. But ultimately, all these differences are expressions or consequences of an objective conception of value. Whether they know it or not (and despite their sometimes mitigating or contradicting it), *this* is the fundamental that differentiates Austrians from the neoclassical school.

I've mentioned Carl Menger as one of the three codiscoverers of the marginal value principle, but it is his unique way of conceptualizing value (fundamentally different from Jevons's) that launches the Austrian school and establishes its distinctive approach to economics. At the outset of his book *Principles of Economics*, Menger establishes his basic conception of value (of a "good"):

> If a thing is to become a good, or in other words, if it is to acquire goods-character, all four of the following prerequisites must be simultaneously present:
>
> 1. A human need.
> 2. Such properties as render the thing capable of being brought into a causal connection with the satisfaction of this need.
> 3. Human knowledge of this causal connection.
> 4. Command of the thing sufficient to direct it to the satisfaction of the need.
>
> Only when all four of these prerequisites are present simultaneously can a thing become a good. When even one of them is absent, a thing cannot acquire goods-character, and a thing already possessing goods-character would lose it at once if but one of the four prerequisites ceased to be present. (1871 [1994], 52)

The concept of a good, for Menger, denotes a *concrete* unit of something, serving a *specific* conceived goal, as *judged* by the individual in question.

Menger's conception of a good falls broadly in Rand's category of objective value: that a good is a particular object pursued by an individual who rationally grasps its causal relation to his needs. For this reason, Menger's is a *conceptual* view of value (versus Jevons's conception of value as "pleasure"), and it accords knowledge a central role in the process of evaluation and in the status of an item as a value. Since value involves knowledge, creative conceptual thought becomes crucial to the process of forming a value (i.e., identifying something as a good).

After defining a good, Menger immediately goes on to discuss "The Causal Connection between Goods" (1871 [1994], 55), and "The Laws concerning Goods-Character" (58), a discussion that is consistently conducted in terms of viewing a good *as* necessarily involving a rational grasp of a causal connection to one's needs. The principles he discusses here do not concern the laws of, or relations among, physical objects; nor do they concern laws or principles of "pleasure," or any other purely conscious phenomena. Rather, they are laws concerning the nature of, and changes in, the four-part *relationship* that his concept of "good" denotes, especially the element of a conceptual grasp of causal connections.

Given his conception of value, there is no dichotomy for Menger between consumer goods and producer goods. Instead, he categorizes goods as "first-order" versus "higher-order", where a higher-order good can be characterized as second-, third-, fourth-order, and so on, depending on its distance in the productive structure from the consumption level. The difference is one of degree, not of kind. All fall under the same basic category of value: they involve a mind's grasp of the causal connection of an object to human needs. This connection can be simple and direct, or complex and indirect, but nevertheless all goods are *valued* in the same way: "It is not a requirement of the goods-character of a thing that it be capable of being placed in direct causal connection with the satisfaction of human needs. It has been shown that goods having an indirect causal relationship with the satisfaction of human needs differ in the closeness of this relationship. But it has also been shown that this difference does not affect the essence of goods-character in any way" (1871 [1994], 56–57).

Moreover, for Menger, even first-order goods are, and only can be, valued in the context of an integrated hierarchy of values—that is, with reference to the role they play in a man's integrated plan of life. Valuing first-order goods involves assessing all the interrelated causal connections involved (not merely experiencing "reactions" of pleasure to isolated objects).

The needs of men are manifold, and their lives and welfare are not assured if they have at their disposal only the means, however ample, for the satisfaction of but one of these needs. Although the manner, and the degree of completeness, of satisfaction of the needs of men can display an almost unlimited variety, a certain harmony in the satisfaction of their needs is nevertheless, up to a certain point, indispensable for the preservation of their lives and welfare. . . . It is clear that even the most complete satisfaction of a single need cannot maintain life and welfare. In this sense, it is not improper to say that all the goods an economizing individual has at his command are mutually interdependent with respect to their goods-character, since each particular good can achieve the end they all serve, the preservation of life and well-being, not by itself, but only in combination with the other goods. . . .

The entire sum of goods at an economizing individual's command for the satisfaction of his needs, we call his property. His property is not, however, an arbitrarily combined quantity of goods, but a direct reflection of his needs, an integrated whole, no essential part of which can be diminished or increased without affecting realization of the end it serves. (1871 [1994], 74–75, 76)

In Jevons's theory, we saw value split from knowledge. We saw that consumer value is conceived as a type of value ("pleasure") that excludes knowledge, and production is conceived purely as a matter of technical knowledge that excludes any value concerns. With Menger, we have a unified conception of value: value conceived as crucially embodying knowledge and applying to *all* goods (consumer and producer). Evaluation is a conceptual perspective on an object that is based on a grasp of its causal connections to man's needs, and it is only as a result of a valuer's taking (and maintaining) this perspective that the object qualifies as a value. It is a view of value that sees value and knowledge as thoroughly integrated, and applying to every instance of a good.

Later Austrians criticized Menger's theory of needs for being too "objective" ("nonsubjective" in their view), and they shifted to a more subjectivist conception of consumer valuations of first-order goods. These criticisms tend to misinterpret Menger; they stem from the limited view that a subjective or intrinsic conception of value are the only two possibilities into which Menger can be slotted. What was missed was the possibility of a third category, Rand's category of "objective value," into which Menger's conception broadly falls. Unfortunately, the move toward conceiving consumer value in subjectivist terms has somewhat muddied the Austrian conception of value, making it harder for Austrians to appreciate the root of their differences from the neoclassical school.

Nevertheless, later thinkers such as Hayek and Mises do preserve crucial elements of Menger's distinctive conception of value (albeit expressed in different terms), which leads them to continue to frame economic issues from the perspective of a conceptual mind conceiving goals and forming plans. This activity of goal-directed thinking cannot be encompassed under a subjective conception of value, which causes the neoclassical school to ignore it and simply assume all goals and plans to be "given." Austrians such as Mises do not ignore it; but because it cannot be subsumed under the category of subjective value Mises came to view it as the subject of a *new* field of inquiry, hitherto unrecognized and unconceptualized: the science of goal-directed human action—that is, *praxeology*.

Mises recognized that certain fundamental concepts and principles about goal-directed action in general are needed to properly ground economics. For Rand, this need is filled by ethics or morality (she uses the terms interchangeably); she views ethics as the fundamental science of values, and values as the objects of goal-directed action. For Rand, *all* of man's goal-directed activity falls squarely under the purview of ethics, which establishes at the most abstract level the fundamental concepts and principles regarding human goals, choices, and actions. She remarks in her marginal comments to *Human Action*: "Isn't it clear by now that 'praxeology' is intended as a substitute for morality? What *is* morality, if it is not the science of 'all human choices'?" (*Marginalia* 133). It is the task of ethics to define the fundamental nature of value. For Rand, value is objective—that is, it crucially involves a conceptual mind creatively grasping means-ends relationships to achieve conceived goals. It is a unified conception of value that, like Menger's, applies to both consumer goods and producer goods. It encompasses the conceptual goal-directed thinking that the neoclassical school ignores and that Mises sees as the subject of praxeology.

In the early part of the twentieth century, the Austrian school was considered one of several allied schools developing the emerging marginal utility ideas, differing from other schools stylistically, but not in essentials; this view changed as a result of the famous socialist calculation debate, when stark differences began to emerge between the Austrian school and the developing mainstream neoclassical school. In 1920 Ludwig von

Mises published his famous paper "Die Wirtschaftsrechnung im Sozial-istischen Gemeinwesen," in which he argued that economic calculation is impossible under socialism.[30] It concluded that socialism is doomed to failure as an economic system, because it is impossible to know how to ra-tionally organize the production of goods, without the price system with which to calculate the best courses of action. Mises gives the example of a mountain lying in the way of a proposed rail line (Mises 1927 [2005], 47–48). Should track be laid around the mountain, or over it, or should a tunnel be dug through it? All these alternatives are *technically* feasible, but the technical knowledge by itself does not dictate which course of ac-tion is best—that is, which plan achieves the most *value*. This can only be determined by calculating the costs and benefits of each plan using mar-ket prices, in order to identify the most profitable route. Such an evalua-tion is impossible to a socialist state, which has no markets for factors of production (since all means of production are owned by the state), hence no prices with which to perform such a calculation. The crux of Mises's argument is that a distinct (but interrelated) process of *evaluation* of the facts and technical possibilities is necessary, which a socialist state simply cannot perform. Technical knowledge alone does not provide the guid-ance needed for the production of *value*.

Neoclassical economists responded that standard neoclassical equi-librium theory could solve the problem—at least in principle. *Given* all the information about consumer preferences, resource availability, and technical recipes, one could construct a huge matrix of simultaneous equations and then solve for the optimal values of prices and quantities. Admittedly, gathering the information, constructing the matrix, and per-forming the calculations might be practically impossible at the present time; but with a large enough computer (it was asserted), the socialist state could organize production just as well as the market economy.[31]

This rejoinder baffled the Austrian side, which led Hayek (the main protagonist for the Austrians in the English language debates) to begin to elaborate elements of the Austrian view that sharply differentiate it from the neoclassical school. Mises also developed his ideas along similar lines, culminating in his monumental treatise *Human Action* (1949 [1996]).[32]

30. The paper is republished in English in Hayek 1935, ch. 3.

31. For a detailed account of the socialist calculation debate, see Lavoie 1985.

32. These ideas in both Mises and Hayek were developed over time, and earlier state-ments of the issue by both were less clear and less focused on the creative element in evalua-tion than their later statements.

Essentially, Hayek brought to the forefront elements from Menger's view of value that made the neoclassical rejoinder seem incoherent. Against the neoclassical assumption that consumer preferences, resource availability, and technical preferences are "given" and "known," Hayek began to elaborate the elements of the process of evaluation by which these things can only *come* to be known, by individuals conceiving productive goals and formulating plans to achieve them. Hayek points out that the neoclassical framework completely ignores this activity. For example, he writes incredulously about Schumpeter's "(to me startling) pronouncement [that] . . . the possibility of a rational calculation in the absence of markets for the factors of production follows for the theorist 'from the elementary proposition that consumers in evaluating ("demanding") consumers' goods ipso facto also evaluate the means of production which enter into the production of these goods.' Taken literally, this statement is simply untrue. The consumers do nothing of the kind" (Hayek 1948, 90). For Hayek, it is only a process of evaluation by individual producers that brings about the integration factors of production, by identifying their value in achieving productive goals. Ignoring this, the neoclassical framework simply assumes that the factors of production are *already* optimally integrated to achieve "given" goals (which are already "known" to be valuable), and therefore consumer utility (value) can be simply mathematically imputed to these known goals and given integrations of factors.

Regarding the overall debate, Hayek writes: "This is not a dispute about whether planning is to be done or not. It is a dispute as to whether planning is to be done centrally, by one authority for the whole economic system, or is to be divided among many individuals. Planning in the specific sense in which the term is used in contemporary controversy necessarily means central planning—direction of the whole economic system according to one unified plan. Competition, on the other hand, means decentralized planning by many separate persons" (Hayek 1948, 79). It is no accident that the concept of "planning," for Hayek's opponents, had only one sense, a sense that did not apply to the individual; for the idea that the individual *plans*, that he conceives goals and creatively forms an integration of means aimed at achieving them, is not part of the neoclassical conception of value. As we saw earlier, Robbinsian man *maximizes*, but he does not plan; all his ends and the available means to them are already given and known; all the integrations are already formed. The neoclassical view leaves no room for conceptual thought, conceptual planning, or conceptual *evaluation*, but only deterministic, mathematical optimizing. Hayek's focus on individual planners stems from Menger's contrary conception of value.

Hayek goes on to outline some of the kinds of knowledge that are relevant to an individual's plans, ridiculing the notion that such knowledge could be collected by and known to the state (to be used in its "planning"):

> Today it is almost heresy to suggest that scientific knowledge is not the sum of all knowledge: But a little reflection will show that there is beyond question a body of very important but unorganized knowledge which cannot possibly be called scientific in the sense of knowledge of general rules: the knowledge of the particular circumstances of time and place. It is with respect to this that practically every individual has some advantage over all others because he possesses unique information of which beneficial use might be made, but of which use can be made only if the decisions depending on it are left to him or are made with his active co-operation. We need to remember only how much we have to learn in any occupation after we have completed our theoretical training, how big a part of our working life we spend learning particular jobs, and how valuable an asset in all walks of life is knowledge of people, of local conditions, and of special circumstances. To know of and put to use a machine not fully employed, or somebody's skill which could be better utilized, or to be aware of a surplus stock which can be drawn upon during an interruption of supplies, is socially quite as useful as the knowledge of better alternative techniques. The shipper who earns his living from using otherwise empty or half-filled journeys of tramp-steamers, or the estate agent whose whole knowledge is almost exclusively one of temporary opportunities, or the arbitrageur who gains from local differences of commodity prices are all performing eminently useful functions based on special knowledge of circumstances of the fleeting moment not known to others. (Hayek 1948, 80)

Hayek thought that the essential issue was that this sort of knowledge is insurmountably "dispersed" (not centralizable, therefore unavailable to the state to use in "planning"). More fundamentally, the kind of knowledge he calls attention to here goes beyond factual, scientific knowledge, encompassing knowledge of what ends can be achieved and what resources might serve as means. "Means" and "ends" are *evaluative* terms that go beyond the factual information. Hayek's "particular knowledge of time and place" is just the sort of knowledge that must be evaluated—that is, integrated by an individual's thought process in conceiving and pursuing goals. This is a process that can only be performed by an individual mind.

It's sometimes expressed in Austrian circles that Hayek and Mises extended the subjectivism of the Austrian paradigm during this period to include "subjective knowledge" (i.e., knowledge as subject-dependent, pertaining only to an individual and his context), to supplement Menger's concept of "subjective value." But these are not two distinct issues; rather, they are inseparable elements of an *objective* conception of value. The kind of knowledge that Mises and Hayek (mis)describe as "subjective" is precisely the kind of knowledge an individual needs in order to form an integrated plan to achieve his specific goals. This sort of knowledge, in contrast to abstract, impersonal, universal scientific knowledge, is subject-dependent, precisely because conceived ends and the mental integration of plans to achieve them are subject-dependent. This category of knowledge was already embedded in Menger's objective conception of value from the start.

In the midst of these discussions, Hayek came to point out that the state of equilibrium at the heart of the neoclassical framework is identical with the state of affairs where all knowledge is given and known; that they are one and the same issue. In the state of equilibrium, all the plans of all individuals dovetail perfectly *because* there is perfect knowledge of all possible ends and means, and perfect knowledge of what everyone else is planning to do. Hayek regarded it as absurd to assume this sort of knowledge as "given." To do so is to assume away the real problem that economics must explain: How is it that all the separate plans of every individual come to be coordinated or integrated?

At root, then, the fundamental problem of economics is a knowledge problem. Each individual, pursuing his own productive goals and plans, needs a method to coordinate his plans and goals with those of others. Otherwise, the expectations embedded in *his* plans will be disappointed. He will be unable to sell what he intended to sell (at the prices he expected), or to buy what he intended to buy (at the prices he expected). He needs to learn what others do value, will value, or could value, in order to integrate his plans with theirs, in order to achieve *his* goals. It is a continuous process of evaluation, learning, and *re*-evaluation; of conceiving goals and formulating plans; and of subsequently reconceiving goals and reformulating plans, as new information comes to light and as circumstances change. This conception of the fundamental problem of economics is basically consistent with the conception that I showed follows from Rand's philosophy.

This coordination of plans is precisely what the market price system enables; the information about what others value is embedded in market prices. The fundamental task of economics, then, is to describe the process by which individual goal-seekers use market prices in evaluating and reevaluating their goals and plans, to progressively coordinate their productive activities. In stark contrast to the neoclassical paradigm with its focus on the unchanging perfect-knowledge equilibrium state, the Austrian framework centers on studying the nature of the evolving *market process*, the ongoing process of the discovery, evaluation, and coordination of knowledge in a nonequilibrium world.

In a nonequilibrium state, supply does not always equal demand, markets may not clear, different prices for the same good may exist in different parts of the market, and so on. This opens the door for entrepreneurial activity: the opportunity to buy lower in one place or time, to sell higher at a different place or time, to create new products and new enterprises, and to capture the difference in prices as entrepreneurial profit. All this sort of activity was systematically excluded from the neoclassical equilibrium framework. But the fundamental reason that any such price discrepancies can exist is because of lack of knowledge that there *is* a price discrepancy. If everyone knows about a price discrepancy, then buying and selling to capture the embedded profit opportunity will already have raised one set of prices and lowered others, such that no profit opportunity remains. At this point, the prices would be fully *integrated*.

The kinds of price discrepancies involved are rarely the "simple" price discrepancies of classic arbitrage opportunities (e.g., buying gold in New York, while instantly selling it higher in London, to capture momentarily different prices for the same good). Such opportunities are infrequent and rapidly disappear. Usually it's necessary to perform a complex *integration* of prices and goods, in order to identify a profit opportunity. This may take the form, for example, of the accounting calculations of a proposed business plan (how a business could buy certain resources, transform them, and sell the output at higher prices, to earn a profit). It may take the form of the formulas of a financial model, to identify situations where assets should trade according to a certain relationship (but perhaps currently do not). It may take the form of the economic forecasts by which large corporations plan their investments to meet future demand to earn higher profits. There are innumerable forms of this sort of creative integration to discover potential price discrepancies and hence profit opportunities. The crucial point is that such integrations *are creative* integrations; they require fresh thought in order to integrate the price information in new ways (including to project and anticipate *future* prices), in order to evaluate alternative goals and identify new profit opportunities. The discovery of profit opportunities is specifically the result of this creative thought process and not merely a quantitative maximization problem.

The market process, then, is driven by individuals creatively seeking profit opportunities in this fashion. Kirzner (following Mises) designates this process of intellectual discovery the "pure" entrepreneurial function.[33] In effect, it is the pure intellectual act of creatively integrating knowledge to evaluate an opportunity.

The entrepreneur is commonly thought of as the figure who starts new businesses, but the "pure" entrepreneurial function, for Mises and Kirzner, is a broader concept that centers on this intellectual act of evaluation, which applies far more broadly than just to the activities of businessmen. Every market decision by anyone in the economy, in Mises's view, necessarily involves an element of creatively seeking to discover value (whether it's the job-seeker looking for better employment, the investor weighing investment decisions, the consumer shopping around, etc.). As Mises puts it: "Economics, in speaking of entrepreneurs, has in view not men, but a definite function. This function is not the particular feature of a special group or class of men; it is inherent in every action and burdens every actor. . . . The capitalists, the landowners, and the laborers are by necessity speculators. So is the consumer in providing for anticipated future needs" (1949 [1996], 253).

In this view, everyone, to the extent he participates in the market at all, engages in the creative discovery of value, guided by market prices.[34] It is nevertheless true that the traditionally labeled entrepreneur is the figure in the economy for whom the pure intellectual act of discovering profit opportunities (and acting to realize them) is the *primary* activity. It's for this reason that Mises views the entrepreneur as the central force at the heart of the economic system: "The driving force of the market, the element tending toward unceasing innovation and improvement, is provided by the restlessness of the promoter and his eagerness to make

---

33. For Kirzner's elaboration of this concept, see Kirzner 1973, ch. 2.

34. Rand would disagree with this view, to the extent that she disagrees with Mises that everyone is engaged in rational, creative goal-seeking action at all times (this point is elaborated in the final section below).

profits as large as possible" (1949 [1996], 255). And "The driving force of the market process is provided . . . by the promoting and speculating entrepreneurs" (328).

The Austrian perspective reaches its culmination and full, systematic presentation with Mises's treatise *Human Action*, where Mises develops in depth the economic calculation perspective (1949 [1996]). For Mises, the concept of economic calculation is the root principle of his entire system of economics.[35] He writes: "Monetary calculation is the guiding star of action under the social system of the division of labor. It is the compass of the man embarking upon production" (229). And "Monetary calculation is the main vehicle of planning and acting in the social setting of a society of free enterprise directed and controlled by the market and its prices" (230).

With this root principle, Mises brings a radically individualistic perspective to economics: the perspective of the individual creatively pursuing his goals and plans, using economic calculation to guide him in identifying a potential value, and then acting to achieve it. Like Rand, then, Mises's fundamental perspective *is* the perspective of the shoemaker trying to make a living. The problem the shoemaker faces is not only that of combining physical elements (tools, machines, leather, labor time, etc.) to make shoes for others; he must figure out how to combine these elements *profitably*, so that the revenue from selling finished shoes exceeds the cost of the resources used to make them, and he must do this continually in the face of constantly changing circumstances. This problem of identifying profit opportunities can *only* be solved by means of economic calculation; and it is this process of economic calculation that shapes and drives which physical, technical combinations of resources will be discovered and employed at all.

By using economic calculation in this way, the shoemaker serves his own goals *by means of* producing value for others. It is only by using economic calculation that he can *know* he is successfully producing value for others (and thus can profit for himself). The process of economic calculation performed by an individual mind, then, is the fundamental solution to the economic problem: how the individual is to know what counts as production under the division of labor.

---

35. Mises's economic calculation concept is viewed by some as a purely polemical point against socialism—but for Mises, it is a polemical point against socialism precisely because it is the root principle of production under the division of labor.

The neoclassical idea that all technical possibilities of production can be given and known, apart from any value considerations, is simply absurd from the Austrian viewpoint. The technical possibilities we now know and use were mainly investigated and selected because they were seen to be *economically* feasible. Vast areas of technical possibility are simply ignored from the start (never investigated or developed) because they are obviously economically impossible. The technological innovator is guided at every step, in every element of his creation, by value considerations. The goal of the innovator is not merely to create something new, but something *better*—that is, more valuable. Essential to this goal is an evaluation that, in the Austrian view, requires economic calculation. The technical integration involved in production plans is first and foremost *value* integration. It represents a process of thought that is essentially evaluative—one that integrates facts (including facts about human needs and one's own circumstances) to form and rank new goals, devise means to them, and integrate these means into coherent plans. This process can only be understood from the perspective of Rand's objective conception of value, since, according to the subjective and intrinsic conceptions, value does not essentially involve knowledge, and means are "given" rather than devised.

In Mises's system, all the fundamental elements of economic theory are rooted in the mental process of an individual creatively conceiving goals and devising plans, guided by economic calculation, to achieve profit. It is this mental process that constitutes the crux of the concept of *production* for Mises (consistent with Rand's view of production) as the creative origination of the ideas that guide a man's productive actions. Mises writes: "Production is not something physical, material, and external; it is a spiritual and intellectual phenomenon. Its essential requisites are not human labor and external natural forces and things, but the decision of the mind to use these factors as means for the attainment of ends. What produces the product are not toil and trouble in themselves, but the fact that the toiling is guided by reason" (1949 [1996], 141–42).

It is this mental process that constitutes the "pure entrepreneurial" function, and it is just this sort of thinking that is the primary role of the entrepreneur in the economy. The standard that guides this creative mental process is profit, the hallmark of successful production. Mises (like Rand) tends to downplay the competitive element, while Hayek and Kirzner discuss it more; in any case it's clear that, for Austrians, competition can only refer to competition in the creative discovery of value opportunities.[36] These elements (creative thought, profit, the entrepreneur, competition), which are absent from the neoclassical framework, are at the *very center* of the Austrians' economic theory.

Mises reconceptualizes all economic concepts in terms of his root principle of economic calculation.[37] Typically it is said, for example, that the Austrians treat "cost" or "profit" as subjective (i.e., "subject-dependent"). More precisely, these concepts denote mental tools used by an individual engaged in a conceptual thought process of evaluation. For Mises, these concepts only arise, and *only have meaning*, within the context of an individual's engagement in economic calculation. The concept of "cost" only has meaning when it refers to the sum of prices of the particular constellation of goods the individual is contemplating using, per his plan. The concept of "profit" denotes the net result of the individual's calculations, validating that his contemplated plan *is* an identification of value. Profit can only arise in, and be viewed from, the context of his plans, his integrations, his goal. Even the concept of "capital", for Mises, arises only as an evaluative tool for the individual engaging in economic calculation: "The concept of capital is the fundamental concept of economic calculation, the foremost mental tool of the conduct of affairs in the market economy. . . . The concept of capital cannot be separated from the context of monetary calculation and from the social structure of a market economy in which alone monetary calculation is possible" (1949 [1996], 260–61).

The view of man embedded in the Austrian economic calculation framework is the opposite of the neoclassical "Robbinsian maximizer." In contrast to the neoclassical view of a passive, deterministic, algorithmic maximizer, the Austrian view of man is that of an open-ended goal-seeker, creatively forming and evaluating new goals and plans by means of economic calculation. Although the exact epistemological nature of this creative thought process is not made clear in the writings of Mises and Kirzner, what's important is that they do recognize it is some form of volitional act of creative conceptual evaluation that must lie at the root of economic theory. Mises emphasizes the uncertainty of the future as the reason that creative thought is required (versus being able to algorithmically deduce the future from current data); and, for the same reason, he

36. This is revealed, for example, in the very title of Hayek's essay "Competition as a Discovery Procedure" (Hayek 1978, ch. 12).

37. In fact, the proper way to read *Human Action* (often missed) is to read it *as* a complete reconceptualization of economic theory from the perspective of economic calculation.

insists that it must be a volitional act (it cannot be mere passive reaction to "given" data). Kirzner designates the unspecified creative thought process "entrepreneurial alertness." In *Discovery, Capitalism, and Distributive Justice* (1989), in which he explores the nature of this process most deeply, Kirzner comes remarkably close to an explicit recognition of the category Rand calls "objective."[38] It's clear that he senses a missing category and struggles to make it explicit. Ultimately, however, it takes much deeper work at a higher epistemological level to fully grasp and understand Rand's concept of "objective."[39]

There is much to be said about all the particular differences between the mainstream neoclassical school and the Austrian school—differences in methodology, analytic concepts and conclusions, policy recommendations, and so on. But all trace back to their different foundational conceptions of value. Perhaps the culmination of these differences is that the neoclassical consensus believed socialist planning to be possible (while Austrians did not), because the absence of an objective conception of value led them to systematically ignore all the essential features of free markets (profit, entrepreneurship, competition). If these elements are dispensable from economic theory, then capitalism itself is dispensable. In fact, these elements were often conceived as *negatives*, sources or expressions of "market failure" or "inefficiency." At the extreme, profits are seen as stemming from pernicious monopoly power, the entrepreneur is viewed as an exploiter who does no real work, and competition is considered wasteful and vicious. Not only were these elements considered dispensable, in many cases it was argued that *they should be dispensed with*. This is the inevitable result of theories that ignore the essential role of the operation of the market process in allowing individuals to discover knowledge relevant to forming and evaluating their own goals and plans (and reformulating as necessary to bring these plans into greater harmony with each other and with the facts). If all plans and goals are assumed known and coordinated in advance, then of course the operation of the market process is superfluous. Many free market institutions whose primary role *is* the dissemination and coordination of value-relevant knowledge (e.g., advertising) have been attacked as useless and wasteful, pre-

38. It does not appear that Kirzner ever encountered or was familiar with Rand's concept of objective value.

39. Rand's concept of "objective" is grounded in her theory of concepts; her theory explains the specific creative act involved in forming a conceptual integration, which underlies all creative thought (see *ITOE*).

cisely because their functions would not be needed (or even possible) in a state of equilibrium.

For Mises, in contrast, the principle of economic calculation (implicitly embodying an objective conception of value) makes socialism impossible and free markets necessary, if there is to be a complex division of labor economy at all. Mises further argues that any government intervention in markets faces the same essential problem as central planning: to the extent the intervention distorts market prices (as it must), it disrupts the ability of individuals to accurately engage in economic calculation, making it impossible therefore for them to *evaluate* properly. Logically, this can only lead to the misperception and misallocation of value—that is, to the destruction of value.[40]

Mises viewed capitalism as the only social system that makes economic calculation possible—that is, which allows the individual to engage in creative, conceptual evaluation to achieve productive goals in the economic realm. At a more abstract philosophical level, Rand's view of capitalism was that it is the only social system that protects the individual's creative, conceptual functioning in discovering, pursuing, and achieving values. Rand states: "Of all the social systems in mankind's history, *capitalism is the only system based on an objective theory of values*" (*CUI* 14). It is no accident that the Austrian school, starting with an implicitly objective conception of value, effectively shares with Rand a conception of capitalism as the only system that protects the functioning of the individual creative mind.

Is Economics Value-Free?

The debate over whether economics is a value-free science has a long history, one impossible to summarize here. On this question, Austrians and neoclassicals agree: economics is indeed value-free. In contrast, Rand emphatically rejected the idea that economics can be separated from morality.[41] Her remarks on this subject were brief (she never elaborated on her view of the exact connection of morality to economic theory), but a few important points can be made.

---

40. This point parallels in economics (and for analogous reasons) Rand's philosophic point that force can never achieve value but only destroy value (Peikoff 1991, 315–18).

41. She once wrote, for example, regarding Ludwig von Mises: "His book, *Omnipotent Government*, had some bad flaws, in that he attempted to divorce economics from morality, which is impossible; but with the exception of his last chapter, which simply didn't make sense, his book was good, and did not betray our cause" (*Letters* 308).

First, the urge to separate economics from morality seemed to originate with the desire to establish economics as a factual science—one that could reach true conclusions apart from any political or moral considerations (just as, e.g., the truth of the principles of physics are grasped independently of one's moral or political views). Whether one views markets as moral or immoral, desirable or undesirable, economics can nevertheless reach factual, objective, scientific conclusions about how, for example, the laws of supply and demand operate. One may not *like* the consequences of the operation of those laws, but one still must acquiesce (in this view) to the *fact* that these laws do operate in the way that economic science describes.

My main purpose, however, has been to show precisely that (and how) a conception of value shapes the entire framework of an economic theory, even if just implicitly. One cannot, in fact, reach true conclusions in economics without a correct conception of value. The root of the fundamental disagreements between the Austrian school and the neoclassical school come down (as I've argued) not to a disagreement on "factual" or "scientific" points but to an implicit disagreement about the fundamental nature of value: an objective versus a subjective conception of value. As a result, the two schools approach economic science from completely different perspectives and reach radically opposed conclusions.

Ethics is indispensable to economics, for it is only in rising to the philosophic level that one can investigate and make explicit any implicit assumptions about the nature of value. It is only at the level of ethical theory that one can identify, define, and validate a proper conception of value.[42] But the fact that ethical conceptions are crucial to economics does not mean thereby that "nonfactual" or "nonscientific" considerations are being imported into economics. For Rand, ethics is a science just as much as economics (or any other science) and itself rests on factual, descriptive, observational data.

There is a long-standing controversy in economics regarding the nature of man and how to reflect it in economic theory. W. C. Mitchell, for example, criticizing theories built on the foundation of a rational view of man, objects that the empirical facts of the matter indicate that most men

42. Some theorists seek to avoid making any assumptions about the nature of value by working merely with "choice" or "revealed preference" as allegedly neutral substitutes for a concept of value. But this is self-deceiving. The elimination of any reference to the conceptual thought processes of the individual is ipso facto to exclude an objective conception of value and to default to a subjective conception of value.

are driven more by habit and custom than by careful rational planning and calculation: "Reason is . . . very imperfectly developed in the case of most people. For the great bulk of mankind it is true from first to last that their activity is determined for them by these instinctive impulses to act, of the source of which very little is known, and that being the case, any account of human conduct, which makes man primarily a rational creature, pursuing a calculated course leading toward some logical end, is not true to the facts" (Mitchell 1969, 288).

Economic theory, in this type of view, must fundamentally reflect the fact of how *most* men are. The neoclassical equilibrium framework does in fact (as we've seen) express a kind of economic system that reflects a view of man as passive, reactive, algorithmic in his thinking (rather than active and creative), as repeating rote activities (rather than seeking goals), and so on—in other words, a view of man as functioning habitually and instinctively. This is the view that a subjective conception of value leads to.

Austrian economics, in contrast, with its implicitly objective conception of value, expresses a view of man as a rational, creative, purposeful goal-seeker. This is the base of Mises's system, his starting concept of "human action." However, in trying to justify this starting point, Mises goes so far as to argue that passive *inaction* also qualifies as a type of purposeful action. Mises seeks to secure the foundation for his system in this way: "Praxeology consequently does not distinguish between 'active' or energetic and 'passive' or indolent man. The vigorous man industriously striving for the improvement of his condition acts neither more nor less than the lethargic man who sluggishly takes things as they come. For to do nothing and to be idle are also action, they too determine the course of events" (1949 [1996], 13).

From Rand's perspective, the choice between the two views of man (rational and purposeful versus passive and unthinking) is not a matter of either/or; both views of man are true. Rand (in contrast to Mises) *does* distinguish between active, energetic man and passive, lethargic, indolent man—and she does so at the most fundamental level. This distinction represents her deepest categorization of men: the conceptual mentality versus the anticonceptual mentality.[43] Both types of men exist: those who exert the effort to use their conceptual faculty (i.e., to be rational), and

43. This is the root difference between the heroes and villains in Rand's novels. She elaborates on the nature and functioning of the anticonceptual mentality in many of her nonfiction writings, starting with her first post–*Atlas Shrugged* essay, "For the New Intellectual" (*FTNI* ch. 1). See also "The Missing Link," and "Selfishness without a Self" (*PWNI* chs. 4, 5).

those who don't. (In her view, most men are in the middle, switching between the two modes of functioning.)

But how are we to decide which view of man is the correct base for economic theory? Particularly if Mitchell is right, that the passive, unthinking types statistically dominate a society? How do we decide whether objective value or subjective value is the right basis for economics?

Rand would argue that the only way to choose is by bringing in *moral* considerations. It may be factually true that a great many men are passive and unthinking. But Rand's view that reason is man's basic means of survival leads her to identify rationality as the primary virtue of her ethics. Man *should* be rational, because he *must* exercise his conceptual faculty, if he is to survive. She emphasizes that even the survival of those who are passive and unthinking (however numerous they may be) depends on the creative thought and production of the rational thinkers: "If some men do not choose to think, they can survive only by imitating and repeating a routine of work discovered by others—but those others had to discover it, or none would have survived. If some men do not choose to think or to work, they can survive (temporarily) only by looting the goods produced by others—but those others had to produce them, or none would have survived" (*CUI* 8).

Mises seeks to coerce agreement with his system by asserting purposeful, goal-directed action as a universal, inescapable *axiom*, arguing for all human activity to be uniformly categorized this way. But for Rand, conceptual, goal-directed functioning is a moral *choice* (and man's fundamental choice); it's a moral achievement for an individual to reach. It is precisely because it is the moral choice necessary for man's survival that Rand would view the rational conception of man as the correct foundation for economic theory.[44]

The objective conception of value is factually descriptive of how men act when they choose to rationally pursue life-serving goals. But it is also *prescriptive*, in that it is the mode in which men morally should function. It is for this reason that Rand advocates capitalism as the only moral social system, since it is the only system that embodies an objective conception of value; it is the only system that protects and rewards a rational mode of

44. Peikoff puts the broad point (not specifically in reference to economics) as follows: "In the Objectivist view, the proposition that man is the rational animal does not mean that men always follow reason; many do not. Nor does it mean merely that man alone possesses the faculty of reason. It means that this faculty is a fundamental of human nature, because man is the organism who survives by its use" (Peikoff 1991, 195).

functioning. But it's also factually true that capitalism is the only *practical* system.[45] Mises's socialist calculation argument showed that production under a division of labor economy is impossible under socialism; pure socialism is thus ultimately doomed to collapse into autarkic production. Rand similarly argues at the ethical and political level that socialism, by thwarting the conditions necessary for men to think and produce, can only end in destruction and collapse.

It is only to the extent that people choose to creatively pursue long-range productive goals (and are free to do so) that a sophisticated division of labor economy can arise and be sustained at all. Thus, in fact, it is free markets (embodying an objective conception of value) *which alone give rise to the complex phenomena which economics studies.* The fundamental to be explained by economics (for Rand and the Austrians) is how rational goal-seeking individuals successfully evaluate and thus produce under the division of labor (i.e., while jointly *forming* the increasingly complex integration that constitutes the division of labor). The subject matter of economics is the description and explanation of the principles and dynamics of the operation of objective value and objective evaluation. In contrast, if everyone were universally passive and unthinking, in the way Mitchell asserts, actuated only by the (intrinsic) values of tradition and authority or by nonrational (subjective) impulses or instincts rather than by long-range goals and plans, there could be no production of any degree of complexity. There would be no division of labor to speak of, merely a primitive level of bare, isolated agricultural production. There would then be nothing for economics to describe or explain.

For Rand, there can be no tension or conflict between morality and economics, since an objective conception of value is both the crux of her morality and the proper base for economics as a science. Any apparent conflict between morality and economics, or between morality and capitalism, or between morality and free market outcomes necessarily stems from an assumed perspective of intrinsic or subjective value. Rand argues (*CUI* 12–15) that both intrinsic and subjective conceptions of value necessarily lead to a collective view of the good—that is, some notion of the "common good," an alleged collective scale of values against which social outcomes can be compared and judged. In contrast, with an objective conception of value there can be no such thing as the "common good,"

---

45. For Rand, since value is based on and derives from facts, there can be no issue of a clash between fact and value or between the moral and the practical.

only the individual good of each individual thinker and goal-seeker. From this perspective, there can be no moral meaning per se to any particular pattern of free market outcomes, other than that it represents the free, voluntary choices of the individual market participants, each pursuing his own goals.

Without an explicit understanding of the objective value perspective, it is all too easy, even for many defenders of capitalism, to implicitly slip into a perspective of viewing market outcomes from a collective ("common good") perspective. It is for this reason that Rand writes: "It is in regard to a free market that the distinction between an intrinsic, subjective, and objective view of values is particularly important to understand" (*CUI* 16). Free market prices and outcomes (profits, sales revenues, incomes, etc.) represent *aggregate* outcomes, to be sure, but not *collective* outcomes—that is, they are not the results of the actions of a collective qua collective, seeking a collective goal according to a collective scale of values. Rand coins the concepts of "socially objective value" and "philosophically objective value" to help sort out the proper way to think about these aggregate economic outcomes, while strictly maintaining the individualistic objective-value perspective, and avoiding falling into collectivist, tribal perspectives on the economy and economic quantities.

Rand writes that "the market value of a product does not reflect its *philosophically objective* value, but only its *socially objective* value" (*CUI* 16). She defines socially objective value as "the sum of the individual judgments of all the men involved in trade at a given time, the sum of what *they* valued, each in the context of his own life." (*CUI* 17). A common confusion regarding "socially objective value" is to assume that Rand is referring to market prices. However, nowhere in the essay introducing this concept ("What Is Capitalism?" *CUI* ch.1) does she use the word "price." She refers to "market value" and seems to have in mind something like the total sales revenue of a good, relative to the economy. She defines socially objective value as "the sum" of what men value. She introduces the concept with the analogy: "Just as the number of its adherents is not a proof of an idea's truth or falsehood, of an art work's merit or demerit, of a product's efficacy or inefficacy. . ." (*CUI* 17). The parallel in markets is the *number* of people who purchase a product—that is, something like sales revenue, not price. As an example of socially objective value, she speaks of a lipstick manufacturer earning greater profits than a microscope manufacturer, which is true not because the *price* of lipstick is higher (obviously), but because total sales revenue is much higher; people spend more in aggregate on lipstick than they do on microscopes.

Viewed from an intrinsic value perspectives, the lipstick/microscope outcome can seem problematic. Even leaving aside some religious perspectives (e.g., that it represents the sin of vanity, angers God, and should be suppressed), a common implicit perspective is to view it as problematic that so much money in society is spent on something that may seem relatively trivial and frivolous, while less is spent on something as "serious" and "important" as microscopes. On this sort of intrinsic-value perspective, spending patterns should reflect what's "best," or "highest," or "noblest" for human life (e.g., producing more Hugo novels and fewer true-confession magazines). Since people aren't voluntarily spending their money in this way, the government "should" redirect spending to these (intrinsically) "better" values.

What lends plausibility to this perspective (and what can make it hard to untangle) is that those products *are* better, in an important sense. On rational, objective grounds, microscopes are *scientifically* more valuable than lipstick and can lead to life-saving discoveries on a large scale; Hugo's novels are *aesthetically* more valuable than true-confession magazines (and people should aspire to enjoying them); and so on. This is the perspective on value that Rand conceptualizes as "philosophically objective value," which she defines as "a value estimated from the standpoint of the best possible to man, i.e., by the criterion of the most rational mind possessing the greatest knowledge, in a given category, in a given period, and in a defined context (nothing can be estimated in an undefined context)" (*CUI* 16–17).

Such products may be objectively "better" in terms of their value (potential or actual) to human life. But "better" to whom, and for what? The objective-value perspective always stays cognizant of these two crucial questions, to keep the concept of value firmly grounded in the *individual*.[46] Such products are only values to those who can and do creatively conceive goals and plans requiring the use of those products for their goal-fulfillment. Forcing an object on someone, simply because it seems intrinsically "better" according to some abstract standard, by no means

---

46. As we saw earlier, classical economists fell prey to this intrinsic-value error by failing to reach the perspective of these two questions, causing them to reify the abstract value of a good to human life as necessarily occurring equally in every concrete instance of the good, regardless of individual context, purpose, knowledge, and so on.

causes an individual to suddenly have, without any cognitive effort, specific goals and plans vis-à-vis that product, which alone would allow *him* to value it and use it. It is this sort of perspective that leads, for example, to an impoverished country building mega-dams and superhighways (using government-granted global development loans), because such things are seen as "intrinsically valuable" to human life—while the population is starving for lack of farm implements and the private property protections that would allow individuals to invest in and acquire such objects as they actually need for the pursuit of their individual productive goals and plans.

The fact that market outcomes merely reflect the sum of what people currently value does not, however, mean that values are subjective. A subjective-value perspective naturally leads to the view that the moral imperative is to maximize subjective "utility" or "preference satisfaction," which becomes a collective standard against which aggregate market outcomes are measured. While many free market advocates try to defend capitalism on this standard (that free markets are what maximize total societal utility), the collective perspective embodied in this viewpoint inevitably undercuts capitalism. Critics of markets argue that there is no reason to suppose that the "arbitrary" pattern of market outcomes is what maximizes aggregate utility; nor is there any reason that some people should get "more" preference satisfaction than others, rather than distributing it equally. Any sort of interpersonal summation or comparison of subjective utility or preference-satisfaction itself is inevitably subjective, so it becomes a matter of subjective preference as to what distribution of subjective utility is deemed to be the "maximum." Moreover, a subjective-value approach leads to the view that collective action can or should be taken in order to realize a collective goal, one that is "subjectively preferred" by the majority. If the majority subjectively "likes" environmental regulation, or the "security" of socialized health care, then the advocate for markets would have to argue to *thwart* the subjective likings of the majority—or else he is relegated to making the rather inconsistent argument that a free market is what people "really" do, or really would, subjectively like, but they just don't know what is good for them.

By conceptualizing aggregate free market values as "socially objective value," Rand cuts off at the root any sort of collective perspective and shows how to interpret the nature of aggregate market outcomes entirely from the individual's perspective. What makes socially objective value "objective" is precisely that these free market values arise under a social system that reflects, protects, and encourages an objective-value mode of functioning: each individual is free, within his own life context and context of knowledge, to creatively conceive his own goals, form his own plans, and achieve them as best he can (while relying only on the *voluntary* cooperation of others who are doing the same with their lives).[47] Rand elaborates, for example, what the value and use of a lipstick could mean to the life of a stenographer, and how it can be more valuable *to her* than the use of a microscope. Or, that someone of modest intelligence might be unable to read Hugo but does enjoy true-confession magazines, and thus in the context of *his* life and goals and enjoyment, it's objectively right that he spends his money on the latter. Market values are the sum of all such evaluations.

Capitalism as a social system provides the *conditions* that alone make objective evaluation possible, but it does not (and cannot) *guarantee* that every member of society will evaluate objectively (no social system can). To call market values "socially objective" is not to assert that they reflect only objective evaluations on the part of every individual. But a crucial part of the objective-value perspective is to view the market as a *process* and not as a static snapshot. (In contrast, intrinsic- and subjective-value perspectives do and must view market outcomes as static snapshots; for example, neoclassical equilibrium theory.) What makes market values socially objective is not only that they arise from the conditions that make objective evaluation possible, but that there is an inbuilt dynamic in free markets that progressively encourages objective evaluation and penalizes its opposite. The free market rewards those who evaluate objectively with greater incomes, greater profits, greater sales revenues—that is, with a greater role in the economy, thus giving their future evaluations a greater impact on aggregate market values. Conversely, those who do not evaluate objectively are penalized and see their role and power in the economy increasingly shrink. While free market values do not (necessarily) reflect "philosophically objective value," they *do* progressively move in this direction, at least within each field: "Within every category of goods and services offered on a free market, it is the purveyor of the best product at the cheapest price who wins the greatest financial rewards in that field—not automatically nor immediately nor by fiat, but by virtue of the

---

47. It's crucial to bear in mind that "socially objective value" pertains only to market value as it arises in a free market; any government interference into markets to that extent diminishes or negates the social objectivity of the resulting distorted market values.

free market, which teaches every participant to look for the objective best within the category of his own competence, and penalizes those who act on irrational considerations" (*CUI* 18). And "The 'philosophically objective' value of a new product serves as the teacher for those who are willing to exercise their rational faculty, each to the extent of his ability. Those who are unwilling remain unrewarded" (18).

In this way, an objective-value perspective explains *the fact* of the continuous progress of free markets. In contrast, a subjective-value perspective is helpless on this score. If market values merely reflect the subjective "likings" of market participants, then any change in subjective values can only be conceptualized as merely a "shift" to reflect a new pattern of subjective likings, not as an "improvement." It would always be akin to, for example, a change in color preferences for shoes, causing the market for brown shoes to decline and the market for black shoes to increase—nothing more significant than that.[48]

Another sense in which economics is traditionally said to be "value-free" is the idea that the economist does not and cannot prescribe *which* particular ends individuals should or will seek. It doesn't matter if the products and services sought are moral or immoral, objective or nonobjective, rational or irrational. Independent of the economist's moral judgments, economics will disinterestedly explain how and why prices for all such goods are formed. In this view, a subjective conception of value is perfectly sufficient as far as economics is concerned. We need only know *that* someone seeks a particular end and is willing to exchange for it; we need not inquire into his motives or the moral status of those ends. However, the discussion above of socially objective value has already shown why this view is inadequate. While people are free to pursue nonobjective values under capitalism, capitalism contains systematic forces that discourage, limit, and progressively diminish the role and influence of nonobjective values (and those who evaluate nonobjectively) in free markets. In this deeper sense, capitalism is decidedly *not* value-neutral; it is morally biased in favor of the pursuit of objective values and against the

48. Not coincidentally, neoclassical economics has long had difficulties incorporating any sort of theory of growth into the main body of economics, typically tacking it on as a sidecar to macroeconomics. Even then, it invariably remains a theory of *growth* (quantitative increases in preexisting goods), rather than a theory of *progress*. See for example, Holcombe (2007, 8): "The neoclassical vantage point leaves out the two central concepts of this book: progress and entrepreneurship. Neoclassical theory analyzes growth, not progress. Output is measured as a homogeneous quantity, which assumes away the possibility for developing new and improved products."

pursuit of nonobjective values. For the same reason, economic theory, in studying and explaining the functioning of markets, is not value-neutral in this deeper sense.[49]

49. I should briefly mention George Reisman's book *Capitalism* (1996), the most prominent and ambitious work in economics by an adherent of Ayn Rand's philosophy. Reisman's stated purpose was to integrate Austrian and Classical schools of economics (an "Austro-classical synthesis"), while also integrating economic theory to Rand's philosophy. Unfortunately, while the book contains some excellent material on certain specific topics, it does not succeed in presenting a valid new *system* of economic theory and, in fact, goes badly awry.

As Kirzner (1999) charges in a review article, Reisman fundamentally misses (or ignores) the uniquely Austrian perspective on economics, and thus his "synthesis" defaults into the intrinsic value framework (which Kirzner calls "objective") of the Classical system, with some Austrian ideas patched on. Such a synthesis has to fail, since the two schools do represent fundamentally different, and fundamentally incompatible, perspectives.

Reisman seems to miss entirely that the Austrian system is built on an (implicitly) objective conception of value, in Rand's sense of objective. This is doubly unfortunate. He not only fails to adopt the essentially correct Austrian approach to economics, but at the same time his own intrinsic value perspective, which pervades his system, only serves to cement in the minds of Austrian thinkers that Rand uses the term "objective" to denote an intrinsic conception of value (cohering with their use and understanding of the term "objective"). The conceptual confusion between the two camps (Austrians and Objectivists) is only thickened and the perceived gulf widened. (Kirzner, for example, mentions at several points in his review that Reisman's view of value presumably derives from Rand's "objective" view.)

All the fundamental elements of the Austrian perspective are missing from Reisman's system. Reisman conceives "wealth" as essentially physical objects, and thus (following Classical economists) views the "economic problem" as the problem of maximizing the aggregate production of these physical goods. He regularly adopts an "aggregate" perspective in his systematic analysis, rather than the fundamental perspective of the individual creatively conceiving goals and forming plans. Production is conceived in efficient-cause terms, with inputs causing output (rather than the teleological view of production of Mises and Rand), and so on.

Mises, Rand, and the
Twentieth Century

PETER J. BOETTKE

T he defining ideology of the twentieth century was collectivism. The *totality project* of collectivism came in a variety of forms—communism, socialism, National Socialism (or socialism in one country) stand out—but one should include various other "isms" as well, such as environmentalism and certain strands of feminism. These animating ideologies all sought to replace the liberal ideology that put the freedom and dignity of the individual front and center in discussions of political and social theory and philosophy. Instead, the concerns of society that these "isms" preach should be placed above that of the individual.

The consequences in the twentieth century of the extreme forms of collectivism was drastic to humanity as they wrought deprivation and death wherever and whenever they were implemented in public policy. In *Death by Government* (1994), R. J. Rummell has estimated that between the period of 1917 and 1987 the Soviet Union was responsible for 61,911,000 deaths at the hands of the government. In his estimates on the People's Republic of China (1949–1987), Rummell calculates an estimated 35 million plus deaths from collectivization, retrenchment, and the Cultural Revolution. Nazi Germany (1933–1945) is responsible for the death of 20,946,000. Let those horrific figures sink in. Stalin, Hitler, and Mao were mass exterminators of humanity in the name of a doctrine that promised to deliver humanity from the Kingdom of Necessity to the Kingdom of Freedom. Instead, the collectivist ideology threatened to destroy civilization.

The two most ardent critics of collectivism in the twentieth century were arguably Ludwig von Mises and Ayn Rand. Mises was a hard-nosed economist and political economist; Rand was a hard-hitting novelist and philosopher.[1] Mises attacked the economic and political workings of collectivism; Rand attacked the morality and aesthetic of collectivism. In this essay I discuss the relationship between the two modes of argumentation. First I will discuss what I term the "head" and the "heart" arguments and the reasons that the "head" must be used to temper the "heart." Both Mises and Rand emphasized the primacy of private property in their defense of individualism. Whereas Mises was using the "head" argument to emphasize the role of private property as the necessary institutional framework for rational economic calculation, Rand appealed to the "heart," emphasizing the role of private property in securing the conditions "necessary for the operation of the most significant asset of human nature—the mind" (Den Uyl and Rasmussen 1984, 166). Then I discuss why a "heart" tempered by the "head" is still nevertheless a beating "heart." I address the relevance of the relationship between technical economics and social philosophy and explain why the abysmal failure of collectivism should be seen not as a weakness of humanity but as a failure with the ideal.

The "Head" and the "Heart" in the Analysis of Socialism

There is an old quip that if you aren't a socialist at the age of twenty then you have no "heart," but if you remain a socialist at the age of thirty you have no "head." But this quip, often attributed to Winston Churchill, concerning young Liberals and old Conservatives, must be read as a product of the nineteenth and early twentieth century. After the experience with socialism in the twentieth century, such a quip should be uttered with a bit more caution. The fact that it isn't speaks to the staying power of socialist ideals even in the face of overwhelming evidence of socialism's inhumanity and destructive consequences at an economic, political, and sociological level whenever and wherever it is put into practice. Answer-

---

1. Rand's use of fiction to communicate her ideas results in a strange citation issue. I will attribute to her the ideas of her central characters when quoting from works of fiction such as *Atlas Shrugged*.

ing why it is so easy for socialist ideology to penetrate the ideological imagination of populations young and old, far and wide, is one of the great mysteries of political economy and social philosophy.

The great political economist James Buchanan (1991) has noted a rather strange intellectual crisis that befell classical liberal political economists in the late nineteenth and early twentieth century. As he put it, never before in history had humanity simultaneously achieved such levels of material progress, individual autonomy, and peaceful social cooperation than the liberal order of free markets, free trade, and constitutionally limited government in the late nineteenth century. Yet it was precisely at this juncture in human history that a forceful critique of the system was being forged based on distributive justice and economic inefficiency. Capitalism was judged seriously wanting—it was regarded as inefficient, unjust, and thus illegitimate as an organizing system for a progressive intellectual. Socialism seemed to offer an alternative. Deirdre McCloskey (2007) more recently has sought to challenge the "clerisy's" presuppositions about the morality of commerce and trade with a strong dose of comparative historical analysis of both the precapitalist era and the socialist experience in terms of human well-being. As she stresses, you cannot answer empirical questions philosophically, yet that is what the secular clerics of socialism are prone to do.

It is all too easy, intellectually speaking, to blame the failures of socialism on the shortcomings of humanity. I want to deny this intellectual move. Rather, I would argue that socialism did not fail as a system because of the shortcomings of humanity but because it is an ideological system that fails to account for the demands of humanity. It is a flawed doctrine, and when put into practice the results are a colossal failure at a political, economic, and sociological level. But we cannot reach this conclusion if we simply dismiss the doctrine out of hand before carefully and fully dissecting it.

As Ludwig von Mises put it on the very first page of his classic work *Socialism: An Economic and Sociological Analysis*: "Socialism is the watchword and catchword of our day. The socialist idea dominates the modern spirit. The masses approve it. It expresses the thoughts and feelings of all; it has set its seal upon our time" (1922 [1951], 25). Socialism, as an animating social philosophy, was able to tap into a dream-aspiration that was deeply embedded in the human psyche. Socialism promised to rid the world of social ills and usher in an era of peace and harmony. The promise made was that "Paradise on Earth" was within our collective will. The exploitation of man by man would be abolished, and for the first time in human history, a just social world would be in the grasp of mortals here on earth. Religious and secular thinkers alike were intellectually seduced by the socialist vision of ending exploitation by transcending alienation and realizing true social harmony as class warfare would disappear. As Mises would state:

> Whatever our view of its utility or its practicability, it must be admit-ted that the idea of Socialism is at once grandiose and simple. Even its most determined opponents will not be able to deny it a detailed exam-ination. We may say, in fact, that it is one of the most ambitious creations of the human spirit. The attempt to erect society on a new basis while breaking with all traditional forms of social organization, to conceive a new world plan and foresee the form which all human affairs must as-sume in the future—this is so magnificent, so daring, that it has rightly aroused the greatest admiration. If we wish to save the world from bar-barism we have to conquer Socialism, but we cannot thrust it carelessly aside. (1922 [1951], 52)

In this intellectual context Mises put pen to paper in an act of intel-lectual courage similar to Martin Luther's pinning of his *The Ninety-Five Theses on the Power and Efficacy of Indulgences* on the All Saints Church in Wittenberg in 1517. But the analogy breaks down. Unlike Luther, Mises did not intend to present a moral indictment of collectivism but, rather, to focus his analysis of the logical problem that a collectivist common-wealth would face because of its inability to engage in rational economic calculation. Mises for the sake of argument, as we have seen, was more than willing to grant the great moral appeal of collectivism. But he sought instead to raise scientific objections to the program as understood by its advocates in the early part of the twentieth century.

In his 1940 memoirs, *Notes and Recollections*, written after his arrival in America after experiencing war-torn Europe and narrowly escaping Nazi persecution, Mises discusses how he arrived at his analysis and why he stressed the strictly scientific nature of his argument in his examina-tion of socialism and systems of social cooperation more generally. "In my publications on social cooperation I have spent much time and ef-fort in dispute against socialists and interventionists of all varieties and trends. . . . It has been objected that I failed to consider the psychological aspects of the organization problem. Man has a soul, and this soul is said to be uncomfortable in a capitalist system; and that there also is willingness to suffer reduction in the living standards in exchange for a more satisfactory labor and employment structure for society" (Mises 2013, 80). But, Mises insists, "It is important, first, to determine whether this argument—let us call it the 'heart [or emotional] argument'—is incongruent with the original argument which we may call the 'head [or intellectual] argument' still being promoted by socialists and interventionists. The latter socialist argument endeavors to justify its programs with the assertion that capitalism reduces the full development of productive capabilities; production is less than the potential. Socialist production methods are expected to increase output immeasurably, and thereby create the conditions necessary for plentiful provision for everybody" (80–81; original brackets).

Mises concludes this discussion by stressing again the role that reason plays in human affairs: "To judge the heart argument, it is of course important to inquire into the extent of the reduction in economic well-being brought about by adopting a socialist production system. . . . [Socialists argue that] Economics is . . . unable to settle the dispute." But, Mises counters, "I dealt with this problem in a way that discredits the use of the heart argument. If the socialist system leads to chaos because economic calculation is impossible, and if interventionism cannot attain the objectives proclaimed by its advocates, then it is pure trifling to arrive at those illogical systems via the heart argument. I have never denied that emotional arguments explain the popularity of anti-capitalist policies. But unsuitable proposals and measures cannot be made suitable by such psychic nonsense" (2013, 81). Mises's analysis of systems of social cooperation is based on a *strict scientific* approach of means-ends analysis. While he may have severely disagreed with the ends sought by collectivists, Mises did not focus his efforts as an economist in that direction. He was deeply committed to the ideal of value-free economic science. In that vision of scientific analysis, the economists' task is to concentrate their critical analysis of the effectiveness of chosen means to the attainment of given ends. With regard to socialist proposals, this meant that the examination was about whether collective ownership of the means of production, or the abolition of private property over the means of production (the means chosen) would be effective at realizing the ends sought (the rationalization of production and the ensuing burst of productive capacity that would enable the social harmony promised). As pointed out, Mises did not engage the "heart argument" directly but, instead, sought to address the "head argument" to temper the appeal of the "heart."

All the dream-aspirations in the world cannot curtail the fundamental problem with socialist organization that Mises had scientifically dissected. Henry Hazlitt pinpointed this in his *New York Times* review of *Socialism*, when it was first translated into English in the early 1930s: "The greatest difficulty to the realization of socialism in Mises's view, in short, is intellectual. It is not a mere matter of goodwill, or of willingness to cooperate energetically without personal reward. 'Even angels, if they were endowed only with human reason, could not form a socialistic community'" (Hazlitt 1938). Socialism must forgo the intellectual division of labor that economic calculation enables under a private-property market economy. Capitalism, in other words, is able to solve the problem of economic calculation and achieve the complex coordination of exchange and production activity. Socialism cannot solve the problem and thus will result in systemic waste and planned chaos.

Mises left the "heart" claims in place and examined with the "head" the effectiveness of the chosen means for obtaining the desired ends of the collectivist. His argument was that collectivism as conceived was an incoherent project and would result not in the attainment of the desired end but in outcomes that would be viewed as abhorrent to the advocates of the system. As Mises's close collaborator on this issue, F. A. Hayek, wrote in *The Road to Serfdom*: "That democratic socialism, the great utopia of the last few generations, is not only unachievable, but that to strive for it produces something so utterly different that few of those who now wish it would be prepared to accept the consequences, many will not believe until the connection has been laid bare in all its aspects" (1944, 31). To Mises and Hayek, the demonstration required a logical examination of the means/ends, with the ends treated as given, and the means subjected to an analysis of the logic of the situation and the organizational logic of the administrative apparatus being proposed. Through this logical economic and political analysis one learns of the fatal flaws of abolishing private property over the means of production: (1) the impossibility of rational economic calculation under socialism; (2) the inability to mobilize and utilize the dispersed knowledge manifested through free pricing and profit/loss accounting; and (3) the tragic loss of political freedom and human dignity as the worst get on top to exercise power.

The "Head" in the Service of the "Heart"—The Economics of *Atlas Shrugged*

Ayn Rand, on the other hand, objected to collectivism as a matter of moral principle. As a youth she had experienced the horrors of collectivism in

Soviet Russia, and her novel *We the Living* (1937) correctly captures her visceral reaction to the hopelessness of the individual squashed under the weight of collectivism and the thuggish morality of those who claim to exercise power in the interests of society. She emerged in the middle of the twentieth century as the strongest and most ardent critic of collectivism in all forms among the intelligentsia. Her medium of communication, unlike Mises, was not scientific nor philosophical treatises but artistic representations of science and philosophy in the form of novels. Besides *We the Living*, Rand's indictment of collectivism was portrayed with great success in *The Fountainhead* (1943) and *Atlas Shrugged* (1957). She also published a novella, *Anthem* (1938), which directly bore on these issues. From the 1960s to her death in the 1980s, Rand also lectured and wrote nonfiction commentary on questions of economic policy, philosophical trends, and current affairs. My focus is on a slice of these endeavors—the relationship between the "heart" and the "head" in her analysis.

As a matter of record, Rand's economic education was a function of common sense and Ludwig von Mises.[2] She was a staunch anticommunist since her youth and a defender of individualism against collectivism. She developed in her own mind an individualist philosophy, which she dubbed Objectivism. In so doing, she claimed originality as a philosopher. But she did not claim originality in economics. She made it clear that her economics came from the leading free-market advocates of her age—Henry Hazlitt (1946) and Ludwig von Mises (e.g., 1949 [1966]).[3] Hazlitt acknowledged Mises as the greatest economist of modern times, and Rand took that endorsement as her own as well. Rand, however, disagreed with Mises (and Hazlitt) on the moral defense of individualism. Both economists subscribed to a form of utilitarianism, whereas Rand built her moral case on an "objectivist" ethics. Rand's case for individual rights flows directly from her claims about what is good for man's survival qua man (Mack 1984, 150). The rightness of man's survival implies the right-

2. Bernice Rosenthal (2004) has argued that the firsthand experience of economic collapse that Rand acquired in Russia—during the First World War, the revolutions, and under communist rule—is the source of Rand's understanding of economics.

3. In a letter to Martin Larson dated July 15, 1960, Rand recommends the following works to dispel the myth that the market economy is depression-prone and to prove that depressions are caused instead by government intervention in the economy: "I refer you to such books as *Capitalism the Creator* by Carl Snyder, *Economics in One Lesson* by Henry Hazlitt, *How Can Europe Survive* by Hans Sennholz, and the works of the great economist Ludwig von Mises" (*Letters* 582).

ness of the institutional conditions (namely, the right to private property) for man's utilization of reason and the creative power of the human mind for its survival. As Rand states: "'Rights' are a moral concept—the concept that provides a logical transition from the principles guiding an individual's actions to the principles guiding his relationship with others—the concept that preserves and protects individual morality in a social context—the link between the moral code of a man and the legal code of a society, between ethics and politics. *Individual rights are a means of subordinating society to moral law*" ("Man's Rights," *VOS* 108/*CUI* 367; original emphasis). We need not go further into the disagreements between Rand and her economist friends for our present purposes.[4]

Instead, I want to focus on the basic principles she learned from Hazlitt and Mises and how she then tried to communicate those ideas in narrative form through the story of *Atlas Shrugged*. These are the basic principles of economics that one would find in Hazlitt and Mises:

1. Bad economics looks only at the immediate consequences of an action or policy, whereas good economics looks at both the immediate consequences and the longer term consequences of any action or policy.

2. Private property and the price system work to coordinate the economic activities of millions of individuals in a harmonious manner through the realization of mutually beneficial exchange.

3. Interference with the price system leads to distortions in the allocation of resources.

4. Taxation discourages production.

5. Inflation is socially destructive because it distorts the pattern of exchange and production and breaches trust in the monetary unit, which links all exchange activity.

Both Hazlitt and Mises thought the project of economic literacy was essential to establishing and maintaining a free and prosperous commonwealth.[5] This task was quite difficult for two reasons: (1) economics re-

4. However, for an excellent discussion of ethics as social science and how the Hazlitt and Mises position need not be confined to moral relativism, as Rand thought it must, see Yeager 2001.

5. A wonderful discussion of what Mises thought were the primary objectives in proper economic education can be found in his memorandum of 1948 to Leonard Read concerning the tasks of the newly founded Foundation for Economic Education, where Mises was an advisor to Read. See Mises 1948 [1990].

quires that the reader follow long chains of logical reasoning to sort out the consequences of any action and policy, and (2) special interest groups are constantly pleading their case. The difficulty of reasoning economically from first principles to logical conclusions combined with unmasking the sophisms of special interest groups led Hazlitt and Mises to devote their lives to economic education through the written and spoken word.

It is my contention that Rand picked up that challenge and attempted to provide economic enlightenment to her readers through the story of *Atlas Shrugged*. The book is no doubt one of the most philosophical novels of the twentieth century—whatever one's judgment of Rand's philosophic thought—but learning philosophy through Rand is not my topic. Instead, my concern is with learning economics through Rand, and here I believe one would be hard-pressed to find a more economically literate novel written by a noneconomist.[6]

Various passages from *Atlas Shrugged* demonstrate the principles that Rand attempts to illuminate in her novel. Her message was that, if men of achievement stopped allowing themselves to be exploited by lesser men, then the social system of exchange and production would come to an abrupt stop. The reader is led to realize that the prime mover of progress is the bold individual living by his reason and pursuing his own self-interest. Collectivism in all aspects of life, Rand informs us, is a false ideal that must be eradicated from our minds and hearts. In the economy, the individuals of achievement are represented by industrialists and entrepreneurs. The government, through its policies of taxation and regulation, attempt to live parasitically off these individuals of achievement, and the masses are deluded by ideologies that justify such theft. Rand postulates that the system only continues to plod along because these men of achievement allow the parasitic system to continue to live off them. If they reject the parasite, the culture of parasitism and all who live by its code will wither away and eventually die. Rand's protagonists are men of achievement who persuade others of the parasitic nature of the culture of redistribution and government control of business, science, law, scholarship, and the arts. Her basic point is unassailable. What indeed would happen if the innovators and wealth creators in a country simply shrugged and stopped allowing themselves to be taxed, regulated, and

6. I make the qualification about a noneconomist only because Breit and Elzinga have used the genre of detective novels (Jevons 1978 [1993], 1985, 1995), and Russell Roberts (2001a, 2001b) has also more recently used the novel form to explicitly teach the principles of economics to their readers.

controlled against their will? A collapse of the economy would indeed ensue.[7]

Atlas Shrugged was first published in 1957. We have to remember the economic and social ideas that were dominant in the post–Second World War period. First, this was the beginning of the Keynesian hegemony in economic theory and public policy. The main idea was that a market economy was not self-regulating and was prone to business cycles caused by irrational swings of pessimism and optimism on the part of business-men. It was for the government's macroeconomic policymakers to ensure full employment, utilizing monetary and fiscal policy tools to make sure that macroeconomic imbalances did not occur. Second, not only was the profession preoccupied with macroeconomic instability, and govern-ment's role in correcting it, but there was little faith left in the efficiency claims of a market economy in a microeconomic analysis. The market economy was said to suffer from problems of wasteful competition, mo-nopolistic tendencies, and externalities—all of which required proactive government policies to correct for the failures of voluntary action to pro-mote a harmony of interests. Finally, in the aftermath of the Great De-pression and the Second World War, socialism was seen not only as a vi-able alternative economic system but also as a morally superior economic system. The classical economic idea of laissez-faire was challenged on ev-ery conceivable front by the academic elite, among the decision makers in Washington, DC, and throughout popular culture. Paul Samuelson, in his popular principles of economics book, summed up the sentiments of the time: "No longer is modern man able to believe 'that government gov-erns best which governs least.' In a frontier society, when a man moved further west as soon as he could hear the bark of his neighbor's dog, there was some validity to the view 'let every man paddle his own canoe.' But today, in our vast interdependent society, the waters are too crowded to make unadulterated 'rugged individualism' tolerable. The emphasis is in-creasingly on 'we're all in the same boat,' 'don't rock the craft,' 'don't spit into the wind,' and 'don't disregard the traffic signals'" (1948, 152).

7. In an irony of timing, one semester while I was having my students read *Atlas Shrugged* we were going over Rearden's trial when Judge Jackson's ruling on Microsoft came down. It made for a great week or two of class. The havoc that antitrust policy can have when based on poor economic reasoning was perhaps best summed up by Judge Robert Bork when he said: "A determined attempt to remake the American economy into a replica of the text-book model of competition would have roughly the same effect on national wealth as several dozen strategically placed nuclear explosions" (1978, 92).

Perhaps nineteenth-century America came as close as any economy ever has to the state of laissez faire, which Carlyle called "anarchy plus the constable." The result was a century of rapid material progress and an environment of individual freedom. There also resulted periodic business cycles, wasteful exhaustion of irreplaceable material resources, extremes of poverty and wealth, corruption of government by vested interest groups, and too often the supplanting of self-regulating competition in favor of all-consuming monopoly.

Samuelson argues that, coming out of the nineteenth-century experience, we learned to apply the methods of Alexander Hamilton to achieve the goals of Thomas Jefferson. In other words, we started to use the powers of the state to secure the public interest. Regulation of utilities and railroads were followed by regulation of commerce between the states and the establishment of antitrust laws. Banking regulations were instituted and a central banking system was established. Food and drug legislation was passed in order to ensure product safety and humanitarian legislation improved the plight of the workingman. Theodore Roosevelt's "Square Deal" was replaced by Franklin Roosevelt's "New Deal," and according to Samuelson, our democracy can never again allow itself to go backward to the nineteenth-century ideal of laissez faire. "Where the complex economic conditions of life necessitate social coordination and planning," Samuelson wrote in a thinly veiled critique of Hayek, "there can sensible men of good will be expected to invoke the authority and creative activity of government" (1948, 153). Samuelson even suggests that our failure to recognize the need to reject laissez faire and adapt to the changing economic conditions of modernity led to the breakdown of democracy in Germany, the rise of Nazism, and the need to fight the most expensive war to that point in human history, the Second World War.

Talk about rhetorical flair being used in economics and the construction of a narrative in attempting to get across a point! Who could possibly argue against Samuelson? Only a handful of economists and intellectuals would resist this line of argument in the post–Second World War intellectual culture of the United States and Europe, and in the world of the literati only Ayn Rand would stand tall. Buttressed by the economic writings of Hazlitt and Mises, Rand was able to challenge every one of the premises—theoretical, historical, and moral—contained in the line of argument summarized by Samuelson. No wonder that one of Rand's favorite lines was "check your premises." *Atlas Shrugged* was her attempt in novel form to challenge each of the Samuelson era's premises and conventional wisdoms.

Consider the scene in *Atlas Shrugged* when Rearden meets with Dr. Potter of the State Science Institute about the introduction of Rearden metal (178–82). The economy is in a precarious position and the introduction of Rearden's superior product could disturb that already precarious position. The competition on the market would throw out of business the steel producers who cannot keep up, and this could lead to serious "social damage." Rearden informs Dr. Potter that he does not worry about the fate of other companies but only for the success of his endeavors as judged in the marketplace. Potter's response to this individualist outlook is to inform Rearden that cooperation between business and government is required in this day and age and that to fight this trend is to create enemies instead of friends in high places. He then offers to buy the rights to Rearden metal with government money. Rearden refuses. Potter ends their conversation by threatening Rearden with government action against his company unless he cooperates.

The scene illustrates important free-market economic principles. The first is that the social responsibility of business is to earn profits— nothing more, nothing less. Second, state involvement in the economy is justified on the nebulous grounds of "social damage." In this instance, the social damage is caused by a superior firm outcompeting the less effective producers of steel in the marketplace. The claim is being made by Potter that the economy's balance requires cooperation, not competition, and that this cooperation will be best maintained via state involvement. Third, once the state is allowed to be involved in economic decision making, Rand quickly stresses that those in positions of power will wield that power to the advantage of themselves and their friends.

The theme of political-pull backed by the threat of violence versus voluntary persuasion on the market is repeated throughout *Atlas Shrugged*. Orren Boyle, a competitor to Rearden who has aligned himself with the state, is described as a man who fails to fulfill contracts, and who spends his time pursuing pet projects for a social cause rather than improving his business (*Atlas* 211). The mutually beneficial aspects of trade are spelled out by Francisco d'Anconia in perhaps the single most sustained discussion of economic principles in the work. He states: "Money is a tool of exchange, which can't exist unless there are goods produced and men able to produce them. Money is the material shape of the principle that men who wish to deal with one another must deal by trade and give value for value. Money is not the tool of the moochers, who claim your products by tears, or of the looters, who take it from you by force. Money is made possible only by the men who produce" (410). Money, as the medium of exchange, links individuals together within the economic system and in so doing guides production and exchange. But it does so because "every man is the owner of his mind and his effort. Money allows no power to prescribe the value of your effort except the voluntary choice of the man who is willing to trade you his effort in return. . . . Money permits no deals except those to mutual benefit by the unforced judgment of the traders" (411). At the end of Francisco's discussion, he sums up the basic point: "Until and unless you discover that money is the root of all good, you ask for your own destruction. When money ceases to be the tool by which men deal with one another, then men become the tools of men. Blood, whips, and guns—or dollars. Take your choice—there is no other—and your time is running out" (415).

The culture of moochers and looters, not that of producers and traders, is what is evil and leads to economic ruin and political tyranny when followed to its ultimate conclusion. Rand uses as a particular target of derision the legend of Robin Hood:

> He is remembered, not as a champion of *property*, but as a champion of *need*, not as a defender of the *robbed*, but as a provider of the *poor*. He is held to be the first man who assumed a halo of virtue by practicing charity with wealth which he did not own, by giving away goods which he had not produced, by making others pay for the luxury of his pity. He is the man who became the symbol of the idea that need, not achievement, is the source of rights, that we don't have to produce, only to want, that the earned does not belong to us, but the unearned does. . . . Until men learn that of all human symbols, Robin Hood is the most immoral and the most contemptible, there will be no justice on earth and no way for mankind to survive. (*Atlas* 577)[8]

The first demonstration of the perverse consequences of pursuing the principle of need over the principle of productivity is the fate of the Twentieth Century Motor Company. Ivy Starnes, the daughter of an industrialist, regarded her father as evil because he cared for little else but business. When she and her brothers took over the factory, they set out to change that and institute a new order of business based on equity and commu-

---

8. As Chris Matthew Sciabarra has pointed out to me, Rand actually saw Ragnar Danneskjöld as an inversion of the Robin Hood legend. Rand's intellectual style was one that often began with a conventional icon, appropriating it, and then inverting it. Ragnar, she writes in a journal entry dated October 30, 1948, is a "Robin Hood who robs the [parasitic] humanitarians and gives to the [productive] rich" (*Journals* 585; brackets added).

nal spirit, not profit. "We brought a great, new plan into the factory. It was eleven years ago. We were defeated by the greed, the selfishness and the base, animal nature of men. It was the eternal conflict between spirit and matter, between soul and body. . . . We put into practice that noble historical precept: From each according to his ability, to each according to his need. . . . It was based on the principle of selflessness. It required men to be motivated, not by personal gain, but by love for their brothers" (*Atlas* 322–23). The plan, we are told, failed miserably.[9] With the incentives for production and innovation absent, the company is led to bankruptcy within a few short years and in the context of Rand's story it is the beginning of the unraveling of the US economy as the men of achievement begin to refuse to submit to the ideology and forceful rule of the looters and moochers. In the process, Rand's main heroic character, John Galt, moves from mythical to concrete status within the book—he was the first to walk out when confronted with the new plan. As Rand would have Galt say later on: "We are on strike against self-immolation. We are on strike against the creed of unearned rewards and unrewarded duties. We are on strike against the dogma that the pursuit of one's happiness is evil" (1010).

Rand's story is one of the alliances of moochers and looters against the producers and traders. In her description of how the alliance between the moochers and looters formed, she explicates many of the basic principles of public choice economics—namely, the concentration of benefits on the well-organized and well-informed and the dispersal of costs among the uninformed masses. The political tug and pull associated with

9. A thorough discussion of the consequences of Ivy Starnes's plan at the Twentieth Century Motor Company is provided in *Atlas Shrugged* when Dagny meets a tramp who was a former employee at the company at the time of its introduction (657–72). In many ways, this discussion is actually the best discussion of economics in the novel. In particular, it provides a logical explanation of how the best of intentions are dashed by the inability of government planning to achieve the purpose because of incentives and the unworkability of state planning of the economy. Thus the cumbersomeness of the tasks is exploited by those who seek power to rule over others. "But when the people are six thousand howling voices, trying to decide without yardstick, rhyme or reason, when there are no rules to the game and each can demand anything, but has a right to nothing, when everybody holds power over everybody's life except his own—then it turns out, as it did, that the voice of the people is Ivy Starnes. By the end of the second year, we dropped the pretense of the 'family meetings'—in the name of 'production efficiency and time economy,' one meeting used to take ten days—and all the petitions of need were simply sent to Miss Starnes' office" (*Atlas* 667). Hayek's thesis from *The Road to Serfdom* (1944) about both how the worst get on top and the limits of democratic agreement could not have been better illustrated than in the treatment in Rand's book. The very unworkability of the ideology of the moochers and the aspirations of planners provides the opportunity for the looters to wield power to their favor for as long as the system lasts.

government interventionism reaches its highest form in the discussion of Directive 10-289 written by Wesley Mouch. Economic freedom had been tried, according to Mouch, and failed. Now force must be introduced to coordinate economic activities and fix the ailing economy. Directive 10-289 would provide the necessary powers and policies to accomplish that goal. Mouch is a creature of the political world, a man of neither academic nor business accomplishment, but he is able to climb up the political ranks through connections and unscrupulous behavior. Now he drafts the directive to be put in place to plan the US economy. In the room to discuss the directive with Mouch are Orren Boyle, James Taggart, Fred Kinnan, and Dr. Ferris. As point after point is introduced, it becomes clear to all who are thinking even a little bit that the plan is completely unworkable and in fact destructive to the economy.

As they jockey with one another to see who is more committed to the ideology of selflessness, labor leader Fred Kinnan finally speaks bluntly and cuts through the haze. "Are we here to talk business or are we here to kid one another?" And then he puts it plainly to all in the room: "All I've got to say is that you'd better staff that Unification Board with my men. . . . Better make sure of it, brother—or I'll blast your Point One to hell" (*Atlas* 540). The others in the room are uncomfortable with Kinnan's forthrightness, but only because he is unmasking the underlying realities. Eventually he gets what he wants. The others in the room are still squeamish about explicit statements of the consequences of their policies and Kinnan does not eliminate their squeamishness when he states: "Well, this, I guess, is the anti-industrial revolution." Ferris counters that "Every expert has conceded long ago that a planned economy achieves the maximum of productive efficiency and that centralization leads to super-industrialization." Boyle chimes in with "Centralization destroys the blight of monopoly," and Kinnan mockingly says "How's that again?"—recognizing that centralization is, in fact, the monopolization of an economy in the hands of the state and its protected parties. As Kinnan points out when he is told that as long as business respects the rights of the workers, he will be expected to respect the rights of the industrialists, but "Which rights of which industrialists?" Directive 10-289 goes into effect with the approval of the men representing business, science, labor, and government—each with their cut of the US economy guaranteed (548–49).

By contrasting the conscious and deliberate planning of industrialists such as Dagny Taggart or Hank Rearden, as they conduct business, with the proposed attempts at comprehensive central planning of the economy by government and a consortium of business, labor, and government, Rand makes the very important point that the critique of socialism was never against rational planning per se. Rather, the question was who was to do the planning and the scope and scale of the plan proposed. Individual-level and firm-level planning is an essential part of the capitalist economy, and the main driver in this planning process is the search for profit. Government planning of the economy centralizes the planning and attempts to shield decisions from the profit and loss calculus of the market economy. In such an environment, the planners will find themselves without the requisite information to rationally calculate the best use of resources and will lack incentives to be efficient in the attempt to produce. Consistent with economic principles and with Rand's story, the politics of pull will substitute for the lure of profits in guiding exchange and production under these circumstances. The slippery slope that Hayek, Hazlitt, and Mises warned about—where one failed intervention begets another failed intervention—is neatly illustrated in Rand's story. Moreover, as in the work of these economists, the reversal of public policy away from statism and toward freedom will not occur until a sea change in the underlying ideology takes place. So one can read in Rand's novel both the dynamics of interventionism and the mechanism of effective social change that a variety of classical liberal economists since Adam Smith have attempted to articulate in their articles and books.

It is also the case that, in Rand's hands, the "heart" and the "head" need not be in contradiction with one another. An appropriate understanding by the "head" should temper and inform matters of the "heart." Our dream-aspirations should be consistent with our working knowledge of how human flourishing is achieved in our individual striving and in our interactions with others in the marketplace, political organization, and social community. Socialism rather than an ideal dream aspiration, must be understood as one of the surest ways to squash those dreams and destroy those aspirations.

Conclusion

In his recent book *The End of Socialism*, James Otteson makes the important point about the project of the political economist:

> Some scholars have mistakenly suggested that Smith's concern for the poor means he must have been on the political left. That is to misunderstand his project—and, I would argue, the project of economics generally,

including the project of this book. Smith's goal—like that of economics, and of my own work—is first to understand how human social institutions work, and then to make recommendations accordingly in the hopes of helping reduce human misery and to promote human prosperity. This is not a partisan project; it is not an ideological project; it is not even overtly a political project. It is a humane project. And, again, certainly a moral one. (2014, 92)

While I completely agree that Mises, as well as Smith before him and Hayek after him, were making a scientific argument about the impact of alternative institutional arrangements on economic performance, I do agree with Otteson that there is a fundamental point for the "social morality for mortals" (a term I use) being made. As political economists, we must, as James Buchanan argued, be willing not only to think through the technical economic principles but also to consider the fundamental philosophical questions. As Buchanan put it: "Political economists stress the technical economic principles that one must understand in order to assess alternative arrangements for promoting peaceful cooperation and productive specialization among free men. Yet political economists go further and frankly try to bring out into the open the philosophical issues that necessarily underlie all discussions of the appropriate functions of government and all proposed economic policy measures" (1958, 5). Socialism, unfortunately, remains an animating ideology—as seen with the "Occupy" movement and the public outcry over perceived growing inequality in the democratic West—perhaps not with the romance associated with central planning as it was once presented, but it is still a powerful ideal to many. The works of Mises and Rand are critical to the ongoing dialogue that must take place between political economy and social philosophy. The socialist debate is far from a "dead-horse" that we keep beating, it is a very real and live issue that we confront every day in the philosophical and practical world. And it is for each generation of political economists and social philosophers to master the technical economic principles not only to engage in comparative institutional analysis but also to engage in the philosophical (and I would add historical) scholarship to be able to talk in a sophisticated way about questions of justice and human betterment.

The Head, the Heart, and the Ethics of Capitalism
Response to Boettke

ROBERT GARMONG

> The head has its reasons which the heart must
> learn to know.
> AYN RAND

A s Peter Boettke notes, there is a strong connection between Ayn Rand and Ludwig von Mises. Both were powerful defenders of the capitalist system, both withstood withering opposition from the intellectual mainstream of their day, and both eventually were (Professor Boettke and I would agree) vindicated by history. Furthermore, Ayn Rand clearly admired Mises's economics. However, the two *were* philosophically at odds, not only on ethics but also on core issues of epistemology and scientific methodology.

Boettke, seeking to be a friend to both thinkers, minimizes their differences; but in so doing, he unintentionally misrepresents important aspects of Ayn Rand's views. Due respect to both Mises and Rand requires that we appreciate not only the ways in which they were fellow-travelers but also their disagreements. As Boettke notes, both Mises and Rand would agree that socialism is not wrong because "human nature is not good enough." Both argue that capitalism is consistent with human nature, whereas socialism is based on misguided theories of human nature, not benign "over-optimism." It is a mistake to think that "what's

The epigraph is from a letter to John Hospers, dated January 3, 1961 (*Letters* 526).

good in theory doesn't work in practice," and thus that socialism is "good in theory, but bad in practice"—all common slogans of the Conservative "Right" during the middle and latter part of the twentieth century.

However, Mises limited and even undercut the effectiveness of his defense of capitalism by eschewing ethical arguments. As Boettke points out, the economist saw himself as focusing on the "head," rather than the "heart." According to Mises, the entire realm of values is subjective: economists must begin with the brute fact that different people wish for different things, and reason accordingly. As Mises wrote in *Human Action*: "There are no such things as eternal, absolute, and unchanging values" (1949 [1966], 229).

Ayn Rand would have emphatically rejected Mises's terminology of the head versus the heart. She rejected any such idea that ethics or esthetics should be relegated to the realm of the mere emotional "heart," exempt from rational thinking. In her view, both ethics and esthetics were fully rational subjects, every bit as objective and scientific as economics or physics. (In these comments, I shall focus primarily on ethics, because that is more directly related to politics, but the same comments could have been applied to Rand's esthetics.)

To Mises's claim that there are no universal values, she responded in a marginal note that this was a "basic contradiction" of his view that "human life *has to* be constant motion. If life *is* motion, then action is man's proper state—and only abstinence from action . . . can cause 'uneasiness.'" (*Marginalia* 132; original emphasis) Like all subjectivists, Mises falls victim to self-exclusion: on the one hand he asserts that there are no universal values, while on the other hand he theorizes about human nature and values.

Early in "The Objectivist Ethics," Rand tackles this very issue. "In the sorry record of the history of mankind's ethics," she writes, "with a few rare, and unsuccessful, exceptions—moralists have regarded ethics as the province of whims, that is: of the irrational" (*VOS* 14). Rand, however, regarded the definition of an objective, rational code of values as a crucial task for philosophy, and she thought the failure to do so had devastating consequences. In typically forceful terms, she laid out the stakes: "If you wonder why the world is now collapsing to a lower and ever lower rung of hell, this is the reason. If you want to save civilization, it is this premise of modern ethics—and of all ethical history—that you must challenge" (*VOS* 15–16). Since this is one of the key differences between their respective philosophies, couching the difference in terms of a "head-heart" distinction begs the question against Rand's view.

The key to Rand's achievements in ethics is her having provided, for the first time, a fully rational basis for ethical values and, thus, for political freedom. All prior attempts to make ethics rational ultimately rested on some nonrational or irrational feelings (which Rand terms "whims"). Utilitarianism, for example, attempted to provide a rational calculus for maximizing "utility," but utility was ultimately defined in terms of pleasure and pain (including both physical and emotional pleasures). Rand's ethics is reason all the way down.

Her approach to politics follows suit: she grounds capitalism, not in an irrational "heart" but in a rational ethics of principled self-interest. But Mises consigning ethics to the "heart," explicitly in contradistinction to the thinking "head," rules out the possibility of any such project from the outset. This terminology itself begs the question against Rand's arguments.

In a telling formulation, Boettke says that "an appropriate understanding by the 'head' should temper and inform matters of the 'heart.'" But Rand argued that reason should not merely "temper and inform" values; it should and does *entirely determine* them. On her view, there are no prior, *nonrational* values for reason to "temper and inform." In her view, *all* values—even wrong-headed values, such as those resulting from altruistic ethics—are the results of reason (albeit, frequently faulty reasoning). Ayn Rand chose to devote her life to philosophy and literature, not to escape from rationality but to bring reason home to those key fields from which it had been exiled.

Another key difference between Mises and Rand regards the contents of ethics. Rand was a rational egoist, believing "that which is proper to the life of a rational being is the good; all that which negates, opposes, or destroys it is the evil" "The Objectivist Ethics" (*VOS* 23). Mises, on the other hand, equates ethics with altruism.

Mises writes in *Socialism*: "The idea of a dualism of motivation assumed by most ethical theorists, when they distinguish between egoistic and altruistic motives of action, cannot . . . be maintained" (1922 [1951], 397). According to Mises, "the social interdependence of individuals" renders any distinction between self-interested and altruistic actions moot. "There is," he writes, "no contrast between moral duty and selfish interests." "In the society based on division of labour and co-operation, the interests of all members are in harmony, and it follows from this basic fact of social life that ultimately action in the interests of myself and action in the interest of others do not conflict, since the interests of individuals come together in the end. Thus the famous scientific dispute as to the possibility of deriving the altruistic from the egoistic motives of action may be regarded as definitely disposed of" (397–98). Notice Mises's equation of "altruistic motives of action," "moral duty," and other-regarding action. This essentially renders ethics redundant to social science. Because Mises sees "moral duties" as the subject of ethics, and he assumes that those duties are other-regarding, he sees the domain of ethics as the same as that of social science (primarily economics). As Rand wrote in her marginalia to Mises's *Human Action*, "for M. von Mises, morality cannot be anything but a form of economics" (*Marginalia* 108).

Just as it is a mistake, in Rand's view, to equate morality with altruism, so it is a mistake to equate altruism with other-regarding action. Altruism, she wrote, means more than merely acting with kindness or respect or justice toward others. As Rand analyzes it, "the basic premise of altruism is that man has no right to live for his own sake, that service to others is the only justification of his existence, and that self-sacrifice is his highest moral duty, virtue and value" ("Faith and Force: Destroyers of the Modern World," *PWNI* 83).

According to egoism, "*concern with his own interests* is the essence of a moral existence, and . . . *man must be the beneficiary of his own moral actions*" ("Introduction," *VOS* x; original emphasis). According to altruism, by contrast: "Apart from such times as he manages to perform some act of self-sacrifice, he possesses no moral significance: morality takes no cognizance of him and has nothing to say to him for guidance in the crucial issues of his life; it is only his own personal, private, 'selfish' life and, as such, it is regarded either as evil or, at best, *amoral*" ("Introduction," *VOS* ix; original emphasis). Nor is this definition of altruism a quirk of Ayn Rand's. Altruism in exactly the form she identified is espoused by cultural leaders from US presidential candidates to academic philosophers. It is inherent in John McCain's claim that "to sacrifice for a cause greater than yourself, and to sacrifice your life to the eminence of that cause, is the noblest activity of all" (quoted in Smidt et al. 2010, 113). Michelle Obama, in 2009, quoted approvingly Marian Wright Edelman's statement that "service is the rent we pay for living," which suggests that one owes "rent" for merely existing.[1] So much for the inalienable rights to life, liberty, and the pursuit of happiness.

1. Wright Edelman 1992, 6; for Michelle Obama's quoting of the line, see https://www.nytimes.com/2009/05/16/us/politics/16text-michelle.html (accessed September 16, 2018).

On a more philosophical plane, John Stuart Mill, in his *Utilitarianism*, argued that ethics consists in the willingness to concede one's own happiness for the sake of others: "the happiness which forms the utilitarian standard of what is right in conduct, is not the agent's own happiness, but that of all concerned. As between his own happiness and that of others, utilitarianism requires him to be as strictly impartial as a disinterested and benevolent spectator" (ch. 2, § 21). Thus, "Though it is only in a very imperfect state of the world's arrangements that any one can best serve the happiness of others by the absolute sacrifice of his own, yet so long as the world is in that imperfect state, I fully acknowledge that the readiness to make such a sacrifice is the highest virtue which can be found in man" (ch. 2, § 19). It is fine, on Mill's view, to pursue one's own self-interest insofar as that self-interest does not impinge on others. However, moral credit is granted only when one sacrifices one's own happiness for the sake of others.

As a social theorist, Mill sought to align political incentives so as to make it the case that one's own self-interest was best pursued by promoting the well-being of society. But the well-being of society, not one's own happiness, was the ultimate moral goal of all Mill's theorizing. In effect, then, Mill's goal was the same as Mises's: to collapse morality into social science, so that the benefit of society would be, to the greatest extent possible, the goal of every individual's actions.

Altruism, thus understood as a theory demanding sacrifice of one's own happiness for the sake of others, is a crucial root of the idea that there are inherent conflicts of interest. If your moral duty is to sacrifice for the sake of others, and I have an unmet need (such as health care), then my interest in getting medical treatment is in direct conflict with your interest in spending your money to further your own well-being. Furthermore, the notion that values are subjective necessitates conflicts of interests. Consider the classic mythology of the Trojan War. If Paris and Menelaus both love Helen, they are commonly considered to be in conflict. However, the conflict exists only insofar as love is considered to be "blind"—that is, irrational.

A rational man may pine for his beloved, may even suffer mighty pain for her—but if she in fact loves another man, not him, then his own rational consideration of her rational/emotional judgment would lead him to accept her choice and to realize that recapturing her by force of arms would not, in fact, be to his self-interest. The pursuit of Helen was not, in fact, a selfish act. It was a massive sacrifice in pursuit of the impossible.

Likewise, consider two businesses pursuing the same market. Commonly, they would be considered to have a conflict of interest. Yet their "conflict" exists only insofar as one assumes that each individual's interest is whatever he personally regards as his interest.

Each one in fact depends on there being a free and open market for competitive enterprises. Each depends on there being a demand for their type of product. And each will benefit from the other's advertising and marketing to expand that demand. Both, if they are rational, will benefit from their competition. Therefore, competition does not entail a real conflict of interest. Conflict of interest arises from the notion that whatever I want is inherently in my self-interest—a subjectivist premise that Mises would have agreed with but Rand would not have.

It is only on the basis of Rand's rational egoism that one can fully defend Mises's view that the interests of all members of society are in harmony. Egoism holds that each of us is responsible for his or her own life and happiness, that none of us has an unchosen moral duty to take care of the others, that I am not "my brother's keeper," and that I must assess my self-interest rationally, not on the basis of mere whims. Therefore it is morally right and proper for us to interact on the basis of mutual self-interest, trading value for value, no one sacrificing himself or herself for the sake of others, and each one applying reason to the best of his or her ability.

In the clash between these two ethical views, it is clear that capitalism is the system compatible with egoism, while socialism comports with altruism. Capitalism is based on the selfish profit motive and the absolute rights of individuals to life, liberty, and property, to be pursued in their own self-interest. Socialism is based on the duty of the individual to sacrifice for the sake of society. Therefore, ceding the moral case to altruism gives up the game to the proponents of socialism.

It's no accident that Mises implicitly accepts both altruism and the "head-heart" distinction. The severing of reason from emotion ("head" from "heart") is fundamental to the acceptance of altruism. As Rand puts it, "there is one word—a single word—which can blast the morality of altruism out of existence and which it cannot understand—the word: 'Why?' Why must man live for the sake of others? Why must he be a sacrificial animal? Why is that the good? There is no earthly reason for it—and, ladies and gentlemen, in the whole history of philosophy no earthly reason has ever been given. . . . What most moralists—and few of their victims—realize is that reason and altruism are incompatible" ("Faith and Force: Destroyers of the Modern World," *PWNI* 61). Hence, as long as Mises accepts the prevailing equation of altruism and ethics, he must likewise accept the cleavage between reason and emotion.

Boettke presents the difference between Rand and Mises as a mere case of division of labor between the economist and the philosopher, but this understates the difference between them. The philosophic case for any social system is more fundamental than the economic case, and to the extent that Mises concedes values to subjectivism and ethics to altruism, he undercuts his attempt to defend capitalism on purely scientific grounds.

If values were truly subjective, then any fundamental value one chose would be just as valid as any other. Thus, an Islamist's desire to rid the world of infidels would be just as valid as the infidels' desire to live. Likewise, a businessman's desire to produce wealth would be no more valid than an egalitarian's desire to end income inequality. A racist's hatred of immigrants would be just as valid as a rancher's desire to hire them. It would do no good to point out that Islamism, egalitarianism, and racism are impractical and destructive views: if values are subjective, then those who hold them will not be swayed by economic arguments.

Economics is, of course, a crucial science. The scientific case for economic freedom is persuasive—but only insofar as its audience already shares the values of reason, man's life, and egoism (even if only implicitly). As Boettke points out, Rand herself clearly relied on economics in writing *Atlas Shrugged*. She also wrote explicitly on economic theory, notably in her "Egalitarianism and Inflation" (*PWNI*). But that economic case can only be successful if firmly grounded in the philosophical case.

It is true that, as Boettke puts it, the socialist planner lacks "incentives to be efficient in the attempt to produce," but Rand argues that he does so intentionally, as a means to evade the ironclad logic of the market. This, indeed, is one of the major points of *Atlas Shrugged*: that statism is not merely an error of knowledge, it is based on irrationalism at its very root. Socialism at root is an attempt to stamp out logic ("profit-and-loss calculations"), individual rights, and indeed the very law of causality. Mises and Boettke fail to appreciate this fundamental level of socialist irrationality.

Ayn Rand wrote that it is a great tragedy of history that the enemies of capitalism understood what its defenders did not: that capitalism necessarily rests on egoism. Any defense of capitalism must be based on the objective moral rights to one's own life, liberty, property, and pursuit of happiness. Anything else will be undercut by statist arguments from the "heart."

French economist Thomas Piketty, in his book *Capital in the Twenty-First Century*, 2014), argued that capitalism is an inherently evil system because it promotes income inequality—and the book made huge waves, despite the fact that his economics was quickly shown to be badly flawed.[2] As long as altruism and egalitarianism are the dominant moral theories, capitalism's enemies will always hold the upper hand. I have been in gatherings of Austrian-school and other procapitalist economists who, in private moments, scratched their heads with incomprehension at the triumph of such easily debunked economic theories as Marxism and Keynesianism, particularly after Hayek and Mises entered the debate. If those economists understood this point from Ayn Rand, the power of altruism to undo economic arguments, they would not have to puzzle at the power of socialism in a culture dominated by altruism.

Indeed, the fundamentality of the philosophical-ethical case for capitalism to the economic one can be seen in some passages from Boettke's chapter. For instance, as part of his discussion of economic lessons in *Atlas Shrugged*, Boettke writes: "Rand's message was that, if men of achievement stopped allowing themselves to be exploited by lesser men, then the social system of exchange and production would come to an abrupt stop. The reader is led to realize that the prime mover of progress is the bold individual living by his reason and pursuing his own self-interest." Yet "men of achievement" is not, per se, an economic concept. There is, of course, the theory of entrepreneurship, to which Israel Kirzner contributed so much, but this theory would scrupulously avoid such morally loaded terms as "achievement." Likewise, the idea that the exploiters are "lesser men" is an ethical judgment, not a directly economic one.

The boldness of that "bold individual" and the fact that he lives by his own reason are not particularly essential to the economic understanding of capitalism, qua scientific understanding. These are value-laden and epistemological terms, not particularly economic ones. The fact that these terms entered Boettke's discussion of Rand as an economic thinker itself suggests the limitations of mere economics. A purely economic defense of capitalism, one that dismisses ethics as the realm of the "heart," is insuf-

2. See N. Smith, "Piketty's Three Big Mistakes," *Bloomberg View* (March 27, 2015), http://www.bloombergview.com/articles/2015-03-27/piketty-s-three-big-mistakes-in-inequality-analysis (last accessed February 4, 2016).

ficient. It must be underpinned by the moral case. Ayn Rand understood this, but Mises did not.

None of my comments is intended to take anything away from Mises's status as a giant of economics. He indeed created a monumental contribution to the understanding of capitalism, from which Ayn Rand unquestionably drew a great deal of her own thinking. Both were heroes of the defense of capitalism, and personal heroes of mine. Nonetheless, Boettke's admirable attempt to highlight what these two champions of capitalism have in common does not do justice to the differences between them.

Imagine if an economist of the genius of Mises had also had a consistent and rational philosophical foundation, one that did not undercut his own message. Imagine if he had gone forth to advocate not merely a heartless head but a consistent, integrated, moral, epistemological, and economic case. Imagine if he had not only drily enjoined us to think with cold-hard reason about economics, but to think the same way all the way down to the depths of ethics and human nature. The history of the twentieth century might have been very different.

The Aristocracy of Pull
An Objectivist Analysis of Cronyism
STEVE SIMPSON

> "We are at the dawn of a new age," said James
> Taggart, from above the rim of his champagne
> glass. "We are breaking up the vicious tyranny
> of economic power. We will set men free of the
> rule of the dollar. We will release our spiritual
> aims from dependence on the owners of material
> means. We will liberate our culture from the
> stranglehold of the profit chasers. We will replace
> the aristocracy of money by—"
>   "—the aristocracy of pull," said a voice
> beyond the group.
> AYN RAND, *ATLAS SHRUGGED*

In recent years, cronyism has become a prominent issue in American politics, as commentators, politicians, and activists from all sides of the political spectrum have criticized special interest influence, money in politics, and a government that regularly favors the well-connected at the expense of everyone else. An oft-cited example of cronyism is the federal Export-Import Bank, which provides government-guaranteed loans to foreign purchasers of American products. The avowed purpose of the bank is to help the economy by spurring American exports, but critics charge that it mainly serves the interests of a handful of well-connected companies—among them, Boeing, whose customers have received over half of the bank's loans. Other examples include the bailout of Wall Street firms during the financial crisis and the waste of billions in TARP funds for pork-barrel projects. Groups as seemingly diverse as Occupy Wall Street and the Tea Party, and politicians such as President Obama, on the Democrat side, and Senator Mike Lee and Congressman Paul Ryan, on the Republican side, have made cronyism a central part of their complaints about government.

Stepping back from complaints about specific laws and programs, the idea behind the charge of cronyism is that our government is corrupt in some significant manner. Instead of serving proper "public" purposes, the argument goes, government ends up serving the private interests of those with money, power, and influence. The result is laws and government programs that unfairly favor some over others and a government that fosters injustice and inequality. The cause is typically seen as corrupt or flawed individuals, either in the private sector or in government itself, who cause government to do too many things or to serve the interests only of the rich and powerful. Proposed solutions to cronyism typically reflect these evaluations, with many on the right advocating smaller government as the solution and many on the left advocating legal reforms such as campaign finance and lobbying laws.

Ayn Rand viewed this issue radically differently from other thinkers and thus approached it in a fundamentally different way. She did not use the term "cronyism" and likely would not have used it, as it implies that the cause of problems such as pressure group warfare, influence peddling, and the unjust laws that result is individual favoritism. Instead, Rand looked for the cause of these problems in mistaken philosophical premises about the nature, purpose, and proper functions of government. In Rand's view, the fundamental cause of these problems is not corrupt individuals but, rather, a flaw in the *ends* that government is held to serve. Increasingly, our laws and policies are based on and justified by altruism and collectivism, Rand argued. These premises lead to a political system that is designed to compel individuals to sacrifice their incomes, their labor, and ultimately their lives for the good of "society." Rand saw any political system based on altruism and collectivism as a form of institutionalized thuggery—a system in which some people possess the legal authority to impose their will by force on others. In any society, this will lead to a form of gang warfare, as different factions fight to control the government and thus the legal authority to sacrifice others. In America, the influence of altruism and collectivism has created a mixed economy, so named for its mixture of freedom and controls. The result is a society increasingly characterized by pressure group warfare, influence peddling, unjust "special interest laws," and many of the other problems of which the critics of cronyism complain. In Rand's view, the solution is not to attack these symptoms but to cure the underlying disease by replacing altruism with egoism and collectivism with individualism. Only egoism and individualism, Rand argued, will enable us to sustain a government limited to its proper purpose of protecting individual rights. Under such a government, the principle is not sacrifice and plunder for the sake of

412 ■ STEVE SIMPSON

those with political connections but, rather, freedom, production, trade, and the pursuit of happiness.

This focus on the philosophical premises sets Rand apart from other political thinkers who have addressed the problems associated with cronyism. Although critics of these problems come from across the political and intellectual spectrum, my focus in this essay will be to compare Rand's approach primarily with free market thinkers on the right, with whom she is often grouped. These thinkers have made a much more comprehensive attack on cronyism than those on the left, and their attack at least purports to share with Rand the goals of limited government and individual freedom. As I will argue, however, Rand's focus on philosophical fundamentals and particularly her embrace of egoism and rejection of altruism make her analysis of these problems and her solutions unique among free market thinkers and allow her to avoid traps into which even the best critics on the right fall.

The Conventional View of Cronyism as Private Interests Corrupting Public Purposes

On the right, today's complaints about cronyism find their most recent roots in free market critiques of government involvement in economics, particularly the critiques from the public choice school. Developed in the mid-twentieth century, public choice is an effort to bring economic thinking to the study of politics (Seldon 2002). In the words of James Buchannan, one of the school's founders, public choice seeks to take the "romance" out of politics by evaluating the way government actually operates rather than the way we might like it to operate (Buchanan 1979). Public choice thinkers are skeptical of the claim that government can solve so-called market failures, responding that government solutions typically make problems worse. Markets don't always do what we would like them to do, a public choice thinker would admit, but government often fails as well, and markets tend to correct themselves more readily than governments do (Seldon 2002; Buchanan 1979). One reason that governments fail to accomplish the goals we set for them, according to public choice thinkers, is that they are operated by the same types of people who operate in the marketplace. "People are people," as Gordon Tullock, another founder of the public choice school, once said. Whether they are shopping at the supermarket, running a business, casting a ballot, or overseeing a bureaucracy, they all act out of their own self-interests rather than some broader public interest. We should therefore expect government to operate consistently with the interests of those who run it rather than for the good of the public (Tullock 2002b, 3–5). Following this line of thinking, public choice thinkers have focused a great deal of their analysis and criticism on "rent seeking," an idea developed by Tullock in the 1960s that is, for all practical purposes, synonymous with the complaint at the core of cronyism: some individuals and groups influence government so they can extract "rents"—that is, the favors, subsidies, and other benefits of which the critics of cronyism complain—at the expense of others (Tullock 2002b).[1]

We can see the similarities in complaints about rent seeking and cronyism in the way the critics describe these phenomena. According to free market economist David Henderson: "People are said to seek rents when they try to obtain benefits for themselves through the political arena. They typically do so by getting a subsidy for a good they produce . . . by getting a tariff on a good they produce, or by getting a special regulation that hampers their competitors" (Henderson n.d.). Veronique de Rugy, a senior research fellow at the Mercatus Center and regular contributor to *Reason* magazine, describes cronyism in the same terms: "A company wants a special privilege from the government in exchange for political support in future elections. If the company is wealthy enough or is backed by powerful-enough interest groups, the company will get its way and politicians will get another private-sector ally. The few cronies 'win' at the expense of everyone else" (Rugy 2014). Timothy Carney, a journalist and fellow at the American Enterprise Institute who has written extensively about cronyism, describes the issue similarly. Seeking subsidies, favorable tax treatment, and laws that restrict competitors, big businesses lobby a government that is all too willing to give them what they want (2006, 3–12).

Whether they label the issue "cronyism" or "rent seeking," critics on the right typically see the cause of the phenomenon as a government with too much power that meddles too much in economic affairs (Lachman 2014; Roberts 2012). For example, according to Republican Senator Mike Lee, "The more power government amasses the more privileges are bestowed on the government's friends, the more businesses invest in influ-

---

1. Many of the current critics of cronyism have noted that "cronyism" is often used synonymously with "rent seeking" and that public choice thinkers such as Tullock are the intellectual forefathers of today's critics of cronyism on the right (*Economist* 2014; Holcombe 2014).

ence instead of innovation, the more advantages accrue to the biggest special interests with the most to spend on politics and the most to lose from fair competition" (quoted in Carney 2014). Tom Borelli of the conservative National Center for Policy Research concurs: "When the government enters the marketplace and picks winners and losers with cash infusions it leads to marketplace distortions and political shenanigans from a feeding frenzy of lobbyists and the politically connected (2011). Henderson (n.d.) argues that, instead of "rent seeking," critics of the phenomenon should use the term "privilege seeking" because that is what is being sought—a privileged status that only government can grant.

But the question that immediately arises is, how do we distinguish an improper "privilege"—that is, something government should not do for or grant to a given individual or group—from those things government should do or provide? As an editorial in the *Los Angeles Times* criticizing Republican efforts to eliminate the Export-Import Bank puts the point: "Governments regularly intervene in markets in the name of public safety, economic growth or consumer protection, drawing squawks of protest whenever one interest is advanced at the expense of others. But a policy that's outrageous to one faction—for example, the government subsidies for wind, solar and battery power that have drawn fire on the right—may in fact be a welcome effort to achieve an important societal objective" (2014).

The *Times* makes a good point. Given the scope of government power today, any governmental action will advance some interests and frustrate others. The complaint that certain groups benefit and not others tells us nothing about whether government is doing the right things or the wrong things. It makes the charge of cronyism sound like a partisan complaint. Thus, to understand whether government is handing out an improper privilege rather than performing a proper function, we need some standard for deciding what government *should do* in the first place. It makes no sense to complain that government is unfairly favoring some groups over others if our conception of government necessitates such favoritism. Nor can we complain about government "privileges" or "benefits" flowing to one group or another without a clear conception of what services government is supposed to provide and to whom. If, for example, government *should* provide welfare for the poor or should help businesses compete, then favoring these groups is not a sign of government failure; it is a sign of government success. Further, if granting these sorts of "benefits" to certain groups is part of our vision of a proper government, then it is senseless to complain when representatives of those groups try to influence government to ensure that they get what they are entitled to. We might complain that government sometimes does a poor job of providing these benefits. But if that is all the charge of cronyism amounts to, then allegations of systemic corruption and injustice are misplaced, and the solution is simply to tinker with specific procedures and personnel.

The *New Republic* makes essentially this point in responding to the criticisms of cronyism from the right: "In principle, clearing out overly cozy and sometimes corrupt relationships between government and business is a worthy goal—one, in fact, that would have plenty of support on the left. Liberals rarely celebrate these arrangements. They merely tolerate them as politically necessary means for achieving broader goals, whether it's helping millions of people to get health insurance or keeping manufacturing jobs in the U.S. If conservatives are up for achieving those same goals without forking over cash to corporations, liberals will stand with them" (Cohn 2014).

Cronyism, on this view, is a problem of the process by which government operates, not its ends. Some individuals might be corrupt, government might waste a bit too much money, and some interest groups may end up profiting too much, but the solution to those problems is to find ways to prevent corruption or to limit the benefits that flow to corporations and other well-connected interests. Not surprisingly, those who take this view of cronyism typically support campaign finance and other "good government" reforms that are intended to limit the amount by which any given group or faction can influence government. And if one accepts the goals of a modern welfare state—that government should provide welfare for the poor and other social services such as health care and retirement plans; that it should manage the economy, create jobs, and promote American businesses—then this position makes sense. *Someone* has to implement all the policies government pursues, after all. Short of government running everything, some private parties (typically businesses in industries like health care, banking and finance, and other areas in which government is heavily involved) are going to be involved and some of them are going to benefit.

One question we must ask, then, is: *do* the critics of cronyism on the right share the same view of government's purpose as their opponents on the left? The answer is debatable. But many of the critics of cronyism on the right at least *seem* to share the same view of government's purpose as their opponents on the left, for they often describe that purpose in the same terms. The widespread view today on both left and right is that government's purpose is to serve "public" ends and goals over "private" ones, and criticisms of cronyism presuppose this view when the problem is couched in terms of government serving private interests rather than public ones.

On the left, we can see that view stated explicitly in the *Los Angeles Times* op-ed quoted above: "What's truly crony capitalism is when the government confuses private interests with public ones" (2014), and it is implicit in the *New Republic* article quoted above (Cohn 2014). On the right, we can see it expressed by the American Enterprise Institute's Timothy Carney, who is one of the most vocal critics of cronyism today: "Naturally, all economic policies will help some interests and hurt others. Just because a company profits from a policy doesn't make it 'crony capitalism.' But when lawmakers go along with lobbyists' requests, they are often subordinating the public interest to private interests—or at least showing more concern about the fate of the well-connected than the fate of the masses" (2013).

Gordon Tullock takes the same fundamental approach to rent seeking. Rent seeking, as he describes it, is "the use of resources for the purpose of obtaining rents for people where the rents themselves come from some activity that has *negative social value*" (2002a, 43; emphasis added). As examples of rent seeking, Tullock cites a car company that lobbies for a tariff on foreign cars and a drug company that convinces Congress to ban a competitor's product (43). The "rents" in both cases would be the profits the companies enjoy as a result of the law for which they lobbied. Tullock then contrasts these with the example of someone who invests a lot of money in cancer research. Most economists, says Tullock, would see only the former two examples as rent seeking, but not the latter. The reason, according to Tullock, lies in the social benefits of the different investments. "If someone is observed receiving a rent," he argues, "the first thought should be to inquire whether society as a whole is better off as a result of the activity or product that generates the rent" (44). Cancer research benefits society as a whole, in Tullock's view, whereas the laws in the other two cases do not.

Before turning to Rand's view, it's worth making two observations.

First, complaints that officials often put private interests ahead of the "public interest" or the "good of society" are no more coherent than complaints about government handing out "privileges" and "benefits" to some groups but not others. Who counts as "the public" after all? Anyone can claim that their pet project and the groups that support them are consistent with the public interest, so almost any policy goal can be characterized as "socially beneficial" or a "public good." American jobs are good for society so we should impose tariffs on foreign goods. More exports are a public good, so government should create an Export-Import Bank to promote the purchase of American goods abroad. Wilderness is in the public interest, so government should restrict private development and logging. Then again, perhaps we should consider the jobs logging creates, the lower prices to consumers that would result if we eliminated tariffs, or the savings to taxpayers from eliminating government-subsidized loans to be in the public interest. The list of policies that might—or might not—be in the public's interest can be multiplied indefinitely. As a result, whether those who try to influence government to support any given policy will be seen as engaging in rent seeking and cronyism, as opposed to pursuing proper public purposes, will depend on which policies one wants the government to pursue.

Second, and relatedly, because anyone can claim to be acting in the public interest, the use of a standard like this exacerbates the very problem the critics of cronyism are targeting. Government obviously cannot achieve all of the goals claimed to be in the public's or society's interest. How, then, do we sort through all of these competing claims? The obvious answer is to defer to the political process and let the electorate or legislatures decide what is in the public interest. But as public choice thinkers have often pointed out, handing unchecked power to democratic institutions, particularly over economic affairs, creates an enormous incentive for individuals to form pressure groups so they can lobby to be the beneficiary of that power rather than the victim. In short, cronyism and rent seeking are a consequence of the idea that our government may do whatever is in the public interest.

There is more to say about both of these observations. The point for now is that the right's argument against cronyism and rent seeking ultimately fails to provide the one thing necessary to sort out competing claims about whose interests government should favor or what sorts of "benefits" or "privileges" it should provide: what is government's proper purpose? Without a clear answer to this question, arguments about cronyism amount to so much partisan bickering.

For Rand Cronyism Is a Problem with the Goals of Government

When we understand the nature of government power as physical force, the problem of cronyism comes into sharper focus. Cronyism, under Rand's approach to government, is a misuse of the force that government possesses. It occurs when government becomes disconnected from any principle or moral standard that guides its actions. Government, for Rand, is not a free-floating entity. It is a human institution, created and operated by individual human beings. Specifically, it is the institution that possesses a legal monopoly on the use of force. Absent some principle for distinguishing proper from improper government action, government reduces simply to a group of men who possess the legal authority to use force against others. If that use of force is not guided by principle, government is no longer based on the rule of law but on the rule of men. In short, government becomes a gang that operates on the principle of might makes right.

The question thus becomes: what is the principle that distinguishes proper from improper government action? For Rand, there is only one answer: the protection of individual rights. Individual rights, for Rand, are the key to understanding the proper purpose of government because they connect that purpose to the moral requirements of an individual's life. Rights ground government in reality and render it moral by answering the question: why have a government at all? Briefly stated, Rand's answer is: because of the type of entity humans are. We are beings who must think and take certain actions to survive, and doing so requires that we be free of physical force. Thinking cannot be compelled; it cannot function under command by others but must be initiated by the individual, who must follow reason to where it leads if he or she wishes to live successfully. "A gun," as Rand once put it, "is not an argument" ("What Is Capitalism?" *CUI* 8). As a result, force can only shut down an individual's ability to think and to act on his or her judgment. It can stop an individual from functioning, but it cannot make that individual think, produce values, live, and flourish.[2]

Rights provide the principle that defines this freedom and connects it to the lives of individual human beings. As Rand puts the point:

2. On Ayn Rand's theory of rights, see "Man's Rights" (*VOS*), Peikoff 1991, 351–69, and the chapters by Wright and by Miller and Mossoff in this volume.

Rights are conditions of existence required by man's nature for his proper survival. If man is to live on earth, it is *right* for him to use his mind, it is *right* to act on his own free judgment, it is *right* to work for his values and to keep the product of his work. If life on earth is his purpose, he has a *right* to live as a rational being: nature forbids him the irrational. Any group, any gang, any nation that attempts to negate man's rights, is *wrong*, which means: is evil, which means: is anti-life. (Galt's speech, reprinted in *FWNI* 182.)

Government is the institution we create to protect our rights so that we may live proper, human lives. Rand thus agreed with the American Founders that, as the Declaration of Independence states, governments are instituted among men to protect their rights to life, liberty, and the pursuit of happiness. But for Rand, this is the *only* proper purpose of government. When government uses the force it possesses for anything beyond this purpose, it necessarily becomes a threat to our lives and welfare rather than our protector. The reason is that, fundamentally, force can be used only in one way: to stop individuals from functioning. Force as such cannot create the values—the food, clothing, shelter, and other things—necessary for our survival. Only individuals applying reason and thought can do so. Government, therefore, can use the force it possesses to protect individual rights—which means, to protect individuals in their effort to think, produce, live, thrive, and be happy. Or it can use the force it possesses to violate individual rights—that is, to threaten individuals, steal the values they create, and ultimately destroy their ability to live.

Cronyism or rent seeking is an aspect of the latter type of government in action. It is a use of force, not to protect rights but to plunder. Different nations (our own included) exhibit this problem to different degrees, based on the extent to which their use of force is disconnected from the protection of rights. The most consistent example (and the worst) is outright statism, which Rand referred to as a kind of institutionalized gang warfare because various factions in these nations constantly fight for control of government and the right to use the law to plunder others ("The Roots of War," *CUI* 31). In a country like America, however, where the government is a mixture of freedom and statism (hence the term "mixed economy"), this conflict takes the form of pressure group warfare, influence peddling (or "pull peddling" in Rand's words), and "special interest" laws, as various factions compete in the political arena for the privilege of using the law for their own benefit and against others.

It is crucial to keep in mind what the various factions are competing *for* in these countries. The answer is: the legal right to use the force of law for whatever ends they choose. When we speak of government providing "benefits" or "privileges" to one group or another, what we mean concretely is that government is using force to provide these things. Since government does not create values, the so-called benefits it provides must come from someone who did create them. Welfare or business subsidies, for example, consist of wealth that was first earned by someone and then transferred by law to someone else. The "privilege" a business enjoys when it is protected from competition consists of government using law to restrain the business's competitors from trading with potential customers. When government "favors" some interests over others, this means it is using force on behalf of those interests and against others. Statist nations and mixed economies differ in the degree to which they use force for these purposes. But the nature of the power in both cases and how it is being used is the same. It is force used against innocent men and on behalf of criminals.[3]

In *Atlas Shrugged*, Rand depicts a mixed economy as it transitions to a fully statist society. It is important to note that cronyism is not the cause of this transition. The cause is fundamentally philosophical—it is altruism and collectivism and the fact that these premises lead inexorably to a government with unlimited power. But cronyism does contribute to the process of disintegration which such a society experiences by creating a dynamic that constantly punishes virtue and rewards vice. Force cannot be used to create but only to take values from those who produce them, so the more any society uses force for the wrong ends the more it

3. For this reason, "cronyism" and "rent seeking" are misnomers. Both terms are far too tame to describe what is really going on, which is the use of government for the purpose of theft and plunder. "Cronyism" suggests the problem is favoritism; "rent seeking" suggests the problem is profit. Both serve to obscure and thereby to excuse the real problem, which is the use of government power (i.e., force) to violate rights rather than to protect them. Rand used the terms "looting" and "plundering" to designate this misuse of government power. She referred to the phenomenon of influencing government to use its power for those ends as "pull peddling" because the individuals involved are trying to survive based on connections and plunder rather than on the kind of sustained, long-term effort that the production of wealth requires. The essential point to recognize is that this misuse of government power is an unavoidable feature of statism. As a result, the closer a nation moves to statism, the more the phenomenon of influence peddling of this sort will occur. A better term for this phenomenon than "cronyism" (or the truly unjust "crony-capitalism") would be "crony-statism." This term would still be redundant, however, as "cronyism" is an unavoidable feature of statism, not a type of statism. I use the term "cronyism" throughout this essay for ease of reference.

stops the best, most productive members from creating and rewards the worst, most parasitic members of that society for stealing. As this process advances, the best individuals are increasingly sacrificed to the worst as the government is increasingly put in the service of the latter and against the former. The rule of law increasingly gives way to the rule of men, the economy falters, then slows, then stops, and civilization reaches a state of barbarism. This is the society depicted in *Atlas Shrugged*. As Rand described that process in the novel:

> But when a society establishes criminals-by-right and looters-by-law—men who use force to seize the wealth of *disarmed* victims—then money becomes its creators' avenger. Such looters believe it safe to rob defenseless men, once they've passed a law to disarm them. But their loot becomes the magnet for other looters, who get it from them as they got it. Then the race goes, not to the ablest at production, but to those most ruthless at brutality. When force is the standard, the murderer wins over the pickpocket. And then that society vanishes, in a spread of ruins and slaughter.
>
> Do you wish to know whether that day is coming? Watch money. Money is the barometer of a society's virtue. When you see that trading is done, not by consent, but by compulsion—when you see that in order to produce, you need to obtain permission from men who produce nothing—when you see that money is flowing to those who deal, not in goods, but in favors—when you see that men get richer by graft and by pull than by work, and your laws don't protect you against them, but protect them against you—when you see corruption being rewarded and honesty becoming a self-sacrifice—you may know that your society is doomed. Money is so noble a medium that it does not compete with guns and it does not make terms with brutality. It will not permit a country to survive as half-property, half-loot. (*Atlas* 413)

A significant part of Rand's purpose in *Atlas* is to make explicit a fact that is too often ignored today in thinking about society and government, which is the supreme importance of thought and production to human life and therefore the supreme importance of the types of individuals—the producers—who embody these virtues. Rand, of course, illustrates their importance in *Atlas* by showing what happens when the producers go on strike against a society that hates and punishes them for their virtues. The primary cause of this hatred is the ethics of altruism—but cronyism, as a feature of the statist/collectivist government that results from altruism, plays an important role in the manner in which producers are punished and ultimately destroyed in such a society. Cronyism, one might say, is a manifestation of the ethics of altruism playing out in the political realm. It is one way in which altruism leads inexorably to producers being punished for their virtues and, thus, one way in which a society operating on altruist/collectivist premises destroys itself. This point is crucial for a full understanding of the evil that an altruist/collectivist regime represents, so it is worth examining in some detail.

For Rand, a prime example of the producer is the businessman. He is the thinking man of action, the man who exercises independent thought and takes the actions necessary to produce the values—the food, clothing, shelter, the appliances, the homes, the cars, the airplanes, the health care, the technology—on which we all depend to live, thrive, and be happy. The producer only requires freedom to thrive. He needs only a government that protects his rights to produce and trade with others.

On the opposite end of the scale are the types of individuals who thrive under statism and a mixed economy. They are essentially parasites—individuals who choose not to think and live independently or to exercise the responsibility to sustain their own lives. Instead, they seek to live off the values created by others. The parasite opposes a limited government because it will not provide him with the opportunity to live off others. Hence, Rand often refers to this type as the "looter" or the "Money-Appropriator." This man, according to Rand,

> is essentially noncreative—and his basic goal is to acquire an unearned share of the wealth created by others. He seeks to get rich, not by conquering nature, but by manipulating men, not by intellectual effort, but by social maneuvering. He does not produce, he redistributes: he merely switches the wealth already in existence from the pockets of its owners to his own.
>
> The Money-Appropriator may become a politician—or a businessman who "cuts corners"—or that destructive product of a "mixed economy": the businessman who grows rich by means of government favors, such as special privileges, subsidies, franchises; that is, grows rich by means of *legalized force*.[4]

Two good examples of producers in *Atlas Shrugged* are Hank Rearden, a self-made steel magnate, and Dagny Taggart, a railroad executive.

---

4. Ayn Rand, "The Money-Making Personality," *Cosmopolitan* (April 1963), reprinted in Ghate and Ralston 2011, 65–74.

A large part of the action in the novel involves their efforts to continue to run their companies in the face of a collapsing economy and a government that has long since passed from basically free into the latter stages of a mixed economy, in which economic controls are the rule rather than the exception. Rand contrasts them with two looters: businessmen Orren Boyle, Rearden's chief competitor in the steel business, and James Taggart, Dagny's conniving brother and the CEO of Taggart Transcontinental. In contrast to Dagny and Rearden, Boyle and James disdain work, typically flee from the responsibility of making decisions, and rely on their political connections to lobby for laws that restrict free trade and hobble their competitors. As noted, Rand referred to this as "pull-peddling" (see "The Pull Peddlers," *CUI* 184–90), but it is also an aspect of what is meant by cronyism and rent seeking.

There are many examples in *Atlas* of laws passed through political pull at the behest of businessmen such as Jim Taggart and Orren Boyle. One is the Anti-dog-eat-dog rule, which Taggart lobbies for in order to put a smaller, more effective railroad out of business. The rule essentially parcels out regional franchises to different railroads based not on merit but on seniority. Not surprisingly, Taggart, who taps his connections with Boyle to obtain passage of the rule, runs the railroad with the most seniority, and the small competitor he uses the rule to destroy has the least (*Atlas* 73–77). Another example is the Equalization of Opportunity Bill, which Taggart agrees to help pass in exchange for the help Boyle provided on the Anti-dog-eat-dog rule. Boyle wants the law, which would prevent any company from owning more than one business concern (130), because it would make Rearden a less effective competitor by requiring him to divest himself of his coal and mining concerns.[5] Ultimately, the Equalization of Opportunity Bill is passed into law when Taggart convinces Rearden's Washington lobbyist, Wesley Mouch, to betray Rearden and lobby for the bill in exchange for Taggart's help in landing Mouch a job in the Bureau of National Planning (212–13, 395).

These episodes, and many others in *Atlas*, read like chronicles of influence peddling, logrolling, and pressure group warfare by today's critics of cronyism, but with one very important distinction.[6] Unlike the critics

5. Both these laws mirror actual laws. The Anti-dog-eat-dog rule is similar to the types of rules adopted under FDR's National Industrial Recovery Act, which allowed the president to adopt as law various codes of "fair competition" submitted by industrial groups. The Equalization of Opportunity bill resembles the antitrust laws.

6. Economist Bryan Caplan cites many of these examples in his article "*Atlas Shrugged* and Public Choice: The Obvious Parallels" (Caplan 2007a). His thesis is that Rand criticizes

of cronyism, Rand never fails to distinguish between the types of individuals who thrive on political pull and those who do not, their respective motives, and the reasons a society based on pull develops. For Rand, producers and the parasites who prey on them can come from any walk of life, and she shows these types among businessmen, scientists, artists, doctors, middle managers, train conductors, and even store clerks. The key for her is not the individuals' occupations or income levels, but how they approach the basic alternative in life. Do they face life independently and choose to think and produce to the best of their ability? Or do they attempt to evade the necessity of independent thought and effort and try to live off of others?

It is just as important to draw a moral distinction between these two types, for Rand, as it is to distinguish between honest men and criminals. Indeed, it is arguably more important to do so, for the criminal has to operate outside of the law, whereas the man who thrives on political pull operates under cover of the law, and he operates against legally disarmed victims. As a result, Rand would never fail to draw a moral distinction between the two types of examples Tullock cites in his discussion of rent seeking (2002a)—the investor in cancer research and the company that procures a law that puts a competitor out of business. In her view, the former is engaging in productive activity; the latter, in theft. They differ in the same way that a businessman who invests in a new venture differs from one who hires a mobster to destroy his competitor's business.

But how do the parasites get away with using law and government for the purposes of plunder? Rand's answer is nonobjective law, which is a feature of a statist or semi-statist society. In a free society, law has two related purposes: it defines the narrow range of actions that constitute violations of men's rights and it defines the power of government to deal with those who violate rights. The principle in both cases is the same: rights can be violated only by the initiation of force. Only force can prevent a man from taking the actions necessary to live his life, so only force can violate his rights. As a result, government's legitimate power is narrow. In a free society, government essentially performs a self-defense function. It may use the force it possesses to defend innocent men by retaliating

many of the same phenomena that public choice thinkers have criticized, and he highlights many more examples from *Atlas Shrugged* than I do here. Although I disagree with aspects of Caplan's argument—most notably his acceptance of the view that self-interested motives are base and suspect and altruistic motives are benevolent and good, his article is well worth reading.

against those who initiate force against them, but its power goes no further than that. The principle may be stated as follows: in a free society, government's power is narrow and individual freedom is broad. Government may act only to redress violations of rights, but individual men enjoy broad freedom to do anything that does not violate rights.

Nonobjective law accomplishes the opposite purpose: it renders government's power broad and indefinite and thus necessarily limits the freedom of individuals. Nonobjective law does not serve the narrow purpose of protecting rights, it serves the broad purpose of granting government unlimited power. To the extent that it exists even in a semi-free society, it transforms a limited government based on the rule of law into a gang limited only by the whims of men. For this reason, among others, Rand refers to nonobjective law in *Atlas* as "humanity's darkest evil" (737).

The hallmark of nonobjective law, in Rand's words, is "the grant of an undefined, and undefinable, non-objective, arbitrary power to some government officials. . . . The worst aspect of it is not that such a power can be used dishonestly, but that *it cannot be used honestly*. The wisest man in the world, with the purest integrity, cannot find a criterion for the just, equitable, rational application of an unjust, inequitable, irrational principle. The best that an honest official can do is to accept no material bribe for his arbitrary decision; but this does not make his decision and its consequences more just or less calamitous" ("The Pull Peddlers," *CUI* 188). Laws such as this are common in America today. The Federal Communications Act, for example, authorizes the FCC to grant broadcast licenses based on the "public convenience, interest, and necessity." The Federal Trade Commission Act authorizes the FTC to prohibit "unfair methods of competition." The Code of the Federal Register is filled with nearly two hundred thousand pages of similar regulations. Nonobjective law empowers those in charge of government to use the force of law in whatever manner they please. The typical manner they please is to use government to threaten, restrict, and plunder innocent men.[7]

One result of a government that exercises this sort of power is pressure group warfare and political pull. It is a system under which the worst types of individuals—Money-Appropriators such as Jim Taggart and Orren Boyle—can use the law to take the values created by the best. And the best—Money-Makers such as Dagny Taggart and Hank Rearden—

7. For a fuller discussion of Rand's views on nonobjective law, see Smith 2009; Smith 2016.

are driven to participate in this system out of self-defense. When law becomes vague and unclear and the difference between lawful and lawless action becomes the interpretation of some bureaucrat, the only way to function is to appeal to and try to please the bureaucrat. Thus, producers like Hank Rearden and Dagny Taggart must hire lobbyists and political fixers, contribute to campaigns, and involve themselves in the regulatory and legislative process, because this becomes the only way to do business and to protect themselves from others who do the same. To be sure, at some point it becomes difficult to tell the producers in a system like this from the looters, and many participants are mixtures of both. But to fail to distinguish between the two types in principle and in appropriate circumstances is a gross injustice, tantamount to treating a businessman who hires a mobster to destroy a competitor's business the same as the businessman who pays for the privilege of not having his business destroyed. Many of the individuals who participate in such a system are certainly corrupt, but there is a much deeper corruption at work. It is a corruption of the purpose of government, and it creates a system that rewards dishonesty and punishes virtue. That is the Aristocracy of Pull.

A social system like this does not develop by accident, however. The final major difference between Rand and other critics of cronyism that I would like to address is her focus on the ethical premises that lead to a society based on pull—namely, altruism and the collectivism it supports. According to altruism, an individual is not an end in himself but, rather, a means to the ends of others ("Faith and Force: The Destroyers of the Modern World," *PWNI* 91). Collectivism is the closely related idea that the group takes precedence over the individual and the individual's supreme duty is to serve the tribe, the collective, "society," the "public," the state, or the nation. Under collectivism, the group always has the moral right, and ultimately the legal authority, to dispose of the individual's time, his labor and productive efforts, and his money and property (see also Peikoff 1991, 362).

Rand argued that America's primary flaw was that its premises were a mixture of egoism and individualism, on the one hand, and altruism and collectivism, on the other. The balance was tipped far more toward the former in the early years of the republic, but this changed over the course of the nineteenth century. Today, America and the capitalist system it embodies are defended almost exclusively on altruist-collectivist grounds. Freedom and capitalism are justified, the argument goes, to the extent that they serve the welfare of society or the public interest or the greatest happiness of the greatest number. As a result, the amazing wealth and technology, the great private fortunes, and the high standard of living enjoyed by most Americans must be justified on the same grounds. Teddy Roosevelt (1910) captured this view in his speech on "The New Nationalism," when he said, "The right to regulate the use of wealth in the public interest is universally admitted" and that the gaining of fortunes should be permitted "only so long as the gaining represents a benefit to the community." The same applies to property, in Roosevelt's view: "every man holds his property subject to the general right of the community to regulate its use to whatever degree the public welfare may require it" (Roosevelt 1910).

This view became embedded in government and legal policy during the New Deal, and it is widespread today. We can see it in the notion that America is a "democracy" under which "the people" have almost unlimited power to adopt whatever social and economic policies they prefer, and in the constant criticisms of the "1 percent." And, of course, we find it in the argument that the proper purpose of government is to serve the "public interest" or "common good."

For Rand, this idea necessarily places individuals in conflict with one another. There is no such thing as "the public," she points out, and the idea is never used to refer literally to *all* members of society. Instead, it acts as cover for allowing the rights and interests of some to take precedence over those of others. In short, the idea that government has the authority to sacrifice some people to others is built right into the concept of the public good. The predictable result is pressure group warfare, as individuals and groups scramble to be considered "the public" so they may be the beneficiaries rather than the victims of laws and policies that sacrifice some to others. Pull peddling, which is the means by which individuals angle to gain an advantage over others in a system like this, amounts to trading on the basis of political favoritism and relationships rather than value. The longer a society functions in this manner, the more cronyism becomes entrenched. As Rand memorably described this process and its results: "A man who is tied cannot run a race against men who are free: he must either demand that his bonds be removed or that the other contestants be tied as well. If men choose the second, the economic race slows down to a walk, then to a stagger, then to a crawl—and then they all collapse at the goal posts of a Very Old Frontier: the totalitarian state. No one is the winner but the government" ("The Cold Civil War," *Column* 18).

Conclusion

Rand's approach to cronyism is certainly consistent with her approach to government in general, but it is much more than that. Her account is also far more convincing than the view presented by any other thinker, for it provides a standard for understanding why cronyism is not just unpleasant or politically unpopular but, in fact, evil. Cronyism is understandable as immoral and corrupt only if we understand that government has a proper purpose that can be corrupted. Only then can we recognize cronyism as a misuse of government power that consists in using the force government possesses for immoral purposes—by punishing the virtuous and rewarding the vicious. Ignoring government's proper role by casting it in the vague terms of the "public interest," as critics on both right and left do, serves only to make a very serious problem seem like nothing more than a matter of preference or partisan politics. When defenders of the free market accept this premise, they undermine their own arguments. The solution to cronyism is not to turn the altruist/collectivist conception of government into an unreachable "romantic" ideal and conclude, cynically, that "people are people" who cannot live up to that moral ideal because they all operate on their base, "self-interested" desires. The solution is to jettison altruism and the collectivist politics to which it leads, to understand what self-interest really means, and to ground government on an egoistic, individualistic foundation. As Rand spent her career arguing, that is the *only* path to capitalism and freedom.

UNIFORM ABBREVIATIONS OF WORKS
BY AYN RAND

(with indication of the editions cited from)

There is no standard edition of Rand's works, and since much of her nonfiction is most readily available in mass-market editions with inconsistent pagination, referring to them can be challenge. We have adapted a set of abbreviations for Rand's works. Find them listed below paired with bibliographic information on the edition (and, when necessary, the printing) that is referenced in this volume.

Most of Rand's nonfiction was initially published in periodicals she edited or coedited, and much of it has been republished in books, some compiled by Rand during her lifetime and others compiled posthumously by other editors. Both Rand's periodicals and some of the books she compiled during her lifetime contain pieces by other authors, and she endorsed this material as representative of her philosophy. Some of the posthumously published collections of her essays contain additional essays written by other authors after her death, which do not share this same endorsement. In the decades since her death, Rand's estate has also brought out editions of her unpublished stories, correspondence, and notes, and several books have been prepared based on material she originally presented orally in various formats. All of this posthumously published material has been edited in various ways by other hands and, in any case, did not necessarily represent Rand's considered views. Volumes marked by a dagger (†) in the list below are comprised of such posthumously published material. Volumes marked by an asterisk (*) include both pieces that Rand published in her lifetime and posthumously published material or pieces written by other authors after her death. (For more on the composition of Rand's corpus and the provenance of various pieces, see Salmieri 2016e.)

Answers†   *Ayn Rand Answers: The Best of Her Q&A*. Edited by Robert Mayhew. London: New American Library, 2005.

Anthem   *Anthem*. Centennial edition. New York: Dutton, 2005.

Anthem38   *Anthem*. London: Cassell, 1938.

AOF†   *The Art of Fiction: A Guide for Writers and Readers*. Edited by T. Boeckmann. New York: Plume, 2000.

AON†   *The Art of Nonfiction: A Guide for Writers and Readers*. Edited by R. Mayhew. New York: Plume, 2000.

ARL   *The Ayn Rand Letter*. Bound edition. New Milford, CT: Second Renaissance Book, 1990.

Atlas   *Atlas Shrugged*. Centennial edition. New York: Dutton, 2005.

Column   *The Ayn Rand Column*. Revised edition. Edited by P. Schwartz. New Milford, CT: Second Renaissance Books, 1998.

CUI   *Capitalism: The Unknown Ideal*. Centennial edition. New York: Signet, 2005.

Fountainhead   *The Fountainhead* (*1943). "Introduction" is the introduction to the twenty-fifth anniversary edition of *The Fountainhead*. New York: Bobbs-Merrill, 1968.

FTNI   *For the New Intellectual: The Philosophy of Ayn Rand*. Centennial edition. New York: Signet, 2005.

Ideal†   *Ideal: The Novel and the Play*. Edited by R. Ralston and L. Peikoff. New York: New American Library, 2015.

ITOE   *Introduction to Objectivist Epistemology*. Expanded second edition. Edited by H. Binswanger and L. Peikoff. New York: Meridian, 1990.

Journals†   *Journals of Ayn Rand*. Edited by D. Harriman. New York: Dutton, 1999.

Letters†   *Letters of Ayn Rand*. Edited by M. Berliner. New York: Dutton, 1997.

Lexicon†   *The Ayn Rand Lexicon: Objectivism from A to Z*, ed. H. Binswanger, The Ayn Rand Library, vol. 4. New York: Plume, 1986.

Marginalia†   *Ayn Rand's Marginalia: Her Critical Comments on the Writings of over 20 Authors*. Edited by R. Mayhew. New Milford, CT: Second Renaissance Books, 1995.

PWNI   *Philosophy: Who Needs It*. Centennial edition. New York: Signet, 2005.

RM   *The Romantic Manifesto: A Philosophy of Literature.* Centennial edition. New York: Signet, 2005.

ROTP   *Return of the Primitive: The Anti-Industrial Revolution.* Edited by P. Schwartz. New York: Meridian, 1999.

Speaking†   *Objectively Speaking: Ayn Rand Interviewed.* Edited by M. Podritske and P. Schwartz. Lanham, MD: Lexington Books, 2009.

TO   *The Objectivist.* Bound edition. New Milford, CT: Second Renaissance Books, 1990.

TOF   *The Objectivist Forum.* Bound edition. New York: TOF Publications, 1990.

TON   *The Objectivist Newsletter.* Bound edition. New Milford, CT: Second Renaissance Books, 1990.

Unconquered†   *The Unconquered with another, earlier adaptation of We The Living.* Edited by R. Mayhew. New York: Palgrave Macmillan, 2014.

VOR   *The Voice of Reason: Essays in Objectivist Thought.* Edited by L. Peikoff. New York: Meridian, 1990.

VOS   *The Virtue of Selfishness: A New Concept of Egoism.* Centennial edition. New York: Signet, 2005.

WTL   *We The Living.* Seventy-fifth anniversary deluxe edition. New York: New American Library, 2011.

WTL36   *We the Living.* London: Macmillan, 1936.

Ackerman, Bruce. 1991. *We the People: Foundations*. Cambridge, MA: Harvard University Press.

Badhwar, Neera K. 1999. "Is Virtue Only a Means to Happiness? An Analysis of Virtue and Happiness in Ayn Rand's Writings." *Reason Papers*, 24.

Badhwar, Neera, and Roderick Long. 2016. "Ayn Rand." *Stanford Encyclopedia of Philosophy*. http://plato.stanford.edu/entries/ayn-rand/.

Ball, Terence, ed. 1992. *James Mill: Political Writings*. Cambridge: Cambridge University Press.

Baumol, William J. 1968. "Entrepreneurship in Economic Theory." *American Economic Review* 58(2): 64–71.

Bentham, Jeremy. 1844. "Anarchical Fallacies." In *Benthamiana: or, Select Extracts from the Works of Jeremy Bentham*, edited by J. H. Burton, 83–107. Philadelphia: Lea & Blanchard.

Bianchi, Milo, and Magnus Henrekson. 2005. "Is Neoclassical Economics Still Entrepreneurless?" *SSE/EFI Working Paper Series in Economics and Finance* no. 584. http://swopec.hhs.se/hastef/papers/hastef0584.pdf.

Binswanger, Harry. 1981. Q & A Department. *The Objectivist Forum* 2(4): 11–14.

Binswanger, Harry. 1990. *The Biological Basis of Teleological Concepts*. Marina Del Rey, CA: Ayn Rand Institute Press.

Binswanger, Harry. 1992. "Life Based Teleology and the Foundations of Ethics." *Monist* 75:1.

Binswanger, Harry. 2005. "Antitrust: 'Free Competition' at Gunpoint." In Hull 2005, 121–42.

Binswanger, Harry. 2011. "The Dollar and the Gun." In Ghate and Ralston 2011, 267–75.

Binswanger, Harry. 2014. *How We Know: Epistemology on an Objectivist Foundation*. New York: TOF Publications.

Blackstone, William. 1765 [1979]. *Commentaries on the Laws of England*. Vol. 1: *Of the Rights of Persons*, with an introduction by Stanley N. Katz. Chicago: University of Chicago Press.

Boeckmann, Tore. 2007. "The Fountainhead as a Romantic Novel." In *Essays on Ayn Rand's* The Fountainhead, edited by Robert Mayhew, 119–154. Lanham, MD: Lexington.

Böhm-Bawerk, Eugen von. 1891 [1930]. *The Positive Theory of Capital*. Translated by William Smart. New York: G. E. Stechert.

Borelli, Tom. 2011. "Occupy Wall Street Should Protest Crony Capitalism." FoxNews.com. October 27. http://www.foxnews.com/opinion/2011/10/27/occupy-wall-street-should-protest-crony-capitalism/.

Bork, Robert H. 1978. *The Antitrust Paradox: A Policy at War with Itself*. New York: Basic Books.

Bou-Habib, Paul. 2003. "Locke, Sincerity and the Rationality of Persecution." *Political Studies* 51(4): 611–26.

Bowles, Chester. 1959. "We Are All Liberals Now." *New York Times Magazine*, April 19.

Brewer, Talbot. 2014. "The Coup That Failed." *Hedgehog Review* 16(2): 64–83.

Browne, Harry. 1973. *How I Found Freedom in an Unfree World: A Handbook for Personal Liberty*. New York: Macmillan.

Buchanan, James M. 1958. "The Thomas Jefferson Center for Studies in Political Economy." *University of Virginia News Letter* 35(2): 5–9.

Buchanan, James M. 1979. "Politics without Romance: A Sketch of Public Choice Theory and Its Normative Implications." *IHS-Journal* 3: B1–11.

Buchanan, James M. 1991. *The Economics and the Ethics of Constitutional Order*. Ann Arbor: University of Michigan Press.

Burke, Edmund. 1890. *The Works of the Right Hon. Edmund Burke*. London: George Bell & Sons. 6 vols.

Burns, Jennifer. 2009. *Goddess of the Market: Ayn Rand and the American Right*. Oxford: Oxford University Press.

Burton, David M. 1995. *Burton's History of Mathematics: An Introduction*. 3rd ed. Dubuque, IA: Wm. C. Brown Publishers.

Caplan, Bryan. 2007a. "*Atlas Shrugged* and Public Choice: The Obvious Parallels." In *Ayn Rand's* Atlas Shrugged: *A Philosophical and Literary Companion*, edited by Edward Younkins, 225–34. Burlington, VT: Ashgate.

Caplan, Bryan. 2007b. *The Myth of the Rational Voter*. Princeton, NJ: Princeton University Press.

Carney, Timothy P. 2006. *The Big Ripoff: How Big Business and Big Government Steal Your Money*. Hoboken, NJ: John Wiley and Sons.

Carney, Timothy P. 2013. "The Case against Cronies: Libertarians Must Stand Up to Corporate Greed." *The Atlantic*, April 30. https://www.aei.org/publication /the-case-against-cronies-libertarians-must-stand-up-to-corporate-greed/.

Carney, Timothy P. 2014. "Mike Lee's Agenda Could Make 2014 Elections about Crony Capitalism." *Washington Examiner*, May 10. http:// washingtonexaminer.com/mike-lees-agenda-could-make-2014-elections -about-crony-capitalism/article/2548297/.

Child, James W. 1994. "Can Libertarianism Sustain a Fraud Standard?" *Ethics* 104(4): 722–38.

Childs, Roy A. 1969. "Objectivism and the State: An Open Letter to Ayn Rand." In *Liberty against Power: Essays by Roy A. Childs, Jr.*, edited by Joan Kennedy Taylor, 145–56. New York: Fox and Wilkes.

Church, Forrest, ed. 2004. *The Separation of Church and State*. Boston: Beacon Press.

Cobb, Thomas. 1858. *An Inquiry into the Law of Negro Slavery in the United States*. Philadelphia: T & W. Johnson.

Cohen, Gerald A. 1989. "On the Currency of Egalitarian Justice." *Ethics* 99: 906–44.

Cohen, Gerald A. 1995. *Self-Ownership, Freedom, and Equality*. Cambridge: Cambridge University Press.

Cohen, Gerald A. 2011. "Freedom and Money." In *On the Currency of Egalitarian Justice and Other Essays in Political Philosophy*, edited by G. A. Cohen and M. Otsuka, 166–99. Princeton, NJ: Princeton University Press.

Cohn, Jonathan. 2014. "The Conservative Crusade against Crony Capitalism Turns Out to Be Another Crusade against the Safety Net." *New Republic*, April 29. http://www.newrepublic.com/ article/117572/ thomas-piketty-crony-capitalism-and-conservatives-inequality/.

Cooke, Jacob, ed. 1961. *The Federalist*. Middletown, CT: Wesleyan University Press.

Daniels, Eric. 2005. "Reversing Course: American Attitudes about Monopolies, 1607–1890." In Hull 2005, 63–94.

Dawidoff, Nicholas. 2009. "The Civil Heretic." *New York Times Magazine*, March 25. http://www.nytimes.com/2009/03/29/magazine/29Dyson-t .html?pagewanted=all&_r=0/.

Den Uyl, Douglas, and Douglas Rasmussen. 1978. "Nozick on the Randian Argument." *The Personalist* 59: 184–205. Reprinted in *Reading Nozick*, edited by Jeffrey Paul, 232–69. Lanham, MD: Rowman and Littlefield, 1981.

Den Uyl, Douglas, and Douglas Rasmussen, eds. 1984. *The Philosophical Thought of Ayn Rand*. Urbana: University of Illinois Press.

Doherty, Brian. 2007. *Radicals for Capitalism: A Freewheeling History of the Modern Libertarian Movement*. New York: Public Affairs.

Dreisbach, Daniel L. 2002. *Thomas Jefferson and the Wall of Separation between Church and State*. New York: New York University Press.

Dressler, Joshua. 2006. *Understanding the Criminal Law*. 4th ed. Newark: LexisNexis.

The Economist (no byline). 2014. "The New Age of Crony Capitalism." March 14. http://www.economist.com/ news/leaders/21598996-political-connections -have-made-many-people-hugely-rich-recent-years-crony-capitalism-may/.

Edmundson, William A. 1998. *Three Anarchical Fallacies: An Essay on Political Authority*. Cambridge: Cambridge University Press.

Feinberg, Joel. 1978. "Voluntary Euthanasia and the Inalienable Right to Life." *Philosophy and Public Affairs* 7: 93–123.

Foot, Philippa. 2001. *Natural Goodness*. Oxford: Oxford University Press.

Fox, Caroline. 1882. *Memories of Old Friends: Being Extracts from the Journals and Letters of Caroline Fox*. Edited by H. Pym. Philadelphia: J. B. Lippincott.

Freeman, Samuel. 2002. "Illiberal Libertarians: Why Libertarianism Is Not a Liberal View." *Philosophy and Public Affairs* 30(2): 106–51.

Friedman, David. 1989. *The Machinery of Freedom*. LaSalle, IL: Open Court.

Friedman, Milton. 1990. *Free to Choose: A Personal Statement*. New York: Harcourt Brace.

Gaus, Gerald. 2012. "Property." In *The Oxford Handbook of Political Philosophy*, edited by David Estlund, 93–112. Oxford: Oxford University Press.

Gay, Peter. 1966. *The Enlightenment: An Interpretation*. Vol. 1: *The Rise of Modern Paganism*. New York: W. W. Norton.

Gay, Peter. 1969. *The Enlightenment: An Interpretation*. Vol. 2: *The Science of Freedom*. New York: W. W. Norton.

Ghate, Debi, and Richard E. Ralston, eds. 2011. *Why Businessmen Need Philosophy*. New York: New American Library.

Ghate, Onkar. 2016. "A Being of Self-Made Soul." In Gotthelf and Salmieri 2016, 105–29.

Ghate, Onkar. 2017. "Individual Rights: The Bridge between Morality and Politics." Recorded Lecture. https://www.youtube.com/watch?v=YuFzT MoodqQ/.

Gobineau, Joseph Arthur, comte de. 1866 [1900]. *Les Religions et Les Philosophies dans L'Asie Centrale*. 3rd ed. Paris: Ernest Leroux.

Goldie, Mark, ed. 1997. *Locke: Political Essays*. Cambridge: Cambridge University Press.

Gotthelf, Allan. 2000. *On Ayn Rand*. Belmont, CA: Wadsworth.

Gotthelf, Allan. 2016. "The Morality of Life." In Gotthelf and Salmieri 2016, 73–104.

Gotthelf, Allan, and James G. Lennox, eds. 2011. *Metaethics, Egoism and Virtue: Studies in Ayn Rand's Normative Theory*. Ayn Rand Society Philosophical Studies. Vol. 1. Pittsburgh, PA: University of Pittsburgh Press.

Gotthelf, Allan, and James G. Lennox, eds. 2013. *Concepts and Their Role in Knowledge: Reflections on Objectivist Epistemology. Ayn Rand Society Philosophical Studies*. Vol. 2. Pittsburgh: University of Pittsburgh Press.

Gotthelf, Allan, and Gregory Salmieri, eds. 2016. *A Companion to Ayn Rand*. Oxford: Wiley-Blackwell.

Grotius, Hugo. 1625 [1925]. *De Jure Belli ac Pacis Libri Tres*. Translated by Francis W. Kelsey. Oxford: Clarendon Press.

Hardin, Garret. 1968. "The Tragedy of the Commons." *Science* 162(3859): 1243–48.

Harriman, David. 2010. *The Logical Leap: Induction in Physics*. New York: New American Library.

Hart, H. L. A. 1982. *Essays on Bentham*. Oxford: Oxford University Press.

Hayek, Friedrich A., ed. 1935. *Collectivist Economic Planning*. London: Routledge and Kegan Paul.

Hayek, Friedrich A. 1944. *The Road to Serfdom*. Foreword by John Chamberlain. Chicago: University of Chicago Press.

Hayek, Friedrich A. 1948. *Individualism and Economic Order*. Chicago: University of Chicago Press.

Hayek, Friedrich A. 1978. *New Studies in Philosophy, Politics, Economics and the History of Ideas*. London: Routledge and Kegan Paul.

Hazlitt, Henry. 1938. "A Revised Attack on Socialism." *New York Times Book Review*, January 9.

Hazlitt, Henry. 1946. *Economics in One Lesson*. New York: Harper and Brothers.

Henderson, David R. n.d. "Rent Seeking." In *The Concise Encyclopedia of Economics*. http://www.econlib.org/library/Enc/RentSeeking.html.

Hobbes, Thomas. 1651 [1996]. *Leviathan*. Edited by Richard Tuck. Cambridge: Cambridge University Press.

Hohfeld. Wesley. 1913. "Fundamental Legal Conceptions as Applied in Judicial Reasoning." *Yale Law Journal* 23(1): 16–59.

Holcombe, Randall G. 2007. *Entrepreneurship and Economic Progress*. New York: Routledge.

Holcombe, Randall G. 2014. "Crony Capitalism: By-Product of Big Government." *Mercatus Center Working Paper* no. 12-32. October. http://mercatus.org/sites/default/files/Crony-Capitalsim-Holcombe-v1-0_0.pdf.

Hsieh, Diana. 2003. "Libertarianism versus libertarianism." *Noodlefood* (web blog), March 27. http://www.philosophyinaction.com/blog/?p=349/.

Huebert, Jacob H. 2010. *Libertarianism Today*. Santa Barbara, CA: Praeger.

Huemer, Michael. 1996. "Why I Am Not an Objectivist." http://spot.colorado.edu/~huemer/rand.htm.

Huemer, Michael. 2002. "Is Benevolent Egoism Coherent?" *Journal of Ayn Rand Studies* 3(2): 259–88.

Huemer, Michael. 2005a. "Critique of the Objectivist Ethics." http://spot.colorado.edu/~huemer/rand5.htm.

Huemer, Michael. 2005b. *Ethical Intuitionism*. New York: Palgrave Macmillan.

Huemer, Michael. 2013. *The Problem of Political Authority: An Examination of the Right to Coerce and the Duty to Obey*. New York: Palgrave Macmillan.

Hull, Gary, ed. 2005. *The Abolition of Antitrust*. New Brunswick, NJ: Transaction Publishers.

Hume, David. 1748 [1975]. *An Enquiry Concerning Human Understanding*. In *Enquiries Concerning Human Understanding and Concerning the Principles of Morals*, edited by L. A. Selby-Bigge. Oxford: Clarendon Press.

Hunt, Lester H. 1997. *Character and Culture*. Lanham, MD: Rowman and Littlefield.

Hunt, Lester H. 2015. *Anarchy, State, and Utopia: An Advanced Guide*. Oxford: Wiley-Blackwell.

Hunt, Lester H. 2016. "Ayn Rand's Evolving View of Friedrich Nietzsche." In Gotthelf and Salmieri 2016, 343–50.

Jevons, Marshall. 1978 [1993]. *Murder on the Margin*. Princeton, NJ: Princeton University Press.

Jevons, Marshall. 1985. *The Fatal Equilibrium*. Cambridge, MA: MIT Press.

Jevons, Marshall. 1995. *A Deadly Indifference*. New York: Carroll and Graf.

Jevons, William Stanley. 1888. *The Theory of Political Economy*. 3rd ed. London: Macmillan.

Kant, Immanuel. 1785 [2002]. *Groundwork for the Metaphysics of Morals*. Translated by Allen W. Wood. New Haven: Yale University Press.

Kinne, Burdette. 1943. "Voltaire Never Said It!" *Modern Language Notes* 58(7): 534–35.

Kinsella, N. Stephan. 2003. "A Libertarian Theory of Contract: Title Transfer, Binding Promises, and Inalienability." *Journal of Libertarian Studies* 17(2): 11–37.

Kirzner, Israel M. 1973. *Competition and Entrepreneurship*. Chicago: University of Chicago Press.

Kirzner, Israel M. 1976. *The Economic Point of View: An Essay in the History of Economic Thought*. Kansas City, MO: Sheed and Ward.

Kirzner, Israel M. 1989. *Discovery, Capitalism, and Distributive Justice*. New York: Basil Blackwell.

Kirzner, Israel M. 1999. "Report on a Treatise." *Review of Austrian Economics* 12: 81–94.

Koch, Adrienne, and William Peden, eds. 1944. *The Life and Selected Writings of Thomas Jefferson*. New York: Random House.

Kymlicka, Will. 2002. *Contemporary Political Philosophy: An Introduction*. 2nd ed. Oxford: Oxford University Press.

Lachman, Desmond. 2014. "America's Crony Capitalism Challenge." July. *American Enterprise Institute*. https://www.aei.org/publication/americas-crony-capitalism-challenge/.

Lavoie, Don. 1985. *Rivalry and Central Planning.* Cambridge: Cambridge University Press.

Leavis, F. R., ed. 1980. *Mill on Bentham and Coleridge.* Cambridge: Cambridge University Press.

Lennox, James G. 2010. "*Bios* and Explanatory Unity in Aristotle's Biology." In *Definition in Greek Philosophy,* edited by David Charles, 328–55. Oxford: Oxford University Press.

Lepp, Stephanie. 2017. "A Paid Climate Skeptic Switches Sides." *Reckonings.* http://www.reckonings.show/episodes/17.

Lewis, John David, and Gregory Salmieri. 2016. "A Philosopher on Her Times: Ayn Rand's Political and Cultural Commentary." In Gotthelf and Salmieri 2016, 352–402.

Lindberg, David C. 1992. *The Beginnings of Western Science.* Chicago: University of Chicago Press.

Little, Margaret Olivia. 1996. "Why a Feminist Approach to Bioethics?" *Kennedy Institute of Ethics Journal* 6:1.

Locke, John. 1689. *A Letter Concerning Toleration.* Translated from the Latin version (published the same year) by W. Popple. London: Awnsham Churchill.

Locke, John. 1689 [1824]. *A Letter Concerning Toleration.* In *The Works of John Locke in Nine Volumes.* 12th ed. Vol. 5. London: Rivington. http://oll.liberty fund.org/titles/locke-the-works-vol-5-four-letters-concerning-toleration/.

Locke, John. 1689 [2010]. *A Letter Concerning Toleration.* Translated by M. Silverthorne. In Vernon 2010, 3–46.

Locke, John. 1690 [1979]. *An Essay Concerning Human Understanding.* Edited by Peter H. Nidditch. Oxford: Clarendon Press.

Locke, John. 1690 [1980]. *Second Treatise of Government.* Indianapolis: Hackett.

Locke, John. 1690 [1988]. *Two Treatises of Government.* Edited by Peter Laslett. Cambridge: Cambridge University Press (student edition).

Locke, John. 1690 [2010]. *A Second Letter Concerning Toleration.* In Vernon 2010, 67–107.

Locke, John. 1693 [1996]. *Some Thoughts Concerning Education and Of the Conduct of the Understanding.* Edited by Ruth W. Grant and Nathan Tarcov. Indianapolis: Hackett.

Locke, John. 1706 [1824]. *Conduct of the Understanding.* In *The Works of John Locke in Nine Volumes.* 12th ed. Vol. 2. London: Rivington.

Loewen, James W. 2005. *Sundown Towns: A Hidden Dimension of American Racism.* New York: The New Press.

Lomasky, Loren. 1991. "Compensation and the Bounds of Rights." *Nomos* 33: 13–44.

Long, Roderick. 2000. *Reason and Value: Aristotle versus Rand.* Washington, DC: The Atlas Society.

Long, Roderick. 2010. "The Winnowing of Ayn Rand." In *Cato Unbound: A Journal of Debate*. http://www.cato-unbound.org/2010/01/20/roderick-t-long/winnowing-ayn-rand/.

Long, Roderick. 2016. "Rational Animals, Productivity, and Constitutive Virtues." In *Cato Unbound: A Journal of Debate*. http://www.cato-unbound.org/2016/11/03/roderick-t-long/rational-animals-productivity-constitutive-virtues/.

Loopis, Louise Ropes, ed. 1943. *Aristotle on Man in the Universe*. Roslyn NY: Walter J. Black.

Los Angeles Times (no byline). 2014. "GOP Is Off Target on Export-Import Bank." August 4. http://www.latimes.com/opinion/editorials/la-ed-ex-im-bank-20140804-story.html.

Machan, Tibor. 1980. "Libertarianism and Conservatives." *Modern Age* 24(1): 21–33.

Machan, Tibor. 1998. *Classical Individualism: The Supreme Importance of Each Human Being*. New York: Routledge.

Mack, Eric. 1984. "The Fundamental Moral Elements of Rand's Theory of Rights." In Den Uyl and Rasmussen 1984, 122–61.

Mack, Eric. 2003. "Problematic Arguments in Randian Ethics." *Journal of Ayn Rand Studies* 5(1).

Mack, Eric. 2013. *John Locke*. Major Conservative and Libertarian Thinkers, vol. 2. New York: Bloomsbury.

Madison, James. 1835 [1910]. "Sovereignty." In *The Writings of James Madison*, edited by Gaillard Hunt, 9:568–73. New York: G. P. Putnam's Sons.

Matthes, Erich Hatala. 2015. "Impersonal Value, Universal Value, and the Scope of Cultural Heritage." *Ethics* 125: 99–127.

Mavrodes, George I. 1972. "Property." *The Personalist* 53: 245–62.

Mayhew, Robert, ed. 2005. *Essays on Ayn Rand's* Anthem. Lanham, MD: Lexington Books.

Mayhew, Robert, ed. 2009. *Essays on Ayn Rand's* Atlas Shrugged. Lanham, MD: Lexington Books.

McCloskey, Deirdre N. 2007. *The Bourgeois Virtues: Ethics for an Age of Commerce*. Chicago: University of Chicago Press.

McKeon, Richard, ed. 1941. *The Basic Works of Aristotle*. New York: Random House.

Meacham, Jon. 2007. *American Gospel: God, the Founding Fathers, and the Making of a Nation*. New York: Random House.

Menger, Carl. 1871 [1994]. *Principles of Economics*. Translated by J. Dingwall and B. Hoselitz. Grove City, PA: Libertarian Press.

Mill, John Stuart. 1848 [1909]. *Principles of Political Economy*. Edited by W. J. Ashley. 7th ed. London: Longmans, Green.

Mill, John Stuart. 1859 [1977]. *On Liberty*. In *The Collected Works of John Stuart Mill*. Vol. XVIII: *Essays on Politics and Society Part I*. Edited by John M. Robson. Toronto: University of Toronto Press.

Mill, John Stuart. 1874. *Autobiography*. 4th ed. London: Longmans, Green, Reader, and Dyer.

Mill, John Stuart. 1875. *Dissertations and Discussions*. Vol. 4, 2nd ed. London: Longmans, Green, Reader, and Dryer.

Miller, Casey, and Kate Swift. 1976. *Words and Women*. Garden City, NY: Anchor Press/Doubleday.

Miller, Fred D. Jr. 2006. "Virtue and Rights in Aristotle's Best Regime." In *Values and Virtues: Aristotelianism in Contemporary Ethics*, edited by T. Chappell, 67–89. Cambridge: Cambridge University Press.

Miller, Fred D. Jr., and Adam Mossoff. 2016. "Political Theory: Radical for Capitalism." In Gotthelf and Salmieri 2016, 187–208.

Milosz, Czeslaw. 1955. *The Captive Mind*. Translated by J. Zielonko. New York: Vintage Books.

Mineka, Francis E., and Dwight N. Lindley, eds. 1972. *The Collected Works of John Stuart Mill*. Vol. 14: *The Later Letters of John Stuart Mill 1849–1873*, Part 1 [1849–1855]. Toronto: University of Toronto Press.

Mises, Ludwig von. 1922 [1951]. *Socialism: An Economic and Sociological Analysis*. Translated by J. Kahane. Expanded ed. New Haven: Yale University Press.

Mises, Ludwig von. 1927 [2005]. *Liberalism*. Indianapolis: Liberty Fund.

Mises, Ludwig von. 1948 [1990]. "The Objectives of Economic Education." Reprinted in *Economic Freedom and Interventionism: An Anthology of Articles and Essays*, edited by B. B. Greaves, 203–11. New York: Foundation for Economic Education.

Mises, Ludwig von. 1949 [1966]. *Human Action: A Treatise on Economics*. 3rd ed. Chicago: Regnery.

Mises, Ludwig von. 1949 [1996]. *Human Action: A Treatise on Economics*. 4th rev. ed. San Francisco: Fox and Wilkes.

Mises, Ludwig von. 2013. *Notes and Recollections* [1940], with *The Historical Setting of the Austrian School of Economics* [1962]. Edited by B. Bien Greaves. Indianapolis: Liberty Fund.

Mitchell, Wesley C. 1967. *Types of Economic Theory*. Vol. 1. New York: Augustus M. Kelley.

Mitchell, Wesley C. 1969. *Types of Economic Theory*. Vol. 2. New York: Augustus M. Kelley.

Moore, G. E. *Principia Ethica*. 1903 [1993]. Rev. ed. Edited and with an introduction by T. Baldwin. Cambridge: Cambridge University Press.

Mossoff, Adam. 2002. "Locke's Labor Lost." *University of Chicago Law School Roundtable* 9(1): 155–64.

Mossoff, Adam. 2013. "Saving Locke from Marx: The Labor Theory of Value in Intellectual Property Theory." *Social Philosophy and Policy* 29: 283–317.

Moulton, Janice. 1981. "The Myth of the Neutral 'Man'." *In Sexist Language: A Modern Philosophical Analysis*, edited by Mary Vetterling-Braggin, 100–116. Totowa, NJ: Littlefield, Adams.

Nagel, Thomas. 1975. "Libertarianism without Foundations." *Yale Law Journal* 85: 136–49.

Nagel, Thomas. 1986. *The View from Nowhere*. Oxford: Oxford University Press.

Narveson, Jan. 1988. *The Libertarian Idea*. Philadelphia: Temple University Press.

Nickson, Elizabeth. 2012. *Eco-Fascists*. New York: Broadside Books.

Nozick, Robert. 1971. "On the Randian Argument." *The Personalist* 52: 282–304. Reprinted in R. Nozick, *Socratic Puzzles*, 249–64. Cambridge, MA: Harvard University Press, 1997.

Nozick, Robert. 1974. *Anarchy, State, and Utopia*. New York: Basic Books.

Nozick, Robert. 1993. *The Nature of Rationality*. Princeton, NJ: Princeton University Press.

Obama, Barack. 2006. "Politicians Need Not Abandon Religion." *USA Today*, July 9. http://usatoday30.usatoday.com/news/opinion/editorials/2006-07-09 -forum-religion-obama_x.htm.

Otteson, James. 2014. *The End of Socialism*. Cambridge: Cambridge University Press.

Packe, Michael St. John. 1954. *The Life of John Stuart Mill*. New York: Macmillan.

Peikoff, Leonard. 1982. *The Ominous Parallels: The End of Freedom in America*. New York: Dutton.

Peikoff, Leonard. 1991. *Objectivism: The Philosophy of Ayn Rand*. New York: Dutton.

Peikoff, Leonard. 1998. *Objectivism through Induction*. Gaylordsville, CT: Second Renaissance Books. Audio recording.

Peikoff, Leonard. 2005. *Induction in Physics and Philosophy*. Irvine, CA: The Ayn Rand Bookstore. Audio recording.

Piketty, Thomas. 2014. *Capital in the Twenty-First Century*. Translated by A. Goldhammer. Cambridge, MA: Harvard University Press.

Proast, Jonas. 1690 [2010]. *The Argument of the Letter concerning Toleration Briefly Considered and Answered*. In Vernon 2010, 54–66.

Pufendorf, Samuel. 1672 [1934]. *De Jure Naturae et Gentium Libri Octo*. Translated by C. H. Oldfather and W. A. Oldfather. Oxford: Clarendon Press.

Rachels, James. 2003. *The Elements of Moral Philosophy*. New York: McGraw-Hill.

Rasmussen, Douglas B. 2002. "Rand on Obligation and Value." *Journal of Ayn Rand Studies* 4(1): 69–86.

Rasmussen, Douglas B. 2006. "Regarding Choice and the Foundations of Morality: Reflection on Rand's Ethics." *Journal of Ayn Rand Studies* 7(2): 309–28.

Rasmussen, Douglas B. 2007a. "The Aristotelian Significance of the Section Titles of *Atlas Shrugged*: A Brief Consideration of Rand's View of Logic and Reality." In *Ayn Rand's Atlas Shrugged: A Philosophical and Literary Companion*, edited by Edward W. Younkins, 33–45. Aldershot, UK: Ashgate.

Rasmussen, Douglas B. 2007b. "Rand's Metaethics: Rejoinder to Hartford." *Journal of Ayn Rand Studies* 8(2): 307–16.

Rasmussen, Douglas, and Douglas Den Uyl. 1991. *Liberty and Nature: An Aristotelian Defense of Liberal Order*. LaSalle, IL: Open Court.

Rasmussen, Douglas, and Douglas Den Uyl. 2005. *Norms of Liberty: A Perfectionist Basis for Non-perfectionist Politics*. University Park: Pennsylvania State University Press.

Rawls, John. 1971 [1999]. *A Theory of Justice*. Revised ed. Cambridge, MA: Harvard University Press.

Raz, Joseph. 1986. *The Morality of Freedom*. Oxford: Clarendon Press.

Raz, Joseph. 2001. *Value, Respect, and Attachment*. Cambridge: Cambridge University Press.

Read, Leonard E. 1958. "I, Pencil: My Family Tree as told to Leonard E. Read." *The Freeman* (December 1958).

Regan, Donald H. 2003. "How to Be a Moorean." *Ethics* 113: 651–77.

Reisman, George. 1996. *Capitalism: A Treatise on Economics*. Ottawa, IL: Jameson Books.

Robbins, Lionel. 1932. *An Essay on the Nature and Significance of Economic Science*. London: Macmillan.

Roberts, Russell A. 2001a. *The Choice: A Fable of Free Trade and Protectionism*. New York: Prentice Hall.

Roberts, Russell A. 2001b. *The Invisible Heart: An Economic Romance*. Cambridge, MA: MIT Press.

Roberts, Russell. 2012. "Stiglitz on Inequality." *EconTalk*, July 9. http://www.econtalk.org/archives/2012/07/stiglitz_on_ine.html.

Robson, Ann P., and John M. Robson, eds. 1986. *The Collected Works of John Stuart Mill*. Vol. 22: *Newspaper Writings, Part I: December 1822–July 1831*. Toronto: University of Toronto Press.

Robson, John M., ed. 1984. *The Collected Works of John Stuart Mill*. Vol. 21: *Essays on Equality, Law, and Education*. Toronto: University of Toronto Press.

Roosevelt, Franklin D. 1941. *Annual Message to Congress on the State of the Union*. January 6. http://www.fdrlibrary.marist.edu/pdfs/fftext.pdf.

Roosevelt, Theodore. 1910. *New Nationalism Speech*. http://teachingamerican history.org/ library/document/new-nationalism-speech/.

Rosenthal, Bernice. 2004. *New Myth, New World: From Nietzsche to Stalinism.* University Park: Pennsylvania State University Press.

Rothbard, Murray N. 1973 [2006]. *For a New Liberty: The Libertarian Manifesto.* 2nd ed. Auburn, AL: Ludwig von Mises Institute.

Rothbard, Murray N. 1982 [2002]. *The Ethics of Liberty.* With a new introduction by H. Hoppe. New York: New York University Press.

Rugy, Veronique de. 2014. "Big Business Rewards Senator Mary Landrieu for Supporting Cronyism." *National Review,* July. http://www.nationalreview .com/corner/big-business-rewards-senator-mary-landrieu-supporting -cronyism-veronique-de-rugy/.

Rummell, R. J. 1994. *Death by Government.* New Brunswick, NJ: Transaction Publishers.

Salmieri, Gregory. 2005. "Prometheus' Discovery: Individualism and the Meaning of the Concept 'I' in *Anthem.*" In Mayhew 2005, 255–84.

Salmieri, Gregory. 2009. "*Atlas Shrugged* on the Role of the Mind in Man's Existence." In Mayhew 2009, 219–52.

Salmieri, Gregory. 2013. "Conceptualization and Justification." In Gotthelf and Lennox 2013, 41–84.

Salmieri, Gregory. 2016a. "The Act of Valuing and the Objectivity of Values." In Gotthelf and Salmieri 2016, 49–72.

Salmieri, Gregory, 2016b. "Annotated Bibliography of Primary and Quasi-Primary Sources." In Gotthelf and Salmieri 2016, 463–69.

Salmieri, Gregory. 2016c. "Egoism and Altruism: Selfishness and Sacrifice." In Gotthelf and Salmieri 2016, 130–56.

Salmieri, Gregory. 2016d. "An Introduction to the Study of Ayn Rand." In Gotthelf and Salmieri 2016, 1–21.

Salmieri, Gregory. 2016e. "The Objectivist Epistemology." In Gotthelf and Salmieri 2016, 272–318.

Salmieri, Gregory. 2016f. "Rational Cognition and Motivation in the Greeks, Kant, and Rand." *Cato Unbound: A Journal of Debate.* http://www .cato-unbound.org/2016/11/02/gregory-salmieri/rational-cognition -motivation-greeks-kant-rand/.

Salmieri, Gregory. 2016g. "What's Wrong with the Concept 'Libertarian'?" *Check Your Premises: The Blog of the Ayn Rand Society,* 9 March. http:// www.borelli.org/2016/03/09/whats-wrong-with-the-concept-libertarian/.

Samuelson, Paul A. 1948. *Economics: An Introductory Analysis.* 1st ed. New York: McGraw-Hill.

Samuelson, Paul A. 1955. *Economics: An Introductory Analysis.* 3rd ed. New York: McGraw-Hill.

Say, Jean-Baptiste. 1803 [1855]. *A Treatise on Political Economy.* Translated by C. R. Prinsep. 6th ed. Philadelphia: Lippincott, Grambo & Co.

Schmidtz, David. 1994. "The Institution of Property." *Social Philosophy and Policy* 11(2): 42–62.

Schumpeter, Joseph. 1942 [1975]. *Capitalism, Socialism and Democracy.* Harper Perennial Modern Thought Edition. New York: Harper and Row.

Seldon, Arthur. 2002. "Introduction: About Public Choice." In Tullock, Seldon, and Brady 2002, ix–xii.

Simon, Michael A. 1971. *The Matter of Life: Philosophical Problems of Biology.* New Haven, CT: Yale University Press.

Skorupski, John. 1989. *John Stuart Mill.* New York: Routledge.

Smidt, C., K. den Dulk, B. Froehle, J. Penning, S. Monsma, and D. Koopman. 2010. *The Disappearing God Gap? Religion in the 2008 Presidential Election.* Oxford: Oxford University Press.

Smith, Adam. 1776 [1981]. *An Inquiry into the Nature and Causes of the Wealth of Nations.* Edited by R.H Campbell, A.S. Skinner, and W.B. Todd. Indianapolis: Liberty Classics.

Smith, Tara. 1995. *Moral Rights and Political Freedom.* Lanham, MD: Roman and Littlefield.

Smith, Tara. 2000. *Viable Values: A Study of Life as the Root and Reward of Morality.* Lanham, MD: Rowman and Littlefield.

Smith, Tara. 2006. *Ayn Rand's Normative Ethics.* Cambridge: Cambridge University Press.

Smith, Tara. 2009. "'Humanity's Darkest Evil': The Lethal Destructiveness of Non-Objective Law." In Mayhew 2009, 335–61.

Smith, Tara. 2013. "Originalism, Vintage or Nouveau: 'He Said, She Said' Law." *Fordham Law Review* 82: 619–39.

Smith, Tara. 2015. *Judicial Review in an Objective Legal System.* Cambridge: Cambridge University Press.

Smith, Tara. 2016. "Objective Law." In Gotthelf and Salmieri 2016, 209–21.

Spinoza, Benedict de. 1677 [1949]. *Ethics.* Edited by James Gutman. New York: Hafner Press.

Tannehill, Morris, and Linda Tannehill. 1970. *The Market for Liberty.* Lansing, MI: Self-published.

Thaler, Richard H., and Cass R. Sunstein. 2009. *Nudge: Improving Decisions about Health, Wealth, and Happiness.* Revised and expanded ed. New York: Penguin.

Thomas, William, and David Kelley. 1999. *The Logical Structure of Objectivism.* https://atlassociety.org/sites/default/files/LSO%20Binder.pdf.

Thompson, Michael. 2008. *Life and Action: Elementary Structures of Practice and Practical Thought.* Cambridge, MA: Harvard University Press.

Tomasi, John. 1998. "The Key to Locke's Proviso." *British Journal for the History of Philosophy* 6(3): 447–54.

Tuccille, Jerome. 1971. *It Usually Begins with Ayn Rand*. 1971. New York: Stein and Day.

Tuck, Richard. 1979. *Natural Rights Theories: Their Origin and Development*. Cambridge: Cambridge University Press.

Tullock, Gordon. 2002a. *The Cost of Rent Seeking*. In Tullock, Seldon, and Brady 2002, 43–52.

Tullock, Gordon. 2002b. "People Are People: The Elements of Public Choice." In Tullock, Seldon, and Brady 2002, 3–15.

Tullock, Gordon, Arthur Seldon, and Gordon L. Brady. 2002. *Government Failure: A Primer in Public Choice*. Washington, DC: Cato Institute.

Unger, Peter. 1975. *Ignorance: A Case for Scepticism*. Oxford: Clarendon Press.

Vernon, Richard, ed. 2010. *Locke on Toleration*. Cambridge: Cambridge University Press.

Waldron, Jeremy. 1979. "Enough and as Good Left for Others." *Philosophical Quarterly* 29(117): 319–28.

Waldron, Jeremy. 1988. "Locke: Toleration and the Rationality of Persecution." In *Justifying Toleration: Conceptual and Historical Perspectives*, edited by Susan Mendus. Cambridge: Cambridge University Press.

Warren, Virginia L. 1986. "Guidelines for Non-sexist Use of Language." *Proceedings and Addresses of the American Philosophical Association*, 59:3.

Weber, Max. 1946. "Politics as a Vocation." In *From Max Weber: Essays in Sociology*, edited by H. H. Gerth and C. Wright Mills, 77–128. Oxford: Oxford University Press.

Wellman, Christopher Heath. 2005. "Samaritanism and the Duty to Obey the Law." In *Is There a Duty to Obey the Law?* edited by Christopher Heath Wellman and A. John Simmons, 1–89. Cambridge: Cambridge University Press.

Williams, Bernard. 1981. *Moral Luck*. Cambridge: Cambridge University Press.

Williams, Bernard. 1985. *Ethics and the Limits of Philosophy*. Cambridge, MA: Harvard University Press.

Wright, Darryl. 2005. "Needs of the *Psyche* in Ayn Rand's Early Ethical Thought." In Mayhew 2005, 190–224.

Wright, Darryl. 2008. "Evaluative Concepts and Objective Values." In *Objectivism, Subjectivism, and Relativism in Ethics*, edited by Ellen Frankel Paul, Fred D. Miller, and Jeffery Paul, 149–81. Cambridge: Cambridge University Press.

Wright, Darryl. 2011a. "Reasoning about Ends." In Gotthelf and Lennox 2011, 3–32.

Wright, Darryl. 2011b. "Virtue and Sacrifice: Response to Swanton." In Gotthelf and Lennox 2011, 101–10.

Wright, Darryl. 2016. "'A Human Society': Rand's Social Philosophy." In Gotthelf and Salmieri 2016, 159–86.

Wright Edelman, Marian. 1992. *The Measure of Our Success: A Letter to My Children and Yours.* Boston: Beacon Press.

Yeager, Leland. 2001. *Ethics as Social Science: The Moral Philosophy of Social Cooperation.* Northampton: Edward Elgar.

Yolton, John. 1958. "Locke on the Law of Nature." *Philosophical Review* 67(4): 477–98.

Zwolinski, Matt. 2013. "Six Reasons Why Libertarians Should Reject the Non-Aggression Principle." Libertarianism.org. April 8. http://www.libertarian ism.org/blog/six-reasons-libertarians-should-reject-non-aggression -principle/.

Zwolinski, Matt. 2016. "The Libertarian Non-Aggression Principle." *Social Philosophy and Policy* 32: 62–90.

Harry Binswanger taught philosophy at Hofstra University, Hunter College (CUNY), and the University of Texas at Austin. He is the author of *The Biological Basis of Teleological Concepts* and *How We Know: Epistemology on an Objectivist Foundation*. He was the publisher and editor of *The Objectivist Forum,* a bimonthly journal that Ayn Rand helped establish and for which she served as "Philosophic Consultant," until her death in 1982. He edited *The Ayn Rand Lexicon* and co-edited, with Leonard Peikoff, the second edition of Rand's *Introduction to Objectivist Epistemology.*

Peter J. Boettke is University Professor of Economics and Philosophy at George Mason University, where he is also the director of the F. A. Hayek Program for Advanced Study in Philosophy, Politics, and Economics and the BB&T Professor for the Study of Capitalism at the Mercatus Center. His many publications include *Why Perestroika Failed* (Routledge 1993) and (as coeditor) *The Oxford Handbook of Austrian Economics* (2015).

Robert Garmong received his PhD in philosophy from the University of Texas, Austin (2002), with a dissertation on John Stuart Mill's political philosophy. For many years he taught business ethics and European civilization at Dongbei University of Finance and Economics in Dalian, China. He is now Deputy Resident Director for Southern China for CMB EB-5 Regional Centers.

Onkar Ghate is a Senior Fellow and Chief Philosophy Officer at the Ayn Rand Institute in Irvine, California. He specializes in Ayn Rand's philosophy of Objectivism and is the institute's senior instructor and editor. He has published and lectured extensively on many aspects of Rand's philosophy and fiction, including the application of the philosophy to cultural and political issues. His current research focuses on religion, morality, and the separation of church and state.

Michael Huemer is Professor of Philosophy at the University of Colorado at Boulder. He is the author of more than sixty academic articles in ethics, epistemology, political philosophy, and metaphysics as well as five amazing books that you should immediately buy: *Skepticism and the Veil of Perception* (2001), *Ethical Intuitionism* (2005), *The Problem of Political Authority* (2013), *Approaching Infinity* (2016), and *Paradox Lost* (2018).

Lester H. Hunt is Professor of Philosophy at the University of Wisconsin–Madison. He is the author of *Nietzsche and the Origins of Virtue* (Routledge, 1990), *Character and Culture* (Rowman and Littlefield, 1997), and *Anarchy, State, and Utopia: An Advanced Guide* (Wiley-Blackwell, 2015). He has also written dozens of scholarly articles on ethics, social and political philosophy, esthetics, and the history of philosophy, including "Nussbaum on Emotion" (*Ethics* 2006) and "Ayn Rand's Evolving View of Friedrich Nietzsche" (in *A Companion to Ayn Rand*).

Robert Mayhew is Professor of Philosophy at Seton Hall University. His primary research interests are in ancient philosophy, and his most recent books in this field are *Aristotle's Lost* Homeric Problems (Oxford University Press, 2019), *Theophrastus of Eresus: On Winds* (Brill, 2018), *Prodicus the Sophist* (Oxford University Press, 2011), and *Aristotle: Problems* (Loeb Classical Library, Harvard University Press, 2011). His most recent publications on Ayn Rand and Objectivism are an annotated edition of her previously unpublished play *The Unconquered* (Palgrave-Macmillan, 2014) and (as editor) *Essays on Ayn Rand's* We the Living (Lexington Books, 2nd ed., 2012).

Fred D. Miller Jr. is Research Professor in the Department of Political Economy and Moral Science at the University of Arizona. He is executive editor of the journal *Social Philosophy & Policy*. He is the author of *Nature, Justice, and Rights in Aristotle's Politics* (Oxford University Press, 1995) and has coedited many collections including *A Companion to Ar-*

istotle's Politics (Blackwell, 1991) and *A History of Philosophy of Law from the Ancient Greeks to the Scholastics* (2nd edition, Springer, 2015). His new translation of Aristotle's *On the Soul and Other Psychological Works* was recently published by Oxford University Press (2018).

Adam Mossoff is a Professor of Law at Antonin Scalia Law School at George Mason University. He is a founder of the Center for the Protection of Intellectual Property, where he is also Director of Academic Programs and a Senior Scholar. He has published extensively in academic journals and in the public policy debates on the theory and history of property and intellectual property rights. His scholarship has been cited by the US Supreme Court, and his article "What Is Property?" (*Arizona Law Review* 45 [2003]) is ranked as a top-twenty-five cited article in property law in law journals.

Gregory Salmieri is a fellow at the Anthem Foundation for Objectivist Scholarship and teaches philosophy at Rutgers University. He is coeditor (with Allan Gotthelf) of *A Companion to Ayn Rand* (Wiley-Blackwell, 2016), cosecretary (with James Lennox) of the Ayn Rand Society, and coeditor of its *Philosophical Studies* series. His writings on Rand include "Discovering Atlantis" (in Mayhew, ed., *Essays on Ayn Rand's* Atlas Shrugged), "Conceptualization and Justification" (in volume 2 of this series), and several chapters in *A Companion to Ayn Rand*. He also writes and lectures on Aristotle and on various philosophical issues.

Steve Simpson is Senior Litigation Counsel at the New Civil Liberties Alliance. As Director of Legal Studies at the Ayn Rand Institute (2013–2018), he edited *Defending Free Speech* (ARI Press, 2016) and lectured and published widely on free speech, campaign finance, and other legal issues. As a litigator for the Institute for Justice (2001–2013), he was involved in many precedent-setting cases in courts across the nation. He has testified in Congress, appeared often on television and radio, and written for many publications. After earning his law degree from New York Law School in 1994, he clerked for a federal district court judge and worked in private practice before moving into constitutional law.

Robert Tarr received an MA in philosophy from the University of Toronto and spent a year in a PhD economics program, before pursuing a career with a large offshore hedge fund in Bermuda. He was a portfolio manager and research group manager, devising systematic strategies across a broad set of asset classes for fifteen years. He retired in early 2008, just prior to the financial crisis. He currently engages in independent research in economics and the philosophy of economics, with a particular interest in the Austrian theory of the business cycle and its application to understanding recent and upcoming crises.

Darryl Wright is Professor of Philosophy and Willard W. Keith Fellow in the Humanities at Harvey Mudd College (The Claremont Colleges). He has published articles on the history of ethics, early analytic philosophy, and most recently, Rand's moral and political philosophy. His essay "Reasoning about Ends: Life as a Value in Ayn Rand's Ethics" appeared in the first volume in this series.

Matt Zwolinski is Professor of Philosophy at the University of San Diego and director of USD's Center for Ethics, Economics, and Public Policy. He is also a codirector of USD's Institute for Law and Philosophy and a Fellow at UCSD'S Center on Global Justice. He is the author of nearly thirty articles focusing on various theoretical and applied aspects of exploitation, the editor of *Arguing about Political Philosophy* (2nd edition, Routledge, 2014) and of *The Politics, Philosophy, and Economics of Exploitation* (Oxford, 2017). With John Tomasi he is the author of *A Brief History of Libertarianism* (Princeton University Press, forthcoming).

abortion, 113, 123, 230, 277, 285n3
abstraction. *See* concepts
aggression. *See* force; non-aggression principle; non-initiation of force principle; violence
altruism, 18n3, 24–25, 72–73, 224, 231, 234, 272; and capitalism, 240, 264–68, 280; and cronyism, 411–12, 420–22, 426, 428; biological, 18n3; defined, 267–69; Locke's views on, 130; von Mises's views on, 403–8; objections to, 266–68, 404–8. *See also* sacrifice
analytic-synthetic distinction, 184n27
anarchism, 8n5, 82n4, 215, 231–34; as collectivist, 233–34; as non-objective, 228–32; criticism of, 207–8, 215, 219–22, 228–36, 242–43, 275–80; defense of, 242–43, 249–60; entailed by non-aggression principle, 245, 258–60. *See also* anarcho-capitalism; anarchy
anarcho-capitalism, 215, 219–22, 228–36, 246, 251, 276n18, 278n23. *See also* anarchism; anarchy; Rothbard, M.
anarchy, 8, 213–16, 249–50, 258–60. *See also* anarchism; anarcho-capitalism
anti-concept, 138
anti-force principle. *See* non-initiation of force principle

arbitrary, 40–41, 48, 62–63, 68, 298n17; uses of force as, 229, 243, 425; socially, 80
aristocracy of pull, 11, 410, 426. *See also* cronyism; mixed economy; Money-Appropriator
Aristotle, 121n7, 134, 163–64, 169n6, 174–75n8
art, 27n14, 28n16, 41, 344
Atlas Shrugged, 60, 74n28, 87, 263n3; characterization 37n23, 183n25, 185n29, 397n7, 410, 422–23, 426; economics in 331–32, 338, 389–99, 407, 420–23; Galt's Speech in, 28–32, 135–37, 140, 153–57, 167n1; themes of, 27, 74n28, 181n20, 210, 223
Austrian economics, 357–73; as based on an objective theory of values, 333, 357–73; and the socialist calculation debate, 362–65; and subjective knowledge, 334, 366; vs. neoclassical economics, 346–61. *See also* economics; Hayek, F.; Menger, C.; methodological individualism; von Mises, L.

Bentham, J., 131, 315, 349
Binswanger, H., 8n5, 222, 243, 250
bios, 174n12. *See also* life
Boeckmann, T., 174n12
Branden, N., 358n28

Brewer, T., 59–60, 63n18, 320

Browne, H., 278n23

Buchanan, J., 386, 400, 412

businessmen, 339, 422. *See also* entrepreneurship; producer

capitalism, 3–8, 117, 235–40, 283, 327–28; as embodying an objective theory of values, 327, 339, 376–78; as the only economic system which protects the creative mind, 373; moral-philosophic base of the defense of, 223n12, 232, 327, 401–3, 406. *See also* free market

Caplan, B., 423n6

Carney, T., 413, 416

causality, 38n25. *See also* production

censorship, 50, 53, 308, 314; self-, 62. *See also* freedom of speech

Child, J., 103–13

church-state separation, 283–303; Jefferson's justification of, 295–97; Locke's justification of, 288–95; popular understanding of, 284–88; religionists on, 284–85, 287; Rand's justification of, 297–303; secularists on, 284–87; wall of separation metaphor, 284, 296. *See also* economy-state separation; intellectual freedom

Civil Rights Act of 1964, 182, 183nn23–24, 317

classical economics, 328, 333–34, 339, 342–46, 350, 357, 379n46, 383n49. *See also* economics; Reisman, G.; Ricardo, D.; Smith, A.

coercion. *See* force

cognitive paralysis, 58–60, 63; latent and occurrent, 66–67, 70

Cohen, G., 162n10

competing governments. *See* anarcho-capitalism

competition, 177, 230, 340, 364, 370–72, 408; theory of perfect competition, 356–57; market, 394–95, 414, 420; state restrictions on, 423–25. *See also* conflicts of interest; cronyism; economics

concepts, 33–37, 336–37

conflicts of interest, 149, 177; as multiplied by altruism, 427; none among rational people, 176; and property acquisition, 160; theoretical presuppositions of belief in, 405–6; and trade, 26–30, 177–78;

consent, 42, 103–6, 110–12, 273; of the governed, 126, 131, 229, 279; informed, 104–5, 112; and rights, 155–56, 184–92. *See also* force; rights

consequentialism, 92n17, 244n14, 313. *See also* Mill, J. S.

conservatism, 4–8, 232, 402, 485

constitutive approach to egoistic justification, 155–57, 168–76

context, 36–41. *See also* objective theory of values; objectivity

contracts, 44; breaches of, 84, 103, 106–9, 123n10; 191, 248–49, 273; necessity, 108; slavery, 80n3. *See also* fraud; force; trade

coordination problem, 366–67, 372, 391, 398

creator. *See* producer

cronyism, 410–28; conventional views of, 410–17; as a misnomer, 418n3; and nonobjective law, 424–27; as a political manifestation of altruism, 421–27; Rand's views on, 411, 418–27. *See also* aristocracy of pull; mixed economy; Money-Appropriator

Crusoe, R., 208, 218, 340

Declaration of Independence, 126n14, 419

defamation, 274

Den Uyl, D., 167n2

diamond-water paradox, 342–47. *See also* classical economics

discrimination, 182–83, 191, 305, 316–18, 321–22. *See also* racism; religious persecution; sexism

division of labor, 80, 190, 271, 340–41; and the purpose of economics, 346, 369, 373, 377; and property, 190. *See also* economics; production; trade

drug use, 242, 252

economic calculation, 362–73. *See also* Austrian economics; economics

economic freedom. *See* free market

economics, 327–409; and coordination problems, 366–67; and ethics, 373–83; fundamental problem of, 366–67; and human nature, 374–77; and mathematics, 349–55, 364–65; rent seeking, 412–24; as a science, 340–41, 407; tribalism in, 341–42, 346, 353, 378. *See also* Austrian economics; capitalism; classical economics; cronyism; economic calculation; economy-state separation; free market; marginal theory of value; methodological individualism; neoclassical economics; values

economic vs. political power, 215n4

economy-state separation, 283, 301–3. *See also* capitalism; free market

egoism, 25, 195, 403, 168–76; criticisms of, 243–54, 264–69; defense of 240–54, 264–70; and rights, 146–49, 155–57, 167, 190, 195

emergencies, 23, 26n12, 86–87, 190–91, 274–76

ends. *See* means-end relationship; ultimate value; value

Enlightenment, 216, 223–25

entrepreneurship, 21, 337–39, 346; as central to the market process, 368–72; difficulty in explaining, 346, 355, 367, 382n48, 408; in market equilibrium and nonequilibrium, 354–57, 367. *See also* Austrian economics; businessmen; economics; Kirzner, I.; production; productiveness

esthetics, 174n12, 402. *See also* art; sense of life

evasion (mental), 17–18, 22–23, 60, 299–230, 331–32, 426

First Amendment, 4, 285–87, 296

force, 28–33, 41–44, 160–65, 178–84, 214–16, 245–49, 272–75; as coercion, 16, 48, 215, 230, 273; as impediment to survival, 30–33, 42, 45–47, 76–81, 87, 180, 278; as impractical, 89–103, 178–80; indirect 42–45, 50–57, 91, 103–12, 248; as monopolistic, 278; moralized concept of, 44n33, 84, 161–63, 185n28, 248; as negating the mind, 28–29, 43, 46–48, 124–25, 163–65, 180, 300; as paralyzing the mind, 28–29, 60–75, 180–81; as only way to violate rights, 123–24, 227; retaliatory, 79–80, 108, 125, 178, 216n5, 220–21, 229–36, 247, 279–80; taxonomy of types of initiation, 42–43; vs. natural harms, 164, 180–81; vs. other putative means of coercion, 180–81, 183, 313–16. *See also* fraud; non-initiation of force principle; threats

Founders of America, 10, 126, 134, 206, 223. *See also* Enlightenment; Jefferson, T.; Locke, J.; Madison, J.

fraud, 44n31, 103–6, 109–12, 124n11

free market, 238, 300–4, 372–73, 377–82; as corollary of free mind, 303; requires government, 230. *See also* capitalism; economy-state separation

free-riding, 23–25, 30. *See also* conflict of interest

freedom, 30, 81, 91, 118–24, 128, 180, 186; Huemer's defense of, 237–40, 251–58; intellectual 295–301, 318–23; political, 84, 122n8, 134; religious, 288–92, 297–99. *See also* church-state separation; free market

freedom of speech, 30, 123n10, 285n4, 296, 313. *See also* censorship; freedom of thought; Mill, J. S.

free trade, 123n10

Friedman, D., 276

frozen abstraction, 109

Ghate, O., 179, 184n26, 195n1

good. *See* value

government, 206–80; as authority of 252, 288; defined, 228, 245n17; form of as driven by citizens' philosophy, 234; functions of, 108, 126, 250, 289, 424; historical record of, 119, 234; justification of 109, 207–18, 228–29, 234;

government (*cont.*): limitations of, 15, 411; minimal, 8n5; as monopoly on physical force, 16, 49, 228, 234, 418; purpose, 49, 78, 80–85, 292, 411, 418–19, virtue theories of, 119n8; voluntary financing of, 90. *See also* anarcho-capitalism; church-state separation; economy-state separation; force; rights state of nature; statism

Grotius, H., 131, 130n26, 132n30

happiness, 20–21, 223, 300–303, 384, 419, 422, 427; as the purpose of life, 99n27, 142; requirements for, 47, 71, 186, 323, 411; right to the pursuit of 83, 123n10, 126, 186, 213–17, 407–8, 413; and trade, 27; utilitarian view of, 347, 405–6

Hayek, F., 90–91, 96, 208, 227, 394–97, 400, 408; as critic of 'perfect competition' theory, 357–58; on the role of knowledge in economic calculation, 362–66, 370–71, 389; *Road to Serfdom*, 96n23, 389, 397n9

Hazlitt, H., 389–91

Hobbes, T., 156, 175–76

Homestead Act of 1862, 83

Hospers, J., 169n4, 401

Huemer, M., 8n5, 118, 134, 146–49, 261–80

human nature, 374–77. *See also* life, man's

immigration law, 242, 252

impersonal good, 92, 103. *See also* intrinsic theory of value

independence (virtue), 28, 322

individual rights. *See* rights

induction, 37, 38n24, 38n25, 41n28, 363n4

instinct, 17, 99

instrumental approach to egoistic justification, 140n41, 155–56, 168–75

instrumental value vs. intrinsic value, 168–71

intellectual freedom. *See under* freedom

intrinsicism. *See* intrinsic theory of value

intrinsic theory of value, 93–97, 132–44, 169n4, 226–27, 332–33, 344–46,

378–80. *See also* classical economics; impersonal theory of good

intuition, 119, 194, 224, 271

irrationality, 22, 31. *See also* evasion (mental); rationality

Jefferson, T., 134, 288–303

Jevons, S., 346–47, 349, 351, 361

Jim Crow laws, 179n18, 183n23, 221

justification (epistemic), 37–39

Kant, I., 94, 120, 140–42, 194, 200, 223n11, 269n12

Kirzner, I., 352–53, 368, 370–72, 383n49. *See also* Austrian economics; entrepreneurship

labor theory of value, 344n18. *See also* classical economics; economics

Lee, M., 410, 413

Lennox, J., 174n12

liberalism, 304–23; Locke's vs. Mill's, 309–16; Mill's vs. Rand's 318–23. *See also* Enlightenment; freedom of thought; Locke, J.; Mill, J. S.; political philosophy

Libertarian movement, 4, 5, 117, 267n8

libertarianism, 7–8, 16, 103, 117, 228; and capitalism, 238; defined, 8n5, 237; and Objectivism, 238n1. *See also* anarcho-capitalism; non-aggression principle

liberty. *See* freedom

life, 17–18, 98–101, 120, 169–75, 185; man's, 19–20, 79–81, 91, 100, 172–73, 199, 334; one's own, 20, 102, 108, 142, 172. *See also* standard of value; ultimate value; value

Locke, J., 10, 46, 69, 157, 159, 160n8, 201n3; compared with Rand, 49–57, 126–34, 297–303; criticisms of, 49–57, 126–34; epistemology of, 127n20, 306–8; *Essay Concerning Human Understanding*, 49–57, 127n20, 223n12, 293–94; on free speech, 306; *Letters Concerning Toleration*, 49–57, 127n18, 288–95,

305–8; as liberal, 305–8; moral theory of, 126–31, 223n12; on property, 79n1, 130, 133; on rights 126–34; *Some Thoughts Concerning Education and of the Conduct of the Understanding*, 130; *Two Treatises of Government*, 126–32

Long, R., 170n7, 173–74

looters, 24, 32, 178, 422, 424. *See also* cronyism; Money-Appropriators

Mack, E., 32, 52n8, 118–49

Madison, J., 10, 288, 295, 297–98

marginal theory of value, 346–73; Menger's as objective, 359–60; comparison of Menger's with Jevons's, 247–348. *See also* Austrian economics; economics; Jevons, S.; Menger, C.; value

means-end relationship, 24, 155–56, 168–70, 173–76, 330; 337, 362, 388. as subject-centric, 347–49; *See also* instrumental value vs. intrinsic value; teleological measurement; value

meta-normative principles, 167n2

methodological individualism, 207–11, 339–42, 369. *See also* methodology; Robinson Crusoe; state of nature

methodology, 36, 40–41, 143, 150, 184n27, 255–56, 261–64. *See also* concepts; induction; objectivity; rationality; reason

Menger, C., 346, 359–62, 364, 366. *See also* marginal theory of value; methodological individualism

Mill, H., 310n7, 311, 311n9

Mill, J., 308, 312–15, 312n10, 312n11, 315n14

Mill, J. S., 10, 305–23, 405; and the Harm Principle, 309, 321–22; on free speech, 309, 313; *On Liberty*, 309–10

Miller, F., 152–65

Milosz, C., 61–73, 75n30

mixed economy, 420. *See also* cronyism; economic freedom; statism

Money-Appropriator, 422, 426. *See also* cronyism; looters; mixed economy

Moore, G., 92n18, 94

moral principles, justification of 17–25

morality, 18, 23, 79, 128, 172, 175, imposed by force 232, 233, 291. *See also* values

Mossoff, A., 152–65

Narveson, J., 199n2

natural law theory, 107, 128n23, 144. *See also* Locke, J.; natural rights

natural resources, 77–79, 132–33, 157–62, 176–77, 187–89, 344. *See* property

natural rights, 126–34. *See also* Locke, J.; natural law theory

neoclassical economics, 333–83; as based on view of values, 333–34, 346–57; equilibrium theory of, 252–59, 366–67; as undermining capitalism, 372. *See also* economics; Jevons, S.

New Deal, 394, 427

non-aggression principle, 123, 137, 144, 160, 168n3, 194, 241–42; criticisms of, 160–65, 247–49; as entailing anarchism, 245; terminology of, 110n35; vs. Rand's non-initiation of force principle, 15n1, 103–13. *See also* anti-force principle; government; libertarianism; non-initiation of force principle; rights

non-initiation of force principle, 31, 33–41, 76–103, 168n3, 176–84, 194; justification of, 76–89, 113–14; presuppositions of, 33–41, 81, 113, 230, 273; as a principle, 90–91, 160, 225; responses to criticisms of, 180–84, 272–75. *See also* non-aggression principle

Nozick, R., 80n3, 82n4, 84n6, 133–35, 159, 193–227; as critic of Objectivism 142–49; criticism of, 211–18; M, 198–204; "On The Randian Argument," 134, 142–43, 149

Obama, B., 285n3, 410

Obama, M., 404, 404n1

objective (vs. intrinsic and subjective) value, 93, 146n50, 157, 361, 377

objective theory of value, 40, 93, 100–103,

objective theory of value (*cont.*), 176, 227, 332–33. *See also* Austrian economics; socially (vs. philosophically) objective value; value

Objectivism: epistemology of, 33–41, 150, 226–27, 336; ethics of, 17–33, 168–84, 240–41, 264–67, 299–300, 402–3; radicalism of, 5–6, 222–27, 254, 283, 341–42; structure of, 4, 16, 19–20, 117–19, 166–68, 193–94, 206–11, 327–28. *See also* capitalism; egoism; non-initiation of force principle; objective theory of value; objectivity; Rand, A.; rights

objectivity, 28, 40–41, 62, 70–71, 98; public, 78–80, 277, 279; role of volition in, 39, 41n28, 53–57, 335–38, 371. *See also* arbitrary; methodology; objective theory of values; objective (vs. intrinsic and subjective) value; rationality; reason; socially (vs. philosophically) objective value

obligation as hypothetical not categorical, 120, 140, 149

pacifism, 232, 278

package-deal, 8n5, 137–38, 305n1

Peikoff, L., 16n2, 41n28, 57, 74n29, 82, 263

perception, 17, 33, 34n18

persecution. *See* religious persecution

Plato, 140, 149, 169, 176, 234, 257

political philosophy, 4, 15–16, 107n33, 117, 194. *See also* liberalism; Locke, J.; Mill, J. S.; Nozick, R.

praxeology, 358, 362, 375. *See also* Austrian economics; von Mises, L.

predation, 179, 276

principles, 19–20, 23, 24, 175; implicit, 85, 88; moral as selfish, 19; necessity of, 19, 32, 85–86, 100; Rand's method of thinking in, 119. *See* methodology; moral principles; virtue

Proast, J., 51n6, 52n8

producer, 26–27, 337–38, 346, 357, 360–62, 395–97, 421–66. *See also* businessman; entrepreneurship

production, 81, 121, 336–38; efficient-cause view of 338, 345–46, 357, 383n49. *See also* economics; productiveness

productiveness, 20–26, 176, 201, 334. *See also* production; rationality; reason; virtue

profit, 223, 339–40 354–57; 367–72. *See also* Austrian economics; capitalism; economics; neoclassical economics

property, 43–44, 77–85, 121–23, 161–62, 184–92; intellectual, 44n32, 83, 190; justification of, 107, 113, 153, 158–60, 187–90; reputation as, 274

Pufendorf, S., 128n23, 131, 132n30

purpose, 20–21, 99n27

racism, 164, 182–83, 191, 230, 285, 317–18, 407

radicals for capitalism, 6, 117

Rand, A.: *Anthem*, 263n3, 389; biography of, 389–90; "Causality Versus Duty," 145; *The Fountainhead*, 210, 174n12, 389; in relation to liberal tradition, 49–57, 126–34, 297–303, 318–23; "Man's Rights," 82; methodology of, 143, 175–76, 184n27, 263–64; *The Moral Basis of Individualism*, 87; "The Nature of Government," 209; "The Objectivist Ethics," 142; reception of, 6–8, 134 152–53, 390; scholarship concerning, 4, 7–8, 33n17; "The Simplest Thing in the World," 74; *We the Living*, 389; "What Is Capitalism?," 92–103. See also *Atlas Shrugged*; Objectivism

Rasmussen, R., 167n2, 170n7, 227n14

rationalism vs. empiricism, 254, 261, 263

rationality, 21–22, 27–28, 33, 60, 196–205, 223n12. *See also* concepts; methodology; reason; virtue

Read, L., 187n30, 391n5

reason, 33–41; as an absolute, 22, 297; as a cardinal value, 21–22; as man's basic means of survival, 20, 22, 119, 121, 172, 329, 334, 376; as man's means of knowledge, 20, 22; as volitional, 39, 299. *See also* objectivity; rationality regulation, 30, 46–47, 87n11, 380, 394. *See also* cronyism; mixed economy; statism

religious persecution, 50–57, 285–86, 295, 302, 319. *See also* church-state separation; freedom, intellectual; freedom, religious

religious toleration. *See* church-state separation; freedom, religious; Locke, J.

rent seeking, 413–24

Reisman, G., 383n49

Ricardo, D., 240, 308

right to a fair trial, 123n10

right to do wrong, 137–39

right to liberty, 121–39, 186–88, 213–17, 223, 302, 308–11. *See also* freedom

right to life, 120–23, 194. *See also* life

right to privacy, 123n10

right to revolution, 222n10

right to self-defense, 123n10, 217–22, 229–30, 234, 279

right to the pursuit of happiness, 83, 123n10, 186, 213, 217, 223, 300–303

right to vote, 123n10

rights, 81–83, 118–26, 144–45, 184–92, 211–19; as claims, 153–57; as constraints on self-interest, 146–149, 155, 195, 204; criticisms of Rand's theory of, 32–33, 84n6, 134–50, 155, 161–65, 184–85; equivocations concerning, 135–42, 154; in relation to force, 161–62, 184–87; justifications of, 126–37, 142–51, 166–76, 190–92, 193–96, 207–11; objectivity of 126–34, 218–19; permissible violations of, 190–92; positive vs. negative, 154; role of in Rand's political theory, 167, 184–87, 211–19; why needed, 43, 81, 108–9, 114, 117–19, 184–92, 222. *See also* force; freedom; government; Locke, J.; non-initiation of force principle; Nozick, R.

rights of children, 103, 112–13

Rothbard, M., 104–14, 124n11, 161n9, 168n3, 207–8, 214–15

Ryan, P., 5, 410

sacrifice, 25, 96n23, 143, 146–49, 197; and trade, 176–84. *See also* altruism

Salmieri, G., 15n0, 263n3

Samuelson, P., 354–55, 393–94

sanction of the victim, 24–25, 73n26. *See also* Atlas Shrugged

Say, J., 345

Schumpeter, J., 237, 240, 238

second-handers, 47, 323. *See also* Rand, A.: *The Fountainhead*

segregation. *See* Jim Crow laws

self, 19, 24

self-defense, 123n10, 221, 229

self-esteem, 19–20, 27

self-exclusion fallacy, 29, 402

self-interest, 19, 21, 24–25, 168. *See also* egoism

self-ownership, 107–8. *See also* right to life

self-sacrifice. *See* altruism; sacrifice

sense of life, 41, 61, 201, 225

sexism, 165, 169–70n6, 182–83, 191n35

side constraints, 144, 195–204, 222. *See also* Nozick, R.

slander, 248

Smith, A., 342–46, 398; "invisible hand" theory of, 208, 211, 215, 219, 227

Smith, T., 170n7

socialism, 385, 407. *See also* socialist calculation debate; statism

socialist calculation debate, 362–63. *See also* Austrian economics; economic calculation; economics; Hayek, F.; Mises, L.; socialism

socially (vs. philosophically) objective value, 378–82. *See also* economics; objective theory of values; objective (vs. intrinsic and subjective) value

society, 80–84, 207–11, 217–18, 229, 279, 341

Socrates, 169n5, 176n16

Spinoza, 256, 271; *Ethics*, 257n28, 271n13

squirms, the, 58, 63, 66–67. *See also* cognitive paralysis

standard of value, 99–100, 169, 172, 175, 328–33

state of nature, 207–11. *See also* Locke, J.;
    Nozick, R.
statism, 419–20
stolen concept, 230
subjective knowledge. *See* Austrian
    economics; Hayek, F.
subjective theory of value, 93–97, 147n50,
    149, 176, 226–27, 270; in economics,
    333, 346–73, 380, 402, 407. *See also*
    Jevons, S.; marginal theory of value;
    objective (vs. intrinsic and subjective)
    value
subpoena power, 90n16
survival, 18–21, 102, 170–74, 210, 266; as
    requiring non-material values, 334; vs.
    flourishing (scholarly controversy),
    20, 169–73. *See also* life; non-initiation
    of force principle; productiveness;
    reason; rights; value

taxation, 90, 131
technology, political implications of 190
teleological measurement, 100, 330–31,
    337–38, 345, 349–51
threats, 42–48, 57–75, 180, 246–48, 273;
    private force as, 229, 279. *See also* force
trade, 26–28, 110–12, 176–84, 215, 271. *See
    also* division of labor; trader principle
trader principle, 26–33, 178. *See also*
    division of labor; trade
tribalism. *See* economics: tribalism in
Tullock, G., 412, 416, 424, 413n1

ultimate value, 17–19, 96n23, 99n27,
    142n45, 169–75, 195, 331
utilitarianism, 197, 403

value, 17–18, 120, 169–75, 328–42;
    achievement of, 98, 100, 121, 171, 330,
    337–40; as chosen, 101–2, 120; concepts
    of, 120, 266–67; defined, 98–99,
    285, 328; human, 17–18, 76, 99–101;
    non-cognitivism about, 94–96;
    non-material, 20, 27n14, 102, 334; as
    objective, 17, 100, 169, 357–73, 402;
    optional, 335; and reason, 329, 403; and
    theories of rationality, 196. *See also*
    economics; life; marginal theory of
    value; standard of value; teleological
    measurement; ultimate value
violence, 109n34, 110n35. *See also* force
virtue, 18–21, 98, 172–74, 184n27; as
    unable to be coerced, 233. *See also*
    independence; moral principles;
    principles; productiveness; rationality;
    virtue ethics
virtue ethics, 19. *See also* virtue
virtue-based theories of civil society,
    122n8
von Böhm-Bawerk, E., 348
von Mises, L., 238n2, 362–63,
    366–77; "Head" and "heart" defense of
    capitalism, 384–409; *Human Action*,
    342, 358, 363, 369, 371n37, 402; Rand's
    differences with, 96–97, 373n41, 401–9;
    Socialism, 386, 403. *See also* Austrian
    economics; economics

Waldron, J., 49–57. *See also* cognitive
    negation; Locke, J.
welfare, 219n6, 242, 252
Wright, D., 8–9, 320

Zwolinski, M., 104n29, 109n34, 166–92